WEBSTER'S
SPANISH - ENGLISH
ENGLISH - SPANISH
DICTIONARY

COMPACT EDITION

© Geddes & Grosset Ltd., New Lanark, Scotland 1990

Published by Russell, Geddes & Grosset, Windsor Court,
New York, N.Y. U.S.A.

Printed in the U.S.A.

This book is not published by the original publishers of
Webster's Dictionary or by their successors.

	Abbreviations	**Abreviaturas**
abrev	abbreviation	abreviatura
adj	adjective	adjectivo
adv	adverb	adverbio
art	article	artículo
auto	automobile	automóvil
aux	auxiliary	auxiliar
bot	botany	botánica
chem	chemistry	química
col	colloquial term	lengua familiar
com	commerce	comercio
compd	in compounds	usado en palabras compuestas
conj	conjunction	conjunción
dep	sport	deporte
excl	exclamation	exclamación
<u>*f*</u>	<u>feminine noun</u>	sustantivo femenino
fam	colloquial term	lengua familiar
ferró	railroad	ferrocarrilero
fig	figurative use	uso figurado
gr	grammar	gramática
imp	impersonal	impersonal
inform	computers	informática
interj	interjection	interjección
invar	invariable	invariable
irr	irregular	irregular
jur	law term	jurisprudencia
law	law term	jurisprudencia
ling	linquistics	lingüística
<u>*m*</u>	<u>masculine noun</u>	sustantivo masculino
mar	marine term	vocablo marítimo
mat, math	mathematics	matemáticas
med	medicine	medicina

mil	military term	lo militar
mus	music	música
n	noun	sustantivo
pej	pejorative	peyorativo
pl	plural	plural
pn	pronoun	pronombre
poet	poetical term	vocablo poético
prep	preposition	preposición
quim	chemistry	química
rad	radio	radio
rail	railroad	ferrocarilero
sl	slang	argot
teat	theater	teatro
tec	technology	técnica, tecnología
TV	television	televisión
vi	intransitive verb	verbo intransitivo
vr	reflexive verb	verbo reflexivo
vt	transitive verb	verbo transitivo

A

a *art* un, uno, una; ● *prep* a, al, en.
aback *adv* detrás, atrás; to be taken ~ *vi* quedar consternado.
abacus *n* ábaco *m*.
abandon *vt* abandonar, dejar.
abandonment *n* abandono *m*; desamparo *m*.
abase *vt* abatir, humillar.
abasement *n* abatimiento *m*; humillación *f*.
abash *vt* avergonzar, causar confusión.
abate *vt* disminuir, rebajar; ● *vi* disminuirse.
abatement *n* rebaja, disminución *f*.
abbess *n* abadesa *f*.
abbey *n* abadía *f*.
abbot *n* abad *m*.
abbreviate *vt* abreviar, acortar.
abbreviation *n* abreviatura *f*.
abdicate *vt* abdicar; renunciar.
abdication *n* abdicación *f*; renuncia *f*.
abdomen *n* abdomen, bajovientre *m*.
abdominal *adj* abdominal.
abduct *vt* secuestrar.
abductor *n* músculo abductor *m*.
abed *adv* en (la) cama.
aberrant *adj* anormal.
aberration *n* error *m*; aberración *f*.
abet *vt*: to aid and ~ ser cómplice de.
abeyance *n* desuso *m*.
abhor *vt* aborrecer, detestar.
abhorrence *n* aborrecimiento, odio *m*.
abhorrent *adj* repugnante.
abide *vt* soportar, sufrir.
ability *n* habilidad, capacidad, aptitud *f*; abilities *pl* talento *m*.
abject *adj* vil, despreciable, bajo; ~ly *adv* vilmente, bajamente.
abjure *vt* abjurar; renunciar.
ablative *n* (*gr*) ablativo *m*.
ablaze *adj* en llamas.
able *adj* capaz, hábil; to be ~ poder.
able-bodied *adj* robusto, vigoroso.
ablution *n* ablución *f*.
ably *adv* con habilidad.
abnegation *n* abnegación, resignación *f*.
abnormal *adj* anormal.
abnormality *n* anormalidad *f*.
aboard *adv* a bordo.
abode *n* domicilio *m*.
abolish *vt* abolir, anular, revocar.
abolition *n* abolición, anulación *f*.
abominable *adj* abominable, detestable; ~bly *adv* abominablemente.
abomination *n* abominación *f*.
aboriginal *adj* aborigen.
aborigines *npl* aborígenes, primeros habitantes de un país *mpl*.
abort *vi* abortar.
abortion *n* aborto *m*.
abortive *adj* fracasado.
abound *vi* abundar; to ~ with abundar de.
about *prep* acerca de, acerca; I carry no money ~ me no traigo dinero; ● *adv* aquí y allá; to be ~ to estar para; to go ~ andar acá y acullá; to go ~ a thing emprender alguna cosa; all ~ en todo lugar.
above *prep* encima; ● *adv* arriba; ~ all sobre todo, principalmente; ~ mentioned ya mencionado.
aboveboard *adj* legítimo.
abrasion *n* abrasión *f*.
abrasive *adj* abrasivo.
abreast *adv* de costado.
abridge *vt* abreviar, compendiar; acortar.
abridgment *n* compendio *m*.

abroad *adv* en el extranjero; to go ~ salir del país.
abrogate *vt* abrogar, anular.
abrogation *n* abrogación, anulación *f*.
abrupt *adj* brusco; ~ly *adv* precipitadamente; bruscamente.
abscess *n* absceso *m*.
abscond *vi* esconderse; huirse.
absence *n* ausencia *f*.
absent *adj* ausente; ● *vi* ausentarse.
absentee *n* ausente *m*.
absenteeism *n* absentismo *m*.
absent-minded *adj* distraído.
absolute *adj* absoluto; categórico; ~ly *adv* totalmente.
absolution *n* absolución *f*.
absolutism *n* absolutismo *m*.
absolve *vt* absolver.
absorb *vt* absorber.
absorbent *adj* absorbente.
absorbent cotton *n* algodón hidrófilo *m*.
absorption *n* absorción *f*.
abstain *vi* abstenerse, privarse.
abstemious *adj* abstemio, sobrio; ~ly *adv* moderadamente.
abstemiousness *n* sobriedad, abstinencia *f*.
abstinence *n* abstinencia *f*; templanza *f*.
abstinent *adj* abstinente, sobrio.
abstract *adj* abstracto; ● *n* extracto *m*; sumario *m*; in the ~ de modo abstracto.
abstraction *n* abstracción *f*.
abstractly *adv* en abstracto.
abstruse *adj* oscuro; ~ly *adv* oscuramente.
absurd *adj* absurdo; ~ly *adv* absurdamente.
absurdity *n* absurdidad *f*.
abundance *n* abundancia *f*.
abundant *adj* abundante; ~ly *adv* abundantemente.
abuse *vt* abusar; maltratar; ● *n* abuso *m*; injurias *fpl*.
abusive *adj* abusivo, ofensivo; ~ly *adv* abusivamente.
abut *vi* confinar.
abysmal *adj* abismal; insondable.
abyss *n* abismo *m*.
acacia *n* acacia *f*.
academic *adj* académico.
academician *n* académico *m*.
academy *n* academia *f*.
accede *vi* acceder.
accelerate *vt* acelerar.
accelerator *n* acelerador *m*.
acceleration *n* aceleración *f*.
accent *n* acento *m*; tono *m*; ● *vt* acentuar.
accentuate *vt* acentuar.
accentuation *n* acentuación *f*.
accept *vt* aceptar; admitir.
acceptable *adj* aceptable.
acceptability *n* aceptabilidad *f*.
acceptance *n* aceptación *f*.
access *n* acceso *m*; entrada *f*.
accessible *adj* accesible.
accession *n* aumento, acrecentamiento *m*; advenimiento *m*; acceso *m*.
accessory *n* accesorio *m*; (*law*) cómplice *m*.
accident *n* accidente *m*; casualidad *f*.
accidental *adj* casual; ~ly *adv* por casualidad.
acclaim *vt* aclamar, aplaudir.
acclamation *n* aclamación *f*; aplauso *m*.
acclimate *vt* aclimatar.
accommodate *vt* alojar; complacer.
accommodating *adj* servicial.
accommodations *npl* alojamiento *m*.
accompaniment *n* (*mus*) acompañamiento *m*.
accompanist *n* (*mus*) acompañante *m*.
accompany *vt* acompañar.
accomplice *n* cómplice *m*.
accomplish *vt* efectuar, completar.
accomplished *adj* elegante, consumado.

accomplishment *n* cumplimiento *m*; ~s *pl* talentos, conocimientos *mpl*.

accord *n* acuerdo, convenio *m*; **with one** ~ unánimemente; **of one's own** ~ espontáneamente.

accordance *n*: **in** ~ **with** de acuerdo con.

according *prep* según, conforme; ~ **as** según que, como; ~**ly** *adv* por consiguiente.

accordion *n* (*mus*) acordeón *m*.

accost *vt* trabar conversación con.

account *n* cuenta *f*; **on no** ~ de ninguna manera; bajo ningún concepto; **on** ~ **of** por motivo de; **to call to** ~ pedir cuenta; **to turn to** ~ hacer provechoso; ● *vt* **to** ~ **for** explicar.

accountability *n* responsabilidad *f*.

accountable *adj* responsable.

accountancy *n* contabilidad *f*.

accountant *n* contable, contador *m*.

account book *n* libro de cuentas *m*.

account number *n* número *m* de cuenta.

accrue *vi* resultar, provenir.

accumulate *vt* acumular; amontonar; ● *vi* crecer.

accumulation *n* acumulación *f*; amontonamiento *m*.

accuracy *n* exactitud *f*.

accurate *adj* exacto; ~**ly** *adv* exactamente.

accursed *adj* maldito.

accusation *n* acusación *f*.

accusative *n* (*gr*) acusativo *m*.

accusatory *adj* acusatorio.

accuse *vt* acusar; culpar.

accused *n* acusado *m*.

accuser *n* acusador *m*; denunciador *m*.

accustom *vt* acostumbrar.

accustomed *adj* acostumbrado, habitual.

ace *n* as *m*; **within an** ~ **of** casi, casi; por poco no . . .

acerbic *adj* mordaz.

acetate *n* (*chem*) acetato *m*.

ache *n* dolor *m*; ● *vi* doler.

achieve *vt* realizar; obtener.

achievement *n* realización *f*; hazaña *f*.

acid *adj* ácido; agrio; ● *n* ácido *m*.

acidity *n* acidez *f*.

acknowledge *vt* reconocer, confesar.

acknowledgment *n* reconocimiento *m*; gratitud *f*.

acme *n* apogeo *m*.

acne *n* acné *m*.

acorn *n* bellota *f*.

acoustics *n* acústica *f*.

acquaint *vt* informar, avisar.

acquaintance *n* conocimiento *m*; conocido *m*.

acquiesce *vi* someterse, consentir, asentir.

acquiescence *n* consentimiento *m*.

acquiescent *adj* deferente.

acquire *vt* adquirir.

acquisition *n* adquisición, obtención *f*.

acquit *vt* absolver.

acquittal *n* absolución *f*.

acre *n* acre *m*.

acrid *adj* acre.

acrimonious *adj* mordaz.

acrimony *n* acrimonia, acritud *f*.

across *adv* de través, de una parte a otra; ● *prep* a través de; **to come** ~ topar con.

act *vt* representar; ● *vi* hacer; ● *n* acto, hecho *m*; acción *f*; ~**s of the apostles** Actos *mpl*.

acting *adj* interino.

action *n* acción *f*; batalla *f*.

action replay *n* repetición *f*.

activate *vt* activar.

active *adj* activo; ~**ly** *adv* activamente.

activity *n* actividad *f*.

actor *n* actor *m*.

actress *n* actriz *f*.

actual *adj* real; efectivo; ~**ly** *adv* en efecto, realmente.

actuary *n* actuario de seguros *m*.

acumen *n* agudeza, perspicacia *f*.

acute *adj* agudo; ingenioso; ~ **accent** *n* acento agudo *m*; ~ **angle** *n* ángulo agudo *m*; ~**ly** *adv* con agudeza.

acuteness *n* perspicacia, sagacidad *f*.

ad *n* aviso *m*.

adage *n* proverbio *m*.

adamant *adj* inflexible.

adapt *vt* adaptar, acomodar; ajustar.

adaptability *n* facilidad de adaptarse *f*.

adaptable *adj* adaptable.

adaptation *n* adaptación *f*.

adaptor *n* adaptador *m*.

add *vt* añadir, agregar; **to** ~ **up** sumar.

addendum *n* suplemento *m*.

adder *n* culebra *f*; víbora *f*.

addict *n* drogadicto *m*.

addiction *n* dependencia *f*.

addictive *adj* que crea dependencia.

addition *n* adición *f*.

additional *adj* adicional; ~**ly** *adv* en *o* por adición.

additive *n* aditivo *m*.

address *vt* dirigir; ● *n* dirección *f*; discurso *m*.

adduce *vt* alegar, aducir.

adenoids *npl* vegetaciones adenoide *fpl*.

adept *adj* hábil.

adequacy *n* suficiencia *f*.

adequate *adj* adecuado; suficiente; ~**ly** *adv* adecuadamente.

adhere *vi* adherir.

adherence *n* adherencia *f*.

adherent *n* adherente, partidario *m*.

adhesion *n* adhesión *f*.

adhesive *adj* pegajoso.

adhesive tape *n* (*med*) esparadrapo *m*.

adhesiveness *n* adhesividad *f*.

adieu *adv* adiós; ● *n* despedida *f*.

adipose *adj* adiposa.

adjacent *adj* adyacente, contiguo.

adjectival *adj* adjetivado; ~**ly** *adv* como adjetivo.

adjective *n* adjetivo *m*.

adjoin *vi* estar contiguo.

adjoining *adj* contiguo.

adjourn *vt* aplazar.

adjournment *n* prórroga *f*.

adjudicate *vt* adjudicar.

adjunct *n* adjunto *m*.

adjust *vt* ajustar, acomodar.

adjustable *adj* ajustable.

adjustment *n* ajustamiento, arreglo *m*.

adjutant *n* (*mil*) ayudante *m*.

ad lib *vt* improvisar.

administer *vt* administrar; gobernar; **to** ~ **an oath** prestar juramento.

administration *n* administración *f*; gobierno *m*.

administrative *adj* administrativo.

administrator *n* administrador *m*.

admirable *adj* admirable; ~**bly** *adv* admirablemente, a maravilla.

admiral *n* almirante *m*.

admiralship *n* almirantía *f*.

admiralty *n* almirantazgo *m*.

admiration *n* admiración *f*.

admire *vt* admirar.

admirer *n* admirador *m*.

admiringly *adv* con admiración.

admissible *adj* admisible.

admission *n* admisión *f*; entrada *f*.

admit *vt* admitir; **to** ~ **to** confesarse culpable de.

admittance *n* entrada *f*.

admittedly *adj* de acuerdo que.

admixture *n* mixtura, mezcla *f*.

admonish *vt* amonestar, reprender.

admonition *n* amonestación *f*; consejo, aviso *m*.
admonitory *adj* exhortatorio.
ad nauseam *adv* hasta el cansancio.
ado *n* dificultad *f*.
adolescence *n* adolescencia *f*.
adopt *vt* adoptar.
adopted *adj* adoptivo.
adoption *n* adopción *f*.
adoptive *adj* adoptivo.
adorable *adj* adorable.
adorably *adv* de modo adorable.
adoration *n* adoración *f*.
adore *vt* adorar.
adorn *vt* adornar.
adornment *n* adorno *m*.
adrift *adv* a la deriva.
adroit *adj* diestro, hábil.
adroitness *n* destreza *f*.
adulation *n* adulación, zalamería *f*.
adulatory *adj* lisonjero.
adult *adj* adulto; ● *n* adulto *m*; adulta *f*.
adulterate *vt* adulterar, corromper; ● *adj* adulterado, falsificado.
adulteration *n* adulteración, corrupción *f*.
adulterer *n* adúltero *m*.
adulteress *n* adúltera *f*.
adulterous *adj* adúltero.
adultery *n* adulterio *m*.
advance *vt* avanzar; promover; pagar por adelantado; ● *vi* hacer progresos;● *n* avance *m*; paga adelantada *f*.
advanced *adj* avanzado.
advancement *n* adelantamiento *m*; progreso *m*; promoción *f*.
advantage *n* ventaja *f*; to take ~ of sacar provecho de.
advantageous *adj* ventajoso; ~ly *adv* ventajosamente.
advantageousness *n* ventaja, utilidad *f*.
advent *n* venida *f*; Advent *n* Adviento *m*.
adventitious *adj* adventicio.
adventure *n* aventura *f*.
adventurer *n* aventurero *m*.
adventurous *adj* intrépido; valeroso; ~ly *adv* arriesgadamente.
adverb *n* adverbio *m*.
adverbial *adj* adverbial; ~ly *adv* como adverbio.
adversary *n* adversario enemigo *m*.
adverse *adj* adverso, contrario.
adversity *n* calamidad *f*; infortunio *m*.
advertise *vt* anunciar.
advertisement *n* aviso *m*.
advertising *n* publicidad *f*.
advice *n* consejo *m*; aviso *m*.
advisability *n* prudencia, conveniencia *f*.
advisable *adj* prudente, conveniente.
advise *vt* aconsejar; avisar.
advisedly *adv* prudentemente, avisadamente.
advisory *adj* consultivo.
advocacy *n* defensa *f*.
advocate *n* abogado *m*; protector *m*; ● *vt* abogar por.
advocateship *n* abogacía *f*.
aerial *n* antena *f*.
aerobics *npl* aerobic *m*.
aerometer *n* aerómetro *m*.
aerosol *n* aerosol *m*.
aerostat *n* globo aerostático *m*.
afar *adv* lejos, distante; from ~ desde lejos.
affability *n* afabilidad, urbanidad *f*.
affable *adj* afable, complaciente; ~bly *adv* afablemente.
affair *n* asunto *m*; negocio *m*.
affect *vt* conmover; afectar.
affectation *n* afectación *f*.
affected *adj* afectado, lleno de afectación; ~ly *adv* con afectación.
affectingly *adv* con afecto.

affection *n* cariño *m*.
affectionate *adj* afectuoso; ~ly *adv* cariñosamente.
affidavit *n* declaración jurada *f*.
affiliate *vt* afiliar.
affiliation *n* afiliación *f*.
affinity *n* afinidad *f*.
affirm *vt* afirmar, declarar.
affirmation *n* afirmación *f*.
affirmative *adj* afirmativo; ~ly *adv* afirmativamente.
affix *vt* pegar; ● *n* (*gr*) afijo *m*.
afflict *vt* afligir.
affliction *n* aflicción *f*; dolor *m*.
affluence *n* abundancia *f*.
affluent *adj* opulento.
afflux *n* confluencia, afluencia *f*.
afford *vt* dar; proveer.
affray *n* asalto *m*; tumulto *m*.
affront *n* afrenta, injuria *f*; ● *vt* afrentar, insultar, ultrajar.
aflame *adv* en llamas.
afloat *adv* flotante, a flote.
afore *prep* antes; ● *adv* primero.
afraid *adj* espantado, tímido; I am ~ temo.
afresh *adv* de nuevo, otra vez.
aft *adv* (*mar*) a popa.
after *prep* después; detrás; según; ● *adv* después; ~ all después de todo.
afterbirth *n* secundinas *fpl*.
after-crop *n* segunda cosecha *f*.
after-effects *npl* consecuencias *fpl*.
afterlife *n* vida venidera *f*.
aftermath *n* consecuencias *fpl*.
afternoon *n* tarde *f*.
afterpains *npl* dolores de sobreparto *mpl*.
aftershave *n* aftershave *m*.
aftertaste *n* resabio *m*.
afterward *adv* después.
again *adv* otra vez; ~ and ~ muchas veces; as much ~ otra vez tanto.
against *prep* contra; ~ the grain a contrapelo; de mala gana.
agate *n* ágata *f*.
age *n* edad *f*; vejez *f*; under ~ menor; ● *vt* envejecer.
aged *adj* viejo, anciano.
agency *n* agencia *f*.
agenda *n* orden del día *m*.
agent *n* agente *m*.
agglomerate *vt* aglomerar.
agglomeration *n* aglomeración *f*.
aggrandizement *n* engrandecimiento *m*.
aggravate *vt* agravar, exagerar.
aggravation *n* agravación *f*.
aggregate *n* agregado *m*.
aggregation *n* agregación *f*.
aggression *n* agresión *f*.
aggressive *adj* ofensivo.
aggressor *n* agresor *m*.
aggrieved *adj* ofendido.
aghast *adj* horrorizado.
agile *adj* ágil; diestro.
agility *n* agilidad *f*; destreza *f*.
agitate *vt* agitar.
agitation *n* agitación *f*; perturbación *f*.
agitator *n* agitador, incitador *m*.
ago *adv* pasado, largo tiempo; después; how long ~? ¿cuánto hace?
agog *adj* emocionado.
agonizing *adj* atroz.
agony *n* agonía *f*.
agrarian *adj* agrario.
agree *vt* convenir; ● *vi* estar de acuerdo.
agreeable *adj* agradable; amable; ~bly *adv* agradablemente; ~ with según, conforme a.
agreeableness *n* amabilidad, gracia *f*.

agreed adj establecido, convenido; ~! adv ¡de acuerdo!
agreement n acuerdo m.
agricultural adj agrario.
agriculture n agricultura f.
agriculturist n agricultor m.
aground adv (mar) encallado.
ah! excl ¡ah! ¡ay!
ahead adv más allá, delante de otro; (mar) por la proa.
ahoy! excl (mar) ¡ohé! ¡ahupa!
aid vt ayudar, socorrer; **to ~ and abet** ser cómplice de; ● n ayuda f; auxilio, socorro m.
aide-de-camp n (mil) ayudante de campo m.
AIDS n SIDA m.
ail vt afligir, molestar.
ailing adj doliente.
ailment n dolencia, indisposición f.
aim vt apuntar aspirar a; intentar; ● n designio m; puntería f.
aimless adj sin designio, sin objeto; ~ly a la deriva.
air n aire m; ● vt airear; ventilar.
air balloon n globo aerostático m.
airborne adj aerotransportado.
air-conditioned adj climatizado.
air-conditioning n aire acondicionado m.
aircraft n avión m.
air cushion n cojinete rellenado de aire m.
air force n fuerzas aéreas fpl.
air freshener n ambientador m.
air gun n escopeta de aire comprimido f.
air hole n respiradero m.
airiness n ventilación f.
airless adj falto de ventilación, sofocado.
airlift n puente aéreo m.
airline n línea aérea f.
airmail n: **by ~** por avión.
airplane n avión m.
airport n aeropuerto m.
air pump n bomba de aire f.
airstick adj mareado.
airstrip n pista de aterrizaje f.
air terminal n terminal f.
airtight adj herméticamente cerrado.
airy adj bien ventilado.
aisle n nave de una iglesia f.
ajar adj entreabierto.
akimbo adj corvo.
akin adj parecido.
alabaster n alabastro m; ● adj alabastrino.
alacrity n presteza f.
alarm n alarma f; ● vt alarmar; inquietar.
alarm bell n timbre de alarma m.
alarmist n alarmista m.
alas adv desgraciadamente.
albeit conj aunque.
album n álbum m.
alchemist n alquimista m.
alchemy n alquimia f.
alcohol n alcohol m.
alcoholic adj alcohólico; ● n alcoholizado m.
alcove n niche m.
alder n aliso m.
ale n cerveza f.
alehouse n cervecería, taberna f.
alert adj vigilante; alerto; ● n alerta f.
alertness n cuidado m; vigilancia f.
algae npl alga f.
algebra n álgebra f.
algebraic adj algebraico.
alias adj alias.
alibi n (law) coartada f.
alien adj ajeno; ● n forastero m.
alienate vt enajenar.
alienation n enajenación f.

alight vi apearse; ● adj encendido.
align vt alinear.
alike adj semejante, igual; ● adv igualmente.
alimentation n alimentación f.
alimony n alimentos mpl.
alive adj vivo, viviente; activo.
alkali n álcali m.
alkaline adj alcalino.
all adj todo; ● adv totalmente; **~ at once ~ of a sudden** de repente; **~ the same** sin embargo; **~ the better** tanto mejor; **not at ~!** ¡no hay de qué!; **once for ~** una vez por todas; ● n todo m.
allay vt aliviar.
all clear n luz verde f.
allegation n alegación f.
allege vt alegar; declarar.
allegiance n lealtad, fidelidad f.
allegorical adj alegórico; ~ly adv alegóricamente.
allegory n alegoría f.
allegro n (mus) alegro m.
allergy n alergia f.
alleviate vt aliviar, aligerar.
alleviation n alivio m; mitigación f.
alley n callejuela f.
alliance n alianza f.
allied adj aliado.
alligator n caimán m.
allitteration n aliteración f.
all-night adj abierto toda la noche.
allocate vt repartir.
allocation n cuota f.
allot vt asignar.
allow vt conceder; permitir; dar, pagar; **to ~ for** tener en cuenta.
allowable adj admisible, permitido.
allowance n concesión f.
alloy n liga, mezcla f.
all-right adv bien.
all-round adj completo.
allspice n pimienta de Jamaica f.
allude vt aludir.
allure n fascinación f.
alluring adj seductor; ~ly adv seductoramente.
allurement n aliciente, atractivo m.
allusion n alusión f.
allusive adj alusivo; ~ly adv de modo alusivo.
alluvial adj aluvial.
ally n aliado m; ● vt aliar.
almanac n almanaque m.
almighty adj omnipotente, todopoderoso.
almond n almendra f.
almond-milk n almendrada f.
almond tree n almendro m.
almost adv casi; cerca de.
alms n limosna f.
aloft prep arriba.
alone adj solo; ● adv solamente, sólo; **to leave ~** dejar en paz.
along adv a lo largo; **~ side** al lado.
aloof adv lejos.
aloud adj en voz alta.
alphabet n alfabeto m.
alphabetical adj alfabético; ~ly adv por orden alfabético.
alpine adj alpino.
already adv ya.
also adv también, además.
altar n altar m.
altarpiece n retablo m.
alter vt modificar.
alteration n alteración f.
altercation n altercado m.
alternate adj alterno; ● vt alternar, variar; ~ly adv alternativamente.

alternating *adj* alterno.
alternation *n* alternación *f*.
alternator *n* alternador *m*.
alternative *n* alternativa *f*; ● *adj* alternative; ~**ly** *adv* si no.
although *conj* aunque, no obstante.
altitude *n* altitud, altura *f*.
altogether *adv* del todo.
alum *n* alumbre *m*.
aluminous *adj* aluminoso.
aluminum *n* aluminio *m*.
always *adv* siempre, constantemente.
a.m. *adv* de la mañana.
amalgam *n* amalgama *f*.
amalgamate *vt vi* amalgamar(se).
amalgamation *n* amalgamación *f*.
amanuensis *n* amanuense, secretario *m*.
amaryllis *n* (*bot*) amarilis *f*.
amass *vt* acumular, amontonar.
amateur *n* aficionado *m*.
amateurish *adj* torpe.
amatory *adj* amatorio; erótico.
amaze *vt* asombrar.
amazement *n* asombro *m*.
amazing *adj* pasmoso; ~**ly** *adv* extraordinariamente.
amazon *n* amazona *f*.
ambassador *n* embajador *m*.
ambassadress *n* embajadora *f*.
amber *n* ámbar *m*; ● *adj* ambarino.
ambidextrous *adj* ambidextro.
ambient *adj* ambiente.
ambiguity *n* ambigüedad, duda *f*.
ambiguous *adj* ambiguo; ~**ly** *adv* ambiguamente.
ambition *n* ambición *f*.
ambitious *adj* ambicioso; ~**ly** *adv* ambiciosamente.
amble *vi* andar sin prisa.
ambulance *n* ambulancia *f*.
ambush *n* emboscada *f*; **to lie in** ~ estar emboscado; ● *vt* tender una emboscada a.
ameliorate *vt* mejorar.
amelioration *n* mejoramiento *m*.
amenable *adj* sensible.
amend *vt* enmendar.
amendable *adj* reparable, corregible.
amendment *n* enmienda *f*.
amends *npl* compensación *f*.
amenities *npl* comodidades *fpl*.
America *n* América *f*.
American *adj* americano.
amethyst *n* amatista *f*.
amiability *n* amabilidad *f*.
amiable *adj* amable.
amiableness *n* amabilidad *f*.
amiably *adv* amablemente.
amicable *adj* amigable, amistoso; ~**bly** *adv* amistasamente.
amid(st) *prep* entre, en medio de.
amiss *adv*: **something's** ~ algo pasa.
ammonia *n* amoníaco *m*.
ammunition *n* municiones *fpl*.
amnesia *n* amnesia *f*.
amnesty *n* amnistía *f*.
among(st) *prep* entre, en medio de.
amoral *adv* amoral.
amorous *adj* amoroso; ~**ly** *adv* amorosamente.
amorphous *adj* informe.
amount *n* importe *m*; cantidad *f*; ● *vi* sumar.
amp(ère) *n* amperio *m*.
amphibian *n* anfibio *m*.
amphibious *adj* anfibio.
amphitheater *n* anfiteatro *m*.
ample *adj* amplio.
ampleness *n* amplitud, abundancia *f*.
amplification *n* amplificación *f*; extensión *f*.

amplifier *n* amplificador *m*
amplify *vt* ampliar, extender.
amplitude *n* amplitud, extensión *f*.
amply *adv* ampliamente.
amputate *vt* amputar.
amputation *n* amputación *f*.
amulet *n* amuleto *m*.
amuse *vt* entretener, divertir.
amusement *n* diversión *f*, pasatiempo, entretenimiento *m*.
amusing *adj* divertido; ~**ly** *adv* entretenidamente.
an *art* un, uno, una.
anachronism *n* anacronismo *m*.
analog *adj* (*comput*) analógico.
analogous *adj* análogo.
analogy *n* analogía *f*.
analysis *n* análisis *m*.
analyst *n* analizador *m*.
analytical *adj* analítico; ~**ly** *adv* analíticamente.
analyze *vt* analizar.
anarchic *adj* anárquico.
anarchist *adj* anarquista.
anarchy *n* anarquía *f*.
anatomical *adj* anatómico; ~**ly** *adv* anatómicamente.
anatomize *vt* anatomizar.
anatomy *n* anatomía *f*
ancestor *n*: ~**s** *pl* antepasados *mpl*.
ancestral *adj* hereditario.
ancestry *n* raza, alcurnia *f*
anchor *n* ancla *f*; ● *vi* anclar.
anchorage *n* ancladero *m*
anchovy *n* anchoa *f*
ancient *adj* antiguo; ~**ly** *adv* antiguamente.
ancientness *n* antigüedad *f*
ancillary *adj* auxiliar.
and *conj* y, e.
anecdotal *adj* anecdótico.
anecdote *n* anécdota *f*
anemia *n* anemia *f*.
anemic *adj* (*med*) anémico.
anemone *n* (*bot*) anémona *f*
anesthetic *n* anestesia *f*.
anew *adv* de nuevo, nuevamente.
angel *n* ángel *m*
angelic *adj* angélico.
anger *n* cólera *f*; ● *vt* enojar, irritar.
angle *n* ángulo *m*; ● *vt* pescar con caña.
angled *adj* anguloso.
angler *n* pescador de caña *m*
anglicism *n* anglicismo *m*.
angling *n* pesca con caña *f*
angrily *adv* enojado.
angry *adj* enojado.
anguish *n* ansia, angustia *f*
angular *adj* angular.
angularity *n* forma angular *f*.
animal *n adj* animal *m*.
animate *vt* animar; ● *adj* viviente.
animated *adj* vivo.
animation *n* animación *f*
animosity *n* rencor *m*.
animus *n* odio *m*
anise *n* anís *m*
aniseed *n* anís *m*
ankle *n* tobillo *m*; ~ **bone** hueso del tobillo *m*
annals *n* anales *mpl*.
annex *vt* anejar; ● *n* anejo *m*.
annexation *n* anexión *f*.
annihilate *vt* aniquilar.
annihilation *n* aniquilación *f*.
anniversary *n* aniversario *m*.
annotate *vi* anotar.
annotation *n* anotación *f*.

announce *vt* anunciar, publicar.
announcement *n* anuncio *m*.
announcer *n* locutor *m*.
annoy *vt* molestar.
annoyance *n* molestia *f*.
annoying *adj* molesto; fastidioso.
annual *adj* anual; ~ly *adv* anualmente, cada año.
annuity *n* renta vitalicia *f*.
annul *vt* anular.
annulment *n* anulación *f*.
annunciation *n* anunciación *f*
anodyne *adj* anodino.
anoint *vt* untar, ungir.
anomalous *adj* anómalo.
anomaly *n* anomalía, irregularidad *f*.
anon *adv* más tarde.
anonymity *n* anonimato *m*.
anonymous *adj* anónimo; ~ly *adj* anónimamente.
anorexia *n* anorexia *f*.
another *adj* otro, diferente; one ~ uno a otro.
answer *vt* responder, replicar; corresponder; to ~ for responder de *o* por; to ~ to corresponder a; • *n* respuesta, réplica *f*.
answerable *adj* responsable.
answering machine *n* contestador automático *m*.
ant *n* hormiga *f*.
antagonism *n* antagonismo *m*; rivalidad *f*.
antagonist *n* antagonista *m*.
antagonize *vt* provocar.
antarctic *adj* antártico.
anteater *n* oso hormiguero *m*
antecedent *n*: ~s *pl* antecedentes *mpl*.
antechamber *n* antecámara *f*
antedate *vt* antedatar.
antelope *n* antílope *m*.
antenna *npl* antena *f*.
anterior *adj* anterior, precedente.
anthem *n* himno *m*.
ant-hill *n* hormiguero *m*.
anthology *n* antología *f*.
anthracite *n* antracita *f*.
anthropology *n* antropología *f*
anti-aircraft *adj* antiaéreo.
antibiotic *n* antibiótico *m*.
antibody *n* anticuerpo *m*.
Antichrist *n* Anticristo *m*.
anticipate *vt* anticipar, prevenir.
anticipation *n* anticipación *f*.
anticlockwise *adv* en sentido contrario a la de las agujas del reloj.
antidote *n* antídoto *m*.
antifreeze *n* anticongelante *m*.
antimony *n* antimonio *m*.
antipathy *n* antipatía *f*.
antipodes *npl* antípodas *fpl*
antiquarian *n* anticuario *m*.
antiquated *adj* antiguo; • *n* antigüedad *f*.
antiquity *n* antigüedad *f*
antiseptic *adj* antiséptico.
antisocial *adj* antisocial.
antithesis *n* antítesis *f*.
antler *n* cuerna *f*.
anvil *n* yunque *m*.
anxiety *n* ansiedad, ansia *f*; afán *m*.
anxious *adj* ansioso; ~ly *adv* ansiosamente.
any *adj pn* cualquier, cualquiera; alguno, alguna; todo; ~body alguno, cualquiera; ~how de cualquier modo que sea; ~more más; ~place en ninguna parte; ~thing algo.
apace *adv* rápidamente.
apart *adv* aparte, separadamente.
apartment *n* departamento *m*.
apartment house *n* casa de apartamentos *f*.

apathetic *adj* apático.
apathy *n* apatía *f*.
ape *n* mono *m*; • *vt* remedar.
aperture *n* abertura *f*.
apex *n* ápice *m*.
aphorism *n* aforismo *m*; máxima *f*.
apiary *n* colmena *f*.
apiece *adv* por cabeza, por persona.
aplomb *n* aplomo *m*.
Apocalypse *n* Apocalípsis *m*.
apocrypha *npl* libros apócrifos *mpl*.
apocryphal *adj* apócrifo, no canónico.
apologetic *adj* de disculpa.
apologist *n* apologista *m*.
apologize *vt* disculpar.
apology *n* apología, defensa *f*.
apoplexy *n* apoplejía *f*
apostle *n* apóstol *m*.
apostolic *adj* apostólico.
apostrophe *n* apóstrofe *m*.
apotheosis *n* apoteosis *f*.
appall *vt* espantar, aterrar.
appalling *adj* espantoso.
apparatus *n* aparato *m*.
apparel *n* traje, vestido *m*.
apparent *adj* evidente, aparente; ~ly *adv* por lo visto.
apparition *n* aparición, visión *f*.
appeal *vi* apelar, recurrir a un tribunal superior; • *n* (*law*) apelación *f*.
appealing *adj* atractivo.
appear *vi* aparecer.
appearance *n* apariencia *f*.
appease *vt* aplacar.
appellant *n* (*law*) apelante *m*.
append *vt* anejar.
appendage *n* cosa accesoria *f*.
appendicitis *n* apendicitis *f*.
appendix *n* apéndice *m*.
appertain *vi* tocar a.
appetite *n* apetito *m*.
appetizing *adj* apetitivo.
applaud *vi* aplaudir.
applause *n* aplausos *mpl*
apple *n* manzana *f*.
apple pie *n* pastelillo de manzanas *m*; in ~ order en sumo orden.
apple tree *n* manzano *m*.
appliance *n* aparato *m*.
applicability *n* aplicabilidad *f*.
applicable *adj* aplicable.
applicant *n* aspirante, candidato *m*.
application *n* aplicación *f*; solicitud *f*.
applied *adj* aplicado.
apply *vt* aplicar; • *vi* dirigirse a, recurrir a.
appoint *vt* nombrar.
appointee *n* persona nombrada *f*.
appointment *n* cita *f*; nombramiento *m*.
apportion *vt* repartir.
apportionment *n* repartición *f*.
apposite *adj* adaptado.
apposition *n* aposición *f*.
appraisal *n* estimación *f*.
appraise *vt* tasar; estimar.
appreciable *adj* sensible.
appreciably *adv* sensiblemente.
appreciate *vt* apreciar; agradecer.
appreciation *n* aprecio *m*.
appreciative *adj* agradecido.
apprehend *vt* arrestar.
apprehension *n* aprensión *f*.
apprehensive *adj* aprensivo, tímido.
apprentice *n* aprendiz *m*; • *vt* poner de aprendiz.

apprenticeship *n* aprendizaje *m*.
apprise, apprize *vt* informar.
approach *vt vi* aproximar(se); ● *n* acceso *m*.
approachable *adj* accesible.
approbation *n* aprobación *f*.
appropriate *vt* apropiarse de; ● *adj* apropiado.
approval *n* aprobación *f*.
approve (of) *vt* aprobar.
approximate *vi* acercarse; ● *adj* aproximativo; ~**ly** *adv* aproximadamente.
approximation *n* aproximación *f*.
apricot *n* damasco, albaricoque *m*.
April *n* abril *m*.
apron *n* delantal *m*.
apse *n* ábside *m*.
apt *adj* apto, idóneo; ~**ly** *adv* oportunamente.
aptitude *n* aptitud *f*.
aqualung *n* escafandra autónoma *f*.
aquarium *n* acuario *m*.
Aquarius *n* Acuario *m*.
aquatic *adj* acuático.
aqueduct *n* acueducto *m*.
aquiline *adj* aguileño.
arabesque *n* arabesco *m*.
arable *adj* labrantío.
arbiter *n* árbitro *m*.
arbitrariness *n* arbitrariedad *f*.
arbitrary *adj* arbitrario.
arbitrate *vt* arbitrar, juzgar como árbitro.
arbitration *n* arbitrio *m*.
arbitrator *n* árbitro *m*.
arbor *n* emparrado *m*; enramada *f*.
arcade *n* galería *f*.
arch *n* arco *m*; ● *adj* malicioso.
archaic *adj* arcaico.
archangel *n* arcángel *m*.
archbishop *n* arzobispo *m*.
archbishopric *n* arzobispado *m*.
archeological *adj* arqueológico.
archeology *n* arqueología *f*.
archer *n* arquero *m*.
archery *n* tiro con arco y flecha *m*.
architect *n* arquitecto *m*.
architectural *adj* arquitectónico.
architecture *n* arquitectura *f*.
archives *npl* archivos *mpl*.
archivist *n* archivero *m*.
archly *adv* maliciosamente.
archway *n* arcada, bóveda *f*.
arctic *adj* ártico.
ardent *adj* apasionado; ~**ly** *adv* con pasión.
ardor *n* ardor *m*; vehemencia *f*; pasión *f*.
arduous *adj* arduo, difícil.
area *n* área *f*; espacio *m*.
arena *n* arena *f*.
arguably *adv* posiblemente.
argue *vi* discutir; ● *vt* sostener.
argument *n* argumento *m*, controversia *f*.
argumentation *n* argumentación *f*.
argumentative *adj* discutidor.
aria *n* (*mus*) aria *f*.
arid *adj* árido, estéril.
aridity *n* sequedad *f*.
Aries *n* Aries *m*.
aright *adv* bien; **to set** ~ rectificar.
arise *vi* levantarse; nacer.
aristocracy *n* aristocracia *f*.
aristocrat *n* aristócrata *m*.
aristocratic *adj* aristocrático; ~**ally** *adv* aristocráticamente.
arithmetic *n* aritmética *f*.
arithmetical *adj* aritmético; ~**ly** *adv* aritméticamente.
ark *n* arca *f*.

arm *n* brazo *m*; arma *f*; ● *vt* (*vi*) armar(se).
armament *n* armamento *m*.
armchair *n* sillón *m*.
armed *adj* armado.
armful *n* brazada *f*.
armhole *n* sobaco *m*.
armistice *n* armisticio *m*.
armor *n* armadura *f*.
armored car *n* carro blindado *m*.
armory *n* arsenal *m*.
armpit *n* sobaco *m*.
armrest *n* apoyabrazos *m invar*.
army *n* ejército *m*; tropas *fpl*.
aroma *n* aroma *m*.
aromatic *adj* aromático.
around *prep* alrededor de; ● *adv* alrededor.
arouse *vt* despertar; excitar.
arraign *vt* acusar.
arraignment *n* acusación *f*; proceso criminal *m*.
arrange *vt* organizar.
arrangement *n* colocación *f*; arreglo.
arrant *adj* consumado.
array *n* serie *f*.
arrears *npl* resto de una deuda *m*; atraso *m*.
arrest *n* arresto *m*; ● *vt* detener, arrestar.
arrival *n* llegada *f*.
arrive *vi* llegar.
arrogance *n* arrogancia, presunción *f*.
arrogant *adj* arrogante, presuntuoso; ~**ly** *adv* arrogantemente.
arrogate *vt* arrogarse.
arrogation *n* arrogación *f*.
arrow *n* flecha *f*.
arsenal *n* (*mil*) arsenal *m*; (*mar*) atarazana, armería *f*.
arsenic *n* arsénico *m*.
arson *n* fuego incendiario *m*.
art *n* arte *m*.
arterial *adj* arterial.
artesian well *n* pozo artesiano *m*.
artery *n* arteria *f*.
artful *adj* ingenioso.
artfulness *n* astucia, habilidad *f*.
art gallery *n* pinacoteca *f*.
arthritis *n* artritis *f*.
artichoke *n* alcachofa *f*.
article *n* artículo *m*. —LOSS
articulate *vt* articular, pronunciar distintamente.
articulated *adj* articulado.
articulation *n* articulación *f*.
artifice *n* artificio, fraude *m*.
artificial *adj* artificial; artificioso; ~**ly** *adv* artificialmente; artificiosamente.
artificiality *n* artificialidad *f*.
artillery *n* artillería *f*.
artisan *n* artesano *m*.
artist *n* artista *m*.
artistic *adj* artístico.
artistry *n* habilidad *f*.
artless *adj* sencillo, simple; ~**ly** *adv* sencillamente, naturalmente.
artlessness *n* sencillez *f*.
art school *n* escuela de bellas artes *f*.
as *conj* como; mientras; también; visto que, puesto que; ~ **for**, ~ **to** en cuanto a.
asbestos *n* asbesto, amianto *m*.
ascend *vi* ascender, subir.
ascendancy, *n* dominio *m*.
ascension *n* ascensión *f*.
ascent *n* subida *f*.
ascertain *vt* establecer.
ascetic *adj* ascético; ● *n* asceta *m*.
ascribe *vt* atribuir.

ash n (bot) fresno m; ceniza f
ashcan n bote de la basura m.
ashamed adj avergonzado.
ashore adv en tierra, a tierra; to go ~ desembarcar.
ashtray n cenicero m.
Ash Wednesday n miércoles de ceniza m.
aside adv a un lado.
ask vt pedir, rogar; to ~ after preguntar por; to ~ for pedir; to ~ out invitar.
askance adv desconfiado.
askew adv de lado.
asleep adj dormido; to fall ~ dormirse.
asparagus n espárrago m.
aspect n aspecto m.
aspen n álamo temblón m.
aspersion n calumnia f.
asphalt n asfalto m.
asphyxia n (med) asfixia f.
asphyxiate vt asfixiar.
asphyxiation n asfixia f.
aspirant n aspirante m.
aspirate vt aspirar, pronunciar con aspiración; • n sonido aspirado m.
aspiration n aspiración f.
aspire vi aspirar, desear.
aspirin n aspirina f.
ass n asno m; she ~ burra f.
assail vt asaltar, atacar.
assailant n asaltador, agresor m.
assassin n asesino m.
assassinate vt asesinar.
assassination n asesinato m.
assault n asalto m; • vt acometer, asaltar.
assemblage n multitud f.
assemble vt reunir, convocar; • vi juntarse.
assembly n asamblea, junta f; congreso m.
assembly line n cadena de montaje f.
assent n asenso m; • vi asentir.
assert vt sostener, mantener; afirmar.
assertion n aserción f.
assertive adj perentorio.
assess vt valorar.
assessment n valoración f.
assessor n asesor m.
assets npl bienes mpl.
assiduous adj diligente, aplicado; ~ly adv diligentemente.
assign vt asignar.
assignation n cita f.
assignment n asignación f; tarea f.
assimilate vt asimilar.
assimilation n asimilación f.
assist vt asistir, ayudar, socorrer.
assistance n asistencia f; socorro m.
assistant n asistente, ayudante m.
associate vt asociar; • adj asociado; • n socio m.
association n asociación, sociedad f.
assonance n asonancia f.
assorted adj surtido.
assortment n surtido m.
assuage vt mitigar, suavizar.
assume vt asumir; suponer.
assumption n supuesto m; Assumption n Asunción f.
assurance n seguro m.
assure vt asegurar.
assuredly adv sin duda.
asterisk n asterisco m.
astern adv (mar) a popa.
asthma n asma f.
asthmatic adj asmático.
astonish vt pasmar, sorprender.
astonishing adj asombroso; ~ly adv asombrosamente.
astonishment n asombro m.

astound vt pasmar.
astraddle adv a horcajadas.
astray adv: to go ~ extraviarse; to lead ~ llevar por mal camino.
astride adv a horcajadas.
astringent adj astringente.
astrologer n astrólogo m.
astrological adj astrológico.
astrology n astrología f.
astronaut n astronauta m.
astronomer n astrónomo m.
astronomical adj astronómico.
astronomy n astronomía f.
astute adj astuto.
asylum n asilo, refugio m.
at prep a; en; ~ once en seguida; ~ all en absoluto; ~ all events en todo caso; ~ first al principio; ~ last por fin.
atheism n ateísmo m.
atheist n ateo m.
athlete n atleta m.
athletic adj atlético.
atlas n atlas m.
atmosphere n atmósfera f.
atmospheric adj atmosférico.
atom n átomo m.
atom bomb n bomba atómica f.
atomic adj atómico.
atone vt expiar.
atonement n expiación f.
atop adv encima.
atrocious adj atroz; ~ly adv atrozmente.
atrocity n atrocidad, enormidad f.
atrophy n (med) atrofia f.
attach vt adjuntar.
attaché n agregado m.
attachment n afecto m.
attack vt atacar; acometer; • n ataque m.
attacker n asaltante m.
attain vt conseguir, obtener.
attainable adj asequible.
attempt vt intentar; probar, experimentar; • n intento m, tentativa f.
attend vt servir; asistir; to ~ to ocuparse de; • vi prestar atención.
attendance n presencia f.
attendant n sirviente m.
attention n atención f; cuidado m.
attentive adj atento; cuidadoso; ~ly adv con atención.
attenuate vt atenuar, disminuir.
attest vt atestiguar.
attic n desván m; guardilla f.
attire n atavío m.
attitude n actitud, postura f.
attorney n abogado m.
attract vt atraer.
attraction n atracción f; atractivo m.
attractive adj atractivo.
attribute vt atribuir; • n atributo m.
attrition n agotamiento m.
auburn adj moreno, castaño.
auction n subasta f.
auctioneer n subastador, rematador m.
audacious adj audaz, temerario; ~ly adv atrevidamente.
audacity n audacia, osadía f.
audible adj perceptible al oído; ~ly adv de modo que se pueda oír.
audience n audiencia f; auditorio m.
audit n auditoría f; • vt auditar.
auditor n censor de cuentas m.
auditory adj auditivo.
augment vt aumentar, acrecentar; • vi crecer.
augmentation n aumentación f; aumento m.

August *n* agosto *m*.
august *adj* majestuoso.
aunt *n* tía *f*.
au pair *n* au pair *f*.
aura *n* aura *f*.
auspices *npl* auspicios *mpl*.
auspicious *adj* propicio; ~**ly** *adv* favorablemente.
austere *adj* austero, severo; ~**ly** *adv* austeramente.
austerity *n* austeridad *f*.
authentic *adj* auténtico; ~**ly** *adv* auténticamente.
authenticate, *vt* autenticar.
authenticity *n* autenticidad *f*.
author *n* autor *m*; escritor *m*.
authoress *n* autora; escritora *f*.
authoritarian *adj* autoritario.
authoritative *adj* autoritativo; ~**ly** *adv* autoritativamente, con autoridad.
authority *n* autoridad *f*.
authorization *n* autorización *f*.
authorize *vt* autorizar.
authorship *n* autoría *f*.
auto *n* carro, coche *m*.
autocrat *n* autócrata *m*.
autocratic *adj* autocrático.
autograph *n* autógrafo *m*.
automated *adj* automatizado.
automatic *adj* automático.
automaton *n* automata *m*.
autonomy *n* autonomía *f*.
autopsy *n* autopsia *f*.
autumn *n* otoño *m*.
autumnal *adj* otoñal.
auxiliary *adj* auxiliar, asistente.
avail *vt*: to ~ oneself of aprovecharse de; • *n*: to no ~ en vano.
available *adj* disponible.
avalanche *n* alud *m*.
avarice *n* avaricia *f*.
avaricious *adj* avaro.
avenge *vt* vengarse, castigar.
avenue *n* avenida *f*.
aver *vt* afirmar, declarar.
average *vt* tomar un término medio; • *n* término medio *m*.
aversion *n* aversión *f*, disgusto *m*.
avert *vt* desviar, apartar.
aviary *n* pajarera *f*.
avoid *vt* evitar, escapar, huir.
avoidable *adj* evitable.
await *vt* aguardar.
awake *vt* despertar; • *vi* despertarse; • *adj* despierto.
awakening *n* el despertar.
award *vt* otorgar; • *n* premio *m*; sentencia, decisión *f*.
aware *adj* consciente; vigilante.
awareness *n* conciencia *f*.
away *adv* ausente, fuera; ~! ¡fuera, quita de ahí, marcha! **far and** ~ de mucho, con mucho.
away game *n* partido de fuera *m*.
awe *n* miedo, temor *m*.
awe-inspiring, awesome *adj* imponente.
awful *adj* tremendo; horroroso; ~**ly** *adv* terriblemente.
awhile *adv* un rato, algún tiempo.
awkward *adj* torpe, rudo, poco diestro; ~**ly** *adv* groseramente, toscamente.
awkwardness *n* tosquedad, grosería, poca habilidad *f*.
awl *n* lesna *f*.
awning *n* (*mar*) toldo *m*.
awry *adv* oblicuamente, torcidamente, al través.
ax *n* hacha *f*; • *vt* despedir; cortar.
axiom *n* axioma *m*.
axis *n* eje *m*.
axle *n* eje *m*.
ay(e) *excl* sí.

B

baa *n* balido *m*; • *vi* balar.
babble *vi* charlar, parlotear; ~, **babbling** *n* charla, cháchara *f*; flujo de hablar *m*.
babbler *n* charlador, charlatán *m*.
babe, baby *n* niño pequeño, nene *m*; infante *m*.
baboon *n* cinocéfalo *m*, mono grande *m*.
babyhood *n* niñez *f*.
babyish *adj* niñero; pueril.
baby carriage *n* cochecito *m*.
baby linen *n* envoltura de una criatura recién nacida *f*.
bachelor *n* soltero *m*; bachiller *m*.
bachelorship *n* soltería *f*; bachillerato *m*.
back *n* dorso *m*; revés de la mano *m*; • *adv* atrás, detrás; **a few years** ~ hace algunos años; • *vt* sostener, apoyar, favorecer.
backbite *vt* hablar mal del que está ausente; difamar.
backbiter *n* detractor *m*.
backbone *n* hueso dorsal, espinazo *m*.
backdate *vt* fechar con atraso.
backdoor *n* puerta trasera *f*.
backer *n* partidario *m*.
backgammon *n* juego de chaquete *o* tablas *m*.
background *n* fondo *m*.
backlash *n* reacción *f*.
backlog *n* trabajo acumulado *m*.
back number *n* número atrasado de algún periódico *m*.
backpack *n* mochila *f*.
back payment *n* paga atrasada *f*.
backside *n* trasero *m*.
back-up lights *npl* (*auto*) luces de marcha atrás *fpl*.
backward *adj* tardo, lento; • *adv* hacia atrás.
bacon *n* tocino *m*.
bad *adj* mal, malo; perverso; infeliz; dañoso; indispuesto; ~**ly** *adv* malamente.
badge *n* señal *f*; símbolo *m*; divisa *f*.
badger *n* tejón *m*; • *vt* fatigar; cansar, atormentar.
badminton *n* bádminton *m*.
badness *n* maldad, mala calidad *f*.
baffle *vt* confundir, hundir; acosar.
bag *n* saco *m*; bolsa *f*.
baggage *n* bagaje, equipaje *m*.
bagpipe *n* gaita *f*.
bail *n* fianza, caución (juratoria) *f*; fiador *m*; • *vt* caucionar, fiar.
bailiff *n* alguacil *m*; mayordomo *m*.
bait *vt* cebar; atraer; • *n* cebo *m*; anzuelo *m*.
baize *n* bayeta *f*.
bake *vt* cocer en horno.
bakery *n* panadería *f*.
baker *n* hornero, panadero *m*; ~**'s dozen** trece piezas.
baking *n* amasar *m*.
baking powder *n* levadura *f*.
balance *n* balanza *f*; equilibrio *m*; saldo de una cuenta *m*; **to lose one's** ~ caerse, dar en tierra; • *vt* pesar en balanza; contrapesar; saldar; considerar, examinar.
balance sheet *n* balance *m*.
balcony *n* balcón *m*.
bald *adj* calvo.
baldness *n* calvicie *f*.
bale *n* bala *f*; • *vt* embalar; tirar el agua del bote.
baleful *adj* triste, funesto; ~**ly** *adv* tristemente; míseramente.
ball *n* bola *f*; pelota *f*; baile *m*.
ballad *n* balada *f*.
ballast *n* lastre *m* • *vt* lastrar.
ballerina *n* bailarina *f*.
ballet *n* ballet *m*.
ballistic *adj* balístico.
balloon *n* globo *m*.
ballot *n* bolilla para votar *f*; escrutinio *m*; • *vi* votar con balotas.

ballpoint (pen) *n* bolígrafo *m*.
ballroom *n* salón de baile *m*.
balm, balsam *n* bálsamo *m*; ● *vt* untar con bálsamo.
balmy *adj* balsámico; fragante.
balustrade *n* balaustrada *f*.
bamboo *n* mimbre *m*.
bamboozle *vt* (*fam*) engañar.
ban *n* prohibición *f*; ● *vt* prohibir.
banal *adj* vulgar.
banana *n* plátano *m*.
band *n* faja *f*; cuadrilla *f*; banda (de soldados) *f*; orquesta *f*.
bandage *n* venda *f*, vendaje *m*; ● *vt* vendar.
bandaid *n* tirita *f*.
bandit *n* bandido *m*.
bandstand *n* quiosco *m*.
bandy *vt* pelotear; discutir.
bandy-legged *adj* patizambo.
bang *n* golpe *m*; ● *vt* golpear; cerrar con violencia.
bangle *n* brazalete *m*.
bangs *npl* fleguillo *m*.
banish *vt* desterrar, echar fuera, proscribir, expatriar.
banishment *n* destierro *m*.
banister(s) *n(pl)* pasamanos *m*.
banjo *n* banjo *m*.
bank *n* orilla (de río) *f*; montón de tierra *m*; banco *m*; dique *m*; escollo *m*; ● *vt* poner dinero en un banco; **to ~ on** contar con.
bank account *n* cuenta de banco *f*.
bank card *n* tarjeta bancaria *f*.
banker *n* banquero *m*.
banking *n* banca *f*.
banknote *n* billete de banco *m*.
bankrupt *adj* insolvente; ● *n* fallido, quebrado *m*.
bankruptcy *n* bancarrota, quiebra *f*.
bank statement *n* detalle de cuenta *m*.
banner *n* bandera *f*; estandarte *m*.
banquet *n* banquete *m*.
baptism *n* bautismo *m*.
baptismal *adj* bautismal.
baptistery *n* bautisterio *m*.
baptize *vt* bautizar.
bar *n* bar *m*; barra *f*; tranca *f*; obstáculo *m*; (*law*) estrados *mpl*; ● *vt* impedir; prohibir; excluir.
barbarian *n* hombre bárbaro *m*; ● *adj* bárbaro, cruel.
barbaric *adj* bárbaro.
barbarism *n* (*gr*) barbarismo *m*; crueldad *f*.
barbarity *n* barbaridad, inhumanidad *f*.
barbarous *adj* bárbaro, cruel.
barbecue *n* barbacoa *f*.
barber *n* peluquero *m*.
bar code *n* código de barras *m*.
bard *n* bardo *m*; poeta *m*.
bare *adj* desnudo, descubierto; simple; puro; ● *vt* desnudar, descubrir.
barefaced *adj* desvergonzado, impudente.
barefoot(ed) *adj* descalzo, sin zapatos.
bareheaded *adj* descubierto.
barelegged *adj* con las piernas desnudas.
barely *adv* apenas, solamente.
bareness *n* desnudez *f*.
bargain *n* ganga *f*; contrato, pacto *m*; ● *vi* pactar; negociar; **to ~ for** esperar.
barge *n* barcaza *f*.
baritone *n* (*mus*) baritono *m*.
bark *n* corteza *f*; ladrido *m* (del perro); ● *vi* ladrar.
barley *n* cebada *f*.
barmaid *n* moza de taberna *f*.
barman *n* barman *m*.
barn *n* granero, pajar *m*.
barnacles *npl* percebe *m*.
barometer *n* barómetro *m*.
baron *n* barón *m*.

baroness *n* baronesa *f*.
baronial *adj* de barón.
barracks *npl* cuartel *m*.
barrage *n* descarga *f*; (*fig*) lluvia *f*.
barrel *n* barril *m*; cañón de escopeta *m*.
barrelled *adj* (of fire-arms) con . . . cañones.
barrel organ *n* organillo de cilindro *m*.
barren *adj* estéril, infructuoso.
barricade *n* barricada *f*; estacada *f*; barrera *f*; ● *vt* cerrar con barreras, empalizar.
barrier *n* barrera *f*; obstáculo *m*.
barring *adv* excepto, fuera de.
barrow *n* carretilla *f*.
bartender *n* barman *m*.
barter *vi* baratar; ● *vt* cambiar, trocar.
base *n* fondo *m*; base *f*; basa *f*; pedestal *m*; contrabajo *m*; ● *vt* apoyar; ● *adj* bajo, vil.
baseball *n* béisbol *m*.
baseless *adj* sin fondo *o* base.
basement *n* sótano *m*.
baseness *n* bajeza, vileza *f*.
bash *vt* golpear.
bashful *adj* vergonzoso, modesto, tímido; **~ly** *adv* vergonzosamente.
basic *adj* básico; **~ally** *adv* básicamente.
basilisk *n* basilisco *m*.
basin *n* jofaina, bacía *f*.
basis *n* base *f*; fundamento *m*.
bask *vi* ponerse a tomar el sol.
basket *n* cesta, canasta *f*.
basketball *n* baloncesto *m*.
bass *n* (*mus*) contrabajo *m*.
bassoon *n* bajón *m*.
bass viol *n* viola *f*.
bass voice *n* bajo cantante *m*.
bastard *n*, *adj* bastardo *m*.
bastardy *n* bastardía *f*.
baste *vt* pringar la carne en el asador; hilvanar.
basting *n* hilván *m*; apaleamiento *m*; paliza *f*.
bastion *n* (*mil*) bastión *m*.
bat *n* murciélago *m*.
batch *n* serie *f*.
bath *n* baño *m*.
bathe *vt* (*vi*) bañar(se).
bathing suit *n* traje de baño *m*.
bathos *n* estilo bajo en la poesía *m*.
bathroom *n* (cuarto de) baño *m*.
baths *npl* piscina *f*.
bathtub *n* baño *m* (la cuba).
baton *n* batuta *f*.
battalion *n* (*mil*) batallón *m*.
batter *vt* apalear; batir, cañonear; ● *n* batido *m*.
battering ram *n* (*mil*) ariete *m*.
battery *n* batería *f*.
battle *n* combate *m*; batalla *f*; ● *vi* batallar, combatir.
battle array *n* orden de batalle *f*.
battlefield *n* campo de guerra *m*.
battlement *n* muralla almenada *f*.
battleship *n* acorazado *m*.
bawdy *adj* indecente.
bawl *vi* gritar, vocear.
bay *n* bahía *f*; laurel, lauro *m*; ● *vi* balar; ● *adj* bayo.
bayonet *n* bayoneta *f*.
bay window *n* ventana salediza *f*.
bazaar *n* bazar *m*.
be *vi* ser; estar.
beach *n* playa, orilla *f*.
beacon *n* almenara *f*.
bead *n* cuenta *f*; **~s** *npl* rosario *m*.
beagle *n* sabueso *m*.
beak *n* pico *m*.
beaker *n* taza con pico *f*.

beam *n* rayo de luz *m*; travesaño *m*; ● *vi* brillar.
bean *n* haba *f*; **French ~** frijol *m*.
beansprouts *npl* brotes de soja *mpl*.
bear *vt* llevar alguna cosa como carga; sostener; soportar; producir; parir; ● *vi* sufrir (algún dolor).
bear *n* oso *m*; **she ~** osa *f*.
bearable *adj* soportable.
beard *n* barba *f*.
bearded *adj* barbado.
bearer *n* portador *m*; árbol fructífero *m*.
bearing *n* relación *f*; modo de portarse en lo exterior *m*.
beast *n* bestia *f*; hombre brutal *m*; **~ of burden** acémila *f*.
beastliness *n* bestialidad, brutalidad *f*.
beastly *adj* bestial, brutal; ● *adv* brutalmente.
beat *vt* golpear; tocar (un tambor); ● *vi* pulsar, palpitar; ● *n* golpe *m*; pulsación *f*.
beatific *adj* beatífico.
beatify *vt* beatificar, santificar.
beating *n* paliza, zurra *f*; pulsación *f*.
beatitude *n* beatitud, felicidad *f*.
beautiful *adj* hermoso, bello; **~ly** *adv* con belleza o perfección.
beautify *vt* hermosear; embellecer; adornar.
beauty *n* hermosura, belleza *f*; **~ salon** *n* salón de belleza *m*; **~ spot** *n* lunar *m*.
beaver *n* castor *m*.
because *conj* porque, a causa de.
beckon *vi* hacer seña con la cabeza o la mano.
become *vt* convenir; estar bien; ● *vi* hacerse, convertirse, venir a parar.
becoming *adj* decente, conveniente.
bed *n* cama *f*.
bedclothes *npl* cobertores *npl*, mantas o colchas *fpl*.
bedding *n* ropa de cama *f*.
bedecked *adj* adornado.
bedlam *n* manicomio *m*.
bed-post *n* pilar de cama *m*.
bedridden *adj* postrado en cama (sea por vejez o enfermedad).
bedroom *n* dormitorio *m*.
bedspread *n* colcha *f*.
bedtime *n* hora de irse a la cama *f*.
bee *n* abeja *f*.
beech *n* haya *f*.
beef *n* carne de vaca *f*.
beefburger *n* hamburguesa *f*.
beefsteak *n* bistec *m*.
beehive *n* colmena *f*.
beeline *n* línea recta *f*.
beer *n* cerveza *f*.
beeswax *n* cera *f*.
beet *n* remolacha *f*.
beetle *n* escarabajo *m*.
befall *vi* suceder, acontecer, sobrevenir.
befit *vt* convenir, acomodarse a.
before *adv*, *prep* antes de; delante, enfrente; ante.
beforehand *adv* de antemano, anticipadamente.
befriend *vt* proteger, amparar.
beg *vt* mendigar, rogar; suplicar; suponer; ● *vi* vivir de limosna.
beget *vt* engendrar.
beggar *n* mendigo *m*.
begin *vt*, *vi* comenzar, empezar.
beginner *n* principiante *m*; novicio *m*.
beginning *n* principio, origen *m*.
begrudge *vt* envidiar.
behalf *n* favor, patrocinio *m*; consideración *f*.
behave *vi* comportarse, portarse bien o mal.
behavior *n* conducta *f*; modo de portarse *m*.
behead *vt* decapitar, cortar la cabeza.
behind *prep* detrás; atrás; ● *adv* atrasadamente; fuera de la vista.
behold *vt* ver, contemplar, observar.

behove *vi* importar, ser útil o necesario.
beige *adj* color beige.
being *n* existencia *f*; estado *m*; ser *m*; persona (que existe) *f*.
belated *adj* trasnochado.
belch *vi* eructar, vomitar; ● *n* eructo *m*.
belfry *n* campanario *m*.
belie *vt* desmentir, calumniar.
belief *n* fe, creencia *f*; opinión *f*; credo *m*.
believable *adj* creible.
believe *vt* creer; ● *vi* pensar, imaginar.
believer *n* creyente, fiel, cristiano *m*.
belittle *vt* minimizar.
bell *n* campana *f*.
bellicose *adj* belicoso.
belligerent *adj* beligerante.
bellow *vi* bramar; rugir; vociferar; ● *n* bramido *m*.
bellows *npl* fuelle *m*.
belly *n* vientre *m*; panza *f*.
bellyful *n* panzada *f*; hartura *f*.
belong *vi* pertenecer.
belongings *npl* pertenencias *fpl*.
beloved *adj* querido, amado.
below *adv*, *prep* debajo, inferior; abajo.
belt *n* cinturón, cinto *m*.
beltway *n* carretera de circunvalación *f*.
bemoan *vt* deplorar, lamentar.
bemused *adj* confundido.
bench *n* banco *m*.
bend *vt* encorvar, inclinar, plegar; hacer una reverencia; ● *vi* encorvarse, inclinarse; ● *n* curva *f*.
beneath *adv*, *prep* debajo, abajo.
benediction *n* bendición *f*.
benefactor *n* bienhechor *m*.
benefice *n* beneficio *m*; beneficio eclesiástico *m*.
beneficent *adj* benéfico.
beneficial *adj* beneficioso, provechoso, útil.
beneficiary *n* beneficiario *m*.
benefit *n* beneficio *m*; utilidad *f*; provecho *m*; ● *vt* beneficiar; ● *vi* utilizarse; prevalerse.
benefit night *n* representación dramática al beneficio de un actor o de una actriz *f*.
benevolence *n* benevolencia *f*; donativo gratuito *m*.
benevolent *adj* benévolo.
benign *adj* benigno; afable; liberal.
bent *n* inclinación *f*.
benzine *n* (*chem*) benzina *f*.
bequeath *vt* legar en testamento.
bequest *n* legado *m*.
bereave *vt* privar.
bereavement *n* pérdida *f*.
beret *n* boina *f*.
berm *n* arcén *m*.
berry *n* baya *f*.
berserk *adj* loco.
berth *n* (*mar*) alojamiento de un navío *m*.
beseech *vt* suplicar, implorar, conjurar, rogar.
beset *vt* acosar.
beside(s) *prep* al lado de; excepto; sobre; fuera de; ● *adv* por otra parte, aun.
besiege *vt* sitiar, bloquear.
best *adj* mejor; ● *adv* (lo) mejor; ● *n* lo mejor *m*.
bestial *adj* bestial, brutal; **~ly** *adv* bestialmente.
bestiality *n* bestialidad, brutalidad *f*.
bestow *vt* dar, conferir; otorgar.
bestseller *n* bestseller *m*.
bet *n* apuesta *f*; ● *vt* apostar.
betray *vt* traicionar; divulgar algún secreto.
betrayal *n* traición *f*.
betroth *vt* contraer esponsales.
betrothal *n* esponsales *mpl*.
better *adj*, *adv* mejor; mejor, más bien; **so much the ~** tanto mejor; ● *vt* mejorar, reformar.

betting n juego m.
between prep entre, en medio de.
bevel n cartabón m.
beverage n bebida f; trago m.
bevy n bandada (de aves) f.
beware vi guardarse.
bewilder vt descaminar; pasmar.
bewilderment n perplejidad f.
bewitch vt encantar, hechizar.
beyond prep más allá, más adelante, fuera de.
bias n propensión, inclinación f; sesgo m; prejuicio m.
bib n babador m.
Bible n Biblia f.
biblical adj bíblico.
bibliography n bibliografía f.
bicarbonate of soda n bicarbonato de soda m.
bicker vi escaramucear, reñir, disputar.
bicycle n bicicleta f.
bid vt mandar, ordenar; ofrecer; ● n oferta f; tentativa f.
bidding n orden f; mandato m; ofrecimiento m.
bide vt sufrir, aguantar.
biennial adj bienal.
bifocals npl anteojos bifocales mpl.
bifurcated adj dividido en dos puntas o dientes.
big adj grande, lleno; inflado.
bigamist n bígamo m.
bigamy n bigamia f.
big dipper n montaña rusa f.
bigheaded adj engreído.
bigness n grandeza f; tamaño bulto m.
bigot n fanático m.
bigoted adj fanático.
bike n bici f.
bikini n bikini m.
bilberry n arándano m.
bile n bilis f.
bilingual adj bilingüe.
bilious adj bilioso.
bill n pico de ave m; billete m; cuenta f.
billboard n cartelera f.
billet n alojamiento m.
billfold n cartera f.
billiards npl billar m.
billiard-table n mesa de billar f.
billion n mil millones m.
billy n porra f.
bin n cubo de la basura m.
bind vt atar; unir; encuadernar.
binder n encuadernador m.
binding n venda, faja f.
binge n juerga f.
bingo n bingo m.
biochemistry n bioquímica f.
binoculars npl prismáticos mpl.
biographer n biógrafo m.
biographical adj biográfico.
biography n biografía f.
biological adj biológico.
biology n biología f.
biped n bípede m.
birch n abedul m.
bird n ave f; pájaro m.
bird's-eye view n vista de pájaro f.
bird-watcher n ornitólogo m.
birth n nacimiento m; origen m; parto m.
birth certificate n partida de nacimiento f.
birth control n control de natalidad m.
birthday n cumpleaños m invar.
birthplace n lugar de nacimiento m.
birthright n derechos de nacimiento mpl; primogenitura f.
biscuit n bizcocho m.
bisect vt dividir en dos partes.

bishop n obispo m.
bison n bisonte m.
bit n bocado m; pedacito m.
bitch n perra f; (fig) zorra f.
bite vt morder; picar; ~ the dust (fam) morder la tierra, morir; ● n mordedura f.
bitter adj amargo, áspero; mordaz, satírico; penoso; ~ly adv amargamente; con pena; severamente.
bitterness n amargor m; rencor m; pena f; dolor m.
bitumen n betún m.
bizarre adj raro, extravagante.
blab vi chismear.
black adj negro, oscuro; funesto; ● n color negro m.
blackberry n zarzamora f.
blackbird n mirlo m.
blackboard n pizarra f.
blacken vt teñir de negro; ennegrecer.
black ice n hielo invisible m.
blackjack n veintiuna f.
blackleg n bribón m.
blacklist n lista negra f.
blackmail n chantaje m; ● vt chantajear.
black market n estraperlo m.
blackness n negrura f.
black pudding n morcilla f.
black sheep n oveja sarnosa f.
blacksmith n herrero m.
blackthorn n endrino m.
bladder n vejiga f.
blade n hoja f; filo m.
blame vt culpar; ● n culpa f.
blameless adj inocente, irreprensible, puro; ~ly adv inocentemente.
blanch vt blanquear.
bland adj blando, suave, dulce, apacible.
blank adj blanco; pálido; ● n blanco m.
blank check n cheque en blanco m.
blanket n cubierta de cama f.
blare vi resonar.
blasé adj indiferente.
blaspheme vt blasfemar, jurar, decir blasfemias.
blasphemous adj blasfematorio.
blasphemy n blasfemia f.
blast n soplo de aire m; carga explosiva f; ● vt volar.
blast-off n lanzamiento m.
blatant adj obvio.
blaze n llama f; ● vi encenderse en llamas; brillar, replandecer.
bleach vt blanquear al sol; ● vi blanquear; ● n lejía f.
bleached adj teñido de rubio; descolorado.
bleachers npl gradas fpl.
bleak adj pálido, descolorido; frío, helado.
bleakness n frialdad f; palidez f.
bleary(-eyed) adj lagañoso.
bleat n balido m; ● vi balar.
bleed vi, vt sangrar.
bleeding n sangría f.
bleeper n busca m.
blemish vt manchar, ensuciar; infamar; ● n tacha f; deshonra, infamia f.
blend vt mezclar.
bless vt bendecir.
blessing n bendición f; favores del cielo mpl.
blight vt arruinar.
blind adj ciego; ~ alley n callejón sin salida m; ● vt cegar; deslumbrar; ● n velo m; (Venetian ~) persiana f.
blinders npl anteojeras fpl.
blindfold vt vendar los ojos; ~ed adj con los ojos vendados.
blindly adv ciegamente, a ciegas.
blindness n ceguedad f.
blind side n el flaco de alguna persona f.
blind spot n mácula f.

blink *vi* parpadear.
blinkers *npl* anteojeras *fpl*.
bliss *n* felicidad (eterna) *f*.
blissful *adj* feliz en sumo grado; beato, bienaventurado; ~ ly *adv* felizmente.
blissfulness *n* suprema felicidad *f*.
blister *n* ampolla *f*; ● *vi* ampollarse.
blitz *n* bombardeo aéreo *m*.
blizzard *n* huracán *m*.
bloated *adj* hinchado.
blob *n* gota *f*.
bloc *n* bloque *m*.
block *n* bloque *m*; obstáculo *m*; manzana *f*; ~ (**up**) *vt* bloquear.
blockade *n* bloqueo *m*; ● *vt* bloquear.
blockage *n* obstrucción *f*.
blockbuster *n* éxito de público *m*.
blockhead *n* bruto, necio, zopenco *m*.
blond *adj* rubio; ● *n* rubio *m*.
blood *n* sangre *f*.
blood donor *n* donante de sangre *m*.
blood group *n* grupo sanguíneo *m*.
bloodhound *n* sabueso *m*.
bloodily *adv* cruelmente, inhumanamente.
bloodiness *n* (*fig*) crueldad *f*.
bloodless *adj* exangüe; sin efusión de sangre.
blood poisoning *n* envenenamiento *m*.
blood pressure *n* presión de sangre *f*.
bloodshed *n* efusión de sangre *f*; matanza *f*.
bloodshot *adj* ensangrentado.
bloodstream *n* corriente sanguínea *f*.
bloodsucker *n* sanguijuela *f*; (*fig*) desollador *m*.
blood test *n* analisis de sangre *m*.
bloodthirsty *adj* sanguinario.
blood transfusion *n* transfusión de sangre *f*.
blood vessel *n* vena *f*; canal de la sangre *m*.
bloody *adj* sangriento, ensangrentado; cruel; ~ minded *adj* sanguinario.
bloom *n* flor *f*; (*also fig*); ● *vi* florecer.
blossom *n* flor *f*.
blot *vt* manchar (lo escrito); cancelar; denigrar; ● *n* mancha *f*.
blotchy *adj* muy manchado.
blotting pad *n* papelería *f*.
blotting paper *n* papel de secar *m*.
blouse *n* blusa *f*.
blow *vi* soplar; sonar; ● *vt* soplar; inflar; **to ~ up** volar(se) por medio de pólvora; ● *n* golpe *m*.
blowout *n* pinchazo *m*.
blowpipe *n* soplete *m*.
blubber *n* grasa de ballena *f*; ● *vi* lloriquear.
bludgeon *n* cachiporra *f*; palocorto *m*.
blue *adj* azul.
bluebell *n* campanilla *f*.
bluebottle *n* (*bot*) campanilla *f*; moscarda *f*.
blueness *n* color azul *m*.
blueprint *n* (*fig*) anteproyecto *m*.
bluff *n* farol *m*; ● *vt* farolear.
bluish *adj* azulado.
blunder *n* desatino *m*; error craso *m*; ● *vi* meter la pata.
blunt *adj* obtuso; grosero; ● *vt* embotar.
bluntly *adv* sin artificio; claramente; obtusamente.
bluntness *n* embotadura, grosería *f*.
blur *n* mancha *f*; ● *vt* manchar.
blurt out *vt* hablar a tontas y a locas.
blush *n* rubor *m*; sonrojo *m*; ● *vi* ponerse colorado (de vergüenza).
blustery *adj* tempestuoso.
boa *n* boa *f* (serpiente).
boar *n* verraco *m*; **wild ~** jabalí *m*.
board *n* tabla *f*; mesa *f*; consejo *m*; ● *vt* embarcarse en; subir a.
boarder *n* pensionista *m*.

boarding card *n* tarjeta de embarque *f*.
boarding house *n* casa de pupilos *f*; casa de huéspedes *f*.
boarding school *n* casa pensión *f*.
boast *vi* jactarse; ● *n* jactancia *f*; ostentación *f*.
boastful *adj* jactancioso.
boat *n* barco *m*; bote *m*; barca *f*.
boating *n* barcaje *m*; paseo en barquilla *m*; regata *f*.
bobsleigh *n* bob *m*.
bode *vt* presagiar, pronosticar.
bodice *n* corsé *m*.
bodily *adj, adv* corpóreo; corporalmente.
body *n* cuerpo *m*; individuo *m*; gremio *m*; **any ~** cualquier; **every ~** cada uno.
body-building *n* culturismo *m*.
bodyguard *n* guardaespaldas *m*.
bodywork *n* (*auto*) carrocería *f*.
bog *n* pantano *m*.
boggy *adj* pantanoso, palustre.
bogus *adj* postizo.
boil *vi* hervir; bullir; hervirle a uno la sangre; ● *vt* cocer; ● *n* furúnculo *m*.
boiled egg *n* huevo cocido *m*.
boiled potatoes *npl* patatas hervidas *fpl*.
boiler *n* marmita *f*; caldero *m*.
boiling point *n* punto de ebullición *m*.
boisterous *adj* borrascoso, tempestuoso; violento; ~ly *adv* tumultuosamente, furiosamente.
bold *adj* ardiente, valiente; audaz; temerario; impudente; ~ly *adv* descaradamente.
boldness *n* intrepidez *f*; valentía *f*; osadía *f*.
bolster *n* travesero *m*; cabezal *m*; ● *vt* reforzar.
bolt *n* cerrojo *m*; ● *vt* cerrar con cerrojo.
bomb *n* bomba *f*; **~ disposal** desmontaje de explosivos *m*.
bombard *vt* bombardear.
bombardier *n* bombardero *m*.
bombardment *n* bombardeo *m*.
bombshell *n* (*fig*) bomba *f*.
bond *n* ligadura *f*; vínculo *m*; vale *m*; obligación *f*.
bondage *n* esclavitud, servidumbre *f*.
bond holder *n* tenedor de unos vales *m*.
bone *n* hueso *m*; ● *vt* desosar.
boneless *adj* sin huesos; desosado.
bonfire *n* hoguera *f*.
bonnet *n* gorra *f*; bonete *m*.
bonny *adj* bonito.
bonus *n* cuota, prima *f*.
bony *adj* osudo.
boo *vt* abuchear.
booby trap *n* trampa explosiva *f*.
book *n* libro *m*; **to bring to ~** *vt* pedir cuentas a alguien.
bookbinder *n* encuadernador de libros *m*.
bookcase *n* armario para libros *m*.
bookkeeper *n* tenedor de libros *m*.
bookkeeping *n* teneduría de libros *f*.
bookmaking *n* apuesta en las carreras de caballos *f*.
bookmarker *n* registro de un libro *m*.
bookseller *n* librero *m*.
bookstore *n* librería *f*.
bookworm *n* polilla que roe los libros *f*; hombre del todo aficionado a los libros *m*.
boom *n* trueno *m*; boom *m*; ● *vi* retumbar.
boon *n* presente, regalo *m*; favor *m*.
boor *n* patán, villano *m*.
boorish *adj* rústico, agreste.
boost *n* estímulo *m*; ● *vt* estimular.
booster *n* reinyección *f*.
boot *n* ganancia *f*; provecho *m*; bota *f*; **to ~** *adv* además.
booth *n* barraca, cabaña *f*.
booty *n* botín *m*; presa *f*; saqueo *m*.
booze *vi* emborracharse; ● *n* bebida *f*.
border *n* orilla *f*; borde *m*; margen *f*; frontera *f*; ● *vt* lindar con.

borderline *n* frontera *f*.
bore *vt* taladrar; barrenar; fastidiar; • *n* taladro *m*; calibre *m*; hombre enfadoso *m*.
boredom *n* aburrimiento *m*.
boring *adj* aburrido.
born *adj* nacido; destinado.
borrow *vt* pedir prestado.
borrower *n* prestamista *m*.
bosom *n* seno, pecho *m*.
bosom friend *n* amigo íntimo *m*.
boss *n* jefe *m*; patrón *m*.
botanic(al) *adj* botánico.
botanist *n* botánico *m*.
botany *n* botánica *f*.
botch *vt* chapuzar.
both *adj* ambos, entrambos; ambas, entrambas; • *conj* tanto como.
bother *vt* preocupar; fastidiar; • *n* molestia *f*.
bottle *n* botella *f*; • *vt* embotellar.
bottleneck *n* embotellamiento *m*.
bottle-opener *n* abrebotellas *m invar*.
bottom *n* fondo *m*; fundamento *m*; • *adj* más bajo; último.
bottomless *adj* insondable; excesivo; impenetrable.
bough *n* brazo del árbol *m*; ramo *m*.
boulder *n* canto rodado *m*.
bounce *vi* rebotar; ser rechazado; • *n* rebote *m*.
bound *n* límite *m*; salto *m*; repercusión *f*; • *vi* resaltar; • *adj* destinado.
boundary *n* límite *m*; frontera *f*.
boundless *adj* ilimitado, infinito.
bounteous, bountiful *adj* liberal, generoso, bienhechor.
bounty *n* liberalidad, bondad *f*.
bouquet *n* ramillete de flores *m*.
bourgeois *adj* burgués.
bout *n* ataque *m*; encuentro *m*.
bovine *adj* bovino.
bow *vt* encorvar, doblar; • *vi* encorvarse; hacer una reverencia; • *n* reverencia, inclinación *f*.
bow *n* arco *m*; arco de violín; corbata *f*; nudo *m*.
bowels *npl* intestinos *mpl*; entrañas *fpl*.
bowl *n* taza; bola *f*; • *vi* jugar a las bochas.
bowling *n* bolos *mpl*.
bowling alley *n* bolera *f*.
bowling-green *n* bolingrín *m*.
bowstring *n* cuerda del arco *f*.
bow tie *n* pajarita *f*.
box *n* caja, cajita *f*; palco de teatro *m*; ~ **on the ear** bofetada *f*; • *vt* meter alguna cosa en una caja; • *vi* boxear.
boxer *n* boxeador *m*.
boxing *n* boxeo *m*.
boxing gloves *npl* guantes de boxeo *mpl*.
boxing ring *n* cuadrilátero *m*.
box office *n* taquilla *f*.
box-seat *n* pescante *m*.
boy *n* muchacho *m*; niño *m*.
boycott *vt* boicotear; • *n* boicot *m*.
boyfriend *n* novio *m*.
boyish *adj* pueril; frívolo.
bra *n* sujetador *m*.
brace *n* abrazadera *f*; corrector *m*.
bracelet *n* brazalete *m*.
bracing *adj* vigorizante.
bracken *n* (*bot*) helecho *m*.
bracket *n* puntal *m*; paréntesis *m*; corchete *m*; • **to** ~ **with** *vt* unir, ligar.
bracing *adj* vigorizante.
brag *n* jactancia *f*; • *vi* jactarse, fanfarronear.
braid *n* trenza *f*; • *vt* trenzar.
brain *n* cerebro *m*; seso, juicio *m*; • *vt* descerebrar, matar a uno.
brainchild *n* parto del ingenio *m*.
brainwash *vt* lavar el cerebro.

brainwave *n* idea luminosa *f*.
brainy *adj* inteligente.
brainless *adj* tonto, insensato.
brake *n* freno *m*; • *vt*, *vi* frenar.
brake fluid *n* líquido de frenos *m*.
brake light *n* luz de frenado *f*.
bramble *n* zarza, espina *f*.
bran *n* salvado *m*.
branch *n* ramo *m*; rama *f*; • *vt* (*vi*) ramificar(se).
branch line *n* (*rail*) empalme, ramal *m*.
brand *n* marca *f*; hierro *m*; • *vt* marcar con un hierro ardiendo.
brandish *vt* blandir, ondear.
brand-new *adj* flamante.
brandy *n* coñac *m*.
brash *adj* tosco; descarado.
brass *n* bronce *m*.
brassière *n* sujetador *m*.
brat *n* crío *m*.
bravado *n* baladronada *f*.
brave *adj* bravo, valiente, atrevido; • *vt* bravear; • *n* bravo *m*; ~**ly** *adv* bravamente.
bravery *n* valor *m*; magnificencia *f*; bravata *f*.
brawl *n* pelea, camorra *f*; • *vi* pelearse.
brawn *n* pulpa *f*; carne de verraco *f*.
bray *vi* rebuznar; • *n* rebuzno (del asno) *m*.
braze *vt* soldar con latón; broncear.
brazen *adj* de bronce; desvergonzado; impudente; • *vi* hacerse descarado.
brazier *n* brasero *m*.
breach *n* rotura *f*; brecha *f*; violación *f*.
bread *n* pan *m*; (*fig*) sustento *m*; **brown** ~ pan moreno *m*.
breadbox *n* panera *f*.
breadcrumbs *npl* migajas *fpl*.
breadth *n* anchura *f*.
breadwinner *n* sostén de la familia *m*.
break *vt* romper; quebrantar; violar; arruinar; interrumpir; • *vi* romperse; ~ **into** forzar; **to** ~ **out** abrirse salida; • *n* rotura, abertura *f*; interrupción *f*; ~ **of day** despuntar del día *m*, aurora *f*.
breakage *n* rotura *f*.
breakdown *n* avería *f*; descalabro *m*.
breakfast *n* desayuno *m*; • *vi* desayunar.
breaking *n* rompimiento *m*; principio de las vacaciones en las escuelas *m*; fractura *f*.
breakthrough *n* avance *m*.
breakwater *n* muelle *m*.
breast *n* pecho, seno *m*; tetas *fpl*; corazón *m*.
breastbone *n* esternón *m*.
breastplate *n* peto *m*; pectoral *m*; coraza *f*.
breaststroke *n* braza de pecho *f*.
breath *n* aliento *m*, respiración *f*; soplo de aire *m*.
breathe *vt*, *vi* respirar; exhalar.
breathing *n* respiración *f*; aliento *m*.
breathing space *n* descanso, reposo *m*.
breathless *adj* falto de aliento; desalentado.
breathtaking *adj* pasmoso.
breed *n* casta, raza *f*; • *vt* procrear, engendrar; producir; educar; • *vi* multiplicarse.
breeder *n* criador *m*.
breeding *n* crianza *f*; buena educación *f*.
breeze *n* brisa *f*.
breezy *adj* refrescado con brisas.
brethren *npl* (*de* **brother**) hermanos *mpl* (en estilo grave).
breviary *n* breviario *m*.
brevity *n* brevedad, concisión *f*.
brew *vt* hacer; tramar; mezclar; • *vi* hacerse; tramarse; • *n* brebaje *m*.
brewer *n* cervecero *m*.
brewery *n* cervecería *f*.
briar, brier *n* zarza *f*, espino *m*.

bribe n cohecho, soborno m; • vt cohechar, corromper, sobornar.
bribery n cohecho, soborno m.
bric-a-brac n baratijas fpl.
brick n ladrillo m; • vt enladrillar.
bricklayer n albañil m.
bridal adj nupcial.
bride n novia f.
bridegroom n novio m.
bridesmaid n madrina de boda f.
bridge n puente m/f; caballete de la nariz m; puente de violín m; to ~ (over) vt construir un puente.
bridle n brida f freno m; • vt embridar; reprimir, refrenar.
brief adj breve, conciso, sucinto; • n compendio m; breve m.
briefcase n cartera f.
briefly adv brevemente, en pocas palabras.
brier n = **briar**
brigade n (mil) brigada f.
brigadier n (mil) general de brigada m.
brigand n bandido m.
bright adj claro, luciente, brillante; ~ly adv espléndidamente.
brighten vt pulir, dar lustre; ilustrar; • vi aclararse.
brightness n esplendor m, brillantez f; agudeza f; claridad f.
brilliance n brillo m.
brilliant adj brilliante; ~ly adv espléndidamente.
brim n borde extremo m; orilla f.
brimful(l) adj lleno hasta el borde.
bring vt llevar, traer; conducir; inducir, persuadir; to ~ about efectuar; to ~ forth producir; parir; to ~ up educar.
brink n orilla f; margen m/f, borde m.
brisk adj vivo, alegre, jovial; fresco.
brisket n pecho (de un animal) m.
briskly adv vigorosamente; alegremente; vivamente.
bristle n cerda, seta f; • vi erizarse.
bristly adj cerdoso, lleno de cerdas.
brittle adj quebradizo, frágil.
broach vt comenzar a hablar de.
broad adj ancho.
broadbeans npl haba gruesa f.
broadcast n emisión f; • vt, vi emitir; transmitir.
broadcasting n radiodifusión f.
broaden vt, vi ensanchar(se).
broadly adv anchamente.
broad-minded adj tolerante.
broadness n ancho m; anchura f.
broadside n costado de navío m; andanada f.
broadways adv a lo ancho, por lo ancho.
brocade n brocado m.
broccoli n brécol m.
brochure n folleto m.
brogue n abarca f; idioma corrompido m.
broil vt asar a la parrilla.
broken adj roto, interrumpido; ~ English inglés mal articulado m.
broker n corredor m.
brokerage n corretaje m.
bronchial adj bronquial.
bronchitis n bronquitis f.
bronze n bronce m; • vt broncear.
brooch n broche m.
brood vi empollar; pensar alguna cosa con cuidado; • n raza f; nidada f.
brood-hen n empolladora f.
brook n arroyo m.
broom n hiniesta f; escoba de hiniesta f.
broomstick n palo de escoba m.
broth n caldo m.
brothel n burdel m.
brother n hermano m.
brotherhood n hermandad f; fraternidad f.
brother-in-law n cuñado m.
brotherly adj, adv fraternal; fraternalmente.

brow n caja f; frente f; cima f.
browbeat vt mirar con ceño.
brown adj moreno; castaño; ~ paper n papel de estraza m; ~ bread n pan moreno m; ~ sugar n azúcar terciado m; • n color moreno m; • vt volver moreno.
browse vi ramonear; • vi pacer la hierba.
bruise vt magullar; • n magulladura, contusión f.
brunch n desayuno-almuerzo m.
brunette n morena f.
brunt n choque m.
brush n cepillo m; escobilla f; combate m; • vt cepillar.
brushwood n breñal, zarzal m.
brusque adj brusco.
Brussels sprout n col de Bruselas f.
brutal adj brutal; ~ly adv brutalmente.
brutality n brutalidad f.
brutalize vt (vi) embrutecer(se).
brute n bruto m; • adj feroz, bestial; irracional.
brutish adj brutal, bestial; feroz; ~ly adv brutalmente.
bubble n burbuja f; • vi burbujear, bullir.
bubblegum n chicle m.
bucket n cubo, pozal m.
buckle n hebilla f; • vt hebillar; afianzar; • vi encorvarse.
bucolic adj bucólico.
bud n pimpollo, botón m; • vi brotar.
Buddhism n Budismo m.
budding adj en ciernes.
buddy n compañero m.
budge vi moverse, menearse.
budgerigar n periquito m.
budget n presupuesto m.
buff n entusiasta m.
buffalo n bisonte m.
buffers npl (rail) parochoques, topes mpl.
buffet n buffet m; • vt abofetear.
buffoon n bufón, chocarrero m.
bug n chinche m.
bugbear n espantajo, coco m.
bugle(horn) n trompa de caza f.
build vt edificar; construir.
builder n arquitecto m; maestro de obras m.
building n edificio m; construcción f.
bulb n bulbo m; cebolla f.
bulbous adj bulboso.
bulge vi combarse; • n bombeo m.
bulk n masa f; volumen m; grosura f; mayor parte f; capacidad de un buque f; in ~ a granel.
bulky adj grueso, grande.
bull n toro m.
bulldog n dogo m.
bulldozer n aplanadora f.
bullet n bala f.
bulletin board n tablón de anuncios m.
bulletproof adj a prueba de balas.
bullfight n corrida de toros f.
bullfighter n torero m.
bullfighting n los toros mpl.
bullion n oro o plata en barras m o f.
bullock n novillo capado m.
bullring n plaza de toros f.
bull's-eye n centro del blanco m.
bully n valentón m; • vt tiranizar.
bulwark n baluarte m.
bum n vagabundo m.
bumblebee n abejorro, zángaro m.
bump n hinchazón f; jiba f; bollo m; barriga f; • vt chocar contra.
bumpkin n patán m; villano m.
bumpy adj bacheado.
bun n bollo m; moño m.
bunch n ramo m; grupo m.

bundle n fard m, haz m (de leña etc); paquete m; rollo m; ● vt atar, hacer un lío.
bung n tapón m; ● vt atarugar.
bungalow n bungalow m.
bungle vt chapucear; ● vi hacer algo chabacanamente.
bunion n juanete c.
bunk n litera f.
bunker n refugio m; búnker m.
buoy n (mar) boya f.
buoyancy n fluctuación f.
buoyant adj boyante.
burden n carga f; ● vt cargar.
bureau n armario m; escritorio m.
bureaucracy n burocracia f.
bureaucrat n burócrata m.
burglar n ladrón m.
burglar alarm n alarma de ladrones f.
burglary n robo de una casa m.
burial n enterramiento m; exequias fpl.
burial place n cementerio m.
burlesque n, adj lengua burlesca f; burlesco m.
burly adj fornido.
burn vt quemar, abrasar, incendiar; ● vi arder; ● n quemadura f.
burner n quemador m; mechero m.
burning adj ardiente.
burrow n conejera f; ● vi esconderse en la conejera.
bursar n tesorero m.
burse n bolsa, lonja f..
burst vi reventar; abrirse; to ~ into tears prorrumpir en lágrimas; to ~ out laughing estallarse de risa; ● vt to ~ into irrumpir en; ● n reventón m; rebosadura f.
bury vt enterrar, sepultar; esconder.
bus n autobús m.
bush n arbusto, espinal m; cola de zorra f.
bushy adj espeso, lleno de arbustos.
busily adv diligentemente, apresuradamente.
business n asunto m; negocios mpl; empleo m; ocupación f.
businesslike adj serio.
businessman n hombre de negocios m.
business trip n viaje de negocios m.
businesswoman n mujer de negocios f.
bust n busto m.
bus-stop n parada de autobuses f.
bustle vi hacer ruido; entremeterse; ● n baraúnda f; ruido m.
bustling adj animado.
busy adj ocupado; entrometido.
busybody n entrometido m.
but conj pero; mas; excepto, menos; solamente.
butcher n carnicero m; ● vt matar atrozmente.
butcher's (shop) n carnicería f.
butchery n matadero m.
butler n mayordomo m.
butt n colilla f; cabo, extremo m; ● vt topar.
butter n mantequilla f; ● vt untar con mantequilla.
buttercup n (bot) amargón, diente de león m.
butterfly n mariposa f.
buttermilk n suero de manteca m.
buttocks npl posaderas fpl.
button n botón m; ● vt abotonar.
buttonhole n ojal m.
buttress n estribo m; apoyo m; ● vt estribar.
buxom adj frescachona, rolliza.
buy vt comprar.
buyer n comprador m.
buzz n susurro, soplo m; ● vi zumbar.
buzzard n ratonero común m.
buzzer n timbre m.
by prep por; a, en; de; cerca, al lado de; ~ and ~ de aquí a poco, ahora; ~ the ~ de paso; ~ much con mucho; ~ all means por supuesto.
bygone adj pasado.

by-law n ley local f.
bypass n carretera de circunvalación f.
by-product n derivado m.
by-road n camino descarriado m.
bystander n mirador m.
byte n (comput) byte m.
byword n proverbio, refrán m.

C

cab n taxi m.
cabbage n berza, col f.
cabin n cabaña, cámara de navío f.
cabinet n consejo de ministros m; gabinete m; escritorio m.
cabinet-maker n ebanista m.
cable n (mar) cable m.
cable car n teleférico m.
cable television n televisión por cable f.
caboose n (mar) cocina f.
cabstand n parada de taxis f.
cache n silo m.
cackle vi cacarear o graznar; ● n cacareo m; charla f.
cactus n cacto m.
cadence n (mus) cadencia f.
cadet n cadete m.
cadge vt mangar.
café n café m.
cafeteria n café m.
caffein(e) n cafeína f.
cage n jaula f; prisión f; ● vt enjaular.
cagey adj cauteloso.
cajole vt lisonjear, adular.
cake n bollo m; tortita f.
calamitous adj calamitoso.
calamity n calamidad, miseria f.
calculable adj calculable.
calculate vt calcular, contar.
calculation n calculación f; cálculo m.
calculator n calculadora f.
calculus n cálculo m.
calendar n calendario m.
calf n ternero m; ternera f; carne de ternero f.
caliber n calibre m.
caligraphy n caligrafía f.
calisthenics npl ejercicios gimnásticos mpl.
call vt llamar, nombrar; llamar por teléfono; convocar, citar; apelar; to ~ for preguntar por alguno, ir a buscarle; to ~ on visitar; to ~ attention llamar la atención; to ~ names injuriar; ● n llamada f; instancia f; invitación f; urgencia f; vocación f; profesión f.
caller n visitador m.
calligraphy n caligrafía f.
calling n profesión, vocación f.
callous adj calloso, endurecido; insensible.
calm n calma, tranquilidad f; ● adj quieto, tranquilo; ● vt calmar; aplacar, aquietar; ~ly adv tranquilamente.
calmness n tranquilidad, calma f.
calorie n caloría f.
calumny n calumnia f.
Calvary n calvario m.
calve vi parir, producir la váca.
Calvinist n calvinista m.
camel n camello m.
cameo n camafeo m.
camera n máquina fotográfica f; camera f.
cameraman n cámara m.
camomile n manzanilla f.
camouflage n camuflaje m.
camp n campo m; ● vi acampar.
campaign n campaña f; ● vi hacer campaña.

campaigner *n* campeador *m.*
camper *n* campista *m.*
camping *n* camping *m.*
camphor *n* alcanfor *m.*
campsite *n* camping *m.*
campus *n* ciudad universitaria *f.*
can *vi* poder; ● *n* lata *f.*
canal *n* estanque *m*; canal *m.*
cancel *vt* cancelar; anular, invalidar.
cancellation *n* cancelación *f.*
cancer *n* cáncer *m.*
Cancer *n* Cáncer *m* (signo del zodíaco).
cancerous *adj* canceroso.
candid *adj* cándido, sencillo, sincero; **~ly** *adv* cándidamente, francamente.
candidate *n* candidato *m.*
candied *adj* bañado de azúcar.
candle *n* candela *f*; vela *f.*
candlelight *n* luz de candela *f.*
candlestick *n* candelero *m.*
candor *n* candor *m*; sinceridad *f.*
candy *n* caramelo *m.*
cane *n* caña *f*; bastón *m.*
canine *adj* canino, perruno.
canister *n* bote *m.*
cannabis *n* marijuana *f.*
cannibal *n* caníbal *m*; antropófago *m.*
cannibalism *n* canibalismo *m.*
cannie *adj* cuerdo, discreto.
cannon *n* cañón *m.*
cannonball *n* bala de artillería *f.*
canoe *n* canoa *f.*
canon *n* canon *m*; regla *f*; **~law** derecho canónico *m.*
canonization *n* canonización *f.*
canonize *vt* canonizar.
can opener *n* abrelatas *m invar.*
canopy *n* dosel, pabellón *m.*
cantankerous *adj* aspero, fastidioso.
canteen *n* cantina *f.*
canter *n* galope corto *m.*
canvas *n* cañamazo *m.*
canvass *vt* escudriñar, examinar; controvertir; ● *vi* solicitar votos; pretender.
canvasser *n* solicitador *m.*
canyon *n* cañón *m.*
cap *n* gorra *f.*
capability *n* capacidad, aptitud, inteligencia *f.*
capable *adj* capaz.
capacitate *vt* hacer capaz.
capacity *n* capacidad *f*; inteligencia, habilidad *f.*
cape *n* cabo, promontorio *m.*
caper *n* cabriola *f*; alcaparra *f*; ● *vi* hacer cabriolas.
capillary *adj* capilar.
capital *adj* capital; principal; ● *n* capital *f* (la ciudad principal); capital, fondo *m*; mayúscula *f.*
capitalism *n* capitalismo *m.*
capitalist *n* capitalista *m.*
capitalize *vt* capitalizer; to ~ **on** aprovechar.
capital punishment *n* pena de muerte *f.*
Capitol *n* Capitolio *m.*
capitulate *vi* capitular.
capitulation *n* capitulación *f.*
caprice *n* capricho *m*; extravagancia *f.*
capricious *adj* caprichoso; **~ly** *adv* caprichosamente.
Capricorn *n* Capricornio *m* (signo del zodíaco).
capsize *vt* (*mar*) trabucar, zozobrar.
capsule *n* cápsula *f.*
captain *n* capitán *m.*
captaincy, captainship *n* capitanía *f.*
captivate *vt* cautivar.
captivation *n* atractivo *m.*
captive *n* cautivo, esclavo *m.*

captivity *n* cautividad, esclavitud *f*, cautiverio *m.*
capture *n* captura *f*; presa *f*; ● *vt* apresar, capturar.
car *n* coche, carro *m*; vagón *m.*
carafe *n* garrafa *f.*
caramel *n* caramelo *m.*
carat *n* quilate *m.*
caravan *n* caravana *f.*
caraway *n* (*bot*) alcaravea *f.*
carbohydrates *npl* hidratos de carbono *mpl.*
carbon *n* carbón dulce *m.*
carbon copy *n* copia al carbón *f.*
carbonize *vt* carbonizar.
carbon paper *n* papel carbón *m.*
carbuncle *n* carbúnculo, rubí *m*; carbunco, tumor maligno *m.*
carburetor *n* carburador *m.*
carcass *n* cadáver *m.*
card *n* naipe *m*; carta *f*; **pack of ~s** baraja *f.*
cardboard *n* cartón *m.*
card game *n* juego de naipes *m.*
cardiac *adj* cardíaco.
cardinal *adj* cardinal, principal; ● *n* cardenal *m.*
card table *n* mesa para jugar *f.*
care *n* cuidado *m*; solicitud *f*; ● *vi* cuidar, tener cuidado *o* pena, inquietarse; **what do I ~?** ¿a mí qué me importa?; to ~ **for** *vt* cuidar a; querer.
career *n* carrera *f*; curso *m*; ● *vi* correr a carrera tendida.
carefree *n* despreocupado.
careful *adj* cuidadoso, diligente, prudente; **~ly** *adv* cuidadosamente.
careless *adj* descuidado, negligente; indolente; **~ly** *adv* descuidadamente.
carelessness *n* negligencia, indiferencia *f.*
caress *n* caricia *f*; ● *vt* acariciar, halagar.
caretaker *n* portero *m.*
car-ferry *n* transbordador para coches *m.*
cargo *n* cargamento de navío *m.*
car hire *n* alquiler de coches *m.*
caricature *n* caricatura *f*; ● *vt* hacer caricaturas, ridiculizar.
caries *n* caries *f.*
caring *adj* humanitario.
Carmelite *n* carmelita *m.*
carnage *n* carnicería, matanza *f.*
carnal *adj* carnal; sensual; **~ly** *adv* carnalmente.
carnation *n* clavel *m.*
carnival *n* carnaval *m.*
carnivorous *adj* carnívoro.
carol *n* villancico *m*, canción de alegría *o* piedad *f.*
carpenter *n* carpintero *m*; **~'s bench** banco de carpintero *m.*
carpentry *n* carpintería *f.*
carpet *n* alfombra *f*; ● *vt* cubrir con alfombras.
carpeting *n* alfombrado *m.*
carriage *n* porte *m*; coche *m*; vehículo *m.*
carriage-free *adj* franco de porte.
carrier *n* portador, carretero *m.*
carrier pigeon *n* paloma correo *o* mensajera *f.*
carrion *n* carroña *f.*
carrot *n* zanahoria *f.*
carry *vt* llevar, conducir; ● *vi* oírse; to ~ **the day** quedar victorioso; to ~ **on** seguir.
cart *n* carro *m*; carreta *f*; ● *vt* llevar (en carro).
cartel *n* cartel *m.*
carthorse *n* caballo de tiro *m.*
Carthusian *n* cartujo (monje) *m.*
cartilage *n* cartílago *m.*
cartload *n* carretada *f.*
carton *n* caja *f.*
cartoon *n* dibujo animado *m*; tira cómica *f.*
cartridge *n* cartucho *m.*
carve *vt* cincelar; trinchar; grabar.
carving *n* escultura *f.*
carving knife *n* cuchillo grande de mesa *m.*
car wash *n* lavado de coches *m.*

case n caja f; maleta f; caso m; estuche m; vaina f; **in ~** por si acaso.
cash n dinero contante m; • vt cobrar.
cash card n tarjeta dinero f.
cash dispenser n cajero automático m.
cashier n cajero m.
cashmere n cachemira f.
casing n forro m; cubierta f.
casino n casino m.
cask n barril, tonel m.
casket n ataúd m.
casserole n cazuela f.
cassette n cassette m.
cassette player, recorder n tocacassettes m invar.
cassock n sotana f.
cast vt tirar, lanzar; modelar; • n reparto m; forma f.
castanets npl castañetas fpl.
castaway n réprobo m.
caste n casta f.
castigate vt castigar.
casting vote n voto decisivo m.
cast iron n hierro colado m.
castle n castillo m; fortaleza f.
castor oil n aceite de ricino m.
castrate vt castrar.
castration n capadura f.
cast steel n acero fundido m.
casual adj casual, fortuito; **~ly** adv casualmente, fortuitamente.
casualty n víctima f; baja f.
cat n gato m; gata f.
catalog n catálogo m.
catalyst n catalizador m.
cataplasm n cataplasma f.
catapult n catapulta f.
cataract n cascada f; catarata f.
catarrh n catarro m; reuma f.
catastrophe n catástrofe f.
catcall n silbido m; reclamo m.
catch vt coger, agarrar, asir; atrapar; pillar; sorprender; **to ~ cold** resfriarse; **to ~ fire** encenderse; • n presa f; captura f; (mus) repetición f; trampa f.
catching adj contagioso.
catchphrase n lema m.
catchword n reclamo m.
catchy adj pegadizo.
catechism n catecismo m.
catechize vt cateqizar, examinar.
categorical adj categórico; **~ly** adv categóricamente.
categorize vt clasificar.
category n categoría f.
cater vi abastecer, proveer.
caterer n proveedor, abastecedor m.
catering n alimentación f.
caterpillar n oruga f.
catgut n cuerda de violón f.
cathedral n catedral f.
catholic adj, n católico m.
Catholicism n catolicismo m.
cattle n ganado m.
cattle show n exposición de ganados f.
caucus n junta electoral f.
cauliflower n coliflor f.
cause n causa f; razón f; motivo m; proceso m; • vt causar.
causeway n arrecife m.
caustic adj, n cáustico m.
cauterize vt cauterizar.
caution n prudencia, precaución f; aviso m; • vt avisar; amonestar; advertir.
cautionary adj de escarmiento.
cautious adj prudente, circunspecto, cauto.
cavalier adj arrogante.

cavalry n caballería f.
cave n caverna f; bodega f.
caveat n aviso m; advertencia f; (law) notificación f.
cavern n caverna f; bodega f.
cavernous adj cavernoso.
caviar n caviar m.
cavity n hueco m.
cease vt parar, suspender; • vi desistir.
ceasefire n alto el fuego m.
ceaseless adj incesante, continuo; **~ly** adv perpetuamente.
cedar n cedro m.
cede vt ceder, transferir.
ceiling n techo m.
celebrate vt celebrar.
celebration n celebración f.
celebrity n celebridad, fama f.
celery n apio m.
celestial adj celeste, divino.
celibacy n celibato m, soltería f.
celibate adj soltero; soltera.
cell n celdilla f; célula f; cueva f.
cellar n sótano m; bodega f.
'cello n violoncelo m.
cellophane n celofán m.
cellular adj celular.
cellulose n (chem) celulosa f.
cement n cemento m; (fig) vínculo m; • vt pegar con cemento.
cemetery n cementerio m.
cenotaph n cenotafio m.
censor n censor m; crítico m
censorious adj severo, crítico.
censorship n censura f.
censure n censura, reprensión f; • vt censurar, reprender; criticar.
census n censo m.
cent n centavo m.
centenarian n centenario m; centenaria f.
centenary n centena f; • adj centenario.
centennial adj centenario.
center n centro m; • vt colocar en un centro; reconcentrar; • vi colocarse en el centro; reconcentrarse.
centigrade n centígrado m.
centiliter n centilitro m.
centimeter n centímetro m.
centipede n escolopendra f.
central adj central; **~ly** adv centralmente, en el centro.
centralize vt centralizar.
centrifugal adj centrífugo.
century n siglo m.
ceramic adj cerámico.
cereals npl cereales fpl.
cerebral adj cerebral.
ceremonial adj, n ceremonial m; rito externo m.
ceremonious adj ceremonioso; **~ly** adv ceremoniosamente.
ceremony n ceremonia f; formulas exteriores fpl.
certain adj cierto, evidente; seguro; **~ly** adv ciertamente, sin duda.
certainty, certitude n certeza f; seguridad f.
certificate n certificado, testimonio m.
certification n certificado m.
certified mail n correo certificado m.
certify vt certificar, afirmar.
cervical adj cervical.
cesarean section, ~ operation n (med) operación cesárea f.
cessation n cesación f.
cesspool n cloaca f; sumidero m.
chafe vt frotar; enojar, irritar.
chaff n paja menuda f.
chaffinch n pinzón m.
chagrin n disgusto m.
chain n cadena f; serie, sucesión f; • vt encadenar, atar con cadena.

chain reaction *n* reacción en cadena *f*.
chainstore *n* gran almacén *m*.
chair *n* silla *f*; • *vt* presidir.
chairman *n* presidente *m*.
chalice *n* cáliz *m*.
chalk *n* creta *f*; tiza *f*.
challenge *n* desafío *m*; • *vt* desafiar.
challenger *n* desafiador *m*.
challenging *adj* desafiante.
chamber *n* cámara *f*; aposento *m*.
chambermaid *n* moza de cámara *f*.
chameleon *n* camaleón *m*.
chamois leather *n* gamuza *f*.
champagne *n* champaña *m*.
champion *n* campeón *m*; • *vt* defender.
championship *n* campeonato *m*.
chance *n* ventura, suerte *f*; oportunidad *f*; **by ~** por acaso; • *vt* arriesgar.
chancellor *n* canciller *m*.
chancery *n* chancillería *f*.
chandelier *n* araña de luces *f*; candelero *m*.
change *vt* cambiar; • *vi* variar, alterarse; • *n* mudanza, variedad *f*; vicisitud *f*; cambio *m*.
changeable *adj* variable, inconstante; mudable.
changeless *adj* constante, inmutable.
changing *adj* cambiante.
channel *n* canal *m* estrecho *m*; • *vt* encauzar.
chant *n* canto (llano) *m*; • *vt* cantar.
chaos *n* caos *m*; confusión *f*.
chaotic *adj* confuso.
chapel *n* capilla *f*.
chaplain *n* capellán *m*.
chapter *n* capítulo *m*.
char *vt* chamuscar.
character *n* carácter *m*; personaje *m*.
characteristic *adj* característico; **~ally** *adv* característicamente.
characterize *vt* caracterizar.
characterless *adj* sin carácter.
charade *n* charada *f*.
charcoal *n* carbón de leña *m*.
charge *vt* cargar; acusar, imputar; • *n* cargo *m*; acusación *f*; (*mil*) ataque *m*; depósito *m*; carga *f*.
chargeable *adj* imputable.
charge card *n* tarjeta de cuenta *f*.
charitable *adj* caritativo; benigno, clemente; **~bly** *adv* caritativamente.
charity *n* caridad, benevolencia *f*; limosna *f*.
charlatan *n* charlatán *m*.
charm *n* encanto *m*; atractivo *m*; • *vt* encantar, embelesar, atraer.
charming *adj* encantado.
chart *n* carta de navegar *f*.
charter *n* carta *f*; privilegio *m*; • *vt* fletar un buque; alquilar.
charter flight *n* vuelo chárter *m*.
chase *vt* cazar; perseguir; • *n* caza *f*.
chasm *n* vacío *m*.
chaste *adj* casto; puro; honesto.
chasten *vt* corregir, castigar.
chastise *vt* castigar, reformar, corregir.
chastisement *n* castigo *m*.
chastity *n* castidad, pureza *f*.
chat *vi* charlar; • *n* charla, cháchara *f*.
chatter *vi* cotorrear; rechinar; charlar; • *n* chirrido *m*; charla *f*.
chatterbox *n* parlero, hablador, gárrulo *m*.
chatty *adj* locuaz, parlanchín.
chauffeur *n* chófer *m*.
chauvinist *n* machista *m*.
cheap *adj* barato; **~ly** *adv* a bajo precio.
cheapen *vt* regatear; abaratar.
heaper *adj* más barato.

cheat *vt* engañar, defraudar; • *n* trampa *f*; fraude, engaño *m*; trampista *m*.
check *vt* comprobar; contar; reprimir, refrenar; regañar; registrar; • *n* cheque *m*; restricción *f*; freno *m*.
checkerboard *n* tablero de ajedrez *m*.
checkered *adj* accidentado.
checking account *n* cuenta corriente *f*.
checkmate *n* mate *m*.
checkout *n* caja *f*.
checkpoint *n* control *m*.
checkroom *n* consigna *f*.
checkup *n* reconocimiento general *m*.
cheek *n* mejilla *f*; (*fam*) desvergüenza *f*; atrevimiento *m*.
cheekbone *n* hueso del carrillo *m*.
cheer *n* alegría *f*; aplauso *m*; buen humor *m*; • *vt* animar, alentar.
cheerful *adj* alegre, vivo, jovial; **~ly** *adv* alegremente.
cheerfulness, cheeriness *n* alegría *f*; buen humor *m*.
cheese *n* queso *m*.
chef *n* jefe de cocina *m*.
chemical *adj* químico.
chemist *n* químico *m*.
chemistry *n* química *f*.
cherish *vt* fomentar, proteger.
cheroot *n* puro *m*.
cherry *n* cereza *f*; • *adj* bermejo.
cherrytree *n* cerezo *m*.
cherub *n* querubín *m*.
chess *n* ajedrez *m*.
chessboard *n* tablero (para jugar al ajedrez) *m*.
chessman *n* pieza de ajedrez *f*.
chest *n* pecho *m*; arca *f*; **~ of drawers** cómoda *f*.
chestnut *n* castaña *f*; color de castaña *m*.
chestnut tree *n* castaño *m*.
chew *vt* mascar, masticar.
chewing gum *n* chicle *m*.
chic *adj* elegante.
chicanery *n* sofistería, quisquilla *f*.
chick *n* polluelo *m*; (*fig*) chica *f*.
chicken *n* pollo *m*.
chickenpox *n* varicela *f*.
chickpea *n* garbanzo *m*.
chicory *n* achicoria *f*.
chide *vt* reprobar, regañar.
chief *adj* principal, capital; **~ly** *adv* principalmente; • *n* jefe, principal *m*.
chief executive *n* director general *m*.
chieftain *n* jefe, comandante *m*.
chiffon *n* gasa *f*.
chilblain *n* sabañón *m*.
child *n* niño *m*; niña *f*; hijo *m*; hija *f*; **from a ~** desde niño; **with ~** preñada, embarazada.
childbirth *n* parto *m*.
childhood *n* infancia, niñez *f*.
childish *adj* frívolo, pueril; **~ly** *adv* puerilmente.
childishness *n* puerilidad *f*.
childless *adj* sin hijos.
childlike *adj* pueril.
children *npl de child* niños *mpl*.
chill *adj* frío, friolero; • *n* frío *m*; • *vt* enfriar; helar.
chilly *adj* friolero, friolento.
chime *n* armonía *f*; clave *m*; • *vi* sonar con armonía; concordar.
chimney *n* chimenea *f*.
chimpanzee *n* chimpancé *m*.
chin *n* barbilla *f*.
china(ware) *n* porcelana *f*.
chink *n* grieta, hendedura *f*; • *vi* resonar.
chip *vt* desmenuzar; • *vi* reventarse; • *n* astilla *f*; chip *m*; patata *o* papa frita.
chiropodist *n* pedicuro *m*.
chirp *vi* chirriar, gorjear; • *n* gorjeo, chirrido *m*.

chirping n canto de las aves m.
chisel n cincel m; • vt cincelar, grabar.
chitchat n charla, parlería f.
chivalrous adj caballeresco.
chivalry n caballería f; hazaña f.
chives npl cebolleta f.
chlorine n cloro m.
chloroform n cloroformo m.
chock-full adj de bote en bote, completamente lleno.
chocolate n chocolate m.
choice n elección, preferencia f; selecto m; • adj selecto, exquisito, excelente.
choir n coro m.
choke vt sufocar; oprimir; tapar.
cholera n cólera m.
choose vt escoger, elegir.
chop vt tajar, cortar; • n chuleta f; ~s pl (sl) quijadas fpl.
chopper n helicóptero m.
chopping block n tajo de cocina m.
chopsticks npl palillos mpl.
chore n faena f.
choral adj coral.
chord n cuerda f.
chorist, chorister n corista m.
chorus n coro m.
Christ n Cristo m.
christen vt bautizar.
Christendom n cristianismo m; cristiandad f.
christening n bautismo m.
Christian adj, n cristiano m; ~ name nombre de pila m.
Christianity n cristianismo m; cristiandad f.
Christmas n Navidad f.
Christmas card n tarjeta de Navidad f.
Christmas Eve n víspera de Navidad f.
chrome n cromo m.
chronic adj crónico.
chronicle n crónica f.
chronicler n cronista m.
chronological adj cronológico; ~ly adv cronológicamente.
chronology n cronología f.
chronometer n cronómetro m.
chubby adj gordo.
chuck vt lanzar.
chuckle vi reírse a carcajadas.
chug vi resoplar.
chum n compañero de cuarto (entre estudiantes) m.
chunk n trozo m.
church n iglesia f.
churchyard n cementerio m.
churlish adj rústico, grosero; tacaño.
churn n mantequera f; • vt batir la leche para hacer manteca.
cider n sidra f.
cigar n cigarro m.
cigarette n cigarrillo m.
cigarette case n pitillera f.
cigarette end n colilla f.
cigarette holder n boquilla f.
cinder n carbonilla f.
cinema n cine m.
cinnamon n canela f.
cipher n cifra f.
circle n círculo m; corrillo m; asamblea f; • vt circundar, cercar; • vi circular.
circuit n circuito m; recinto m.
circuitous adj circular.
circular adj circular, redondo; • n carta circular f.
circulate vi circular; moverse alrededor.
circulation n circulación f.
circumcise vt circuncidar.
circumcision n circuncisión f.
circumference n circunferencia f; circuito m.
circumflex n acento circunflejo m.

circumlocution n circunlocución f.
circumnavigate vt circunnavegar.
circumnavigation n circunnavegación f.
circumscribe vt circunscribir.
circumspect adj circunspecto, prudente, reservado.
circumspection n circunspección, prudencia f.
circumstance n circunstancia, condición f; incidente m.
circumstantial adj accidental; accesorio.
circumstantiate vt circunstanciar, detallar.
circumvent vt burlar.
circumvention n engaño m; trampa f; embrollo m.
circus n circo m.
cistern n cisterna f.
citadel n ciudadela, fortaleza f.
citation n citación, cita f.
cite vt citar (a juicio); alegar; referirse a.
citizen n ciudadano m.
citizenship n ciudadanía f.
city n ciudad f.
civic adj cívico.
civil adj civil, cortés; ~ly adv civilmente.
civil defense n protección civil f.
civil engineer n ingeniero civil m.
civilian n paisano m.
civility n civilidad, urbanidad, cortesía f.
civilization n civilización f.
civilize vt civilizar.
civil law n derecho civil m.
civil war n guerra civil f.
clad adj vestido, cubierto.
claim vt pedir en juicio, reclamar; • n demanda f; derecho m.
claimant n reclamante m; demandador m.
clairvoyant n clarividente m.
clam n almeja f.
clamber vi gatear, trepar.
clammy adj viscoso.
clamor n clamor, grito m; • vi vociferar, gritar.
clamp n abrazadera f; • vt afianzar; to ~ down on reforzar la lucha contra.
clan n familia, tribu, raza f.
clandestine adj clandestino, oculto.
clang n rechino, sonido desapacible m; • vi rechinar.
clap vt aplaudir.
clapping n palmada f; aplauso, palmoteo m.
claret n clarete m.
clarification n clarificación f.
clarify vt clarificar, aclarar.
clarinet n clarinete m.
clarity n claridad f.
clash vi chocar; • n estruendo m; choque m.
clasp n broche m; hebilla f; abrazo m; • vt abrochar; abrazar.
class n clase f; orden f; • vt clasificar, coordinar.
classic(al) adj clásico; • n autor clásico m.
classification n clasificación f.
classified advertisement n anuncio por palabras m.
classify vt clasificar.
classmate n compañero de clase m.
classroom n aula f.
clatter vi resonar; hacer ruido; • n ruido m.
clause n cláusula f; artículo m; estipulación f.
claw n garra f; • vt desgarrar, arañar.
clay n arcilla f.
clean adj limpio; casto; • vt limpiar.
cleaning n limpieza f.
cleanliness n limpieza f.
cleanly adj limpio; • adv limpiamente, aseadamente.
cleanness n limpieza f; pureza f.
cleanse vt limpiar, purificar; purgar.
clear adj claro; neto; diáfano; evidente; • adv claramente; • vt clarificar, aclarar; justificar, absolver; • vi aclararse.
clearance n despeje m; acreditación f.
clear-cut adj bien definido.

clearly adv claramente, evidentemente.
cleaver n cuchillo de carnicero m.
clef n clave f.
cleft n hendedura, abertura f.
clemency n clemencia f.
clement adj clemente, benigno.
clenched adj cerrado.
clergy n clero m.
clergyman n eclesiástico m.
clerical adj clerical, eclesiástico.
clerk n dependiente m; oficinista m.
clever adj listo; hábil, mañoso; ~ly adv diestramente, hábilmente.
click vt chasquear; • vi taconear.
client n cliente m.
cliff n acantilado m.
climate n clima m; temperatura f.
climatic adj climático.
climax n clímax m.
climb vt escalar, trepar; • vi subir.
climber n alpinista m.
climbing n alpinismo m.
clinch vt cerrar; remachar.
cling vi colgar, adherirse, pegarse.
clinic n clínica f.
clink vt hacer resonar; • vi resonar; • n retintín m.
clip vt cortar; • n clip m; horquilla f.
clipping n recorte m.
clique n camarilla f.
cloak n capa f; pretexto m; • vi encapotar.
cloakroom n guardarropa m.
clock n reloj m.
clockwork n mecanismo de un reloj m; • adj sumamente exacto y puntual.
clod n terrón m.
clog n zueco m; • vi coagularse.
cloister n claustro, monasterio m.
close vt cerrar; concluir, terminar; • vi cerrarse; • n fin m; conclusión f; • adj cercano; estrecho; ajustado; denso; reservado; • adv de cerca; ~ by muy cerca; junto.
closed adj cerrado.
closely adv estrechamente; de cerca.
closeness n proximidad f; estrechez, espesura, reclusión f.
closet n armario m.
close-up n primer plano m.
closure n cierre m; conclusión f.
clot n grumo m; embolia f.
cloth n paño m; mantel m; vestido m; lienzo m.
clothe vt vestir, cubrir.
clothes npl ropa f; ropaje m; ropa de cama f; bed ~ cobertores mpl.
clothes basket n cesta grande f.
clotheshorse n enjugador m.
clothesline n cuerda (para la ropa) f.
clothespin n pinza f.
clothing n vestidos mpl.
cloud n nube f; nublado m; (fig) adversidad f; • vt anublar; oscurecer; • vi anublarse; oscurecerse.
cloudiness n nublosidad f; oscuridad f.
cloudy adj nublado, nubloso; oscuro; sombrío, melancólico.
clout n tortazo m.
clove n clavo m.
clover n trébol m.
clown n payaso m.
club n cachiporra f; club m.
club car n coche salón m.
clue n pista f, indicios m; idea f.
clump n grupo m.
clumsily adv torpemente.
clumsiness n torpeza f.
clumsy adj tosco, pesado; sin arte.

cluster n racimo m; manada f; pelotón m; • vt agrupar; • vi arracimarse.
clutch n embrague m; apretón m; • vt empuñar.
clutter vt atestar.
coach n autocar, autobus m; vagón m; entrenador m; • vt entrenar; enseñar.
coach trip n excursión en autocar f.
coagulate vt coagular, cuajar; • vi coagularse, cuajarse, espesarse.
coal n carbón m.
coalesce vi juntarse, incorporarse.
coalfield n yacimiento de carbón m.
coalition n coalición, confederación f.
coalman n carbonero m.
coalmine n mina de carbón, carbonería f.
coarse adj basto; grosero; ~ly adv groseramente.
coast n costa f.
coastal adj costero.
coastguard n guardacostas m invar.
coastline n litoral m.
coat n chaqueta f; abrigo m; capa f; • vt cubrir.
coat hanger n percha f.
coating n revestimiento m.
coax vt lisonjear.
cob n mazorca de maíz f.
cobbler n zapatero m.
cobbles, cobblestones npl adoquines mpl.
cobweb n telaraña f.
cocaine n cocaína f.
cock n gallo m; macho m; • vt armar el sombrero; amartillar, montar una escopeta.
cock-a-doodle-doo n canto del gallo m.
cockcrow n canto del gallo m.
cockerel n gallito m.
cockfight(ing) n pelea de gallos f.
cockle n caracol de mar m.
cockpit n cabina f.
cockroach n cucaracha f.
cocktail n cóctel m.
cocoa n coco m; cacao m.
coconut n coco m.
cocoon n capullo del gusano de seda m.
cod n bacalao m.
code n código m; prefijo m.
cod-liver oil n aceite de hígado de bacalao m.
coefficient n coeficiente m.
coercion n coerción f.
coexistence n coexistencia f.
coffee n café m.
coffee break n descanso m.
coffee house n café m.
coffeepot n cafetera f.
coffee table n mesita f.
coffer n cofre m; caja f.
coffin n ataúd m.
cog n diente (de rueda) m.
cogency n fuerza, urgencia f.
cogent adj convincente, urgente; ~ly adv de modo convincente.
cognac n coñac m.
cognate adj cognado.
cognition n conocimiento m; convicción f.
cognizance n conocimiento m; competencia f.
cognizant adj informado; (law) competente.
cogwheel n rueda dentada f.
cohabit vi cohabitar.
cohabitation n cohabitación f.
cohere vi pegarse; unirse.
coherence n coherencia, conexión f.
coherent adj coherente; consiguiente.
cohesion n coherencia f.
cohesive adj coherente.

coil *n* rollo *m*; bobina *f*; ● *vt* enrollar.

coin *n* moneda *f*; ● *vt* acuñar.

coincide *vi* coincidir, concurrir, convenir.

coincidence *n* coincidencia *f*.

coincident *adj* coincidente.

coke *n* coque *m*.

colander *n* colador, pasador *m*.

cold *adj* frío; indiferente, insensible; reservado; ~ly *adv* fríamente; indiferentemente; ● *n* frío *m*; frialdad *f*; resfriado *m*.

cold-blooded *adj* impasible.

coldness *n* frialdad *f*; indiferencia, insensibilidad, apatía *f*.

cold sore *n* herpes labial *m*.

coleslaw *n* ensalada de col *f*.

colic *n* cólico *m*.

collaborate *vt* cooperar.

collaboration *n* cooperación *f*.

collapse *vi* hundirse; ● *n* hundimiento; (*med*) colapso *m*.

collapsible *adj* plegable.

collar *n* cuello *m*.

collarbone *n* clavícula *f*.

collate *vt* comparar, confrontar.

collateral *adj* colateral; ● *n* garantía subsidiaria *f*.

collation *n* colación *f*.

colleague *n* colega, compañero *m*.

collect *vt* recoger; coleccionar.

collection *n* colección *f*; compilación *f*.

collective *adj* colectivo, congregado; ~ly colectivamente.

collector *n* coleccionista *m*.

college *n* colegio *m*.

collide *vi* chocar.

collision *n* choque *m*, colisión *f*.

colloquial *adj* familiar; íntimo; ~ly *adv* familiarmente.

colloquialism *n* lengua usual *f*.

collusion *n* colusión *f*.

colon *n* dos puntos *mpl*; (*med*) colon *m*.

colonel *n* (*mil*) coronel *m*.

colonial *adj* colonial.

colonist *n* colono *m*.

colonize *vt* colonizar.

colony *n* colonia *f*.

color *n* color *m*; pretexto *m*; ~s *pl* bandera *f*; ● *vt* colorar; paliar; ● *vi* ponerse colorado.

color-blind *adj* que tiene daltonismo.

colorful *adj* lleno de color.

coloring *n* colorido *m*.

colorless *adj* descolorido, sin color.

color television *n* televisión en color *f*.

colossal *adj* colosal.

colossus *n* coloso *m*.

colt *n* potro *m*.

column *n* columna *f*.

columnist *n* columnista *m*.

coma *n* coma *f*.

comatose *adj* comatoso.

comb *n* peine *m*; ● *vt* peinar.

combat *n* combate *m*; batalla *f*; single ~ duelo *m*; ● *vt* combatir.

combatant *n* combatiente *m*.

combative *adj* combativo.

combination *n* combinación, coordinación *f*.

combine *vt* combinar; ● *vi* unirse.

combustion *n* combustión *f*.

come *vi* venir; to ~ across/upon *vt* topar con; dar con; to ~ by *vt* conseguir; to ~ down *vi* bajar; ser derribado; to ~ from *vt* ser de; to ~ in for *vt* merecer; to ~ into *vt* heredar; to ~ round/to *vi* volver en sí; to ~ up with *vt* sugerer.

comedian *n* comediante, cómico *m*.

comedienne *n* cómica *f*.

comedy *n* comedia *f*.

comet *n* cometa *f*.

comfort *n* confort *m*; ayuda *f*; consuelo *m*; comodidad *f*; ● *vt* confortar; alentar, consolar.

comfortable *adj* cómodo, consolatorio.

comfortably *adv* agradablemente; cómodamente.

comforter *n* chupete *m*.

comic(al) *adj* cómico, burlesco; ~ly *adv* cómicamente.

coming *n* venida, llegada *f*; ● *adj* venidero.

comma *n* (*gr*) coma *f*.

command *vt* comandar, ordenar; ● *n* orden *f*.

commander *n* comandante *m*.

commandment *n* mandamiento, precepto *m*.

commando *n* comando *m*.

commemorate *vt* conmemorar; celebrar.

commemoration *n* conmemoración *f*.

commence *vt, vi* comenzar.

commencement *n* principio *m*.

commend *vt* encomendar; alabar; enviar.

commendable *adj* recomendable.

commendably *adv* loablemente.

commendation *n* recomendación *f*.

commensurate *adj* proporcionado.

comment *n* comentario *m*; ● *vt* comentar; glosar.

commentary *n* comentario *m*; interpretación *f*.

commentator *n* comentador *m*.

commerce *n* comercio, tráfico, trato, negocio *m*.

commercial *adj* comercial.

commiserate *vt* compadecer, tener compasión.

commiseration *n* conmiseración, piedad *f*.

commissariat *n* comisaría *f*.

commission *n* comisión *f*; ● *vt* comisionar; encargar.

commissioner *n* comisionado, delegado *m*.

commit *vt* cometer; depositar; encargar.

commitment *n* compromiso *m*.

committee *n* comité *m*.

commodity *n* comodidad *f*.

common *adj* común; bajo; in ~ comunmente; ● *n* pastos comunales *mpl*.

commoner *n* plebeyo *m*.

common law *n* ley municipal *f*; costumbre que tiene fuerza de ley *f*.

commonly *adv* comunmente, frecuentemente.

commonplace *n* lugares comunes *mpl*; ● *adj* trivial.

common sense *n* sentido común *m*.

commonwealth *n* república *f*.

commotion *n* tumulto *m*; perturbación del ánimo *f*.

commune *vi* conversar, conferir.

communicable *adj* comunicable, impartible.

communicate *vt* comunicar, participar; ● *vi* comunicarse.

communication *n* comunicación *f*.

communicative *adj* comunicativo.

communion *n* comunión *f*.

communiqué *n* comunicado *m*.

communism *n* comunismo *m*.

communist *n* comunista *m*.

community *n* comunidad *f*; república *f*.

community center *n* centro social *m*.

community chest *n* arca comunitaria *f*.

commutable *adj* conmutable, cambiable.

commutation ticket *n* billete de abono *m*.

commute *vt* conmutar.

compact *adj* compacto, sólido, denso; ● *n* pacto, convenio *m*; ~ly *adv* estrechamente; en pocas palabras.

compact disc *n* compact disc *m*.

companion *n* compañero, socio, compinche *m*.

companionship *n* sociedad, compañía *f*.

company *n* compañía, sociedad *f*; compañía de comercio *f*.

comparable *adj* comparable.

comparative *adj* comparativo; ~ly *adv* comparativamente.

compare *vt* comparar.

comparison *n* comparación *f*.

compartment *n* compartimiento *m*.

compass *n* brújula *f*.

compassion *n* compasión, piedad *f*.

compassionate *adj* compasivo.

compatibility *n* compatibilidad *f*.
compatible *adj* compatible.
compatriot *n* compatriota *m*.
compel *vt* compeler, obligar, constreñir.
compelling *adj* convicente.
compensate *vt* compensar.
compensation *n* compensación *f*; resarcimiento *m*.
compère *n* presentador *m*.
compete *vi* concurrir, competir.
competence *n* competencia *f*; suficiencia *f*.
competent *adj* competente, bastante; ~**ly** *adv* competente-
mente.
competition *n* competencia *f*; concurrencia *f*.
competitive *adj* que compete.
competitor *n* competidor, rival *m*.
compilation *n* compilación *f*.
compile *vt* compilar.
complacency *n* auto-satisfacción *f*.
complacent *adj* complaciente.
complain *vi* quejarse, lamentarse, lastimarse, dolerse.
complaint *n* queja *f*; reclamación *f*.
complement *n* complemento *m*.
complementary *adj* complementario.
complete *adj* completo, perfecto; ~**ly** *adv* completamente; •
vt completar, acabar.
completion *n* terminación *f*.
complex *adj* complejo.
complexion *n* tez *f*; aspecto *m*.
complexity *n* complejidad *f*.
compliance *n* complacencia, sumisión *f*.
compliant *adj* complaciente, oficioso.
complicate *vt* complicar.
complication *n* complicación *f*.
complicity *n* complicidad *f*.
compliment *n* cumplido *m*; • *vt* cumplimentar; hacer cum-
plidos.
complimentary *adj* cumplimentero, ceremonioso.
comply *vi* cumplir; condescender, conformarse.
component *adj* componente.
compose *vt* componer; sosegar.
composed *adj* compuesto, moderado.
composer *n* autor *m*; compositor *m*.
composite *adj* compuesto.
composition *n* composición *f*.
compositor *n* cajista *m*.
compost *n* abono, estiércol *m*.
composure *n* composición *f*; tranquilidad, sangre fría *f*.
compound *vt* componer, combinar; • *adj*, *n* compuesto *m*.
comprehend *vt* comprender, contener; entender.
comprehensible *adj* comprensible; ~**ly** *adv* comprensible-
mente.
comprehension *n* comprensión *f*; inteligencia *f*.
comprehensive *adj* comprensivo; ~**ly** *adv* compren-
sivamente.
compress *vt* comprimir, estrechar; • *n* cabezal *m*.
comprise *vt* comprender, incluir.
compromise *n* compromiso *m*; • *vt* comprometer.
compulsion *n* compulsión *f*; apremio *m*.
compulsive *adj* compulsivo; ~**ly** *adv* por fuerza.
compulsory *adj* obligatorio.
compunction *n* compunción, contrición *f*.
computable *adj* computable, calculable.
computation *n* computación, cuenta hecha *f*.
compute *vt* computar, calcular.
computer *n* ordenador *m*.
computerize *vt* computerizar.
computer programing *n* programación *f*.
computer science *n* informática *f*.
comrade *n* camarada, compañero *m*.
comradeship *n* compañerismo *m*.
con *vt* estafar; • *n* estafa *f*.
concave *adj* cóncavo.

concavity *n* concavidad *f*.
conceal *vt* ocultar, esconder.
concealment *n* ocultación *f*; encubrimiento *m*.
concede *vt* conceder, asentir.
conceit *n* concepción *f*; capricho *m*; pensamiento *m*; presunción *f*.
conceited *adj* afectado, vano, presumido.
conceivable *adj* concebible, inteligible.
conceive *vt* concebir, comprender; • *vi* concebir.
concentrate *vt* concentrar.
concentration *n* concentración *f*.
concentration camp *n* campo de concentración *m*.
concentric *adj* concéntrico.
concept *n* concepto *m*.
conception *n* concepción *f*; sentimiento *m*.
concern *vt* concernir, importar; • *n* negocio *m*; asunto *m*;
preocupación *f*.
concerning *prep* tocante a.
concert *n* concierto *m*.
concerto *n* concierto *m*.
concession *n* concesión *f*; privilegio *m*.
conciliate *vt* conciliar.
conciliation *n* conciliación *f*.
conciliatory *adj* conciliativo.
concise *adj* conciso, sucinto; ~**ly** *adv* concisamente.
conclude *vt* concluir; decidir; determinar.
conclusion *n* conclusión, determinación *f*; fin *m*.
conclusive *adj* decisivo, conclusivo; ~**ly** *adv* concluyente-
mente.
concoct *vt* cocer, digerir.
concoction *n* confección *f*; cocción *f*.
concomitant *adj* concomitante.
concord *n* concordia, armonía *f*.
concordance *n* concordancia *f*.
concordant *adj* concordante, conforme.
concourse *n* concurso *m*; multitud *f*; gentío *m*.
concrete *n* concreto *m*; • *vt* concretar.
concubine *n* concubina *f*.
concur *vi* concurrir; juntarse.
concurrence *n* concurrencia *f*; unión *f*; asistencia *f*.
concurrently *adv* al mismo tiempo.
concussion *n* concusión *f*.
condemn *vt* condenar; desaprobar; vituperar.
condemnation *n* condenación *f*.
condensation *n* condensación *f*.
condense *vt* condensar.
condescend *vi* condescender; consentir.
condescending *adj* condescendiente.
condescension *n* condescendencia *f*.
condiment *n* condimento *m*; salsa *f*.
condition *vt* condicionar; •*n* situación, condición, calidad *f*;
estado *m*.
conditional *adj* condicional, hipotético; ~**ly** *adv* condicional-
mente.
conditioned *adj* condicionado.
conditioner *n* acondicionador *m*.
condolences *npl* pésame *m*.
condom *n* condón *m*.
condominium *n* condominio *m*,
condone *vt* perdonar.
conducive *adj* conducente, oportuno.
conduct *n* conducta *f*; manejo, proceder *m*; • *vt* conducir,
guiar.
conductor *n* conductor *m*; guía, director *m*; conductor de
electricidad *m*.
conduit *n* conducto *m*; caño *m*.
cone *n* cono *m*.
confection *n* confitura *f*; confección *f*.
confectioner *n* confitero *m*.
confectioner's (shop) *n* pastelería *f*; confitería *f*.
confederacy *n* confederación *f*.
confederate *vi* confederarse; • *adj*, *n* confederado *m*.

confer vi conferenciar; • vt conferir, comparar.
conference n conferencia f.
confess vt, vi confesar(se).
confession n confesión f.
confessional n confesionario m.
confessor n confesor m.
confetti n confeti m.
confidant n confidente, amigo íntimo m.
confide vt, vi confiar; fiarse.
confidence n confianza, seguridad f.
confidence trick n timo m.
confident adj cierto, seguro; confiado.
confidential adj confidencial.
configuration n configuración f.
confine vt limitar; aprisionar.
confinement n prisión f; estreñimiento m.
confirm vt confirmar; ratificar.
confirmation n confirmación f; ratificación f; prueba f.
confirmed adj empedernido.
confiscate vt confiscar.
confiscation n confiscación f.
conflagration n conflagración f; incendio general m.
conflict n conflicto m; combate m; pelea f.
conflicting adj contradictorio.
confluence n confluencia f; concurso m.
conform vt, vi conformar(se).
conformity n conformidad, conveniencia f.
confound vt turbar, confundir.
confront vt afrontar; confrontar; comparar.
confrontation n enfrentamiento m.
confuse vt confundir; desordenar.
confusing adj confuso.
confusion n confusión f; perturbación f; desorden m.
congeal vt, vi helar, congelar(se).
congenial adj congenial.
congenital adj congénito.
congested adj atestado.
congestion n congestión f; acumulación f.
conglomerate vt conglomerar, aglomerar; • adj aglomerado; • n (com) conglomerado m.
conglomeration n aglomeración f.
congratulate vt congratular, felicitar.
congratulations npl felicidades fpl.
congratulatory adj congratulatorio.
congregate vt congregar, reunir.
congregation n congregación, reunión f.
congress n congreso m; conferencia f.
congressman n miembro del Congreso m.
congruity n congruencia f.
congruous adj idóneo, congruo, apto.
conic(al) adj cónico.
conifer n conífera f.
coniferous adj (bot) conífero.
conjecture n conjetura, apariencia f; • vt conjeturar; pronosticar.
conjugal adj conyugal, matrimonial.
conjugate vt (gr) conjugar.
conjugation n conjugación f.
conjunction n conjunción f; unión f.
conjuncture n coyuntura f; ocasión f; tiempo crítico m.
conjure vi conjurar, exorcizar.
conjurer n conjurador, encantador m.
con man n timador m.
connect vt juntar, unir, enlazar.
connection n conexión f.
connivance n connivencia f.
connive vi tolerar.
connoisseur n conocedor m.
conquer vt conquistar; vencer.
conqueror n vencedor, conquistador m.
conquest n conquista f.
conscience n conciencia f; escrúpulo m.

conscientious adj concienzudo, escrupuloso; ~ly adv según conciencia.
conscious adj sabedor, convencido; ~ly adv a sabiendas.
consciousness n conciencia f.
conscript n conscripto m.
conscription n reclutamiento m.
consecrate vt consagrar; dedicar.
consecration n consagración f.
consecutive adj consecutivo; ~ly adv consecutivamente.
consensus n consenso m.
consent n consentimiento m; aprobación f; • vi consentir; aprobar.
consequence n consecuencia f; importancia f.
consequent adj consecutivo, concluyente; ~ly adv consiguientemente.
conservation n conservación f.
conservative adj conservativo.
conservatory n conservatorio m.
conserve vt conservar; • n conserva f.
consider vt considerar, examinar; • vi pensar, deliberar.
considerable adj considerable; importante; ~bly adv considerablemente.
considerate adj considerado, prudente, discreto; ~ly adv juiciosamente; prudentemente.
consideration n consideración f; deliberación f; importancia f; valor, mérito m.
considering conj en vista de; ~ that a causa de; visto que, en razon a.
consign vt consignar.
consignment n consignación f.
consist vi consistir.
consistency n consistencia f.
consistent adj consistente; conveniente, conforme; sólido, estable; ~ly adv conformemente.
consolable adj consolable.
consolation n consolación f; consuelo m.
consolatory adj consolatorio.
console vt consolar.
consolidate vt, vi consolidar(se).
consolidation n consolidación f.
consonant adj consonante, conforme; • n (gr) consonante f.
consort n consorte, socio m.
conspicuous adj conspicuo, aparente; notable; ~ly adv claramente.
conspiracy n conspiración f.
conspirator n conspirador m.
conspire vi conspirar, maquinar.
constancy n constancia, perseverancia, persistencia f.
constant adj constante; perseverante; ~ly adv constantemente.
constellation n constelación f.
consternation n consternación f; terror m.
constipated adj estreñido.
constituency n junta electoral f.
constituent n constitutivo m; • adj constituyente.
constitute vt constituir; establecer.
constitution n constitución f; estado m; temperamento m.
constitutional adj constitucional, legal.
constrain vt constreñir, forzar; restringir.
constraint n constreñimiento m; fuerza, violencia f.
constrict vt constreñir, estrechar.
construct vt construir, edificar.
construction n construcción f.
construe vt construir; interpretar.
consul n cónsul m.
consular adj consular.
consulate, consulship n consulado m.
consult vt, vi consultar(se); aconsejar(se).
consultation n consulta, deliberación f.
consume vt consumir; disipar; • vi consumirse.
consumer n consumidor m.
consumer goods npl bienes de consumo mpl.

consumerism n consumismo m.

consumer society n sociedad de consumo f.

consummate vt consumar, acabar, perfeccionar; ● adj cumplido, consumado.

consummation n consumación, perfección f.

consumption n consumo m.

contact n contacto m.

contact lenses npl lentes de contacto mpl.

contagious adj contagioso.

contain vt contener, comprender; caber, reprimir, refrenar.

container n recipiente m.

contaminate vt contaminar; corromper; ~d adj contaminado, corrompido.

contamination n contaminación f.

contemplate vt contemplar.

contemplation n contemplación f.

contemplative adj contemplativo.

contemporaneous, contemporary adj contemporáneo.

contempt n desprecio, desdén m.

contemptible adj despreciable, vil; ~bly adv vilmente.

contemptuous adj desdeñoso, insolente; ~ly adv con desdén.

contend vi contender, disputar, afirmar.

content adj contento, satisfecho; ● vt contentar, satisfacer; ● n contenido m; ~s pl contenido m; tabla de materias f.

contentedly adv de un modo satisfecho; con paciencia.

contention n contención, altercación f.

contentious adj contencioso, litigioso; ~ly adv contenciosamente.

contentment n contentamiento, placer m.

contest vt contestar, disputar, litigar; ● n concurso m; contestación, altercación f.

contestant n concursante m.

context n contexto m; contextura f.

contiguous adj contiguo, vecino.

continent adj continente; ● n continente m.

continental adj continental.

contingency n contingencia f; acontecimiento m; eventualidad f.

contingent n contingente m; cuota f; ● adj contingente, casual; ~ly ad casualmente.

continual adj continuo; ~ly adv continuamente.

continuation n continuación, serie f.

continue vt continuar; ● vi durar, perseverar, persistir.

continuity n continuidad f.

continuous adj continuo, unido; ~ly adv continuadamente.

contort vt torcer.

contortion n contorsión f.

contour n contorno m.

contraband n contrabando m; ● adj prohibido, ilegal.

contraception n contracepción f.

contraceptive n anticonceptivo m; ● adj anticonceptivo.

contract vt contraer; abreviar; contratar; ●vi contraerse; ● n contrato, pacto m.

contraction n contracción f; abreviatura f.

contractor n contratante m.

contradict vt contradecir.

contradiction n contradicción, oposición f.

contradictory adj contradictorio.

contraption n artilugio m.

contrariness n contrariedad, oposición f.

contrary adj contrario, opuesto; ● n contrario m; **on the** ~ al contrario.

contrast n contraste m; oposición f; ● vt contrastar, oponer.

contrasting adj opuesto.

contravention n contravención f.

contributary adj contributario.

contribute vt contribuir, ayudar.

contribution n contribución f; tributo m.

contributor n contribuidor m.

contributory adj contribuyente.

contrite adj contrito, arrepentido.

contrition n penitencia, contrición f.

contrivance n designio m; invención f; concepto m.

contrive vt inventar, trazar, maquinar; manejar; combinar.

control n control m; inspección f; ● vt controlar; manejar; restringir; gobernar.

control room n sala de mando f.

control tower n torre de control f.

controversial adj polémico.

controversy n controversia f.

contusion n contusión f, magullamiento m.

conundrum n problema m.

conurbation n urbanización f.

convalesce vi convalecer.

convalescence n convalecencia f.

convalescent adj convaleciente.

convene vt convocar; juntar, unir; ● vi convenir, juntarse.

convenience n conveniencia, comodidad, conformidad f.

convenient adj conveniente, apto, cómodo, propio; ~ly adv cómodamente, oportunamente.

convent n convento, claustro, monasterio m.

convention n convención f; contrato, tratado m.

conventional adj convencional, estipulado.

converge vi convergir.

convergence n convergencia f.

convergent adj convergente.

conversant adj versado en; íntimo.

conversation n conversación f.

converse vi conversar; platicar.

conversely adv mutuamente, recíprocamente.

conversion n conversión, transmutación f.

convert vt, vi convertir(se); ● n converso, convertido m.

convertible adj convertible, transmutable; ● n descapotable m.

convex adj convexo.

convexity n convexidad f.

convey vt transportar; transmitir, transferir.

conveyance n transporte m; conducción f; escritura de traspaso f.

conveyancer n notario m.

convict vt probar un delito; ● n convicto m.

conviction n convicción f.

convince vt convencer, poner en evidencia.

convincing adj convincente.

convincingly adv de modo convincente.

convivial adj sociable; hospitalario.

conviviality n sociabilidad f.

convoke vt convocar, reunir.

convoy n convoy m.

convulse vt conmover, trastornar.

convulsion n convulsión f; conmoción f; tumulto m.

convulsive adj convulsivo; ~ly adv convulsivamente.

coo vi arrullar.

cook n cocinero m; cocinera f; ● vt cocinar; ● vi cocinar; guisar.

cookbook n libro de cocina m.

cooker n cocina f.

cookery n arte culinario m.

cookie n galleta f.

cool adj fresco; indiferente; ● n frescura f; ● vt enfriar, refrescar.

coolly adv frescamente; indiferentemente.

coolness n fresco m; frialdad, frescura f.

cooperate vi cooperar.

cooperation n cooperación f.

cooperative adj cooperativo; cooperante.

coordinate vt coordinar.

coordination n coordinación, elección f.

cop n (fam) poli m.

copartner n compañero, socio m.

cope vi arreglárselas.

copier n copiadora f.

copious adj copioso, abundante; ~ly adv en abundancia.

copper n cobre m.

coppice, copse n monte bajo m.
copulate vi copularse.
copy n copia f; original m; ejemplar de algún libro m; • vt copiar; imitar.
copybook n copiador de cartas (libro) m.
copying machine n copiadora f.
copyist n copista m.
copyright n propiedad de una obra literaria f; derechos de autor mpl.
coral n coral m.
coral reef n arrecife de coral m.
cord n cuerda f; cable m.
cordial adj cordial, de corazón, amistoso; ~**ly** adv cordialmente.
corduroy n pana f.
core n cuesco m; interior, centro, corazón m; materia f.
cork n alcornoque m; corcho m; • vt tapar botellas con corchos.
corkscrew n tirabuzón m.
corn n maíz m; grano m; callo m.
corncob n mazorca f.
cornea n córnea f.
corned beef n carne acecinada f.
corner n rincón m; esquina f.
cornerstone n piedra angular f.
cornet n corneta f.
cornfield n maizal m.
cornflakes npl copos de maíz mpl.
cornice n cornisa f.
cornstarch n harina de maíz f.
corollary n corolario m.
coronary n infarto m.
coronation n coronación f.
coroner n oficial que hace la inspección jurídica de los cadáveres m.
coronet n corona pequeña f.
corporal n caporal m.
corporate adj corporativo.
corporation n corporación f; gremio m.
corporeal adj corpóreo.
corps n cuerpo de ejército m; regimiento m.
corpse n cadáver m.
corpulent adj corpulento, gordo.
corpuscle n corpúsculo, átomo m.
corral n corral m.
correct vt corregir; enmendar; • adj correcto, justo; ~**ly** adv correctamente.
correction n corrección f; enmienda f; censura f.
corrective adj correctivo; • n correctivo m; restricción f.
correctness n exactitud f.
correlation n correlación f.
correlative adj correlativo.
correspond vi corresponder; corresponderse.
correspondence n correspondencia f.
correspondent adj correspondiente, conforme; • n corresponsal m.
corridor n pasillo m.
corroborate vt corroborar.
corroboration n corroboración f.
corroborative adj corroborativo.
corrode vt corroer.
corrosion n corrosión f.
corrosive adj, n corrosivo m.
corrugated iron n chapa ondulada f.
corrupt vt corromper; sobornar; • vi corromperse, pudrirse; • adj corrompido; depravado.
corruptible adj corruptible.
corruption n corrupción f; depravación f.
corruptive adj corruptivo.
corset n corsé, corpiño m.
cortège n cortejo m.
cosily adv cómodamente, con facilidad.

cosmetic adj, n cosmético m.
cosmic adj cósmico.
cosmonaut n cosmonauta m.
cosmopolitan adj cosmopolita.
cosset vt mimar.
cost n coste, precio m; • vi costar.
costly adj costoso, caro.
costume n traje m.
cottage n casita, casucha f.
cotton n algodón m.
cotton candy n algodón azucarado m.
cotton mill n hilandería de algodón.
cotton wool n algodón hidrófilo m.
couch n sofá m.
couchette n litera f.
cough n tos f; • vi toser.
council n concilio, consejo m.
councilor n concejal, individuo del concejo m.
counsel n consejo, aviso m; abogado m.
counselor n consejero m; abogado m.
count vt contar, numerar; calcular; **to ~ on** contar con; • n cuenta f; cálculo m; conde m.
countdown n cuenta atrás f.
countenance n rostro m; aspecto m; (buena o mala) cara f.
counter n mostrador m; ficha f.
counteract vt contrariar, impedir, estorbar; frustrar.
counterbalance vt contrapesar; igualar, compensar; • n contrapeso m.
counterfeit vt contrahacer, imitar, falsear; • adj falsificado; fingido.
countermand vt contramandar; revocar.
counterpart n parte correspondiente f.
counterproductive adj contraproducente.
countersign vt refrendar; firmar un decreto.
countess n condesa f.
countless adj innumerable.
countrified adj rústico; tosco, rudo.
country n país m; campo m; región f; patria f; • adj rústico; campestre, rural.
country house n casa de campo, granja f.
countryman n paisano m; compatriota m.
county n condado m.
coup n golpe m.
coupé n cupé m.
couple n par m; lazo m; • vt unir, parear; casar.
couplet n copla f; par m.
coupon n cupón m.
courage n coraje, valor f.
courageous adj corajudo, valeroso; ~**ly** adv valerosamente.
courier n correo, mensajero, expreso m.
course n curso m; carrera f; camino m; ruta f; método m; **of ~** por supuesto, sin duda.
court n corte f; palacio m; tribunal de justicia m; • vt cortejar; solicitar, adular.
courteous adj cortés; benévolo; ~**ly** adv cortésmente.
courtesan n cortesana f.
courtesy n cortesía f; benignidad f.
courthouse n palacio de justicia m.
courtly adj cortesano, elegante.
court martial n consejo militar m.
courtroom n sala de justicia f.
courtyard n patio m.
cousin n primo m; prima f; **first ~** primo hermano m.
cove n (mar) ensenada, caleta f.
covenant n contrato m; convención f; • vi pactar, estipular.
cover n cubierta f; abrigo m; pretexto m; • vt cubrir; tapar; ocultar; proteger.
coverage n alcance m.
coveralls npl mono m.
covering n ropa f; vestido m.
cover letter n carta de explicación f.
covert adj cubierto; oculto, secreto; ~**ly** adv secretamente.

cover-up *n* encubrimiento *m*.
covet *vt* codiciar, desear con ansia.
covetous *adj* avariento, sórdido.
cow *n* vaca *f*.
coward *n* cobarde *m*.
cowardice *n* cobardía, timidez *f*.
cowardly *adj, adv* cobarde; pusilánime; cobardemente.
cowboy *n* vaquero *m*.
cower *vi* agacharse.
cowherd *n* vaquero *m*.
coy *adj* recatado, modesto; esquivo; ~**ly** *adv* con esquivez.
coyness *n* esquivez, modestia *f*.
cozy *adj* cómodo.
crab *n* cángrejo *m*; manzana silvestre *f*.
crab apple *n* manzana silvestre *f*; **crab-apple tree** *n* manzano silvestre *m*.
crack *n* crujido *m*; hendedura, quebraja *f*; ● *vt* hender, rajar; romper; **to ~ down on** reprimandar fuertemente; ● *vi* reventar.
cracker *n* buscapiés *m invar*; galleta *f*.
crackle *vi* crujir, chillar.
crackling *n* estallido, crujido *m*.
cradle *n* cuna *f*; ● *vt* mecer la cuna.
craft *n* arte *m*; artificio *m*; barco *m*.
craftily *adv* astutamente.
craftiness *n* astucia, estratagema *f*.
craftsman *n* artífice, artesano *m*.
craftsmanship *n* artesanía *f*.
crafty *adj* astuto, artificioso.
crag *n* despeñadero *m*.
cram *vt* embutir; engordar; empujar; ● *vi* empollar.
crammed *adj* atestado.
cramp *n* calambre *m*; ● *vt* constreñir.
cramped *adj* apretado.
crampon *n* crampón *m*.
cranberry *n* arandilla *f*.
crane *n* grulla *f*; grúa *f*.
crash *vi* estallar; ● *n* estallido *m*; choque *m*.
crash helmet *n* casco *m*.
crash landing *n* aterrizaje forzado *m*.
crass *adj* craso, grueso, basto, tosco, grosero.
crate *n* cesta grande *f*.
crater *n* cráter *m*; boca de volcán *f*.
cravat *n* pañuelo *m*.
crave *vt* rogar, suplicar.
craving *adj* insaciable, pedigüeño; ● *n* deseo ardiente *m*.
crawfish *n* ástaco *m*.
crawl *vi* arrastrar; **to ~ with** hormiguear.
crayfish *n* cangrejo de río *m*.
crayon *n* lápiz *m*.
craze *n* manía *f*.
craziness *n* locura *f*.
crazy *adj* loco.
creak *vi* crujir, estallar.
cream *n* crema *f*; ● *adj* color crema.
creamy *adj* lleno de crema.
crease *n* pliegue *m*; ● *vt* plegar.
create *vt* crear; causar.
creation *n* creación *f*; elección *f*.
creative *adj* creativo.
creator *n* criador *m*.
creature *n* criatura *f*.
credence *n* creencia, fe *f*; renombre *m*.
credentials *npl* (cartas) credenciales *fpl*.
credibility *n* credibilidad *f*.
credible *adj* creíble.
credit *n* crédito *m*; reputación *f*; autoridad *f*; ● *vt* creer, fiar, acreditar.
creditable *adj* estimable, honorífico; ~**bly** *adv* honorablemente.
credit card *n* tarjeta de crédito *f*.
creditor *n* acreedor *m*.

credulity *n* credulidad *f*.
credulous *adj* crédulo; ~**ly** *adv* con credulidad.
creed *n* credo *m*.
creek *n* arroyo *m*.
creep *vi* arrastrar, serpear; complacer bajamente.
creeper *n* (*bot*) enredadera *f*.
creepy *adj* horripilante.
cremate *vt* incinerar cadáveres.
cremation *n* cremación *f*.
crematorium *n* crematorio *m*.
crescent *adj* creciente; ● *n* creciente *f* (fase de la luna).
cress *n* berro *m*.
crest *n* cresta *f*.
crested *adj* crestado.
crestfallen *adj* acobardado, abatido de espíritu.
crevasse *n* grieta *f*.
crevice *n* raja, hendedura *f*.
crew *n* banda, tropa *f*; tripulación *f*.
crib *n* cuna *f*; pesebre *m*.
cricket *n* grillo *m*; críquet *m*.
crime *n* crimen *m*; culpa *f*.
criminal *adj* criminal, reo; ~**ly** *adv* criminalmente; ● *n* criminal *m*.
criminality *n* criminalidad *f*.
crimson *adj, n* carmesí *m*.
cripple *n, adj* cojo *m*; ● *vt* lisiar; (*fig*) estropear.
crisis *n* crisis *f*.
crisp *adj* fresco.
crispness *n* encrespadura *f*.
criss-cross *adj* entrelazado.
criterion *n* criterio *m*.
critic *n* crítico *m*; crítica *f*.
critic(al) *adj* crítico; exacto; delicado; ~**ally** *adv* exactamente, rigurosamente.
criticism *n* crítica *f*.
criticize *vt* criticar, censurar.
croak *vi* graznar.
crochet *n* ganchillo *m*; ● *vt, vi* hacer ganchillo.
crockery *n* loza *f*; vasijas de barro *fpl*.
crocodile *n* cocodrilo *m*.
crony *n* amigo (o conocido) antiguo *m*.
crook *n* (*fam*) ladrón *m*; cayado *m*.
crooked *adj* torcido; perverso.
crop *n* cultivo *m*; cosecha *f*; ● *vt* recortar.
cross *n* cruz *f*; carga *f*; ● *adj* mal humorado; ● *vt* atravesar, cruzar; **to ~ over** traspasar.
crossbar *n* travesaño *m*.
crossbreed *n* raza cruzada *f*.
cross-country *n* carrera a campo traviesa *f*.
cross-examine *vt* preguntar a un testigo.
crossfire *n* fuego cruzado *m*.
crossing *n* cruce *m*; paso a nivel *m*.
cross-purpose *n* disposición contraria *f*; contradicción *f*; **to be at ~s** entenderse mal.
cross-reference *n* contrarreferencia *f*.
crossroad *n* encrucijada *f*.
crosswalk *n* paso de peatones *m*.
crotch *n* entrepierna *f*.
crouch *vi* agacharse, bajarse.
crow *n* cuervo *m*; canto del gallo *m*; ● *vi* cantar el gallo.
crowd *n* público *m*; muchedumbre *f*; ● *vt* amontonar; ● *vi* reunirse.
crown *n* corona *f*; colmo *m*; ● *vt* coronar.
crown prince *n* príncipe real *m*.
crucial *adj* crucial.
crucible *n* crisol *m*.
crucifix *n* crucifijo *m*.
crucifixion *n* crucifixión *f*.
crucify *vt* crucificar; atormentar.
crude *adj* crudo, imperfecto; ~**ly** *adv* crudamente.
cruel *adj* cruel, inhumano; ~**ly** *adv* cruelmente.
cruelty *n* crueldad *f*.

cruet *n* vinagrera *f.*

cruise *n* crucero *m;* • *vi* hacer un crucero.

cruiser *n* crucero *m.*

crumb *n* miga *f.*

crumble *vt* desmigajar, desmenuzar; • *vi* desmigajarse.

crumple *vt* arrugar.

crunch *vt* ronzar; • *n* (*fig*) crisis *f.*

crunchy *adj* crujiente.

crusade *n* cruzada *f.*

crush *vt* apretar, oprimir; • *n* choque *m.*

crust *n* costra *f;* corteza *f.*

crusty *adj* costroso; bronco, áspero.

crutch *n* muleta *f.*

crux *n* lo esencial.

cry *vt, vi* gritar; exclamar; llorar; • *n* grito *m;* lloro *m;* clamor *m.*

crypt *n* cripta (bóveda subterránea) *f.*

cryptic *adj* enigmático.

crystal *n* cristal *m.*

crystal-clear *adj* claro como el agua.

crystalline *adj* cristalino; transparente.

crystallize *vt, vi* cristalizar(se).

cub *n* cachorro *m.*

cube *n* cubo *m.*

cubic *adj* cúbico.

cuckoo *n* cuclillo, cuco *m.*

cucumber *n* pepino *m.*

cud *n:* **to chew the ~** rumiar; (*fig*) reflexionar.

cuddle *vt* abrazar; • *vi* abrazarse; • *n* abrazo *m.*

cudgel *n* garrote, palo *m.*

cue *n* taco (de billar) *m.*

cuff *n* puñada *f;* vuelta *f.*

culinary *adj* culinario, de la cocina.

cull *vt* escoger, elegir.

culminate *vi* culminar.

culmination *n* colmo *m.*

culpability *n* culpabilidad *f.*

culpable *adj* culpable, criminal; **~bly** *adv* culpablemente, criminalmente, por la vía criminal.

culprit *n* culpable *m.*

cult *n* culto *f.*

cultivate *vi* cultivar, mejorar; perfeccionar.

cultivation *n* cultivación *f;* cultivo *m.*

cultural *adj* cultural.

culture *n* cultura *f.*

cumbersome *adj* engorroso, pesado, confuso.

cumulative *adj* cumulativo.

cunning *adj* astuto; intrigante; **~ly** *adv* astutamente; expertamente; • *n* astucia, sutileza *f.*

cup *n* taza, jícara *f;* (*bot*) cáliz *m.*

cupboard *n* armario *m.*

curable *adj* curable.

curate *n* teniente de cura *m;* párroco *m.*

curator *n* curador *m;* guardián *m.*

curb *n* freno *m;* bordillo *m;* • *vt* refrenar, contener, moderar.

curd *n* cuajada *f.*

curdle *vt* (*vi*) cuajar(se), coagular(se).

cure *n* cura *f;* remedio *m;* • *vt* curar, sanar.

curfew *n* toque de queda *m.*

curing *n* curación *f.*

curiosity *n* curiosidad *f;* rareza *f.*

curious *adj* curioso; **~ly** *adv* curiosamente.

curl *n* rizo de pelo *m;* • *vt* rizar; ondear; • *vi* rizarse.

curling iron *n,* **curling tongs** *npl* tenacillas de rizar *fpl.*

curly *adj* rizado.

currant *n* pasa *f.*

currency *n* moneda *f;* circulación *f;* duración *f.*

current *adj* corriente, común; • *n* curso, progreso *m;* marcha *f;* corriente *f.*

current affairs *npl* actualidades *fpl.*

currently *adv* corrientemente; a la moda.

curriculum vitae *n* currículum *m.*

curry *n* curry *m.*

curse *vt* maldecir; • *vi* imprecar; blasfemar; • *n* maldición *f.*

cursor *n* cursor *m.*

cursory *adj* precipitado, inconsiderado.

curt *adj* sucinto.

curtail *vt* cortar; mutilar.

curtain *n* cortina *f;* telón en los teatros *m.*

curtain rod *n* varilla de cortinaje *f.*

curtsy *n* reverencia *f;* • *vi* hacer una reverencia.

curvature *n* curvatura *f.*

curve *vt* encorvar; • *n* curva *f.*

cushion *n* cojín *m;* almohada *f.*

custard *n* natillas *fpl.*

custodian *n* custodio *m.*

custody *n* custodia *f;* prisión *f.*

custom *n* costumbre *f*, uso *m.*

customary *adj* usual, accostumbrado, ordinario.

customer *n* cliente *m.*

customs *npl* aduana *f.*

customs duty *n* derechos de aduana *mpl.*

customs officer *n* aduanero *m.*

cut *vt* cortar; separar; herir; dividir; alzar los naipes; **to ~ short** interrumpir, cortar la palabra; **to ~ teeth** nacerle los dientes (a un niño); • *vi* traspasar; cruzarse; • *n* corte *m;* cortadura *f;* herida *f;* **~ and dry** *adj* pronto.

cutback *n* reducción *f.*

cute *adj* lindo.

cutlery *n* cuchillería *f.*

cutlet *n* costilla asada de carnero *f.*

cut-rate *adj* a precio reducido.

cut-throat *n* asesino *m;* • *adj* encarnizado.

cutting *n* cortadura *f;* • *adj* cortante; mordaz.

cyanide *n* cianuro *m.*

cycle *n* ciclo *m;* bicicleta *f;* • *vi* ir en bicicleta.

cycling *n* ciclismo *m.*

cyclist *n* ciclista *m.*

cyclone *n* ciclón *m.*

cygnet *n* pollo del cisne *m.*

cylinder *n* cilindro *m;* rollo *m.*

cylindric(al) *adj* cilíndrico.

cymbals *n* címbalo *m.*

cynic(al) *adj* cínico; obsceno; • *n* cínico *m* (filósofo).

cynicism *n* cinismo *m.*

cypress *n* ciprés *m.*

cyst *n* quiste *m.*

czar *n* zar *m.*

D

dab *n* pedazo pequeño *m;* toque *m.*

dabble *vi* chapotear.

Dacron *n* terylene *m.*

dad(dy) *n* papá *m.*

daddy-long-legs *n* zancudo *m.*

daffodil *n* narciso *m.*

dagger *n* puñal *m.*

daily *adj* diario, cotidiano; • *adv* diariamente, cada día; • *n* diario *m.*

daintily *adv* delicadamente.

daintiness *n* elegancia *f;* delicadeza *f.*

dainty *adj* delicado; elegante.

dairy *n* lechería *f.*

dairy farm *n* granja *f.*

dairy produce *n* productos lácteos *mpl.*

daisy *n* margarita, maya *f.*

daisy wheel *n* margarita *f.*

dale *n* valle *m.*

dally *vi* tardar.

dam *n* presa *f;* • *vt* represar.

damage *n* daño *m;* perjuicio *m;* • *vt* dañar; perjudicar.

damask *n* damasco *m*; ● *adj* de damasco.
dame *n* chica *f*.
damn *vt* condenar; ● *adj* maldito.
damnable *adj* maldito; **~bly** *adv* terriblemente.
damnation *n* perdición *f*.
damning *adj* irrecusable.
damp *adj* húmedo; ● *n* humedad *f*; ● *vt* mojar.
dampen *vt* mojar.
dampness *n* humedad *f*.
damson *n* damascena *f* (ciruela).
dance *n* danza *f*; baile *m*; ● *vi* bailar.
dance hall *n* salón de baile *m*.
dancer *n* bailarín *m*.
dandelion *n* diente de león *m*.
dandruff *n* caspa *f*.
dandy *adj* mono.
danger *n* peligro, riesgo *m*.
dangerous *adj* peligroso; **~ly** *adv* peligrosamente.
dangle *vi* estar colgado.
dank *adj* húmedo.
dapper *adj* apuesto.
dappled *adj* rodado.
dare *vi* atreverse; ● *vt* desafiar.
daredevil *n* atrevido *m*.
daring *n* osadía *f*; ● *adj* atrevido; **~ly** *adv* atrevidamente, osadamante.
dark *adj* oscuro; ● *n* oscuridad *f*; ignorancia *f*.
darken *vt*, *vi* oscurecer(se).
dark glasses *npl* anteojos de sol *mpl*.
darkness *n* oscuridad *f*.
darkroom *n* cuarto oscuro *m*.
darling *n*, *adj* querido *m*.
darn *vt* zurcir.
dart *n* dardo *m*.
dartboard *n* diana *f*.
dash *vi* irse de prisa; ● *n* pizca *f*; **at one ~** de un golpe.
dashboard *n* tablero de instrumentos *m*.
dashing *adj* gallardo.
dastardly *adj* cobarde.
data *n* datos *mpl*.
database *n* base de datos *f*.
data processing *n* proceso de datos *m*.
date *n* fecha *f*; cita *f*; (*bot*) dátil *m*; ● *vt* fechar; salir con.
dated *adj* anticuado.
dative *n* dativo *m*.
daub *vt* manchar.
daughter *n* hija *f*; **~ in-law** nuera *f*.
daunting *adj* desalentador.
dawdle *vi* gastar tiempo.
dawn *n* alba *f*; ● *vi* amanecer.
daybreak *n* alba *f*.
day laborer *n* jornalero *m*.
daylight *n* luz del día, luz natural *f*; **~ saving time** *n* hora de verano *f*.
daytime *n* día *m*.
daze *vt* aturdir.
dazed *adj* aturdido.
dazzle *vt* deslumbrar.
dazzling *adj* deslumbrante.
deacon *n* diácono *m*.
dead *adj* muerto; marchito; **~wood** *n* lastre *m*; **~ silence** *n* silencio profundo *m*; **the ~** *npl* los muertos.
dead-drunk *adj* borracho como una cuba.
deaden *vt* amortiguar.
dead heat empate *m*.
deadline *n* fecha tope *f*.
deadlock *n* punto muerto *m*.
deadly *adj* mortal; ● *adv* terriblemente.
dead march *n* marcha fúnebre *f*.
deadness *n* inercia *f*.
deaf *adj* sordo.

deafen *vt* ensordecer.
deaf-mute *n* sordomudo *m*.
deafness *n* sordera *f*.
deal *n* convenio *m*; transacción *f*; **a great ~** mucho; **a good ~** bastante; ● *vt* distribuir; dar; ● *vi* comerciar; **to ~ in/with** tratar con.
dealer *n* comerciante *m*; traficante *m*; mano *f*.
dealings *npl* trato *m*.
dean *n* deán *m*.
dear *adj* querido; caro, costoso; **~ly** *adv* caro.
dearness *n* carestía *f*.
dearth *n* carestía *f*.
death *n* muerte *f*.
deathbed *n* lecho de muerte *m*.
deathblow *n* golpe mortal *m*.
death certificate *n* partida de difunción *f*.
death penalty *n* pena de muerte *f*.
death throes *npl* agonía *f*.
death warrant *n* sentencia de muerte *f*.
debacle *n* desastre *m*.
debar *vt* excluir, no admitir.
debase *vt* degradar.
debasement *n* degradación *f*.
debatable *adj* discutible.
debate *n* debate *m*; polémica *f*; ● *vt* discutir; examinar.
debauched *adj* vicioso.
debauchery *n* libertinaje *m*.
debilitate *vt* debilitar.
debit *n* debe *m*; ● *vt* (*com*) cargar en una cuenta.
debt *n* deuda *f*; obligación *f*; **to get into ~** contraer deudas.
debtor *n* deudor *m*.
debunk *vt* desacreditar.
decade *n* década *f*.
decadence *n* decadencia *f*.
decaffeinated *adj* descafeinado.
decanter *n* garrafa *f*.
decapitate *vt* decapitar, degollar.
decapitation *n* decapitación *f*.
decay *vi* decaer; pudrirse; ● *n* decadencia *f*; caries *f*.
deceased *adj* muerto.
deceit *n* engaño *m*.
deceitful *adj* engañoso; **~ly** *adv* falsamente.
deceive *vt* engañar.
December *n* diciembre *m*.
decency *n* decencia *f*; modestia *f*.
decent *adj* decente, razonable; **~ly** *adv* decentemente.
deception *n* engaño *m*.
deceptive *adj* engañoso.
decibel *n* decibelio *m*.
decide *vt*, *vi* decidir; resolver.
decided *adj* decidido.
decidedly *adv* decididamente.
deciduous *adj* (*bot*) de hoja caduca.
decimal *adj* decimal.
decimate *vt* diezmar.
decipher *vt* descifrar.
decision *n* decisión, determinación *f*.
decisive *adj* decisivo; **~ly** *adv* de modo decisivo.
deck *n* cubierta *f*; ● *vt* adornar.
deckchair *n* tumbona *f*.
declaim *vi* declamar.
declamation *n* declamación *f*.
declaration *n* declaración *f*.
declare *vt* declarar, manifestar.
declension *n* declinación *f*.
decline *vt* (*gr*) declinar; evitar; ● *vi* decaer; ● *n* decadencia *f*.
declutch *vi* desembragar.
decode *vt* descifrar.
decompose *vt* descomponer.
decomposition *n* descomposición *f*.
décor *n* decoración *f*.
decorate *vt* decorar, adornar.

decoration *n* decoración *f*.
decorative *adj* decorativo.
decorator *n* pintor decorador *m*.
decorous *adj* decoroso; ~ly *adv* decorosamente.
decorum *n* decoro, garbo *m*.
decoy *n* señuelo *m*.
decrease *vt* disminuir; • *n* disminución *f*.
decree *n* decreto *m*; • *vt* decretar; ordenar.
decrepit *adj* decrépito.
decry *vt* desacreditar, censurar.
dedicate *vt* dedicar; consagrar.
dedication *n* dedicación *f*; dedicatoria *f*.
deduce *vt* deducir; concluir.
deduct *vt* restar.
deduction *n* deducción *f*; descuento *m*.
deed *n* acción *f*; hecho *m*; hazaña *f*.
deem *vi* juzgar.
deep *adj* profundo.
deepen *vt* profundizar.
deep-freeze *n* congeladora *f*.
deeply *adv* profundamente.
deepness *n* profundidad *f*.
deer *n* ciervo *m*.
deface *vt* desfigurar, afear.
defacement *n* desfiguración *f*.
defamation *n* difamación *f*.
default *n* defecto *m*; falta *f*; • *vi* faltar.
defaulter *n* (*law*) moroso *m*.
defeat *n* derrota *f*; • *vt* derrotar; frustrar.
defect *n* defecto *m*; falta *f*.
defection *n* deserción *f*.
defective *adj* defectuoso.
defend *vt* defender; proteger.
defendant *n* acusado *m*.
defense *n* defensa *f*; protección *f*.
defenseless *adj* indefenso.
defensive *adj* defensivo; ~ly *adv* de modo defensivo.
defer *vt* aplazar.
deference *n* deferencia *f*; respeto *m*.
deferential *adj* respetuoso.
defiance *n* desafío *m*.
defiant *adj* insolente.
deficiency *n* defecto *m*; falta *f*.
deficient *adj* insuficiente.
deficit *n* déficit *m*.
defile *vt* ensuciar.
definable *adj* definible.
define *vt* definir.
definite *adj* definido; preciso; ~ly *adv* no cabe duda.
definition *n* definición *f*.
definitive *adj* definitivo; ~ly *adv* definitivamente.
deflate *vt* desinflar.
deflect *vt* desviar.
deflower *vt* desvirgar.
deform *vt* desfigurar.
deformity *n* deformidad *f*.
defraud *vt* estafar.
defray *vt* costear.
defrost *vt* deshelar; descongelar.
defroster *n* eliminador de vaho *m*.
deft *adj* diestro; ~ly *adv* hábilmente.
defunct *adj* difunto.
defuse *vt* desactivar.
degenerate *vi* degenerar; • *adj* degenerado.
degeneration *n* degeneración *f*.
degradation *n* degradación *f*.
degrade *vt* degradar.
degree *n* grado *m*; título *m*.
dehydrated *adj* deshidratado.
de-ice *vt* deshelar.
deign *vi* dignarse.
deity *n* deidad, divinidad *f*.

dejected *adj* desanimado.
dejection *n* desaliento *m*.
delay *vt* demorar; • *n* retraso *m*.
delectable *adj* deleitoso.
delegate *vt* delegar; • *n* delegado *m*.
delegation *n* delegación *f*.
delete *vt* tachar; borrar.
deliberate *vt* deliberar; • *adj* intencionado; ~ly *adv* a propósito.
deliberation *n* deliberación *f*.
deliberative *adj* deliberativo.
delicacy *n* delicadeza *f*.
delicate *adj* delicado; exquisito; ~ly *adv* delicadamente.
delicious *adj* delicioso; exquisito; ~ly *adv* deliciosamente.
delight *n* delicia *f*; gozo, encanto *m*; • *vt*, *vi* deleitar(se).
delighted *adj* encantado.
delightful *adj* encantador, ~ly *adv* en forma encantadora.
delineate *vt* delinear.
delineation *n* delineación *f*.
delinquency *n* delincuencia *f*.
delinquent *n* delincuente *m*.
delirious *adj* delirante.
delirium *n* delirio *m*.
deliver *vt* entregar; pronunciar.
deliverance *n* liberación.
delivery *n* entrega *f*; parto *m*.
delude *vt* engañar.
deluge *n* diluvio *m*.
delusion *n* engaño *m*; ilusión *f*.
delve *vi* hurgar.
demagog(ue) *n* demagogo *m*.
demand *n* demanda *f*; reclamación *f*; • *vt* exigir; reclamar.
demanding *adj* exigente.
demarcation *n* demarcación *f*.
demean *vi* rebajarse.
demeanor *n* conducta *f*.
demented *adj* demente.
demise *n* desaparición *f*.
democracy *n* democracia *f*.
democrat *n* demócrata *m*.
democratic *adj* democrático.
demolish *vt* demoler.
demolition *n* demolición *f*.
demon *n* demonio, diablo *m*.
demonstrable *adj* demostrable; ~bly *adv* manifiestamente.
demonstrate *vt* demostrar, probar; • *vi* manifestarse.
demonstration *n* demostración *f*; manifestación *f*.
demonstrative *adj* demostrativo.
demonstrator *n* manifestante *m*.
demoralization *n* desmoralización *f*.
demoralize *vt* desmoralizar.
demote *vi* degradar.
demur *vi* objetar.
demure *adj* modesto; ~ly *adv* modestamente.
den *n* guarida *f*.
denatured alcohol *n* alcohol desnaturalizado *m*.
denial *n* negación *f*.
denims *npl* vaqueros *mpl*.
denomination *n* valor *m*.
denominator *n* (*math*) denominador *m*.
denote *vt* denotar, indicar.
denounce *vt* denunciar.
dense *adj* denso, espeso.
density *n* densidad *f*.
dent *n* abolladura *f*; • *vt* abollar.
dental *adj* dental.
dentifrice *n* dentífrico *m*.
dentist *n* dentista *m*.
dentistry *n* odontología *f*.
denture *npl* dentadura postiza *f*.
denude *vt* desnudar, despojar.
denunciation *n* denuncia *f*.

deny *vt* negar.
deodorant *n* desodorante *m*.
deodorize *vt* desdorizar.
depart *vi* partir(se).
department *n* departamento *m*.
department store *n* gran almacén *m*.
departure *n* partida *f*.
departure lounge *n* sala de embarque *f*.
depend *vi* depender; ~ **on/upon** contar con.
dependable *adj* seguro; serio.
dependant *n* dependiente *m*.
dependency *n* dependencia *f*.
dependent *adj* dependiente.
depict *vt* pintar, retratar; describir.
depleted *adj* reducido.
deplorable *adj* deplorable, lamentable; ~**bly** *adv* deplorable-
mente.
deplore *vt* deplorar, lamentar.
deploy *vt* (*mil*) desplegar.
depopulated *adj* despoblado.
depopulation *n* despoblación *f*.
deport *vt* deportar.
deportation *n* deportación *f*; destierro *m*.
deportment *n* conducta *f*.
deposit *vt* depositar; • *n* depósito *m*.
deposition *n* deposición *f*.
depositor *n* depositante *m*.
depot *n* depósito *m*.
deprave *vt* depravar, corromper.
depraved *adj* depravado.
depravity *n* depravación *f*.
deprecate *vt* lamentar.
depreciate *vi* depreciarse.
depreciation *n* depreciación *f*.
depredation *n* pillaje *m*.
depress *vt* deprimir.
depressed *adj* deprimido.
depression *n* depresión *f*.
deprivation *n* privación *f*.
deprive *vt* privar.
deprived *adj* necesitado.
depth *n* profundidad *f*.
deputation *n* diputación *f*.
depute *vt* diputar, delegar.
deputize *vi* suplir a.
deputy *n* diputado *m*.
derail *vt* descarrilar.
deranged *adj* trastornado.
derby *n* hongo *m*.
derelict *adj* abandonado.
deride *vt* burlar.
derision *n* mofa *f*.
derisive *adj* irrisorio.
derivable *adj* deducible.
derivation *n* derivación *f*.
derivative *n* derivado *m*.
derive *vt, vi* derivar(se).
derogatory *adj* despectivo.
derrick *n* torre de perforación *f*.
descant *n* (*mus*) discante *m*.
descend *vi* descender.
descendant *n* descendiente *m*.
descent *n* descenso *m*.
describe *vt* describir.
description *n* descripción *f*.
descriptive *adj* descriptivo.
descry *vt* divisar.
desecrate *vt* profanar.
desecration *n* profanación *f*.
desert *n* desierto *m*; • *adj* desierto.
desert *vt* abandonar; desertar; • *n* mérito *m*.
deserter *n* desertor *m*.

desertion *n* deserción *f*.
deserve *vt* merecer; ser digno.
deservedly *adv* merecidamente.
deserving *adj* meritorio.
deshabille *n* desabillé *m*.
desideratum *n* desiderátum *m*.
design *vt* diseñar; • *n* diseño *m*; dibujo *m*.
designate *vt* nombrar; designar.
designation *n* designación *f*.
designedly *adv* de propósito.
designer *n* diseñador *m*; modisto *m*.
desirability *n* conveniencia *f*.
desirable *adj* deseable.
desire *n* deseo *m*; • *vt* desear.
desirous *adj* deseoso, ansioso.
desist *vi* desistir.
desk *n* escritorio *m*.
desolate *adj* desierto.
desolation *n* desolación *f*.
despair *n* desesperación *f*; • *vi* desesperarse.
despairingly *adj* desesperadamente.
despatch = **dispatch**.
desperado *n* bandido *m*.
desperate *adj* desesperado; ~**ly** *adv* desesperadamente; sumamente.
desperation *n* desesperación *f*.
despicable *adj* despreciable.
despise *vt* despreciar.
despite *prep* a pesar de.
despoil *vt* despojar.
despondency *n* abatimiento *m*.
despondent *adj* abatido.
despot *n* déspota *m*.
despotic *adj* despótico, absoluto; ~**ally** *adv* despóticamente.
despotism *n* despotismo *m*.
dessert *n* postre *m*.
destination *n* destino *m*.
destine *vt* destinar.
destiny *n* destino *m*; suerte *f*.
destitute *adj* indigente.
destitution *n* miseria *f*.
destroy *vt* destruir, arruinar.
destruction *n* destrucción, ruina *f*.
destructive *adj* destructivo.
desultory *adj* irregular; sin método.
detach *vt* separar.
detachable *adj* desmontable.
detachment *n* (*mil*) destacamento *m*.
detail *n* detalle *m*; **in** ~ detalladamente; • *vt* detallar.
detain *vt* retener; detener.
detect *vt* detectar.
detection *n* descubrimiento *m*.
detective *n* detective *m*.
detector *n* detector *m*.
detention *n* detención *f*.
deter *vt* disuadir.
detergent *n* detergente *m*.
deteriorate *vt* deteriorar.
deterioration *n* deterioro *m*.
determination *n* resolución *f*.
determine *vt* determinar, decidir.
determined *adj* resuelto.
deterrent *n* fuerza de disuasión *f*.
detest *vt* detestar, aborrecer.
detestable *adj* detestable, abominable.
dethrone *vt* destronar.
dethronement *n* destronamiento *m*.
detonate *vi* detonar.
detonation *n* detonación *f*.
detour *n* desviación *f*.
detract *vt* desvirtuar.
detriment *n* perjuicio *m*.

detrimental *adj* perjudicial.
deuce *n* deuce *m*.
devaluation *n* devaluación *f*.
devastate *vt* devastar.
devastating *adj* devastador.
devastation *n* devastación, ruina *f*.
develop *vt* desarrollar.
development *n* desarrollo *m*.
deviate *vi* desviarse.
deviation *n* desviación *f*.
device *n* mecanismo *m*.
devil *n* diablo, demonio *m*.
devilish *adj* diabólico; ~ly *adv* diabólicamente.
devious *adj* taimado.
devise *vt* inventar; idear.
devoid *adj* desprovisto.
devolve *vt* delegar.
devote *vt* dedicar; consagrar.
devoted *adj* fiel.
devotee *n* partidario *m*.
devotion *n* devoción *f*.
devotional *adj* devoto.
devour *vt* devorar.
devout *adj* devoto, piadoso; ~ly *adv* piadosamente.
dew *n* rocío *m*.
dewy *adj* rociado.
dexterity *n* destreza *f*.
dexterous *adj* diestro, hábil.
diabetes *n* diabetes *f*.
diabetic *n* diabético *m*.
diabolic *adj* diabólico; ~ally *adv* diabólicamente.
diadem *n* diadema *f*.
diagnosis *n* (*med*) diagnosis *f*.
diagnostic *adj*, *n* diagnóstico (*m*); ~s *pl* diagnóstica *f*.
diagonal *adj*, *n* diagonal (*f*); ~ly *adv* diagonalmente.
diagram *n* diagrama *m*.
dial *n* cuadrante *m*.
dial code *n* prefijo *m*.
dialect *n* dialecto *m*.
dialog(ue) *n* diálogo *m*.
dial tone *n* tono de marcar *m*.
diameter *n* diámetro *m*.
diametrical *adj* diametral; ~ly *adv* diametralmente.
diamond *n* diamante *m*.
diamond-cutter *n* diamantista *m*.
diamonds *npl* (*cards*) diamantes *mpl*.
diaper *n* pañal *m*.
diaphragm *n* diafragma *m*.
diarrhea *n* diarrea *f*.
diary *n* diario *m*.
dice *npl* dados *mpl*.
dictate *vt* dictar; • *n* dictado *m*.
dictation *n* dictado *m*.
dictatorial *adj* autoritativo; magistral.
dictatorship *n* dictadura *f*.
diction *n* dicción *f*
dictionary *n* diccionario *m*.
didactic *adj* didáctico.
die *vi* morir; to ~ away perderse; to ~ down apagarse.
die *n* dado *m*.
diehard *n* reaccionario *m*.
diesel *n* diesel *m*.
diet *n* dieta *f*; régimen *m*; • *vi* estar a dieta.
dietary *adj* dietético.
differ *vi* diferenciarse.
difference *n* diferencia, disparidad *f*.
different *adj* diferent; ~ly *adv* diferentemente.
differentiate *vt* diferenciar.
difficult *adj* difícil.
difficulty *n* dificultad *f*.
diffidence *n* timidez *f*.
diffident *adj* desconfiado; ~ly *adv* desconfiadamente.

diffraction *n* difracción *f*.
diffuse *vt* difundir, esparcir; • *adj* difuso.
diffusion *n* difusión *f*.
dig *vt* cavar; • *n* empujón *m*.
digest *vt* digerir.
digestible *adj* digerible.
digestion *n* digestión *f*.
digestive *adj* digestivo.
digger *n* excavadora *f*.
digit *n* digito *m*.
digital *adj* digital.
dignified *adj* grave.
dignitary *n* dignatario *m*.
dignity *n* dignidad *f*.
digress *vi* hacer digresión.
digression *n* digresión *f*.
dike *n* dique *m*.
dilapidated *adj* desmoronado.
dilapidation *n* ruina *f*.
dilate *vt*, *vi* dilatar(se).
dilemma *n* dilema *m*.
diligence *n* diligencia *f*.
diligent *adj* diligente, asiduo; ~ly *adv* diligentemente.
dilute *vt* dilvir.
dim *adj* turbio; lerdo; oscuro; • *vt* bajar.
dime *n* moneda de diez centavos *f*.
dimension *n* dimensión, extensión *f*.
diminish *vt*, *vi* disminuir(se).
diminution *n* disminución *f*.
diminutive *n* diminutivo *m*.
dimly *adv* indistintamente.
dimmer *n* interruptor *m*.
dimple *n* hoyuelo *m*.
din *n* alboroto *m*.
dine *vi* cenar.
diner *n* restaurante (económico) *m*.
dinghy *n* lancha neumática *f*.
dingy *adj* sombrío.
dinner *n* cena *f*.
dinner time *n* hora de comer *f*.
dinosaur *n* dinosaurio *m*.
dint *n*: by ~ of a fuerza de.
diocese *n* diócesis *f*.
dip *vt* mojar.
diphtheria *n* difteria *f*.
diphthong *n* diptongo *m*.
diploma *n* diploma *m*.
diplomacy *n* diplomacia *f*.
diplomat *n* diplomático *m*.
diplomatic *adj* diplomático.
dipsomania *n* dipsomanía *f*.
dipstick *n* (*auto*) varilla de nivel *f*.
dire *adj* calamitoso.
direct *adj* directo; • *vt* dirigir.
direction *n* dirección *f*; instrucción *f*.
directly *adv* directamente; inmediatamente.
director *n* director *m*.
directory *n* guía *f*.
dirt *n* suciedad *f*.
dirtiness *n* suciedad *f*.
dirty *adj* sucio; vil, bajo.
disability *n* incapacidad *f*.
disabled *adj* minusválido.
disabuse *vt* desengañar.
disadvantage *n* desventaja *f*; • *vt* perjudicar.
disadvantageous *adj* desventajoso.
disaffected *adj* descontento.
disagree *vi* no estar de acuerdo.
disagreeable *adj* desagradable; ~bly *adv* desagradablemente.
disagreement *n* desacuerdo *m*.
disallow *vt* rechazar.
disappear *vi* desaparecer; ausentarse.

disappearance *n* desaparición *f*.
disappoint *vt* decepcionar.
disappointed *adj* decepcionado.
disappointing *adj* decepcionante.
disappointment *n* decepción *f*.
disapproval *n* desaprobación, censura *f*.
disapprove *vt* desaprobar.
disarm *vt* desarmar.
disarmament *n* desarme *m*.
disarray *n* desarreglo *m*.
disaster *n* desastre *m*.
disastrous *adj* desastroso, calamitoso.
disband *vt* disolver.
disbelief *n* incredulidad.
disbelieve *vt* desconfiar.
disburse *vt* desembolsar, pagar.
discard *vt* descartar.
discern *vt* discernir, percibir.
discernible *adj* perceptible.
discerning *adj* perspicaz.
discernment *n* perspicacia *f*.
discharge *vt* descargar; pagar (una deuda); cumplir; ● *n* descarga *f*; descargo *m*.
disciple *n* discípulo *m*.
discipline *n* disciplina *f*; ● *vt* disciplinar.
disclaim *vt* negar.
disclaimer *n* negación *f*.
disclose *vt* revelar.
disclosure *n* revelación *f*.
disco *n* discoteca *f*.
discolor *vt* descolorar.
discoloration *n* descoloramiento *m*.
discomfort *n* incomodidad *f*.
disconcert *vt* desconcertar.
disconnect *vt* desconectar.
disconsolate *adj* inconsolable; ~ly *adv* desconsoladamente.
discontent *n* descontento *m*; ● *adj* malcontento.
discontented *adj* descontento.
discontinue *vi* interrumpir.
discord *n* discordia *f*.
discordant *adj* incongruo.
discount *n* descuento *m*; rebaja *f*; ● *vt* descontar.
discourage *vt* desalentar, desanimar.
discouraged *adj* desalentado.
discouragement *n* desaliento *m*.
discouraging *adj* desalentador.
discourse *n* discurso *m*.
discursive *adj* discursivo.
discourteous *adj* descortés, grosero; ~ly *adv* descortesmente.
discourtesy *n* descortesía *f*.
discover *vt* descubrir.
discovery *n* descubrimiento *m*; revelación *f*.
discredit *vt* desacreditar.
discreditable *adj* ignominioso.
discreet *adj* discreto; ~ly *adv* discretamente.
discrepancy *n* discrepancia, diferencia *f*.
discretion *n* discreción *f*.
discretionary *adj* discrecional.
discriminate *vt* distinguir.
discrimination *n* discriminación *f*.
discuss *vt* discutir.
discussion *n* discusión *f*.
disdain *vt* desdeñar; ● *n* desdén, desprecio *m*.
disdainful *adj* desdeñoso; ~ly *adv* desdeñosamente.
disease *n* enfermedad *f*.
diseased *adj* enfermo.
disembark *vt, vi* desembarcar.
disembarkation *n* (*mil*) desembarco de tropas *m*.
disenchant *vt* desencantar.
disenchanted *adj* desilusionado.
disenchantment *n* desilusión *f*.
disengage *vt* soltar.

disentangle *vt* desenredar.
disfigure *vt* desfigurar, afear.
disgrace *n* ignominia *f*; escándalo *m*; ● *vt* deshonrar.
disgraceful *adj* ignominioso; ~ly *adv* vergonzosamente.
disgruntled *adj* descontento.
disguise *vt* disfrazar; ● *n* disfraz *m*.
disgust *n* aversión *f*; ● *vt* repugnar.
disgusting *adj* repugnante.
dish *n* fuente *f*; plato *m*; taza *f*; ● *vt* servir la vianda en fuente; to ~ up servir.
dishcloth *n* paño de cocina *m*.
dishearten *vt* desalentar.
disheveled *adj* desarreglado.
dishonest *adj* deshonesto; ~ly *adv* deshonestamente.
dishonesty *n* falta de honradez *f*.
dishonor *vt* deshonra, ignominia *f*; ● *vt* deshonrar.
dishonorable *adj* deshonroso; ~bly *adv* ignominiosamente.
dishtowel *n* trapo de fregar *m*.
dishwarmer *n* escalfador *m*.
dishwasher *n* lavaplatos *m*.
disillusion *vt* desilusionar.
disillusioned *adj* desilusionado.
disincentive *n* desincentivo *m*.
disinclination *n* aversión *f*.
disinclined *adj* reacio.
disinfect *vt* desinfectar.
disinfectant *n* desinfectante *m*.
disinherit *vt* desheredar.
disintegrate *vi* disgregarse.
disinterested *adj* desinteresado; ~ly *adv* desinteresadamente.
disjointed *adj* inconexo.
disk *n* disco, disquete *m*.
diskette *n* disco, disquete *m*.
dislike *n* aversión *f*; ● *vt* tener antipatía.
dislocate *vt* dislocar.
dislocation *n* dislocación *f*.
dislodge *vt, vi* desalojar.
disloyal *adj* desleal; ~ly *adv* deslealmente.
disloyalty *n* deslealtad *f*.
dismal *adj* triste.
dismantle *vt* desmontar.
dismay *n* consternación *f*.
dismember *vt* despedazar.
dismiss *vt* despedir.
dismissal *n* despedida *f*.
dismount *vt* desmontar; ● *vi* apearse.
disobedience *n* desobediencia *f*.
disobedient *adj* desobediente.
disobey *vt* desobedecer.
disorder *n* desorden *m*; confusión *f*.
disorderly *adj* desarreglado, confuso.
disorganization *n* desorganización *f*.
disorganized *adj* desorganizado.
disorientated *adj* desorientado.
disown *vt* desconocer.
disparage *vt* despreciar.
disparaging *adj* despreciativo.
disparity *n* disparidad *f*.
dispassionate *adj* desapasionado.
dispatch *vt* enviar; ● *n* envío *m*; informe *m*.
dispel *vt* disipar.
dispensary *n* dispensario *m*.
dispense *vt* dispensar; distribuir.
disperse *vt* disipar.
dispirited *adj* desalentado.
displace *vt* desplazar.
display *vt* exponer; ● *n* ostentación *f*; despliegue *m*.
displeased *adj* disgustado.
displeasure *n* disgusto *m*.
disposable *adj* desechable.
disposal *n* disposición *f*.
dispose *vt* disponer; arreglar.

disposed *adj* dispuesto.
disposition *n* disposición *f*.
dispossess *vt* desposeer.
disproportionate *adj* desproporcionado.
disprove *vt* refutar.
dispute *n* disputa, controversia *f*; ● *vt* disputar.
disqualify *vt* incapacitar.
disquiet *n* inquietud *f*.
disquieting *adj* inquietante.
disquisition *n* disquisición *f*.
disregard *vt* desatender; ● *n* desdén *m*.
disreputable *adj* de mala fama.
disrespect *n* irreverencia *f*.
disrespectful *adj* irreverente; ~**ly** *adv* irreverentemente.
disrobe *vt* desnudar.
disrupt *vt* interrumpir.
disruption *n* interrupción *f*.
dissatisfaction *n* descontento, disgusto *m*.
dissatisfied *adj* insatisfecho.
dissect *vt* disecar.
dissection *n* disección.
disseminate *vt* sembrar.
dissension *n* disensión *f*.
dissent *vi* disentir; ● *n* disensión *f*.
dissenter *n* disidente *m*.
dissertation *n* disertación *f*.
dissident *n* disidente *m*.
dissimilar *adj* heterogéneo.
dissimilarity *n* heterogeneidad *f*.
dissimulation *n* disimulación *f*.
dissipate *vt* disipar.
dissipation *n* disipación *f*.
dissociate *vt* disociar.
dissolute *adj* libertino.
dissolution *n* disolución *f*.
dissolve *vt* disolver; ● *vi* disolverse, derretirse.
dissonance *n* disonancia *f*.
dissuade *vt* disuadir.
distance *n* distancia *f*; **at a** ~ de lejos; ● *vt* apartar.
distant *adj* distante.
distaste *n* disgusto *m*.
distasteful *adj* desagradable.
distend *vt* hinchar.
distil *vt* destilar.
distillation *n* destilación *f*.
distillery *n* destilería *f*.
distinct *adj* distinto, diferente; claro; ~**ly** *adv* distintamente.
distinction *n* distinción *f*.
distinctive *adj* distintivo.
distinctness *n* claridad *f*.
distinguish *vt* distinguir; discernir.
distort *vt* retorcer.
distorted *adj* distorsionado.
distortion *n* distorción *f*.
distract *vt* distraer.
distracted *adj* distraído; ~**ly** *adj* distraídamente.
distraction *n* distracción *f*; confusión *f*.
distraught *adj* enloquecido.
distress *n* angustia *f*; ● *vt* angustiar.
distressing *adj* penoso.
distribute *vt* distribuir, repartir.
distribution *n* distribución *f*.
distributor *n* distribuidor *m*.
district *n* distrito *m*.
district attorney *n* fiscal *m*.
distrustful *adj* desconfiado; sospechoso.
disturb *vt* molestar.
disturbance *n* disturbio *m*.
disturbed *adj* preocupado.
disturbing *adj* inquietante.
disuse *n* desuso *m*.
disused *adj* abandonado.

ditch *n* zanja *f*.
dither *vi* vacilar.
ditto *adv* ídem.
ditty *n* cancioneta *f*.
diuretic *adj* (*med*) diurético.
dive *vi* sumergirse; bucear.
diver *n* buzo *m*.
diverge *vi* divergir.
divergence *n* divergencia *f*.
divergent *adj* divergente.
diverse *adj* diverso, diferente; ~**ly** *adv* diversamente.
diversion *n* diversión *f*.
diversity *n* diversidad *f*.
divert *vt* desviar; divertir.
divest *vt* desnudar; despojar.
divide *vt* dividir; ● *vi* dividirse.
dividend *n* dividendo *m*.
dividers *npl* (*math*) compás de puntas *m*.
divine *adj* divino.
divinity *n* divinidad *f*.
diving *n* salto *m*; buceo *m*.
diving board *n* trampolín *m*.
divisible *adj* divisible.
division *n* (*math*) división *f*; desunión *f*.
divisor *n* (*math*) divisor *m*.
divorce *n* divorcio *m*; ● *vi* divorciarse.
divorced *adj* divorciado.
divulge *vt* divulgar, publicar.
dizziness *n* vértigo *m*.
dizzy *adj* mareado.
DJ *n* pinchadiscos *m*.
do *vt* hacer, obrar.
docile *adj* dócil, apacible.
dock *n* muelle *m*; ● *vi* atracar al muelle.
docker *n* trabajador portuario *m*.
dockyard *n* (*mar*) astillero *m*.
doctor *n* médico *m*.
doctrinal *adj* doctrinal.
doctrine *n* doctrina *f*.
document *n* documento *m*.
documentary *adj* documental.
dodge *vt* esquivar.
doe *n* gama *f*; ~ **rabbit** coneja *f*.
dog *n* perro *m*.
dogged *adj* tenaz; ~**ly** *adv* tenazmente.
dog kennel *n* perrera *f*.
dogmatic *adj* dogmático; ~**ly** *adv* dogmáticamente.
doings *npl* hechos *mpl*; eventos *mpl*.
do-it-yourself *n* bricolaje *m*.
doleful *adj* lúgubre, triste.
doll *n* muñeca *f*.
dollar *n* dólar *m*.
dolphin *n* delfín *m*.
domain *n* campo *m*.
dome *n* cúpula *f*.
domestic *adj* doméstico.
domesticate *vt* domesticar.
domestication *n* domesticación *f*.
domesticity *n* domesticidad *f*.
domicile *n* domicilio *m*.
dominant *adj* dominante.
dominate *vi* dominar.
domination *n* dominación *f*.
domineer *vi* dominar.
domineering *adj* dominante.
dominion *n* dominio *m*.
dominoes *npl* dominó *m*.
donate *vt* donar.
donation *n* donación *f*.
done *p*, *adj* hecho; cocido.
donkey *n* asno, borrico *m*.
donor *n* donante *m*.

doodle *vi* garabatear.

doom *n* suerte *f*.

door *n* puerta *f*.

doorbell *n* timbre *m*.

door handle *n* tirador *m*.

doorman *n* portero *m*.

doormat *n* felpudo *m*.

doorplate *n* planchuela *f*.

doorstep *n* peldaño *m*.

doorway *n* entrada *f*.

dormant *adj* latente.

dormer window *n* buhardilla *f*.

dormitory *n* dormitorio *m*.

dormouse *n* lirón *m*.

dosage *n* dosis *f*.

dose *n* dosis *f*; ● *vt* disponer la dosis de.

dossier *n* expediente *m*.

dot *n* punto *m*.

dote *vi* adorar.

dotingly *adv* con cariño excesivo.

double *adj* doble; ● *vt* doblar; duplicar; ● *n* doble *m*.

double bed *n* cama matrimonial *f*.

double-breasted *adj* cruzado.

double chin *n* papada *f*.

double-dealing *n* duplicidad *f*.

double-edged *adj* con dos filas.

double entry *n* (*com*) partida doble *f*.

double-lock *vt* echar segunda vuelta a la llave.

double room *n* habitación doble *f*.

doubly *adj* doblemente.

doubt *n* duda, sospecha *f*; ● *vt* dudar; sospechar.

doubtful *adj* dudoso.

doubtless *adv* sin duda.

dough *n* masa *f*.

douse *vt* apagar.

dove *n* paloma *f*.

dovecot *n* palomar *m*.

dowdy *adj* mal vestido.

down *n* plumón *m*; flojel *m*; ● *prep* abajo; to sit ~ sentarse; upside ~ al revés.

downcast *adj* cabizbajo.

downfall *n* ruina *f*.

downhearted *adj* desanimado.

downhill *adv* cuesta abajo.

down payment *n* entrada *f*.

downpour *n* aguacero *m*.

downright *adj* manifiesto.

downstairs *adv* abajo.

down-to-earth *adj* práctico.

downtown *adv* al centro (de la ciudad).

downward(s) *adv* hacia abajo.

dowry *n* dote *f*.

doze *vi* dormitar.

dozen *n* docena *f*.

dozy *adj* soñoliento.

drab *adj* gris.

draft *n* borrador *m*; quinta *f*; corriente de aire *f*.

drafts *npl* juego de damas *m*.

drafty *adj* expuesto al aire.

drag *vt* arrastrar; tirar con fuerza; ● *n* lata *f*.

dragnet *n* red barredera *f*.

dragon *n* dragón *m*.

dragonfly *n* libélula *f*.

drain *vt* desaguar; secar; ● *n* desaguadero *m*.

drainage *n* desagüe *m*.

drainboard *n* escurridor *m*.

drainpipe *n* desagüe *m*.

drake *n* ánade macho *m*.

dram *n* traguito *m*.

drama *n* drama *m*.

dramatic *adj* dramático; ~ally *adv* dramáticamente.

dramatist *n* dramático *m*.

dramatize *vt* dramatizar.

drape *vt* cubrir.

drapes *npl* cortinas *fpl*.

drastic *adj* drástico.

draw *vt* tirar; dibujar; to ~ nigh acercarse.

drawback *n* desventaja *f*.

drawer *n* cajón *m*.

drawing *n* dibujo *m*.

drawing board *n* tabla para dibujar *f*.

drawing room *n* salón *m*.

drawl *vi* hablar con pesadez.

dread *n* terror, espanto *m*; ● *vt* temer.

dreadful *adj* espantoso; ~ly *adv* terriblemente.

dream *n* sueño *m*; ● *vi* soñar.

dreary *adj* triste.

dredge *vt* dragar.

dregs *npl* heces *fpl*.

drench *vt* empapar.

dress *vt* vestir; vendar; ● *vi* vestirse; ● *n* vestido *m*.

dresser *n* aparador *m*.

dressing *n* vendaje *m*; aliño *m*.

dressing gown *n* bata *f*.

dressing room *n* tocador *m*.

dressing table *n* tocador *m*.

dressmaker *n* modista *f*.

dressy *adj* elegante.

dribble *vi* caer gota a gota.

dried *adj* seco.

drift *n* montón *m*; ventisquero *m*; significado *m*; ● *vi* ir a la deriva.

driftwood *n* madera de deriva *f*.

drill *n* taladro *m*; (*mil*) instrucción *f*; ● *vt* taladrar.

drink *vt*, *vi* beber; ● *n* bebida *f*.

drinkable *adj* potable.

drinker *n* bebedor *m*.

drinking bout *n* borrachera *f*.

drinking water *n* agua potable *f*.

drip *vi* gotear; ● *n* gota *f*; goteo *m*.

dripping *n* pringue *m*/*f*.

drive *vt* manejar; empujar; ● *vi* pasearse en coche; ● *n* paseo en coche *m*; entrada *f*.

drivel *n* baba *f*; ● *vi* babear.

driver *n* conductor *m*; chófer *m*.

driver's license *n* carnet *m* de manejar.

driveway *n* entrada *f*.

driving *n* el manejar.

driving instructor *n* instructor de manejo *m*.

driving school *n* autoescuela *f*.

driving test *n* examen de manejo *m*.

drizzle *vi* lloviznar.

droll *adj* gracioso.

drone *n* zumbido *m*.

droop *vi* decaer.

drop *n* gota *f*; ● *vt* dejar caer; ● *vi* bajar; to ~ out retirarse.

drop-out *n* marginado *m*.

dropper *n* cuentagotas *m*.

dross *n* escoria *f*.

drought *n* sequía *f*.

drove *n*: in ~s en tropel.

drown *vt* anegar; ● *vi* anegarse.

drowsiness *n* somnolencia *f*.

drowsy *adj* soñoliento.

drudgery *n* trabajo monótono *m*.

drug *n* droga *f*; ● *vt* drogar.

drug addict *n* drogadicto *m*.

druggist *n* farmacéutico *m*.

drugstore *n* farmacia *f*.

drum *n* tambor *m*; ● *vi* tocar el tambor.

drum majorette *n* batonista *f*.

drummer *n* batería *m*.

drumstick *n* palillo de tambor *m*.

drunk *adj* borracho.

drunkard *n* borracho *m*.
drunken *adj* borracho.
drunkenness *n* borrachera *f*.
dry *adj* seco; ● *vt* secar; ● *vi* secarse.
dry-clearning *n* lavado en seco *m*.
dry-goods store *n* mercería *f*.
dryness *n* sequedad *f*.
dry rot *n* podredumbre *f*.
dual *adj* doble.
dual-purpose *adj* de doble uso.
dubbed *adj* doblado.
dubious *adj* dudoso.
duck *n* pato *m*; ● *vt* (*vi*) zambullir(se).
duckling *n* patito *m*.
dud *adj* estropeado.
due *adj* debido, apto; ● *adv* exactamente; ● *n* derecho *m*.
duel *n* duelo *m*.
duet *n* (*mus*) dúo *m*.
dull *adj* lerdo; insípido; gris; ● *vt* aliviar.
duly *adv* debidamente; puntualmente.
dumb *adj* mudo; ~ly *adv* sin chistar.
dumbbell *n* pesa *f*.
dumbfounded *adj* pasmado.
dummy *n* maniquí *m*; imbécil *m*.
dump *n* montón *m*; ● *vt* dejar.
dumping *n* (*com*) dumping *m*.
dumpling *n* bola de masa *f*.
dumpy *adj* gordito.
dunce *n* zopenco *m*.
dune *n* duna *f*.
dung *n* estiércol *m*.
dungarees *npl* mono *m*.
dungeon *n* calabozo *m*.
dupe *n* bobo *m*; ● *vt* engañar, embaucar.
duplex *n* dúplex *m*.
duplicate *n* duplicado *m*; copia *f*; ● *vt* multicopiar.
duplicity *n* duplicidad *f*.
durability *n* durabilidad *f*.
durable *adj* duradero.
duration *n* duración *f*.
during *prep* mientras, durante el tiempo que.
dusk *n* crepúsculo *m*.
dust *n* polvo *m*; ● *vt* desempolvar.
duster *n* plumero *m*.
dusty *adj* polvoriento.
dutch courage *n* valor fingido *m*.
duteous *adj* fiel, leal.
dutiful *adj* obediente, sumiso; ~ly *adv* obedientemente.
duty *n* deber *m*; obligación *f*.
duty-free *adj* libre de derechos de aduana.
dwarf *n* enano *m*; enana *f*; ● *vt* empequeñecer.
dwell *vi* habitar, morar.
dwelling *n* habitación *f*; domicilio *m*.
dwindle *vi* mermar, disminuirse.
dye *vt* teñir; ● *n* tinte *m*.
dyer *n* tintorero *m*.
dyeing *n* tintorería *f*; tintura *f*.
dye-works *npl* taller del tintorero *m*.
dying *p, adj* agonizante, moribundo; ● *n* muerte *f*.
dynamic *adj* dinámico.
dynamics *n* dinámica *f*.
dynamite *n* dinamita *f*.
dynamiter *n* dinamitista *m*.
dynamo *n* dinamo *f*.
dynasty *n* dinastía *f*.
dysentery *n* disentería *f*.
dyspepsia *n* (*med*) dispepsia *f*.
dyspeptic *adj* dispéptico.

E

each *pn* cada uno; ~ other unos a otros, mutuamente.
eager *adv* entusiasmado; ~ly *adv* con entusiasmo.
eagerness *n* ansia *f*; anhelo *m*.
eagle *n* águila *f*.
eagle-eyed *adj* de vista de lince.
eaglet *n* aguilucho *m*.
ear *n* oreja *f*; oído *m*; espiga *f*; by ~ de oreja.
earache *n* dolor de oídos *m*.
eardrum *n* tímpano (del oído) *m*.
early *adj* temprano; *adv* temprano.
earmark *vt* destinar a.
earn *vt* ganar; conseguir.
earnest *adj* serio; en serio; ~ly *adv* seriamente.
earnestness *n* seriedad *f*.
earnings *npl* ingresos *mpl*.
earphones *npl* auriculares *mpl*.
earring *n* zarcillo, pendiente *m*.
earth *n* tierra *f*; ● *vt* conectar a tierra.
earthen *adj* de tierra.
earthenware *n* loza de barro *f*.
earthquake *n* terremoto *m*.
earthworm *n* lombriz *f*.
earthy *adj* sensual.
earwig *n* tijereta *f*.
ease *n* comodidad *f*; facilidad *f*; at ~ con desahogo; ● *vt* aliviar; mitigar.
easel *n* caballete *m*.
easily *adv* fácilmente.
easiness *n* lo fácil.
east *n* este *m*; oriente *m*.
Easter *n* Pascua de resurrección *f*.
Easter egg *n* huevo de Pascua *m*.
easterly *adj* del este.
eastern *adj* del este, oriental.
eastward(s) *adv* hacia el este.
easy *adj* fácil; cómodo, ~ going acomodadizo.
easy chair *n* sillón *m*.
eat *vt* comer; ● *vi* alimentarse.
eatable *adj* comestible; ● ~s *npl* víveres *mpl*.
eaves *npl* alero *m*.
eau de Cologne *n* agua de Colonia *f*.
eavesdrop *vt* escuchar a escondidas.
ebb *n* reflujo *m*; ● *vi* menguar; decaer, disminuir.
ebony *n* ébano *m*.
eccentric *adj* excéntrico.
eccentricity *n* excentricidad *f*.
ecclesiastic *adj* eclesiástico.
echo *n* eco *m*; ● *vi* resonar, repercutir.
eclectic *adj* ecléctico.
eclipse *n* eclipse *m*; ● *vt* eclipsar.
ecology *n* ecología *f*.
economic(al) *adj* económico, frugal, moderado.
economics *npl* economía *f*.
economist *n* economista *m*.
economize *vt* economizar.
economy *n* economía *f*; frugalidad *f*.
ecstasy *n* éxtasis *m*.
ecstatic *adj* extático; ~ally *adv* en éxtasis.
eczema *n* eczema *m*.
eddy *n* reflujo de agua *m*; remolino *m*; ● *vi* arremolinarse.
edge *n* filo *m*; punta *f*; margen *m/f*; acrimonia *f*; ● *vt* ribetear; introducir.
edgeways, edgewise *adv* de lado.
edging *n* orla, orilla *f*.
edgy *adj* nervioso.
edible *adv* comedero, comestible.
edict *n* edicto, mandato *m*.
edification *n* edificación *f*.
edifice *n* edificio *m*; fábrica *f*.

edify vt edificar.
edit vt dirigir; redactar; cortar.
edition n edición f; publicación f; impresión f.
editor n director m; redactor m.
editorial adj, n editorial m.
educate vt educar; enseñar.
education n educación f.
eel n anguila f.
eerie adj espeluznante.
efface vt borrar, destruir.
effect n efecto m; realidad f; ~s npl efectos, bienes mpl; • vt efectuar, ejecutar.
effective adj eficaz; efectivo; ~ly adv efectivamente, en efecto.
effectiveness n eficacia f.
effectual adj eficiente, eficaz; ~ly adv eficazmente.
effeminacy n afeminación f.
effeminate adj afeminado.
effervescence n efervescencia f; hervor m.
effete adj estéril.
efficacy n eficacia f.
efficiency n eficiencia, virtud f.
efficient adj eficaz.
effigy n efigie, imagen f; retrato m.
effort n esfuerzo, empeño m.
effortless adj sin esfuerzo.
effrontery n descaro m; impudencia, desvergüenza f.
effusive adj efusivo.
egg n huevo m; • to ~ on vt animar.
eggcup n huevera f.
eggplant n berenjena f.
eggshell n cáscara de huevo f.
ego(t)ism n egoísmo m.
ego(t)ist n egoísta m.
ego(t)istical adj egoístico.
eiderdown n edredón m.
eight adj, n ocho.
eighteen adj, n dieciocho.
eighteenth adj, n decimoctavo.
eighth adj, n octavo.
eightieth adj, n octogésimo.
eighty adj, n ochenta.
either pn cualquiera, uno de dos; • conj o, sea, ya.
ejaculate vt exclamar; eyacular.
ejaculation n exclamación f; eyaculación f.
eject vt expeler, desechar.
ejection n expulsión f.
ejector seat n asiento proyectable m.
eke vt aumentar; alargar; prolongar; hacer crecer.
elaborate vt elaborar; • adj elaborado; ~ly adv cuidadosamente.
elapse vi pasar, correr (el tiempo).
elastic adj elástico.
elasticity n elasticidad f.
elated adj regocijado.
elation n regocijo m.
elbow n codo m; • vt codear.
elbow-room n anchura f; espacio suficiente m; (fig) libertad, latitud f.
elder n saúco m (árbol); • adj mayor.
elderly adj de edad ya madura.
elders npl ancianos, antepasados mpl.
eldest adj el, la mayor.
elect vt elegir; • adj elegido, escogido.
election n elección f.
electioneering n maniobras electorales fpl.
elective adj facultativo.
elector n elector m.
electoral adj electoral.
electorate n electorado m.
electric(al) adj eléctrico.
electric blanket n manta eléctrica f.

electric cooker n cocina eléctrica f.
electric fire n estufa eléctrica f.
electrician n electricista m.
electricity n electricidad f.
electrify vt electrizar.
electron n electrón m.
electronic adj electrónico; ~s npl electrónica f.
elegance n elegancia f.
elegant adj elegante, delicado; ~ly adv elegantemente.
elegy n elegía f.
element n elemento m; fundamento m.
elemental, elementary adj elemental.
elephant n elefante m.
elephantine adj inmenso.
elevate vt elevar, alzar, exaltar.
elevation n elevación f; altura f; alteza (de pensamientos) f.
elevator n ascensor m.
eleven adj, n once.
eleventh adj, n onceno, undécimo.
elf n duende m.
elicit vt sacar de.
eligibility n elegibilidad f.
eligible adj elegible.
eliminate vt eliminar, descartar.
elk n alce m.
elliptic(al) adj elíptico.
elm n olmo m.
elocution n elocución f.
elocutionist n profesor de elocución m.
elongate vt alargar.
elope vi escapar, huir, evadirse.
elopement n fuga, huída, evasión f.
eloquence n elocuencia f.
eloquent adj elocuente; ~ly adv elocuentemente.
else pn otro.
elsewhere adv en otra parte.
elucidate vt explicar.
elucidation n elucidación, explicación f.
elude vt eludir, evitar.
elusive, elusory adj esquivo.
emaciated adj demacrado.
emanate (from) vi emanar.
emancipate vt emancipar; dar libertad.
emancipation n emancipación f.
embalm vt embalsamar.
embankment n terraplén m.
embargo n prohibición f.
embark vt embarcar.
embarkation n embarcación f.
embarrass vt avergonzar.
embarrassed adj azorado.
embarrassing adj violento; embarazoso.
embarrassment n desconcierto m.
embassy n embajada f.
embed vt empotrar; clavar.
embellish vt hermosear, adornar.
embellishment n adorno m.
embers npl rescoldo m.
embezzle vt desfalcar.
embezzlement n desfalco.
embitter vt amargar.
emblem n emblema m.
emblematic(al) adj emblemático, simbólico.
embodiment n incorporación f.
embody vt incorporar.
embrace vt abrazar; contener; • n abrazo m.
embroider vt bordar.
embroidery n bordado m; bordadura f.
embroil vt embrollar; confundir.
embryo n embrión m.
emendation n enmienda, corrección f.
emerald n esmeralda f.

emerge *vi* salir, proceder.
emergency *n* emergencia *f*; necesidad urgente *f*.
emergency cord *n* timbre de alarma *m*.
emergency exit *n* salida de emergencia *f*.
emergency landing *n* aterrizaje forzoso *m*.
emergency meeting *n* reunión extraordinaria *f*.
emery *n* esmeril *m*.
emigrant *n* emigrado *m*.
emigrate *vi* emigrar.
emigration *n* emigración *f*.
eminence *n* altura *f*; eminencia, excelencia *f*.
eminent *adj* eminente, elevado; distinguido; ~ly *adv* eminentemente.
emission *n* emisión *f*.
emit *vt* emitir; arrojar, despedir.
emolument *n* emolumento, provecho *m*.
emotion *n* emoción *f*.
emotional *adj* emocional.
emotive *adj* emotivo.
emperor *n* emperador *m*.
emphasis *n* énfasis *m*.
emphasize *vt* hablar con énfasis.
emphatic *adj* enfático; ~ally *adv* enfáticamente.
empire *n* imperio *m*.
employ *vt* emplear, ocupar.
employee *n* empleado *m*.
employer *n* patrón *m*; empresario *m*.
employment *n* empleo *m*; trabajo *m*.
emporium *n* emporio *m*.
empress *n* emperatriz *f*.
emptiness *n* vaciedad *f*; futilidad *f*.
empty *adj* vacío; vano; ignorante; • *vt* vaciar, evacuar.
empty-handed *adj* con las manos vacías.
emulate *vt* emular, competir; imitar.
emulsion *n* emulsión *f*.
enable *vt* capacitar.
enact *vt* promulgar; representar; hacer.
enamel *n* esmalte *m*; • *vt* esmaltar.
enamor *vt* enamorar.
encamp *vi* acamparse.
encampment *n* campamento *m*.
encase *vt* encajar, encajonar.
enchant *vt* encantar.
enchanting *adj* encantador.
enchantment *n* encanto *m*.
encircle *vt* cercar, circundar.
enclose *vt* cercar, circunvalar, circundar; incluir.
enclosure *n* cercamiento *m*; cercado *m*.
encompass *vt* abarcar.
encore *adv* otra vez, de nuevo.
encounter *n* encuentro *m*; duelo *m*; pelea *f*; • *vt* encontrar.
encourage *vt* animar, alentar.
encouragement *n* estímulo, patrocinio *m*.
encroach *vt* usurpar, avanzar gradualmente.
encroachment *n* usurpación, intrusión *f*.
encrusted *adj* incrustado.
encumber *vt* embarazar, cargar.
encumbrance *n* embarazo, impedimento *m*.
encyclical *adj* encíclico, circular.
encyclopedia *n* enciclopedia *f*.
end *n* fin *m*; extremidad *f*; término *m*; resolución *f*; to the ~ that para que; to no ~ en vano; on ~ en pie, de pie; • *vt* terminar, concluir, fenecer; • *vi* acabar, terminar.
endanger *vt* peligrar, arriesgar.
endear *vt* encarecer.
endearing *adj* simpático.
endearment *n* encarecimiento *m*.
endeavor *vi* esforzarse; intentar; • *n* esfuerzo *m*.
ending *adj* endémico.
ending *n* conclusión; *f*; desenlace *m*; terminación *f*.
endive *n* (*bot*) endibia *f*.

endless *adj* infinito, perpetuo; ~ly *adv* sin fin, perpetuamente.
endorse *vt* endosar; aprobar.
endorsement *n* endoso *m*; aprobación *f*.
endow *vt* dotar.
endowment *n* dote, dotación *f*.
endurable *adj* sufrible, tolerable.
endurance *n* duración *f*; paciencia *f*; sufrimiento *m*.
endure *vt* sufrir, soportar; • *vi* durar.
endways, endwise *adv* de punta, derecho.
enemy *n* enemigo, antagonista *m*.
energetic *adj* enérgico, vigoroso.
energy *n* energía, fuerza *f*.
enervate *vt* enervar, debilitar.
enfeeble *vt* debilitar.
enfold *vt* envolver.
enforce *vt* hacer cumplir.
enforced *adj* forzoso.
enfranchise *vt* emancipar.
engage *vt* llamar; abordar; contratar.
engaged *adj* prometido.
engagement *n* empeño *m*; combate *m*; pelea *f*; obligación *f*.
engagement ring *n* anillo de prometida *m*.
engaging *adj* atractivo.
engender *vt* engendrar; producir.
engine *n* motor *m*; locomotora *f*.
engine driver *n* maquinista *m*.
engineer *n* ingeniero *m*; maquinista *m*.
engineering *n* ingeniería *f*.
engrave *vi* grabar; esculpir; tallar.
engraving *n* grabado *m*; estampa *f*.
engrossed *adj* absorto.
engulf *vt* sumergir.
enhance *vt* aumentar, realzar.
enigma *n* enigma *m*.
enjoy *vt* gozar; poseer.
enjoyable *adj* agradable; divertido.
enjoyment *n* disfrute *m*; placer *m*; fruición *f*.
enlarge *vt* engrandecer, dilatar, extender.
enlargement *n* aumento *m*; ampliación *f*, soltura *f*.
enlighten *vt* iluminar; instruir.
enlightened *adj* iluminado.
Enlightenment *n*: the ~ el siglo de las luces *m*.
enlist *vt* alistar.
enlistment *n* alistamiento *m*.
enliven *vt* animar; avivar; alegrar.
enmity *n* enemistad *f*; odio *m*.
enormity *n* enormidad *f*; atrocidad *f*.
enormous *adj* enorme; ~ly *adv* enormemente.
enough *adv* bastante; basta; • *n* bastante *m*.
enounce *vt* declarar.
enquire *vt* = **inquire**.
enrage *vt* enfurecer, irritar.
enrapture *vt* arrebatar, entusiasmar; encantar.
enrich *vt* enriquecer; adornar.
enrichment *n* enriquecimiento *m*.
enrol *vt* registrar; arrollar.
enrolment *n* inscripción *f*.
en route *adv* durante el viaje.
ensign *n* (*mil*) bandera *f*; abanderado *m*; (*mar*) alférez *m*.
enslave *vt* esclavizar, cautivar.
ensue *vi* seguirse; suceder.
ensure *vt* asegurar.
entail *vt* suponer.
entangle *vt* enmarañar, embrollar.
entanglement *n* enredo *m*.
enter *vt* entrar; admitir; registrar; to ~ for presentarse para; to ~ into establecer; formar parte de/en; firmar.
enterprise *n* empresa *f*.
enterprising *adj* emprendedor.
entertain *vt* divertir; hospedar; mantener.
entertainer *n* artista *m*.

entertaining *adj* divertido.

entertainment *n* entretenimiento, pasatiempo *m*.

enthralled *adj* encantado.

enthralling *adj* cautivador.

enthrone *vt* entronizar.

enthusiasm *n* entusiasmo *m*.

enthusiast *n* entusiasta *m*.

enthusiastic *adj* entusiasta.

entice *vt* tentar; seducir.

entire *adj* entero, completo, perfecto; ~**ly** *adv* enteramente.

entirety *vt* intitular; conferir algún derecho.

entitled *adj* titulado.

entity *n* entidad, existencia *f*.

entourage *n* séquito *m*.

entrails *npl* entrañas *fpl*; asadura *f*.

entrance *n* entrada *f*; admisión *f*; principio *m*.

entrance examination *n* examen de ingreso *m*.

entrance fee *n* cuota *f*.

entrance hall *n* pórtico, vestíbulo *m*.

entrance ramp *n* rampa de acceso *f*.

entrant *n* participante *m*; candidato *m*.

entrap *vt* enredar; engañar.

entreat *vt* rogar, suplicar.

entreaty *n* petición, súplica, instancia *f*.

entrepreneur *n* empresario *m*.

entrust *vt* confiar.

entry *n* entrada *f*.

entry phone *n* portero automático *m*.

entwine *vt* entrelazar, encroscar, torcer.

enumerate *vt* enumerar, numerar.

enunciate *vt* enunciar, declarar.

enunciation *n* enunciación *f*.

envelop *n* envolver.

envelope *vt* sobre *m*.

enviable *adj* envidiable.

envious *adj* envidioso; ~**ly** *adv* envidiosamente.

environment *n* medio ambiente *m*.

environmental *adj* ambiental.

environs *npl* vecindad *f*; contornos *mpl*.

envisage *vt* prever; concebir.

envoy *n* enviado *m*; mensajero *m*.

envy *n* envidia, malicia *f*; ● *vt* envidiar.

ephemeral *adj* efímero.

epic *adj* épico; ● *n* épica *f*.

epidemic *adj* epidémico; ● *n* epidemia *f*.

epilepsy *n* epilepsia *f*.

epileptic *adj* epiléptico.

epilog(ue) *n* epílogo *m*.

Epiphany *n* Epifanía *f*.

episcopacy *n* episcopado *m*.

episcopal *adj* episcopal.

episcopalian *n* anglicano *m*.

episode *n* episodio *m*.

epistle *n* epístola *f*.

epistolary *adj* epistolar.

epithet *n* epíteto *m*.

epitome *n* epítome, compendio *m*.

epitomize *vt* epitomar, abreviar.

epoch *n* época *f*.

equable *adj* uniforme; ~**bly** *adv* uniformemente.

equal *adj* igual; justo; semejante; ● *n* igual *m*; compañero *m*; ● *vt* igualar; compensar.

equalize *vt* igualar.

equalizer *n* igualada *f*.

equality *n* igualdad, uniformidad *f*.

equally *adv* igualmente.

equanimity *n* ecuanimidad *f*.

equate *vt* equiparar (*con*).

equation *n* ecuación *f*.

equator *n* ecuador *m*.

equatorial *adj* ecuatorial, ecuatorio.

equestrian *adj* ecuestre.

equilateral *adj* equilátero.

equilibrium *n* equilibrio *m*.

equinox *n* equinoccio *m*.

equip *vt* equipar, pertrechar.

equipment *n* equipaje *m*.

equitable *adj* equitativo, imparcial; ~**bly** *adv* equitativamente.

equity *n* equidad, justicia, imparcialidad *f*.

equivalent *adj*, *n* equivalente *m*.

equivocal *adj* equívoco, ambiguo; ~**ly** *adv* equivocadamente, ambiguamente.

equivocate *vt* equivocar, usar equívocos.

equivocation *n* equívoco *m*.

era *n* era *f*.

eradicate *vt* desarraigar, extirpar.

eradication *n* extirpación *f*.

erase *vt* borrar.

eraser *n* goma de borrar *f*.

erect *vt* erigir; establecer; ● *adj* derecho, levantado hacia arriba.

erection *n* establecimiento *m*; estructura *f*; erección *f*.

ermine *n* armiño *m*.

erode *vt* erosionar; corroer.

erotic *adj* erótico.

err *vi* vagar, errar; desviarse.

errand *n* recado, mensaje *m*.

errand boy *n* recadero *m*.

errata *npl* fe de erratas *f*.

erratic *adj* errático, errante; irregular.

erroneous *adj* erróneo; falso; ~**ly** *adv* erróneamente.

error *n* error *m*.

erudite *adj* erudito.

erudition *n* erudición *f*; doctrina *f*.

erupt *vi* entrar en erupción; hacer erupción.

eruption *n* erupción *f*.

escalate *vi* extenderse.

escalation *n* intensificación *f*.

escalator *n* escalera móvil *f*.

escapade *n* travesura *f*.

escape *vt* evitar; escapar; ● *vi* evadirse, salvarse; ● *n* escapada, huida, fuga *f*; inadvertencia *f*; **to make one's ~** poner los pies en polvorosa.

escapism *n* escapismo *m*.

eschew *vt* huir, evitar, evadir.

escort *n* escolta *f*; ● *vt* escoltar.

esoteric *adj* esotérico.

especial *adj* especial; ~**ly** *adv* especialmente.

espionage *n* espionaje *m*.

esplanade *n* (*mil*) esplanada *f*.

espouse *vt* desposar.

essay *n* ensayo *m*.

essence *n* esencia *f*.

essential *n* esencia *f*; ● *adj* esencial, substancial, principal; ~**ly** *adv* esencialmente.

establish *vt* establecer, fundar, fijar; confirmar.

establishment *n* establecimiento *m*; fundación *f*; institución *f*.

estate *n* estado *m*; hacienda *f*; bienes *mpl*.

esteem *vt* estimar, apreciar; pensar; ● *n* estima *f*; consideración *f*.

esthetic *adj* estético; ~**s** *npl* estética *f*.

estimate *vt* estimar, apreciar, tasar.

estimation *n* estimacion, valuación *f*; opinión *f*.

estrange *vt* extrañar, apartar, enajenar.

estranged *adj* separado.

estrangement *n* enajenamiento *m*; extrañeza, distancia *f*.

estuary *n* estuario, brazo de mar *m*; desembocadura de lago o río *f*.

etch *vt* grabar al aguafuerte.

etching *n* grabado al aguafuerte *m*.

eternal *adj* eterno, perpetuo, inmortal; ~**ly** *adv* eternamente.

eternity *n* eternidad *f*.

ether *n* éter *m*.

ethical *adj* ético; **~ly** *adv* moralmente.
ethics *npl* ética *f*.
ethnic *adj* étnico.
ethos *n* genio *m*.
etiquette *n* etiqueta *f*.
etymological *adj* etimológico.
etymologist *n* etimologista *m*.
etymology *n* etimología *f*.
Eucharist *n* Eucaristía *f*.
eulogy *n* elogio, encomio *m*; alabanza *f*.
eunuch *n* eunoco *m*.
euphemism *n* eufemismo *m*.
evacuate *vt* evacuar.
evacuation *n* evacuación *f*.
evade *vt* evadir, escapar, evitar.
evaluate *vt* evaluar; interpretar.
evangelic(al) *adj* evangelico.
evangelist *n* evangelista *m*.
evaporate *vt* evaporar; ● *vi* evaporarse; disiparse.
evaporated milk *n* leche evaporada *f*.
evaporation *n* evaporación *f*.
evasion *n* evasión *f*; escape *m*.
evasive *adj* evasivo; **~ly** *adv* sofísticamente.
eve *n* víspera *f*.
even *adj* llano, igual; par, semejante; ● *adv* aun; aun cuando, supuesto que; no obstante; ● *vt* igualar, allanar; *vi:* **to ~ out** nivelarse.
even-handed *adj* imparcial, equitativo.
evening *n* tarde *f*.
evening class *n* clase nocturna *f*.
evening dress *n* traje de etiqueta *m*; traje de noche *m*.
evenly *adv* igualmente, llanamente.
evenness *n* igualdad *f*; uniformidad *f*; llanura *f*; imparcialidad *f*.
event *n* acontecimiento, evento *m*; éxito *m*.
eventful *adj* lleno de acontecimientos.
eventual *adj* final; **~ly** *adv* por fin.
eventuality *n* eventualidad *f*.
ever *adv* siempre; **for ~ and ~** siempre jamás, eternamente; **~ since** después.
evergreen *adj* de hoja verde; ● *n* siempreviva (planta) *f*.
everlasting *adj* eterno.
evermore *adv* eternamente, para siempre jamás.
every *adj* cada uno *o* cada una; **~ where** en *o* por todas partes; **~ thing** todo; **~ one**, **~ body** cada uno, cada una.
evict *vt* desahuciar.
eviction *n* desahucio *m*.
evidence *n* evidencia *f*; testimonio *m*; prueba *f*; ● *vt* evidenciar.
evident *adj* evidente; patente, manifiesto; **~ly** *adv* evidentemente.
evil *adj* malo, depravado, pernicioso; dañoso; ● *n* mal *m*; maldad *f*.
evil-minded *adj* malicioso, mal intencionado.
evocative *adj* sugestivo.
evoke *vt* evocar.
evolution *n* evolución *f*.
evolve *vt, vi* evolucionar; desenvolver; desplegarse.
ewe *n* oveja *f*.
exacerbate *vt* exasperar.
exact *adj* exacto; ● *vt* exigir.
exacting *adj* exigente.
exaction *n* exacción, extorsión *f*.
exactly *adj* exactamente.
exactness, exactitude *n* exactitud *f*.
exaggerate *vt* exagerar.
exaggeration *n* exageración *f*.
exalt *vt* exaltar, elevar; alabar; realzar.
exaltation *n* exaltación, elevación *f*.
exalted *adj* exaltado; muy animado.
examination *n* examen *m*.
examine *vt* examinar; escudriñar.

examiner *n* inspector *m*.
example *n* ejemplar *m*; ejemplo *m*.
exasperate *vt* exasperar, irritar, enojar, provocar; agravar; amargar.
exasperation *n* exasperación, irritación *f*.
excavate *vt* excavar, ahondar.
excavation *n* excavación *f*.
exceed *vt* exceder; sobrepujar.
exceedingly *adv* extremamente, en sumo grado.
excel *vt* sobresalir, exceder.
excellence *n* excelencia *f*; preeminencia *f*.
Excellency *n* Excelencia (título) *f*.
excellent *adj* excelente; **~ly** *adv* excelentemente.
except *vt* exceptuar, excluir; **~(ing)** *prep* excepto, a excepción de.
exception *n* excepción, exclusión *f*.
exceptional *adj* excepcional.
excerpt *n* extracto *m*.
excess *n* exceso *m*.
excessive *adj* excesivo; **~ly** *adv* excesivamente.
exchange *vt* cambiar; trocar, permutar; ● *n* cambio *m*; bolsa *f*.
exchange rate *n* tipo de cambio *m*.
excise *n* impuestos sobre el comercio interior *mpl*.
excitability *n* excitabilidad *f*.
excitable *adj* excitable.
excite *vt* excitar; estimular.
excited *adj* emocionado.
excitement *n* estímulo, incitamiento *m*.
exciting *adj* emocionante.
exclaim *vi* exclamar.
exclamation *n* exclamación *f*; clamor *m*.
exclamation mark *n* punto de admiración *m*.
exclamatory *adj* exclamatorio.
exclude *vt* excluir; exceptuar.
exclusion *n* exclusión, exclusiva, excepción *f*.
exclusive *adj* exclusivo; **~ly** *adv* exclusivamente.
excommunicate *vt* excomulgar.
excommunication *n* excomunión *f*.
excrement *n* excremento *m*.
excruciating *adj* atroz, enorme, grave.
exculpate *vt* disculpar; justificar.
excursion *n* excursión *f*; digresión *f*.
excusable *adj* excusable.
excuse *vt* disculpar; perdonar; ● *n* disculpa, excusa *f*.
execute *vt* ejecutar.
execution *n* ejecución *f*.
executioner *n* ejecutor *m*; verdugo *m*.
executive *adj* ejecutivo.
executor *n* testamentario, albacea *m/f*.
exemplary *adj* ejemplar.
exemplify *vt* ejemplificar.
exempt *adj* exento.
exemption *n* exención *f*.
exercise *n* ejercicio *m*; ensayo *m*; tarea *f*; práctica *f*; ● *vi* hacer ejercicio; ● *vt* ejercer; valerse de.
excercise book *n* cuaderno *m*.
exert *vt* emplear; **to ~ oneself** esforzarse.
exertion *n* esfuerzo *m*.
exhale *vt* exhalar.
exhaust *n* escape *m*; ● *vt* agotar.
exhausted *adj* agotado.
exhaustion *n* agotamiento *m*; extenuación *f*.
exhaustive *adj* comprensivo.
exhibit *vt* exhibir; mostrar; ● *n* (*law*) objeto expuesto *m*.
exhibition *n* exposición, presentación *f*.
exhilarating *adj* estimulante.
exhilaration *n* alegría *f*; buen humor, regocijo *m*.
exhort *vt* exhortar, excitar.
exhortation *n* exhortación *f*.
exhume *vt* exhumar, desenterrar.
exile *n* destierro *m*; ● *vt* desterrar, deportar.

exist *vi* existir.
existence *n* existencia *f.*
existent *adj* existente.
existing *adj* actual, presente.
exit *n* salida *f;* ● *vi* hacer mutis.
exit ramp *n* vía de acceso *f.*
exodus *n* éxodo *m.*
exonerate *vt* exonerar, descargar.
exoneration *n* exoneración *f.*
exhorbitant *adj* exorbitante, excesivo.
exorcise *vt* exorcizar, conjurar.
exorcism *n* exorcismo *m.*
exotic *adj* exótico, extranjero.
expand *vt* extender, dilatar.
expanse *n* extensión de lugar *f.*
expansion *n* expansión *f.*
expansive *adj* expansivo.
expatriate *vt* expatriar.
expect *vt* esperar, aguardar.
expectance, expectancy *n* expectación, esperanza *f.*
expectant *adj* expectante.
expectant mother *n* mujer encinta *f.*
expectation *n* expectación, expectativa *f.*
expediency *n* conveniencia, oportunidad *f.*
expedient *adj* oportuno, conveniente; ● *n* expediente *m;* ~ly *adv* convenientemente.
expedite *vt* acelerar; expedir.
expedition *n* expedición *f.*
expeditious *adj* pronto, expedito; ~ly *adv* prontamente.
expel *vt* expeler, desterrar.
expend *vt* expender; desembolsar.
expendable *adj* prescindible.
expenditure *n* gasto, desembolso *m.*
expense *n* gasto *m;* coste *m.*
expense account *n* cuenta de gastos *f.*
expensive *adj* caro; costoso; ~ly *adv* costosamente.
experience *n* experiencia *f;* práctica *f;* ● *vt* experimentar.
experienced *adj* experimentado.
experiment *n* experimento *m;* ● *vt* experimentar.
experimental *adj* experimental; ~ly *adv* experimentalmente.
expert *adj* experto, diestro.
expertise *n* pericia *f.*
expiration *n* expiración *f;* muerte *f.*
expire *vi* expirar.
explain *vt* explanar, explicar.
explanation *n* explanación, explicación *f.*
explanatory *adj* explicativo.
expletive *adj* expletivo.
explicable *adj* explicable.
explicit *adj* explícito; ~ly *adv* explícitamente.
explode *vt, vi* estallar, explotar.
exploit *vt* explotar; ● *n* hazaña *f;* hecho heroico *m.*
exploitation *n* explotación *f.*
exploration *n* exploración *f;* examen *m.*
exploratory *adj* exploratorio.
explore *vt* explorar, examinar; sondear.
explorer *n* explorador *m.*
explosion *n* explosión *f.*
explosive *adj, n* explosivo *m.*
exponent *n* (*math*) exponente *m.*
export *vt* exportar.
export, exportation *n* exportación *f.*
exporter *n* exportador *m.*
expose *vt* exponer; mostrar; descubrir; poner en peligro.
exposed *adj* expuesto.
exposition *n* exposición *f;* interpretación *f.*
expostulate *vi* debatir, contender.
exposure *n* exposición *f;* velocidad de obturación *f;* fotografía *f.*
exposure meter *n* fotómetro *m.*
expound *vt* exponer; interpretar.

express *vt* exprimir; representar; ● *adj* expreso, claro; a propósito; ● *n* expreso, correo *m;* (*rail*) tren expreso *m.*
expression *n* expresión *f;* locución *f.*
expressionless *adj* sin expresión (cara).
expressive *adj* expresivo; ~ly *adv* expresivamente.
expressly *adv* expresamente.
expressway *n* autopista *f.*
expropriate *vt* expropiar (por causa de utilidad pública).
expropriation *n* (*law*) expropiación *f.*
expulsion *n* expulsión *f.*
expurgate *vt* expurgar.
exquisite *adj* exquisito, perfecto, excelente; ~ly *adv* exquisitamente.
extant *adj* existente.
extempore *adv* de improviso.
extemporize *vi* improvisar.
extend *vt* extender; amplificar; ● *vi* extenderse.
extension *n* extensión *f.*
extensive *adj* extenso, dilatado; ~ly *adv* extensivamente.
extent *n* extensión *f.*
extenuate *vt* extenuar, disminuir, atenuar.
extenuating *adj* atenuante.
exterior *adj, n* exterior *m.*
exterminate *vt* exterminar; extirpar.
extermination *n* exterminación, extirpación *f.*
external *adj* externo; ~ly *adv* exteriormente; ~s *npl* exterior *m.*
extinct *adj* extinto; abolido.
extinction *n* extinción *f;* abolición *f.*
extinguish *vt* extinguir; suprimir.
extinguisher *n* extintor *m.*
extirpate *vt* extirpar.
extol *vt* alabar, magnificar, alzar, exaltar.
extort *vt* sacar por fuerza.
extortion *n* extorsión *f.*
extortionate *adj* excesivo.
extra *adv* extra; ● *n* extra *m.*
extract *vt* extraer; extractar; ● *n* extracto *m;* compendio *m.*
extraction *n* extracción *f;* descendencia *f.*
extracurricular *adj* extraescolar.
extradite *vt* extraditar.
extradition *n* (*law*) extradición *f.*
extramarital *adj* extramatrimonial.
extramural *adj* extraescolor.
extraneous *adj* extraño, exótico.
extraordinarily *adv* extraordinariamente.
extraordinary *adj* extraordinario.
extravagance *n* extravagancia *f;* gastos, excesivos *mpl.*
extravagant *adj* extravagante, exorbitante; pródigo; ~ly *adv* extravagantemente.
extreme *adj* extremo, supremo; último; ● *n* extremo *m;* ~ly *adv* extremamente.
extremist *adj, n* extremista *m.*
extremity *n* extremidad *f.*
extricate *vt* desembarazar, desenredar.
extrinsic(al) *adj* extrínseco, exterior.
extrovert *adj, n* extrovertido *m.*
exuberance *n* exuberancia, suma abundancia *f.*
exuberant *adj* exuberante, abundantísimo; ~ly *adv* abundantemente.
exude *vi* transpirar.
exult *vt* exultar, regocijarse, triunfar.
exultation *n* exultación *f;* regocijo *m.*
eye *n* ojo *m;* ● *vt* ojear, contemplar, observar.
eyeball *n* globo del ojo *m.*
eyebrow *n* ceja *f.*
eyelash *n* pestaña *f.*
eyelid *n* párpado *m.*
eyesight *n* vista *f.*
eyesore *n* monstruosidad *f.*
eyetooth *n* colmillo *m.*
eyewitness *n* testigo ocular *m.*

eyrie *n* nido de ave de rapiña *m*.

F

fable *n* fábula *f*; ficción *f*.
fabric *n* tejido *m*.
fabricate *vt* fabricar, edificar.
fabrication *n* fabricación *f*.
fabulous *adj* fabuloso; ~ly *adv* fabulosamente.
façade *n* fachada *f*.
face *n* cara, faz *f*; superficie *f*; fachada *f*; aspecto *m*; apariencia *f*; • *vt* encararse; hacer frente; to ~ up to hacer frente a.
face cream *n* crema (de belleza) *f*.
face-lift *n* estirado facial *m*.
face powder *n* polvillos *mpl*.
facet *n* faceta *f*.
facetious *adj* chistoso, alegre, gracioso; ~ly *adv* chistosamente.
face value *n* valor nominal *m*.
facial *adj* facial.
facile *adj* fácil, afable.
facilitate *vt* facilitar.
facility *n* facilidad, ligereza *f*; afabilidad *f*.
facing *n* paramento *m*; • *prep* enfrente.
facsimile *n* facsímile *m*; telefax *m*.
fact *n* hecho *m*; realidad *f*; in ~ en efecto.
faction *n* facción *f*; disensión *f*.
factor *n* factor *m*.
factory *n* fábrica *f*.
factual *adj* basado en los hechos.
faculty *n* facultad *f*; personal docente *m*.
fad *n* moda *f*.
fade *vi* decaer, marchitarse, fallecer.
fail *vt* suspender, reprobar; fallar a; • *vi* suspender; fracasar; fallar.
failing *n* falta *f*; defecto *m*.
failure *n* falta *f*; culpa *f*; descuido *m*; quiebra, bancarrota *f*.
faint *vi* desmayarse, debilitarse; • *n* desmayo *m*; • *adj* débil; ~ly *adv* débilmente.
fainthearted *adj* cobarde, medroso, pusilánime.
faintness *n* flaqueza *f*; desmayo *m*.
fair *adj* hermoso, bello; blanco; rubio; claro, sereno; favorable; recto, justo; franco; • *adv* limpio; • *n* feria *f*.
fairly *adv* justamente; completamente.
fairness *n* hermosura *f*; justicia *f*.
fair play *n* juego limpio *m*.
fairy *n* hada *f*.
fairy tale *n* cuento de hadas *m*.
faith *n* fe *f*; dogma de fe *m*; fidelidad *f*.
faithful *adj* fiel, leal; ~ly *adv* fielmente.
faithfulness *n* fidelidad, lealtad *f*.
fake *n* falsificación *f*; impostor *m*; • *adj* falso; • *vt* fingir; falsificar.
falcon *n* halcón *m*.
falconry *n* halconería *f*.
fall *vi* caer(se); perder el poder; disminuir, decrecer en precio; to ~ asleep dormirse; to ~ back retroceder; to ~ back on recurrir a; to ~ behind quedarse atrás; to ~ down caerse; to ~ for dejarse engañar; enamorarse de; to ~ in hundirse; to ~ short faltar; to ~ sick enfermar; to ~ in love enamorarse; to ~ off caerse; disminuir; to ~ out reñir, disputar; • *n* caída *f*; otoño *m*.
fallacious *adj* falaz, fraudulento; ~ly *adv* falazmente.
fallacy *n* falacia, sofistería *f*; engaño *m*.
fallibility *n* falibilidad *f*.
fallible *adj* falible.
fallout *n* lluvia radioactiva *f*.
fallout shelter *n* refugio antiatómico *m*.
fallow *adj* en barbecho; ~ deer *n* corzo *m*; corza *f*.
false *adj* falso; ~ly *adv* falsamente.

false alarm *n* falsa alarma *f*.
falsehood, falseness *n* falsedad *f*.
falsify *vt* falsificar.
falsity *n* falsedad, mentira *f*.
falter *vi* tartamudear; faltar.
faltering *adj* vacilante.
fame *n* fama *f*; renombre *m*.
famed *adj* celebrado, famoso.
familiar *adj* familiar; casero; ~ly *adv* familiarmente.
familiarity *n* familiaridad *f*.
familiarize *vt* familiarizar.
family *n* familia *f*; linaje *m*; clase, especie *f*.
family business *n* negocio familiar *m*.
family doctor *n* médico de cabecera *m*.
famine *n* hambre *f*; carestía *f*.
famished *adj* hambriento.
famous *adj* famoso, afamado; ~ly *adv* famosamente.
fan *n* abanico *m*; aficionado *m*; • *vt* abanicar; atizar.
fanatic *adj*, *n* fanático *m*.
fanaticism *n* fanatismo *m*.
fan belt *n* correa de ventilador *f*.
fanciful *adj* imaginativo, caprichoso; ~ly *adv* caprichosamente.
fancy *n* fantasía, imaginación *f*; capricho *m*; • *vt* tener ganas de; imaginarse.
fancy-goods *npl* novedades, modas *fpl*.
fancydress ball *n* baile de disfraces *m*.
fanfare *n* (*mus*) fanfarria *f*.
fang *n* colmillo *m*.
fantastic *adj* fantástico; caprichoso; ~ally *adv* fantásticamente.
fantasy *n* fantasía *f*.
far *adv* lejos, a una gran distancia; • *adj* lejano, distante, remoto; ~ and away con mucho, de mucho; ~ off lejano.
faraway *adj* remoto.
farce *n* farsa *f*.
farcical *adj* burlesco.
fare *n* precio *m*; tarifa *f*; comida *f*; viajero *m*; pasaje *m*.
farewell *n* despedida *f*; ~! *excl* ¡adiós!
farm *n* finca *f*, granja *f*; • *vt* cultivar.
farmer *n* estanciero *m*; granjero *m*.
farmhand *n* peón *m*.
farmhouse *n* casa de hacienda *f*.
farming *n* agricultura *f*.
farmland *n* tierra de cultivo *f*.
farmyard *n* corral *m*.
far-reaching *adj* de gran alcance.
fart *n* (*sl*) pedo; • *vi* tirarse un pedo.
farther *adv* más lejos; más adelante; • *adj* más lejos, ulterior.
farthest *adv* lo más lejos; lo más tarde; a lo más.
fascinate *vt* fascinar, encantar.
fascinating *adj* fascinante.
fascination *n* fascinación *f*; encanto *m*.
fascism *n* fascismo.
fashion *n* moda *f*; forma, figura *f*; uso *m*; manera *f*; estilo *m*; people of ~ gente de tono *f*; • *vt* formar, amoldar.
fashionable *adj* a la moda; elegante; the ~ world el gran mundo; ~bly *adv* a o según la moda.
fashion show *n* desfile de modelos *m*.
fast *vi* ayunar; • *n* ayuno *m*; • *adj* rápido; firme, estable; • *adv* rápidamente; firmemente; estrechamente.
fasten *vt* abrochar; afirmar, asegurar, atar; fijar; • *vi* fijarse, establecerse.
fastener, fastening *n* cierre *m*; cerrojo *m*.
fast food *n* comida rápida *f*.
fastidious *adj* fastidioso, desdeñoso; ~ly *adv* fastidiosamente.
fat *adj* gordo; • *n* grasa *f*.
fatal *adj* fatal; funesto; ~ly *adv* fatalmente.
fatalism *n* fatalismo *m*.
fatalist *n* fatalista *m*.
fatality *n* fatalidad, predestinación *f*.
fate *n* hado, destino *m*.

fateful *adj* fatídico.
father *n* padre *m*.
fatherhood *n* paternidad *f*.
father-in-law *n* suegro *m*.
fatherland *n* patria *f*.
fatherly *adj* (*adv*) paternal(mente).
fathom *n* braza (medida) *f*; • *vt* sondar; penetrar.
fatigue *n* fatiga *f*; • *vt* fatigar, sansar.
fatten *vt, vi* engordar.
fatty *adj* graso.
fatuous *adj* fatuo, tonto, imbécil.
faucet *n* grifo *m*, llave *f*.
fault *n* falta, culpa *f*; delito *m*; defecto *m*.
faultfinder *n* censurador *m*.
faultless *adj* perfecto, cumplido.
faulty *adj* defectuoso.
fauna *n* fauna *f*.
faux pas *n* plancha *f*.
favor *n* favor, beneficio *m*; patrocinio *m*; blandura *f*; • *vt* favorecer, proteger.
favorable *adj* favorable, propicio; ~**bly** *adv* favorablemente.
favored *adj* favorecido.
favorite *n* favorito *m*; • *adj* favorecido.
favoritism *n* favoritismo *m*.
fawn *n* cervato *m*; • *vi* adular servilmente.
fawningly *adv* lisonjeramente, con adulación servil.
fax *n* facsímil(e) *m*; telefax *m*; • *vt* mandar por telefax.
fear *vi* temer; • *n* miedo *m*.
fearful *adj* medroso, temeroso; tímido; ~**ly** *adv* medrosamente, temerosamente.
fearless *adj* intrépido, atrevido; ~**ly** *adv* sin miedo.
fearlessness *n* intrepidez *f*.
feasibility *n* posibilidad *f*.
feasible *adj* factible, hacedero.
feast *n* banquete, festín *m*; fiesta *f*; • *vi* banquetear.
feat *n* hecho *m*; acción, hazaña *f*.
feather *n* pluma *f*;.
feather bed *n* plumón *m*.
feature *n* característica *f*; rasgo *m*; forma *f*; • *vi* figurar.
feature film *n* largometraje *m*.
February *n* febrero *m*.
federal *adj* federal.
federalist *n* federalista *m*.
federate *vt, vi* confederar(se).
federation *n* confederación *f*.
fed-up *adj* harto.
fee *n* honorarios *mpl*; cuota *f*.
feeble *adj* flaco, débil.
feebleness *n* debilidad *f*.
feebly *adv* débilmente.
feed *vt* nutrir; alimentar; **to** ~ **on** alimentarse de; • *vi* nutrirse; engordar; • *n* comida *f*; pasto *m*.
feedback *n* reacción *f*.
feel *vt* sentir; tocar; creer; **to** ~ **around** tantear; • *n* sensación *f*; tacto, sentido *m*.
feeler *n* antenas *fpl*; (*fig*) tentativa *f*.
feeling *n* tacto *m*; sensibilidad *f*.
feelingly *adv* sensiblemente.
feign *vt* inventar, fingir; disimular.
feline *adj* gatuno.
fellow *n* tipo, tío *m*; socio *m*.
fellow citizen *n* conciudadano *m*.
fellow countryman *n* compatriota *m*.
fellow feeling *n* simpatía *f*.
fellow men *npl* semejantes *mpl*.
fellowship *n* compañerismo *m*; beca (en un colegio) *f*.
fellow student *n* compañero de curso *m*.
fellow traveler *n* compañero de viaje *m*.
felon *n* criminal *m*.
felony *n* crimen *m*.
felt *n* fieltro *m*.
felt-tip pen *n* rotulador *m*.

female *n* hembra *f*; • *adj* femenino.
feminine *adj* femenino.
feminist *n* feminista *f*.
fen *n* pantano *m*.
fence *n* cerca *f*; defensa *f*; • *vt* cercar; • *vi* esgrimir.
fencing *n* esgrima *f*.
fender *n* parachoques *m invar*.
fennel *n* (*bot*) hinojo *m*.
ferment *n* agitación *f*; • *vi* fermentar.
fern *n* (*bot*) helecho *m*.
ferocious *adj* ferviente; fiero; ~**ly** *adv* ferozmente.
ferocity *n* ferocidad, fiereza *f*.
ferret *n* hurón *m*; • *vt* huronear; **to** ~ **out** descubrir, echar fuera.
ferry *n* barca de pasaje *f*; embarcadero *m*; • *vt* transportar.
fertile *adj* fértil, fecundo.
fertility *n* fertilidad, fecundidad *f*.
fertilize *vt* fertilizar.
fertilizer *n* abono *m*.
fervent *adj* ferviente; fervoroso; ~**ly** *adv* con fervor.
fervid *adj* ardiente, vehemente.
fervor *n* fervor, ardor *m*.
fester *vi* enconarse, inflamarse.
festival *n* fiesta *f*; festival *m*.
festive *adj* festivo.
festivity *n* festividad *f*.
fetch *vt* ir a buscar.
fetching *adj* atractivo.
fête *n* fiesta *f*.
fetid *adj* fétido, hediondo.
fetus *n* feto *m*.
feud *n* riña, contienda *f*.
feudal *adj* feudal.
feudalism *n* feudalismo *m*.
fever *n* fiebre *f*.
feverish *adj* febril.
few *adj* poco; **a** ~ algunos; ~ **and far between** pocos.
fewer *adj* menor; • *adv* menos.
fewest *adj* los menos.
fiancé *n* novio *m*.
fiancée *n* novia *f*.
fib *n* mentira *f*; • *vi* mentir.
fiber *n* fibra, hebra *f*.
fiberglass *n* fibra de vidrio *f*.
fickle *adj* voluble, inconstante, mudable, ligero.
fiction *n* ficción *f*; invención *f*.
fictional *adj* novelesco.
fictitious *adj* ficticio; fingido; ~**ly** *adv* fingidamente.
fiddle *n* violín *m*; trampa *f*; • *vi* tocar el violín.
fiddler *n* violinista *m*.
fidelity *n* fidelidad, lealtad *f*.
fidget *vi* inquietarse.
fidgety *adj* inquieto, impaciente.
field *n* campo *m*; campaña *f*; espacio *m*.
field day *n* (*mil*) día de la revista *m*.
fieldmouse *n* turón *m*.
fieldwork *n* trabajo de campo *m*.
fiend *n* enemigo *m*; demonio *m*.
fiendish *adj* demoniaco.
fierce *adj* fiero, feroz; cruel, furioso; ~**ly** *adv* furiosamente.
fierceness *n* fiereza, ferocidad *f*.
fiery *adj* ardiente; apasionado.
fifteen *adj, n* quince.
fifteenth *adj, n* decimoquinto.
fifth *adj, n* quinto; ~**ly** *adv* en quinto lugar.
fiftieth *adj, n* quincuagésimo.
fifty *adj, n* cincuenta.
fig *n* higo *m*.
fight *vt, vi* reñir; batallar; combatir; • *n* batalla *f*; combate *m*; pelea *f*.
fighter *n* combatiente *m*; luchador *m*; caza *m*.
fighting *n* combate *m*.

fig-leaf *n* hoja de higuera *f*.
fig tree *n* higuera *f*.
figurative *adj* figurativo; **~ly** *adv* figuradamente.
figure *n* figura, forma *f*; imagen *f*; cifra *f*; • *vi* figurar; ser lógico; **to ~ out** comprender.
figurehead *n* testaferro *m*.
filament *n* filamento *m*; fibra *f*.
filch *vi* ratear.
filcher *n* ratero, ladroncillo *m*.
file *n* hilo *m*; lista *f*; (*mil*) fila, hilera *f*; lima *f*; carpeta *f*; fichero *m*; • *vt* enhilar; limar; clasificar; presentar; • *vi* **to ~ in/out** entrar/salir en fila; **to ~ past** desfilar ante.
filing cabinet *n* archivo *m*.
fill *vt* llenar; hartar; **to ~ in** rellenar; **to ~ up** llenar (hasta el borde).
fillet *n* filete *m*.
fillet steak *n* filete de ternera *m*.
filling station *n* estación de servicio *f*.
fillip *n* (*fig*) estímulo *m*.
filly *n* potranca *f*.
film *n* película *f*; film *m*; capa *f*; • *vt* filmar; • *vi* rodar.
film star *n* estrella de cine *f*.
filmstrip *n* tira de película *f*.
filter *n* filtro *m*; • *vt* filtrar.
filter-tipped *adj* con filtro.
filth(iness) *n* inmundicia, porquería *f*; fango, lodo *m*.
filthy *adj* sucio, puerco.
fin *n* aleta *f*.
final *adj* final, último; **~ly** *adv* finalmente.
finale *n* final *m*.
finalist *n* finalista *m*.
finalize *vt* concluir.
finance *n* fondos *mpl*.
financial *adj* financiero.
financier *n* financiero *m*.
find *vt* hallar, descubrir; **to ~ out** averiguar; descubrir; **to ~ one's self** hallarse; • *n* hallazgo *m*.
findings *npl* fallo *m*; recomendaciones *fpl*.
fine *adj* fino; agudo, cortante; claro, trasparente; delicado; astuto; elegante; bello; • *n* multa *f*; • *vt* multar.
fine arts *npl* bellas artes *fpl*.
finely *adv* con elegancia.
finery *n* adorno, atavío *m*.
finesse *n* sutileza *f*.
finger *n* dedo *m*; • *vt* tocar, manosear; manejar.
fingernail *n* uña *f*.
fingerprint *n* huella dactilar *f*.
fingertip *n* yema del dedo *f*.
finicky *adj* delicado.
finish *vt* acabar, terminar, concluir; **to ~ off** acabar (con); **to ~ up** terminar; • *vi*: **to ~ up** ir a parar.
finishing line *n* línea de llegado *f*.
finishing school *n* academia para señoritas *f*.
finite *adj* finito; conjugado.
fir (tree) *n* abeto *m*
fire *n* fuego *m*; incendio *m*; • *vt* disparar; incendiar; despertar; • *vi* encenderse.
fire alarm *n* alarma de incendios *f*.
firearm *n* arma de fuego *f*.
fireball *n* meteóro, meteoro *m*.
fire department *n* bomberos *mpl*.
fire engine *n* coche de bomberos *m*.
fire escape *n* escalera de incendios *f*.
fire extinguisher *n* extintor *m*.
firefly *n* luciérnaga *f*.
fireman *n* bombero *m*.
fireplace *n* hogar, fogón *m*.
fireproof *adj* a prueba de fuego.
fireside *n* chimenea *f*.
fire station *n* parque de bomberos *m*.
firewater *n* aguardiente *m*.
firewood *n* leña *f*.

fireworks *npl* fuegos artificiales *mpl*.
firing *n* disparos *mpl*.
firing squad *n* pelotón de ejecución *m*.
firm *adj* firme, estable, constante; • *n* (*com*) firma *f*; **~ly** *adv* firmemente.
firmament *n* firmamento *m*.
firmness *n* firmeza *f*; constancia *f*.
first *adj* primero; • *adv* primeramente; **at ~** al principio; **~ly** *adv* en primer lugar.
first aid *n* primeros auxilios *mpl*.
first-aid kit *n* botiquín *m*.
first-class *adj* de primera (clase).
first-hand *adj* de primera mano.
First Lady *n* primera dama *f*.
first name *n* nombre de pila *m*.
first-rate *adj* de primera (clase).
fiscal *adj* fiscal.
fish *n* pez *m*; • *vi* pescar.
fishbone *n* espina *f*.
fisherman *n* pescador *m*.
fish farm *n* criadero de peces *m*.
fishing *n* pesca *f*.
fishing line *n* sedal *m*.
fishing rod *n* caña de pescar *f*.
fishing tackle *n* aparejo *m*.
fish market *n* pescadería *f*.
fishseller *n* pescadero *m*.
fishstore *n* pescadería *f*.
fishy *adj* (*fig*) sospechoso.
fissure *n* grieta, hendedura *f*.
fist *n* puño *m*.
fit *n* paroxismo *m*; convulsión *f*; • *adj* en forma; apto, idóneo, justo; • *vt* ajustar, acomodar, adaptar; **to ~ out** proveer; • *vi* convenir; **to ~ in** encajarse; llevarse bien (con todos).
fitment *n* módulo adosable *m*.
fitness *n* salud *f*; aptitud, conveniencia *f*.
fitted carpet *n* moqueta *f*.
fitted kitchen *n* cocina amueblada *f*.
fitter *n* ajustador *m*.
fitting *adj* conveniente, idóneo, justo; • *n* conveniencia *f*; **~s** *pl* guarnición *f*.
five *adj*, *n* cinco.
five spot *n* (*sl*) billete de cinco dólares *m*.
fix *vt* fijar, establecer; **to ~ up** arreglar.
fixation *n* obsesión *f*.
fixed *adj* fijo.
fixings *npl* equipajes *mpl*; pertrechos *mpl*; ajuar *m*.
fixture *n* encuentro *m*.
fizz(le) *vi* silbar.
fizzy *adj* gaseoso.
flabbergasted *adj* pasmado.
flabby *adj* blando, flojo, lacio.
flaccid *adj* flojo, flaco; flácido.
flag *n* bandera *f*; losa *f*; • *vi* debilitarse.
flagpole *n* asta de bandera *f*.
flagrant *adj* flagrante; notorio.
flagship *n* navío almirante *m*.
flagstop *n* parada a petición *f*.
flair *n* aptitud especial *f*.
flak *n* fuego antiaéreo *m*; lluvia de críticas.
flake *n* copo *m*; lámina *f*; • *vi* romperse en láminas.
flaky *adj* roto en pequeñas laminillas.
flamboyant *adj* vistoso.
flame *n* llama *f*; fuego (del amor) *m*.
flamingo *n* flamenco *m*.
flammable *adj* inflamable.
flank *n* ijada *f*; (*mil*) flanco *m*; • *vt* flanquear.
flannel *n* franela, flanela *f*.
flap *n* solapa *f*; hoja *f*; aletazo *m*; • *vt* aletear; • *vi* ondear.
flare *vi* lucir, brillar; **to ~ up** encenderse; encolerizarse; estallar; • *n* llama *f*.
flash *n* flash *m*; relámpago *m*; • *vt* encender y apagar.

flashbulb *n* bombilla fusible *f.*
flash cube *n* cubo de flash *m.*
flashlight *n* linterna *f.*
flashy *adj* superficial.
flask *n* frasco *m*; botella *f.*
flat *adj* llano, plano; insípido; ● *n* llanura *f*; plano *m*; (*mus*) bemol *m*; **~ly** *adv* horizontalmente; llanamente; enteramente; de plano, de nivel; francamente.
flatness *n* llanura *f*; insipidez *f.*
flatten *vt* allanar; abatir.
flatter *vt* adular, lisonjear.
flattering *adj* halagüeño.
flattery *n* adulación, lisonja *f.*
flatulence *n* (*med*) flatulencia *f.*
flaunt *vt* ostentar.
flavor *n* sabor *m*; ● *vt* sazonar.
flavored *adj* con sabor (a).
flavorless *adj* soso.
flaw *n* falta, tacha *f*; defecto *m.*
flawless *adj* sin defecto.
flax *n* lino *m.*
flea *n* pulga *f.*
flea bite *n* picadura de pulga *f.*
fleck *n* mota *f*; punto *m.*
flee *vt* huir de; ● *vi* escapar; huir.
fleece *n* vellón *m*; ● *vt* (*sl*) pelar.
fleet *n* flota *f*; escuadra *f.*
fleeting *adj* pasajero, fugitivo.
flesh *n* carne *f.*
flesh wound *n* herida superficial *f.*
fleshy *adj* carnoso, pulposo.
flex *n* cordón *m*; ● *vt* tensar.
flexibility *n* flexibilidad *f.*
flexible *adj* flexible.
flick *n* golpecito *m*; ● *vt* dar un golpecito a.
flicker *vt* aletear; fluctuar.
flier *n* aviador *m.*
flight *n* vuelo *m*; huída, fuga *f*; bandada (de pájaros) *f*; (*fig*) elevación *f.*
flight attendant *n* tripulante auxiliar *m.*
flight deck *n* cabina de mandos *f.*
flimsy *adj* débil; fútil.
flinch *vi* encogerse.
fling *vt* lanzar, echar.
flint *n* pedernal *m.*
flip *vt* arrojar, lanzar.
flippant *adj* petulante, locuaz.
flipper *n* aleta *f.*
flirt *vi* coquetear; ● *n* coqueta *f.*
flirtation *n* coquetería *f.*
flit *vi* volar, huir; aletear.
float *vt* hacer flotar; lanzar; ● *vi* flotar; ● *n* flotador *m*; carroza *f*; reserva *f.*
flock *n* manada *f*; rebaño *m*; gentío *m*; ● *vi* congregarse.
flog *vt* azotar.
flogging *n* tunda, zurra *f.*
flood *n* diluvio *m*; inundación *f*; flujo *m*; ● *vt* inundar.
flooding *n* inundación *f.*
floodlight *n* foco *m.*
floor *n* suelo, piso *m*; piso de una casa; ● *vt* dejar sin respuesta.
floorboard *n* tabla *f.*
floor lamp *n* lámpara de pie *f.*
floor show *n* cabaret *m.*
flop *n* fracaso *m.*
floppy *adj* flojo; ● *n* floppy *m.*
flora *n* flora *f.*
floral *adj* floral.
florescence *n* florescencia *f.*
florid *adj* florido.
florist *n* florista *m.*
florist's (shop) *n* florería *f.*

flotilla *n* (*mar*) flotilla *f.*
flounder *n* platija (pez de mar) *f*; ● *vi* tropezar.
flour *n* harina *f.*
flourish *vi* florecer; gozar de prosperidad; ● *n* belleza *f*; floreo de palabras *m*; lazo *m*; (*mus*) floreo, preludio *m.*
flourishing *adj* floreciente.
flout *vt* burlarse de.
flow *vi* fluir, manar; crecer la marea; ondear; ● *n* creciente de la marea *f*; abundancia *f*; flujo *m.*
flow chart *n* organigrama *m.*
flower *n* flor *f*; ● *vi* florear; florecer.
flowerbed *n* cuadro (en un jardín) *m.*
flowerpot *n* tiesto de flores *m.*
flowery *adj* florido.
flower show *n* exposición de flores *f.*
fluctuate *vi* fluctuar.
fluctuation *n* fluctuación *f.*
fluency *n* fluidez *f.*
fluent *adj* fluido; fácil; **~ly** *adv* con fluidez.
fluff *n* pelusa *f*; **~y** *adj* velloso.
fluid *adj*, *n* fluido *m.*
fluidity *n* fluidez *f.*
fluke *n* (*sl*) chiripa *f.*
fluoride *n* fluoruro *m.*
flurry *n* ráfaga *f*; agitación *f.*
flush *vt*: **to ~ out** levantar; desalojar; ● *vi* ponerse colorado; ● *n* rubor *m*; resplandor *m.*
flushed *adj* ruborizado.
fluster *vt* confundir.
flustered *adj* aturdido.
flute *n* flauta *f.*
flutter *vi* revolotear; estar en agitación; ● *n* cofusión *f*; agitación *f.*
flux *n* flujo *m.*
fly *vt* pilotar; transportar; ● *vi* volar; huir, escapar; **to ~ away/off** emprender el vuelo; ● *n* mosca *f*; bragueta *f.*
flying *n* volar *m.*
flying saucer *n* platillo volante *m.*
flypast *n* desfile aéreo *m.*
flysheet *n* doble techo *m.*
foal *n* potro *m.*
foam *n* espuma *f*; ● *vi* espumar.
foam rubber *n* espuma de caucho *f.*
foamy *adj* espumoso.
focus *n* foco, el punto céntrico *m.*
fodder *n* forraje *m.*
foe *n* adversario, enemigo *m.*
fog *n* niebla *f.*
foggy *adj* nebuloso, brumoso.
fog light *n* faro antiniebla *m.*
foible *n* debilidad, parte flaca *f.*
foil *vt* frustrar; ● *n* hoja *f*; florete *m.*
fold *n* redil *m*; pliegue *m*; ● *vt* plegar; ● *vi*: **to ~ up** plegarse, doblarse; quebrar.
folder *n* carpeta *f*; folleto *m.*
folding *adj* plegable.
folding chair *n* silla de tijera *f.*
foliage *n* follaje *m.*
folio *n* folio *m.*
folk *n* gente *f.*
folklore *n* folklore *m.*
folk song *n* canción folklórica *f.*
follow *vt* seguir; acompañar; imitar; **to ~ up** responder a; investigar; ● *vi* seguir, resultar, provenir.
follower *rr* seguidor *m*; imitador *m*; secuaz, partidario *m*; adherente *m*; compañero *m.*
following *adj* siguiente; ● *n* afición *f.*
folly *n* extravagancia, bobería *f.*
foment *vt* fomentar; proteger.
fond *adj* cariñoso; **~ly** *adv* cariñosamente.
fondle *vt* acariciar.
fondness *n* gusto *m*; cariño *m.*

font n pila bautismal f.
food n comida f.
food mixer n batidora f.
food poisoning n botulismo m.
food processor n robot de cocina m.
foodstuffs npl comestibles mpl.
fool n loco, tonto m; • vt engañar.
foolhardy adj temerario.
foolish adj bobo, tonto; ~ly adv tontamente.
foolproof adj infalible.
foolscap n papel tamaño folio m.
foot n pie m; pata f; paso m; on o by ~ a pie.
footage n imágenes fpl.
football n balón m; fútbol m.
footballer n futbolista m; jugador de fútbol m.
footbrake n freno de pie m.
footbridge n puentecilla f.
foothills npl estribaciones fpl.
foothold n pie firme m.
footing n base f; estado m; condición f; fundamento m.
footlights npl lámparas del proscenio fpl.
footman n lacayo m; soldado de infantería m.
footnote n nota de pie f.
footpath n senda f.
footprint n huella, pisada f.
footsore adj con los pies doloridos.
footstep n paso m; huella f.
footwear n calzado m.
for prep por, a causa de; para; • conj porque, para que; por cuanto; as ~ me tocante a mí; what ~? ¿para qué?
forage n forraje m; • vt forrajear; saquear.
foray n incursión f.
forbid vt prohibir, vedar; impedir; God ~! ¡Dios no quiera!
forbidding adj inhóspito; severo.
force n fuerza f; poder, vigor m; violencia f; necesidad f; ~s pl tropas fpl; • vt forzar, violentar; esforzar; constreñir.
forced adj forzado.
forced march n (mil) marcha forzada f.
forceful adj enérgico.
forceps n fórceps m.
forcible adj fuerte, eficaz, poderoso; ~bly adv fuertemente, forzadamente.
ford n vado m; • vt vadear.
fore n: to the ~ en evidencia.
forearm n antebrazo m.
foreboding n presentimiento m.
forecast vt pronosticar; • n pronóstico m.
forecourt n patio m.
forefather n abuelo, antecesor m.
forefinger n índice m.
forefront n: in the ~ of en la vanguardia de.
forego vt ceder, abandonar; preceder.
foregone adj pasado; anticipado.
foreground n delantera f.
forehead n frente f; insolencia f.
foreign adj extranjero; extraño.
foreigner n extranjero, forastero m.
foreign exchange n divisas fpl.
foreleg n pata delantera f.
foreman n capataz m; (law) presidente del jurado m.
foremost adj principal.
forenoon n mañana f.
forensic adj forense.
forerunner n precursor m; predecesor m.
foresee vt prever.
foreshadow vt pronosticar; simbolizar.
foresight n previsión f; presciencia f.
forest n bosque m; selva f.
forestall vt anticipar; prevenir.
forester n guardabosque m.
forestry n silvicultura f.
foretaste n muestra f.

foretell vt predecir, profetizar.
forethought n providencia f; premeditación f.
forever adv para siempre.
forewarn vt prevenir de antemano.
foreword n prefacio m.
forfeit n confiscación f; • vt perder derecho a.
forge n fragua f; fábrica de metales f; • vt forjar; falsificar; inventar; • vi: to ~ ahead avanzar constantemente.
forger n falsificador m.
forgery n falsificación f.
forget vt olvidar; • vi olvidarse.
forgetful adj olvidadizo; descuidado.
forgetfulness n olvido m; negligencia f.
forget-me-not n (bot) no-me-olvides m.
forgive vt perdonar.
forgiveness n perdón m; remisión f.
fork n tenedor m; horca f; • vi bifurcarse; to ~ out (sl) desembolsar.
forked adj horcado.
fork-lift truck n máquina elevadora f.
forlorn adj abandonado, perdido.
form n forma f; modelo m; modo m; formalidad f; método m; molde m; • vt formar.
formal adj formal, metódico; cermonioso; ~ly adv formalmente.
formality n formalidad f; ceremonia f.
format n formato m; • vt formatear.
formation n formación f.
formative adj formativo.
former adj precedente; anterior, pasado; ~ly adv antiguamente, en tiempos pasados.
formidable adj formidable, terrible.
formula n fórmula f.
formulate vt formular, articular.
forsake vt dejar, abandonar.
fort n castillo m; fortaleza f.
forte n fuerte m.
forthcoming adj venidero.
forthright adj franco.
forthwith adj inmediatamente, sin tardanza.
fortieth adj, n cuadragésimo m.
fortification n fortificación f.
fortify vt fortificar; corroborar.
fortitude n fortaleza f; valor m.
fortnight n quince días mpl; dos semanas fpl; ~ly adj, adv cada quince días.
fortress n (mil) fortaleza f.
fortuitous adj impensado; casual; ~ly adv fortuitamente.
fortunate adj afortunado; ~ly adv felizmente.
fortune n fortuna, suerte f.
fortune-teller n sortílego, adivino m.
forty adj, n cuarenta.
forum n foro m.
forward adj avanzado; delantero; presumido; ~(s) adv adelante, más allá; • vt remitir; promover, patrocinar.
forwardness n precocidad f; audacia f.
fossil adj, n fósil n.
foster vt criar, nutrir.
foster child n hijo adoptivo m.
foster father n padre adoptivo m.
foster mother n madre adoptiva f.
foul adj sucio, puerco; impuro, detestable; ~ copy n borrador m; ~ly adv suciamente; ilegítimamente; • vt ensuciar.
foul play n mala jugada f; muerte violenta f.
found vt fundar, establecer; edificar; fundir.
foundation n fundación f; fundamento m.
founder n fundador m; fundidor m; • vi (mar) irse a pique.
foundling n niño expósito m.
foundry n fundería f.
fount, fountain n fuente f.
fountainhead n origen de fuente m.
four adj, n cuatro.

fourfold *adj* cuádruple.

four-poster (bed) *n* cama de dosel *f*.

foursome *n* grupo de cuatro personas *m*.

fourteen *adj*, *n* catorce.

fourteenth *adj*, *n* decimocuarto.

fourth *adj* cuarto; • *n* cuarto *m*; ~**ly** *adv* en cuarto lugar.

fowl *n* ave *f*.

fox *n* zorra *f*; (*fig*) zorro *m*.

foyer *n* vestíbulo *m*.

fracas *n* riña *f*.

fraction *n* fracción *f*.

fracture *n* fractura *f*; • *vt* fracturar, romper.

fragile *adj* frágil; débil.

fragility *n* fragilidad *f*; debilidad, flaqueza *f*.

fragment *n* fragmento *m*.

fragmentary *adj* fragmentario.

fragrance *n* fragancia *f*.

fragrant *adj* fragante, oloroso; ~**ly** *adv* con fragancia.

frail *adj* frágil, débil.

frailty *n* fragilidad *f*; debilidad *f*.

frame *n* armazón *m*; marco, cerco *m*; cuadro de vidriera *m*; estructura *f*; montura *f*; • *vt* encuadrar; componer, construir, formar.

frame of mind *n* estado de ánimo *m*.

framework *n* labor hecha en el bastidor *o* telar *f*; armazón *f*.

franchise *n* sufragio *m*; concesión *f*.

frank *adj* franco, liberal.

frankly *adv* francamente.

frankness *n* franqueza *f*.

frantic *adj* frenético, furioso.

fraternal *adj*, ~**ly** *adv* fraternal(mente).

fraternity *n* fraternidad *f*.

fraternize *vi* hermanarse.

fratricide *n* fratricidio *m*; fratricida *m*.

fraud *n* fraude, engaño *m*.

fraudulence *n* fraudulencia *f*.

fraudulent *adj* fraudulento; ~**ly** *adv* fraudulentamente.

fraught *adj* cargado, lleno.

fray *n* riña, disputa, querella *f*.

freak *n* fantasía *f*; fenómeno *m*.

freckle *n* peca *f*.

freckled *adj* pecoso.

free *adj* libre; liberal; suelto; exento; desocupado; • *vt* soltar; librar; eximir.

freedom *n* libertad *f*.

freehold *n* propiedad vitalicia *f*.

free-for-all *n* riña general *f*.

free gift *n* prima *f*.

free kick *n* tiro libre *m*.

freelance *adj*, *adv* por cuenta propia.

freely *adv* libremente; espontáneamente; liberalmente.

freemason *n* francmasón *m*.

freemasonry *n* francmasonería *f*.

freepost *n* porte pagado *m*.

free-range *adj* de granja.

freethinker *n* libertino *m*.

freethinking *n* incredulidad *f*.

free trade *n* libre comercio.

freeway *n* autopista *f*.

freewheel *vi* ir en punto muerto.

free will *n* libre albedrío *m*.

freeze *vi* helar(se); • *vt* congelar; helar.

freeze-dried *adj* liofilizado.

freezer *n* congeladora *f*.

freezing *adj* helado.

freezing point *n* punto de congelación *m*.

freight *n* carga *f*; flete *m*.

freighter *n* fletador *m*.

freight train *n* tren de mercancías *m*.

French bean *n* judía verde *f*.

French fries *npl* patatas *o* papas fritas *fpl*.

French window *n* puertaventana *f*.

frenzied *adj* loco, delirante.

frenzy *n* frenesí *m*; locura *f*.

frequency *n* frecuencia *f*.

frequent *adj*, ~**ly** *adv* frecuente(mente); • *vt* frecuentar.

fresco *n* fresco *m*.

fresh *adj* fresco; nuevo, reciente; ~ **water** *n* agua dulce *f*.

freshen *vt*, *vi* refrescar(se).

freshly *adv* nuevamente; recientemente.

freshman *n* novicio *m*.

freshness *n* frescura *f*; fresco *m*.

freshwater *adj* de agua dulce.

fret *vi* agitarse, enojarse.

friar *n* fraile *m*.

friction *n* fricción *f*.

Friday *n* viernes *m*; **Good ~** Viernes Santo *m*.

friend *n* amigo *m*; amiga *f*.

friendless *adj* sin amigos.

friendliness *n* amistad, benevolencia, bondad *f*.

friendly *adj* amistoso.

friendship *n* amistad *f*.

frieze *n* friso *m*.

frigate *n* (*mar*) fragata *f*.

fright *n* espanto, terror *m*.

frighten *vt* espantar.

frightened *adj* asustado.

frightening *adj* espantoso.

frightful *adj* espantoso, horrible; ~**ly** *adv* espantosamente, terriblemente.

frigid *adj* frío, frígido; ~**ly** *adv* fríamente.

fringe *n* franja *f*.

fringe benefits *npl* ventajas supletorias *fpl*.

frisk *vt* cachear.

frisky *adj* juguetón.

fritter *vt*: **to ~ away** desperdiciar.

frivolity *n* frivolidad *f*.

frivolous *adj* frívolo, vano.

frizz(le) *vt* frisar; rizar.

frizzy *adj* rizado.

fro *adv*: **to go to and ~** ir y venir.

frock *n* vestido *m*.

frog *n* rana *f*.

frolic *vi* juguetear.

frolicsome *adj* juguetón, travieso.

from *prep* de; después; desde.

front *n* parte delantera *f*; fachada *f*; paseo marítimo *m*; frente *m*; apariencias *fpl*; • *adj* delantero; primero.

frontal *adj* de frente.

front door *n* puerta principal *f*.

frontier *n* frontera *f*.

front page *n* primera plana *f*.

front-wheel drive *n* (*auto*) tracción delantera *f*.

frost *n* helada *f*; hielo *m*; • *vt* escarchar.

frostbite *n* congelación *f*.

frostbitten *adj* helado, quemado del hielo.

frosted *adj* deslustrado.

frosty *adj* helado, frío como el hielo.

froth *n* espuma (de algún líquido) *f*; • *vi* espumar.

frothy *adj* espumoso.

frown *vi* mirar con ceño; • *n* ceño *m*; enojo *m*.

frozen *adj* helado.

frugal *adj* frugal; económico; sobrio; ~**ly** *adv* frugalmente.

fruit *n* fruta *f*; fruto *m*; producto *m*.

fruiterer *n* frutero *m*.

fruiterer's (shop) *n* frutería *f*.

fruitful *adj* fructífero, fértil; provechoso, útil; ~**ly** *adv* con fertilidad.

fruitfulness *n* fertilidad *f*.

fruition *n* realización *f*.

fruit juice *n* jugo de fruta *m*.

fruitless *adj* estéril; inútil; ~**ly** *adv* vanamente, inútilmente.

fruit salad *n* ensalada de frutas *f*.

fruit tree *n* frutal *m*.

frustrate *vt* frustrar; anular.
frustrated *adj* frustrado.
frustration *n* frustración *f*.
fry *vt* freir.
frying pan *n* sartén *f*.
fuchsia *n* (*bot*) fuchsia *f*.
fudge *n* caramelo blando *m*.
fuel *n* combustible *m*.
fuel tank *n* déposito *m*.
fugitive *adj*, *n* fugitivo *m*.
fugue *n* (*mus*) fuga *f*.
fulcrum *n* fulcro *m*.
fulfill *vt* cumplir; realizar.
fulfillment *n* cumplimiento *m*.
full *adj* lleno, repleto, completo; perfecto; ● *adv* enteramente, del todo.
full-blown *adj* hecho y derecho.
full-fledged *adj* hecho y derecho.
full-length *adj* de cuerpo entero; completo.
full moon *n* plenilunio *m*; luna llena *f*.
fullness *n* plenitud, abundancia *f*.
full-scale *adj* en gran escala; de tamaño natural.
full-time *adj* de tiempo completo.
fully *adv* llenamente, enteramente, ampliamente.
fulsome *adj* exagerado.
fumble *vi* manejar torpemente.
fume *vi* humear; encolerizarse; ● **~s** *npl* humo *m*.
fumigate *vt* perfumar, sahumar.
fun *n* diversión *f*; alegría *f*.
function *n* función *f*.
functional *adj* funcional.
fund *n* fondo *m*; fondos públicos *mpl*; ● *vt* costear.
fundamental *adj* fundamental; **~ly** *adv* fundamentalmente.
funeral service *n* misa de difuntos *f*.
funeral *n* funeral *m*.
funereal *adj* funeral, fúnebre.
fungus *n* hongo *m*; seta *f*.
funnel *n* embudo *m*; cañón (de chimenea) *m*.
funny *adj* divertido; curioso.
fur *n* piel *f*.
fur coat *n* abrigo de pieles *m*.
furious *adj* furioso, frenético; **~ly** *adv* con furia.
furlong *n* estadio *m*; (octava parte de una milla).
furlough *n* (*mil*) licencia *f*; permiso *m*.
furnace *n* horno *m*; hornaza *f*.
furnish *vt* amueblar; facilitar; suministrar.
furnishings *npl* muebles *mpl*.
furniture *n* muebles *mpl*.
furrow *n* surco *m*; ● *vt* surcar; estriar.
furry *adj* peludo.
further *adj* nuevo; más lejano; ● *adv* más lejos, más allá; aun; además; ● *vt* adelantar, promover, ayudar.
further education *n* educación superior *f*.
furthermore *adv* además.
furthest *adv* lo más lejos, lo más remoto.
furtive *adj* furtivo; secreto; **~ly** *adv* furtivamente.
fury *n* furor *m*; furia *f*; ira *f*.
fuse = fuze
fusion *n* fusión *f*.
fuss *n* lío *m*; alboroto *m*.
fussy *adj* jactancioso.
futile *adj* fútil, frívolo.
futility *n* futilidad, vanidad *f*.
future *adj* futuro; ● *n* futuro *m*; porvenir *m*.
fuze *vt*, *vi* fundir; derretirse; ● *n* fusible *m*; *n* mecha *f*.
fuze box *n* caja de fusibles *f*.
fuzzy *adj* borroso; muy rizado.

G

gab *n* (*fam*) charla *f*.
gabble *vi* charlar, parlotear; ● *n* algarabía *f*.
gable *n* aguilón *m*.
gadget *n* dispositivo *m*.
gaffe *n* plancha *f*.
gag *n* mordaza *f*; chiste *m*; ● *vt* tapar la boca con mordaza.
gaiety *n* alegría *f*.
gaily *adv* alegremente.
gain *n* ganancia *f*; interés, provecho *m*; ● *vt* ganar; conseguir.
gait *n* marcha *f*; porte *m*.
gala *n* fiesta *f*.
galaxy *n* galaxia, vía láctea *f*.
gale *n* vendaval *m*.
gall *n* hiel *f*.
gallant *adj* galante.
gall bladder *n* vesícula biliar *f*.
gallery *n* galería *f*.
galley *n* cocina *f*; galera *f*.
gallon *n* galón *m* (medida).
gallop *n* galope *m*; ● *vi* galopar.
gallows *n* horca *f*.
gallstone *n* cálculo biliario *m*.
galore *adv* en abundancia.
galvanize *vt* galvanizar.
gambit *n* estrategia *f*.
gamble *vi* jugar; especular; ● *n* riesgo *m*; apuesta *f*.
gambler *n* jugador *n*.
gambling *n* juego *m*.
game *n* juego *m*; pasatiempo *m*; partido *m*; partida *f*; caza *f*; ● *vi* jugar.
gamekeeper *n* guardabosques *m*.
gaming *n* juego *m*.
gammon *n* jamón *m*.
gamut *n* (*mus*) gama *f*.
gander *n* ganso *m*.
gang *n* pandilla, banda *f*.
gangrene *n* gangrena *f*.
gangster *n* gángster *m*.
gangway *n* pasarela *f*.
gap *n* hueco *m*; claro *m*; intervalo *m*.
gape *vi* boquear; estar con la boca abierta.
gaping *adj* muy abierto.
garage *n* garaje *m*.
garbage *n* basura *f*.
garbage can *n* bote de la basura *m*.
garbage man *n* basurero *m*.
garbled *adj* falsificado.
garden *n* jardín *m*.
garden-hose *n* regadera *f*.
gardener *n* jardinero *m*.
gardening *n* jardinería *f*.
gargle *vi* hacer gárgaras.
gargoyle *n* gárgola *f*.
garish *adj* ostentoso.
garland *n* guirnalda *f*.
garlic *n* ajo *m*.
garment *n* prenda *f*.
garnish *vt* guarnecer, adornar; ● *n* guarnición *f*; adorno *m*.
garret *n* guardilla *f*; desván *m*.
garrison *n* (*mil*) guarnición *f*; ● *vt* (*mil*) guarnecer.
garrote *vt* estrangular.
garrulous *adj* gárrulo, locuaz, charlador.
garter *n* liga *f*.
gas *n* gas *m*; gasolina *f*.
gas burner *n* mechero de gas *m*.
gas cylinder *n* bombona de gas *f*.
gaseous *adj* gaseoso.
gas fire *n* estufa de gas *f*.
gash *n* cuchillada *f*; raja *f*; ● *vt* acuchillar.

gasket n junta de culata f.
gasp vi jadear; • n respiración difícil f.
gas mask n careta antigás f.
gas meter n contador de gas m.
gasoline n gasolina f.
gas pedal n acelerador f.
gas ring n hornillo de gas m.
gas station n gasolinera f.
gassy adj gaseoso.
gas tap n llave del gas f.
gastric adj gástrico.
gastronomic adj gastronómico.
gasworks npl fábrica de gas f.
gate n puerta f.
gateway n puerta f.
gather vt recoger, amontonar; entender; plegar; • vi juntarse.
gathering n reunión f; colecta f.
gauche adj torpe.
gaudy adj chillón.
gauge n calibre m; entrevía f; indicador m; • vt medir.
gaunt adj, n flaco, delgado m.
gauze n gasa f.
gay adj alegre; vivo; gay.
gaze vi contemplar, considerar; • n mirada f.
gazelle n gacela f.
gazette n gaceta f.
gazetteer n gacetero m; diccionario geográfico m.
gear n atavío m; vestido m; aparejo m; tirantes mpl; velocidad f.
gearbox n caja de cambios f.
gear shift n palanca de cambio f.
gear wheel n rueda dentada f.
gel n gel m.
gelatin(e) n jaletina, jalea f.
gelignite n gelignita f.
gem n joya f.
Gemini n Géminis m (signo del zodíaco).
gender n género m.
gene n gen m.
genealogical adj genealógico.
genealogy n genealogía f.
general adj general, común, usual; in ~ por lo común; ~ly adv generalmente; • n general m; generala f.
general delivery n lista de correos f.
general election n elecciones generales fpl.
generality n generalidad, mayor parte f.
generalization n generalización f.
generalize vt generalizar.
generate vt engendrar; producir; causar.
generation n generación f.
generator n generador m.
generic adj genérico.
generosity n generosidad, liberalidad f.
generous adj generoso.
genetics npl genética f.
genial adj genial, natural; alegre.
genitals npl genitales mpl.
genitive n genitivo m.
genius n genio m.
genteel adj gentil, elegante.
gentile n gentil, pagano m.
gentle adj suave, dócil, manso, moderado; benigno.
gentleman n caballero m.
gentleness n dulzura, suavidad f.
gently adv suavemente.
gentry n alta burguesía f.
gents n aseos mpl.
genuflexion n genuflexión f.
genuine adj genuino, puro; ~ly adv puramente, naturalmente.
genus n género m.
geographer n geógrafo m.

geographical adj geográfico.
geography n geografía f.
geological adj geológico.
geologist n geólogo m.
geology n geología f.
geometric(al) adj geométrico.
geometry n geometría f.
geranium n (bot) geranio m.
geriatric n, adj geriátrico m.
germ n (bot) germen m.
germinate vi brotar.
gesticulate vi gesticular.
gesture n gesto, movimiento expresivo m.
get vt ganar; conseguir, obtener, alcanzar; coger; agarrar; • vi hacerse, ponerse; prevalecer; introducirse; to ~ the better salir vencedor, sobrepujar.
geyser n géiser m; calentador de agua m.
ghastly adj espantoso.
gherkin n pepinillo, cohombrillo m.
ghost n fantasma m; espectro m.
ghostly adj fantasmal.
giant n gigante m.
gibberish n jerigonza f.
gibe vi escarnecer, burlarse, mofar; • n mofa, burla f.
giblets npl despojos y menudillos (de aves) mpl.
giddiness n vértigo m.
giddy adj vertiginoso.
gift n regalo m; don m; dádiva f; talento m.
gifted adj dotado.
gift voucher n vale para regalo m.
gigantic adj gigantesco.
giggle vi reírse tontamente.
gild vt dorar.
gilding, gilt n doradura f.
gill n cuarta parte de pinta f; ~s pl agallas de los peces fpl.
gilt-edged adj de máxima garantía.
gimmick n truco m.
gin n ginebra f.
ginger n jengibre m.
gingerbread n pan de jengibre m.
ginger-haired adj pelirrojo.
giraffe n jirafa f.
girder n viga f.
girdle n faja f; cinturón m.
girl n muchacha, chica f.
girlfriend n amiga f; novia f.
girlish adj de niña.
giro n giro postal m.
girth n cincha f; circunferencia f.
gist n punto principal m.
give vt, vi dar, donar; conceder; abandonar; pronunciar; aplicarse, dedicarse; to ~ away regalar; traicionar; revelar; to ~ back devolver; to ~ in vi ceder; vt entregar; to ~ off despedir; to ~ out distribuir; to ~ up vi rendir; vt renunciar a.
gizzard n molleja f.
glacial adj glacial.
glacier n glaciar m.
glad adj alegre, contento, agradable; I am ~ to see me alegro de ver; ~ly adv alegremente.
gladden vt alegrar.
gladiator n gladiator m.
glamor n encanto, atractivo m.
glamorous adj atractivo.
glance n ojeada f, • vi mirar; echar una ojeada.
glancing adj oblicuo.
gland n glándula f.
glare n deslumbramiento m; mirada feroz y penetrante f; • vi deslumbrar, brillar; echar miradas de indignación.
glaring adj deslumbrante; manifiesto; que clama al cielo.
glass n vidrio m; telescopio m; vaso m; espejo m; ~es pl gafas fpl; • adj vítreo.

glassware n cristalería f.
glassy adj vítreo, cristalino, vidrioso.
glaze vt vidriar; embarnizar.
glazier n vidriero m.
gleam n relámpago, rayo m; • vi relampaguear, brillar.
gleaming adj reluciente.
glean vt espigar; recoger.
glee n alegría f; gozo m; jovialidad f.
glen n valle m; llanura f.
glib adj liso, resbaladizo; ~ly adv corrientemente, voluble-
mente.
glide vi resbalar; planear.
gliding n vuelo sin motor m.
glimmer n vislumbre f; • vi vislumbrarse.
glimpse n vislumbre f; relámpago m; ojeada f; • vt descubrir,
percibir.
glint vi centellear.
glisten, glitter vi relucir, brillar.
gloat vi ojear con admiración.
global adj mundial.
globe n globo m; esfera f.
gloom, gloominess n oscuridad f; melancolía, tristeza f; ~ily
adv oscuramente; tristemente.
gloomy adj sombrío, oscuro; cubierto de nubes; triste, melancólico.
glorification n glorificación, alabanza f.
glorify vt glorificar, celebrar.
glorious adj glorioso, ilustre; ~ly adv gloriosamente.
glory n gloria, fama, celebridad f.
gloss n glosa f; lustre m; • vt glosar, interpretar; to ~ over
encubrir.
glossary n glosario m.
glossy adj lustroso, brillante.
glove n guante m.
glove compartment n guantera f.
glow vi arder; inflamarse; relucir; • n color vivo m; viveza de
color f; vehemencia de una pasión f.
glower vi mirar con ceño.
glue n cola f; cemento m; • vt pegar.
gluey adj viscoso, pegajoso.
glum adj abatido, triste.
glut n hartura, abundancia f.
glutinous adj glutinoso, viscoso.
glutton n glotón, tragón m.
gluttony n glotonería f.
glycerine n glicerina f.
gnarled adj nudoso.
gnash vt, vi chocar; crujir los dientes.
gnat n mosquito m.
gnaw vt roer.
gnome n gnomo m.
go vi ir, irse, andar, caminar; partir(se), marchar; huir; pasar;
to ~ ahead seguir adelante; to ~ away marcharse; to ~
back volver; to ~ by pasar; to ~ for ir por; gustar; to ~ in
entrar; to ~ off irse; pasarse; to ~ on seguir; pasar; to ~ out
salir; apagarse; to ~ up subir.
goad n aguijada, aijada f; • vt aguijar; estimular, incitar.
go-ahead adj emprendedor; • n luz verde f.
goal n meta f; fin m.
goalkeeper n portero m.
goalpost n poste de la portería m.
goatherd n cabrero m.
gobble vt engullir, tragar.
go-between n mediador m.
goblet n copa f.
goblin n espíritu ambulante, duende m.
God n Dios m.
godchild n ahijado, hijo de pila m.
goddaughter n ahijada, hija de pila f.
goddess n diosa f.
godfather n padrino m.
godforsaken adj dejado de la mano de Dios.

godhead n deidad, divinidad f.
godless adj infiel, impío, sin Dios, ateo.
godlike adj divino.
godliness n piedad, devoción, santidad f.
godly adj piadoso, devoto, religioso; recto, justificado.
godmother n madrina f.
godsend n don del cielo m.
godson n ahijado m.
goggle-eyed adj bizco.
goggles npl anteojos mpl; gafas submarinas fpl.
going n ~ida f; salida f; partida f; progreso m.
gold n oro m.
golden adj áureo, de oro; excelente; ~ rule n regla de oro f.
goldfish n pez de colores m.
gold-plated adj chapado en oro.
goldsmith n orfebre m.
golf n golf m.
golf ball n pelota de golf f.
golf club n club de golf m.
golf course n campo de golf m.
golfer n golfista m.
gondolier n gondolero m.
gone adj ido; perdido; pasado; gastado; muerto.
gong n atabal chino m.
good adj bueno, benévolo, cariñoso; conveniente, apto; • adv
bien; • n bien m; prosperidad, ventaja f; ~s pl bienes
· muebles mpl; mercaderías fpl.
goodbye ! excl ¡adiós!
Good Friday n Viernes Santo m.
goodies npl golosinas fpl.
good-looking adj guapo.
good nature n bondad f.
good-natured adj bondadoso.
goodness n bondad f.
goodwill n benevolencia, bondad f.
goose n ganso m; oca f.
gooseberry n grosella espinosa f.
goosebumps npl carne de gallina f.
goose-step n paso de ganso m.
gore n sangre cuajada f; • vt cornear.
gorge n barranco m; • vt engullir, tragar.
gorgeous adj maravilloso.
gorilla n gorila m.
gorse n aulaga f.
gory adj sangriento.
goshawk n azor m.
gospel n evangelio m.
gossamer n vello m; pelusa (de frutas) f.
gossip n charla f; • vi charlar.
gothic adj gótico.
gout n gota f (enfermedad).
govern vt gobernar, dirigir, regir.
governess n gobernadora f.
government n gobierno m; administración pública f.
governor n gobernador m.
gown n toga f; vestido de mujer m; bata f.
grab vt agarrar.
grace n gracia f; favor m; merced f; perdón m; gracias fpl; to
say ~ bendecir la mesa; • vt adornar; agraciar.
graceful adj gracioso, primoroso; ~ly adv elegantemente, con
gracia.
gracious adj gracioso; favorable; ~ly adv graciosamente.
gradation n graduación f.
grade n grado m; curso m.
grade crossing n paso a nivel m.
grade school n escuela primaria f.
gradient n (rail) pendiente.
gradual adj gradual; ~ly adv gradualmente.
graduate vi graduarse.
graduation n graduación f.
graffiti n pintadas fpl.
graft n injerto m; • vt injertar, ingerir.

grain *n* grano *m*; semilla *f*; cereales *mpl*.
gram *n* gramo *m* (peso).
grammar *n* gramática *f*.
grammatical *adj*, ~ly *adv* gramatical(mente).
granary *n* granero *m*.
grand *adj* grande, ilustre.
grandchild *n* nieto *m*; nieta *f*.
grandad *n* abuelo *m*.
granddaughter *n* nieta *f*; great ~ biznieta *f*.
grandeur *n* grandeza *f*; pompa *f*.
grandfather *n* abuelo *m*; great ~ bisabuelo *m*.
grandiose *adj* grandioso.
grandma *n* abuelita *f*.
grandmother *n* abuela *f*; great ~ bisabuela *f*.
grandparents *npl* abuelos *mpl*.
grand piano *n* piano de cola *m*.
grandson *n* nieto *m*; great ~ bisnieto *m*.
grandstand *n* tribuna *f*.
granite *n* granito *m*.
granny *n* abuelita *f*.
grant *vt* conceder; to take for ~ed presuponer; • *n* beca *f*;
    concesión *f*.
granulate *vt* granular.
granule *n* gránulo *m*.
grape *n* uva *f*; bunch of ~s racimo de uvas *m*.
grapefruit *n* toronja *f*.
graph *n* gráfica *f*.
graphic(al) *adj* gráfico; pintoresco; ~ally *adv* gráficamente.
graphics *n* artes gráficas *fpl*; gráficos *mpl*.
grapnel *n* (*mar*) arpeo *m*.
grasp *vt* empuñar, asir, agarrar; • *n* puño *m*; comprensión *f*;
    poder *m*.
grasping *adj* avaro.
grass *n* hierba *f*.
grasshopper *n* saltamontes *m*.
grassland *n* pampa *f*.
grass-roots *adj* popular.
grass snake *n* culebra *f*.
grassy *adj* herboso.
grate *n* reja, verja, rejilla *f*; • *vt* rallar; rechinar (los dientes);
    enrejar.
grateful *adj* grato, agradecido; ~ly *adv* agradecidamente.
gratefulness *n* gratitud *f*.
gratification *n* gratificación *f*.
gratify *vt* contentar; gratificar.
gratifying *adj* grato.
grating *n* rejado *m*; • *adj* áspero; ofensivo.
gratis *adv* gratis.
gratitude *n* gratitud *f*.
gratuitous *adj* gratuito, voluntario; ~ly *adv* gratuitamente.
gratuity *n* gratificación, recompensa *f*.
grave *n* sepultura *f*; • *adj* grave, serio; ~ly *adv* con gravedad,
    seriamente.
grave digger *n* sepulturero *m*.
gravel *n* cascajo *m*.
gravestone *n* piedra sepulcral *f*.
graveyard *n* cementerio *m*.
gravitate *vi* gravitar.
gravitation *n* gravitación *f*.
gravity *n* gravedad *f*.
gravy *n* jugo de la carne *f*; salsa *f*.
gray *adj* gris; cano; • *n* gris *m*.
gray-haired *adj* canoso.
grayish *adj* pardusco; entrecano.
grayness *n* color gris *m*.
graze *vt* pastorear; tocar ligeramente; • *vi* pacer.
grease *n* grasa *f*; • *vt* untar.
greaseproof *adj* a prueba de grasa.
greasy *adj* grasiento.
great *adj* gran, grande; principal; ilustre; noble, magnánimo;
    ~ly *adv* muy, mucho.
greatcoat *n* sobretodo *m*.

greatness *n* grandeza *f*; dignidad *f*; poder *m*; magnanimidad *f*.
greedily *adv* vorazmente, ansiosamente.
greediness, greed *n* gula *f*; codicia *f*.
greedy *adj* hambriento; ansioso, deseoso; insaciable.
Greek *n* griego (idioma) *m*.
green *adj* verde, fresco, reciente; no maduro; • *n* verde *m*;
    llanura verde *f*; ~s *pl* verduras *fpl*.
greenback *n* billete *m*.
green belt *n* zona verde *f*.
green card *n* carta verde *f*.
greenery *n* verdura *f*.
greengrocer *n* verdulero *m*.
greenhouse *n* invernadero *m*.
greenish *adj* verdoso.
greenness *n* verdor, vigor *m*; frescura, falta de experiencia *f*;
    novedad *f*.
green room *n* camerino *m*.
greet *vt* saludar, congratular.
greeting *n* saludo *m*.
greeting(s) card *n* tarjeta de felicitaciones *f*.
grenade *n* (*mil*) granada *f*.
grenadier *n* granadero *m*.
greyhound *n* galgo *m*.
grid *n* reja *f*; red *f*.
gridiron *n* parrilla *f*; campo de fútbol *m*.
grief *n* dolor *m*; aflicción, pena *f*.
grievance *n* pesar *m*; molestia *f*; agravio *m*; injusticia *f*; perju-
    icio *m*.
grieve *vt* agraviar, afligir; • *vi* afligirse; llorar.
grievous *adj* doloroso; enorme, atroz; ~ly *adv* penosamente;
    cruelmente.
griffin *n* grifo *m*.
grill *n* parrilla *f*; • *vt* interrogar.
grille *n* reja *f*.
grim *adj* feo; horrendo; ceñudo.
grimace *n* visaje *m*; mueca *f*.
grime *n* porquería *f*.
grimy *adj* ensuciado.
grin *n* mueca *f*; • *vi* hacer visajes.
grind *vt* moler; pulverizar; afilar; picar; rechinar los dientes.
grinder *n* molinero *m*; molinillo *m*; amolador *m*.
grip *n* asimiento *m*; asidero *m*; maletín *m*; • *vt* agarrar.
gripping *adj* absorbente.
grisly *adj* horroroso.
gristle *n* tendón, nervio *m*.
gristly *adj* tendinoso, nervioso.
grit *n* gravilla *f*; valor *m*.
groan *vi* gemir, suspirar; • *n* gemido, suspiro *m*.
grocer *n* tendero, abarrotero *m*.
groceries *npl* comestibles *mpl*.
grocer's (shop) *n* tienda de abarrotes *f*.
groggy *adj* atontado.
groin *n* ingle *f*.
groom *n* establero *m*; criado *m*; novio *m*; • *vt* cuidar los
    caballos.
groove *n* ranura *f*.
grope *vt, vi* tentar, buscar a oscuras; andar a tientas.
gross *adj* grueso, corpulento, espeso; grosero; estúpido; ~ly
    adv enormemente.
grotesque *adj* grotesco.
grotto *n* gruta *f*.
ground *n* tierra *f*; país *m*; terreno, suelo, pavimento *m*; funda-
    mento *m*; razón fundamental *f*; campo (de batalla) *m*; fondo
    m; • *vt* mantener en tierra; conectar con tierra.
ground floor *n* planta baja *f*.
grounding *n* conocimientos básicos *mpl*.
groundless *adj* infundado; ~ly *adv* sin motivo.
ground staff *n* personal de tierra *m*.
groundwork *n* preparación *f*.
group *n* grupo *m*; • *vt* agrupar.
grouse *n* urogallo *m*; • *vi* quejarse.
grove *n* arboleda *f*.

grovel *vi* arrastrarse.
grow *vt* cultivar; ● *vi* crecer, aumentarse; ~ up crecer.
grower *n* cultivador *m*; productor *m*.
growing *adj* creciente.
growl *vi* regañar, gruñir; ● *n* gruñido *m*.
grown-up *n* adulto *m*.
growth *n* crecimiento *m*.
grub *n* gusano *m*.
grubby *adj* sucio.
grudge *n* rencor, odio *m*; envidia *f*; ● *vt, vi* envidiar.
grudgingly *adv* de mala gana.
grueling *adj* penoso, duro.
gruesome *adj* horrible.
gruff *adj* brusco; ~ly *adv* bruscamente.
gruffness *n* aspereza, severidad *f*.
grumble *vi* gruñir; murmurar.
grumpy *adj* regañón.
grunt *vi* gruñir; ● *n* gruñido *m*.
G-string *n* taparrabo *m*.
guarantee *n* garantía *f*; ● *vt* garantizar.
guard *n* guardia *f*; ● *vt* guardar; defender.
guarded *adj* cauteloso, mesurado.
guardroom *n* (*mil*) cuarto de guardia *m*.
guardian *n* tutor *m*; curador *m*; guardián *m*.
guardianship *n* tutela *f*.
guerrilla *n* guerrillero *m*.
guerrilla warfare *n* guerra de guerrillas *f*.
guess *vt, vi* conjeturar; adivinar; suponer; ● *n* conjetura *f*.
guesswork *n* conjeturas *fpl*.
guest *n* huésped; convidado *m*.
guest room *n* cuarto de huéspedes *m*.
guffaw *n* carcajada *f*.
guidance *n* gobierno *m*; dirección *f*.
guide *vt* guiar, dirigir; ● *n* guía *m*.
guide dog *n* perro pastor *m*.
guidelines *npl* directiva *f*.
guidebook *n* guía *f*.
guild *n* gremio *m*; corporación *f*.
guile *n* astucia *f*.
guillotine *n* guillotina *f*; ● *vt* guillotinar.
guilt *n* culpabilidad *f*.
guiltless *adj* inocente, libre de culpa.
guilty *adj* reo, culpable.
guinea pig *n* cobayo *m*.
guise *n* manera *f*.
guitar *n* guitarra *f*.
gulf *n* golfo *m*; abismo *m*.
gull *n* gaviota *f*.
gullet *n* esófago *m*.
gullibility *n* credulidad *f*.
gullible *adj* crédulo.
gully *n* barranco *m*.
gulp *n* trago *m*; ● *vi* tragar saliva; ● *vt* tragarse.
gum *n* goma *f*; cemento *m*; encía *f*; chicle *m*; ● *vt* pegar con goma.
gum tree *n* árbol gomero *m*.
gun *n* pistola *f*; escopeta *f*.
gunboat *n* cañonera *f*.
gun carriage *n* cureña *f*.
gunfire *n* disparos *mpl*.
gunman *n* pistolero *m*.
gunmetal *n* bronce de cañones *m*.
gunner *n* artillero *m*.
gunnery *n* artillería *f*.
gunpoint *n*: at ~ a punta de pistola; a mano armada.
gunpowder *n* pólvora *f*.
gunshot *n* escopetazo *m*.
gunsmith *n* armero *m*.
gurgle *vi* gorgotear.
guru *n* gurú *m*.
gush *vi* brotar; chorrear; ● *n* chorro *m*.
gushing *adj* superabundante.

gusset *n* escudete *m*.
gust *n* ráfaga *f*; soplo de aire *m*.
gusto *n* entusiasmo *m*.
gusty *adj* tempestuoso.
gut *n* intestino *m*; ~s *npl* valor *m*; ● *vt* destripar.
gutter *n* canalón *m*; arroyo *m*.
guttural *adj* gutural.
guy *n* tío *m*; tipo *m*.
guzzle *vt* engullir.
gym(nasium) *n* gimnasio *m*.
gymnast *n* gimnasta *m*.
gymnastic *adj* gimnástico; ~s *npl* gimnástica *f*.
gynecologist *n* ginecólogo *m*.
gypsy *n* gitano *m*.
gyrate *vi* girar.

H

haberdasher *n* camisero *m*.
haberdashery *n* camisería *f*; prendas de caballero *fpl*.
habit *n* costumbre *f*.
habitable *adj* habitable.
habitat *n* habitat *m*.
habitual *adj* habitual; ~ly *adv* por costumbre.
hack *n* corte *m*; escritor a sueldo *m*; ● *vt* tajar, cortar.
hackneyed *adj* trillado.
haddock *n* especie de merluza *f*.
hag *n* bruja *f*.
haggard *adj* ojeroso.
haggle *vi* regatear.
hail *n* granizo *m*; ● *vt* saludar; ● *vi* granizar.
hailstone *n* piedra de granizo *f*.
hair *n* pelo; cabello *m*.
hairbrush *n* cepillo *m*.
haircut *n* corte de pelo *m*.
hairdresser *n* peluquero *m*.
hairdryer *n* secador de pelo *m*.
hairless *adj* calvo.
hairnet *n* redecilla *f*.
hairpin *n* horquilla *f*.
hairpin curve *n* curva de horquilla *f*.
hair remover *n* depilatorio *m*.
hairspray *n* laca *f*.
hairstyle *n* peinado *m*.
hairy *adj* peludo, cabelludo.
hale *adj* sano, vigoroso.
half *n* mitad *f*; ● *adj* medio.
half-caste *adj* mestizo.
half-hearted *adj* indiferente.
half-hour *n* media hora *f*.
half-moon *n* media luna *f*.
half-price *adj* a mitad de precio.
half-time *n* descanso *m*.
halfway *adv* a medio camino.
hall *n* vestíbulo *m*.
hallmark *n* contraste *m*.
hallow *vt* consagrar, santificar.
hallucination *n* alucinación *f*.
halo *n* halo *m*.
halt *vi* parar; ● *n* parada *f*; alto *m*.
halve *vt* partir en dos mitades.
ham *n* jamón *m*.
hamburger *n* hamburguesa *f*.
hamlet *n* aldea *f*.
hammer *n* martillo *m*; ● *vt* martillar.
hammock *n* hamaca *f*.
hamper *n* cesto *f*; ● *vt* estorbar.
hamstring *vt* desjarretar.
hand *n* mano *f*; obrero *m*; aguja *f*; at ~ a mano; ● *vt* alargar.
handbag *n* cartera *f*.

handbell *n* campanilla *f.*
handbook *n* manual *m.*
handbrake *n* freno de mano *m.*
handcuff *n* esposa *f.*
handful *n* puñado *m.*
handicap *n* desventaja *f.*
handicapped *adj* minusválido.
handicraft *n* artesanía *f.*
handiwork *n* obra *f.*
handkerchief *n* pañuelo *m.*
handle *n* mango, puño *m*; asa; manija *f*; ● *vt* manejar; tratar.
handlebars *npl* manillar *m.*
handling *n* manejo *m.*
handrail *n* pasamanos *m.*
handshake *n* apretón de manos *m.*
handsome *adj* guapo; ~ly *adv* primorosamente.
handwriting *n* letra *f.*
handy *adj* práctico; diestro.
hang *vt* colgar; ahorcar; ● *vi* colgar; ser ahorcado.
hanger *n* percha *f.*
hanger-on *n* parásito *m.*
hangings *npl* tapicería *f.*
hangman *n* verdugo *m.*
hangover *n* resaca *f.*
hang-up *n* complejo *m.*
hanker *vi* ansiar, apetecer.
haphazard *adj* fortuito.
hapless *adj* desgraciado.
happen *vi* pasar; acontecer, acaecer.
happening *n* suceso *m.*
happily *adv* felizmente.
happiness *n* felicidad *f.*
happy *adj* feliz.
harangue *n* arenga *f*; ● *vi* arengar.
harass *vt* cansar, fatigar.
harbinger *n* precursor *m.*
harbor *n* puerto *m*; ● *vt* albergar.
hard *adj* duro, firme; difícil; penoso; severo, rígido; ~ of hearing medio sordo; ~ by muy cerca.
harden *vt, vi* endurecer(se). .
hard-headed *adj* realista.
hard-hearted *adj* duro de corazón, insensible.
hardiness *n* robustez *f.*
hardly *adv* apenas.
hardness *n* dureza *f*; dificultad *f*; severidad *f.*
hardship *n* penas *fpl.*
hard-up *adj* sin plata.
hardware *n* hardware *m*; quinquillería *f.*
hardwearing *adj* resistente.
hardy *adj* fuerte, robusto.
hare *n* liebre *f.*
hare-brained *adj* atolondrado.
hare-lipped *adj* labihendido.
haricot *n* alubia *f.*
harlequin *n* arlequín *m.*
harm *n* mal, daño *m*; perjuicio *m*; ● *vt* dañar.
harmful *adj* perjudicial.
harmless *adj* inocuo.
harmonic *adj* armónico.
harmonious *adj* armonioso; ~ly *adv* armoniosamente.
harmonize *vt* armonizar.
harmony *n* armonía *f.*
harness *n* arreos de un caballo *mpl*; ● *vt* enjaezar.
harp *n* arpa *f.*
harpist *n* arpista *m.*
harpoon *n* arpón *m.*
harpsichord *n* clavicordio *m.*
harrow *n* grada *f.*
harry *vt* hostigar.
harsh *adj* duro; austero; ~ly *adv* severamente.
harshness *n* aspereza, dureza *f*; austeridad *f.*
harvest *n* cosecha *f*; ● *vt* cosechar.

harvester *n* cosechadora *f.*
hash *n* hachís *m*; picadillo *m.*
hassock *n* cojín de paja *m.*
haste *n* apuro *m*; to be in ~ estar apurado.
hasten *vt* acelerar, apresurar; ● *vi* tener prisa.
hastily *adv* precipitadamente.
hastiness *n* precipitación *f.*
hasty *adj* apresurado.
hat *n* sombrero *m.*
hatbox *n* sombrerera *f.*
hatch *vt* incubar; tramar; ● *n* escotilla *f.*
hatchback *n* (*auto*) tres (*o* cinco) puertas *m.*
hatchet *n* hacha *f.*
hatchway *n* (*mar*) escotilla *f.*
hate *n* odio, aborrecimiento *m*; ● *vt* odiar, detestar.
hateful *adj* odioso.
hatred *n* odio, aborrecimiento *m.*
hatter *n* sombrerero *m.*
haughtily *adv* orgullosamente.
haughtiness *n* orgullo *m*; altivez *f.*
haughty *adj* altanero, orgulloso.
haul *vt* tirar; ● *n* botín *m.*
hauler *n* transportista *m.*
haunch *n* anca *f.*
haunt *vt* frecuentar, rondar; ● *n* guarida *f*; costumbre *f.*
have *vt* haber; tener, poseer.
haven *n* asilo *m.*
haversack *n* mochila *f.*
havoc *n* estrago *m.*
hawk *n* halcón *m*; ● *vi* cazar con halcón.
hawthorn *n* espino blanco *m.*
hay *n* heno *m.*
hay fever *n* fiebre del heno *f.*
hayloft *n* henil *m.*
hayrick, haystack *n* almiar *m.*
hazard *n* riesgo *m*; ● *vt* arriesgar.
hazardous *adj* arriesgado, peligroso.
haze *n* niebla *f.*
hazel *n* avellano *m*; ● *adj* castaño.
hazelnut *n* avellana *f.*
hazy *adj* oscuro.
he *pn* él.
head *n* cabeza *f*; jefe *m*; juicio *m*; ● *vt* encabezar; to ~ for dirigirse a.
headache *n* dolor de cabeza *m.*
headdress *n* cofia *f*; tocado *m.*
headland *n* promontorio *m.*
headlight *n* faro *m.*
headline *n* titular *m.*
headlong *adv* precipitadamente.
headmaster *n* director *m.*
head office *n* oficina central *f.*
headphones *npl* auriculares *mpl.*
headquarters *npl* (*mil*) cuartel general *m*; sede central *f.*
headroom *n* altura *f.*
headstrong *adj* testarudo, cabezudo.
headwaiter *n* maître *m.*
headway *n* progresos *mpl.*
heady *adj* cabezón.
heal *vt, vi* curar.
health *n* salud *f*; brindis *m.*
healthiness *n* sanidad *f.*
healthy *adj* sano.
heap *n* montón *m*; ● *vt* amontonar.
hear *vt* oir; escuchar; ● *vi* oir; escuchar.
hearing *n* oído *m.*
hearing aid *n* audífono *m.*
hearsay *n* rumor *m*; fama *f.*
hearse *n* coche fúnebre *m.*
heart *n* corazón *m*; by ~ de memoria; with all my ~ con toda mi alma.
heart attack *n* infarto *m.*

heartbreaking *adj* desgarrador.
heartburn *n* acedía *f*.
heart failure *n* fallo cardíaco *m*.
heartfelt *adj* más sentido.
hearth *n* hogar *m*.
heartily *adv* sinceramente, cordialmente.
heartiness *n* cordialidad, sinceridad *f*.
heartless *adj* cruel; ~**ly** *adv* cruelmente.
hearty *adj* cordial.
heat *n* calor *m*; • *vt* calentar.
heater *n* calentador *m*.
heather *n* (*bot*) brezo *m*.
heathen *n* pagano *m*; ~**ish** *adj* salvaje.
heating *n* calefacción *f*.
heatwave *n* ola de calor *f*.
heave *vt* alzar; tirar; • *n* tirón *m*.
heaven *n* cielo *m*.
heavenly *adj* divino.
heavily *adv* pesadamente.
heaviness *n* pesadez *f*.
heavy *adj* pesado; opresivo.
Hebrew *n* hebreo *m*.
heckle *vt* interrumpir.
hectic *adj* agitado.
hedge *n* seto *m*; • *vt* cercar con seto.
hedgehog *n* erizo *m*.
heed *vt* hacer caso de; • *n* cuidado *m*; atención *f*.
heedless *adj* descuidado, negligente; ~**ly** *adv* negligentemente.
heel *n* talón *m*; **to take to one's ~s** apretar los talones, huir.
hefty *adj* grande.
heifer *n* ternera *f*.
height *n* altura *f*; altitud *f*.
heighten *vt* realzar; adelantar, mejorar; exaltar.
heinous *adj* atroz.
heir *n* heredero *m*; ~ **apparent** heredero forzoso *m*.
heiress *n* heredera *f*.
heirloom *n* reliquia de familia *f*.
helicopter *n* helicóptero *m*.
hell *n* infierno *m*.
hellish *adj* infernal.
helm *n* (*mar*) timón *m*.
helmet *n* casco *m*.
help *vt*, *vi* ayudar, socorrer; **I cannot ~ it** no puedo remedi-
arlo; no puedo dejar de hacerlo; • *n* ayuda *f*; socorro, remedio *m*.
helper *n* ayudante *m*.
helpful *adj* útil.
helping *n* ración *f*.
helpless *adj* indefenso; ~**ly** *adv* irremediablemente.
helter-skelter *adv* a trochemoche en desorden.
hem *n* ribete *m*; • *vt* ribetear.
he-man *n* macho *m*.
hemisphere *n* hemisferio *m*.
hemorrhage *n* hemorragia *f*.
hemorrhoids *npl* hemorroides *mpl*.
hemp *n* cáñamo *m*.
hen *n* gallina *f*.
henchman *n* secuaz *m*.
henceforth, henceforward *adv* de aquí en adelante.
hen-house *n* gallinero *m*.
hepatitis *n* hepatitis *f*.
her *pn* su; ella; de ella; a ella.
herald *n* heraldo *m*.
heraldry *n* heráldica *f*.
herb *n* hierba *f*; ~**s** *pl* hierbas *fpl*.
herbaceous *adj* herbáceo.
herbalist *n* herbolario *m*.
herbivorous *adj* herbívoro.
herd *n* rebaño *m*.
here *adv* aquí, acá.
hereabout(s) *adv* aquí alrededor.

hereafter *adv* en el futuro.
hereby *adv* por esto.
hereditary *adj* hereditario.
heredity *n* herencia *f*.
heresy *n* herejía *f*.
heretic *n* hereje *m*; • *adj* herético.
herewith *adv* con esto.
heritage *n* patrimonio *m*.
hermetic *adj* hermético; ~**ly** *adv* herméticamente.
hermit *n* ermitaño *m*.
hermitage *n* ermita *f*.
hernia *n* hernia *f*.
hero *n* héroe *m*.
heroic *adj* heroico; ~**ally** *adv* heroicamente.
heroine *n* heroína *f*.
heroism *n* heroísmo *m*.
heron *n* garza *f*.
herring *n* arenque *m*.
hers *pn* suyo, de ella.
herself *pn* ella misma.
hesitant *adj* vacilante.
hesitate *vt* dudar; tardar.
hesitation *n* duda, irresolución *f*.
heterogeneous *adj* heterogéneo.
heterosexual *adj*, *n* heterosexual *m*.
hew *vt* tajar; cortar; picar.
heyday *n* apogeo *m*.
hi *excl* ¡hola!
hiatus *n* (*gr*) hiato *m*.
hibernate *vi* invernar.
hiccup *n* hipo *m*; • *vi* tener hipo.
hickory *n* noguera americana *f*.
hide *vt* esconder; • *n* cuero *m*; piel *f*.
hideaway *n* escondite *m*.
hideous *adj* horrible; ~**ly** *adv* horriblemente.
hiding-place *n* escondite, escondrijo *m*.
hierarchy *n* jerarquía *f*.
hieroglyphic *adj*, *n* jeroglífico *m*.
hi-fi *n* estéreo, hi-fi *m*.
higgledy-piggledy *adv* confusamente.
high *adj* alto; elevado.
high altar *n* altar mayor *m*.
highchair *n* silla alta *f*.
high-handed *adj* despótico.
highlands *npl* tierras montañosas *fpl*.
highlight *n* punto culminante *m*.
highly *adj* en sumo grado.
highness *n* altura *f*; alteza *f*.
high school *n* centro de enseñanza secundaria *m*.
high-strung *adj* hipertenso.
high water *n* marea alta *f*.
highway *n* carretera *f*.
hike *vi* ir de excursión.
hijack *vt* secuestrar.
hijacker *n* secuestrador *m*.
hilarious *adj* alegre.
hill *n* colina *f*.
hillock *n* colina *f*.
hillside *n* ladera *f*.
hilly *adj* montañoso.
hilt *n* puño de espada *m*.
him *pn* le, lo, él.
himself *pn* él mismo, se, sí mismo.
hind *adj* trasero, posterior; • *n* cierva *f*.
hinder *vt* impedir.
hindrance *n* impedimento, obstáculo *m*.
hindmost *adj* postrero.
hindquarter *n* cuarto trasero *m*.
hindsight *n*: **with ~** en retrospectiva.
hinge *n* bisagra *f*.
hint *n* indirecta *f*; • *vt* insinuar; sugerir.
hip *n* cadera *f*.

hippopotamus *n* hipopótamo *m*.
hire *vt* alquilar; • *n* alquiler *m*.
his *pn* su, suyo, de él.
Hispanic *adj* hispano; hispánico.
hiss *vt*, *vi* silbar.
historian *n* historiador *m*.
historic(al) *adj* histórico; ~ally *adv* históricamente.
history *n* historia *f*.
histrionic *adj* teatral.
hit *vt* golpear; alcanzar; • *n* golpe *m*; éxito *m*.
hitch *vt* atar; • *n* problema *m*.
hitch-hike *vi* hacer autostop.
hitherto *adv* hasta ahora, hasta aquí.
hive *n* colmena *f*.
hoard *n* montón *m*; tesoro escondido *m*; • *vt* acumular.
hoar-frost *n* escarcha *f*.
hoarse *adj* ronco; ~ly *adv* roncamente.
hoarseness *n* ronquera, carraspera *f*.
hoax *n* trampa *f*; • *vt* engañar, burlar.
hobble *vi* cojear.
hobby *n* pasatiempo *m*.
hobbyhorse *n* caballo de batalla *m*.
hobo *n* vagabundo *m*.
hockey *n* hockey *m*.
hodge-podge *n* mezcolanza *f*.
hoe *n* azadón *m*; • *vt* azadonar.
hog *n* cerdo, puerco *m*.
hoist *vt* alzar; • *n* grúa *f*.
hold *vt* tener; detener; contener; celebrar; **to ~ on to** agarrarse a; • *vi* valer; • *n* presa *f*; poder *m*.
holder *n* poseedor *m*; titular *m*.
holding *n* tenencia, posesión *f*.
holdup *n* atraco *m*; retraso *m*.
hole *n* agujero *m*.
holiday *n* día de fiesta *m*; ~s *pl* vacaciones *fpl*.
holiness *n* santidad *f*.
hollow *adj* hueco; • *n* hoyo *m*; • *vt* excavar, ahuecar.
holly *n* (*bot*) acebo *m*.
hollyhock *n* malva hortense *f*.
holocaust *n* holocausto *m*.
holster *n* pistolera *f*.
holy *adj* santo, pío; consagrado.
holy water *n* agua bendita *f*.
holy week *n* semana santa *f*.
homage *n* homenaje *m*.
home *n* casa *f*; patria *f*; domicilio *m*; ~ly *adj* casero.
home address *n* domicilio *m*.
homeless *adj* sin casa.
homeliness *n* simpleza *f*.
homely *adj* casero.
home-made *adj* casero.
homeopathist *n* homeopatista *m*.
homeopathy *n* homeopatía *f*.
homesick *adj* nostálgico.
homesickness *n* nostalgia *f*.
hometown *n* ciudad natal *f*.
homeward *adj* hacia casa; hacia su país.
homework *n* deberes *mpl*.
homicidal *adj* homicida.
homicide *n* homicidio *m*; homicida *m*.
homogeneous *adj* homogéneo.
homosexual *adj*, *n* homosexual *m*.
honest *adj* honrado; ~ly *adv* honradamente.
honesty *n* honradez *f*.
honey *n* miel *f*.
honeycomb *n* panal *m*.
honeymoon *n* luna de miel *f*.
honeysuckle *n* (*bot*) madreselva *f*.
honor *n* honra *f*; honor *m*; • *vt* honrar.
honorable *adj* honorable; ilustre.
honorably *adv* honorablemente.
honorary *adj* honorario.

hood *n* capó *m*; capucha *f*.
hoodlum *n* matón *m*.
hoof *n* pezuña *f*.
hook *n* gancho *m*; anzuelo *m*; **by ~ or by crook** de un modo u otro; • *vt* enganchar.
hooked *adj* encorvado.
hooligan *n* gamberro *m*.
hoop *n* aro *m*.
hooter *n* sirena *f*.
hop *n* (*bot*) lúpulo *m*; salto *m*; • *vi* saltar, brincar.
hope *n* esperanza *f*; • *vi* esperar.
hopeful *adj* esperanzado; ~ly *adv* con esperanza.
hopefulness *n* buena esperanza *f*.
hopeless *adj* desesperado; ~ly *adv* sin esperanza.
horde *n* horda *f*.
horizon *n* horizonte *m*.
horizontal *adj* horizontal; ~ly *adv* horizontalmente.
hormone *n* hormona *f*.
horn *n* cuerno *m*.
horned *adj* cornudo.
hornet *n* avispón *m*.
horny *adj* calloso.
horoscope *n* horóscopo *m*.
horrendous *adj* horrendo.
horrible *adj* horrible, terrible.
horribly *adv* horriblemente; enormemente.
horrid *adj* horrible.
horrific *adj* horroroso.
horrify *vt* horrorizar.
horror *n* horror, terror *m*.
horror film *n* película de horror *f*.
hors d'oeuvre *n* entremeses *mpl*.
horse *n* caballo *m*; caballete *m*.
horseback *adv*: **on ~** a caballo.
horse-breaker *n* domador de caballos *m*.
horse chesnut *n* castaño de Indias *m*.
horsefly *n* moscarda *f*; moscardón *m*.
horseman *n* jinete *m*.
horsemanship *n* equitación *f*.
horsepower *n* caballo de fuerza *m*.
horse race *n* carrera de caballos *f*.
horseradish *n* rábano silvestre *m*.
horseshoe *n* herradura de caballo *f*.
horsewoman *n* jineta *f*.
horticulture *n* horticultura, jardinería *f*.
horticulturist *n* jardinero *m*.
hose-pipe *n* manga *f*.
hosiery *n* calcetería *f*.
hospitable *adj* hospitalario.
hospitably *adv* con hospitalidad.
hospital *n* hospital *m*.
hospitality *n* hospitalidad *f*.
host *n* anfitrión *m*; hostia *f*.
hostage *n* rehén *m*.
hostess *n* anfitriona *f*.
hostile *adj* hostil.
hostility *n* hostilidad *f*.
hot *adj* caliente; cálido.
hotbed *n* semillero *m*.
hotdog *n* perro caliente *m*.
hotel *n* hotel *m*.
hotelier *n* hotelero *m*.
hotheaded *adj* exaltado.
hot-house *n* invernadero *m*.
hotline *n* teléfono rojo *m*.
hotplate *n* hornillo *m*.
hotly *adv* con calor; violentamente.
hound *n* perro de caza *m*.
hour *n* hora *f*.
hour-glass *n* reloj de arena *m*.
hourly *adv* cada hora.
house *n* casa *f*; familia *f*; • *vt* alojar.

houseboat *n* casa flotante *f.*
housebreaker *n* ladrón de casa *m.*
housbreaking *n* allanamiento de morada *m.*
household *n* familia *f.*
householder *n* amo de casa, padre de familia *m.*
housekeeper *n* ama de llaves *f.*
houskeeping *n* trabajos domésticos *mpl.*
houseless *adv* sin casa.
house-warming party *n* fiesta dada para estrenar una casa *f.*
housewife *n* ama de casa *f.*
housework *n* faenas de la casa *fpl.*
housing *n* vivienda *f.*
housing development *n* urbanización *f.*
hovel *n* choza, cabaña *f.*
hover *vi* flotar.
how *adv* cómo, como; ~ **do you do**! encantado.
however *adv* comoquiera, comoquiera que sea; aunque; no obstante.
howl *vi* aullar; ● *n* aullido *m.*
hub *n* centro *m.*
hubbub *n* barullo *m.*
hubcap *n* tapacubos *m.*
hue *n* color *m*; matiz *m.*
huff *n*: in a ~ picado.
hug *vt* abrazar; ● *n* abrazo *m.*
huge *adj* vasto, enorme; ~**ly** *adv* inmensamente.
hulk *n* (*mar*) casco de la embarcación *m*; armatoste *m.*
hull *n* (*mar*) casco de un buque *m.*
hum *vi* canturrear.
human *adv* humano.
humane *adv* humano; benigno; ~**ly** *adv* humanamente.
humanist *n* humanista *m.*
humanitarian *adj* humanitario.
humanity *n* humanidad *f.*
humanize *vt* humanizar.
humanly *adv* humanamente.
humble *adj* humilde, modesto; ● *vt* humillar, postrar.
humbleness *n* humildad *f.*
humbly *adv* con humildad.
humbug *n* tonterías *fpl.*
humdrum *adj* monótono.
humid *adj* húmedo.
humidity *n* humedad *f.*
humiliate *vt* humillar.
humiliation *n* humillación *f.*
humility *n* humildad *f.*
humming-bird *n* colibrí *m.*
humor *n* sentido del humor *m*, humor *m*; ● *vt* complacer.
humorist *n* humorista *m.*
humorous *adj* gracioso; ~**ly** *adv* con gracia.
hump *n* jiba, joroba *f.*
hunch *n* corazonada *f*; ~**backed** *adj* jorobado, jiboso.
hundred *adj* ciento; ● *n* centenar *m*; un ciento.
hundredth *adj* centésimo.
hundredweight *n* quintal *m.*
hunger *n* hambre *f*; ● *vi* hambrear.
hunger strike *n* huelga de hambre *f.*
hungrily *adv* con apetito.
hungry *adj* hambriento.
hunt *vt* cazar; perseguir; buscar; ● *vi* andar a caza; ● *n* caza *f.*
hunter *n* cazador *m.*
hunting *n* caza *f.*
huntsman *n* cazador *m.*
hurdle *n* valla *f.*
hurl *vt* tirar con violencia; arrojar.
hurricane *n* huracán *m.*
hurried *adj* hecho de prisa; ~**ly** *adv* con prisa.
hurry *vt* acelerar, apresurar; ● *vi* apresurarse; ● *n* prisa *f.*
hurt *vt* hacer daño; ofender; ● *n* mal, daño *m.*
hurtful *adj* dañoso; ~**ly** *adv* dañosamente.
husband *n* marido *m.*
husbandry *n* agricultura *f.*

hush ! ¡chitón!, ¡silencio!; ● *vt* hacer callar; ● *vi* estar quieto.
husk *n* cáscara *f.*
huskiness *n* ronquedad *f.*
husky *adj* ronco.
hustings *n* tribuna para las elecciones *f.*
hustle *vt* empujar con fuerza.
hut *n* cabaña, barraca *f.*
hutch *n* conejera *f.*
hyacinth *n* jacinto *m.*
hydrant *n* boca de incendios *f.*
hydraulic *adj* hidráulico; ~**s** *npl* hidráulica *f.*
hydroelectric *adj* hidroeléctrico.
hydrofoil *n* aerodeslizador *m.*
hydrogen *n* hidrógeno *m.*
hydrophobia *n* hidrofobia *f.*
hyena *n* hiena *f.*
hygiene *n* higiene *f.*
hygienic *adj* higiénico.
hymn *n* himno *m.*
hyperbole *n* hipérbole *f*; exageración *f.*
hypermarket *n* hipermercado *m.*
hyphen *n* (*gr*) guión *m.*
hypochondria *n* hipocondría *f.*
hypochondriac *adj*, *n* hipocondríaco *m.*
hypocrisy *n* hipocresía *f.*
hypocrite *n* hipócrita *m.*
hypocritical *adj* hipócrita.
hypothesis *n* hipótesis *f.*
hypothetical *adj* hipotético; ~**ly** *adv* hipotéticamente.
hysterical *adj* histérico.
hysterics *npl* histeria *f.*

I

I (*pn*) yo.
ice *n* hielo *m*; ● *vt* helar.
ice-ax *n* piqueta *f.*
iceberg *n* iceberg *m.*
ice-bound *adj* rodeado de hielos.
icebox *n* nevera *f.*
ice cream *n* helado *m.*
ice rink *n* pista de hielo *f.*
ice skating *n* patinaje sobre hielo *m.*
icicle *n* carámbano *m.*
iconoclast *n* iconoclasta *m.*
icy *adj* helado; frío.
idea *n* idea *f.*
ideal *adj* ideal; ~**ly** *adv* idealmente.
idealist *n* idealista *m.*
identical *adj* idéntico.
identification *n* identificación *f.*
identify *vt* identificar.
identity *n* identidad *f.*
ideology *n* ideología *f.*
idiom *n* idioma *m.*
idiomatic *adj* idiomático.
idiosyncrasy *n* idiosincrasia *f.*
idiot *n* idiota, necio *m.*
idiotic *adj* tonto, bobo.
idle *adj* desocupado; holgazán; inútil.
idleness *n* pereza *f.*
idler *n* holgazán *m.*
idly *adv* ociosamente; vanamente.
idol *n* ídolo *m.*
idolatry *n* idolatría *f.*
idolize *vt* idolatrar.
idyllic *adj* idílico.
i.e. *adv* esto es.
if *conj* si, aunque, supuesto que; ~ **not** si no.
igloo *n* iglú *m.*

ignite *vt* encender.
ignition *n* (*chem*) ignición *f*; encendido *m*.
ignition key *n* llave de contacto *f*.
ignoble *adj* innoble; bajo.
ignominious *adj* ignominioso; ~ly *adv* ignominiosamente.
ignominy *n* ignominia, infamia *f*.
ignoramus *n* ignorante, tonto *m*.
ignorance *n* ignorancia *f*.
ignorant *adj* ignorante; ~ly *adv* ignorantemente.
ignore *vt* no hacer caso de.
ill *adj* malo, enfermo; ● *n* mal, infortunio *m*; ● *adv* mal.
ill-advised *adj* imprudente.
illegal *adj* ~ly *adv* ilegal(mente).
illegality *n* ilegalidad *f*.
illegible *adj* ilegible.
illegibly *adv* de modo ilegible.
illegitimacy *n* ilegitimidad *f*.
illegitimate *adj* ilegítimo; ~ly *adv* ilegítimamente.
ill feeling *n* rencor *m*.
illicit *adj* ilícito.
illiterate *adj* analfabeto.
illness *n* enfermedad *f*.
illogical *adj* ilógico.
ill-timed *adj* inoportuno.
ill-treat *vt* maltratar.
illuminate *vt* iluminar.
illumination *n* iluminación *f*.
illusion *n* ilusión *f*.
illusory *adj* ilusorio.
illustrate *vt* ilustrar; explicar.
illustration *n* ilustración *f*; elucidación *f*.
illustrative *adj* explicativo.
illustrious *adj* ilustre, insigne.
ill-will *n* rencor *m*.
image *n* imagen *f*.
imagery *n* imágenes *fpl*.
imaginable *adj* concebible.
imaginary *adj* imaginario.
imagination *n* imaginación *f*.
imaginative *adj* imaginativo.
imagine *vt* imaginarse; idear, inventar.
imbalance *n* desequilibrio *m*.
imbecile *adj* imbécil, necio.
imbibe *vt* beber.
imbue *vt* infundir.
imitate *vt* imitar, copiar.
imitation *n* imitación, copia *f*.
imitative *adj* imitativo, imitado.
immaculate *adj* inmaculado, puro.
immaterial *adj* poco importante.
immature *adj* inmaduro.
immeasurable *adj* inconmensurable.
immeasurably *adv* inmensamente.
immediate *adj* inmediato; ~ly *adv* inmediatamente.
immense *adj* inmenso; vasto; ~ly *adv* inmensamente.
immensity *n* inmensidad *f*.
immerse *vt* sumergir.
immersion *n* inmersión *f*.
immigrant *n* inmigrante *m*.
immigration *n* inmigración *f*.
imminent *adj* inminente.
immobile *adj* inmóvil.
immobility *n* inmovilidad *f*.
immoderate *adj* inmoderado, excesivo; ~ly *adv* inmoderadamente.
immodest *adj* inmodesto.
immoral *adj* inmoral.
immorality *n* inmoralidad *f*.
immortal *adj* inmortal.
immortality *n* inmortalidad *f*.
immortalize *vt* inmortalizar, eternizar.
immune *adj* inmune.

immunity *n* inmunidad *f*.
immunize *vt* inmunizar.
immutable *adj* inmutable.
imp *n* diablillo, duende *m*.
impact *n* impacto *m*.
impair *vt* disminuir.
impale *vt* empalar.
impalpable *adj* impalpable.
impart *vt* comunicar.
impartial *adj* ~ly *adv* imparcial(mente).
impartiality *n* imparcialidad *f*.
impassable *adj* impracticable.
impasse *n* punto muerto *m*.
impassive *adj* impasible.
impatience *n* impaciencia *f*.
impatient *adj* ~ly *adv* impaciente(mente).
impeach *vt* acusar, denunciar.
impeccable *adj* impecable.
impecunious *adj* indigente.
impede *vt* estorbar.
impediment *n* obstáculo *m*.
impel *vt* impeler.
impending *adj* inminente.
impenetrable *adj* impenetrable.
imperative *adj* imperativo.
imperceptible *adj* imperceptible.
imperceptibly *adv* imperceptiblemente.
imperfect *adj* imperfecto, defectuoso; ~ly imperfectamente; ● *n* (*gr*) pretérito imperfecto *m*.
imperfection *n* imperfección *f*, defecto *m*.
imperial *adj* imperial.
imperialism *n* imperialismo *m*.
imperious *adj* imperioso; arrogante; ~ly *adv* imperiosamente, arrogantemente.
impermeable *adj* impermeable.
impersonal *adj*, ~ly *adv* impersonal(mente).
impersonate *vt* hacerse parsar por.
impertinence *n* impertinencia *f*; descaro *m*.
impertinent *adj* impertinente; ~ly *adv* impertinentemente.
imperturbable *adj* imperturbable.
impervious *adj* impermeable.
impetuosity *n* impetuosidad *f*.
impetuous *adj* impetuoso; ~ly *adv* impetuosamente.
impetus *n* ímpetu *m*.
impiety *n* irreligión *f*.
impinge (on) *vt* tener influjo en.
impious *adj* impío, irreligioso.
implacable *adj* implacable.
implacably *adv* implacablemente.
implant *vt* implantar.
implement *n* herramienta *f*; utensilio *m*.
implicate *vt* implicar.
implication *n* implicación *f*.
implicit *adj* implícito; ~ly *adv* implícitamente.
implore *vt* suplicar.
imply *vt* suponer.
impolite *adj* maleducado.
impoliteness *n* falta de educación *f*.
impolitic *adj* imprudente; impolítico.
import *vt* importar; ● *n* importación *f*.
importance *n* importancia *f*.
important *adj* importante.
importation *n* importación *f*.
importer *n* importador *m*.
importunate *adj* importuno.
importune *vt* importunar.
importunity *n* importunidad *f*.
impose *vt* imponer.
imposing *adj* imponente.
imposition *n* imposición, carga *f*.
impossibility *n* imposibilidad *f*.
impossible *adj* imposible.

impostor *n* impostor *m.*
impotence *n* impotencia *f.*
impotent *adj* impotente; ~ly *adv* sin poder.
impound *vt* embargar.
impoverish *vt* empobrecer.
impoverished *adj* necesitado.
impoverishment *n* empobrecimiento *m.*
impracticability *n* imposibilidad *f.*
impracticable *adj* irrealizable.
impractical *adj* poco práctico.
imprecation *n* imprecación, maldición *f.*
imprecise *adj* impreciso.
impregnable *adj* inexpugnable.
impregnate *vt* impregnar.
impregnation *n* fecundación *f*; impregnación *f.*
impress *vt* impresionar.
impression *n* impresión *f*; edición *f.*
impressionable *adj* impresionable.
impressive *adj* impresionante.
imprint *n* sello *m*; ● *vt* imprimir; estampar.
imprison *vt* encarcelar.
imprisonment *n* encarcelamiento *m.*
improbability *n* improbabilidad *f.*
improbable *adj* improbable.
impromptu *adj* de improviso.
improper *adj* impropio, indecente; ~ly *adv* impropiamente.
impropriety *n* impropiedad *f.*
improve *vt, vi* mejorar.
improvement *n* progreso, mejoramiento *m.*
improvident *adj* impróvido.
improvise *vt* improvisar.
imprudence *n* imprudencia *f.*
imprudent *adj* imprudente.
impudence *n* impudencia *f.*
impudent *adj* impudente; ~ly *adv* desvergonzadamente.
impugn *vt* impugnar.
impulse *n* impulso *m.*
impulsive *adj* impulsivo.
impunity *n* impunidad *f.*
impure *adj* impuro; ~ly *adv* impuramente.
impurity *n* impureza *f.*
in *prep* en.
inability *n* incapacidad *f.*
inaccessible *adj* inaccesible.
inaccuracy *n* inexactitud *f.*
inaccurate *adj* inexacto.
inaction *n* inacción *f.*
inactive *adj* flojo, perezoso.
inactivity *n* inactividad *f.*
inadequate *adj* inadecuado, defectuoso.
inadmissible *adj* inadmisible.
inadvertently *adv* sin querer.
inalienable *adj* inalienable.
inane *adj* necio.
inanimate *adj* inanimado.
inapplicable *adj* inaplicable.
inappropriate *adj* impropio.
inasmuch *adv* visto *o* puesto que.
inattentive *adj* desatento.
inaudible *adj* inaudible, que no se puede oir.
inaugural *adj* inaugural.
inaugurate *vt* inaugurar.
inauguration *n* inauguración *f.*
inauspicious *adj* poco propicio.
in-between *adj* intermedio.
inborn, inbred *adj* innato.
incalculable *adj* incalculable.
incandescent *adj* incandescente.
incantation *n* encantamiento *m.*
incapable *adj* incapaz.
incapacitate *vt* inhabilitar.
incapacity *n* incapacidad *f.*

incarcerate *vt* encarcelar.
incarnate *adj* encarnado.
incarnation *n* encarnación *f.*
incautious *adj* incauto; ~ly *adv* incautamente.
incendiary *n* bomba incendiaria *f.*
incense *n* incienso *m*; ● *vt* exasperar.
incentive *n* incentivo *m.*
inception *n* principio *m.*
incessant *adj* incesante, constante; ~ly *adv* continuamente.
incest *n* incesto *m.*
incestuous *adj* incestuoso.
inch *n* pulgada *f*; ~ by ~ palmo a palmo.
incidence *n* frecuencia *f.*
incident *n* incidente *m.*
incidental *adj* casual; ~ly *adv* a propósito.
incinerator *n* incinerador *m.*
incipient *adj* incipiente.
incise *vt* tajar, cortar.
incision *n* incisión *f.*
incisive *adj* incisivo.
incisor *n* incisivo *m.*
incite *vt* incitar, estimular.
inclement *adj* feo.
inclination *n* inclinación, propensión *f.*
incline *vt, vi* inclinar(se).
include *vt* incluir, comprender.
including *prep* incluso.
inclusion *n* inclusión *f.*
inclusive *adj* inclusivo.
incognito *adv* de incógnito.
incoherence *n* incoherencia *f.*
incoherent *adj* incoherente, inconsecuente; ~ly *adv* de modo incoherente.
income *n* renta *f*; beneficio *m.*
income tax *n* impuesto sobre la renta *m.*
incoming *adj* entrante.
incomparable *adj* incomparable.
incomparably *adv* incomparablemente.
incompatibility *n* incompatibilidad *f.*
incompatible *adj* incompatible.
incompetence *n* incompetencia *f.*
incompetent *adj* ~ly *adv* incompetente(mente).
incomplete *adj* incompleto.
incomprehensibility *n* incomprehensibilidad *f.*
incomprehensible *adj* incomprehensible.
inconceivable *adj* inconcebible.
inconclusive *adj* no concluyente; ● *adv* sin conclusión.
incongruity *n* incongruencia *f.*
incongruous *adj* incongruo; ~ly *adv* incongruamente.
inconsequential *adj* inconsecuente.
inconsiderate *adj* desconsiderado; ~ly *adv* desconsideradamente.
inconsistency *n* inconsecuencia *f.*
inconsistent *adj* inconsecuente.
inconsolable *adj* inconsolable.
inconspicuous *adj* discreto.
incontinence *n* incontinencia *f.*
incontinent *adj* incontinente.
incontrovertible *adj* incontrovertible.
inconvenience *n* incomodidad *f*; ● *vt* incomodar.
inconvenient *adj* incómodo; ~ly *adv* incómodamente.
incorporate *vt, vi* incorporar(se).
incorporated company *n* sociedad anónima *f.*
incorporation *n* incorporación *f.*
incorrect *adj* incorrecto; ~ly *adv* de modo incorrecto.
incorrigible *adj* incorregible.
incorruptibility *n* incorruptibilidad *f.*
incorruptible *adj* incorruptible.
increase *vt* acrecentar, aumentar; ● *vi* crecer; ● *n* aumento *m.*
increasing *adj* creciente; *adv* ~ly cada vez más.
incredible *adj* increíble.
incredulity *n* incredulidad *f.*

incredulous *adj* incrédulo.
increment *n* incremento *m*.
incriminate *vt* incriminar.
incrúst *vt* incrustar.
incubate *vi* incubar.
incubator *n* incubadora *f*.
inculcate *vt* inculcar.
incumbent *adj* obligatorio; • *n* beneficiado *m*.
incur *vt* incurrir.
incurability *n* lo incurable.
incurable *adj* incurable.
incursion *n* incursión, invasión *f*.
indebted *adj* agradecido.
indecency *n* indecencia *f*.
indecent *adj* indecente; ~ly *adv* indecentemente.
indecision *n* irresolución *f*.
indecisive *adj* indeciso.
indecorous *adj* indecente.
indeed *adv* verdaderamente, de veras.
indefatigable *adj* incansable.
indefinite *adj* indefinido; ~ly *adv* indefinidamente.
indelible *adj* indeleble.
indelicacy *n* falta de delicadeza, grosería *f*.
indelicate *adj* poco delicado.
indemnify *vt* indemnizar.
indemnity *n* indemnidad *f*.
indent *vt* mellar.
independence *n* independencia *f*.
independent *adj* independiente; ~ly *adv* independiente-
mente.
indescribable *adj* indescriptible.
indestructible *adj* indestructible.
indeterminate *adj* indeterminado.
index *n* índice *m*.
index card *n* ficha *f*.
indexed *adj* indexado.
index finger *n* dedo índice *m*.
indicate *vt* indicar.
indication *n* indicación *f*; indicio *m*.
indicative *adj*, *n* (*gr*) indicativo *m*.
indicator *n* indicador *m*.
indict *vt* acusar.
indictment *n* acusación *f*.
indifference *n* indiferencia *f*.
indifferent *adj* indiferente; ~ly *adv* indiferentemente.
indigenous *adj* indígena.
indigent *adj* indigente.
indigestible *adj* indigestible.
indigestion *n* indigestión *f*.
indignant *adj* airado.
indignation *n* indignación *f*.
indignity *n* indignidad *f*.
indigo *n* añil *m*.
indirect *adj* indirecto; ~ly *adv* indirectamente.
indiscreet *adj* indiscreto; ~ly *adv* indiscretamente.
indiscretion *n* indiscreción *f*.
indiscriminate *adj* indistinto; ~ly *adv* sin distinción.
indispensable *adj* indispensable.
indisposed *adj* indispuesto.
indisposition *n* indisposición *f*.
indisputable *adj* indiscutible.
indisputably *adv* indisputablemente.
indistinct *adj* indistinto, confuso; ~ly *adv* indistintamente.
indistinguishable *adj* indistinguible.
individual *adj* individual; ~ly *adv* individualmente; • *n* individuo *m*.
individuality *n* individualidad *f*.
indivisible *adv* indivisible; ~bly *adv* indivisiblemente.
indoctrinate *vt* adoctrinar.
indoctrination *n* adoctrinamiento *m*.
indolence *n* indolencia, pereza *f*.
indolent *adj* indolente; ~ly *adv* con negligencia.

indomitable *adj* indomable.
indoors *adv* dentro.
indubitably *adv* indudablemente.
induce *vt* inducir, persuadir; causar.
inducement *n* aliciente *m*.
induction *n* inducción *f*.
indulge *vt*, *vi* conceder; ser indulgente.
indulgence *n* indulgencia *f*.
indulgent *adj* indulgente; ~ly *adv* de modo indulgente.
industrial *adj* industrial.
industrialist *n* industrial *m*.
industrialize *vt* industrializar.
industrial park *n* polígono industrial *m*.
industrious *adj* trabajador.
industry *n* industria *f*.
inebriated *vt* embriagado.
inebriation *n* embriaguez *f*.
inedible *adj* no comestible.
ineffable *adj* inefable.
ineffective, ineffectual *adj* ineficaz; ~ly *adv* sin efecto.
inefficiency *n* ineficacia *f*.
inefficient *adj* ineficaz.
ineligible *adj* ineligible.
inept *adj* incompetente.
ineptitude *n* incompetencia *f*.
inequality *n* desigualdad *f*.
inert *adj* inerte, perezoso.
inertia *n* inercia *f*.
inescapable *adj* ineludible.
inestimable *adj* inestimable, inapreciable.
inevitable *adj* inevitable.
inevitably *adv* inevitablemente.
inexcusable *adj* inexcusable.
inexhaustible *adj* inagotable.
inexorable *adj* inexorable.
inexpedient *adj* imprudente.
inexpensive *adj* económico.
inexperience *n* inexperiencia *f*.
inexperienced *adj* inexperto.
inexpert *adj* inexperto.
inexplicable *adj* inexplicable.
inexpressible *adj* indecible.
inextricably *adv* indisolublemente.
infallibility *n* infalibilidad *f*.
infallible *adj* infalible.
infamous *adj* vil, infame; ~ly *adv* infamemente.
infamy *n* infamia *f*.
infancy *n* infancia *f*.
infant *n* niño *m*.
infanticide *n* infanticidio *m*; infanticida *m/f*.
infantile *adj* infantil.
infantry *n* infantería *f*.
infatuated *adj* loco.
infatuation *n* infatuación *f*.
infect *vt* infectar.
infection *n* infección *f*.
infectious *adj* contagioso; infeccioso.
infer *vt* inferir.
inference *n* inferencia *f*.
inferior *adj* inferior; • *n* subordinado *m*.
inferiority *n* inferioridad *f*.
infernal *adj* infernal.
inferno *n* infierno *m*.
infest *vt* infestar.
infidel *n* infiel, pagano *m*.
infidelity *n* infidelidad *f*.
infiltrate *vi* infiltrarse.
infinite *adj* infinito; ~ly *adv* infinitamente.
infinitive *n* infinitivo *m*.
infinity *n* infinito *m*; infinidad *f*.
infirm *adj* enfermo, débil.
infirmary *n* enfermería *f*.

infirmity *n* fragilidad, enfermedad *f*.
inflame *vt, vi* inflamar(se).
inflammation *n* inflamación *f*.
inflammatory *adj* inflamatorio.
inflatable *adj* inflable.
inflate *vt* inflar, hinchar.
inflation *n* inflación *f*.
inflection *n* inflexión *f*; modulación de la voz *f*.
inflexibility *n* inflexibilidad *f*.
inflexible *adj* inflexible.
inflexibly *adv* inflexiblemente.
inflict *vt* imponer.
influence *n* influencia *f*; • *vt* influir.
influential *adj* influente.
influenza *n* gripe *f*.
influx *n* afluencia *f*.
inform *vt* informar.
informal *adj* informal.
informality *n* informalidad *f*.
informant *n* informante *m*.
information *n* información *f*.
infraction *n* infracción *f*.
infra-red *adj* infrarrojo.
infrastructure *n* infraestructura *f*.
infrequent *adj* raro; ~ly *adv* raramente.
infringe *vt* contravenir a.
infringement *n* infracción *f*.
infuriate *vt* enfurecer.
infuse *vt* infundir.
infusion *n* infusión *f*.
ingenious *adj* ingenioso; ~ly *adv* ingeniosamente.
ingenuity *n* ingeniosidad *f*.
ingenuous *adj* ingenuo, sincero; ~ly *adv* ingenuamente.
inglorious *adj* ignominioso, vergonzoso; ~ly *adv* ignominiosamente.
ingot *n* barra de metal *f*.
ingrained *adj* inveterado.
ingratiate *vi* congraciarse.
ingratitude *n* ingratitud *f*.
ingredient *n* ingrediente *m*.
inhabit *vt, vi* habitar.
inhabitable *adj* habitable.
inhabitant *n* habitante *m*.
inhale *vt* inhalar.
inherent *adj* inherente.
inherit *vt* heredar.
inheritance *n* herencia *f*.
inheritor *n* heredero *m*.
inhibit *vt* inhibir.
inhibited *adj* cohibido.
inhibition *n* cohibición *f*.
inhospitable *adj* inhospitalario.
inhospitality *n* inhospitalidad *f*.
inhuman *adj* inhumano, cruel; ~ly *adv* inhumanamente.
inhumanity *n* inhumanidad, crueldad *f*.
inimical *adj* enemigo.
inimitable *adj* inimitable.
iniquitous *adj* inicuo, injusto.
iniquity *n* iniquidad, injusticia *f*.
initial *adj* inicial; • *n* inicial *f*.
initially *adv* al principio.
initiate *vt* iniciar.
initiation *n* principio *m*; iniciación *f*.
initiative *n* iniciativa *f*.
inject *vt* inyectar.
injection *n* inyección *f*.
injudicious *adj* poco juicioso.
injunction *n* entredicho *m*.
injure *vt* herir.
injury *n* daño *m*.
injury time *n* descuento *m*.
injustice *n* injusticia *f*.

ink *n* tinta *f*.
inkling *n* sospecha *f*.
inkstand *n* tintero *m*.
inlaid *adj* taraceado.
inland *adj* interior; • *adv* tierra adentro.
in-laws *npl* suegros *mpl*.
inlay *vt* taracear.
inlet *n* entrada *f*.
inmate *n* preso *m*.
inmost *adj* más íntimo.
inn *n* posada *f*; mesón *m*.
innate *adj* innato.
inner *adj* interior.
innermost *adj* más íntimo.
inner tube *n* cámara *f*.
innkeeper *n* posadero, mesonero *m*.
innocence *n* inocencia *f*.
innocent *adj* inocente; ~ly *adv* inocentemente.
innocuous *adj* inocuo; ~ly *adv* inocentemente.
innovate *vt* innovar.
innovation *n* innovación *f*.
innuendo *n* indirecta, insinuación *f*.
innumerable *adj* innumerable.
inoculate *vt* inocular.
inoculation *n* inoculación *f*.
inoffensive *adj* inofensivo.
inopportune *adj* inconveniente, no oportuno.
inordinately *adv* desmesuradamente.
inorganic *adj* inorgánico.
inpatient *n* paciente interno *m*.
input *n* entrada *f*.
inquest *n* encuesta judicial *f*.
inquire *vt, vi* preguntar; to ~ about informarse de; to ~ after *vt* preguntar por; to ~ into *vt* investigar, indagar, inquirir.
inquiry *n* pesquisa *f*.
inquisition *n* inquisición *f*.
inquisitive *adj* curioso.
inroad *n* incursión, invasión *f*.
insane *adj* loco, demente.
insanity *n* locura *f*.
insatiable *adj* insaciable.
inscribe *vt* inscribir; dedicar.
inscription *n* inscripción *f*; dedicatoria *f*.
inscrutable *adj* inescrutable.
insect *n* insecto *m*.
insecticide *n* insecticida *m*.
insecure *adj* inseguro.
insecurity *n* inseguridad *f*.
insemination *n* inseminación *f*.
insensible *adj* inconsciente.
insensitive *adj* insensible.
inseparable *adj* inseparable.
insert *vt* introducir.
insertion *n* inserción *f*.
inshore *adj* costero.
inside *n* interior *m*; • *adv* dentro.
inside out *adv* al revés; a fondo.
insidious *adj* insidioso; ~ly insidiosamente.
insight *n* perspicacia *f*.
insignia *npl* insignias *fpl*.
insignificant *adj* insignificante, frívolo.
insincere *adj* poco sincero.
insincerity *n* falta de sinceridad *f*.
insinuate *vt* insinuar.
insinuation *n* insinuación *f*.
insipid *adj* insípido; insulso.
insist *vi* insistir.
insistence *n* insistencia *f*.
insistent *adj* insistente.
insole *n* plantilla *f*.
insolence *n* insolencia *f*.
insolent *adj* insolente; ~ly *adv* insolentemente.

insoluble *adj* insoluble.
insolvency *n* insolvencia *f.*
insolvent *adj* insolvente.
insomnia *n* insomnio *m.*
insomuch *conj* puesto que.
inspect *vt* examinar, inspeccionar.
inspection *n* inspección *f.*
inspector *n* inspector, superintendente *m.*
inspiration *n* inspiración *f.*
inspire *vt* inspirar.
instability *n* inestabilidad *f.*
instal *vt* instalar.
installation *n* instalacion *f.*
installment *n* instalación *f*; plazo *m.*
installment plan *n* compra a plazos *f.*
instance *n* ejemplo *m*; **for ~** por ejemplo.
instant *adj* immediato; **~ly** *adv* en seguida; ● *n* instante, momento *m.*
instantaneous *adj* instantáneo; **~ly** *adv* instantáneamente.
instead (of) *pr* por, en lugar de, en vez de.
instep *n* empeine *m.*
instigate *vt* instigar.
instigation *n* instigación *f.*
instill *vt* inculcar.
instinct *n* instinto *m.*
instinctive *adj* instintivo; **~ly** *adv* por instinto.
institute *vt* establecer; ● *n* instituto *m.*
institution *n* institución *f.*
instruct *vt* instruir, enseñar.
instruction *n* instrucción *f.*
instructive *adj* instructivo.
instructor *n* instructor *m.*
instrument *n* instrumento *m.*
instrumental *adj* instrumental.
insubordinate *adj* insubordinado.
insubordination *n* insubordinación *f.*
insufferable *adj* insoportable.
insufferably *adv* de modo insoportable.
insufficiency *n* insuficiencia *f.*
insufficient *adj* insuficiente; **~ly** *adv* insuficientemente.
insular *adj* insular.
insulate *vt* aislar.
insulating tape *n* cinta aislante *f.*
insulation *n* aislamiento *m.*
insulin *n* insulina *f.*
insult *vt* insultar; ● *n* insulto *m.*
insulting *adj* insolente.
insuperable *adj* insuperable.
insurance *n* (*com*) seguro *m.*
insurance policy *n* póliza de seguros *f.*
insure *vt* asegurar.
insurgent *n* insurgente, rebelde *m.*
insurmountable *adj* insuperable.
insurrection *n* insurrección *f.*
intact *adj* intacto.
intake *n* admisión *f*; entrada *f.*
integral *adj* íntegro; (*chem*) integrante; ● *n* todo *m.*
integrate *vt* integrar.
integration *n* integración *f.*
integrity *n* integridad *f.*
intellect *n* intelecto *m.*
intellectual *adj* intelectual.
intelligence *n* inteligencia *f.*
intelligent *adj* inteligente.
intelligentsia *n* intelectualidad *f.*
intelligible *adj* inteligible.
intelligibly *adv* inteligiblemente.
intemperate *adj* immoderado; **~ly** *adv* inmoderadamente.
intend *vi* tener intención.
intendant *n* intendente *m.*
intended *adj* deseado.
intense *adj* intenso; **~ly** *adv* intensamente.

intensify *vt* intensificar.
intensity *n* intensidad *f.*
intensive *adj* intensivo.
intensive care unit *n* unidad de vigilancia intensiva *f.*
intent *adj* atento, cuidadoso; **~ly** *adv* con aplicación; ● *n* designio *m.*
intention *n* intención *f*; designio *m.*
intentional *adj* intencional; **~ly** *adv* a propósito.
inter *vt* enterrar.
interaction *n* interacción *f.*
intercede *vi* interceder.
intercept *vt* interceptar.
intercession *n* intercesión, mediación *f.*
interchange *n* intercambio *m.*
intercom *n* interfono *m.*
intercourse *n* relaciones sexuales *fpl.*
interest *vt* interesar; ● *n* interés *m.*
interesting *adj* interesante.
interest rate *n* tipo de interés *m.*
interfere *vi* entrometerse.
interference *n* interferencia *f.*
interim *adj* provisional.
interior *adj* interior.
interior designer *n* interiorista *m.*
interjection *n* (*gr*) interjección *f.*
interlock *vi* endentarse.
interlocutor *n* interlocutor *m.*
interloper *n* intruso *m.*
interlude *n* intermedio *m.*
intermarriage *n* matrimonio mixto *m.*
intermediary *n* intermediario *m.*
intermediate *adj* intermedio.
interment *n* entierro *m*; sepultura *f.*
interminable *adj* inacabable.
intermingle *vt, vi* entremezclar; mezclarse.
intermission *n* descanso *m.*
intermittent *adj* intermitente.
intern *n* interno *m.*
internal *adj* interno; **~ly** *adv* internamente.
international *adj* internacional.
interplay *n* interacción *f.*
interpose *vt* interponer.
interpret *vt* interpretar.
interpretation *n* interpretación *f.*
interpreter *n* intérprete *m.*
interregnum *n* interregno *m.*
interrelated *adj* interrelacionado.
interrogate *vt* interrogar.
interrogation *n* interrogatorio *m.*
interrogative *adj* interrogativo.
interrupt *vt* interrumpir.
interruption *n* interrupción *f.*
intersect *vi* cruzarse.
intersection *n* cruce *m.*
intersperse *vt* esparcir.
intertwine *vt* entretejer.
interval *n* intervalo *m.*
intervene *vi* intervenir; ocurrir.
intervention *n* intervención *f.*
interview *n* entrevista *f*; ● *vt* entrevistar.
interviewer *n* entrevistador *m.*
interweave *vt* entretejer.
intestate *adj* intestado.
intestinal *adj* intestinal.
intestine *n* intestino *m.*
intimacy *n* intimidad *f.*
intimate *n* amigo íntimo *m*; ● *adj* íntimo; **~ly** *adv* íntimamente; ● *vt* insinuar, dar a entender.
intimidate *vt* intimidar.
into *prep* en, dentro, adentro.
intolerable *adj* intolerable.
intolerably *adv* intolerablemente.

intolerance *n* intolerancia *f*.
intolerant *adj* intolerante.
intonation *n* entonación *f*.
intoxicate *vt* embriagar.
intoxication *n* embriaguez *f*.
intractable *adj* intratable.
intransitive *adj* (*gr*) intransitivo.
intravenous *adj* intravenoso.
in-tray *n* bandeja de entrada *f*.
intrepid *adj* intrépido; ~ly *adv* intrépidamente.
intrepidity *n* intrepidez *f*.
intricacy *n* complejidad *f*.
intricate *adj* intricado, complicado; ~ly *adv* intricadamente.
intrigue *n* intriga *f*; ● *vi* intrigar.
intriguing *adj* fascinante.
intrinsic *adj* intrínseco; ~ally *adv* intrínsecamente.
introduce *vt* introducir.
introduction *n* introducción *f*.
introductory *adj* introductorio.
introspection *n* introspección *f*.
introvert *n* introvertido *m*.
intrude *vi* entrometerse.
intruder *n* intruso *m*.
intrusion *n* invasión *f*.
intuition *n* intuición *f*.
intuitive *adj* intuitivo.
inundate *vt* inundar.
inundation *n* inundación *f*.
inure *vt* acostumbrar, habituar.
invade *vt* invadir.
invader *n* invasor *m*.
invalid *adj* invalido, nulo; ● *n* minusválido *m*.
invalidate *vt* invalidar, anular.
invaluable *adj* inapreciable.
invariable *adj* invariable.
invariably *adv* invariablemente.
invasion *n* invasión *f*.
invective *n* invectiva *f*.
inveigle *vt* seducir, persuadir.
invent *vt* inventar.
invention *n* invento *m*.
inventive *adj* inventivo.
inventor *n* inventor *m*.
inventory *n* inventario *m*.
inverse *adj* inverso.
inversion *n* inversión *f*.
invert *vt* invertir.
invest *vt* invertir.
investigate *vt* investigar.
investigation *n* investigación, pesquisa *f*.
investigator *n* investigador *m*.
investment *n* inversión *f*.
inveterate *adj* inveterado.
invidious *adj* odioso.
invigilate *vt* vigilar.
invigorating *adj* vigorizante.
invincible *adj* invencible.
invincibly *adv* invenciblemente.
inviolable *adj* inviolable.
invisible *adj* invisible.
invisibly *adv* invisiblemente.
invitation *n* invitación *f*.
invite *vt* invitar.
inviting *adj* atractivo.
invoice *n* (*com*) factura *f*.
invoke *vt* invocar.
involuntarily *adv* involuntariamente.
involuntary *adj* involuntario.
involve *vt* implicar.
involved *adj* complicado.
involvement *n* compromiso *m*.
invulnerable *adj* invulnerable.

inward *adj* interior; interno; ~, ~s *adv* hacia dentro.
iodine *n* (*chem*) yodo *m*.
I.O.U. (I owe you) *n* vale *m*.
irascible *adj* irascible.
irate, ireful *adj* enojado.
iris *n* iris *m*.
irksome *adj* fastidioso.
iron *n* hierro *m*; ● *adj* férreo; ● *vt* planchar.
ironic *adj* irónico; ~ly *adv* con ironía.
ironing *n* planchado *m*.
ironing board *n* tabla de planchar *f*.
iron ore *n* mineral de hierro *m*.
ironwork *n* herraje *m*; ~s *pl* herrería *f*.
irony *n* ironía *f*.
irradiate *vt* irradiar.
irrational *adj* irracional.
irreconcilable *adj* irreconciliable.
irregular *adj* ~ly *adv* irregular(mente).
irregularity *n* irregularidad *f*.
irrelevant *adj* impertinente.
irreligious *adj* irreligioso.
irreparable *adj* irreparable.
irreplaceable *adj* irremplazable.
irrepressible *adj* incontenible.
irreproachable *adj* irreprensible.
irresistible *adj* irresistible.
irresolute *adj* irresoluto; ~ly *adv* irresolutamente.
irresponsible *adj* irresponsable.
irretrievably *adv* irreparablemente.
irreverence *n* irreverencia *f*.
irreverent *adj* irreverente; ~ly *adv* irreverentemente.
irrigate *vt* regar.
irrigation *n* riego *m*.
irritability *n* irritabilidad *f*.
irritable *adj* irritable.
irritant *n* (*med*) irritante *m*.
irritate *vt* irritar.
irritating *adj* fastidioso.
irritation *n* fastidio *m*; picazón *f*.
Islam *n* islam *m*.
island *n* isla *f*.
islander *n* isleño *m*.
isle *n* isla *f*.
isolate *vt* aislar.
isolation *n* aislamiento *m*.
issue *n* asunto *m*; ● *vt* expedir; publicar; repartir.
isthmus *n* istmo *m*.
it *pn* él, ella, ello, lo, la, le.
italic *n* cursiva *f*.
itch *n* picazón *f*; ● *vi* picar.
item *n* artículo *m*.
itemize *vt* detallar.
itinerant *n* ambulante, errante *m*.
itinerary *n* itinerario *m*.
its *pn* su, suyo.
itself *pn* el mismo, la misma, lo mismo.
ivory *n* marfil *m*.
ivy *n* hiedra *f*.

J

jab *vt* clavar.
jabber *vi* farfullar.
jack *n* gato *m*; sota *f*.
jackal *n* chacal *m*.
jackboots *npl* botas militares *fpl*.
jackdaw *n* grajo *m*.
jacket *n* chaqueta, jaqueta *f*.
jack-knife *vi* colear.
jack plug *n* enchufe de clavija *m*.

jackpot *n* premio gordo *m*.
jade *n* jade *m*.
jagged *adj* dentado.
jaguar *n* jaguar *m*.
jail *n* cárcel *f*.
jailbird *n* preso *m*.
jailer *n* carcelero *m*.
jam *n* conserva *f*; mermelada de frutas *f*.
jangle *vi* sonar.
janitor *n* portero *m*.
January *n* enero *m*.
jar *vi* chocar; (*mus*) discordar; reñir; • *n* jarra *f*.
jargon *n* jerigonza *f*.
jasmine *n* jazmín *m*.
jaundice *n* ictericia *f*.
jaunt *n* excursión *f*.
jaunty *adj* alegre.
javelin *n* jabalina *f*.
jaw *n* mandíbula *f*.
jay *n* arrendajo *m*.
jazz *n* jazz *m*.
jealous *adj* celoso; envidioso.
jealousy *n* celos *mpl*; envidia *f*.
jeans *npl* vaqueros *mpl*.
jeep *n* jeep *m*.
jeer *vi* befar, mofar; • *n* burla *f*.
jelly *n* jalea, gelatina *f*.
jelly-fish *n* aguamar *m*; medusa *f*.
jeopardize *vt* arriesgar, poner en riesgo.
jerk *n* sacudida *f*; • *vt* tirar.
jerky *adj* espasmódico.
jersey *n* jersey *m*.
jest *n* broma *f*.
jester *n* bufón *m*.
jestingly *adv* de burlas.
Jesuit *n* jesuíta *m*.
Jesus *n* Jesús *m*.
jet *n* avión a reacción *m*; azabache *m*.
jet engine *n* motor a reacción *m*.
jettison *vt* desechar.
jetty *n* muelle *m*.
Jew *n* judío *m*.
jewel *n* joya *f*.
jeweler *n* joyero *m*.
jewelry *n* joyería *f*.
jewelry store *n* joyería *f*.
Jewess *n* judía *f*.
Jewish *adj* judío.
jib *n* (*mar*) foque *m*.
jibe *n* mofa *f*.
jig *n* giga *f*.
jigsaw *n* rompecabezas *m*.
jilt *vt* dejar.
jinx *n* gafe *m*.
job *n* trabajo *m*.
jockey *n* jinete *m*.
jocular *adj* jocoso, alegre.
jog *vi* hacer footing.
jogging *n* footing *m*.
join *vt* juntar, unir; to ~ in participar en; • *vi* unirse, juntarse.
joiner *n* carpintero *m*.
joinery *n* carpintería *f*.
joint *n* articulación *f*; • *adj* común.
jointly *adv* conjuntamente.
joint-stock company *n* (*com*) sociedad por acciones *f*.
joke *n* broma *f*; • *vi* bromear.
joker *n* comodín *m*.
jollity *n* alegría *f*.
jolly *adj* alegre.
jolt *vt* sacudir; • *n* sacudida *f*.
jostle *vt* codear.

journal *n* revista *f*.
journalism *n* periodismo *m*.
journalist *n* periodista *m*.
journey *n* viaje *m*; • *vt* viajar.
jovial *adj* jovial, alegre; ~ly *adv* con jovialidad.
joy *n* alegría *f*; júbilo *m*.
joyful, joyous *adj* alegre, gozoso; ~ly *adv* alegremente.
joystick *n* palanca de control *f*.
jubilant *adj* jubiloso.
jubilation *n* júbilo, regocijo *m*.
jubilee *n* jubileo *m*.
Judaism *n* judaísmo *m*.
judge *n* juez *m*; • *vt* juzgar.
judgment *n* juicio *m*.
judicial *adj* ~ly *adv* judicial(mente).
judiciary *n* poder judicial *m*.
judicious *adj* prudente.
judo *n* judo *m*.
jug *n* jarro *m*.
juggle *vi* hacer juegos malabares.
juggler *n* malabarista *m*.
juice *n* jugo *m*; suco *m*.
juicy *adj* jugoso.
jukebox *n* gramola *f*.
July *n* julio *m*.
jumble *vt* mezclar; • *n* revoltijo *m*.
jump *vi* saltar, brincar; • *n* salto *m*.
jumper *n* mandil *m*.
jumpy *adj* nervioso.
juncture *n* coyuntura *f*.
June *n* junio *m*.
jungle *n* selva *f*.
junior *adj* más joven.
juniper *n* (*bot*) enebro *m*.
junk *n* basura *f*; baratijas *fpl*.
junta *n* junta *f*.
jurisdiction *n* jurisdicción *f*.
jurisprudence *n* jurisprudencia *f*.
jurist *n* jurista *m*.
juror, juryman *n* jurado *m*.
jury *n* jurado *m*.
just *adj* justo; • *adv* justamente, exactamente; ~ as como; ~ now ahora mismo.
justice *n* justicia *f*.
justifiably *adv* con justificación.
justification *n* justificación *f*.
justify *vt* justificar.
justly *adv* justamente.
justness *n* justicia *f*.
jut *vi*; to ~ out sobresalir.
jute *n* jute *m*.
juvenile *adj* juvenil.
juxtaposition *n* yuxtaposición *f*.

K

kaleidoscope *n* kaleidoscopio *m*.
kangaroo *n* canguro *m*.
karate *n* karate *m*.
kebab *n* pincho *m*.
keel *n* (*mar*) quilla *f*.
keen *adj* agudo; vivo.
keenness *n* entusiasmo *m*.
keep *vt* mantener; guardar; conservar.
keeper *n* guardián *m*.
keepsake *n* recuerdo *m*.
keg *n* barril *m*.
kennel *n* perrera *f*.
kernel *n* fruta *f*; meollo *m*.
kerosene *n* keroseno *m*.

ketchup *n* catsup *m*.
kettle *n* hervidor *m*.
kettle-drum *n* timbal *m*.
key *n* llave *f*; (*mus*) clave *f*; tecla *f*.
keyboard *n* teclado *m*.
keyhole *n* ojo de la cerradura *m*.
keynote *n* (*mus*) tónica *f*.
key ring *n* llavero *m*.
keystone *n* piedra clave *f*.
khaki *n* caqui *m*.
kick *vt, vi* patear; ● *n* puntapié *m*; patada *f*.
kid *n* chico *m*.
kidnap *vt* secuestrar.
kidnaper *n* secuestrador *m*.
kidnaping *n* secuestro *m*.
kidney *n* riñón *m*.
killer *n* asesino *m*.
killing *n* asesinato *m*.
kiln *n* horno *m*.
kilo *n* kilo *m*.
kilobyte *n* kiloocteto *m*.
kilogram *n* kilo *m*.
kilometer *n* kilómetro *m*.
kilt *n* falda escocesa *f*.
kin *n* parientes *mpl*; **next of ~** pariente próximo *m*.
kind *adj* cariñoso; ● *n* género *m*.
kindergarten *n* jardín de infantes *m*.
kind-hearted *adj* bondadoso.
kindle *vt, vi* encender.
kindliness *n* benevolencia *f*.
kindly *adj* bondadoso.
kindness *n* bondad *f*.
kindred *adj* emparentado.
kinetic *adj* cinético.
king *n* rey *m*.
kingdom *n* reino *m*.
kingfisher *n* martín pescador *m*.
kiosk *n* quiosco *m*.
kiss *n* beso *m*; ● *vt* besar.
kissing *n* beso *m*.
kit *n* equipo *m*.
kitchen *n* cocina *f*.
kitchen garden *n* huerta *f*.
kite *n* cometa *f*.
kitten *n* gatillo *m*.
knack *n* don *m*.
knapsack *n* mochila *f*.
knave *n* bribón, pícaro *m*; (cards) sota *f*.
knead *vt* amasar.
knee *n* rodilla *f*.
knee-deep *adj* metido hasta las rodillas.
kneel *vi* arrodillarse.
knell *n* toque de difuntos *m*.
knife *n* cuchillo *m*.
knight *n* caballero *m*.
knit *vt, vi* tejer, tricotear; **to ~ the brows** fruncir las cejas.
knitter *n* calcetero, mediero *m*.
knitting-pin *n* aguja de tejer *f*.
knitwear *n* prendas de punto *fpl*.
knob *n* bulto *m*; nudo en la madera *m*; botón de las flores *m*.
knock *vt, vi* golpear, tocar; **to ~ down** derribar; ● *n* golpe *m*.
knocker *n* aldaba *f*.
knock-kneed *adj* patizambo.
knock-out *n* K.O. *m*.
knoll *n* cima de una colina *f*.
knot *n* nudo *m*; lazo *m*; ● *vt* anudar.
knotty *adj* escabroso.
know *vt, vi* conocer; saber.
know-all *n* sabelotodo *m*.
know-how *n* conocimientos *mpl*.
knowing *adj* entendido; **~ly** *adv* a sabiendas.
knowledge *n* conocimiento *m*.

knowledgeable *adj* bien informado.
knuckle *n* nudillo *m*.

L

label *n* etiqueta *f*.
labor *n* trabajo *m*; **to be in ~** estar de parto; ● *vt* trabajar.
laboratory *n* laboratorio *m*.
laborer *n* peón *m*.
laborious *adj* laborioso; difícil; **~ly** *adv* laboriosamente.
labor union *n* sindicato *m*.
labyrinth *n* laberinto *m*.
lace *n* cordón; encaje *m*; ● *vt* abrochar.
lacerate *vt* lacerar.
lack *vt, vi* faltar algo; ● *n* falta *f*.
lackadaisical *adj* descuidado.
lackey *n* lacayo *m*.
laconic *adj* lacónico.
lacquer *n* laca *f*.
lad *n* muchacho *m*.
ladder *n* escalera *f*.
ladle *n* cucharón *m*.
ladleful *n* chucharada *f*.
lady *n* señora *f*.
ladybug *n* mariquita *f*.
ladykiller *n* ladrón de corazones *m*.
ladylike *adj* fino.
ladyship *n* señoría *f*.
lag *vi* quedarse atrás.
lager *n* cerveza (rubia) *f*.
lagoon *n* laguna *f*.
laidback *adj* relajado.
lair *n* guarida *f*.
laity *n* laicado *m*.
lake *n* lago *m*; laguna *f*.
lamb *n* cordero *m*; ● *vi* parir.
lambswool *n* lana de cordero *f*.
lame *adj* cojo.
lament *vt, vi* lamentar(se); ● *n* lamento *m*.
lamentable *adj* lamentable, deplorable.
lamentation *n* lamentación *f*.
laminated *adj* laminado.
lamp *n* lámpara *f*.
lampoon *n* sátira *f*.
lampshade *n* pantalla *f*.
lance *n* lanza *f*; ● *vt* hacer una operación quirúrgica con lanceta.
lancet *n* lanceta *f*.
land *n* país *m*; tierra *f*; ● *vt, vi* desembarcar.
land forces *npl* tropas de tierra *fpl*.
landholder *n* hacendado *m*.
landing *n* desembarco *m*.
landing strip *n* pista de aterrizaje *f*.
landlady *n* propietaria *f*.
landlord *n* propietario *m*.
landlubber *n* marinero de agua dulce *m*.
landmark *n* lugar conocido *m*.
landowner *n* terrateniente *m*.
landscape *n* paisaje *m*.
landslide *n* corrimiento de un terreno *m*.
lane *n* callejuela *f*.
language *n* lengua *f*; lenguaje *m*.
languid *adj* lánguido, débil; **~ly** *adv* lánguidamente, débilmente.
languish *vi* languidecer.
lank *adj* lacio.
lanky *adj* alto y delgado.
lantern *n* linterna *f*; farol *m*.
lap *n* regazo *m*; ● *vt* lamer.
lapdog *n* perro de faldas *m*.

lapel *n* solapa *f.*
lapse *n* lapso *m;* ● *vi* transcurrir.
larceny *n* latrocinio *m.*
larch *n* alerce *m.*
lard *n* manteca de cerdo *f.*
larder *n* despensa *f.*
large *adj* grande; **at ~** en libertad; **~ly** *adv* en gran parte.
large-scale *adj* en gran escala.
largesse *n* liberalidad *f.*
lark *n* alondra *f.*
larva *n* larva, oruga *f.*
laryngitis *n* laringitis *f.*
larynx *n* laringe *f.*
lascivious *adj* lascivo; **~ly** *adv* lascivamente.
laser *n* láser *m.*
lash *n* latigazo *m;* ● *vt* dar latigazos; atar.
lasso *n* lazo *m.*
last *adj* último; pasado; **at ~** por fin; **~ly** *adv* finalmente; ● *n* horma de zapatero *f;* ● *vi* durar.
last ditch *adj* último.
lasting *adj* duradero, permanente; **~ly** *adv* perpetuamente.
last-minute *adj* de última hora.
latch *n* picaporte *m.*
latch-key *n* llave maestra *f.*
late *adj* tarde; difunto; *(rail)* **the train is ten minutes ~** el tren tiene un retraso de diez minutos; ● *adv* tarde; **~ly** *adv* recientemente.
latecomer *n* recién llegado *m.*
latent *adj* latente.
lateral *adj* **~ly** *adv* lateral(mente).
lathe *n* torno *m.*
lather *n* espuma *f.*
latitude *n* latitud *f.*
latrine *n* letrina *f.*
latter *adj* último; **~ly** *adv* últimamente, recientemente.
lattice *n* celosía *f.*
laudable *adj* loable.
laudably *adv* loablemente.
laugh *vi* reír; **to ~ at** *vt* reírse de; ● *n* risa *f.*
laughable *adj* absurdo.
laughing stock *n* hazmerreír *m.*
laughter *n* risa *f.*
launch *vt, vi* lanzar(se); ● *n (mar)* lancha *f.*
launching *n* lanzamiento *m.*
launching pad *n* plataforma de lanzamiento *f.*
launder *vt* lavar.
laundromat *n* lavandería automática *f.*
laundry *n* lavandería *f.*
laurel *n* laurel *m.*
lava *n* lava *f.*
lavatory *n* wáter *m.*
lavender *n (bot)* espliego *m,* lavándula *f.*
lavish *adj* pródigo; **~ly** *adv* pródigamente; ● *vt* disipar.
law *n* ley *f;* derecho *m.*
law-abiding *adj* respectuoso de la ley.
law and order *n* orden público *m.*
law court *n* tribunal *m.*
lawful *adj* legal; legítimo; **~ly** *adv* legalmente.
lawless *adj* anárquico.
lawlessness *n* anarquía *f.*
lawmaker *n* legislador *m.*
lawn *n* pasto *m.*
lawnmower *n* cortacésped *m.*
law school *n* facultad de derecho *f.*
law suit *n* proceso *m.*
lawyer *n* abogado *m.*
lax *adj* laxo; flojo.
laxative *n* laxante *m.*
laxity *n* laxitud *f;* flojedad *f.*
lay *vt* poner; **to ~ claim** reclamar; pretender; ● *vi* poner.
layabout *n* vago *m.*
layer *n* capa *f.*

layette *n* ajuar de niño *m.*
layman *n* lego, seglar *m.*
layout *n* composición *f.*
laze *vi* holgazanear.
lazily *adv* perezosamente; lentamente.
laziness *n* pereza *f.*
lazy *adj* perezoso.
lead *n* plomo *m;* ● *vt* conducir, guiar; ● *vi* mandar.
leader *n* jefe *m.*
leadership *n* dirección *f.*
leading *adj* principal; capital; **~ article** *n* artículo de fondo *m.*
leaf *n* hoja *f.*
leaflet *n* folleto *m.*
leafy *adj* frondoso.
league *n* liga, alianza *f;* legua *f.*
leak *n* escape *m;* ● *vi (mar)* hacer agua.
leaky *adj* agujereado.
lean *vt, vi* apoyar(se); ● *adj* magro.
leap *vi* saltar; ● *n* salto *m.*
leapfrog *n* pídola *f.*
leap year *n* año bisiesto *m.*
learn *vt, vi* aprender.
learned *adj* docto.
learner *n* aprendiz *m.*
learning *n* erudición *f.*
lease *n* arriendo *m;* ● *vt* arrendar.
leasehold *n* arriendo *m.*
leash *n* correa *f.*
least *adj* mínimo; **at ~** por lo menos; **not in the ~** en absoluto.
leather *n* cuero *m.*
leathery *adj* correoso.
leave *n* licencia *f;* permiso *m;* **to take ~** despedirse; ● *vt* dejar, abandonar.
leaven *n* levadura *f;* ● *vt* fermentar.
leavings *npl* sobras *fpl.*
lecherous *adj* lascivo.
lecture *n* conferencia *f;* ● *vt* dar una conferencia.
lecturer *n* conferenciante *m.*
ledge *n* reborde *m.*
ledger *n (com)* libro mayor *m.*
lee *n (mar)* sotavento *m.*
leech *n* sanguijuela *f.*
leek *n (bot)* puerro *m.*
leer *vt* mirar de manera lasciva.
lees *npl* sedimento, poso *m.*
leeward *adj (mar)* sotavento.
leeway *n* libertad de acción *f.*
left *adj* izquierdo; **on the ~** a la izquierda.
left-handed *adj* zurdo.
leftovers *npl* sobras *fpl.*
leg *n* pierna *f;* pie *m.*
legacy *n* herencia *f.*
legal *adj* legal, legítimo; **~ly** *adv* legalmente.
legal holiday *n* fiesta oficial *f.*
legality *n* legalidad, legitimidad *f.*
legalize *vt* legalizar.
legal tender *n* moneda de curso legal *f.*
legate *n* legado *m.*
legatee *n* legado *m.*
legation *n* legación *f.*
legend *n* leyenda *f.*
legendary *adj* legendario.
legible *adj* legible.
legibly *adv* legiblemente.
legion *n* legión *f.*
legislate *vt* legislar.
legislation *n* legislación *f.*
legislative *adj* legislativo.
legislator *n* legislador *m.*
legislature *n* cuerpo legislativo *m.*
legitimacy *n* legitimidad *f.*

legitimate *adj* legítimo; ~**ly** *adv* legítimamente; • *vt* legitimar.
leisure *n* ocio *m*; ~**ly** *adj* sin prisa; **at** ~ desocupado.
lemon *n* limón *m*.
lemonade *n* limonada *f*.
lemon tea *n* té con limón *m*.
lemon tree *n* limonero *m*.
lend *vt* prestar.
length *n* largo *m*; duración *f*; **at** ~ finalmente.
lengthen *vt* alargar; • *vi* alargarse.
lengthways, lengthwise *adv* a lo largo.
lengthy *adj* largo.
lenient *adj* indulgente.
lens *n* lente *f*.
Lent *n* Cuaresma *f*.
lentil *n* lenteja *f*.
leopard *n* leopardo *m*.
leotard *n* leotardo *m*.
leper *n* leproso *m*.
leprosy *n* lepra *f*.
lesbian *n* lesbiana *f*.
less *adj* menor; • *adv* menos.
lessen *vt* disminuir; • *vi* disminuirse.
lesser *adj* más pequeño.
lesson *n* lección *f*.
lest *conj* para que no.
let *vt* dejar, permitir; alquilar.
lethal *adj* mortal.
lethargic *adj* letárgico.
lethargy *n* letargo *m*.
letter *n* letra *f*; carta *f*.
letter bomb *n* carta-bomba *f*.
lettering *n* letras *fpl*.
letter of credit *n* carta de crédito *f*.
lettuce *n* lechuga *f*.
leukemia *n* leucemia *f*.
level *adj* llano, igual; nivelado; • *n* nivel *m*; • *vt* allanar; nivelar.
level-headed *adj* sensato.
lever *n* palanca *f*.
leverage *n* influencia *f*.
levity *n* ligereza *f*.
levy *n* leva (de tropas) *f*; • *vt* recaudar.
lewd *adj* obsceno.
lexicon *n* diccionario *m*.
liability *n* responsabilidad *f*.
liable *adj* sujeto; responsable.
liaise *vi* enlazar.
liaison *n* enlace *m*.
liar *n* embustero *m*.
libel *n* difamación *f*; • *vt* difamar.
libelous *adj* difamatorio.
liberal *adj* liberal, generoso; ~**ly** *adv* liberalmente.
liberality *n* liberalidad, generosidad *f*.
liberate *vt* libertar.
liberation *n* liberación *f*.
libertine *n* libertino *m*.
liberty *n* libertad *f*.
Libra *n* Libra *f*.
librarian *n* bibliotecario *m*.
library *n* biblioteca *f*.
libretto *n* libreto *m*.
license *n* licencia *f*; permiso *m*.
license plate *n* placa de matrícula *f*.
licentious *adj* licencioso.
lichen *n* (*bot*) liquen *m*.
lick *vt* lamer.
lid *n* tapa *f*.
lie *n* mentira *f*; • *vi* mentir; echarse.
lieu *n*: **in** ~ **of** en vez de.
lieutenant *n* lugarteniente *m*.
life *n* vida *f*; **for** ~ por toda la vida.

lifeboat *n* lancha de socorro *f*.
life-guard *n* guardia de corps *f*.
life jacket *n* chaleco salvavidas *m*.
lifeless *adj* muerto; sin vida.
lifelike *adj* natural.
lifeline *n* cordón umbilical *m*.
life preserver *n* macana *f*.
life sentence *n* cadena perpetua *f*.
life-sized *adj* de tamaño natural.
lifespan *n* vida *f*.
lifestyle *n* estilo de vida *f*.
life support system *n* sistema de respiración asistida *m*.
lifetime *n* vida *f*.
lift *vt* levantar.
ligament *n* ligamento *m*.
light *n* luz *f*; • *adj* ligero; claro; • *vt* encender; alumbrar.
light bulb *n* foco *m*; bombilla *f*.
lighten *vi* relampaguear; • *vt* iluminar; aligerar.
lighter *n* encendedor *m*.
light-headed *adj* mareado.
lighthearted *adj* alegre.
lighthouse *n* (*mar*) faro *m*.
lighting *n* iluminación *f*.
lightly *adv* ligeramente.
lightning *n* relámpago *m*.
lightning-rod *n* pararrayos *m*.
light pen *n* lápiz optico *m*.
lightweight *adj* ligero.
light year *n* año luz *m*.
ligneous *adj* leñoso.
like *adj* semejante; igual; • *adv* como, del mismo modo que; • *vt*, *vi* gustar.
likeable *adj* simpático.
likelihood *n* probabilidad *f*.
likely *adj* probable, verosímil.
liken *vt* comparar.
likeness *n* semejanza *f*.
likewise *adv* igualmente.
liking *n* agrado *m*.
lilac *n* lila *f*.
lily *n* lirio *m*; ~ **of the valley** lirio de los valles.
limb *n* miembro *m*.
limber *adj* flexible.
lime *n* cal *f*; lima *f*; ~ **tree** tilo *m*.
limestone *n* piedra caliza *f*.
limit *n* límite, término *m*; • *vt* restringir.
limitation *n* limitación *f*; restricción *f*.
limitless *adj* inmenso.
limo(usine) *n* limusina *f*.
limp *vi* cojear; • *n* cojera *f*; • *adj* flojo.
limpet *n* lapa *f*.
limpid *adj* claro, transparente.
line *n* línea *f*; raya *f*; • *vt* forrar; revestir.
lineage *n* linaje *m*.
linear *adj* lineal.
lined *adj* rayado; arrugado.
linen *n* lino *m*.
liner *n* transatlántico *m*.
linesman *n* juez de línea *m*.
linger *vi* persistir.
lingerie *n* ropa interior *f*.
lingering *adj* lento.
linguist *n* lingüista *m*.
linguistic *adj* lingüístico.
linguistics *n* lingüística *f*.
liniment *n* linimento *m*.
lining *n* forro *m*.
link *n* eslabón *m*; • *vt* enlazar.
linnet *n* pardillo *m*.
linoleum *n* linóleo *m*.
linseed *n* linaza *f*.
lint *n* hilas *fpl*.

LOS = ARTICLE

lintel *n* dintel, tranquero *m*.
lion *n* león *m*.
lioness *n* leona *f*.
lip *n* labio *m*; borde *m*.
lip read *vi* leer los labios.
lip salve *n* crema protectora para labios *f*.
lipstick *n* lápiz de labios *m*.
liqueur *n* aguardiente *m*.
liquid *adj* líquido; • *n* líquido *m*.
liquidate *vt* liquidar.
liquidation *n* liquidación *f*.
liquidize *vt* licuar.
liquor *n* licor *m*.
liquorice *n* orozuz *m*; regalicia *f*.
liquor store *n* bodega *f*.
lisp *vi* cecear; • *n* ceceo *m*.
list *n* lista *f*; • *vt* hacer una lista de.
listen *vi* escuchar.
listless *adj* indiferente.
litany *n* letanía *f*.
liter *n* litro *m*.
literal *adj* ~ly *adv* literal(mente).
literary *adj* literario.
literate *adj* culto.
literature *n* literatura *f*.
lithe *adj* ágil.
lithograph *n* litografía *f*.
lithography *n* litografía *f*.
litigation *n* litigio *m*.
litigious *adj* litigioso.
litter *n* litera *f*; camada *f*; • *vt* parir.
little *adj* pequeño, poco; by ~ poco a poco; • *n* poco *m*.
liturgy *n* liturgia *f*.
live *vi* vivir; habitar; to ~ on alimentarse de; to ~ up to *vt* cumplir con; • *adj* vivo.
livelihood *n* vida *f*.
liveliness *n* vivacidad *f*.
lively *adj* vivo.
liven up *vt* animar.
liver *n* hígado *m*.
livery *n* librea *f*.
livestock *n* ganado *m*.
livid *adj* lívido, cárdeno.
living *n* vida *f*; • *adj* vivo.
living room *n* sala de estar *f*.
lizard *n* lagarto *m*.
load *vt* cargar; • *n* carga *f*.
loaded *adj* cargado.
loaf *n* pan *m*.
loafer *n* holgazán, gandul *m*.
loam *n* marga *f*.
loan *n* préstamo *m*.
loathe *vt* aborrecer; tener hastío; • *vi* fastidiar.
loathing *n* aversión *f*.
loathsome *adj* asqueroso.
lobby *n* vestíbulo *m*.
lobe *n* lóbulo *m*.
lobster *n* langosta *f*.
local *adj* local.
local anesthetic *n* anestesia local *f*.
local government *n* gobierno municipal *m*.
locality *n* localidad *f*.
localize *vt* localizar.
locally *adv* en la vecindad.
locate *vt* localizar.
location *n* situación *f*.
loch *n* lago *m*.
lock *n* cerradura *f*; • *vt* cerrar con llave.
locker *n* vestuario *m*.
locket *n* medallón *m*.
lockout *n* paro patronal *m*.
locksmith *n* cerrajero *m*.

lock-up *n* cochera *f*.
locomotive *n* locomotora *f*.
locust *n* langosta *f*.
lodge *n* casa del guarda *f*; • *vi* alojarse.
lodger *n* inquilino *m*.
loft *n* desván *m*.
lofty *adj* alto.
log *n* leño *m*.
logbook *n* (*mar*) diario de a bordo *m*.
logic *n* lógica *f*.
logical *adj* lógico.
logo *n* logotipo *m*.
loin *n* lomo *m*.
loiter *vi* merodear.
loll *vi* repantigarse.
lollipop *n* pirulí *m*.
lonely, lonesome *adj* solitario; solo.
loneliness *n* soledad *f*.
long *adj* largo; • *vi* anhelar.
long-distance *n*: ~ **call** llamada interurbana *f*.
longevity *n* longevidad *f*.
long-haired *adj* de pelo largo.
longing *n* anhelo *m*.
longitude *n* longitud *f*.
longitudinal *adj* longitudinal.
long jump *n* salto de longitud *m*.
long-playing record *n* elepé *m*.
long-range *adj* de gran alcance.
long-term *adj* a largo plazo.
long wave *n* onda larga *f*.
long-winded *adj* prolijo.
look *vi* mirar; parecer; to ~ **after** *vt* cuidar; to ~ **for** *vt* buscar; to ~ **forward to** *vt* esperar con impaciencia; to ~ **out for** *vt* aguardar; • *n* aspecto *m*; mirada *f*.
looking glass *n* espejo *m*.
look-out *n* (*mil*) centinela *f*; vigía *f*.
loom *n* telar *m*; • *vi* amenazar.
loop *n* lazo *m*.
loophole *n* escapatoria *f*.
loose *adj* suelto; flojo; ~ly *adv* aproximadamente; ~, **loosen** *vt* aflojar.
loot *vt* saquear; • *n* botín *m*.
lop *vt* desmochar.
lop-sided *adj* desequilibrado.
loquacious *adj* locuaz.
loquacity *n* locuacidad *f*.
lord *n* señor *m*.
lore *n* saber popular *m*.
lose *vt* perder; • *vi* perder.
loss *n* pérdida *f*; to be at a ~ no saber qué hacer.
lost and found *n* objetos perdidos *mpl*.
lot *n* suerte *f*; lote *m*; a ~ mucho.
lotion *n* loción *f*.
lottery *n* lotería, rifa *f*.
loud *adj* fuerte; ~ly *adv* fuerte.
loudspeaker *n* altavoz *m*.
lounge *n* salón *m*.
louse (*pl* **lice**) *n* piojo *m*.
lousy *adj* vil.
lout *n* gamberro *m*.
lovable *adj* amable.
love *n* amor, cariño *m*; to **fall in** ~ enamorarse; • *vt* amar; gustar.
love letter *n* carta de amor *f*.
love life *n* vida sentimental *f*.
liveliness *n* belleza *f*.
lovely *adj* hermoso.
lover *n* amante *m*.
love-sick *adj* enamorado.
loving *adj* amoroso.
low *adj* bajo; • *vi* mugir.
low-cut *adj* escotado.

lower *adj* más bajo; ● *vt* bajar.
lowest *adj* más bajo, ínfimo.
lowland *n* tierra baja *f*.
lowliness *n* humildad *f*.
lowly *adj* humilde.
low-water *n* baja mar *f*.
loyal *adj* leal; fiel; ~ly *adv* lealmente.
loyalty *n* lealdad *f*; fidelidad *f*.
lozenge *n* pastilla *f*.
lubricant *n* lubricante *m*.
lubricate *vt* lubricar.
lucid *adj* lúcido.
luck *n* suerte *f*; fortuna *f*.
luckily *adv* afortunadamente.
luckless *adj* desdichado.
lucky *adj* afortunado.
lucrative *adj* lucrativo.
ludicrous *adj* absurdo.
lug *vt* arrastrar.
luggage *n* equipaje *m*.
lugubrious *adj* lúgubre, triste.
lukewarm *adj* tibio.
lull *vt* acunar; ● *n* tregua *f*.
lullaby *n* nana *f*.
lumbago *n* lumbago *m*.
lumberjack *n* maderero *m*.
lumber room *n* trastera *f*.
luminous *adj* luminoso.
lump *n* terrón *m*; bulto *m*; chichón *m*; ● *vt* juntar.
lump sum *n* suma global *f*.
lunacy *n* locura *f*.
lunar *adj* lunar.
lunatic *adj* loco.
lunch, luncheon *n* merienda *f*.
lungs *npl* pulmones *mpl*.
lurch *n* sacudida *f*.
lure *n* señuelo *m*; cebo *m*; ● *vt* inducir.
lurid *adj* sensacional.
lurk *vi* esconderse.
luscious *adj* delicioso.
lush *adj* exuberante.
lust *n* lujuria, sensualidad *f*; concupiscencia *f*; ● *vi* lujuriar; to ~ after *vt* codiciar.
luster *n* lustre *m*.
lustful *adj* lujurioso, voluptuoso; ~ly *adv* lujuriosamente.
lustily *adv* vigorosamente.
lusty *adj* fuerte, vigoroso.
lute *n* laúd *m*; luten *m*.
Lutheran *n* luterano *m*.
luxuriance *n* exuberancia, superabundancia *f*.
luxuriant *adj* exuberante, superabundante.
luxuriate *vi* crecer con exuberancia.
luxurious *adj* lujurioso; exuberante; ~ly *adv* voluptuosamente.
luxury *n* lujuria, voluptuosidad *f*; exuberancia *f*.
lying *n* acto de mentir *m*; mentira *f*.
lymph *n* linfa *f*.
lynch *vt* ajusticiar al reo en el acto el populacho.
lynx *n* lince *m*.
lyrical *adj* lírico.
lyrics *npl* letra *f*.

M

macaroni *n* macarrones *mpl*.
macaroon *n* almendrado *m*.
mace *n* maza *f*; macis *f*.
macerate *vt* macerar; mortificar el cuerpo.
machination *n* maquinación, trama *f*.
machine *n* máquina *f*.

machine gun *n* ametralladora *f*.
machinery *n* maquinaria, mecánica *f*.
mackerel *n* escombro *m*.
mad *adj* loco, furioso, rabioso, insensato.
madam *n* madama, señora *f*.
madden *vt* enloquecer.
madder *n* (*bot*) rubia *f*.
madhouse *n* casa de locos *f*.
madly *adv* como un loco.
madman *n* loco *m*.
madness *n* locura *f*.
magazine *n* revista *f*; almacén *m*.
maggot *n* gusano *m*.
magic *n* magia *f*; ● *adj* mágico; ~ally *adv* mágicamente.
magician *n* mago *m*; prestidigitador *m*.
magisterial *adj* magistral; ~ly *adv* magistralmente.
magistracy *n* magistratura *f*.
magistrate *n* magistrado *m*.
magnanimity *n* magnanimidad *f*.
magnanimous *adj* magnánimo; ~ly *adv* magnánimamente.
magnet *n* imán *m*.
magnetic *adj* magnético.
magnetism *n* magnetismo *m*.
magnificence *n* magnificencia *f*.
magnificent *adj* magnífico; ~ly *adv*.
magnify *vt* aumentar; exagerar.
magnifying glass *n* lupa *f*.
magnitude *n* magnitud *f*.
magpie *n* urraca *f*.
mahogany *n* caoba *f*.
maid *n* criada *f*.
maiden *n* doncella *f*.
maiden name *n* nombre de soltera *m*.
mail *n* correo *m*.
mailbox *n* buzón *m*.
mail coach *n* diligencia *f*.
mailing list *n* lista de direcciones *f*.
mail-order *n* venta por correo *f*.
mail train *n* (*rail*) tren correo *m*.
maim *vt* mutilar.
main *adj* principal; esencial; in the ~ en general.
mainland *n* continente *m*.
main-line *n* (*rail*) línea principal *f*.
mainly *adv* principalmente.
main street *n* calle mayor *f*.
maintain *vt* mantener; sostener.
maintenance *n* mantenimiento *m*.
maize *n* maíz *m*.
majestic *adj* majestuoso; ~ally *adv* majestuosamente.
majesty *n* majestad *f*.
major *adj* principal; ● *n* (*mil*) comandante *m*.
majority *n* mayoría *f*.
make *vt* hacer, crear; to ~ for dirigirse a; to ~ up inventar; to ~ up for compensar; ● *n* marca *f*.
make-believe *n* invención *f*.
makeshift *adj* improvisado.
make-up *n* maquillaje *m*.
make-up remover *n* desmaquillador *m*.
malady *n* enfermedad *f*.
malaise *n* malestar *m*.
malaria *n* malaria *f*.
malcontent *adj*, *n* malcontento *m*.
male *adj* masculino; ● *n* macho *m*.
malevolence *n* malevolencia *f*.
malevolent *adj* malévolo; ~ly *adv* malignamente.
malfunction *n* mal funcionamiento *m*.
malice *n* malicia *f*.
malicious *adj* malicioso; ~ly *adv* maliciosamente.
malign *adj* maligno; ● *vt* calumniar.
malignant *adj* maligno; ~ly *adv* malignamente.
mall *n* centro comercial *m*.
malleable *adj* maleable.

mallet *n* mazo *m*.
mallows *n* (*bot*) malva *f*.
malnutrition *n* desnutrición *f*.
malpractice *n* negligencia *f*.
malt *n* malta *f*.
maltreat *vt* maltratar.
mammal *n* mamífero *m*.
mammoth *adj* gigantesco.
man *n* hombre *m*; ● *vt* (*mar*) tripular.
manacle *n* manilla *f*; ~s *pl* esposas *fpl*.
manage *vt*, *vi* manejar, dirigir.
manageable *adj* manejable.
management *n* dirección *f*.
manager *n* director *m*.
manageress *n* directora *f*.
managerial *adj* directivo.
managing director *n* director general *m*.
mandarin *n* mandarina *f*.
mandate *n* mandato *m*.
mandatory *n* obligatorio.
mane *n* crines del caballo *fpl*.
maneuver *n* maniobra *f*.
manfully *adv* valerosamente.
manger *n* pesebre *m*.
mangle *n* rodillo *m*; ● *vt* mutilar.
mangy *adj* sarnoso.
manhandle *vt* maltratar.
manhood *n* edad viril *f*.
man-hour *n* hora hombre *f*.
mania *n* manía *f*.
maniac *n* maníaco *m*.
manic *adj* frenético.
manicure *n* manicura *f*.
manifest *adj* manifiesto, patente; ● *vt* manifestar.
manifestation *n* manifestación *f*.
manifesto *n* manifiesto *m*.
manipulate *vt* manejar.
manipulation *n* manipulación *f*.
mankind *n* género humano *m*.
manlike *adj* varonil.
manliness *n* valentía *f*; valor *m*.
manly *adj* varonil.
man-made *n* artificial.
manner *n* manera *f*; modo *m*; forma *f*; ~s *pl* modales *mpl*.
manpower *n* mano de obra *f*.
mansion *n* palacio *m*.
manslaughter *n* homicidio (sin premeditación) *m*.
mantelpiece *n* repisa de chimenea *f*.
manual *adj*, *n* manual *m*.
manufacture *n* fabricación *f*; ● *vt* fabricar.
manufacturer *n* fabricante *m*.
manure *n* abono *m*; estiércol *m*; fiemo *m*; ● *vt* abonar.
manuscript *n* manuscrito *m*.
many *adj* muchos, muchas; ~ a time muchas veces; how ~?
¿cuántos? as ~ as tantos como.
map *n* mapa *m*; ● *vt* planear, trazar el mapa de; to ~ out
proyectar.
maple *n* arce *m*.
mar *vt* estropear.
marathon *n* maratón *m*.
marauder *n* merodeador *m*.
marble *n* mármol *m*; ● *adj* marmóreo.
March *n* marzo *m*.
march *n* marcha *f*; ● *vi* marchar.
marchpast *n* desfile *m*.
mare *n* yegua *f*.
margarine *n* margarina *f*.
margin *n* margen *m*; borde *m*.
marginal *adj* marginal.
marigold *n* (*bot*) caléndula *f*.
marijuana *n* marijuana *f*.
marinate *vt* adobar.

marine *adj* marino; ● *n* soldado de marina *m*.
mariner *n* marinero *m*.
marital *adj* marital.
maritime *adj* marítimo.
marjoram *n* mejorana *f*.
mark *n* marca *f*; señal *f*; ● *vt* marcar.
marker *n* registro *m*.
market *n* mercado *m*.
marketable *adj* vendible.
marketing *n* márketing *m*.
marketplace *n* mercado *m*.
market research *n* análisis de mercados *m*.
market value *n* valor en el mercado *m*.
marksman *n* tirador *m*.
marmalade *n* mermelada de naranja *f*.
maroon *adj* marrón.
marquee *n* entoldado *m*.
marriage *n* matrimonio *m*; casamiento *m*.
marriageable *adj* casadero.
marriage certificate *n* partida de casamiento *f*.
married *adj* casado; conyugal.
marrow *n* médula *f*.
marry *vi* casar(se).
marsh *n* pantano *m*.
marshal *n* mariscal *m*.
marshy *adj* pantanoso.
marten *n* marta *f*.
martial *adj* marcial; ~ law *n* ley marcial *f*.
martyr *n* mártir *m*.
martyrdom *n* martirio *m*.
marvel *n* maravilla *f*; ● *vi* maravillar(se).
marvelous *adj* maravilloso; ~ly *adv* maravillosamente.
marzipan *n* mazapán *m*.
máscara *n* rímel *m*.
masculine *adj* masculino, varonil.
mash *n* mezcla *f*.
mask *n* máscara *f*; ● *vt* enmascarar.
masochist *n* masoquista *m*.
mason *n* albañil *m*.
masonry *n* mampostería *f*.
masquerade *n* mascarada *f*.
mass *n* masa *f*; misa *f*; montón *m*.
massacre *n* carnicería, matanza *f*; ● *vt* hacer una carnicería.
massage *n* masaje *m*.
masseur *n* masajista *m*.
masseuse *n* masajista *f*.
massive *adj* enorme.
mass-media *npl* medios de comunicación masiva *mpl*.
mast *n* mástil *m*.
master *n* amo, dueño *m*; maestro *m*; ● *vt* dominar.
masterly *adj* magistral.
mastermind *vt* dirigir.
masterpiece *n* obra maestra *f*.
mastery *n* maestría *f*.
masticate *vt* masticar.
mastiff *n* mastín *m*.
mat *n* estera *f*; felpudo *m*.
match *n* fósforo *m*, cerilla *f*; partido *m*; ● *vt* igualar; ● *vi* hacer
juego.
matchbox *n* caja de fósforos *f*.
matchless *adj* incomparable, sin par.
matchmaker *n* casamentero *m*.
mate *n* compañero *m*; ● *vt* acoplar.
material *adj* ~ly *adv* material(mente).
materialism *n* materialismo *m*.
maternal *adj* maternal.
maternity dress *n* vestido premamá *m*.
maternity hospital *n* hospital de maternidad *m*.
math *n* = mathematics.
mathematical *adj* matemático; ~ly *adv* matemáticamente.
mathematician *n* matemático *m*.
mathematics *npl* matemáticas *fpl*.

matinée n función de la tarde f.
mating n aparejamiento m.
matins npl maitines mpl.
matriculate vt matricular.
matriculation n matriculación f.
matrimonial adj matrimonial.
mat(t) adj mate.
matted adj enmarañado.
matter n materia, substancia f; asunto m; cuestión f; **what is the ~?** ¿qué pasa? **a ~ of fact** un hecho; ● vi importar.
mattress n colchón m.
mature adj maduro; ● vt madurar.
maturity n madurez f.
maul vt magullar.
mausoleum n mausoleo m.
mauve adj de color malva.
maxim n máxima f.
maximum n máximo m.
may vi poder; **~ be** acaso, quizá.
May n mayo m.
Mayday n primero de mayo m.
mayonnaise n mayonesa f.
mayor n alcalde m.
mayoress n alcaldesa f.
maze n laberinto m.
me pn me; mí.
meadow n pradera f; prado m.
meager adj pobre.
meagerness n escasez f.
meal n comida f; harina f.
mealtime n hora de comer f.
mean adj tacaño; **in the ~time, ~while** mientras tanto; **~s** npl medios mpl; ● vt, vi significar.
meander vi serpentear.
meaning n sentido, significado m.
meaningful adj significativo.
meaningless adj sin sentido.
meanness n tacañería f.
meantime, meanwhile adv mientras tanto.
measles npl sarampión m.
measure n medida f; (mus) compás m; ● vt medir.
measurement n medida f.
meat n carne f.
meatball n albóndiga f.
meaty adj sustancioso.
mechanic n mecánico m.
mechanical adj mecánico; **~ly** adv mecánicamente.
mechanics npl mecánica f.
mechanism n mecanismo m.
medal n medalla f.
medalist n medallero m.
medallion n medallón m.
meddle vi entrometerse.
meddler n entrometido m.
media npl medios de comunicación mpl.
median (strip) n mediana f.
mediate vi mediar.
mediation n mediación, interposición f.
mediator n intermediario m.
medical adj médico.
medicate vt medicinar.
medicated adj medicinal.
medicinal adj medicinal.
medicine n medicina f, medicamento m.
medieval adj medieval.
mediocre adj mediocre.
mediocrity n mediocridad f.
meditate vi meditar.
meditation n meditación f.
meditative adj contemplativo.
Mediterranean adj mediterráneo.
medium n medio m; ● adj mediano.

medium wave n onda media f.
medley n mezcla m.
meek adj manso; **~ly** adv mansamente.
meekness n mansedumbre f.
meet vt encontrar; **to ~ with** reunirse con; ● vi encontrarse; juntarse.
meeting n reunión f; congreso m.
megaphone n megáfono m.
melancholy n melancolía f; ● adj melancólico.
mellow adj maduro; suave; ● vi madurar.
mellowness n madurez f.
melodious adj melodioso; **~ly** adv melodiosamente.
melody n melodía f.
melon n melón m.
melt vt derretir; ● vi derretirse.
melting point n punto de fusión m.
member n miembro m.
membership n número de miembros m.
membrane n membrana f.
memento n memento m.
memo n memorándum m.
memoir n memoria f.
memorable adj memorable.
memorandum n memorándum m.
memorial n monumento conmemorativo m.
memorize vt aprender de memoria.
memory n memoria f; recuerdo m.
menace n amenaza f; ● vt amenazar.
menacing adj amenazador.
menagerie n casa de fieras f.
mend vt reparar.
mending n reparación f.
menial adj doméstico.
meningitis n meningitis f.
menopause n menopausia f.
menstruation n menstruación f.
mental adj mental, intelectual.
mentality n mentalidad f.
mentally adv mentalmente, intelectualmente.
mention n mención f; ● vt mencionar.
mentor n mentor m.
menu n menú m; carta f.
mercantile adj mercantil.
mercenary adj, n mercenario m.
merchandise n mercancía f.
merchant n comerciante m.
merchantman n navío mercantil m.
merchant marine n marina mercante f.
merciful adj compasivo.
merciless adj despiadado; **~ly** adv despiadadamente.
mercury n mercurio m.
mercy n compasión f.
mere adj mero; **~ly** adv simplemente.
merge vt fundir.
merger n fusión f.
meridian n meridiano m.
meringue n merengue m.
merit n mérito m; ● vt merecer.
meritorious adj meritorio.
mermaid n sirena f.
merrily adv alegremente.
merriment n diversión f; regocijo m.
merry adj alegre.
merry-go-round n tiovivo m.
mesh n malla f.
mesmerize vt hipnotizar.
mess n lío m; (mil) comedor m; **to ~ up** vt desordenar.
message n mensaje m.
messenger n mensajero m.
metabolism n metabolismo n.
metal n metal m.
metallic adj metálico.

metallurgy *n* metalurgia *f.*
metamorphosis *n* metamorfosis *f.*
metaphor *n* metáfora *f.*
metaphoric(al) *adj* metafórico.
metaphysical *adj* metafísico.
metaphysics *npl* metafísica *f.*
mete (out) *vt* imponer.
meteor *n* meteoro *m.*
meteorological *adj* meteorológico.
meteorology *n* meteorología *f.*
meter *n* medidor *m*; metro *m.*
method *n* método *m.*
methodical *adj* metódico; ~ly *adv* metódicamente.
Methodist *n* metodista *m.*
metric *adj* métrico.
metropolis *n* metrópoli *f.*
metropolitan *adj* metropolitano.
mettle *n* valor *m.*
mettlesome *adj* brioso.
mew *vi* maullar.
mezzanine *n* entresuelo *m.*
microbe *n* microbio *m.*
microphone *n* micrófono *m.*
microchip *n* microplaqueta *f.*
microscope *n* microscopio *m.*
microscopic *adj* microscópico.
microwave *n* horno microondas *m.*
mid *adj* medio.
mid-day *n* mediodía *m.*
middle *adj* medio; ● *n* medio, centro *m.*
middle name *n* segundo nombre *m.*
middleweight *n* peso medio *m.*
middling *adj* mediano.
midge *n* mosca *f.*
midget enano *m.*
midnight *n* medianoche *f.*
midriff *n* diafragma *m.*
midst *n* medio, centro *m.*
midsummer *n* pleno verano *m.*
midway *adv* a medio camino.
midwife *n* partera *f.*
midwifery *n* obstetricia *f.*
might *n* poder *m*; fuerza *f.*
mighty *adj* fuerte.
migraine *n* jaqueca *f.*
migrate *vi* emigrar.
migration *n* emigración *f.*
migratory *adj* migratorio.
mike *n* micrófono *m.*
mild *adj* apacible; suave; ~ly *adv* suavemente.
mildew *n* moho *m.*
mildness *n* dulzura *f.*
mile *n* milla *f.*
mileage *n* kilometraje *m.*
milieu *n* ambiente *m.*
militant *adj* militante.
military *adj* militar.
militate *vi* militar.
militia *n* milicia *f.*
milk *n* leche *f*; ● *vt* ordeñar.
milkshake *n* batido *m*, malteada *f.*
milky *adj* lechoso; M~ Way *n* Vía Láctea *f.*
mill *n* molino *m*; ● *vt* moler.
millennium *n* milenio *m.*
miller *n* molinero *m.*
millet *n* (*bot*) mijo *m.*
milligram *n* miligramo *m.*
milliliter *n* mililitro *m.*
millimeter *n* milímetro *m.*
milliner *n* sombrerero.
millinery *n* sombrerería *f.*
million *n* millón *m.*

millionaire *n* millonario *m.*
millionth *adj*, *n* millonésimo.
millstone *n* piedra de molino *f.*
mime *n* mimo *m.*
mimic *vt* imitar.
mimicry *n* mímica *f.*
mince *vt* picar.
mind *n* mente *f*; ● *vt* cuidar; ● *vi* molestar.
minded *adj* dispuesto.
mindful *adj* consciente.
mindless *adj* sin motivo.
mine *pn* mío, mía, mi; ● *n* mina; ● *vi* minar.
minefield *n* campo de minas *m.*
miner *n* minero *m.*
mineral *adj*, *n* mineral *m.*
mineralogy *n* mineralogía *f.*
mineral water *n* agua mineral *f.*
minesweeper *n* dragaminas *m.*
mingle *vt* mezclar.
miniature *n* miniatura *f.*
minimal *adj* mínimo.
minimize *vt* minimizar.
minimum *n* mínimum *m.*
mining *n* explotación minera *f.*
minion *n* favorito *m.*
minister *n* ministro *m*; ● *vt* servir.
ministerial *adj* ministerial.
ministry *n* ministerio *m.*
mink *n* visón *m.*
minnow *n* vario *m* (pez).
minor *adj* menor; ● *n* menor (de edad) *m.*
minority *n* minoría *f.*
minstrel *n* juglar *m.*
mint *n* (*bot*) menta *f*; casa de la moneda *f*; ● *vt* acuñar.
minus *adv* menos.
minute *adj* diminuto; ~ly *adv* minuciosamente.
minute *n* minuto *m.*
miracle *n* milagro *m.*
miraculous *adj* milagroso.
mirage *n* espejismo *m.*
mire *n* fango *m.*
mirky *adj* turbio.
mirror *n* espejo *m.*
mirth *n* alegría *f.*
mirthful *adj* alegre.
misadventure *n* desgracia *f.*
misanthropist *n* misántropo *m.*
misapply *vt* aplicar mal.
misapprehension *n* error *m.*
misbehave *vi* portarse mal.
misbehavior *n* mala conducta *f.*
miscalculate *vt* calcular mal.
miscarriage *n* aborto *m.*
miscarry *vi* abortar; malograrse.
miscellaneous *adj* varios, varias.
miscellany *n* miscelánea *f.*
mischief *n* mal, daño *m.*
mischievous *adj* dañoso; travieso.
misconception *n* equivocación *f.*
misconduct *n* mala conducta *f.*
misconstrue *vt* interpretar mal.
miscount *vt* contar mal.
miscreant *n* malvado *m.*
misdeed *n* delito *m.*
misdemeanor *n* delito *m.*
misdirect *vt* dirigir mal.
miser *n* avaro *m.*
miserable *adj* miserable, infeliz.
miserly *adj* mezquino, tacaño.
misery *n* miseria *f.*
misfit *n* inadaptado *m.*
misfortune *n* desgracia *f.*

misgiving n recelo m; presentimiento m.
misgovern vt gobernar mal.
misguided adj equivocado.
mishandle vt manejar mal.
mishap n desgracia f.
misinform vt informar mal.
misinterpret vt interpretar mal.
misjudge vi juzgar mal.
mislay vt extraviar.
mislead vt engañar.
mismanage vt manejar mal.
mismanagement n mala administración f.
misnomer n nombre inapropiado m.
misogynist n misógino m.
misplace vt extraviar.
misprint vt imprimir mal; • n errata f.
misrepresent vt representar mal.
Miss n señorita f.
miss vt perder; echar de menos.
missal n misal m.
misshape n, adj deforme.
missile n mísil m.
missing adj perdido; ausente.
mission n misión f.
missionary n misionero m.
misspent adj disipado.
mist n niebla f.
mistake vt entender mal; • vi equivocarse, engañarse; to be
   mistaken equivocarse; • n equivocación f; error m.
Mister n Señor m.
mistletoe n (bot) muérdago m.
mistress n amante f.
mistrust vt desconfiar; • n desconfianza f.
mistrustful adj desconfiado.
misty adj nebuloso.
misunderstand vt entender mal.
misunderstanding n malentendido m.
misuse vt maltratar; abusar de.
miter n mitra f.
mitigate vt mitigar.
mitigation n mitigación f.
mittens npl manoplas fpl.
mix vt mezclar.
mixed adj surtido; mixto.
mixed-up adj confuso.
mixer n licuadora f.
mixture n mezcla f.
mix-up n confusión f.
moan n gemido m; • vi gemir; quejarse.
moat n foso m.
mob n multitud f.
mobile adj móvil.
mobile home n caravana f.
mobility n movilidad f.
mobilize vt (mil) movilizar.
moccasin n mocasín m.
mock vt burlarse.
mockery n mofa f.
mode n modo m.
model n modelo m; • vt modelar.
moderate adj moderado; ~ly adv medianamente; • vt
   moderar.
moderation n moderación f.
modern adj moderno.
modernize vt modernizar.
modest adj modesto; ~ly adv modestamente.
modesty n modestia f.
modicum n mínimo m.
modification n modificación f.
modify vt modificar.
modulate vt modular.
modulation n (mus) modulación f.

module n módulo m.
mogul n magnate m.
mohair n mohair m.
moist adj húmedo.
moisten vt humedecer.
moisture n humedad f.
molars npl muelas fpl.
molasses npl melaza f.
mold n molde m; moho m; • vt moldear.
molder vi decaer.
moldy adj enmohecido.
mole n topo m.
molecule n molécula f.
molehill n topera f.
molest vt importunar.
mollify vt apaciguar.
mollusk n molusco m.
mollycoddle vt mimar.
molt vt mudar la piel.
molten adj derretido.
mom n mamá f.
moment n momento m.
momentarily adv momentáneamente.
momentary adj momentáneo.
momentous adj importante.
momentum n ímpetu m.
mommy n mamá f.
monarch n monarca m.
monarchy n monarquía f.
monastery n monasterio m.
monastic adj monástico.
Monday n lunes m.
monetary adj monetario.
money n moneda f; dinero m.
money order n giro m.
mongol n mongólico m.
mongrel adj, n mestizo m.
monitor n monitor m.
monk n monje m.
monkey n mono m.
monochrome adj monocromo.
monocle n monóculo m.
monologue n monólogo m.
monopolize vt monopolizar.
monopoly n monopolio m.
monosyllable n monosílabo m.
monotonous adj monótono.
monotony n monotonía f.
monsoon n (mar) monzón m.
monster n monstruo m.
monstrosity n monstruosidad f.
monstrous adj monstruoso; ~ly adv monstruosamente.
montage n montaje m.
month n mes m.
monthly adj, adv mensual(mente).
monument n monumento m.
monumental adj monumental.
moo vi mugir.
mood n humor m.
moodiness n mal humor m.
moody adj malhumorado.
moon n luna f.
moonbeams npl rayos lunares mpl.
moonlight n luz de la luna f.
moor n páramo; • vt (mar) echar las amarras.
moorland n páramo m.
moose n alce m.
mop n fregona f; • vt fregar.
mope vi estar triste.
moped n ciclomotor m.
moral adj, ~ly adv moral(mente); ~s npl moralidad f.
morale n moral f.

moralist *n* moralista *m*.
morality *n* ética, moralidad *f*.
moralize *vt, vi* moralizar.
morass *n* pantano *m*.
morbid *adj* morboso.
more *adj, adv* más; **never** ~ nunca más; **once** ~ otra vez; ~ **and** ~ más y más, cada vez más; **so much the** ~ cuanto más.
moreover *adv* además.
morgue *n* depósito de cadáveres *m*.
morning *n* mañana *f*; **good** ~ buenos días *mpl*.
moron *n* imbécil *m*.
morose *adj* hosco.
morphine *n* morfina *f*.
morse *n* morse *m*.
morsel *n* bocado *m*.
mortal *adj* mortal; ~**ly** *adv* mortalmente; ● *n* mortal *m*.
mortality *n* mortalidad *f*.
mortar *n* mortero *m*.
mortgage *n* hipoteca *f*; ● *vt* hipotecar.
mortgage company *n* banco hipotecario *m*.
mortgager *n* deudor hipotecario *m*.
mortification *n* mortificación *f*.
mortify *vt* mortificar.
mortuary *n* depósito de cadáveres *m*.
mosaic *n* mosaico *m*.
mosque *n* mezquita *f*.
mosquito *n* mosquito *m*.
moss *n* (*bot*) musgo *m*.
mossy *adj* mohoso.
most *adj* la mayoría de; ● *adv* sumamente; **at** ~ a lo sumo; ~**ly** *adv* principalmente.
motel *n* motel *m*.
moth *n* polilla *f*.
mothball *n* bola de naftalina *f*.
mother *n* madre *f*.
motherhood *n* maternidad *f*.
mother-in-law *n* suegra *f*.
motherless *adj* sin madre.
motherly *adj* maternal.
mother-of-pearl *n* nácar *m*.
mother-to-be *n* futura madre *f*.
mother tongue *n* lengua materna *f*.
motif *n* tema *m*.
motion *n* movimiento *m*.
motionless *adj* inmóvil.
motion picture *n* película *f*.
motivated *adj* motivado.
motive *n* motivo *m*.
motley *adj* abigarrado.
motor *n* motor *m*.
motorbike *n* moto *f*.
motorboat *n* lancha motora *f*.
motorcycle *n* motocicleta *f*.
motor vehicle *n* automóvil *m*.
mottled *adj* multicolor.
motto *n* lema *m*.
mound *n* montón *m*.
mount *n* monte *m*; ● *vt* subir.
mountain *n* montaña *f*.
mountaineer *n* andinista *m*.
mountaineering *n* andinismo *m*.
mountainous *adj* montañoso.
mourn *vt* lamentar.
mourner *n* doliente *m*.
mournful *adj* triste; ~**ly** *adv* tristemente.
mourning *n* luto *m*.
mouse *n* (*pl* **mice**) ratón *m*.
mousse *n* mousse *f*.
mouth *n* boca *f*; desembocadura *f*.
mouthful *n* bocado *m*.
mouth organ *n* harmónica *f*.
mouthpiece *n* boquilla *f*.

mouthwash *n* enjuague *m*.
mouthwatering *adj* apetitoso.
movable *adj* movible.
move *vt* mover; proponer; ● *vi* moverse; ● *n* movimiento *m*.
movement *n* movimiento *m*.
movie *n* película *f*.
movie camera *n* cámara cinematográfica *f*.
moving *adj* conmovedor.
mow *vt* segar.
mower *n* cortacésped *m*; moción *f*.
Mrs *n* señora *f*.
much *adj, adv* mucho; con mucho.
muck *n* suciedad *f*.
mucous *adj* mocoso.
mucus *n* moco *m*.
mud *n* barro *m*.
muddle *vt* confundir *m*; confusión *f*.
muddy *adj* fangoso.
mudguard *n* guardabarros *m*.
muffle *vt* embozar.
mug *n* jarra *f*.
muggy *adj* bochornoso.
mulberry *n* mora *f*; ~ **tree** morera *f*.
mule *n* mulo *m*, mula *f*.
mull *vt* meditar.
multifarious *adj* múltiple.
multiple *adj* múltiplo *m*.
multiplication *n* multiplicación *f*; ~ **table** tabla de multiplicar *f*.
multiply *vt* multiplicar.
multitude *n* multitud *f*.
mumble *vt, vi* refunfuñar.
mummy *n* momia *f*.
mumps *npl* paperas *fpl*.
munch *vt* mascar.
mundane *adj* trivial.
municipal *adj* municipal.
municipality *n* municipalidad *f*.
munificence *n* munificencia *f*.
munitions *npl* municiones *fpl*.
mural *n* mural *m*.
murder *n* asesinato *m*; homicidio *m*; ● *vt* asesinar.
murderer *n* asesino *m*.
murderess *n* asesina *f*.
murderous *adj* homicida.
murky *adj* sombrío.
murmur *n* murmullo, murmurio *m*; ● *vi* murmurar.
muscle *n* músculo *m*.
muscular *adj* muscular.
muse *vi* meditar.
museum *n* museo *m*.
mushroom *n* (*bot*) seta *f*; champiñón *m*.
music *n* música *f*.
musical *adj* musical; melodioso.
musician *n* músico *m*.
musk *n* musco *m*.
muslin *n* muselina *f*.
mussel *n* marisco *m*.
must *v aux* estar obligado; ser menester, ser necesario, convenir.
mustache *n* bigote *m*.
mustard *n* mostaza *f*.
muster *vt* agregar.
musty *adj* mohoso, añejo.
mute *adj* mudo, silencioso.
muted *adj* callado.
mutilate *vt* mutilar.
mutilation *n* mutilación *f*.
mutiny *n* motín, tumulto *m*; ● *vi* amotinarse, rebelarse.
mutter *vt, vi* murmurar, musitar; ● *n* murmuración *f*.
mutton *n* carnero *m*.

mutual *adj* mutuo, mutual, recíproco; ~**ly** *adv* mutuamente, recíprocamente.
muzzle *n* bozal *m*; hocico *m*; ● *vt* embozar.
my *pn* mi, mis; mío, mía; míos, mías.
myriad *n* miriada *f*; gran número *m*.
myrrh *n* mirra *f*.
myrtle *n* mirto, arrayán *m*.
myself *pn* yo mismo.
mysterious *adj* misterioso; ~**ly** *adv* misteriosamente.
mystery *n* misterio *m*.
mystic(al) *adj* místico.
mystify *vt* dejar perplejo.
mystique *n* misterio *m*.
myth *n* mito *m*.
mythology *n* mitología *f*.

N

nab *vt* agarrar.
nag *n* jaca *f*; ● *vt* regañar.
nagging *adj* persistente; ● *npl* quejas *fpl*.
nail *n* uña *f*; garra *f*; clavo *m*; ● *vt* clavar.
nailbrush *n* cepillo para las uñas *m*.
nailfile *n* lima para las uñas *f*.
nail polish *n* esmalte para las uñas *m*.
nail scissors *npl* tijeras para las uñas *fpl*.
naïve *adj* ingenuo.
naked *adj* desnudo; evidente; puro, simple.
name *n* nombre *m*; fama, reputación *f*; ● *vt* nombrar; mencionar.
nameless *adj* anónimo.
namely *adv* a saber.
namesake *n* tocayo *m*.
nanny *n* niñera *f*.
nap *n* sueño ligero *m*.
napalm *n* nápalm *m*.
nape *n* nuca *f*.
napkin *n* servilleta *f*.
narcissus *n* (*bot*) narciso *m*.
narcotic *adj*, *n* narcótico *m*.
narrate *vt* narrar, relatar.
narrative *adj* narrativo; ● *n* narrativa *f*.
narrow *adj* angosto, estrecho; ~**ly** *adv* estrechamente; ● *vt* estrechar; limitar.
narrow-minded *adj* estrecho de miras.
nasal *adj* nasal.
nasty *adj* sucio, puerco; obsceno; sórdido.
natal *adj* nativo; natal.
nation *n* nación *f*.
national *adj*, ~**ly** *adv* nacional(mente).
nationalism *n* nacionalismo *m*.
nationalist *adj*, *n* nacionalista *m*.
nationality *n* nacionalidad *f*.
nationalize *vt* nacionalizar.
nationwide *adj* a nivel nacional.
native *adj* nativo; ● *n* natural *m*.
native language *n* lengua materna *f*.
Nativity *n* Navidad *f*.
natural *adj* natural; sencillo; ~**ly** *adv* naturalmente.
natural gas *n* gas natural *m*.
naturalist *n* naturalista *m*.
naturalize *vt* naturalizar.
nature *n* naturaleza *f*; índole *f*.
naught *n* cero *m*.
naughty *adj* malo, malvado.
nausea *n* náusea, gana de vomitar *f*.
nauseate *vt* dar náuseas a.
nauseous *adj* fastidioso.
nautic(al), naval *adj* náutico, naval.
nave *n* nave (de la iglesia) *f*.

navel *n* ombligo *m*.
navigate *vi* navegar.
navigation *n* navegación *f*.
navy *n* marina *f*; armada *f*.
Nazi *n* nazi *m*.
near *prep* cerca de, junto a; ● *adv* casi; cerca, cerca de; ● *adj* cercano, próximo.
nearby *adj* cercano.
nearly *adv* casi.
near-sighted *adj* miope.
neat *adj* hermoso, pulido; puro; neto; ~**ly** *adv* elegantemente.
nebulous *adj* nebuloso.
necessarily *adv* necesariamente.
necessary *adj* necesario.
necessitate *vt* necesitar.
necessity *n* necesidad *f*.
neck *n* cuello *m*; ● *vi* besuquearse.
necklace *n* collar *m*.
necktie *n* corbata *f*.
nectar *n* néctar *m*.
née *adj*: ~ **Brown** de soltera Brown.
need *n* necesidad *f*; probreza *f*; ● *vt* necesitar.
needle *n* aguja *f*.
needless *adj* superfluo, inútil.
needlework *n* costura *f*; bordado de aguja *m*; obra de punto *m*.
needy *adj* necesitado, pobre.
negation *n* negación *f*.
negative *adj* negativo; ~**ly** *adv* negativamente; ● *n* negativa *f*.
neglect *vt* descuidar, desatender; ● *n* negligencia *f*.
negligee *n* salto de cama *m*.
negligence *n* negligencia *f*; descuido *m*.
negligent *adj* negligente, descuidado; ~**ly** *adv* negligentemente.
negligible *adj* insignificante.
negotiate *vt*, *vi* negociar (con).
negotiation *n* negociación *f*; negocio *m*.
Negress *n* negra *f*.
Negro *adj*, *n* negro *m*.
neigh *vi* relinchar; ● *n* relincho *m*.
neighbor *n* vecino *m*; ● *vt* confinar.
neighborhood *n* vecindad *f*; vecindario *m*.
neighboring *adj* vecino.
neighborly *adj* sociable.
neither *conj* ni; ● *pn* ninguno, ni uno ni otro.
neon *n* neón *m*.
neon light *n* luz de neón *f*.
nephew *n* sobrino *m*.
nepotism *n* nepotismo *m*.
nerve *n* nervio *m*; valor *m*.
nerve-racking *adj* espantoso.
nervous *adj* nervioso; nervudo.
nervous breakdown *n* crisis nerviosa *f*.
nest *n* nido *m*; nidada *f*.
nest egg *n* (*fig*) ahorros *mpl*.
nestle *vt* anidarse.
net *n* red *f*.
netball *n* básquet *m*.
net curtain *n* visillo *m*.
netting *n* mallado *m*.
nettle *n* ortiga *f*.
network *n* red *f*.
neurosis *n* neurosis *f invar*.
neurotic *adj*, *n* neurótico *m*.
neuter *adj* (*gr*) neutro.
neutral *adj* neutral.
neutrality *n* neutralidad *f*.
neutralize *vt* neutralizar.
neutron *n* neutrón *m*.
neutron bomb *n* bomba de neutrones *f*.
never *adv* nunca, jamás; ~ **mind** no importa.
never-ending *adj* sin fin.
nevertheless *adv* no obstante.

new *adj* nuevo, fresco, reciente; **~ly** *adv* nuevamente.
newborn *adj* recién nacido.
newcomer *n* recién llegado *m.*
new-fangled *adj* inventado por novedad.
news *npl* novedad, noticias *fpl.*
news agency *n* agencia de noticias *f.*
newscaster *n* presentador *m.*
newsdealer *n* vendedor de periódicos *m.*
news flash *n* noticia de última hora *f.*
newsletter *n* boletín *m.*
newspaper *n* periódico *m.*
newsreel *n* noticiario *m.*
New Year *n* Año Nuevo *m;* **~'s Day** *n* Día de Año Nuevo *m;* **~'s Eve** Nochevieja *f.*
next *adj* próximo; **the ~ day** el día siguiente; ● *adv* luego, inmediatamente después.
nib *n* pico *m;* punta *f.*
nibble *vt* picar, mordiscar.
nice *adj* simpático; agradable; lindo; **~ly** *adv* bien.
nice-looking *adj* guapo.
niche *n* nicho *m.*
nick *n* mella *f;* ● *vt (sl)* robar.
nickel *n* níquel *m;* moneda de cinco centavos *f.*
nickname *n* mote, apodo *m;* ● *vt* poner apodos.
nicotine *n* nicotina *f.*
niece *n* sobrina *f.*
niggling *adj* insignificante.
night *n* noche *f;* **by ~** de noche; **good ~** buenas noches.
nightclub *n* cabaret *m.*
nightfall *n* anochecer *m.*
nightingale *n* ruiseñor *m.*
nightly *adv* por las noches, todas las noches; ● *adj* nocturno.
nightmare *n* pesadilla *f.*
night school *n* clases nocturnas *fpl.*
night shift *n* turno de noche *m.*
nighttime *n* noche *f.*
nihilist *n* nihilista *m.*
nimble *adj* ligero, activo, listo, ágil.
nine *adj, n* nueve.
nineteen *adj, n* diez y nueve.
nineteenth *adj, n* decimonono.
ninetieth *adj, n* nonagésimo.
ninety *adj, n* noventa.
ninth *adj, n* nono, noveno.
nip *vt* pellizcar; morder.
nipple *n* pezón *m;* tetilla *f.*
nit *n* liendre *f.*
nitrogen *n* nitrógeno *m.*
no *adv* no; ● *adj* ningún, ninguno.
nobility *n* nobleza *f.*
noble *adj* noble; insigne; ● *n* noble *m.*
nobleman *n* noble *m.*
nobody *n* nadie, ninguna persona *f.*
nocturnal *adj* nocturnal, nocturno.
nod *n* cabeceo *m;* señal *f;* ● *vi* cabecear; amodorrarse.
noise *n* ruido, estruendo *m;* rumor *m.*
noisily *adv* con ruido.
noisiness *n* ruido, tumulto, alboroto *m.*
noisy *adj* ruidoso, turbulento.
nominal *adj,* **~ly** *adv* nominal(mente).
nominate *vt* nombrar.
nomination *n* nominación *f.*
nominative *n (gr)* nominativo *m.*
nominee *n* candidato *m.*
non-alcoholic *adj* no alcohólico.
non-aligned *adj* no alineado.
nonchalant *adj* indiferente.
non-committal *adj* reservado.
nonconformist *n* heterodoxo *m.*
nondescript *adj* no descrito.
none *adj* nadie, ninguno.
nonentity *n* nulidad *f.*

nonetheless *adv* sin embargo.
non-existent *adj* inexistente.
non-fiction *n* literatura no novelesca *f.*
nonplused *adj* confuso.
nonsense *n* disparate, absurdo *m.*
nonsensical *adj* absurdo.
non-smoker *n* no fumador *m.*
non-stick *adj* antiadherente.
non-stop *adj* directo; ● *adv* sin parar.
noodles *npl* fideos *mpl.*
noon *n* mediodía *m.*
noose *n* lazo corredizo *m.*
nor *conj* ni.
normal *adj* normal.
north *n* norte *m;* ● *adj* del norte.
North America *n* América del Norte *f.*
northeast *n* nor(d)este *m.*
northerly, northern *adj* norteño.
north pole *n* polo ártico *m.*
northward(s) *adv* hacia el norte.
northwest *n* nor(d)oeste *m.*
nose *n* nariz *f;* olfato *m.*
nosebleed *n* hemorragia nasal *f.*
nosedive *n* picado vertical *m.*
nostalgia *n* nostalgia *f.*
nostril *n* ventana de la nariz *f.*
not *adv* no.
notable *adj* notable; memorable.
notably *adv* especialmente.
notary *n* notario *m.*
notch *n* muesca *f;* ● *vt* hacer muescas.
note *n* nota, marca *f;* señal *f;* aprecio *m;* billete *m;* consecuencia *f;* noticia *f;* indirecta *f;* ● *vt* notar, marcar; observar.
notebook *n* librito de apuntes *m.*
noted *adj* afamado, célebre.
notepad *n* bloc *m.*
notepaper *n* papel de cartas *m.*
nothing *n* nada *f;* **good for ~** lo que sirve para nada.
notice *n* noticia *f;* aviso *m;* ● *vt* observar.
noticeable *adj* notable, reparable.
notification *n* notificación *f.*
notify *vt* notificar.
notion *n* noción *f;* opinión *f;* idea *f.*
notoriety *n* notoriedad *f.*
notorious *adj* notorio; **~ly** *adv* notoriamente.
notwithstanding *conj* no obstante, aunque.
nougat *n* turrón *m.*
nought *n* cero *m.*
noun *n (gr)* sustantivo *m.*
nourish *vt* nutrir, alimentar.
nourishing *adj* nutritivo.
nourishment *n* nutrimiento, alimento *m.*
novel *n* novela *f.*
novelist *n* novelista *m.*
novelty *n* novedad *f.*
November *n* noviembre *m.*
novice *n* novicio *m.*
now *adv* ahora, en el tiempo presente; **~ and then** de vez en cuando.
nowadays *adv* hoy (en) día.
nowhere *adv* en ninguna parte.
noxious *adj* nocivo, dañoso.
nozzle *n* boquilla *f.*
nuance *n* matiz *m.*
nuclear *adj* nuclear.
nucleus *n* núcleo *m.*
nude *adj* desnudo, en carnes, en cueros, sin vestido.
nudge *vt* dar un codazo a.
nudist *n* nudista *m.*
nudity *n* desnudez *f.*
nuisance *n* daño, perjuicio *m;* incomodidad *f.*
nuke *n (col)* bomba atómica *f;* ● *vt* atacar con arma nuclear.

null adj nulo, inválido.
nullify vt anular, invalidar.
numb adj entorpecido; ● vt entorpecer.
number n número m; cantidad f; ● vt numerar.
numbness n torpor m.
numeral n número m.
numerical adj numérico.
numerous adj numeroso.
nun n monja, religiosa f.
nunnery n convento de monjas m.
nuptial adj nupcial; ~s npl nupcias fpl.
nurse n enfermera f; ● vt cuidar; amamantar.
nursery n guardería infantil f; criadero m.
nursery rhyme n canción infantil f.
nursery school n parvulario m.
nursing home n clínica de reposo f.
nurture vt criar, educar.
nut n nuez f.
nutcrackers npl cascanueces m.
nutmeg n nuez moscada f.
nutritious adj nutritivo.
nut shell n cáscara de nuez f.
nylon n nilón m; ● adj de nilón.

O

oak n roble m.
oar n remo m.
oasis n oasis f.
oat n avena f.
oath n juramento m.
oatmeal n harina de avena f.
oats npl avena f.
obedience n obediencia f.
obedient adj, ~ly adv obediente(mente).
obese adj obeso, gordo.
obesity n obesidad f.
obey vt obedecer.
obituary n necrología f.
object n objeto m; ● vt objetar.
objection n oposición, objeción, réplica f.
objectionable adj desagradable.
objective adj, n objetivo m.
obligation n obligación f.
obligatory adj obligatorio.
oblige vt obligar; complacer, favorecer.
obliging adj servicial.
oblique adj oblicuo; indirecto; ~ly adv oblicuamente.
obliterate vt borrar.
oblivion n olvido m.
oblivious adj olvidadizo.
oblong adj oblongo.
obnoxious adj odioso.
oboe n oboe m.
obscene adj obsceno, impúdico.
obscenity n oscenidad f.
obscure adj oscuro; ~ly adv oscuramente; ● vt oscurecer.
obscurity n oscuridad f.
observance n observancia f; reverencia f.
observant adj observante, respetuoso.
observation n observación f.
observatory n observatorio m.
observe vt observar, mirar.
observer n observador m.
observingly adv cuidadosamente, atentamente.
obsess vt obsesionar.
obsessive adj obsesivo.
obsolete adj en desuso.
obstacle n obstáculo m.
obstinate adj obstinado; ~ly adv obstinadamente.

obstruct vt obstruir; impedir.
obstruction n obstrucción f; impedimento m.
obtain vt obtener, adquirir.
obtainable adj asequible.
obtrusive adj intruso, importuno.
obtuse adj obtuso, sin punta; lerdo, torpe.
obvious adj obvio, evidente; ~ly adv naturalmente.
occasion n ocasión f; tiempo oportuno m; ● vt ocasionar, causar.
occasional adj ocasional, casual; ~ly adv ocasionalmente.
occupant, occupier n ocupador m; poseedor m; inquilino m.
occupation n ocupación f; empleo m.
occupy vt ocupar, emplear.
occur vi pasar, ocurrir.
occurrence n incidente m.
ocean n océano m; alta mar f.
ocean-going adj de alta mar.
oceanic adj oceánico.
ocher n ocre m.
octave n octava f.
October n octubre m.
octopus n pulpo m.
odd adj impar; particular; extravagante; extraño; ~ly adv extrañamente.
oddity n singularidad, particularidad, rareza f.
odd jobs npl bricolaje m.
oddness n desigualdad f; singularidad f.
odds npl puntos de ventaja mpl.
odious adj odioso.
odometer n cuentakilómetros m invar.
odor n olor m; fragancia f.
odorous adj odorífero.
of prep de; tocante; según.
off adv desconectado; apagado; cerrado; cancelado; ~! excl ¡fuera!
offend vt ofender, irritar; injuriar; ● vi pecar.
offender n delincuente m.
offense n ofensa f; injuria f.
offensive adj ofensivo; injurioso; ~ly adv ofensivamente.
offer vt ofrecer; ● n oferta f.
offering n sacrificio m; oferta f.
offhand adj descortés; ● adv de repente.
office n oficina f; oficio, empleo m; servicio m.
office automation n ofimática f.
office building n bloque de oficinas m.
office hours npl horas de consulta fpl.
officer n oficial, empleado m.
office worker n oficinista m.
official adj oficial; ~ly adv de oficio; ● n empleado m.
officiate vi oficiar.
officious adj oficioso; ~ly adv oficiosamente.
off-line adj, adv fuera de línea.
off-peak adj de temporada baja.
off-season adj, adv fuera de temporada.
offset vt contrarrestar.
offshoot n ramificación.
offshore adj costera.
offside adj fuera de juego.
offspring n prole f; linaje m; descendencia f.
offstage adv entre bastidores.
off-the-rack adj confeccionado.
ogle vt mirar al soslayo.
oil n aceite m; óleo m; ● vt engrasar.
oilcan n lata de aceite f.
oilfield n campo petrolífero m.
oil filter n filtro de aceite m.
oil painting n pintura al óleo f.
oil rig n torre de perforación f.
oil tanker n petrolero m.
oil well n pozo m.
oily adj aceitoso; grasiento.
ointment n ungüento m.

O.K., okay *excl* O.K., vale; ● *adj* bien; ● *vt* dar el visto bueno a.

old *adj* viejo; antiguo.

old age *n* vejez *f*.

old-fashioned *adj* pasado de moda.

olive *n* olivo *m*; oliva *f*.

olive oil *n* aceite de oliva *m*.

omelet(te) *n* tortilla de huevos *f*.

omen *n* agüero, presagio *m*.

ominous *adj* ominoso.

omission *n* omisión *f*; descuido *m*.

omit *vt* omitir.

omnipotence *n* omnipotencia *f*.

omnipotent *adj* omnipotente, todopoderoso.

on *prep* sobre, encima, en; de; a; ● *adj* encendido; prendido; abierto; puesto.

once *adv* una vez; **at ~** en seguida; **all at ~** de una vez, en seguida; **~ more** otra vez.

oncoming *adj* que viene de frente.

one *adj* un, uno; **~ by ~** uno a uno, uno por uno.

one-day excursion *n* billete de ida y vuelta en un día *m*.

one-man *adj* individual.

onerous *adj* oneroso, molesto.

oneself *pn* sí mismo; sí misma.

one-sided *adj* parcial.

one-to-one *adj* de dos.

ongoing *adj* continuo.

onion *n* cebolla *f*.

on-line *adj, adv* en línea.

onlooker *n* espectador *m*.

only *adj* único, solo; ● *adv* solamente.

onset, onslaught *n* primer ímpetu *m*; ataque *m*.

onus *n* responsabilidad *f*.

onward(s) *adv* adelante.

ooze *vi* manar *o* correr algún líquido suavemente.

opaque *adj* opaco.

open *adj* abierto; patente, evidente; sincero, franco; **~ly** *adv* con franqueza; ● *vt, vi* abrir(se); descubrir(se); **to ~ on to** dar a; **to ~ up** *vt* abrir; *vi* abrirse.

opening *n* abertura *f*; (*com*) salida *f*; principio *m*.

open-minded *adj* imparcial.

openness *n* claridad *f*; franqueza, sinceridad *f*.

opera *n* ópera *f*.

opera house *n* teatro de la ópera *m*.

operate *vi* obrar, operar.

operation *n* operación *f*; efecto *m*.

operational *adj* operacional.

operative *adj* operativo.

operator *n* operario *m*; operador *m*.

ophthalmic *adj* oftálmico.

opine *vi* opinar, juzgar.

opinion *n* opinión *f*; juicio *m*.

opinionated *adj* testarudo.

opinion poll *n* sondeo *m*.

opponent *n* antagonista *m*; adversario *m*.

opportune *adj* oportuno.

opportunist *n* oportunista *m*.

opportunity *n* oportunidad *f*.

oppose *vt* oponerse.

opposing *adj* opuesto.

opposite *adj* opuesto; contrario; ● *adv* enfrente; *prep* frente a; ● *n* lo contrario.

opposition *n* oposición *f*; resistencia *f*; impedimento *m*.

oppress *vt* oprimir.

oppression *n* opresión *f*.

oppressive *adj* opresivo, cruel.

oppressor *n* opresor *m*.

optic(al) *adj* óptico; **~s** *npl* óptica *f*.

optician *n* óptico *m*.

optimist *n* optimista *m*.

optimistic *adj* optimista.

optimum *adj* óptimum.

option *n* opción *f*; deseo *m*.

optional *adj* facultativo.

opulent *adj* opulento.

or *conj* o; u.

oracle *n* oráculo *m*.

oral *adj* oral, vocal; **~ly** *adv* verbalmente, de palabra.

orange *n* naranja *f*.

orator *n* orador *m*.

orbit *n* órbita *f*.

orchard *n* huerto *m*.

orchestra *n* orquesta *f*.

orchestral *adj* de orquesta.

orchid *n* orquídea *f*.

ordain *vt* ordenar; establecer.

ordeal *n* prueba rigurosa *f*.

order *n* orden *mf*; regla *f*; mandato *m*; serie, clase *f*; ● *vt* ordenar, arreglar; mandar.

order form *n* hoja de pedido *f*.

orderly *adj* ordenado, regular.

ordinarily *adv* ordinariamente.

ordinary *adj* ordinario.

ordination *n* ordenación *f*.

ordnance *n* artillería *f*.

ore *n* mineral *m*.

organ *n* órgano *m*.

organic(al) *adj* orgánico.

organism *n* organismo *m*.

organist *n* organista *m*.

organization *n* organización *f*.

organize *vt* organizar.

orgasm *n* orgasmo *m*.

orgy *n* orgía *f*.

oriental *adj* oriental.

orifice *n* orificio *m*.

origin *n* origen, principio *m*.

original *adj* original, primitivo; **~ly** *adv* originalmente.

originality *n* originalidad *f*.

originate *vi* originar.

ornament *n* ornamento *m*; ● *vt* ornamentar, adornar.

ornamental *adj* lo que sirve de adorno.

ornate *adj* adornado, ataviado.

orphan *adj, n* huérfano *m*.

orphanage *n* orfandad *f*.

orthodox *adj* ortodoxo.

orthodoxy *n* ortodoxia *f*.

orthography *n* ortografía *f*.

orthopedic *adj* ortopédico.

oscillate *vi* oscilar, vibrar.

osprey *n* águila marina *f*.

ostensibly *adv* aparentemente.

ostentatious *adj* ostentoso.

osteopath *n* osteópata *m*.

ostracize *vt* desterrar por medio del ostracismo.

ostrich *n* avestruz *m*.

other *pn* otro.

otherwise *adv* de otra manera, por otra parte.

otter *n* nutria *f*.

ouch *excl* ¡ay!

ought *v aux* deber, ser menester.

ounce *n* onza *f*.

our, ours *pn* nuestro, nuestra, nuestros, nuestras.

ourselves *pn pl* nosotros mismos.

oust *vt* quitar; desposeer.

out *adv* fuera, afuera; apagado.

outback *n* interior *m*.

outboard *adj*: **~ motor** (motor) fuera-bordo *m*.

outbreak *n* erupción *f*.

outburst *n* explosión *f*.

outcast *n* paria *m*.

outcome *n* resultado *m*.

outcry *n* clamor *m*; gritería *f*.

outdated *adj* fuera de moda.

outdo *vt* exceder a otro, sobrepujar.
outdoor *adj*, ~s *adv* al aire libre.
outer *adj* exterior.
outermost *adj* extremo; lo más exterior.
outer space *n* espacio exterior *m*.
outfit *n* vestidos *mpl*; ropa *f*.
outfitter *n* confeccionador *m*.
outgoing *adj* extrovertido.
outgrow *vt* sobrecrecer.
outhouse *n* dependencia de una casa *f*.
outing *n* excursión *f*.
outlandish *adj* estrafalario.
outlaw *n* bandido *m*; ● *vt* proscribir.
outlay *n* despensa *f*, gastos *mpl*.
outlet *n* salida *f*.
outline *n* contorno *m*; bosquejo *m*.
outlive *vt* sobrevivir.
outlook *n* perspectiva *f*.
outlying *adj* distante, lejos.
outmoded *adj* anticuado.
outnumber *vt* exceder en número.
out-of-date *adj* caducado; pasado de moda.
outpatient *n* paciente externo *m*.
outpost *n* puesto avanzado *m*.
output *n* rendimiento *m*; salida *f*.
outrage *n* ultraje *m*; ● *vt* ultrajar.
outrageous *adj* ultrajoso; atroz; ~ly *adv* injuriosamente; enormemente.
outright *adv* absolutamente; ● *adj* completo.
outrun *vt* correr más que otro.
outset *n* principio *m*.
outshine *vt* exceder en brillantez, eclipsar.
outside *n* superficie *f*; exterior *m*; apariencia *f*; ● *adv* fuera; ● *prep* fuera de.
outsider *n* forastero *m*.
outsize *adj* de talla grande.
outskirts *npl* alrededores *mpl*.
outspoken *adj* muy franco.
outstanding *adj* excepcional; pendiente.
outstretch *vt* extenderse, alargar.
outstrip *vt* dejar atrás; sobrepujar.
out-tray *n* bandeja de salida *f*.
outward *adj* exterior, externo; de ida; ~ly *adv* por fuera; exteriormente.
outweigh *vt* pesar más que.
outwit *vt* engañar a uno a fuerza de tretas.
oval *n* óvalo *m*; ● *adj* oval.
ovary *n* ovario *m*.
oven *n* horno *m*.
ovenproof *adj* resistente al horno.
over *prep* sobre, encima; más de; durante; **all ~** por todos lados; ● *adj* terminado; de sobra; **~ again** otra vez; **~ and ~** repetidas veces.
overall *adj* total; ● *adv* en conjunto; ~s *npl* overol *m*.
overawe *vt* imponer respeto.
overbalance *vi* perder el equilibrio.
overbearing *adj* despótico.
overboard *adv* (*mar*) encima de bordo, al mar.
overbook *vt* sobrereservar.
overcast *adj* encapotado.
overcharge *vt* sobrecargar; poner alguna cosa a precio muy subido.
overcoat *n* abrigo *m*.
overcome *vt* vencer; superar.
overconfident *adj* demasiado atrevido.
overcrowded *adj* atestado; superpoblado.
overdo *vi* hacer más de lo necesario.
overdose *n* sobredosis *f invar*.
overdraft *n* saldo deudor *m*.
overdrawn *adj* en descubierto.
overdress *vt* engalanar con exceso.
overdue *adj* retrasado.

overeat *vi* atracarse.
overestimate *vt* sobreestimar.
overflow *vt*, *vi* inundar; rebosar; ● *n* inundación *f*;superabundancia *f*.
overgrown *adj* invadido.
overgrowth *n* vegetación exuberante *f*.
overhang *vt* estar colgando sobre alguna cosa; salir algo fuera del nivel de un edificio.
overhaul *vt* revisar; ● *n* revisión *f*.
overhead *adv* sobre la cabeza, en lo alto.
overhear *vt* oír algo por casualidad.
overjoyed *adj* muy gozoso.
overkill *n* exceso de medios *m*.
overland *adj*, *adv* por tierra.
overlap *vi* traslaparse.
overleaf *adv* al dorso.
overload *vt* sobrecargar.
overlook *vt* mirar desde lo alto; examinar; repasar; pasar por alto, tolerar; descuidar.
overnight *adv* durante la noche; ● *adj* de noche.
overpass *n* paso superior *m*.
overpower *vt* predominar, oprimir.
overpowering *adj* agobiante.
overrate *vt* apreciar *o* valuar alguna cosa en más de lo que vale.
override *vt* no hacer caso de.
overriding *adj* predominante.
overrule *vt* denegar.
overrun *vt* inundar; infestar; rebasar.
overseas *adv* en ultramar; ● *adj* extranjero.
oversee *vt* inspeccionar.
overseer *n* superintendente *m*.
overshadow *vt* eclipsar.
overshoot *vt* excederse.
oversight *n* yerro *m*; equivocación *f*.
oversleep *vi* dormir demasiado.
overspill *n* exceso de población *m*.
overstate *vi* exagerar.
overstep *vt* pasar más allá.
overt *adj* abierto; público; ~ly *adv* abiertamente.
overtake *vt* sobrepasar.
overthrow *vt* trastornar; demoler; destruir; ● *n* trastorno *m*; ruina, derrota *f*.
overtime *n* horas extra *fpl*.
overtone *n* tono *m*.
overture *n* abertura *f*; (*mus*) obertura *f*.
overturn *vt* subvertir, trastornar.
overweight *adj* demasiado pesado.
overwhelm *vt* abrumar; oprimir; sumergir.
overwhelming *adj* arrollador; irresistible.
overwork *vi* trabajar demasiado.
owe *vt* deber, tener deudas; estar obligado.
owing *adj* que es debido; **~ to** por causa de.
owl *n* búho *m*.
own *adj* propio; **my ~** mío, mía; ● *vt* tener; poseer; **to ~ up** *vi* confesar.
owner *n* dueño, propietario *m*.
ownership *n* posesión *f*.
ox *n* buey *m*; **~en** *pl* ganado vacuno *m*.
oxidize *vt* oxidar.
oxygen *n* oxígeno *m*.
oxygen mask *n* máscara de oxígeno *f*.
oxygen tent *n* tienda de oxígeno *f*.
oyster *n* ostra *f*.
ozone *n* ozono *m*.

P

pa *n* papá *m*.
pace *n* paso *m*; ● *vt* medir a pasos; ● *vi* pasear.

pacemaker n marcapasos m invar.
pacific(al) adj pacífico.
pacification n pacificación f.
pacify vt pacificar.
pack n lío, fardo m; baraja de naipes f; cuadrilla f; • vt empaquetar; hacer la maleta; llenar.
package n paquete m; acuerdo m.
package tour n viaje organizado m.
packet n paquete m.
packing n embalaje m.
pact n pacto m.
pad n bloc m; plataforma f; (sl) casa f; • vt rellenar.
padding n relleno m; paja f.
paddle vi remar; chapotear; • n canalete m.
paddle steamer n vapor de ruedas m.
paddock n corral m.
paddy n arrozal m.
pagan adj, n pagano m.
page n página f; paje m.
pageant n espectáculo público m.
pageantry n pompa f.
pail n cubo, pozal m.
pain n pena f; castigo m; dolor m; • vt afligir.
pained adj afligido.
painful adj dolorido; penoso; ~ly adv dolorosamente, con pena.
painkiller n analgésico m.
painless adj sin pena; sin dolor.
painstaking adj laborioso, incansado.
paint vt pintar.
paintbrush n pincel m; brocha f.
painter n pintor m.
painting n pintura f.
paintwork n pintura f.
pair n par m.
pajamas npl pijama m.
pal n compañero m.
palace n palacio m.
palatable adj sabroso.
palate n paladar m; gusto m.
palatial adj palatino.
palaver n lío m.
pale adj pálido; claro.
palette n paleta f.
paling n estacada, palizada f.
pall n capa de humo f; • vi perder el sabor.
pallet n pallet m.
palliative adj, n paliativo m.
pallid adj pálido.
pallor n palidez f.
palm n (bot) palma f.
palmistry n quiromancia f.
Palm Sunday n Domingo de Ramos m.
palpable adj palpable; evidente.
palpitation n palpitación f.
paltry adj irrisorio; mezquino.
pamper vt mimar.
pamphlet n folleto m.
pan n cazuela f; sartén f.
panacea n panacea f.
panache n estilo m.
pancake n buñuelo m.
pandemonium n jaleo m.
pane n cristal m.
panel n panel m; paño m.
paneling n paneles mpl.
pang n angustia, congoja f.
panic adj, n pánico m.
panicky adj asustadizo.
panic-stricken adj preso de pánico.
pansy n (bot) pensamiento m.
pant vi jadear.

panther n pantera f.
panties npl bragas fpl.
pantihose n pantimedias fpl.
pantry n despensa f.
pants npl pantalones mpl.
papacy n papado m.
papal adj papal.
paper n papel m; periódico m; examen m; estudio m; ~s pl escrituras fpl; (com) fondos mpl; • adj de papel; • vt empapelar; tapizar.
paperback n libro de bolsillo m.
paper bag n bolsa de papel f.
paper clip n clip m.
paperweight n sujetapapeles m.
paperwork n papeleo m.
paprika n pimienta húngara f.
par n equivalencia f; igualdad f; par m; at ~ (com) a la par.
parable n parábola f.
parachute n paracaídas m invar; • vi lanzarse en paracaídas.
parade n ostentación, pompa f; (mil) parada f; • vt, vi formar, parada; pasear; hacer gala.
paradise n paraíso m.
paradox n paradoja f.
paradoxical adj paradójico.
paragon n modelo perfecto m.
paragraph n párrafo m.
parallel adj paralelo; • n línea paralela f; • vt paralelizar; parangonar.
paralysis n parálisis f.
paralytic(al) adj paralítico.
paralyze vt paralizar.
paramedic n ambulanciero m.
paramount adj supremo, superior.
paranoid adj paranoico.
paraphernalia n avíos mpl.
parasite n gorrista m.
parasol n parasol, quitasol m.
paratrooper n paracaidista m.
parcel n paquete m; porción, cantidad f; equipajes, bultos mpl; • vt empaquetar, embalar.
parch vt resecar.
parched adj muerto de sed.
parchment n pergamino m.
pardon n perdón m; • vt perdonar.
parent n padre m; madre f.
parentage n parentela f; extracción f.
parental adj paternal.
parenthesis n paréntesis m.
parish n parroquia f; • adj parroquial.
parishioner n parroquiano m.
parity n paridad f.
park n parque m; • vt aparcar, estacionar; vi aparcar, estacionarse.
parking n aparcamiento, estacionamiento m.
parking lot n párking m.
parking meter n parquímetro m.
parking ticket n multa de estacionamiento f.
parlance n lenguaje m.
parliament n parlamento m.
parliamentary adj parlamentario.
parlor n sala de recibimiento f.
parody n parodia f; • vt parodiar.
parole n: on ~ libre bajo palabra.
parricide n parricidio m; parricida m.
parrot n papagayo m.
parry vt parar.
parsley n (bot) perejil m.
parsnip n (bot) chirivía f.
part n parte f; partido m; oficio m; papel (de un actor) m; obligación f; raya f; ~s pl partes fpl; paraje, distrito m; • vt partir, separar, desunir; • vi partirse, separarse; to ~ with entregar; pagar; deshacerse de; ~ly adv en parte.

partial *adj*, ~ly *adv* parcial(mente).
participant *n* concursante *m*.
participate *vi* participar (en).
participation *n* participación *f*.
participle *n* (*gr*) participio *m*.
particle *n* partícula *f*.
particular *adj* particular, singular; ~ly *adv* particularmente;
 ● *n* particular *m*; particularidad *f*.
parting *n* separación, partida *f*; raya (en los cabellos) *f*.
partisan *n* partidario *m*.
partition *n* partición, separación ·*f*; ● *vt* partir, dividir en
 varias partes.
partner *n* socio, compañero *m*.
partnership *n* compañía, sociedad de comercio *f*.
partridge *n* perdiz *f*.
party *n* partido *m*; fiesta *f*.
pass *vt* pasar; traspasar; transferir; adelantarse a; ● *vi* pasar,
 aprobar; ● *n* permiso *m*; puerto *m*; to ~ away *vi* fallecer; to
 ~ by *vi* pasar; *vt* pasar por alto; to ~ on *vt* transmitir; pase
 m.
passable *adj* pasadero, transitable.
passage *n* pasaje *m*; travesía *f*; pasadizo *m*.
passbook *n* libreta de dépositos *f*.
passenger *n* pasajero *m*.
passer-by *n* transeúnte *m*.
passing *adj* pasajero.
passion *n* pasión *f*; amor *m*; celo, ardor *m*.
passionate *adj* apasionado; ~ly *adv* apasionadamente; ardientemente.
passive *adj* pasivo; ~ly *adv* pasivamente.
passkey *n* llava maestra *f*.
Passover *n* Pascua *f*.
passport *n* pasaporte *m*.
passport control *n* control de pasaporte *m*.
password *n* contraseña *f*.
past *adj* pasado; gastado; ● *n* (*gr*) pretérito *m*; el pasado; ●
 prep más allá de; después de.
pasta *n* pasta *f*.
paste *n* pasta *f*; engrudo *m*; ● *vt* engrudar.
pasteurized *adj* pasteurizado.
pastime *n* pasatiempo *m*; diversión *f*.
pastor *n* pastor *m*.
pastoral *adj* pastoril; pastoral.
pastry *n* pastelería *f*.
pasture *n* pasto *m*.
pasty *adj* pastoso; pálido.
pat *vt* dar golpecillos.
patch *n* remiendo *m*; parche *m*; terreno *m*; ● *vt* remendar; to
 ~ up reparar; hacer las paces en.
patchwork *n* obra de retacitos *f*; chapucería *f*.
pâté *n* paté *m*.
patent *adj* patente; privilegiado; ● *n* patente *f*; ● *vt* privilegiar.
patentee *n* el que posee un privilegio de invención.
patent leather *n* charol *m*.
paternal *adj* paternal.
paternity *n* paternidad *f*.
path *n* senda *f*.
pathetic *adj* patético; ~ally *adv* patéticamente.
pathological *adj* patológico.
pathology *n* patología *f*.
pathos *n* patetismo *m*.
pathway *n* sendero *m*.
patience *n* paciencia *f*.
patient *adj* paciente, sufrido; ~ly *adv* con paciencia; ● *n*
 enfermo *m*.
patio *n* patio *m*.
patriarch *adj* patriarca *m*.
patriot *n* patriota *m*.
patriotic *adj* patriótico.
patriotism *n* patriotismo *m*.
patrol *n* patrulla *f*; ● *vi* patrullar.

patrol car *n* coche patrulla *m*.
patrolman *n* policía *m*.
patron *n* patrón, protector *m*.
patronage *n* patrocinio *m*; patronato, patronazgo *m*.
patronize *vt* patrocinar, proteger.
patter *n* golpeteo *m*; labia *f*; ● *vi* tamborilear.
pattern *n* patrón *m*; dibujo *m*.
paunch *n* panza *f*; vientre *m*.
pauper *n* pobre *m*.
pause *n* pausa *f*; ● *vt* pausar; deliberar.
pave *vt* empedrar; enlosar, embaldosar.
pavement *n* calzada *f*.
pavilion *n* pabellón *m*.
paving stone *n* ladrillo *m*; losa *f*.
paw *n* pata *f*; garra *f*; ● *vt* manosear.
pawn *n* peón *m*; ● *vt* empeñar.
pawn broker *n* prendero *m*.
pawnshop *n* monte de piedad *m*.
pay *vt* pagar; sufrir por; to ~ back *vt* reembolsar; to ~ for
 pagar; to ~ off *vt* liquidar; *vi* dar resultados; ● *n* paga *f*;
 salario *m*.
payable *adj* pagadero.
pay day *n* día de paga *m*.
payee *n* portador *m*.
pay envelope *n* sobre (de paga) *m*.
paymaster *n* pagador *m*.
payment *n* paga *f*; pagamento, pago *m*.
pay-phone *n* teléfono público *m*.
payroll *n* nómina *f*.
pea *n* guisante *m*.
peace *n* paz *f*.
peaceful *adj* tranquilo, pacífico.
peach *n* melocotón, durazno *m*.
peacock *n* pavón, pavo real *m*.
peak *n* cima *f*.
peak hours, peak period *n* horas punta *fpl*.
peal *n* campaneo *m*; estruendo *m*.
peanut *n* cacahuete *m*; maní *m*.
pear *n* pera *f*.
pearl *n* perla *f*.
peasant *n* campesino *m*.
peat *n* turba *f*.
pebble *n* guija *f*; guijarro *m*.
peck *n* picotazo *m*; ● *vt* picotear; picar.
pecking order *n* orden de jerarquía *m*.
peculiar *adj* peculiar, particular, singular; ~ly *adv* peculiar-
 mente.
peculiarity *n* particularidad, singularidad *f*.
pedal *n* pedal *m*; ● *vi* pedalear.
pedant *n* pedante *m*.
pedantic *adj* pedante.
peddler *n* vendedor ambulante *m*.
pedestal *n* pedestal *m*.
pedestrian *n* peatón *m*; ● *adj* pedestre.
pediatrics *n* pediatría *f*.
pedigree *n* genealogía *f*; ● *adj* de raza.
peek *vi* mirar de soslayo.
peel *vt* pelar; ● *vi* desconcharse; ● *n* piel *f*; cáscara *f*.
peer *n* compañero *m*; par *m*.
peerless *adj* incomparable.
peeved *adj* enojado.
peevish *adj* regañón, bronco; enojadizo.
peg *n* clavija *f*; gancho *m*; ● *vt* clavar.
pelican *n* pelícano *m*.
pellet *n* bolita *f*.
pelt *n* pellejo, cuero *m*; ● *vt* arrojar; ● *vi* llover a cántaros.
pen *n* bolígrafo *m*; pluma *f*; redil *m*.
penal *adj* penal.
penalty *n* pena *f*; castigo *m*; multa *f*.
penance *n* penitencia *f*.
pence *n* = *pl* of penny.
pencil *n* lápiz *m*; lapicero *m*.

pencil case *n* estuche *m*.
pendant *n* pendiente *f*.
pending *adj* pendiente.
pendulum *n* péndulo *m*.
penetrate *vt* penetrar.
penguin *n* pingüino *m*.
penicillin *n* penicilina *f*.
peninsula *n* península *f*.
penis *n* pene *m*.
penitence *n* penitencia *f*.
penitent *adj*, *n* penitente *m*.
penitentiary *n* penitenciario *m*.
penknife *n* navaja *f*.
pennant *n* banderola *f*.
penniless *adj* sin dinero.
penny *n* penique *m*.
penpal *n* amigo por carta *m*.
pension *n* pensión *f*; • *vt* dar alguna pensión.
pensive *adj* pensativo; ~ly *adv* melancólicamente.
pentagon *n*: the P~ el Pentágono.
Pentecost *n* Pentecostés *m*.
penthouse *n* ático *m*.
pent-up *adj* reprimido.
penultimate *adj* penúltimo.
penury *n* penuria, carestía *f*.
people *n* pueblo *m*; nación *f*; gente *f*; • *vt* poblar.
pep *n* energía *f*; to ~ up *vt* animar.
pepper *n* pimienta *f*; • *vt* sazonar con pimienta.
peppermint *n* menta *f*.
per *prep* por.
per annum *adv* al año.
per capita *adj*, *adv* per cápita.
perceive *vt* percibir, comprender.
percentage *n* porcentaje *m*.
perception *n* percepción, idea, noción *f*.
perch *n* percha *f*.
perchance *adv* acaso, quizá.
percolate *vt* colar; filtrar.
percolator *n* cafetera de filtro *f*.
percussion *n* percusión *f*; golpe *m*.
perdition *n* pérdida, ruina *f*.
peremptory *adj* perentorio; decisivo.
perennial *adj* perenne; perpetuo.
perfect *adj* perfecto, acabado; puro; ~ly *adv* perfectamente;
　• *vt* perfeccionar, acabar.
perfection *n* perfección *f*.
perforate *vt* horadar.
perforation *n* perforación *f*.
perform *vt* ejecutar; efectuar; • *vi* representar, hacer papel.
performance *n* ejecución *f*; cumplimiento *m*; obra *f*; represen-
　tación teatral, función *f*.
performer *n* ejecutor *m*; actor *m*.
perfume *n* perfume *m*; fragancia *f*; • *vt* perfumar.
perhaps *adv* quizá, quizás.
peril *n* peligro, riesgo *m*.
perilous *adj* peligroso; ~ly *adv* peligrosamente.
perimeter *n* perímetro *m*.
period *n* período *m*; época *f*; regla *f*.
periodic(al) *adj* periódico; ~ally *adv* periódicamente.
periodical *n* jornal, periódico *m*.
peripheral *adj* periférico; • *n* unidad periférica *f*.
perish *vi* perecer.
perishable *adj* perecedero.
perjure *vt* perjurar.
perjury *n* perjurio *m*.
perk *n* extra *m*.
perky *adj* animado.
perm *n* permanente *f*.
permanent *adj*, ~ly *adv* permanente(mente).
permeate *vt* penetrar, atravesar.
permissible *adj* lícito, permiso.
permission *n* permiso *m*.

permissive *adj* permisivo.
permit *vt* permitir; • *n* permiso *m*.
permutation *n* permutación *f*.
perpendicular *adj*, ~ly *adv* perpendicular(mente); • *n* línea
　perpendicular *f*.
perpetrate *vt* perpetrar, cometer algún delito.
perpetual *adj* perpetuo; ~ly *adv* perpetuamente.
perpetuate *vt* perpetuar, eternizar.
perplex *vt* confundir.
persecute *vt* perseguir, importunar.
persecution *n* persecución *f*.
perseverance *n* perseverancia *f*.
persevere *vi* perseverar.
persist *vi* persistir.
persistence *adj* persistencia *f*.
persistent *adj* persistente.
person *n* persona *f*.
personable *adj* atractivo.
personage *n* personaje *m*.
personal *adj*, ~ly *adv* personal(mente).
personal assistant *n* ayudante personal *m*.
personal column *n* anuncios personales *mpl*.
personal computer *n* computadora personal *f*.
personality *n* personalidad *f*.
personification *n* prosopopeya *f*.
personify *vt* personificar.
personnel *n* personal *m*.
perspective *n* perspectiva *f*.
perspiration *n* transpiración *f*.
perspire *vi* transpirar.
persuade *vt* persuadir.
persuasion *n* persuasión *f*.
persuasive *adj* persuasivo; ~ly *adv* de modo persuasivo.
pert *adj* listo, vivo; petulante.
pertaining : ~ to *prep* relacionado con.
pertinent *adj* pertinente; ~ly *adv* oportunamente.
pertness *n* impertinencia *f*; vivacidad *f*.
perturb *vt* perturbar.
perusal *n* lectura, lección *f*.
peruse *vt* leer; examinar atentamente.
pervade *vt* atravesar, penetrar.
perverse *adj* perverso, depravado; ~ly *adv* perversamente.
pervert *vt* pervertir, corromper.
pessimist *n* pesimista *m*.
pest *n* insecto nocivo *m*; molestia *f*.
pester *vt* molestar, cansar.
pestilence *n* pestilencia *f*.
pet *n* animal doméstico *m*; favorito *m*; • *vt* mimar; • *vi*
　besuquearse.
petal *n* (*bot*) pétalo *m*.
petite *adj* chiquito.
petition *n* presentación, petición *f*; • *vt* suplicar; requerir en
　justicia.
petrified *adj* horrorizado.
petroleum *n* petróleo *m*.
petticoat *n* enaguas *fpl*.
pettiness *n* pequeñez *f*.
petty *adj* mezquino; insignificante.
petty cash *n* dinero para gastos menores *m*.
petty officer *n* contramaestre *m*.
petulant *adj* petulante.
pew *n* banco *m*.
pewter *n* peltre *m*.
phantom *n* fantasma *m*.
Pharisee *n* fariseo *m*.
pharmaceutic(al) *adj* farmacéutico.
pharmacist *n* farmacéutico *m*.
pharmacy *n* farmacia *f*.
phase *n* fase *f*.
pheasant *n* faisán *m*.
phenomenal *adj* fenomenal.
phenomenon *n* fenómeno *m*.

phial n redomilla f.
philanthropic adj filantrópico.
philanthropist n filántropo m.
philanthropy n filantropía f.
philologist n filólogo m.
philology n filología f.
philosopher n filósofo m.
philosophic(al) adj filosófico; ~ally adv filosóficamente.
philosophize vi filosofar.
philosophy n filosofía f; natural ~ física f.
phlegm n flema f.
phlegmatic(al) adj flemático.
phobia n fobia f.
phone n teléfono m; ● vt telefonear; to ~ back vt, vi volver a llamar; to ~ up llamar por teléfono.
phone book n guía telefónica f.
phone box, phone booth n cabina telefónica f.
phone call n llamada (telefónica) f.
phosphorus n fósforo m.
photocopier n fotocopiadora f.
photocopy n fotocopia f.
photograph n fotografía f; ● v: fotografiar.
photographer n fotógrafo m.
photographic adj fotográfico.
photography n fotografía f.
phrase n frase f; estilo m; ● vt expresar.
phrase book n libro de frases m.
physical adj físico; ~ly adv físicamente.
physical education n educación física f.
physician n médico m.
physicist n físico m.
physiological adj fisiológico.
physiologist n fisiologista, fisiólogo m.
physiology n fisiología f.
physiotherapy n fisioterapia f.
physique n físico m.
pianist n pianista m, f.
piano n piano m.
piccolo n flautín m.
pick vt escoger, elegir; recoger; mondar, limpiar; to ~ on vt meterse con; to ~ out vt escoger; to ~ up vi ir mejor; recobrarse; ● vt recoger; comprar; aprender; ● n pico m; lo escogido.
pickax n pico m.
picket n piquete m.
pickle n escabeche m; ●vt escabechar.
pickpocket n carterista m.
pickup n (auto) furgoneta f.
picnic n comida, merienda f.
pictorial adj pictórico.
picture n pintura f; retrato m; ● vt pintar; figurar.
picture book n libro de dibujos m.
picturesque adj pintoresco.
pie n pastel m; tarta f; empanada f.
piece n pedazo m; pieza, obra f; ● vt remendar.
piecemeal adv en pedazos; ● adj dividido.
piecework n trabajo a destajo m.
pier n estribo de puente m; muelle m.
pierce vt penetrar, agujerear, taladrar.
piercing adj penetrante.
piety n piedad, devoción f.
pig n cerdo m; (sl) cochino m.
pigeon n paloma f.
pigeonhole n cajita para guardar cartas f.
piggy bank n hucha f.
pigheaded adj terco.
pigsty n pocilga f.
pigtail n trenza f.
pike n lucio m; pica f.
pile n estaca f; pila f; montón m; pelo m; pelillo (en las telas de lana) m; ~s pl almorranas fpl; ● vt amontonar, apilar.
pile-up n accidente múltiple m.

pilfer vt ratear.
pilgrim n peregrino, romero m.
pilgrimage n peregrinación f.
pill n píldora f.
pillage vt pillar, hurtar.
pillar n pilar m.
pillion n asiento trasero m.
pillow n almohada f.
pillow case n funda f.
pilot n piloto m; ● vt pilotar; (fig) guiar.
pilot light n piloto m.
pimp n chulo, cafiche m.
pimple n grano m.
pin n alfiler m; ~s and needles npl hormigueo m; ● vt prender con alfileres; fijar con clavija.
pinafore n delantal m.
pinball n fliper m.
pincers n pinzas, tenazuelas fpl.
pinch vt pellizcar; (sl) birlar; ● vi apretar; ● n pellizco m.
pincushion n acerico m.
pine n (bot) pino m; ● vi ansiar alguna cosa.
pineapple n piña f, ananás m.
ping n sonido agudo m.
pink n rosa f; ● adj color de rosa.
pinnacle n cumbre f.
pinpoint vt precisar.
pint n pinta f.
pioneer n pionero m.
pious adj pío, devoto; ~ly adv piadosamente.
pip n pepita f.
pipe n tubo, caño m; pipa para fumar f; ~s cañería f.
pipe cleaner n limpiapipas m invar.
pipe dream n sueño imposible m.
pipeline n tubería f; oleoducto m; gasoducto m.
piper n gaitero, flautista m.
piping adj hirviente.
pique n pique m; desazón f; ojeriza f.
piracy n piratería f.
pirate n pirata m.
pirouette n pirueta; vi piruetear.
Pisces n Piscis m (signo del zodíaco).
piss n (sl) meados mpl; ● vi mear.
pistol n pistola f.
piston n émbolo m.
pit n hoyo m; mina f.
pitch n lanzamiento m; tono m; ● vt tirar, arrojar; ● vi caerse; caer de cabeza.
pitchblack adj negro como boca de lobo.
pitcher n cántaro m.
pitchfork n horca f.
pitfall n trampa f.
pithy adj meduloso.
pitiable adj lastimoso.
pitiful adj lastimoso, compasivo; ~ly adv lastimosamente.
pittance n pitanza, ración f; porcioncilla f.
pity n piedad, compasión f; ● vt compadecer.
pivot n eje m.
pizza n pizza f.
placard n pancarta f.
placate vt apaciguar.
place n lugar, sitio m; rango, empleo m; ● vt colocar; poner.
placid adj plácido, quieto; ~ly adv apaciblemente.
plagiarism n plagio m.
plague n peste, plaga f; ● vt atormentar; infestar, apestar.
plaice n platija f (pez).
plaid n tartán m.
plain adj liso, llano, abierto; sincero; puro, simple, común; claro, evidente, distinto; ~ly adv llanamente; claramente; ● n llano m.
plaintiff n (law) demandador m.
plait n pliegue m; trenza f; ● vt plegar; trenzar.
plan n plano m; plan m; ● vt proyectar.

plane n avión m; plano m; cepillo m; • vt allanar; acepillar.
planet n planeta m.
planetary adj planetario.
plank n tabla f.
planner n planificador m.
planning n planificación f.
plant n planta f; fábrica f; maquinaria f; • vt plantar.
plantation n plantación f; colonia f.
plaque n placa f.
plaster n yeso m; emplasto m; • vt enyesar; emplastar.
plastered adj (sl) borracho.
plasterer n yesero m.
plastic adj plástico.
plastic surgery n cirujía plástica f.
plate n plato m; lámina f; placa f.
plateau n meseta f.
plate glass n vidrio cilindrado m.
platform n plataforma f.
platinum n platino m.
platitude n tópico m.
platoon n (mil) pelotón m.
platter n fuente f; plato grande m.
plaudit n aplauso m.
plausible adj plausible.
play n juego m; comedia f; • vt, vi jugar; juguetear; representar; (mus) tocar; to ~ **down** vt quitar importancia a.
playboy n playboy m.
player n jugador m; comediante, actor m.
playful adj juguetón, travieso; ~**ly** adv juguetonamente, retozando.
playmate n camarada m.
playground n patio m.
playgroup n parvulario m.
play-off n desempate m.
playpen n corral m.
plaything n juguete m.
playwright n dramaturgo m.
plea n defensa f; excusa f; pretexto m.
plead vt defender en juicio; alegar.
pleasant adj agradable; placentero, alegre; ~**ly** adv alegremente, placenteramente.
please vt agradar, complacer.
pleased adj contento.
pleasing adj agradable, placentero.
pleasure n gusto, placer m; arbitrio m.
pleat n pliegue m.
pledge n prenda f; fianza f; • vt empeñar, prometer.
plentiful adj copioso, abundante.
plenty n copia, abundancia f.
plethora n plétora, repleción f.
pleurisy n pleuresía f.
pliable, pliant adj flexible, dócil.
pliers npl alicates mpl.
plight n estado difícil m.
plinth n plinto m.
plod vi afanarse mucho, ajetrearse.
plot n pedazo pequeño de terreno m; plano m; conspiración, trama f; estratagema f; • vi trazar; conspirar; tramar.
plow n arado m; • vt arar, labrar la tierra; to ~ **back** vt reinvertir; to ~ **through** abrirse paso; roer.
ploy n truco m.
pluck vt tirar con fuerza; arrancar; desplumar; • n ánimo m.
plucky adj gallardo.
plug n tapón m; enchufe m; bujía f; • vt tapar.
plum n ciruela f.
plumage n plumaje m.
plumb n plomada f; • adv a plomo; • vt aplomar.
plumber n plomero m.
plume n pluma f.
plump adj gordo, rollizo.
plum tree n ciruelo m.

plunder vt saquear, pillar, robar; • n pillaje, botín m; bagaje m.
plunge vi sumergir(se), precipitarse.
plunger n desatascador m.
pluperfect n (gr) pluscuamperfecto m.
plural adj, n plural m.
plurality n pluralidad f.
plus n signo de más m; • prep más, y, además de.
plush adj de felpa.
plutonium n plutonio m.
ply vt trabajar con ahinco; • vi aplicarse; (mar) ir y venir.
plywood n madera contrachapada f.
pneumatic adj neumático.
pneumatic drill n martillo neumático m.
pneumonia n pulmonía f.
poach vt escalfar; cazar en vedado; • vi cazar en vedado.
poached adj escalfado.
poacher n cazador furtivo m.
poaching n caza furtiva f.
pocket n bolsillo m; bolsa f; • vt embolsar.
pocketbook n cartera f.
pocket money n dinero para los gastos menudos m.
pod n vaina f.
podgy adj gordinflón.
poem n poema m.
poet n poeta m.
poetess n poetisa f.
poetic adj poético.
poetry n poesía f.
poignant adj punzante.
point n punta f; punto m; promontorio m; puntillo m; estado m; ~ **of view** n punto de vista m; • vt apuntar; aguzar; puntuar.
point-blank adv directamente.
pointed adj puntiagudo; epigramático; ~**ly** adv sútilmente.
pointer n apuntador m; perro de punta y vuelta m.
pointless adj sin sentido.
poise n peso m; equilibrio m.
poison n veneno m; • vt envenenar.
poisoning n envenenamiento m.
poisonous adj venenoso.
poke vt hurgar la lumbre; empujar.
poker n atizador m; póker m.
poker-faced adj de cara impasible.
poky adj estrecho.
polar adj polar.
pole n polo m; palo m; pértiga f.
pole bean n judía trepadora f.
pole vault n salto con pértiga m.
police n policía f.
police car n coche-patrulla m.
policeman n policía m.
police state n estado policial m.
police station n comisaría f.
policewoman n mujer policía f.
policy n política f.
polio n polio f.
polish vt pulir, alisar; limar; to ~ **off** vt terminar; despachar; • n pulimento m.
polished adj elegante, pulido.
polite adj pulido, cortés; ~**ly** adv cortésmente.
politeness n cortesía f.
politic adj político; astuto.
political adj político.
politician n político m.
politics npl política f.
polka n polca f; ~ **dot** n lunar m.
poll n lista de los que votan en alguna elección f; voto m; sondeo m.
pollen n (bot) polen m.
pollute vt ensuciar; corromper.
pollution n polución, contaminación f.

polo n polo m.
polyester n poliéster m.
polyethylene n politeno m.
polygamy n poligamia f.
polystyrene n poliestireno m.
polytechnic n politécnico m.
pomegranate n granada f.
pomp n pompa f; esplendor m.
pompom n borla f.
pompous adj pomposo.
pond n estanque de agua m.
ponder vt ponderar, considerar.
ponderous adj ponderoso, pesado.
pontiff n pontífice, papa m.
pontoon n pontón m.
pony n jaca f; potro m.
ponytail n cola de caballo f.
pool n charca f; piscina, alberca f; • vt juntar.
poor adj pobre; humilde; de poco valor; ~ly adv pobremente; the ~ n los pobres mpl.
pop n pop m; papá m; gaseosa f; chasquido m; • to ~ in/off vi entrar o salir un momento.
pop concert n concierto pop m.
popcorn n palomitas fpl.
Pope n papa m.
poplar n álamo m.
poppy n (bot) amapola f.
popsicle n polo m.
populace n populacho m.
popular adj, ~ly adv popular(mente).
popularity n popularidad f.
popularize vt popularizar.
populate vi poblar.
population n población f.
populous adj populoso.
porcelain n porcelana, china, loza fina f.
porch n pórtico, vestíbulo m.
porcupine n puerco espín m.
pore n poro m.
pork n carne de puerco f.
pornography n pornografía f.
porous adj poroso.
porpoise n marsopa f.
porridge n gachas de avena fpl.
port n puerto m; (mar) babor m; vino de Oporto m.
portable adj portátil.
portal n portal m; portada f.
porter n portero m; mozo m.
portfolio n cartera f.
porthole n portilla f.
portico n pórtico, portal m.
portion n porción, parte f.
portly adj rollizo.
portrait n retrato m.
portray vt retratar.
pose n postura f; pose f; • vi posar; • vt plantear.
posh adj elegante.
position n posición, situación f; • vt colocar.
positive adj positivo, real, verdadero; ~ly adv positivamente; ciertamente.
posse n pelotón m.
possess vt poseer; gozar.
possession n posesión f.
possessive adj posesivo.
possibility n posibilidad f.
possible adj posible; ~ly adv quizá, quizás.
post n correo m; puesto m; empleo m; poste m; • vt apostar; fijar.
postage n porte m.
postage stamp n sello m; estampilla f.
postcard n tarjeta postal f.
postdate vt posfechar.

poster n cartel m.
posterior n trasero m.
posterity n posteridad f.
postgraduate n posgraduado m.
posthumous adj póstumo.
postman n cartero m.
postmark n matasellos m.
postmaster n administrador de correos m.
post office n correos m.
postpone vt diferir, suspender; posponer.
postscript n posdata f.
posture n postura f.
postwar adj de posguerra.
posy n ramillete de flores m.
pot n marmita f; olla f; (sl) marihuana f; • vt preservar en marmitas.
potato n patata f; papa f.
potato peeler n pelapatatas m.
potbellied adj panzudo.
potent adj potente, poderoso, eficaz.
potential adj potencial, poderoso.
pothole n bache m.
potion n poción, bebida medicinal f.
potted adj en conserva; en tiesto.
potter n alfarero m.
pottery n cerámica f.
potty adj cerámica f.
pouch n bolsa f; petaca f.
poultice n cataplasma f.
poultry n aves caseras fpl.
pound n libra f; libra esterlina f; corral m; • vt machacar; • vi dar golpes.
pour vt echar; servir; • vi fluir con rapidez; llover a cántaros.
pout vi ponerse ceñudo.
poverty n pobreza f.
powder n polvo m; pólvora f; • vt polvorear.
powder compact n polvera f.
powdered milk n leche en polvo f.
powder puff n borla f.
powder room n aseos mpl.
powdery adj polvoriento.
power n poder m; potestad f; imperio m; potencia f; autoridad f; fuerza f; • vt impulsar.
powerful adj poderoso; ~ly adv poderosamente, con mucha fuerza.
powerless adj impotente.
power station n central eléctrica f.
practicable adj practicable; hacedero.
practical adj práctico; ~ly adv prácticamente.
practicality n factibilidad f.
practical joke n broma pesada f.
practice n práctica f; uso m; costumbre f; ~s pl intrigas fpl; • vi practicar, ejercer.
practitioner n médico m.
pragmatic adj pragmático.
prairie n pampa f.
praise n renombre m; alabanza f; • vt celebrar, alabar.
praiseworthy adj digno de alabanza.
prance vi cabriolar.
prank n travesura, extravagancia f.
prattle vi charlar; • n charla f.
prawn n gamba f.
pray vi rezar; rogar; orar.
prayer n oración, súplica f.
prayer book n libro de devociones m.
preach vi predicar.
preacher n pastor m.
preamble n preámbulo m.
precarious adj precario, incierto; ~ly adv precariamente.
precaution n precaución f.
precautionary adj preventivo.
precede vt anteceder, preceder.

precedence n precedencia f.
precedent adj, n precedente m.
precinct n límite, lindero m; barrio m; distrito electoral m.
precious adj precioso.
precipice n precipicio m.
precipitate vt precipitar; • adj precipitado m.
precise n preciso, exact; ~ly adv precisamente, exactamente.
precision n precisión, limitación exacta f.
preclude vt prevenir, impedir.
precocious adj precoz, temprano, prematuro.
preconceive vt opinar o imaginar con antelación.
preconception n preocupación f.
precondition n condición previa f.
precursor n precursor m.
predator n animal de rapiña m.
predecessor n predecesor, antecesor m.
predestination n predestinación f.
predicament n predicamento m.
predict vt predecir.
predictable adj previsible.
prediction n predicción f.
predilection n predilección f.
predominant adj predominante.
predominate vt predominar.
preen vt limpiarse (las plumas).
prefab n casa prefabricada f.
preface n prefacio m.
prefer vt preferir.
preferable adj preferible.
preferably adv de preferencia.
preference n preferencia f.
preferential adj preferente.
preferment n promoción f; preferencia f.
prefix vt prefijar; • n (gr) prefijo m.
pregnancy n embarazo m.
pregnant adj embarazada.
prehistoric adj prehistórico.
prejudice n perjuicio, daño m; • vt perjudicar, hacer daño.
prejudiced adj predispuesto; parcial.
prejudicial adj perjudicial, dañoso.
preliminary adj preliminar.
prelude n preludio m.
premarital adj premarital.
premature adj prematuro; ~ly adv anticipadamente.
premeditation n premeditación f.
premier n primer ministro m.
première n estreno m.
premise n premisa f.
premises npl establecimiento m.
premium n premio m; remuneración f; prima f.
premonition n presentimiento m.
preoccupied adj preocupado; ensimismado.
prepaid adj porte pagado.
preparation n preparación f; cosa preparada f.
preparatory adj preparatorio.
prepare vt preparar(se).
preponderance n preponderancia f.
preposition n preposición f.
preposterous adj prepóstero; absurdo.
prerequisite n requisito m.
prerogative n prerrogativa f.
prescribe vi prescribir; recétar.
prescription n prescripción f; receta medicinal f.
presence n presencia f; asistencia f.
present n regalo m; • adj presente; ~ly adv al presente; • vt ofrecer, presentar; regalar; acusar.
presentable adj decente, decoroso.
presentation n presentación f.
present-day adj actual.
presenter n locutor m.
presentiment n presentimiento m.
preservation n preservación f.

preservative n preservativo m.
preserve vt preservar, conservar; hacer conservas de frutas; • n conserva, confitura f.
preside vi presidir; dirigir.
presidency n presidencia f.
president n presidente m.
presidential adj presidencial.
press vt empujar; apretar; compeler; • vi apretar; • n prensa f; armario m; apretón m; imprenta f.
press agency n agencia de prensa f.
press conference n rueda de prensa f.
pressing adj, ~ly adv urgente(mente).
pressure n presión f; opresión f.
pressure cooker n olla a presión f.
pressure group n grupo de presión m.
pressurized adj a presión.
prestige n prestigio m.
presumable adj presumible.
presumably adv es de suponer que.
presume vt presumir, suponer.
presumption n presunción f.
presumptuous adj presuntuoso.
presuppose vt presuponer.
pretend vi pretender; presumir.
pretender n pretendiente m.
pretense n pretexto m; pretensión f.
pretension n pretensión f.
pretentious adj presumido; ostentoso.
preterite n pretérito m.
pretext n pretexto m.
pretty adj lindo, bien parecido; hermoso; • adv algo, un poco.
prevail vi prevalecer, predominar.
prevailing adj dominante (uso, costumbre).
prevalent adj predominante, eficaz.
prevent vt prevenir; impedir.
prevention n prevención, preocupación f.
preventive adj preventivo.
preview n preestreno m.
previous adj previo; antecedente; ~ly adv antes.
prewar adj de antes de la guerra.
prey n presa f.
price n precio m; premio m.
priceless adj inapreciable.
price list n tarifa f.
prick vt punzar, picar; apuntar; excitar; • n puntura f; picadura f; punzada f.
prickle n pincho m; espina f.
prickly adj espinoso.
pride n orgullo m; vanidad f; jactancia f.
priest n sacerdote m.
priestess n sacerdotisa f.
priesthood n sacerdocio m.
priestly adj sacerdotal.
priggish adj afectado.
prim adj peripuesto, afectado.
primacy n primacía f.
primarily adv primariamente, sobre todo.
primary adj primario, principal, primero.
primate n primado m.
prime n (fig) flor, nata f; primavera f; principio m; • adj primero; primoroso, excelente; • vt cebar.
Prime Minister n primer ministro m.
primeval adj primitivo.
priming n cebo m; imprimación f.
primitive adj primitivo; ~ly adv primitivamente.
primrose n (bot) prímula f.
prince n príncipe m.
princess n princesa f.
principal adj, ~ly adv principal(mente); • n principal, jefe m.
principality n principado m.
principle n principio m; causa primitiva f; fundamento, motivo m.

print *vt* imprimir; ● *n* impresión, estampa, edición *f*; impreso *m*; out of ~ vendido, agotado (libros).
printed matter *n* impresos *mpl*.
printer *n* impresor *m*; indianero *m*.
printing *n* imprenta *f*.
prior *adj* anterior, precedente; ● *n* prior (prelado) *m*.
priority *n* prioridad *f*.
priory *n* priorato *m*.
prism *n* prisma *m*.
prison *n* prisión, cárcel *f*.
prisoner *n* prisionero *m*.
pristine *adj* prístino, antiguo.
privacy *n* soledad *f*.
private *adj* secreto, privado; particular; ~ soldier *n* soldado raso *m*; ~ly *adv* en secreto.
private eye *n* detective privado *m*.
privet *n* alheña *f*.
privilege *n* privilegio *m*.
prize *n* premio *m*; presa *f*; ● *vt* apreciar, valuar; to ~ open abrir por fuerza.
prize-giving *n* distribución de premios *f*.
prizewinner *n* premiado *m*.
pro *prep* para.
probability *n* probabilidad, verosimilitud *f*.
probable *adj* probable, verosímil; ~bly *adv* probablemente.
probation *n* prueba *f*.
probationary *adj* probatorio.
probe *n* sonda *f*; encuesta *f*; ● *vt* sondar; investigar.
problem *n* problema *m*.
problematical *adj* problemático; ~ly *adv* problemáticamente.
procedure *n* procedimiento *m*; progreso, proceso *m*.
proceed *vi* proceder; provenir, originarse; ~s *npl* producto *m*; rédito *m*; gross ~s producto íntegro; net ~s producto neto.
proceedings *n* procedimiento *m*; proceso *m*; conducta *f*.
process *n* proceso *m*; progreso *m*.
procession *n* procesión *f*.
proclaim *vt* proclamar, promulgar; publicar.
proclamation *n* proclamación *f*; decreto *m*.
procrastinate *vt* diferir, retardar.
proctor *n* censor *m*.
procure *vt* procurar.
procurement *n* procuración *f*.
prod *vt* empujar.
prodigal *adj* pródigo.
prodigious *adj* prodigioso; ~ly *adv* prodigiosamente.
prodigy *n* prodigio *m*.
produce *vt* producir, criar; causar; ● *n* producto *m*.
produce dealer *n* verdulero *m*.
producer *n* producente *m*.
product *n* producto *m*; obra *f*; efecto *m*.
production *n* producción *f*; producto *m*.
production line *n* línea de producción *f*.
productive *adj* productivo.
productivity *n* productividad *f*.
profane *adj* profano.
profess *vt* profesar; ejercer; declarar.
profession *n* profesión *f*.
professional *adj* profesional.
professor *n* profesor, catedrático *m*.
proficiency *n* capacidad *f*.
proficient *adj* proficiente, adelantado.
profile *n* perfil *m*.
profit *n* ganancia *f*; provecho *m*; ventaja *f*; ● *vi* aprovechar.
profitability *n* rentabilidad *f*.
profitable *adj* provechoso, ventajoso.
profiteering *n* explotación *f*.
profound *adj* profundo; ~ly *adv* profundamente.
profuse *adj* profuso, pródigo; ~ly *adv* profusamente.
program *n* programa *m*.
programing *n* programación *f*.
programmer *n* programador *m*.

progress *n* progreso *m*; curso *m*; ● *vi* hacer progresos.
progression *n* progresión *f*; adelantamiento *m*.
progressive *adj* progresivo; ~ly *adv* progresivamente.
prohibit *vt* prohibir, vedar; impedir.
prohibition *n* prohibición *f*.
project *vt* proyectar, trazar; ● *n* proyecto *m*.
projectile *m* proyectil *m*.
projection *n* proyección *f*; proyectura *f*.
projector *n* proyector *m*.
proletarian *adj* proletario.
proletariat *n* proletariado *m*.
prolific *adj* prolífico, fecundo.
prolix *adj* prolijo, difuso.
prolog *n* prólogo *m*.
prolong *vt* prolongar; diferir.
prom *n* baile de gala *m*.
promenade *n* paseo *m*.
prominence *n* prominencia *f*.
prominent *adj* prominente, saledizo.
promiscuous *adj* promiscuo.
promise *n* promesa *f*; ● *vt* prometer.
promising *adj* prometedor.
promontory *n* promontorio *m*.
promote *vt* promover.
promoter *n* promotor, promovedor *m*.
promotion *n* promoción *f*.
prompt *adj* pronto; ~ly *adv* prontamente; ● *vt* sugerir, insinuar; apuntar (en el teatro).
prompter *n* apuntador de teatro *m*.
prone *adj* inclinado.
prong *n* diente *m*.
pronoun *n* pronombre *m*.
pronounce *vt* pronunciar; recitar.
pronounced *adj* marcado.
pronouncement *n* declaración *f*.
pronunciation *n* pronunciación *f*.
proof *n* prueba *f*; ● *adj* impenetrable; de prueba.
prop *vt* sostener; ● *n* apoyo, puntal *m*; sostén *m*.
propaganda *n* propaganda *f*.
propel *vt* impeler.
propeller *n* hélice *f*.
propensity *n* propensión, tendencia *f*.
proper *adj* propio; conveniente; exacto; bien parecido; ~ly *adv* propiamente, justamente.
property *n* propiedad *f*.
prophecy *n* profecía *f*.
prophesy *vt* profetizar; predicar.
prophet *n* profeta *m*.
prophetic *adj* profético.
proportion *n* proporción *f*; simetría *f*.
proportional *adj* proporcional.
proportionate *adj* proporcionado.
proposal *n* propuesta, proposición *f*; oferta *f*.
propose *vt* proponer.
proposition *n* proposición, propuesta *f*.
proprietor *n* propietario *m*.
propriety *n* propiedad *f*.
pro rata *adv* a prorrateo.
prosaic *adj* prosaico, en prosa.
prose *n* prosa *f*.
prosecute *vt* proseguir.
prosecution *n* prosecución *f*; acusación *f*.
prosecutor *n* acusador *m*.
prospect *n* perspectiva *f*; esperanza *f*; ● *vt* explorar; ● *vi* buscar.
prospecting *n* prospección *f*.
prospective *adj* probable; futuro.
prospector *n* explorador *m*.
prospectus *n* prospecto *m*.
prosper *vi* prosperar.
prosperity *n* prosperidad *f*.
prosperous *adj* próspero, feliz.

prostitute n prostituta f.
prostitution n prostitución f.
prostrate adj postrado.
protagonist n protagonista m.
protect vt proteger; amparar.
protection n protección f.
protective adj protectorio.
protector n protector, patrono m.
protégé n protegido m.
protein n proteína f.
protest vi protestar; ● n protesta f.
Protestant n protestante m.
protester n manifestante m.
protocol n protocolo m.
prototype n prototipo m.
protracted adj prolongado.
protrude vi sobresalir.
proud adj soberbio, orgulloso; ~ly adv soberbiamente.
prove vt probar, justificar; ● vi resultar; salir (bien o mal).
proverb n proverbio m.
proverbial adj, ~ly adv proverbial(mente).
provide vt proveer; to ~ for mantener a; tener en cuenta.
provided conj: ~ that con tal que.
providence n providencia f.
province n provincia f; obligación particular f.
provincial adj, n provincial m.
provision n provisión f; precaución f.
provisional adj, ~ly adv provisional(mente).
proviso n estipulación f.
provocation n provocación f; apelación f.
provocative adj provocativo.
provoke vt provocar; apelar.
prow n (mar) proa f.
prowess n proeza, valentía f.
prowl vi rondar, vagar.
prowler n merodeador m.
proximity n proximidad f.
proxy n poder m; apoderado m.
prudence n prudencia f.
prudent adj prudente, circunspecto; ~ly adv con juicio.
prudish adj gazmoño, mojigato.
prune vt podar; ● n ciruela pasa f.
prussic acid n ácido azul m.
pry vi espiar, acechar; to ~ open vt abrir por fuerza.
psalm n salmo m.
pseudonym n seudónimo m.
psyche n psique f.
psychiatric adj psiquiátrico.
psychiatrist n psiquiatra m.
psychiatry n psiquiatría f.
psychic adj psíquico.
psychoanalysis n psicoanálisis m.
psychoanalyst n psicoanalista m.
psychological adj psicológico.
psychologist n psicólogo m.
psychology n psicología f.
puberty n pubertad f.
public adj público; común; notorio; ~ly adv públicamente; ● n público m.
public address system n megafonía f.
publican n publicano m; tabernero m.
publication n publicación f; edición f.
publicity n publicidad f.
publicize vt publicitar; hacer propaganda para.
public opinion n opinión pública f.
public school n instituto m.
publish vt publicar.
publisher n publicador, editor m.
publishing n industria del libro f.
pucker vt arrugar, hacer pliegues.
pudding n pudín m; morcilla f.
puddle n charco m.

puerile adj pueril.
puff n soplo m; bocanada f; resoplido m; ● vt chupar; ● vi bufar; resoplar.
puff pastry n hojaldre m.
puffy adj hinchado, entumecido.
pull vt tirar; coger; rasgar, desgarrar; to ~ down derribar; to ~ in parar; llegar a la estación; to ~ off cerrar; to ~ out vi irse; salir; ● vt arrancar; to ~ through salir adelante; recobrar salud; to ~ up vi parar; ● vt arrancar; parar; ● n tirón m; sacudida f.
pulley n polea, garrucha f.
pullover n jersey m.
pulp n pulpa f; pasta f.
pulpit n púlpito m.
pulsate vi pulsar, latir.
pulse n pulso m; legumbres fpl.
pulverize vt pulverizar.
pumice n piedra pómez f.
pummel vt aporrear.
pump n bomba f; ● vt dar a la bomba; sondear; sonsacar.
pumpkin n calabaza f.
pun n equívoco, chiste m; ● vi jugar del vocablo, decir equívocos.
punch n puñetazo m; punzón m; taladro m; ponche m; ● vt golpear; perforar.
punctual adj puntual, exacto; ~ly adv puntualmente.
punctuate vi puntuar.
punctuation n puntuación f.
pundit n experto m.
pungent adj picante, acre, mordaz.
punish vt castigar.
punishment n castigo m; pena f.
punk n punki m; música punk f; rufián m.
punt n barco llano m.
puny adj joven, pequeño; inferior.
pup n cachorro m; ● vi parir la perra.
pupil n alumno m; pupila f.
puppet n títere, muñeco m.
puppy n perrito m.
purchase vt comprar; ● n compra f; adquisición f.
purchaser n comprador m.
pure adj puro; ~ly adv puramente.
purée n puré m.
purge vt purgar.
purification n purificación f.
purify vt purificar.
purist n purista m.
puritan n puritano m.
purity n pureza f.
purl n punto del revés m.
purple adj purpúreo; ● n púrpura f.
purport vi: to ~ to dar a entender que.
purpose n intención f; designio, proyecto m; to the ~ al propósito; to no ~ inútilmente; on ~ a propósito.
purposeful adj resuelto.
purr vi ronronear.
purse n bolsa f; cartera f.
purser n comisario m.
pursue vi perseguir; seguir, acosar.
pursuit n perseguimiento m; ocupación f.
purveyor n abastecedor m.
push vt empujar; estrechar, apretar; to ~ aside apartar; to ~ off (sl) largarse; to ~ on seguir adelante; ● n impulso m; empujón m; esfuerzo m; asalto m.
pusher n traficante de drogas m.
push-up n plancha f.
put vt poner, colocar; proponer; imponer, obligar; to ~ away guardar; to ~ down poner en el suelo; sacrificar; apuntar; sofocar; to ~ forward adelantar; to ~ off aplazar; desanimar; to ~ on ponerse; encender; presentar; ganar; echar; to ~ out apagar; extender; molestar; to ~ up alzar; aumentar; alojar.

putrid adj podrido.
putt n putt m; vt hacer un putt.
putty n masilla f.
puzzle n acertijo m; rompecabezas m inv ar.
puzzling adj extraño.
pylon n torre de conducción eléctrica f.
pyramid n pirámide f.
python n pitón atigrado m.

Q

quack vi graznar; • n graznido m; (sl) curandero m.
quadrangle n cuadrángulo m.
quadrant n cuadrante m.
quadrilateral adj cuadrilátero.
quadruped n cuadrúpedo m.
quadruple adj cuádruplo.
quadruplet n cuatrillizo m.
quagmire n tremedal m.
quail n codorniz f.
quaint adj pulido; exquisito.
quake vi temblar; tiritar.
Quaker n cuáquero m.
qualification n calificación f; título m.
qualified adj capacitado; titulado.
qualify vt calificar; modificar; • vi clasificarse.
quality n calidad f.
qualm n escrúpulo m.
quandary n incertidumbre, duda f.
quantitative adj cuantitativo.
quantity n cantidad f.
quarantine n cuarentena f.
quarrel n riña, contienda f; • vi reñir, disputar.
quarrelsome adj pendenciero.
quarry n cantera f.
quarter n cuarto m; cuarta parte f; ~ **of an hour** un cuarto de hora; • vt cuartear.
quarterly adj trimestral; • adv una vez cada trimestre.
quartermaster n (mil) comisario m.
quartet n (mus) cuarteto m.
quartz n (min) cuarzo m.
quash vt fracasar; anular, abrogar.
quay n muelle m.
queasy adj nauseabundo; fastidioso.
queen n reina f; dama f.
queer adj extraño; ridículo; (sl) maricón m.
quell vt calmar; sosegar.
quench vt apagar; extinguir.
query n cuestión, pregunta f; • vt preguntar.
quest n pesquisa, inquisición, busca f.
question n pregunta f; cuestión f; asunto m; duda f; • vt dudar de; interrogar.
questionable adj cuestionable, dudoso.
questioner n inquiridor, preguntador m.
question mark n punto de interrogación m.
questionnaire n cuestionario m.
quibble vi buscar evasivas.
quick adj rápido; vivo; pronto; ágil; ~**ly** adv rápidamente.
quicken vt apresurar; • vi darse prisa.
quicksand n arena movediza f.
quicksilver n azogue, mercurio m.
quick-witted adj agudo, perspicaz.
quiet adj callado; ~**ly** adv tranquilamente.
quietness n tranquilidad f.
quinine n quinina f.
quintet n (mus) quinteto m.
quintuple adj quíntuplo.
quintuplet n quintillizo m.
quip n indirecta f; • vt echar pullas.
quirk n peculiaridad f.

quit vt dejar; desocupar; • vi renunciar; irse; • adj libre, descargado.
quite adv bastante; totalmente, enteramente, absolutamente.
quits adv ¡en paz!
quiver vi temblar.
quixotic adj quijotesco.
quiz n concurso m; programa-concurso m; • vt interrogar.
quizzical adj burlón.
quota n cuota f.
quotation n citación, cita f.
quotation marks npl comillas fpl.
quote vt citar.
quotient n cociente m.

R

rabbi n rabí, rabino m.
rabbit n conejo m.
rabbit hutch n conejera f.
rabble n gentuza f.
rabid adj rabioso, furioso.
rabies n rabia f.
race n raza, casta f; carrera f; • vt hacer correr; competir contra; acelerar; • vi correr; competir; latir rápidamente.
racer n caballo de carreras m.
racial adj racial; ~**ist** adj, n racista m/f.
raciness n vivacidad f.
racing n carreras fpl.
rack n rejilla f; estante m; • vt atormentar; trasegar.
racket n ruido m; raqueta f.
rack-rent n arrendamiento exorbitante m.
racy adj picante, vivo.
radiance n brillantez f, resplandor m.
radiant adj radiante, brillante.
radiate vt, vi radiar, irradiar.
radiation n radiación f.
radiator n radiador m.
radical adj ~**ly** adv radical(mente).
radicalism n radicalismo m.
radio n radio f.
radioactive adj radioactivo.
radish n rábano m.
radius n radio f.
raffle n rifa f (juego); • vt rifar.
raft n balsa, almadía f.
rafter n par m; viga f.
rag n trapo, andrajo m.
ragamuffin n granuja, galopín m.
rage n rabia f; furor m; • vi rabiar; encolerizarse.
ragged adj andrajoso.
raging adj furioso, rabioso.
rag-man, ~ **picker** n trapero m.
raid n incursión f; • vt invadir.
raider n invasor m.
rail n baranda, barandilla f; (rail) raíl, carril m; • vt cercar con barandillas.
raillery n burlas fpl.
railroad, railway n ferrocarril m.
raiment n vestido m.
rain n lluvia f; • vi llover.
rainbow n arco iris m.
rainwater n agua llovediza f.
rainy adj lluvioso.
raise vt levantar, alzar; fabricar, edificar; elevar.
raisin n pasa f (uva seca).
rake n rastro, rastrillo m; libertino m; • vt rastrillar.
rakish adj libertino, disoluto.
rally vt (mil) reunir; • vi reunirse.
ram n carnero, morueco m; ariete m; • vt chocar con.

ramble *vi* divagar; salir de excursión a pie; ● *n* excursión a pie, caminata *f*.
rambler *n* excursionista a pie *m*.
ramification *n* ramificación *f*.
ramify *vi* ramificarse.
ramp *n* rampa *f*.
rampant *adj* exuberante.
rampart *n* terraplén *m*; (*mil*) muralla *f*.
ramrod *n* baqueta *f*; atacador *m*.
ramshackle *adj* en ruina.
ranch *n* hacienda, estancia *f.* 5-29-20
rancid *adj* rancio.
rancor *n* rencor *m*.
random *adj* fortuito, sin orden; **at ~** al azar.
range *vt* colocar, ordenar; ●*vi* vagar; ● *n* clase *f*; orden *m*; hilera *f*; cordillera *f*; campo de tiro *m*; reja de cocina *f*.
ranger *n* guardabosques *m invar*.
rank *adj* exuberante; rancio; fétido; ● *n* fila, hilera, clase *f*.
rankle *vi* doler.
rankness *n* exuberancia *f*; olor *o* gusto rancio *m*.
ransack *vt* saquear, pillar.
ransom *n* rescate *m*.
rant *vi* divagar.
rap *vi* dar un golpecito; ● *n* golpecito *m*.
rapacious *adj* rapaz; **~ly** *adv* con rapacidad.
rapacity *n* rapacidad *f*.
rape *n* violación *f*; estupro *m*; (*bot*) colza *f*; ● *vt* violar.
rapid *adj* rápido; **~ly** *adv* rápidamente.
rapidity *n* rapidez *f*.
rapier *n* espadín *m*.
rapist *n* violador *m*.
rapt *adj* arrebatado; absorto.
rapture *n* rapto *m*; éxtasis *m*.
rapturous *adj* maravilloso.
rare *adj* raro, extraordinario; **~ly** *adv* raramente.
rarity *n* raridad, rareza *f*.
rascal *n* pícaro *m*.
rash *adj* precipitado, temerario; **~ly** *adv* temerariamente; ● *n* salpullido *m*; erupción (cutánea) *f*.
rashness *n* temeridad *f*.
rasp *n* raspador *m*; ● *vt* raspar, escofinar.
raspberry *n* frambuesa *f*; **~ bush** frambueso *m*.
rat *n* rata *f*.
rate *n* tasa *f*, precio, valor *m*; grado *m*; manera *f*; ● *vt* tasar, apreciar.
rather *adv* más bien; antes.
ratification *n* ratificación *f*.
ratify *vt* ratificar.
rating *n* tasación *f*; clasificación *f*; índice *m*.
ratio *n* razón *f*.
ration *n* ración *f*; (*mil*) víveres *mpl*.
rational *adj* racional; razonable; **~ly** *adv* racionalmente.
rationality *n* racionalidad *f*.
rattan *n* (*bot*) rota *f*.
rattle *vi* golpear; traquetear; ● *vt* sacudir; ● *n* traqueteo *m*; sonajero *m*.
rattlesnake *n* culebra de cascabel *f*.
ravage *vt* saquear, pillar; estragar; ● *n* saqueo *m*.
rave *vi* delirar.
raven *n* cuervo *m*.
ravenous *adj* **~ly** *adv* voraz(mente).
ravine *n* barranco *m*.
ravish *vt* encantar; raptar.
ravishing *adj* encantador.
raw *adj* crudo; puro; novato *m*.
rawboned *adj* huesudo; magro.
rawness *n* crudeza *f*; falta de experiencia *f*.
ray *n* rayo de luz *m*; raya *f* (pez).
raze *vt* arrasar.
razor *n* navaja; máquina de afeitar *f*.
reach *vt* alcanzar; llegar hasta; ● *vi* extenderse, llegar; alcanzar, penetrar; ● *n* alcance *m*.

react *vi* reaccionar.
reaction *n* reacción *f*.
read *vt* leer; ● *vi* estudiar.
readable *adj* legible.
reader *n* lector *m*.
readily *adv* pronto; de buena gana.
readiness *n* voluntad, gana *f*; prontitud *f*.
reading *n* lectura *f*.
reading room *n* sala de lectura *f*.
readjust *vt* reajustar.
ready *adj* listo, pronto; inclinado; fácil.
real *adj* real, verdadero; **~ly** *adv* realmente.
reality *n* realidad *f*.
realization *n* realización *f*.
realize *adv* darse cuenta de; realizar.
realm *n* reino *m*.
ream *n* resma *f*.
reap *vt* segar.
reaper *n* segador *m*.
reappear *vi* reaparecer.
rear *n* parte trasera *f*; retaguardia *f*; ● *vt* levantar, alzar.
rearmament *n* rearme *m*.
reason *n* razón *f*; causa *f*; ● *vt, vi* razonar.
reasonable *adj* razonable.
reasonableness *n* lo razonable.
reasonably *adv* razonablemente.
reasoning *n* razonamiento *m*.
reassure *vt* tranquilizar, alentar; (*com*) asegurar.
rebel *n* rebelde *m/f*; ● *vi* rebelarse.
rebellion *n* rebelión *f*.
rebellious *adj* rebelde.
rebound *vi* rebotar.
rebuff *n* desaire *m*; ● *vt* rechazar.
rebuild *vt* reedificar.
rebuke *vt* reprender; ● *n* reprensión *f*.
rebut *vi* repercutir.
recalcitrant *adj* recalcitrante.
recall *vt* recordar; retirar; ● *n* retirada *f*.
recant *vt* retractar, desdecirse.
recantation *n* retractación *f*.
recapitulate *vt, vi* recapitular.
recapitulation *n* recapitulación *f*.
recapture *n* recobra *f*.
recede *vi* retroceder.
receipt *n* recibo *m*; recepción *f*; **~s** *npl* ingresos *mpl*.
receivable *adj* recibidero.
receive *vt* recibir; aceptar, admitir.
recent *adj* reciente, nuevo; **~ly** *adv* recientemente.
receptacle *n* receptáculo *m*.
reception *n* recepción *f*.
recess *n* descanso *m*; recreo *m*; hueco *m*.
recession *n* retirada *f*; (*com*) recesión *f*.
recipe *n* receta *f*.
recipient *n* recipiente *m*.
reciprocal *adj* recíproco; **~ly** *adv* recíprocamente.
reciprocate *vi* reciprocar.
reciprocity *n* reciprocidad *f*.
recital *n* recital *m*.
recite *vt* recitar; referir, relatar.
reckless *adj* temerario; **~ly** *adv* temerariamente.
reckon *vt* contar, computar; ● *vi* calcular.
reckoning *n* cuenta *f*; cálculo *m*.
reclaim *vt* reformar; reclamar.
reclaimable *adj* reclamable.
recline *vt, vi* reclinar(se); recotar(se).
recluse *n* recluso/a *m/f*.
recognition *n* reconocimiento; recuerdo *m*.
recognize *vt* reconocer.
recoil *vi* recular.
recollect *vt* acordarse de; recordar.
recollection *n* recuerdo *m*.
recommence *vt* empezar de nuevo.

recommend vt recomendar.
recommendation n recomendación f.
recompense n recompensa f; • vt recompensar.
reconcilable adj reconciliable.
reconcile vt reconciliar.
reconciliation n reconciliación f.
recondite adj recóndito, reservado.
reconnoiter vt (mil) reconocer.
reconsider vt considerar de nuevo.
reconstruct vt reedificar.
record vt registrar; grabar; • n registro, archivo m; disco; récord m; ~s pl anales mpl.
recorder n registrador, archivero m; (mus) flauta de pico f.
recount vt contar de nuevo.
recourse n recurso m.
recover vt recobrar; recuperar; restablecer; • vi convalecer, restablecerse.
recoverable adj recuperable.
recovery n convalecencia f; recobro m.
recreation n recreación f; recreo m.
recriminate vi recriminar.
recrimination n recriminación f.
recruit vt reclutar; • n (mil) recluta m.
recruiting n recluta f.
rectangle n rectángulo m.
rectangular adj rectangular.
rectification n rectificación f.
rectify vt rectificar.
rectilinear adj rectilíneo.
rectitude n rectitud f.
rector n rector m.
recumbent adj recostado, reclinado.
recur vi repetirse.
recurrence n repetición f.
recurrent adj repetido.
red adj rojo; tinto; • n rojo m.
redden vt teñir de color rojo; • vi ponerse colorado.
reddish adj rojizo.
redeem vt redimir, rescatar.
redeemable adj redimible.
redeemer n redentor m.
redemption n redención f.
redeploy vt reorganizar.
redhanded adj to catch sb ~ pillar a uno con las manos en la masa.
redhot adj candente, ardiente.
red-letter day n día señalado m.
redness n rojez, bermejura f.
redolent adj fragante, oloroso.
redouble vt, vi redoblar(se).
redress vt corregir; reformar; rectificar; • n reparación, compensación f.
redskin n piel roja m/f.
red tape n (fig) trámites mpl.
reduce vt reducir; disminuir; rebajer.
reducible adj reducible.
reduction n reducción f; rebaja f.
redundancy n desempleo.
redundant adj superfluo.
reed n caña f.
reedy adj lleno de cañas.
reef n (mar) rizo m; arrecife m.
reek n mal olor; m; • vi humear; vahear.
reel n carrete m; bobina f; rollo m; • vi tambalear(se).
re-election n reelección f.
re-engage vt empeñar de nuevo.
re-enter vt volver a entrar.
re-establish vt restablecer, volver a establecer una cosa.
re-establishment n restablecimiento m; restauración f.
refectory n refectorio m.
refer vt, vi referir, remitir; referirse.
referee n árbitro m.

reference n referencia, relación f.
refine vt refinar, purificar.
refinement n refinación f; refinadura f; cultura f.
refinery n refinería f.
refit vt reparar; (mar) reparar.
reflect vt, vi reflejar; reflexionar.
reflection n reflexión, meditación f.
reflector n reflector m; captafaros m invar.
reflex adj reflejo.
reform vt, vi reformar(se).
reform, reformation n reformación f.
reformer n reformador m.
reformist n reformista m.
refract vt refractar.
refraction n refracción f.
refrain vi: to ~ from something abstenerse de algo.
refresh vt refrescar.
refreshment n refresco, refrigerio m.
refrigerator n nevera f; refrigerador m.
refuel vi repostar (combustible).
refuge n refugio, asilo m.
refugee n refugiado m/f.
refund vt devolver; • n reembolso m.
refurbish vt restaurar, renovar.
refusal n negativa f.
refuse vt rehusar; • n basura f.
refute vt refutar.
regain vt recobrar, recuperar.
regal adj real.
regale vt regalar.
regalia n insignias fpl.
regard vt estimar; considerar; • n consideración f; respeto m.
regarding pr en cuanto a.
regardless adv a pesar de todo.
regatta n regata f.
regency n regencia f.
regenerate vt regenerar; • adj regenerado.
regeneration n regeneración f.
regent n regente m.
regime n régimen m.
regiment n regimiento m.
region n región f.
register n registro m; • vt registrar; ~ed letter n carta certificada f.
registrar n registrador m.
registration n registro m.
registry n registro m.
regressive adj regresivo.
regret n sentimiento m; remordimiento m; • vt sentir.
regretful adj pesaroso.
regular adj regular; ordinario; ~ly adv regularmente; • n regular m.
regularity n regularidad f.
regulate vt regular, ordenar.
regulation n regulación f; arreglo m.
regulator n regulador m.
rehabilitate vt rehabilitar.
rehabilitation n rehabilitación f.
rehearsal n repetición f; ensayo m (de una obra de teatro).
rehearse vt repetir; ensayar.
reign n reinado, reino m; • vi reinar; prevalecer.
reimburse vt reembolsar.
reimbursement n reembolso m.
rein n rienda f; • vt refrenar.
reindeer n reno m.
reinforce vt reforzar.
reinstate vt reintegrar.
reinsure vt (com) reasegurar.
reissue n nueva edición f.
reiterate vt reiterar.
reiteration n reiteración, repetición f.
reject vt rechazar.

rejection *n* rechazo *m*.
rejoice *vt, vi* regocijar(se).
rejoicing *n* regocijo *m*.
relapse *vi* recaer; • *n* reincidencia *f*; recaída *f*.
relate *vt, vi* relatar, referirse.
related *adj* emparentado.
relation *n* relación *f*; pariente *m*.
relationship *n* parentesco *m*; relación *f*; relaciones *fpl*.
relative *adj* relativo; ~ly *adv* relativamente; • *n* pariente *m/f*.
relax *vt, vi* relajar; descansar.
relaxation *n* relajación *f*; descanso *m*.
relay *n* parada *o* posta *f*; • *vt* retransmitir.
release *vt* soltar, libertar; • *n* liberación *f*; descargo *m*.
relegate *vt* relegar.
relegation *n* relegación *f*.
relent *vi* ablandarse.
relentless *adj* implacable.
relevant *adj* pertinente.
reliable *adj* fiable, de confianza.
reliance *n* confianza *f*.
relic *n* reliquia *f*.
relief *n* relieve *m*; alivio *m*.
relieve *vt* aliviar, consolar; socorrer.
religion *n* religión *f*.
religious *adj* religioso; ~ly *adv* religiosamente.
relinquish *vt* abandonar, dejar.
relish *n* sabor *m*; gusto *m*; salsa *f*; • *vt* gustar de, agradar.
reluctance *n* repugnancia *f*.
reluctant *adj* renuente.
rely *vi* confiar en; contar con.
remain *vi* quedar, restar, permanecer, durar.
remainder *n* resto, residuo *m*.
remains *npl* restos, residuos *mpl*; sobras *fpl*.
remand *vt*: to ~ in custody mantener bajo custodia.
remark *n* observación, nota *f*; • *vt* notar, observar.
remarkable *adj* notable, interesante.
remarkably *adv* notablemente.
remarry *vi* volver a casarse.
remedial *adv* curativo.
remedy *n* remedio, recurso *m*; • *vt* remediar.
remember *vt* acordarse de; recordar.
remembrance *n* memoria *f*; recuerdo *m*.
remind *vt* recordar.
reminiscence *n* reminiscencia *f*.
remiss *adj* negligente.
remission *n* remisión *f*.
remit *vt, vi* remitir, perdonar; disminuir.
remittance *n* remesa *f*.
remnant *n* resto, residuo *m*.
remodel *vt* remodelar.
remonstrate *vi* protestar.
remorse *n* remordimiento *m*; compunción *f*.
remorseless *adj* implacable.
remote *adj* remoto, lejano; ~ly *adv* remotamente, lejos.
remoteness *n* alejamiento *m*; distancia *f*.
removable *adj* amovible.
removal *n* remoción *f*; mudanza *f*.
remove *vt* quitar; • *vi* mudarse.
remunerate *vt* remunerar.
remuneration *n* remuneración *f*.
render *vt* devolver, restituir; traducir; rendir.
rendezvous *n* cita *f*; lugar señalado para encontrarse *m*.
renegade *n* renegado *m*.
renew *vt* renovar, restablecer.
renewal *n* renovación *f*.
rennet *n* cuajo *m*.
renounce *vt* renunciar.
renovate *vt* renovar.
renovation *n* renovación *f*.
renown *n* renombre *m*; celebridad *f*.
renowned *adj* célebre.
rent *n* renta *f*; arrendamiento *m*; alquiler *m*; • *vt* alquilar.

rental *n* alquiler *m*.
renunciation *n* renuncia, renunciación *f*.
reopen *vt* abrir de nuevo.
reorganization *n* reorganización *f*.
reorganize *vt* reorganizar.
repair *vt* reparar; resarcir; • *n* reparación *f*.
reparable *adj* reparable.
reparation *n* reparación *f*.
repartee *n* réplica aguda *o* picante *f*.
repatriate *vt* repatriar.
repay *vt* devolver; pagar, restituir.
repayment *n* pago *m*.
repeal *vt* abrogar, revocar; • *n* revocación, anulación *f*.
repeat *vt* repetir.
repeatedly *adv* repetidamente.
repeater *n* reloj de repetición *m*.
repel *vt* repeler, rechazar.
repent *vi* arrepentirse.
repentance *n* arrepentimiento *m*.
repentant *adj* arrepentido.
repertory *n* repertorio *m*.
repetition *n* repetición, reiteración *f*.
replace *vt* reemplazar; reponer.
replant *vt* replantar.
replenish *vt* llenar, surtir.
replete *adj* repleto, lleno.
reply *n* respuesta *f*; • *vi* responder.
report *vt* referir, contar; dar cuenta de; • *n* informe *m*; reportaje *m*; relación *f*.
reporter *n* reportero *m/f*.
repose *vt, vi* reposar; • *n* reposo *m*.
repository *n* depósito *m*.
repossess *vt* reobrar.
reprehend *vt* reprender.
reprehensible *adj* reprensible.
represent *vt* representar.
representation *n* representación *f*.
representative *adj* representativo; • *n* representante *m*.
repress *vt* reprimir, domar.
repression *n* represión *f*.
repressive *adj* represivo.
reprieve *vt* suspender una ejecución; dar espera; • *n* dilación *f* (de algún castigo).
reprimand *vt* reprender, corregir; • *n* reprensión *f*; reprimenda *f*.
reprint *vt* reimprimir.
reprisal *n* represalia *f*.
reproach *n* improperio, oprobio *m*; • *vt* improperar; vituperar.
reproachful *adj* ignominioso; ~ly *adv* ignominiosamente.
reproduce *vt* reproducir.
reproduction *n* reproducción *f*.
reptile *n* reptil *m*.
republic *n* república *f*.
republican *adj, n* republicano/a *m/f*.
republicanism *n* republicanismo *m*.
repudiate *vt* repudiar.
repugnance *n* repugnancia, desgana *f*.
repugnant *adj* repugnante; ~ly *adv* de muy mala gana.
repulse *vt* repulsar, desechar; • *n* repulsa *f*; rechazo *m*.
repulsion *n* repulsión, repulsa *f*.
repulsive *adj* repulsivo.
reputable *adj* honroso.
reputation *n* reputación *f*.
repute *vt* reputar.
request *n* petición, súplica *f*; • *vt* rogar, suplicar.
require *vt* requerir, demandar.
requirement *n* requisito *m*; exigencia *f*.
requisite *adj* necesario, indispensable; • *n* requisito *m*.
requisition *n* petición, demanda *f*.
requite *vt* recompensar.
rescind *vt* rescindir, abrogar.

rescue *vt* librar, rescatar; • *n* libramiento, recobro *m*.
research *vt* investigar; • *n* investigaciones *fpl*.
resemblance *n* semejanza *f*.
resemble *vt* asemejarse.
resent *vt* resentirse.
resentful *adj* resentido; vengativo; ~ly *adv* con resentimiento.
resentment *n* resentimiento *m*.
reservation *n* reservación, reserva *f*; restricción mental *f*.
reserve *vt* reservar; • *n* reserva *f*.
reservedly *adv* con reserva.
reservoir *n* depósito *m*; pantano *m*.
reside *vi* residir, morar.
residence *n* residencia, morada *f*.
resident *adj* residente.
residuary *adj* sobrado; ~ legatee *n* (*law*) legatario universal *m*.
residue *n* residuo, resto *m*.
residuum *n* (*chem*) residuo *m*.
resign *vt, vi* resignar, renunciar, ceder; resignarse, rendirse.
resignation *n* resignación *f*.
resin *n* resina *f*.
resinous *adj* resinoso.
resist *vt* resistir, oponerse.
resistance *n* resistencia *f*.
resolute *adj* resuelto; ~ly *adv* resueltamente.
resolution *n* resolución *f*.
resolve *vt, vr* resolver(se).
resonance *n* resonancia *f*.
resonant *adj* resonante.
resort *vi* recurrir, frecuentar; • *n* concurso *m*; resorte *m*.
resound *vi* resonar.
resource *n* recurso *m*; expediente *m*.
respect *n* respecto *m*; respeto *m*; motivo *m*; ~s *pl* enhorabuena *f*; • *vt* apreciar; respetar; venerar.
respectability *n* consideración *f*; carácter respetable *m*.
respectable *adj* respetable; considerable; ~bly *adv* notablemente.
respectful *adj* respetuoso; ~ly *adv* respetuosamente.
respecting *prep* con respecto a.
respective *adj* respectivo, relativo; ~ly *adv* respectivamente.
respirator *n* respirador *m*.
respiratory *adj* respiratorio.
respite *n* suspensión *f*; respiro *m*; • *vt* suspender, diferir.
resplendence *n* resplandor, brillo *m*.
resplendent *adj* resplandeciente.
respond *vt* responder; corresponder.
respondent *n* (*law*) defensor *m*.
response *n* respuesta, réplica *f*.
responsibility *n* responsabilidad *f*.
responsible *adj* responsable.
responsive *adj* conforme.
rest *n* reposo *m*; sueño *m*; quietud *f*; (*mus*) pausa *f*; resto, residuo *m*; • *vt* descansar; apoyar; • *vi* dormir, reposar; descansarse.
resting place *n* descansadero *m*.
restitution *n* restitución *f*.
restive *adj* repropio; obstinado.
restless *adj* insomne; inquieto.
restoration *n* restauración *f*.
restorative *adj* restaurativo.
restore *vt* restaurar, restituir.
restrain *vt* restringir, restriñir.
restraint *n* refrenamiento, constreñimiento *m*.
restrict *vt* restringir, limitar.
restriction *n* restricción *f*.
restrictive *adj* restricto.
rest room *n* aseos *mpl*.
result *vi* resultar; • *n* resultado *m*.
resume *vt* resumir; empezar de nuevo.
resurrection *n* resurrección *f*.
resuscitate *vt* resucitar.

retail *vt* revender, regatonear; • *n* venta por menor *f*.
retain *vt* retener, guardar.
retainer *n* adherente, partidario *m*; ~s *pl* comitiva *f*; séquito *m*.
retake *vt* volver a tomar.
retaliate *vt* tomar represalias.
retaliation *n* represalias *fpl*.
retardation *n* retardación *f*.
retarded *adj* retrasado.
retch *vi* esforzarse a vomitar.
retention *n* retención *f*.
retentive *adj* retentivo.
reticence *n* reticencia *f*.
reticule *n* retículo.
retina *n* retícula *f* (del ojo).
retire *vt, vi* retirar(se); jubilar(se).
retired *adj* apartado, retirado; jubilado.
retirement *n* retiro, retiramiento *m*.
retort *vt* replicar; • *n* réplica *f*.
retouch *vt* retocar.
retrace *vt* volver a trazar.
retract *vt* retraer; retractar.
retrain *vt* reciclar.
retraining *n* readaptación profesional *f*.
retreat *n* retirada *f*; • *vi* retirarse.
retribution *n* retribución, recompensa *f*.
retrievable *adj* recuperable; reparable.
retrieve *vt* recuperar, recobrar.
retriever *n* sabueso *m*.
retrograde *adj* retrógrado.
retrospect, retrospection *n* reflexión *f*.
retrospective *adj* retrospectivo.
return *vt* retribuir; restituir; devolver; • *n* retorno *m*; vuelta *f*; recompensa, retribución *f*; recaída *f*.
reunion *n* reunión *f*.
reunite *vt, vi* reunir(se).
reveal *vt* revelar.
revel *vi* andar de juerga.
revelation *n* revelación *f*.
reveler *n* juerguista *m*.
revelry *n* juerga *f*.
revenge *vt* vengar; • *n* venganza *f*.
revengeful *adj* vengativo.
revenue *n* renta *f*; rédito *m*.
reverberate *vt, vi* reverberar; resonar, retumbar.
reverberation *n* rechazo *m*; reverberación *f*.
revere *vt* reverenciar, venerar.
reverence *n* reverencia *f*; • *vt* reverenciar.
reverend *adj* reverendo; venerable; • *n* padre *m*.
reverent, reverential *adj* reverencial, respetuoso.
reversal *n* revocación de una sentencia *f*; cambio total *m*.
reverse *vt* trastrocar; abolir; poner en marcha atrás; • *n* vicisitud *f*; contrario *m*; reverso *m* (de una moneda).
reversible *adj* revocable; reversible.
reversion *n* reversión *f*.
revert *vt, vi* trastrocar; volverse atrás.
review *vt* rever; (*mil*) revistar; • *n* revista *f*; reseña *f*.
reviewer *n* revisor *m*; redactor de una revista.
revile *vt* ultrajar; difamar.
revise *vt* rever; repasar.
reviser *n* revisor *m*.
revision *n* revisión *f*.
revisit *vt* volver a visitar.
revival *n* restauración *f*; restablecimiento *m*.
revive *vt* avivar; restablecer; • *vi* revivir.
revocation *n* revocación *f*.
revoke *vt* revocar, anular.
revolt *vi* rebelarse; • *n* rebelión *f*.
revolting *adj* asqueroso.
revolution *n* revolución *f*.
revolutionary *adj, n* revolucionario/a *m/f*.
revolve *vt* revolver; meditar; • *vi* girar.

revolver n revólver m.
revolving adj giratorio.
revue n revista f.
revulsion n revulsión f.
reward n recompensa f; ● vt recompensar.
rhapsody n rapsodia f.
rhetoric n retórica f.
rhetorical adj retórico.
rheumatic adj reumático.
rheumatism n reumatismo m.
rhinoceros n rinoceronte m.
rhombus n rombo m.
rhomboid n romboide m.
rhubarb n ruibarbo m.
rhyme n rima f; poema m; ● vi rimar.
rhythm n ritmo m.
rhythmical adj rítmico.
rib n costilla f.
ribald adj escabroso.
ribbon n listón m; cinta f.
rice n arroz m.
rich adj rico; opulento; abundante; ~**ly** adv ricamente.
riches npl riqueza f.
richness n riqueza f; abundancia f.
rickets n raquitis f.
rickety adj raquítico.
rid vt librar, desembarazar.
riddance n: good ~! ¡enhoramala!
riddle n enigma m; criba f; ● vt cribar.
ride vi cabalgar; andar en coche; ● n paseo a caballo o en coche m.
rider n caballero, cabalgador m.
ridge n espinazo, lomo m; cumbre f; ● vt formar lomos o surcos.
ridicule n ridiculez f; ridículo m; ● vt ridiculizar.
ridiculous adj ridiculoso; ~**ly** adv ridículamente.
riding n acción de andar a caballo o en coche f; paseo a caballo o en coche m.
riding habit n traje de amazona m.
riding school n picadero m.
rife adj común, frecuente.
riffraff n desecho, desperdicio m.
rifle vt robar, pillar; estriar, rayar; ● n rifle m.
rifleman n escopetero m.
rig vt ataviar; (mar) aparejar; ● n torre de perforación f; plataforma petrolera f.
rigging n (mar) aparejo m.
right adj derecho, recto; justo; honesto; ~! ¡bien!, ¡bueno! ~**ly** adv rectamente, justamente; ● n justicia f; razón f; derecho m; mano derecha f; ● vt hacer justicia.
righteous adj justo, honrado; ~ **ly** adv justamente.
righteousness n equidad f; honradez f.
rigid adj rígido; austero, severo; ~**ly** adv con rigidez.
rigidity n rigidez, austeridad f.
rigmarole n galimatías m.
rigorous adj rigoroso; ~**ly** adv rigorosamente.
rigor n rigor m; severidad f.
rim n margen m/f; orilla f.
rind n corteza f.
ring n círculo, cerco m; anillo m; campaneo m; ● vt sonar; ● vi retiñir, retumbar; **to ~ the bell** pulsar el timbre.
ringer n campanero m.
ringleader n cabeza de partido o bando f.
ringlet n anillejo m.
ringworm n (med) tiña favosa f.
rink n (also ice ~) pista de hielo f.
rinse vt lavar, limpiar.
riot n tumulto, bullicio m; ● vi amotinarse.
rioter n amotinado/a m/f.
riotous adj bullicioso, sedicioso; disoluto; ~**ly** adv disolutamente.
rip vt rasgar, lacerar; descoser.

ripe adj maduro, sazonado.
ripen vt, vi madurar.
ripeness n madurez f.
rip-off n (sl): **it's a ~!** ¡es una estafa!
ripple vi rizarse; ● vt rizar; ● n onda f, rizo m.
rise vi levantarse; nacer, salir; rebelarse; ascender; hincharse; elevarse; resucitar; ● n levantamiento m; elevación f; subida f; salida (del sol) f; causa f.
rising n salida del sol f; fin de una junta o sesión m.
risk n riesgo, peligro m; ● vt arriesgar.
risky adj peligroso.
rissole n croqueta f.
rite n rito m.
ritual adj, n ritual m.
rival adj émulo; ● n rival m; ● vt competir, emular.
rivalry n rivalidad f.
river n río m.
rivet n remache m; ● vt remachar, roblar.
rivulet n riachuelo m.
roach n raya f.
road n camino m.
roadsign n señal de tráfico f.
roadstead n (mar) rada f.
roadworks npl obras fpl.
roam vt, vi corretear; vagar.
roan adj roano, ruano.
roar vi rugir, aullar; bramar; ● n rugido m; bramido, truendo m, mugido m.
roast vt asar; tostar.
roast beef n asado de vaca m.
rob vt robar, hurtar.
robber n robador, ladrón m.
robbery n robo m.
robe n manto m; toga f; ● vt vestir de gala.
robin (redbreast) n petirrojo m.
robust adj robusto.
robustness n robustez f.
rock n roca f; escollo m; rueca f; ● vt mecer; arrullar; apedrear; ● vi bambolear.
rock and roll n rocanrol m.
rock crystal n cuarzo m.
rocking chair n mecedora f.
rocket n cohete m.
rock salt n sal gema f.
rocky adj peñascoso.
rod n varilla, verga, caña f.
rodent n roedor m.
roe n corzo m; hueva f.
roebuck n corzo m.
rogation n rogaciones fpl.
rogue n bribón, pícaro, villano m.
roguish adj pícaro.
roll vt rodar; volver; arrollar; ● vi rodar; girar; ● n rodadura f; rollo m; lista f; catálogo m; bollo m; panecillo m.
roller n rodillo, cilindro m.
roller skates npl patines de rueda mpl.
rolling pin n rodillo de pastelero m.
Roman Catholic adj, n católico/a m/f (romano/a).
romance n romance m; ficción f; cuento m; fábula f.
romantic adj romántico.
romp vi retozar.
roof n tejado m; paladar m; ● vt techar.
roofing n techado, tejado m.
rook n corneja de pico blanco f; roque m (en el juego de ajedrez).
room n habitación, sala f; lugar, espacio m; aposento m.
roominess n espaciosidad, capacidad f.
rooming house n pensión f.
roomy adj espacioso.
roost n pértiga del gallinero f; ● vi dormir las aves en una pértiga.
root n raíz f; origen m; ● vt, vi; **to ~ out** desarraigar; arraigar.

rooted *adj* inveterado.
rope *n* cuerda *f*; cordel *m*; ● *vi* hacer hebras.
ropemaker *n* cordelero *m*.
rosary *n* rosario *m*.
rose *n* rosa *f*.
rosebed *n* campo de rosales *m*.
rosebud *n* capullo de rosa *m*.
rosemary *n* (*bot*) romero *m*.
rose tree *n* rosal *m*.
rosette *n* roseta *f*.
rosé wine *n* vino rosado *m*.
rosewood *n* palo de rosa *m*.
rosiness *n* color róseo *m*.
rosy *adj* róseo.
rot *vi* pudrirse; ● *n* putrefacción *f*.
rotate *vt*, *vi* girar.
rotation *n* rotación *f*.
rote *n* uso *m*; práctica *f*.
rotten *adj* podrido, corrompido.
rottenness *n* podredumbre, putrefacción *f*.
rotund *adj* rotundo, redondo, circular, esférico.
rouble *n* rublo *m*.
rouge *n* arrebol, colorete *m*.
rough *adj* áspero, tosco; bronco, bruto, brusco; tempestuoso; ~ly *adv* rudamente.
roughcast *n* mezcla gruesa *f*.
roughen *vt* poner áspero.
roughness *n* aspereza *f*; rudeza, tosquedad *f*; tempestad *f*.
roulette *n* ruleta *f*.
round *adj* redondo; cabal; franco, sincero; ● *n* círculo *m*; redondez *f*; vuelta *f*; giro *m*; escalón *m*; ronda *f*; andanada de cañones *f*; descarga *f*; ● *adv* redondamente; por todos lados; ~ly *adv* redondamente; francamente; ● *vi* cercar, rodear; redondear.
roundabout *adj* amplio; indirecto, vago; ● *n* jubón *m*.
roundness *n* redondez *f*.
rouse *vt* despertar; excitar.
rout *n* rota, derrota *f*; ● *vt* derrotar.
route *n* ruta *f*; camino *m*.
routine *adj* rutinario; ● *n* rutina *f*; número.
rove *vi* vagar, vaguear.
rover *n* vagamundo *m*; pirata *m*.
row *n* camorra *f*; riña *f*.
row *n* (line) hilera, fila *f*; ● *vt* (*mar*) remar, bogar.
rowdy *n* alborotador, bullanguero *m*.
rower *n* remero *m*.
royal *adj* real; regio; ~ly *adv* regiamente.
royalist *n* realista *m*.
royalty *n* realiza, dignidad real *f*; honorarios que paga el editor al autor por cada ejemplar vendido de su obra *mpl*; royalties *pl* regalías *fpl*; insignias de la corona *f*.
rub *vt* estregar, fregar, frotar; raspar; ● *n* frotamiento *m*; (*fig*) embarazo *m*; dificultad *f*.
rubber *n* caucho *m*, goma *f*; condón *m*.
rubber-band *n* goma, gomita *f*.
rubbish *n* basura *f*; tonterías *fpl*; escombro *m*; ruinas *fpl*.
rubric *n* rúbrica *f*.
ruby *n* rubí *m*.
rucksack *n* mochila *f*.
rudder *n* timón *m*.
ruddiness *n* tez lustrosa y encendida *f*.
ruddy *adj* colorado, rubio.
rude *adj* rudo, brutal, rústico, grosero; tosco; ~ly *adv* rudamente, groseramente.
rudeness *n* descortesía *f*; rudeza, insolencia *f*.
rudiment *n* rudimentos *mpl*.
rue *vi* compadecerse; ● *n* (*bot*) ruda *f*.
rueful *adj* lamentable, triste.
ruffian *n* malhechor, bandolero *m*; ● *adj* brutal.
ruffle *vt* desordenar, desazonar; rizar.
rug *n* alfombra *f*.
rugby *n* rugby *m*.

rugged *adj* áspero, tosco; brutal; peludo.
ruin *n* ruina *f*; perdición *f*; escombros *mpl*; ● *vt* arruinar; destruir.
ruinous *adj* ruinoso.
rule *n* mando *m*; regla *f*; regularidad *f*; dominio *m*; ● *vt* gobernar; reglar, arreglar, dirigir.
ruler *n* gobernador *m*; regla *f*.
rum *n* ron *m*.
rumble *vi* crujir, rugir.
ruminate *vt* rumiar.
rummage *vt* trastornar.
rumor *n* rumor *m*; ● *vt* divulgar alguna noticia.
rump *n* ancas *fpl*.
run *vt* dirigir; organizar; llevar; pasar; to ~ the risk aventurar, arriesgar; ● *vi* correr; fluir, manar; pasar rápidamente; proceder; ir; desteñirse; ser candidato; ● *n* corrida, carrera *f*; paseo *m*; curso *m*; serie *f*; moda *f*; ataque *m*.
runaway *n* fugitivo, desertor *m*.
rung *n* escalón, peldaño *m* (de escalera de mano).
runner *n* corredor *m*; correo, mensajero *m*.
running *n* carrera, corrida *f*; curso *m*.
runway *n* pista de aterrizaje *f*.
rupture *n* rotura *f*; hernia, quebradura *f*; ● *vt* reventar, romper.
rural *adj* rural, campestre, rústico.
ruse *n* astucia, maña *f*.
rush *n* junco *m*; ráfaga *f*; ímpetu *m*; ● *vt* apresurar; ● *vi* abalanzarse, tirarse.
rusk *n* galleta *f*.
russet *adj* bermejo.
rust *n* herrumbre *f*; ● *vi* enmohecerse.
rustic *adj* rústico; ● *n* patán, rústico *f*.
rustiness *n* herrumbre *f*.
rustle *vi* crujir, rechinar; ● *vt* hacer crujir.
rustling *n* estruendo *m*; crujido *m*.
rusty *adj* oriniento, mohoso; rancio.
rut *n* celo *m*; carril *m*.
ruthless *adj* cruel, insensible; ~ly *adv* inhumanamente.
rye *n* (*bot*) centeno *m*.

S

Sabbath *n* sábado *m*.
saber *n* sable *m*.
sable *n* cebellina *f*.
sabotage *n* sabotaje *m*.
saccharin *n* sacarina *f*.
sachet *n* sobrecito *m*.
sack *n* saco *m*; ● *vt* despedir; sequear.
sacrement *n* sacramento *m*; Eucaristía *f*.
sacramental *adj* sacremental.
sacred *adj* sagrado, sacro; inviolable.
sacredness *n* santidad *f*.
sacrifice *n* sacrificio *m*; ● *vt*, *vi* sacrificar.
sacrificial *adj* perteneciente a los sacrificios.
sacrilege *n* sacrilegio *m*.
sacrilegious *adj* sacrílego.
sad *adj* triste, melancólico; infausto; obscuro; ~ly *adv* tristemente.
sadden *vt* entristecer.
saddle *n* silla *f*; sillín *m*; ● *vt* ensillar.
saddlebag *n* saco para dinero *m*.
saddler *n* sillero *m*.
sadness *n* tristeza *f*.
safari *n* safari *m*.
safe *adj* seguro; ileso; fuera de peligro; de fiar; ~ly *adv* seguramente; ~ and sound sano y salvo; ● *n* caja fuerte *f*.
safe-conduct *n* salvoconducto *m*.
safeguard *n* salvaguardia *f*; ● *vt* proteger, defender.
safety *n* seguridad *f*; salvamento *m*.

safety belt *n* cinturón (de seguridad) *m*.
safety pin *n* imperdible, seguro *m*.
saffron *n* azafrán *m*.
sage *n* (*bot*) salvia *f*; sabio *m*; ● *adj* sabio; ~**ly** *adv* sabiamente.
Sagittarius *n* Sagitario *m* (signo del zodíaco).
sago *n* (*bot*) zagú *m*.
sail *n* vela *f*; ● *vt* gobernar; ● *vi* dar a la vela, navegar.
sailing *n* navegación *f*.
sailor *n* marinero *m*.
saint *n* santo *m*; santa *f*.
sainted, saintly *adj* santo.
sake *n* causa, razón *f*; **for God's ~** por amor de Dios.
salad *n* ensalada *f*.
salad bowl *n* ensaladera *f*.
salad dressing *n* aliño *m*.
salad oil *n* aceite de olivas *m*.
salamander *n* salamandra *f*.
salary *n* sueldo *m*.
sale *n* venta *f*; liquidación *f*.
saleable *adj* vendible.
salesman *n* vendedor *m*.
saleswoman *n* vendedora *f*.
salient *adj* saliente, saledizo.
saline *adj* salino.
saliva *n* saliva *f*.
sallow *adj* cetrino, pálido.
sally *n* (*mil*) salida, surtida *f*; ● *vi* salir.
salmon *n* salmón *m*.
salmon trout *n* trucha salmonada *f*.
saloon *n* bar *m*.
salt *n* sal *f*; ● *vt* salar.
salt cellar *n* salero *m* (en la mesa).
saltness *n* saladura *f*.
saltpeter *n* nitro, salitre *m*.
saltworks *npl* salina *f*.
salubrious *adj* salubre, saludable.
salubrity *n* salubridad *f*.
salutary *adj* salubre, salutífero.
salutation *n* salutación *f*.
salute *vt* saludar; ● *n* saludo *m*.
salvage *n* (*mar*) derecho de salvamento *m*.
salvation *n* salvación *f*.
salve *n* emplasto, ungüento *m*.
salver *n* salvilla, bandeja *f*.
salvo *n* reservación, excusa *f*.
same *adj* mismo, idéntico.
sameness *n* identidad *f*.
sample *n* muestra *f*; ejemplo *m*; ● *vt* probar.
sampler *n* muestra *f*; dechado, modelo *m*.
sanctify *vt* santificar.
sanctimonious *adj* semejante a santo.
sanction *n* sanción *f*; ● *vt* sancionar.
sanctity *n* santidad *f*.
sanctuary *n* santuario *m*; asilo *m*.
sand *n* arena *f*; ● *vt* lijar.
sandal *n* sandalia *f*.
sandbag *n* (*mil*) saco de tierra *m*.
sandpit *n* arenal *m*.
sandstone *n* piedra arenisca *f*.
sandwich *n* bocadillo, sandwich *m*.
sandy *adj* arenoso, arenisco.
sane *adj* sapo.
sanguinary *adj* sanguinario.
sanguine *adj* sanguíneo.
sanitarium *n* sanatorio *m*.
sanitary napkin *n* paño higiénico *m*, compresa *f*.
sanity *n* juicio sano, sentido común *m*.
sap *n* savia *f*; ● *vt* minar.
sapient *adj* sabio, cuerdo.
sapling *n* renuevo *m*.
sapphire *n* zafir, zafiro *m*.
sarcasm *n* sarcasmo *m*.

sarcastic *adj* mordaz, cáustico; ~**ally** *adv* mordazmente.
sarcophagus *n* sarcófago, sepulcro *m*.
sardine *n* sardina *f*.
sash *n* cíngulo *m*, cinta *f*.
sash window *n* ventana *o* vidriera corrediza *f*.
sassy *adj* fresco.
Satan *n* Sátanas *m*.
satanic(al) *adj* diabólico.
satchel *n* mochila *f*.
satellite *n* satélite *m*.
satiate, sate *vt* saciar, hartar.
satin *n* raso *m*; ● *adj* de raso.
satire *n* sátira *f*.
satiric(al) *adj* satírico; ~**ly** *adv* satíricamente.
satirist *n* autor satírico *m*.
satirize *vt* satirizar.
satisfaction *n* satisfacción *f*.
satisfactorily *adv* satisfactoriamente.
satisfactory *adj* satisfactorio.
satisfy *vt* satisfacer; convencer.
saturate *vt* saturar.
Saturday *n* sábado *m*.
saturnine *adj* saturnino, melancólico.
satyr *n* sátiro *m*.
sauce *n* salsa *f*; crema *f*; ● *vt* condimentar.
saucepan *n* cazo *m*.
saucer *n* platillo *m*.
saucily *adv* desvergonzadamente.
sauciness *n* insolencia, impudencia *f*.
saucy *adj* insolente.
saunter *vi* callejear, corretear.
sausage *n* salchicha *f*.
savage *adj* salvaje, bárbaro; ~**ly** *adv* bárbaramente; ● *n* salvaje *m*.
savageness *n* salvajería, *f*; crueldad *f*.
savagery *n* crueldad *f*.
savannah *n* sábana *f*.
save *vt* salvar; economizar; ahorrar; evitar; conservar; ● *adv* salvo, excepto; ● *n* parada *f*.
saveloy *n* chorizo *m*.
saver *n* libertador *m*; ahorrador *m*.
saving *adj* frugal, económico; ● *prep* fuera de, excepto; ● *n* salvamiento *m*; ~**s** *pl* ahorro *m*, economía *f*.
savings account *n* cuenta de ahorros *f*.
savings and loan association *n* sociedad de préstamo inmobiliario *f*.
savings bank *n* caja de ahorros *f*.
Savior *n* Redentor *m*.
savor *n* olor *m*; sabor *m*; ● *vt* gustar, saborear.
savoriness *n* paladar *m*; fragrancia *f*.
savory *adj* sabroso.
saw *n* sierra *f*; ● *vt* serrar.
sawdust *n* aserrín *m*.
sawfish *n* priste *m*.
sawmill *n* molino de aserrar *m*.
sawyer *n* aserrador *m*.
saxophone *n* saxófono *m*.
say *vt* decir, hablar.
saying *n* dicho, proverbio *m*.
scab *n* roña *f*; roñoso *m*.
scabbard *n* vaina de espada *f*; cobertura *f*.
scabby *adj* sarnoso.
scaffold *n* tablado *m*; cadalso *m*.
scaffolding *n* andamio *m*.
scald *vt* escaldar; ● *n* escaladura *f*.
scale *n* balanza *f*; escama *f*; escala *f*; gama *f*; ● *vt*, *vi* escalar; descostrarse.
scallion *n* cebolleta *f*.
scallop *n* festón *m*; ● *vt* festonear.
scalp *n* cráneo *m*; ● *vt* escalpar.
scamp *n* bribón, ladrón *m*.
scamper *vi* escapar, huir.

scampi *npl* gambas *fpl*.

scan *vt* escudriñar; registrar: medir las sílabas de un verso.

scandal *n* escándalo *m*; infamia *f*.

scandalize *vt* escandalizar.

scandalous *adj* escandaloso; ~ly *adv* escandalosamente.

scant, scanty *adj* escaso, parco.

scantily *adv* escasamente, estrechamente.

scantiness *n* estrechez, escasez *f*.

scapegoat *n* chivo emisario *m*.

scar *n* cicatriz *f*; ● *vt* hacer alguna cicatriz.

scarce *adj* raro; ~ly *adv* apenas.

scarcity *n* escasez *f*; raridad *f*.

scare *vt* espantar; ● *n* susto *m*.

scarecrow *n* espantajo *m*.

scarf *n* bufanda *f*.

scarlatina *n* escarlatina *f*.

scarlet *n* escarlata *f*; ● *adj* de color de escarlata.

scarp *n* escarpa *f*.

scat *interj, sl* ¡zape!

scatter *vt* esparcir; disipar.

scavenger *n* basurero *m*.

scenario *n* argumento *m*; guión *m*; (*fig*) escenario *m*.

scene *n* escena *f*; panorama *m*; escándalo *m*; paisaje *m*.

scenery *n* vista *f*; decoración (de teatro) *f*.

scenic *adj* escénico.

scent *n* olfato *m*; olor *m*; rastro *m*; ● *vt* oler.

scent bottle *n* frasquito con agua de olor *m*.

scentless *adj* sin olfato; inodoro.

scepter *n* cetro *m*.

schedule *n* horario *m*; programa *m*; lista *f*.

scheme *n* proyecto, plan *m*; esquema *m*; sistema *m*; modelo *m*; ● *vt* proyectar; ● *vi* intrigar.

schemer *n* proyectista, invencionero *m*.

schism *n* cisma *m*.

schismatic *n* cismático *m*.

scholar *n* estudiante *m*; erudito *m*.

scholarship *n* ciencia *f*; educación literaria *f*.

scholastic *adj* escolástico.

school *n* escuela *f*; ● *vt* enseñar.

schoolboy *n* alumno *m*.

schoolgirl *n* alumna *f*.

schooling *n* instrucción *f*.

schoolmaster *n* maestro de escuela *m*.

schoolmistress *n* maestra de niños *o* niñas *f*.

schoolteacher *n* maestro, tra *m/f*; profesor, ra *m/f*.

schooner *n* (*mar*) goleta *f*.

sciatic *n* ciática *f*.

science *n* ciencia *f*.

scientific *adj* científico; ~ally *adv* científicamente.

scientist *n* científico, ca *m/f*.

scimitar *n* cimitarra *f*.

scintillate *vi* chispear, centellar.

scintillating *adj* brillante, ingenioso.

scission *n* separación, partición *f*.

scissors *npl* tijeras *fpl*.

scoff *vi* mofarse, burlarse.

scold *vt, vi* regañar, reñir, refunfuñar.

scoop *n* cucharón *m*; pala *f*; exclusiva *f*; ● *vt* cavar, socavar.

scooter *n* moto *f*; patinete *m*.

scope *n* objeto, intento, designio, blanco, espacio *m*; alcance *m*; libertad *f*.

scorch *vt* quemar; tostar; ● *vi* quemarse, secarse.

score *n* muesca, canalita *f*; consideración *f*; cuenta *f*; puntuación *f*; razón *f*; motivo *m*; veintena *f*; ● *vt* ganar; señalar con una línea; ● *vi* marcar un tanto.

scoreboard *n* marcador *m*.

scorn *vt, vi* despreciar; mofar; ● *n* desdén, menosprecio *m*.

scornful *adj* desdeñoso; ~ly *adv* con desdén.

Scorpio *n* Escorpión *m* (signo del zodíaco).

scorpion *n* escorpión *m*.

scotch *vt* descartar.

Scotch *n* whisky escocés *m*.

Scotch tape *n* scotch *m*.

scoundrel *n* pícaro *m*.

scour *vt* fregar, estregar; limpiar; ● *vi* corretear.

scourge *n* azote *m*; castigo *m*; ● *vt* azotar, castigar.

scout *n* (*mil*) batidor de la campaña *m*; centinela avanzada *f*; espía *m*; ● *vi* reconocer secretamente los movimientos del enemigo.

scowl *vi* mirar con ceño; ● *n* ceño, semblante ceñudo *m*.

scragginess *n* flaqueza, extenuación *f*; aspereza *f*.

scraggy *adj* áspero; macilento.

scramble *vi* arrapar; trepar; disputar; ● *n* disputa *f*; subida *f*.

scrap *n* migaja *f*; sobras *fpl*; pedacito *m*; riña *f*; chatarra *f*.

scrape *vt, vi* raer, raspar; arañar; tocar mal un instrumento; ● *n* embarazo *m*; dificultad *f*.

scraper *n* rascador *m*.

scratch *vt* rascar, raspar; raer, garrapatear; ● *n* rasguño *m*.

scrawl *vt, vi* garrapatear; ● *n* garabatos *mpl*.

scream, screech *vi* chillar, dar alaridos; ● *n* chillido, grito, alarido *m*.

screen *n* pantalla *f*; biombo *m*; mampara *f*; abanico de chimenea *m*; ● *vt* abrigar, esconder; proyectar; cribar, cerner.

screenplay *n* guión *m*.

screw *n* tornillo *m*; ● *vt* atornillar; forzar, apretar, estrechar.

screwdriver *n* destornillador *m*.

scribble *vt* escarabajear; ● *n* escrito de poco mérito *m*.

scribe *n* escritor *m*; escriba *m*.

scrimmage *n* turbamulta *f*.

script *n* guión *m*; letra *f*.

scriptural *adj* bíblico.

Scripture *n* Escritura sagrada *f*.

scroll *n* rollo (de papel *o* pergamino) *m*.

scrub *vt* estregar con un estropajo; anular; ● *n* maleza *f*.

scruffy *adj* desaliñado.

scruple *n* escrúpulo *m*.

scrupulous *adj* escrupuloso; ~ly *adv* escrupulosamente.

scrutinize *vt* escudriñar, examinar.

scrutiny *n* escrutinio, examen *m*.

scuffle *n* quimera, riña *f*; ● *vi* reñir, pelear.

scull *n* barquillo *m*.

scullery *n* fregadero *m*.

sculptor *n* escultor, ra *m/f*.

sculpture *n* escultura *f*; ● *vt* esculpir.

scum *n* espuma *f*; escoria *f*; canalla *m*.

scurrilous *adj* vil, bajo; injurioso; ~ly *adv* injuriosamente.

scurvy *n* escorbuto *m*; ● *adj* escorbútico; vil, despreciable.

scuttle *n* banasta *f*; ● *vt* barrenar.

scythe *n* guadaña *f*.

sea *n* mar *m/f*; ● *adj* de mar; heavy ~ oleada *f*.

sea breeze *n* viento de mar *m*.

seacoast *n* costa marítima *f*.

sea fight *n* combate naval *m*.

seafood *n* mariscos *mpl*.

sea front *n* paseo marítimo *m*.

seagreen *adj* verdemar.

seagull *n* gaviota *f*.

sea horse *n* morso *m*.

seal *n* sello *m*; foca *f*; ● *vt* sellar.

sealing wax *n* lacre *m*.

seam *n* costura *f*; ● *vt* coser.

seaman *n* marinero *m*.

seamanship *n* pericia en la navegación *m*.

seamstress *n* costurera *f*.

seamy *adj* sórdido.

sea plane *n* hidroavión *m*.

seaport *n* puerto de mar *m*.

sear *vt* cauterizar.

search *vt* examinar; escudriñar; inquirir, tentar; investigar, buscar; ● *n* pesquisa *f*; busca *f*; buscada *f*.

searchlight *n* reflector eléctrico *m*.

seashore *n* ribera *f*, litoral *m*.

seasick *adj* mareado.

seasickness n mareamiento, mareo m.
seaside n orilla o ribera del mar f.
season n estación f; tiempo oportuno m; sazón f; ● vt sazonar; imbuir.
seasonable adj oportuno, a propósito.
seasonably adv en sazón.
seasoning n condimento m.
season ticket n abono m.
seat n asiento m; silla f; culo m; escaño m; situación f; ● vt situar; colocar; asentar.
seat belt n cinturón de seguridad m.
seaward adj del litoral; ~ s adv hacia el mar.
seaweed n alga márina f.
seaworthy adj a propósito para navegar.
secede vi apartarse, separarse.
secession n apartamiento m; separación f.
seclude vt apartar, excluir.
seclusion n separación f; exclusión f.
second adj segundo; ~(ly) adv en segundo lugar; ● n defensor m; segundo m; (mus) segunda f; ● vt ayudar; segundar.
secondary adj secundario.
secondary school n escuela secundaria f.
secondhand n segunda mano f (en las compras).
secrecy n secreto, silencio cuidadoso m.
secret adj, n secreto m; ~ly adv secretamente.
secretary n secretario, ria m/f.
secrete vt esconder; (med) secretar.
secretion n secreción f.
secretive adj misterioso.
sect n secta f.
sectarian n sectario m.
section n sección f.
sector n sector m.
secular adj secular, seglar.
secularize vt secularizar.
secure adj seguro; salvo ~ly adv seguramente; ● vt asegurar; salvar.
security n seguridad f; defensa f; confianza f; fianza f.
sedan n sedán m.
sedate adj sosegado, tranquilo; ~ly adv tranquilamente.
sedateness n tranquilidad f.
sedative n sedativo m.
sedentary adj sedentario.
sedge n (bot) lirio espadañal m.
sediment n sedimento m; hez f; poso m.
sedition n sedición f; tumulto, alboroto, motín m; revuelta f.
seditious adj sedicioso.
seduce vt seducir; engañar.
seducer n seductor m.
seduction n seducción f.
seductive adj seductivo.
sedulous adj asiduo; ~ly adv diligentemente.
see vt, vi ver, observar, descubrir; advertir; conocer, juzgar; comprender; ~! ¡mira!
seed n semilla, simiente f; ● vi granar.
seedling n planta de semillero f.
seedsman n tratante en semillas m.
seed time n sementera, siembra f.
seedy adj desaseado.
seeing conj: ~ that visto que.
seek vt, vi buscar; pretender.
seem vi parecer, semejarse.
seeming n apariencia f; ~ly adv al parecer.
seemliness n decensia f.
seemly adj decente, propio.
seer n profeta m.
seesaw n vaivén m; ● vi balancear.
seethe vi hervir, bullir.
segment n segmento m.
seize vt asir, agarrar; secuestrar (bienes o efectos).
seizure n captura f; secuestro m.

seldom adv raramente, rara vez.
select vt elegir, escoger; ● adj selecto, escogido.
selection n selección f.
self n uno mismo; the ~ el yo; ● pref auto. . . .
self-command n imperio sobre sí mismo m.
self-conceit n presunción f.
self-confident adj que tiene confianza en sí mismo.
self-defense n defensa propia f.
self-denial n abnegación de sí mismo f.
self-employed adj autónomo (en el trabajo).
self-evident adj obvio.
self-governing adj autónomo.
self-interest n propio interés m.
selfish adj egoísta; ~ly adv interesadamente.
selfishness n egoísmo m.
self-pity n lástima de sí mismo f.
self-portrait n autorretrato m.
self-possession n sangre fría, tranquilidad de ánimo f.
self-reliant adj independiente.
self-respect n estima de sí mismo f.
selfsame adj idéntico, el mismo o lo mismo exactamente.
self-satisfied adj pagado de sí mismo.
self-seeking adj egoístico.
self-service adj de autoservicio.
self-styled adj titulado.
self-sufficient adj autosuficiente.
self-taught adj autodidacto.
self-willed adj obstinado.
sell vt, vi vender; traficar.
seller n vendedor, ra m/f.
selling-off n venta pública f.
semblance n semejanza, apariencia f.
semen n semen m.
semester n semestre m.
semicircle n semicírculo m.
semicircular adj semicircular.
semicolon n punto y coma m.
semiconductor n semiconductor m.
seminary n seminario m.
semitone n (mus) semitono m.
senate n senado m.
senator n senador, ra m/f.
senatorial adj senatorio.
send vt enviar, despachar, mandar; enviar; producir.
sender n remitente m.
senile adj senil.
senility n senectud; vejez f.
senior n mayor m; ● adj mayor; superior.
seniority n antigüedad, ancianidad f.
senna n (bot) sena f.
sensation n sensación f.
sense n sentido m; entendimiento m; razón f; juicio m; sentimiento m.
senseless adj insensible; insensato; ~ly adv insensatamente.
senselessness n tontería, insensatez f.
sensibility n sensibilidad f.
sensible adj sensible, sensitivo; juicioso.
sensibly adv sensiblemente.
sensitive adj sensitivo.
sensual, sensuous adj, ~ly adv sensual(mente).
sensuality n sensualidad f.
sentence n oración f; sentencia f; ● vt sentenciar, condenar.
sententious adj sentencioso; ~ly adv sentenciosamente.
sentient adj sensitivo.
sentiment n sentimiento m; opinión f.
sentimental adj sentimental.
sentinel, sentry n centinela m.
sentry box n garita de centinela f.
separable adj separable.
separate vt (vi) separar(se); ● adj separado; distinto; ~ly adv separadamente.
separation n separación f.

September *n* se(p)tiembre *m*.
septennial *adj* sieteñal.
septuagenarian *n* septuagenario *m*.
sepulcher *n* sepulcro *m*.
sequel *n* continuación *f*; consecuencia *f*.
sequence *n* serie, continuación *f*.
sequester, sequestrate *vt* secuestrar.
sequestration *n* secuestro *m*.
seraglio *n* seraIlo *m*.
seraph *n* serafín *m*.
serenade *n* serenata *f*; ● *vt* dar serenatas.
serene *adj* seneno; ~ly *adv* serenamente.
serenity *n* serenidad *f*.
serf *n* siervo, esclavo *m*.
serge *n* sarga *f* (tela de lana fina).
sergeant *n* sargento *m*; alguacil *m*; abogado de primera clase *m*.
serial *adj* consecutivo, en serie; ● *n* serial *m*; telenovela *f*.
series *n* serie *f*.
serious *adj* serio, grave; ~ly *adv* seriamente.
sermon *n* sermón *f*; oración evangélica *f*.
serious *adj* seroso, acuoso.
serpent *n* serpiente, sierpe *f*.
serpentine *adj* serpentino; ● *n* (*chem*) serpentina *f*.
serrated *adj* serrado.
serum *n* suero *m*.
servant *n* criado *m*; criada *f*.
servant-girl *n* criada *f*.
serve *vt, vi* servir; asistir (a la mesa); hacer; cumplir; sacar; ser a propósito; to ~ a warrant ejecutar un auto de prisión.
service *n* servicio *m*; servidumbre, utilidad *f*; culto divino *m*; acomodo *m*; ● *vt* mantener; reparar.
service station *n* estación de servicio *f*.
serviceable *adj* serviable; oficioso.
servile *adj* servil.
servitude *n* servidumbre, esclavitud *f*.
session *n* junta *f*; sesión *f*.
set *vt* poner, colocar, fijar; establecer, determinar; ● *vi* ponerse (el sol o los astros); cuajarse; aplicarse; ● *n* juego, conjunto de buenas cartas *m*; servicio (de plata) *m*; conjunto o agregado de muchas cósas *m*; decorado *m*; set *m*; cuadrilla, bandada *f*; ● *adj* puesto, fijo; listo; decidido.
settee *n* sofá *m*.
setter *n* perro de muestra *m*.
setting *n* establecimiento *m*; marco *m*; montadura *f*; ~ of the sun puesta del sol *f*.
settle *vt* colocar, fijar, afirmar; arreglar; calmar; ● *vi* reposarse; establecerse; sosegarse.
settlement *n* establecimiento *m*; domicilio *m*; contrato *m*; empleo *m*; poso *m*; colonia *f*.
settler *n* colono, na *m/f*.
set-to *n* riña *f*; combate *m*.
seven *adj, n* siete.
seventeen *adj, n* diez y siete, diecisiete.
seventeenth *adj, n* decimoséptimo.
seventh *adj, n* séptimo.
seventieth *adj, n* septuagésimo.
seventy *adj, n* setenta.
sever *vt, vi* separar.
several *adj, pn* varios, algunos.
severance *n* separación *f*.
severe *adj* severo, riguroso, áspero, duro; ~ly *adv* severamente.
severity *n* severidad *f*.
sew *vt, vi* coser.
sewer *n* albañal *m*.
sewerage *n* construcción de albañales *f*; agua de sumidero *f*.
sex *n* sexo *m*.
sewing machine *n* máquina de coser *f*.
sexist *adj, n* sexista *m/f*.
sextant *n* sextante *m*.
sexton *n* sepulturero *m*.

sexual *adj* sexual.
sexy *adj* sexy.
shabbily *adv* vilmente, mezquinamente.
shabbiness *n* miseria *f*.
shabby *adj* desharrapado.
shackle *vt* encadenar; ~s *npl* grillos *mpl*.
shade *n* sombra, oscuridad *f*; matiz *m*; sombrilla *f*; ● *vt* dar sombra a; abrigar; proteger.
shadiness *n* sombraje *m*; umbría *f*.
shadow *n* sombra *f*; protección *f*.
shadowy *adj* umbroso; oscuro; quimérico.
shady *adj* opaco, oscuro, sombrío.
shaft *n* flecha, saeta *f*; fuste de columna *m*; pozo *m*; hueco *m*; rayo *m*.
shag *n* tabaco picado *m*; cormorán moñudo *m*.
shaggy *adj* afelpado.
shake *vt* sacudir; agitar; ● *vi* vacilar; temblar; to ~ hands darse las manos; ● *n* sacudida *f*; vibración *f*.
shaking *adj* sacudimiento; temblor *m*.
shaky *adj* titubeante.
shallow *adj* somero, superficial; trivial.
shallowness *n* poca profundidad *f*; necedad *f*.
sham *vt* engañar; ● *n* fingimiento *m*; impostura *f*; ● *adj* fingido, disimulado.
shambles *npl* confusión *f*.
shame *n* vergüenza *f*; deshonra *f*; ● *vt* avergonzar, deshonrar.
shamefaced *adj* vergonzoso, pudoroso.
shameful *adj* vergonzoso; deshonroso; ~ly *adv* ignominiosamente.
shameless *adj* desvergonzado; ~ly *adv* desvergonzadamente.
shamelessness *n* desvergüenza, impudencia *f*.
shammy *n* gamuza *f*.
shampoo *vt* lavar con champú; ● *n* champú *m*.
shamrock *n* trébol *m*.
shank *n* pierna *f*; asta *f*; asta de ancla *f*; cañón de pipa *m*.
shanty *n* chabola *f*.
shanty town *n* barrio de chabolas *m*.
shape *n, vi* formar; proporcionar; concebir; ● *n* forma, figura *f*; modelo *m*.
shapeless *adj* informe.
shapely *adj* bien hecho.
share *n* parte, porción *f*; (*com*) acción *f*; reja del arado *f*; ● *vt, vi* repartir; compartir.
sharer *n* partícipe *m*.
shark *n* tiburón *m*.
sharp *adj* agudo, aguzado; astuto; perspicaz; penetrante; acre, mordaz, severo, rígido; vivo, violento; ● *n* (*mus*) becuadro *m*; ● *adv* en punto.
sharpen *vt* afilar, aguzar.
sharply *adv* con filo; severamente, agudamente; ingeniosamente.
sharpness *n* agudeza *f*; sutileza, perspicacia *f*; acrimonia *f*.
shatter *vt* destrozar, estrellar; ● *vi* hacerse pedazos.
shave *vt* afeitar, rasurar; ● *vi* afeitarse, rasurarse; *n* afeite *m*.
shaver *n* máquina de afeitar *f*.
shaving *n* rasurado *m*.
shaving brush *n* brocha (de afeitar) *f*.
shaving cream *n* crema (de afeitar) *f*.
shawl *n* chal *m*.
she *pn* ella.
sheaf *n* gavilla *f*; haz *m*.
shear *vt* atusar; tundir; ~s *npl* tijeras grandes *fpl*.
sheath *n* vaina *f*.
shed *vt* verter, derramar; esparcir; ● *n* tejadillo *m*; cabaña *f*.
sheen *n* resplandor *m*.
sheep *n* oveja *f*.
sheepfold *n* redil *m*.
sheepish *adj* vergonzoso; tímido.
sheepishness *n* timidez, cortedad de genio *f*.
sheep-run *n* dehesa *f*; carneril, pasto de ovejas *m*.
sheepskin *n* piel de carnero *m*.

sheer *adj* puro, claro, sin mezcla; escarpado; • *adv* verticalmente.

sheet *n* sábana *f*; lámina *f*; pliego de papel *f*; (*mar*) escota *f*.

sheet anchor *n* áncora mayor de un navío *f*.

sheeting *n* tela para sábanas *f*.

sheet iron *n* plancha de hierro batido *f*.

sheet lightning *n* relampagueamiento *m*.

shelf *n* anaquel *m*; (*mar*) arrecife *m*; escollera *f*; **on the ~** desecho.

shell *n* cáscara *f*; proyectil *m*; concha *f*; corteza *f*; • *vt* descascarar, descortezar; bombardear; • *vi* descascararse.

shellfish *npl invar* crustáceo *m*; mariscos *mpl*.

shelter *n* guardia *f*; amparo, abrigo *m*; asilo, refugio *m*; • *vt* guarecer, abrigar; acoger; • *vi* abrigarse.

shelve *vt* echar a un lado, arrinconar.

shelving *n* estantería *f*.

shepherd *n* pastor *m*.

shepherdess *n* pastora *f*.

sherbet *n* sorbete *m*.

sheriff *n* sherif *m*.

sherry *n* jerez *m*.

shield *n* escudo *m*; patrocinio *m*; • *vt* defender.

shift *vi* cambiarse; moverse; • *vt* mudar, cambiar; transportar; • *n* cambio *m*; turno *m*.

shinbone *n* espinilla *f*.

shine *vi* lucir, brillar, resplandecer; • *vt* lustrar; • *n* brillo *m*.

shingle *n* guijarras *fpl*; **~s** *pl* (*med*) herpes *m/fpl*.

shining *adj* resplandeciente; • *n* esplendor *m*.

shiny *adj* brillante, luciente.

ship *n* nave *f*; barco *m*; navío, buque *m*; • *vt* embarcar; transportar.

shipbuilding *n* arquitectura naval *f*.

shipmate *n* (*mar*) ayudante *m*.

shipment *n* cargazón *f*.

shipowner *n* naviero *m*.

shipwreck *n* naufragio *m*.

shirt *n* camisa *f*.

shit *excl* (*sl*) ¡mierda!

shiver *vi* tiritar de frío.

shoal *n* banco *m*.

shock *n* choque *m*; descarga *f*; susto *m*; • *vt* asustar; ofender.

shock absorber *n* amortiguador *m*.

shoddy *adj* de pacotilla.

shoe *n* zapato *m*; herradura de caballo *f*; • *vt* calzar; herrar un caballo.

shoeblack *n* limpiabotas *m*.

shoehorn *n* calzador *m*.

shoelace *n* correa de zapato *f*.

shoemaker *n* zapatero *m*.

shoestring *n* lazo de zapato *m*.

shoot *vt* tirar, arrojar, lanzar, disparar; • *vi* brotar, germinar; sobresalir; lanzarse; • *n* vástago *m*.

shooter *n* tirador *m*.

shooting *n* caza con escopeta *f*; tiro *m*.

shop *n* tienda *f*; taller *m*.

shopfront *n* escaparate *m*.

shoplifter *n* ladrón de tiendas *m*.

shopper *n* comprador, ra *m/f*.

shopping *n* compras *fpl*.

shopping center *n* centro comercial *m*.

shore *n* costa, ribera, playa *f*.

short *adj* corto breve, sucinto, conciso; **~ly** *adv* brevemente; pronto; en pocas palabras.

shortcoming *n* insuficiencia *f*; déficit *m*.

shorten *vt* acortar; abreviar.

shortness *n* cortedad *f*; brevedad *f*.

short-sighted *adj* corto de vista.

short-sightedness *n* cortedad de vista *f*.

shortwave *n* onda corta *f*.

shot *n* tiro *m*; alcance *m*; perdigones *mpl*; tentativa *f*; toma *f*.

shotgun *n* escopeta *f*.

shoulder *n* hombro *m*; brazuelo *m*; • *vt* cargar al hombro.

shout *vi* gritar, aclamar; • *vt* gritar; • *n* aclamación, grito *m*.

shouting *n* gritos *mpl*.

shove *vt, vi* empujar; impeler; • *n* empujón *m*.

shovel *n* pala *f*; • *vt* traspalar.

show *vt* mostrar; descubrir, manifestar; probar; enseñar, explicar; • *vi* parecer; • *n* espectáculo *m*; muestra *f*; exposición, parada *f*.

show business *n* el mundo del espectáculo *m*.

shower *n* nubada *f*; llovizna *f*; ducha *f*; (*fig*) abundancia *f*; • *vi* llover.

showery *adj* lluvioso.

showroom *n* sala de muestras *f*.

showy *adj* ostentoso, suntuoso.

shred *n* cacho, pedazo pequeño *m*; • *vt* hacer trizas.

shrew *n* mujer de mal genio *f*; musgaño *m*.

shrewd *adj* astuto; maligno; **~ly** *adv* astutamente.

shrewdness *n* astucia *f*.

shriek *vt, vi* chillar; • *n* chillido *m*.

shrill *adj* agudo, penetrante.

shrillness *n* aspereza del sonido *o* de la voz *f*.

shrimp *n* camarón *m*; enano, hombrecillo *m*.

shrine *n* relicario *m*.

shrink *vi* encogerse; angostarse, acortarse.

shrivel *vi* arrugarse, encogerse; • *vt* encoger.

shroud *n* cubierta *f*; mortaja *f*; • *vt* cubrir, defender; amortajar; proteger.

Shrove Tuesday *n* martes de carnaval *m*.

shrub *n* arbusto *m*.

shrubbery *n* plantío de arbustos *m*.

shrug *vt* encogerse de hombros; • *n* encogimiento de hombros *m*.

shudder *vi* estremecerse; • *n* temblor *m*.

shuffle *vt* desordenar; barajar los naipes.

shun *vt* huir, evitar.

shunt *vt* (*rail*) maniobrar.

shut *vt* cerrar, encerrar; *vi* cerrarse.

shutter *n* contraventana *f*.

shuttle *n* lanzadera *f*.

shuttlecock *n* volante, rehilete *m*.

shy *adj* tímido; reservado; vergonzoso, contenido; **~ly** *adv* tímidamente.

shyness *n* timidez *f*.

sibling *n* hermano, na *m/f*.

sibyl *n* sibila, profetisa *f*.

sick *adj* malo, enfermo; disgustado.

sicken *vt* enfermar; • *vi* caer enfermo.

sickle *n* hoz *f*.

sick leave *n* baja por enfermedad *f*.

sickliness *n* indisposición habitual *f*.

sickly *adj* enfermizo.

sickness *n* enfermedad *f*.

sick pay *n* subsidio por enfermedad *m*.

side *n* lado *m*; costado *m*; facción *f*; partido *m*; • *adj* lateral; oblicuo; • *vi* unirse con alguno.

sideboard *n* aparador *m*; alacena *f*.

sidelight *n* luz lateral *f*.

sidelong *adj* lateral.

sidewalk *n* acera *f*.

sideways *adv* de lado, al través.

siding *n* toma de partido *f*; (*rail*) aguja *f*.

sidle *vi* ir de lado.

siege *n* (*mil*) sitio *m*.

sieve *n* tamiz *m*; criba *f*; cribo *m*; • *vt* cribar.

sift *vt* cerner; cribar; examinar; investigar.

sigh *vi* suspirar, gemir; • *n* suspiro *m*.

sight *n* vista *f*; mira *f*; espectáculo *m*.

sightless *adj* ciego.

sightly *adj* vistoso, hermoso.

sightseeing *n* excursionismo, turismo *m*.

sign *n* señal *f*, indicio *m*; letrero *m*; signo *m*; firma *f*; seña *f*; • *vt* firmar.

signal *n* señal *f*, aviso *m*; • *adj* insigne, señalado.

signalize vt señalar.
signal lamp n (rail) reflector de señales m.
signalman n (rail) guardavía m.
signature n firma f.
signet n sello m.
significance n importancia f.
significant adj significante.
signify vt significar.
signpost n indicador m.
silence n silencio m; ● vt imponer silencio.
silent adj silencioso; ~ly adv silenciosamente.
silex n guijarro m.
silicon chip n plaqueta de silico f.
silk n seda f.
silken adj hecho de seda; sedeño.
silkiness n blandura, molicie f.
silkworm n gusano de seda m.
silky adj hecho de seda; sedeño.
sill n repisa f; umbral de puerta m.
silliness n simpleza, bobería, tontería, necedad f.
silly adj tonto, imbécil.
silver n plata f; ● adj de plata.
silversmith n platero m.
silvery adj plateado.
similar adj similar; semejante; ~ly adv del mismo modo.
similarity n semejanza f.
simile n símil m.
simmer vi hervir a fuego lento.
simony n simonía f.
simper vi sonreirse; ● n sonrisa f.
simple adj simple, puro, sencillo.
simpleton n simplón, simplonazo m.
simplicity n sencillez f; simpleza f.
simplification n simplificación f.
simplify vt simplificar.
simply adv sencillamente; solo.
simulate vt simular, fingir.
simulation n simulación f.
simultaneous adj simultáneo.
sin n pecado m; ● vi pecar, faltar.
since adv desde, entonces, después; ● prep desde; ● conj desde que; ya que.
sincere adj sencillo; sincero; ~ly adv sinceramente; yours ~ly le saluda atentamente.
sincerity n sinceridad f.
sinecure n sueldo sin empleo m.
sinew n tendón m; nervio m.
sinewy adj nervoso, robusto.
sinful adj pecaminoso, malvado; ~ly adv malvadamente.
sinfulness n corrupción f.
sing n, vt cantar; gorjear los pájaros; (poet) celebrar.
singe vt chamuscar.
singer n cantor m; cantora f.
singing n canto m.
single adj sencillo, simple, solo; soltero, soltera; ● n billete sencillo m; sencillo m; ● vt singularizar; separar.
singly adv separadamente.
singular adj singular, peculiar; ● n singular m; ~ly adv singularmente.
singularity n singularidad f.
sinister adj siniestro, izquierdo; infeliz, funesto.
sink vi hundirse; sumergirse; bajarse; arruinarse, decaer; ● vt hundir, echar a lo hondo; destruir; ● n fregadero m.
sinking fund n caja de amortización f.
sinner n pecador m; pecadora f.
sinuosity n sinuosidad f.
sinuous adj sinuoso.
sinus n seno m.
sip vt sorber; ● n sorbo m.
siphon n sifón m.
sir n señor m.
sire n caballo padre m.

siren n sirena f.
sirloin n lomo de buey o vaca m.
sister n hermana f.
sister-in-law n cuñada f.
sisterhood n hermandad f.
sisterly adj con hermandad.
sit vi sentarse; estar situado; ● vt presentarse a.
site n sitio m; situación f.
sit-in n ocupación f.
sitting n sesión, junta f; sentada f.
sitting room n sala de estar f.
situated adj situado.
situation n situación f.
six adj, n seis.
sixteen adj, n diez y seis, dieciséis.
sixteenth adj, n decimosexto.
sixth adj, n sexto.
sixtieth adj, n sexagésimo.
sixty adj, n sesenta.
size n tamaño, talle m; calibre m; dimensión f; estatura f; condición f.
sizeable adj considerable.
skate n patín m; ● vi patinar.
skateboard n monopatín m.
skating n patinaje m.
skating rink n pista de patinaje f.
skein n madeja f.
skeleton n esqueleto m.
skeleton key n llave maestra f.
skeptic n escéptico.
skeptic(al) adj escéptico.
skepticism n escépticismo m.
sketch n esbozo m; esquicio m; ● vt esquiciar, bosquejar.
skewer n aguja de lardear f; espetón m; ● vt espetar.
ski n esquí m; ● vi esquiar.
ski boot n bota de esquí f.
skid n patinazo m; ● vi patinar.
skier n esquiador, ra m/f.
skiing n esquí m.
skill n destreza, arte, pericia f.
skilled adj práctico, instruído.
skillful adj práctico, diestro; ~ly adv diestramente.
skillfulness n destreza f.
skim vt espumar; tratar superficialmente.
skimmed milk n leche desnatada f.
skimmer n espumadera f.
skin n piel f; cutis m/f; ● vt desollar.
skin diving n buceo m.
skinned adj desollado.
skinny adj flaco, macilento.
skip vi saltar, brincar; ● vt pasar, omitir; ● n salto, brinco m; cuba f.
ski pants npl pantalones de esquí mpl.
skipper n capitán m.
skirmish n escaramuza f; ● vi escaramuzar.
skirt n falda, orla f; ● vt orillar.
skit n burla, zumba f.
skittish adj espantadizo, retozón; terco; inconstante; ~ly adv caprichosamente.
skittle n bolo m.
skulk vi escuchar, acechar.
skull n cráneo m.
skullcap n gorro m.
sky n cielo, firmamento m.
skylight n claraboya f.
skyrocket n cohete m.
skyscraper n rascacielos m invar.
slab n losa f.
slack adj flojo, perezoso, negligente, lento.
slack(en) vt, vi aflojar; ablandar; entibiarse; decaer; relajar; aliviar.
slackness n flojedad, remisión f; descuido m.

slag *n* escoria *f*.
slam *vt* empujar con violencia; ● *vi* cerrarse de golpe.
slander *vt* calumniar, infamar; ● *n* calumnia *f*.
slanderer *n* calumniador, maldiciente *m*.
slanderous *adj* calumnioso; ~**ly** *adv* calumniosamente.
slang *n* argot *m*; jerigonza *f*.
slant *vi* pender oblicuamente; ● *n* sesgo *m*; interpretación *f*.
slanting *adj* sesgado, oblicuo.
slap *n* manotada *f*; (**on the face**) bofetada *f*; ● *adv* directamente; ● *vt* golpear, dar una bofetada.
slash *vt* acuchillar; ● *n* cuchillada *f*.
slate *n* pizarra *f*.
slater *n* pizarrero *m*.
slating *n* techo de pizarras *m*.
slaughter *n* carnicería, matanza *f*; ● *vt* matar atrozmente; matar en la carnicería.
slaughterer *n* matador, asesino *m*.
slaughterhouse *n* matadero *m*.
slave *n* esclavo *m*; esclava *f*; ● *vi* trabajar como esclavo.
slaver *n* baba *f*; ● *vi* babosear.
slavery *n* esclavitud *f*.
slavish *adj* servil, humilde; ~**ly** *adv* servilmente.
slavishness *n* bajeza, servidumbre *f*.
slay *vt* matar, quitar la vida.
slayer *n* matador *m*.
sleazy *adj* de mala fama.
sled, sleigh *n* trineo *m*.
sledgehammer *n* macho *m*.
sleek *adj* liso, bruñido.
sleep *vi* dormir; ● *n* sueño *m*.
sleeper *n* durmiente *m*.
sleepily *adv* con somnolencia *o* torpeza.
sleepiness *n* sueño *m*.
sleeping bag *n* saco de dormir *m*.
sleeping pill *n* somnífero *m*.
sleepless *adj* desvelado.
sleepwalking *n* sonambulismo *m*.
sleepy *adj* soñoliento.
sleet *n* aguanieve *f*.
sleeve *n* manga *f*.
sleight *n*: ~ **of hand** escamoteo *m*.
slender *adj* delgado, débil, pequeño, escaso; ~**ly** *adv* delgadamente.
slenderness *n* delgadez *f*; tenuidad *f*; pequeñez *f*.
slice *n* rebanada *f*; espátula *f*; ● *vt* rebanar.
slide *vi* resbalar, deslizarse; correr por encima del hielo; ● *n* resbalón *m*; corredera *f*; diapositiva *f*; tobogán *m*.
sliding *adj* corredizo.
slight *adj* ligero, leve, pequeño; ● *n* descuido *m*; ● *vt* despreciar.
slightly *adv* ligeramente.
slightness *n* debilidad *f*; negligencia *f*.
slim *adj* delgado; ● *vi* adelgazar.
slime *n* lodo *m*; substancia viscosa *f*.
sliminess *n* viscosidad *f*.
slimming *n* adelgazamiento *m*.
slimy *adj* viscoso, pegajoso.
sling *n* honda *f*; cabestrillo *m*; ● *vt* tirar.
slink *vi* escaparse; esconderse.
slip *vi* resbalar; escapar, huirse; ● *vt* deslizar; ● *n* resbalón *m*; tropiezo *m*; escapada *f*; papelito *m*.
slipper *n* zapatilla *f*.
slippery *adj* resbaladizo.
slipshod *adj* descuidado.
slipway *n* grada *f*, gradas *fpl*.
slit *vt* rajar, hender; ● *n* raja, hendedura *f*.
slobber *n* baba *f*.
sloe *n* endrina *f*.
slogan *n* eslogan, lema *m*.
sloop *n* (*mar*) balandra *f*.
slop *n* aguachirle *f*; lodazal *m*; ~**s** *pl* gachas *fpl*.
slope *n* cuesta *f*; sesgo *m*; declivio *m*; escarpa *f*; ● *vt* sesgar.

sloping *adj* oblicuo; en declive.
sloppy *adj* descuidado; desaliñado.
sloth *n* pereza *f*.
slouch *vt*, *vi* estar cabizbajo; bambolearse pesadamente.
slovenliness *n* desaliño *m*; porquería *f*.
slovenly *adj* desaliñado, puerco, sucio.
slow *adj* tardío, lento, torpe, perezoso; ~**ly** *adv* lentamente, despacio.
slowness *n* lentitud, tardanza, pesadez *f*.
slow worm *n* cecilia *f*.
slug *n* holgazán, zángano *m*; babosa *f*; ficha *f*; trago *m*.
sluggish *adj* perezoso; lento; ~**ly** *adv* perezosamente.
sluggishness *n* pereza *f*.
sluice *n* compuerta *f*; ● *vt* soltar la compuerta de un canal *etc*.
slum *n* tugurio *m*; barrio bajo *m*.
slumber *vi* dormitar; ● *n* sueño ligero *m*.
slump *n* depresión *f*.
slur *vt* ensuciar; calumniar; pronunciar mal; ● *n* calumnia *f*.
slush *n* lodo, barro, cieno *m*.
slut *n* marrana *f*.
sly *adj* astuto; ~**ly** *adv* astutamente.
slyness *n* astucia, maña *f*.
smack *n* sabor, gusto *m*; beso fuerte (que se oye) *m*; chasquido de látigo *m*; ● *vi* saber; besar con ruido; ● *vt* golpear.
small *adj* pequeño, menudo.
smallish *adj* algo pequeño.
smallness *n* pequeñez *f*.
smallpox *n* viruelas *fpl*.
smalltalk *n* charla, prosa *f*.
smart *adj* elegante; listo, ingenioso; vivo; ● *vi* escocer.
smartly *adv* agudamente, vivamente; elegantemente; inteligentemente.
smartness *n* agudeza, viveza, sutileza *f*.
smash *vt* romper, quebrantar; estrellar; batir; ● *vi* hacerse pedazos; estrellarse; ● *n* fracaso *m*; choque *m*.
smattering *n* conocimiento superficial *m*.
smear *n* (*med*) frotis *m invar*; ● *vt* untar; difamar.
smell *vt*, *vi* oler; ● *n* olfato *m*; olor *m*; hediondez *f*.
smelly *adj* maloliente.
smelt *n* espirenque de mar *m*; ● *vt* fundir (el metal).
smelter *n* fundidor *m*.
smile *vi* sonreírse; ● *n* sonrisa *f*.
smirk *vi* sonreírse.
smite *vt* herir; afligir.
smith *n* forjador de metales *m*.
smithy *n* herrería *f*.
smock *n* camisa de mujer *f*.
smoke *n* humo *m*; vapor *m*; ● *vt*, *vi* ahumar; humear; fumar.
smokeless *adj* sin humo.
smoker *n* fumador, ra *m/f*.
smoke shop *n* estanco *m*, tabaquería *f*.
smoking : 'no ~' 'prohibido fumar'.
smoky *adj* humeante; humoso.
smolder *vi* arder debajo la ceniza.
smooth *adj* liso, pulido, llano; suave; afable; ● *vt* allanar; alisar; lisonjear.
smoothly *adv* llanamente; con blandura.
smoothness *n* lisura; llanura; suavidad *f*.
smother *vt* sufocar; suprimir.
smudge *vt* manchar; ● *n* mancha *f*.
smug *adj* presumido.
smuggle *vt* pasar de contrabando.
smuggler *n* contrabandista *m/f*.
smuggling *n* contrabando *m*.
smut *n* tiznón *m*; suciedad *f*.
smuttiness *n* tizne *m*; obscenidad *f*.
smutty *adj* tiznado; obsceno.
snack *n* bocado, bocadillo *m*.
snack bar *n* cafetería *f*.
snag *n* problema *m*.
snail *n* caracol *m*.
snake *n* culebra *f*.

snaky *adj* serpentino.
snap *vt, vi* romper; agarrar; morder; insultar; **to ~ one's fingers** castañetear; ● *n* estallido *m*; foto *f*.
snapdragon *n* (*bot*) antirrino *m*.
snap fastener *n* botón de presión *m*.
snare *n* lazo *m*; trampa *f*.
snarl *vi* regañar, gruñir.
snatch *vt* arrebatar; agarrar; ● *n* arrebatamiento *m*; robo *m*; bocado *m*.
sneak *vi* arrastrar; ● *n* hombre servil *m*.
sneakers *npl* zapatos de lona *mpl*.
sneer *vi* hablar con desprecio; fisgarse.
sneeringly *adv* con desprecio.
sneeze *vi* estornudar.
sniff *vt* oler; ● *vi* resollar con fuerza.
snigger *vi* reír a menudo.
snip *vt* tijeretear; ● *n* tijeretada *f*, pedazo pequeño *m*; porción *f*.
snipe *n* agachadiza *f*; zopenco *m*.
sniper *n* francotirador, ra *m/f*.
snivel *n* moquita *f*; *vi* moquear.
sniveler *n* lloraduelos *m*.
snob *n* (e)snob *m/f*.
snobbish *adj* esnob.
snooze *n* sueño ligero *m*; ● *vi* echar una siesta.
snore *vi* roncar.
snorkel *n* (tubo)respirador *m*.
snort *vi* resoplar.
snout *n* hocico *m*; trompa de elefante *f*.
snow *n* nieve *f*; ● *vi* nevar.
snowball *n* bola de nieve *f*.
snowdrop *n* (*bot*) campanilla blanca *f*.
snowman *n* figura de nieve *f*.
snowplow *n* quitanieves *m invar*.
snowy *adj* nevoso; nevado.
snub *vt* reprender, regañar.
snub-nosed *adj* chato.
snuff *n* rapé *m*.
snuffbox *n* tabaquera *f*.
snuffle *vi* ganguear, hablar gangoso.
snug *adj* abrigado; conveniente, cómodo, agradable, grato.
so *adv* así; de este modo; tan.
soak *vi, vt* remojarse; calarse; empapar, remojar.
soap *n* jabón *m*; ● *vt* jabonar.
soap bubble *n* ampolla de jabón *f*.
soap opera *n* telenovela *f*.
soap powder *n* jabón en polvo *m*.
soapsuds *n* jabonaduras *fpl*.
soapy *adj* jabonoso.
soar *vi* remontarse, sublimarse.
sob *n* sollozo *m*; ● *vi* sollozar.
sober *adj* sobrio; serio; **~ly** *adv* sobriamente; juiciosamente.
sobriety *n* sobriedad *f*; seriedad, sangre fría *f*.
soccer *n* fútbol *m*.
sociability *n* sociabilidad *f*.
sociable *adj* sociable, comunicativo.
sociably *adv* sociablemente.
social *adj* social, sociable; **~ly** *adv* sociablemente.
socialism *n* socialismo *m*.
socialist *n* socialista *m/f*.
social work *n* asistencia social *f*.
social worker *n* asistente, ta social *m/f*.
society *n* sociedad *f*; compañía *f*.
sociologist *n* sociólogo, ga *m/f*.
sociology *n* sociología *f*.
sock *n* calcetín *m*; media *f*.
socket *n* enchufe *m*.
sod *n* césped *m*.
soda *n* sosa *f*; gaseosa *f*.
sofa *n* sofá *m*.
soft *adj* blando, suave; benigno, tierno; afeminado; **~ly** *adv* suavemente; paso a paso.

soften *vt* ablandar, mitigar; enternecer.
soft-hearted *adj* compasivo.
softness *n* blandura, dulzura *f*.
soft-spoken *adj* afable.
software *n* software *m*.
soil *vt* ensuciar, emporcar; ● *n* mancha, porquería *f*; terreno *m*; tierra *f*.
sojourn *vi* residir, morar; ● *n* morada *f*; residencia *f*.
solace *vt* solazar, consolar; ● *n* consuelo *m*.
solar *adj* solar.
solder *vt* soldar; ● *n* soldadura *f*.
soldier *n* soldado *m*.
soldierly *adj* soldadesco.
sole *n* planta del pie *f*; suela del zapato *f*; lenguado *m*; ● *adj* único, solo.
solecism *n* (*gr*) solecismo *m*.
solemn *adj*, **~ly** *adv* solemne(mente).
solemnity *n* solemnidad *f*.
solemnize *vt* solemnizar.
solicit *vt* solicitar; implorar.
solicitation *n* solicitación *f*.
solicitor *n* representante, agente *m/f*.
solicitous *adj* solícito, diligente; **~ly** *adv* solícitamente.
solicitude *n* solicitud *f*.
solid *adj* sólido, compacto; ● *n* sólido *m*; **~ly** *adv* sólidamente.
solidify *vt* solidificar.
solidity *n* solidez *f*.
soliloquy *n* soliloquio *m*.
solitaire *n* solitario *m*; grueso diamante *m*.
solitary *adj* solitario, retirado; ● *n* ermitaño *f*.
solitude *n* soledad *f*; vida solitaria *f*.
solo *n* (*mus*) solo *m*.
solstice *n* solsticio *m*.
soluble *adj* soluble.
solution *n* solución *f*.
solve *vt* resolver.
solvency *n* solvencia *f*.
solvent *adj* solvente; *n* (*chem*) solvente *m*.
some *adj* algo de, un poco, algún, alguno, alguna, unos, pocos, ciertos.
somebody *n* alguien *m*.
somehow *adv* de algún modo.
someplace *adv* en alguna parte; a alguna parte.
something *n* alguna cosa, algo.
sometime *adv* algún día.
sometimes *adv* a veces.
somewhat algo; algún tanto, un poco.
somewhere *adv* en alguna parte; a alguna parte.
somnambulism *n* somnambulismo *m*.
somnambulist *n* somnámbulo *m*.
somnolence *n* somnolencia *f*.
somnolent *adj* somnolente.
son *n* hijo *m*.
sonata *n* (*mus*) sonata *f*.
song *n* canción.
son-in-law *n* yerno *m*.
sonnet *n* soneto *m*.
sonorous *adj* sonoro.
soon *adv* pronto; **as ~ as** luego que.
sooner *adv* antes, más pronto.
soot *n* hollín *m*.
soothe *vt* adular; calmar.
soothsayer *n* adivino *m*.
sop *n* sopa *f*.
sophism *n* sofisma *m*.
sophist *n* sofista.
sophistical *adj* sofístico.
sophisticate *vt* sofisticar; falsificar.
sophisticated *adj* sofisticado.
sophistry *n* sofistería *f*.
sophomore *n* estudiante de segundo año *m/f*.

soporific *adj* soporífero.

sorcerer *n* hechicero *m*.

sorceress *n* hechicera *f*.

sorcery *n* hechizo, encanto *m*.

sordid *adj* sórdido, sucio; avariento.

sordidness *n* sordidez, mezquindad *f*.

sore *n* llaga, úlcera *f*; ● *adj* doloroso, penoso; resentido; ~ly *adv* penosamente.

sorrel *n* (*bot*) acedera *f*; ● *adj* alazán rojo.

sorrow *n* pesar *m*; tristeza *f*; ● *vi* entristecerse.

sorrowful *adj* pesaroso, afligido; ~ly *adv* con aflicción.

sorry *adj* triste, afligido; arrepentido; I am ~ lo siento.

sort *n* suerte *f*; género *m*; especie *f*; calidad *f*; manera *f*; ● *vt* separar en distintas clases; escoger, elegir.

soul *n* alma *f*; esencia *f*; persona *f*.

sound *adj* sano; entero; puro; firme; ~ly *adv* sanamente, vigorosamente; ● *n* sonido, ruido *m*; estrecho *m*; ● *vt* sonar; tocar; celebrar; sondar; ● *vi* sonar, resonar; parecer.

sounding board *n* diapasón *m*; sombrero de púlpito *m*.

sound effects *npl* efectos sonoros *mpl*.

soundings *npl* (*mar*) sondeo *m*; (*mar*) surgidero profundo *m*.

soundness *n* sanidad *f*; fuerza, solidez *f*.

soundtrack *n* banda sonora *f*.

soup *n* sopa *f*.

sour *adj* agrio, ácido; cortado; áspero; ~ly *adv* agriamente; ● *vt*, *vi* agriar, acedar; agriarse.

source *n* manantial *m*; principio *m*.

sourness *n* acedía, agrura *f*; acrimonia *f*.

souse *n* (*sl*) borracho, cha *m/f*; ● *vt* escabechar; chapuzar.

souvenir *n* recuerdo *m*.

south *n* sur *m*; ● *adj* del sur; ● *adv* al sur.

southerly, southern *adj* del sur, meridional.

southward(s) *adv* hacia el sur.

southwester *n* (*mar*) viento de sudoeste *m*; sombrero grande de los marineros *m*.

sovereign *adj*, *n* soberano, na (*m/f*).

sovereignty *n* soberanía *f*.

sow *n* puerca, marrana *f*.

sow *vt* sembrar; esparcir.

sowing-time *n* sementera, siembra *f*.

soy *n* soja *f*.

space *n* espacio *m*; intersticio *m*; ● *vt* espaciar.

spacecraft *n* nave espacial *f*.

spaceman/woman *n* astronauta *m/f*.

spacious *adj* espacioso, amplio; ~ly *adv* con bastante espacio.

spaciousness *n* espaciosidad *f*.

spade *n* laya, azada *f*; espadas *fpl* (en los naipes).

spaghetti *n* espaguetis, fideos *mpl*.

span *n* palmo *m*; envergadura *f*; ● *vt* cruzar; abarcar.

spangle *n* lentejuela *f*; ● *vt* adornar con lentejuelas.

spaniel *n* perro de aguas *m*.

Spanish *adj* español(a); ● *n* español *m*.

spar *n* palo *m*; ● *vi* entrenarse.

spare *vt*, *vi* ahorrar, economizar; perdonar; pasarse sin; vivir con economía; ● *adj* de más; de reserva.

sparing *adj* escaso, raro, económico; ~ly *adv* parcamente, frugalmente.

spark *n* chispa *f*.

sparkle *n* centella, chispa *f*; ● *vi* chispear; espumar.

spark plug *n* bujía *f*.

sparrow *n* gorrión *m*.

sparrowhawk *n* hembra del gavilán *f*.

sparse *adj* delgado; tenue; ~ly *adv* tenuemente.

spasm *n* espasmo *m*.

spasmodic *adj* espasmódico.

spatter *vt* salpicar, manchar.

spatula *n* espátula *f*.

spawn *n* freza *f*; ● *vt*, *vi* desovar; engendrar.

spawning *n* freza *f*.

speak *vt*, *vi* hablar; decir; conversar; pronunciar.

speaker *n* altavoz; bafle *m*; orador, ra *m/f*.

spear *n* lanza *f*; arpón *m*; ● *vt* herir con lanza.

special *adj* especial, particular; ~ly *adv* especialmente.

specialty *n* especialidad *f*.

species *n* especie *f*.

specific *adj* específico; ● *n* específico *m*.

specifically *adv* en especie.

specification *n* especificación *f*.

specify *vt* especificar.

specimen *n* muestra *f*; prueba *f*.

specious *adj* especioso.

speck(le) *n* mácula, tacha *f*; ● *vt* abigarrar, manchar.

spectacle *n* espectáculo *m*.

spectator *n* espectador, ra *m/f*.

specter *n* espectro *m*.

spectral *adj* aduendado; espectométrico; ~ analysis *n* análisis del espectro solar *f*.

speculate *vi* especular; reflexionar.

speculation *n* especulación *f*; especulativa *f*; meditación *f*.

speculative *adj* especulativo, teórico.

speculum *n* espejo *m*.

speech *n* habla *m*; discurso *m*; lenguaje *m*; conversación *f*.

speechify *vi* arengar.

speechless *adj* mudo.

speed *n* prisa *f*; velocidad *f*; ● *vt* apresurar; despachar; ● *vi* darse prisa.

speedboat *n* lancha motora *f*.

speedily *adv* aceleradamente, de prisa.

speediness *n* celeridad, prontitud, precipitación *f*.

speed limit *n* límite de velocidad *m*, velocidad máxima *f*.

speedometer *n* velocímetro *m*.

speedway *n* pista de carrera *f*.

speedy *adj* veloz, pronto, diligente.

spell *n* hechizo, encanto *m*; período *m*; ● *vt*, *vi* escribir correctamente; deletrear; hechizar, encantar.

spelling *n* ortografía *f*.

spend *vt* gastar; pasar; disipar; consumir.

spendthrift *n* pródigo *m*.

spent *adj* alcanzado de fuerzas.

sperm *n* esperma *f*.

spermaceti *n* espermaceti *m*.

spew *vi* (*sl*) vomitar.

sphere *n* esfera *f*.

spherical *adj* esférico; ~ly *adv* en forma esférica.

spice *n* especia *f*; ● *vt* especiar.

spick-and-span *adj* aseado, (bien) arreglado.

spicy *adj* aromático.

spider *n* araña *f*.

spigot *n* llave de fuente *f*.

spike *n* espiga de grano *f*; espigón *m*; ● *vi* clavar con espigones.

spill *vt* derramar, verter; ● *vi* derramarse.

spin *vt* hilar; alargar, prolongar; girar; ● *vi* dar vueltas; ● *n* vuelta *f*; paseo (en coche) *m*.

spinach *n* espinaca *f*.

spinal *adj* espinal.

spindle *n* huso *m*; quicio *m*.

spine *n* espinazo *m*, espina *f*.

spinet *n* (*mus*) espineta *f*.

spinner *n* hilador *m*; hilandera *f*.

spinning wheel *n* torno de hilar *m*.

spin-off *n* derivado, producto secundario *m*.

spinster *n* soltera *f*.

spiral *adj* espiral; ~ly *adv* en figura de espiral.

spire *n* espira *f*; pirámide *m*; aguja *f* (de una torre).

spirit *n* aliento *m*; espíritu *m*; ánimo, valor *m*; brío *m*; humor *m*; fantasma *m*; ● *vt* incitar, animar; to ~ away quitar secretamente.

spirited *adj* vivo, brioso; ~ly *adv* con espíritu.

spirit lamp *n* velón *o* quinqué alimentado con alcohol *m*.

spiritless *adj* abatido, sin espíritu.

spiritual *adj*, ~ly *adv* espiritual(mente).

spiritualist *n* espiritualista *m*.

spirituality *n* espiritualidad *f*.

spit n asador m; saliva f; ● vt, vi espetar; escupir.

spite n rencor m, malevolencia f; in ~ of a pesar de, a despecho; ● vt dar pesar.

spiteful adj rencoroso, malicioso; ~ly adv malignamente, con tirria.

spitefulness n malicia f; rencor m.

spittle n saliva f; esputo m.

splash vt salpicar, enlodar; ● vi chapotear; ● n chapoteo m; mancha f.

spleen n bazo m; esplín m.

splendid adj espléndido, magnífico; ~ly adv espléndidamente.

splendor n esplendor m; pompa f.

splice vt (mar) empalmar, empleitar.

splint n tablilla f.

splinter n cacho m; astilla f; brisna f; ● vt (vi) hender(se).

split n hendedura f; división f; ● vt hender, rajar; ● vi henderse.

spoil vt despojar; arruinar; mimar.

spoiled adj pasado; cortado.

spoke n rayo de la rueda m.

spokesman n portavoz m.

spokeswoman n portavoz f.

sponge n esponja f; ● vt limpiar con esponja; ● vi meterse de mogollón.

sponger n mogollón m.

sponginess n calidad esponjosa f.

spongy adj esponjoso.

sponsor n fiador m; padrino m; madrina f.

sponsorship n patrocinio m.

spontaneity n espontaneidad, voluntariedad f.

spontaneous adj espontáneo; ~ly adv espontáneamente.

spool n carrete m; canilla, broca f.

spoon n cuchara f.

spoonful n cucharada f.

sporadic(al) adj esporádico.

sport n deporte m; juego, retozo m; juguete, divertimiento, recreo, pasatiempo m.

sport jacket n chaqueta deportiva f.

sports car n coche sport m.

sportsman n deportista m.

sportswear n trajes de deporte o sport mpl.

sportswoman n deportista f.

spot n mancha f; borrón m; sitio, lugar m; grano m; ● vt notar; manchar.

spotless adj limpio, inmaculado.

spotlight n foco, reflector m.

spotted, spotty adj lleno de manchas; con granos.

spouse n esposo m; esposa f.

spout vi arrojar agua con mucho ímpetu; borbotar; chorrear; ● vt llave de fuente f; gárgola f; bomba marina f.

sprain adj descoyuntar; ● n dislocación f.

sprat n meleta, nuesa f (pez).

sprawl vi revolcarse.

spray n rociada f; espray m; ramita f; espuma de la mar f.

spread vt extender, desplegar; esparcir, divulgar; ● vi extenderse, desplegarse; ● n extensión, dilatación f.

spree n fiesta f; juerga f.

sprig n ramito m.

sprightliness n alegría, vivacidad f.

sprightly adj alegre, despierto, vivaracho.

spring vi brotar, arrojar; nacer, provenir; dimanar, originarse; saltar, brincar; ● n primavera f; elasticidad f; muelle, resorte m; salto m; manantial m.

springiness n elasticidad f.

springtime n primavera f.

springwater n agua de fuente f.

springy adj elástico.

sprinkle vt rociar.

sprinkling n rociadura f.

sprout n vástago, renuevo m; ~s npl coles de Bruselas fpl; ● vi brotar.

spruce adj pulido, gentil; ~ly adv bellamente, lindamente; ● vr vestirse con afectación.

spruceness n lindeza, hermosura f.

spur n espuela f; espolón (del gallo) m; estímulo m; ● vt espolear; estimular.

spurious adj espurio, falso; contrahecho; supuesto; bastardo.

spurn vt despreciar.

sputter vi escupir con frecuencia; babosear; barbotar.

spy n espía m; ● vt, vi espiar; columbrar.

squabble vi reñir, disputar; ● n riña, disputa f.

squad n escuadra de soldados f; brigada f; equipo m.

squadron n (mil) escuadrón m.

squalid adj sucio, puerco.

squall n ráfaga f; chubasco m; ● vi chillar.

squally adj borrascoso.

squalor n porquería, suciedad f.

squander vt malgastar, disipar.

square adj cuadrado, cuadrángulo; exacto; cabal; ● n cuadro m; plaza f; escuadra f; ● vt cuadrar; ajustar, arreglar; ● vi ajustarse.

squareness n cuadratura f.

squash vt aplastar; ● n squash, frontenis m.

squat vi agacharse; ● adj agachado; rechoncho.

squatter n colono usurpador m.

squaw n hembra de un indiano f.

squeak vi plañir, chillar; ● n grito, plañido m.

squeal vi plañir, gritar.

squeamish adj fastidioso; demasiado delicado.

squeeze vt apretar, comprimir; estrechar; ● n presión f; apretón m; restricción f.

squid n calamar m.

squint adj bizco; ● vi bizquear; ● n estrabismo.

squirrel n ardilla f.

squirt vt jeringar; ● n jeringa f; chorro m; pisaverde m.

stab vt apuñalar; ● n puñalada f.

stability n estabilidad, solidez f.

stable n establo m; ● vt poner en el establo; ● adj estable.

stack n pila f; ● vt hacinar.

staff n personal m, plantilla f; palo m; apoyo m.

stag n ciervo m.

stage n etapa f; escena f; tablado m; teatro m; parada f; escalón m.

stagger vi vacilar, titubear; estar incierto; ● vt asustar; escalonar.

stagnation n estancamiento m.

stagnant adj estancado.

stagnate vi estancarse.

staid adj grave, serio.

stain vt manchar; empañar la reputación; ● n mancha f; deshonra f.

stainless adj limpio; inmaculado.

stair n escalón m; ~s pl escalera f.

staircase n escalera f.

stake n estaca f; apuesta f (en el juego); ● vt estacar; apostar.

stale adj añejo, viejo, rancio.

staleness n vejez f; rancidez f.

stalk vi andar con paso majestuoso; ● n tallo, pie, tronco m; troncho m (de ciertas hortalizas).

stall n pesebre m; tienda portátil f; tabanco m; emplazamiento m; ● vt parar; ● vi pararse; buscar evasivas.

stallion n semental m.

stalwart n partidario leal m.

stamen n estambre m; fundamento m.

stamina n resistencia f.

stammer vi tartamudear; ● n tartamudeo m.

stamp vt patear; estampar, imprimir; acuñar; andar con mucha pesadez; ● vi patear; ● n cuño m; sello m; impresión f; huella f; estampilla f.

stampede n estampida f.

stand vi estar de pie o derecho; sostenerse; permanecer; pararse, hacer alto, estar situado; hallarse; erizarse el pelo; ● vt poner; aguantar; sostener, defender; ● n puesto, sitio m;

posición, situación *f*; parada *f*; estado *m* (fijo); tribuna *f*; stand *m*.

standard *n* estandarte *m*; modelo *m*; precio ordinario *m*; norma *f*; ● *adj* normal.

standing *adj* permanente, fijado, establecido; de pie; estancado; ● *n* duración *f*; posición *f*; puesto *m*.

standstill *n* pausa *f*; alto *m*.

staple *n* grapa *f*; ● *adj* ajustado, establecido; ● *vt* engrapar.

star *n* estrella *f*; asterisco *m*.

starboard *n* estribor *m*.

starch *n* almidón *m*; ● *vt* almidonar.

stare *vi*: to ~ at clavar la vista; ● *n* mirada fija *f*.

stark *adj* fuerte, áspero; puro; ● *adv* del todo.

starling *n* estornino *m*.

starry *adj* estrellado.

start *vi* empezar; sobrecogerse, sobresaltarse; levantarse de repente; salir los caballos en las carreras; ● *vt* empezar; causar; fundar; poner en marcha; ● *n* principio *m*; salida *f*; sobresalto *m*; ímpetu *m*; paso primero *m*.

starter *n* estárter *m*; el oficial que da la salida en las carreras.

starting point *n* punto de partida *m*.

startle *vt* sobresaltar.

startling *adj* alarmante.

starvation *n* hambre, inanición *f*.

starve *vi* pasar hambre.

state *n* estado *m*; condición *f*; estado (político); pompa, grandeza *f*; the S~s los Estados Unidos *mpl*; ● *vt* afirmar; exponer.

stateliness *n* grandeza, pompa *f*.

stately *adj* augusto, majestuoso.

statement *n* afirmación, cuenta *f*.

statesman *n* estadista, político *m*.

statesmanship *n* política *f*.

static *adj* estático; ● *n* parásitos *mpl*.

station *n* estación *f*; emisora *f*; empleo, puesto *m*; situación *f*; condición *f*; (*rail*) estación *f*; ● *vt* apostar.

stationary *adj* estacionario, fijo.

stationer *n* papelero *m*.

stationery *n* papelería *f*.

station wagon *n* furgoneta *f*.

statistical *adj* estadístico.

statistics *npl* estadística *f*.

statuary *n* estatuario, escultor *m*.

statue *n* estatua *f*.

stature *n* estatura, talla *f*.

statute *n* estatuto *m*; reglamento *m*.

stay *n* estancia *f*; ~s *npl* corsé, justillo *m*; ● *vi* quedarse, estarse; detenerse; esperarse; to ~ in quedarse en casa; to ~ on quedarse; to ~ up velar.

stead *n* lugar, sitio, paraje *m*.

steadfast *adj* firme, estable, sólido; ~ly *adv* firmemente, con constancia.

steadily *adv* firmemente; invariablemente.

steadiness *n* firmeza, estabilidad *f*.

steady *adj* firme, fijo; ● *vt* hacer firme.

steak *n* filete *m*; bistec *m*.

steal *vt*, *vi* robar.

stealth *n* hurto *m*; by ~ a hurtadillas.

stealthily *adv* furtivamente.

stealthy *adj* furtivo.

steam *n* vapor *m*; humo *m*; ● *vt* cocer al vapor; ● *vi* echar humo.

steam-engine *n* máquina de vapor *f*.

steamer, steamboat *n* vapor, buque de vapor *m*.

steel *n* acero *m*; ● *adj* de acero.

steelyard *n* romana *f*.

steep *adj* escarpado; excesivo; ● *vt* empapar.

steeple *n* torre *f*; campanario *m*.

steeplechase *n* carrera ciega *f*.

steepness *n* precipicio *m*; escarpa *f*.

steer *n* novillo *m*; ● *vt* manejar, conducir; dirigir; gobernar; ● *vi* conducir.

steering *n* dirección *f*.

steering wheel *n* volante *m*.

stellar *adj* estrellado.

stem *n* vástago, tallo *m*; estirpe *f*; pie *m*; cañón *m*; ● *vt* cortar la corriente.

stench *n* hedor *m*.

stencil *n* cliché *m*.

stenographer *n* taquígrafo, fa *m/f*.

stenography *n* taquigrafía *f*.

step *n* paso, escalón *m*; huella *f*; ● *vi* dar un paso; andar.

stepbrother *n* medio hermano *m*.

stepdaughter *n* hijastra *f*.

stepfather *n* padrastro *m*.

stepmother *n* madrastra *f*.

stepping stone *n* pasadera *f*.

stepsister *n* media hermana *f*.

stepson *n* hijastro *m*.

stereo *n* estéreo *m*.

stereotype *n* estereotipo *m*; ● *vt* estereotipar.

sterile *adj* estéril.

sterility *n* esterilidad *f*.

sterling *adj* esterlín, genuino, verdadero; ● *n* libras esterlinas *fpl*.

stern *adj* austero, rígido, severo; ● *n* (*mar*) popa *f*; ~ly *adv* austeramente.

stethoscope *n* (*med*) estetoscopio *m*.

stevedore *n* (*mar*) estivador *m*.

stew *vt* estofar; ● *n* estufa *f*.

steward *n* mayordomo *m*; (*mar*) despensero *m*.

stewardess *n* azafata *f*.

stewardship *n* mayordomía *f*.

stick *n* palo, palillo, bastón *m*; vara *f*; ● *vt* pegar, hincar; aguantar; picar; ● *vi* pegarse; detenerse; perseverar; dudar.

stickiness *n* viscosidad *f*.

stick-up *n* asalto, atraco *m*.

sticky *adj* viscoso, tenaz.

stiff *adj* tieso; duro, torpe; rígido; obstinado; ~ly *adv* obstinadamente.

stiffen *vt* atiesar, endurecer; ● *vi* endurecerse.

stiff neck *n* torticolis *m*.

stiffness *n* tesura, rigidez *f*; obstinación *f*.

stifle *vt* sufocar.

stifling *adj* bochornoso.

stigma *n* estigma *m*.

stigmatize *vt* infamar, manchar.

stile *n* portillo con escalones *m* (para pasar de un cercado a otro).

stiletto *n* estilete *m*; tacón de aguja *m*.

still *vt* aquietar, aplacar; destilar; ● *adj* silencioso, tranquilo; ● *n* alambique *m*; ● *adv* todavía; hasta ahora; no obstante; aun así.

stillborn *adj* nacido muerto.

stillness *n* calma, quietud *f*.

stilts *npl* zancos *mpl*.

stimulant *n* estimulante *m*.

stimulate *vt* estimular, aguijonear.

stimulation *n* estímulo *m*; estimulación *f*.

stimulus *n* estímulo *m*.

sting *n* picar *o* morder (un insecto); ● *vi* escocer; ● *n* aguijón *m*; punzada, picadura, picada *f*; remordimiento de conciencia *m*.

stingily *adv* avaramente.

stinginess *n* tacañería, avaricia *f*.

stingy *adj* mezquino, tacaño, avaro.

stink *vi* heder; ● *n* hedor *m*.

stint *n* tarea *f*.

stipulate *vt* estipular.

stipulation *n* estipulación *f*; contrato mutuo *m*.

stir *vt* remover; agitar; incitar; ● *vi* moverse; ● *n* tumulto *m*; turbulencia *f*.

stirrup *n* estribo *m*.

stitch *vt* coser; ● *n* punzada *f*; punto *m*.

stoat n comadreja f.

stock n existencias fpl; ganado m; caldo m; estirpe f, linaje m; capital, principal m; fondo m; ~s (pl) acciones en los fondos públicos fpl; • vt proveer, abastecer.

stockade n prisión militar f.

stockbroker n agente de bolsa m/f.

stock exchange n bolsa f.

stockholder n accionista m.

stocking n media f.

stock market n bolsa f.

stoic n estoico m.

stoical adj estoico; ~ly adv estoicamente.

stoicism n estoicismo m.

stole n estola f.

stomach n estómago m; apetito m; • vt aguantar.

stone n piedra f; pepita f; hueso de fruta m; • adj de piedra; • vt apedrear; quitar los huesos de las frutas; empedrar; trabajar de albañilería.

stone deaf adj sordo como una tapia.

stoning n apedreamiento m.

stony adj de piedra, pétreo; duro.

stool n banquillo, taburete m; cámara, evacuación f.

stoop vi encorvarse, inclinarse; bajarse; • n inclinación hacia abajo f.

stop vt detener, parar; tapar; • vi pararse, hacer alto; • n parada f; punto m; pausa f; obstáculo m.

stopover n parada; rescala f.

stoppage, stopping n obstrucción f; impedimento m; (rail) alto m.

stopwatch n cronómetro m.

storage n almacenamiento m; almacenaje m.

store n abundancia f; provisión f; almacén m, tienda f; • vt surtir, proveer, abastecer.

storekeeper n tendero, ra m/f.

stork n cigüeña f.

storm n tempestad, borrasca f; asalto m; • vt tomar por asalto; • vi rabiar.

stormily adj violentamente.

stormy adj tempestuoso; violento.

story n historia f; chiste m; piso m (de una casa).

stout adj robusto, corpulento, vigoroso; terco; ~ly adv valientemente; obstinadamente.

stoutness n valor m; fuerza f; corpulencia f.

stove n cocina f; estufa f.

stow vt ordenar, colocar; (mar) estibar.

straggle vi rezagarse.

straggler n rezagado m.

straight adj derecho; estrecho; franco; • adv luego; directamente.

straightaway adv inmediatamente, luego.

straighten vt enderezar.

straightforward adj derecho; franco; leal.

straightforwardness n derechura f.

strain vt colar, filtrar; apretar (a uno contra sí); forzar, violentar; • vi esforzarse; • n tensión f; retorcimiento m; raza f; linaje m; estilo m; sonido m; armonía f.

strainer n colador m; coladera f.

strait n estrecho; aprieto, peligro m; penuria f.

strait-jacket n camisa de fuerza f.

strand n hebra f; costa, playa f.

strange adj extranjero; extraño; ~ly adv extrañamente, extraordinariamente.

strangeness n extranjería f; extrañeza f.

stranger n desconocido m; extranjero, ra m/f.

strangle vt ahogar.

strangulation n ahogamiento m.

strap n correa, tira de cuero f; tirante de bota m; • vt atar con correa.

strapping adj abultado, corpulento.

stratagem n estratagema f; astucia f.

strategic adj estratégico m.

strategy n estrategia f.

stratum n estrato m.

straw n paja m; pajita f.

strawberry n fresa f.

stray vi extraviarse; perder el camino; • adj extraviado; perdido.

streak n raya, lista f; vena f; • vt rayar.

stream n arroyo, río, torrente m; • vi correr.

streamer n serpentina f.

street n calle f.

streetcar n tranvía f.

strength n fuerza, robustez f; vigor m; fortaleza f.

strengthen vt fortificar; corroborar.

strenuous adj arduo; ágil.

stress n presión f; estrés m; fuerza f; peso m; importancia f; acento m; • vt subrayar; acentuar.

stretch vt, vi extender, alargar; estirar; extenderse; esforzarse; • n extensión f; trecho m; estirón m.

stretcher n camilla f.

strew vt esparcir; sembrar.

strict adj estricto, estrecho; exacto, riguroso, severo; ~ly adv exactamente, con severidad.

strictness n exactitud f; severidad f.

stride n tranco m; • vi atrancar.

strife n contienda, disputa f.

strike vt, vi golpear; herir; castigar; tocar; chocar; sonar; cesar de trabajar; • n ataque m; descubrimiento m; huelga f.

striker n huelguista m/f.

striking adj llamativo; notorio; ~ly adv de modo sorprendente.

string n cordón m; hilo m; cuerda f; hilera f; fibra f; • vt encordar; enhilar; estirar.

stringent adj astringente.

stringy adj fibroso.

strip vt desnudar, despojar; • vi desnudarse; • n tira f; franja f; cinta f.

stripe n raya, lista f; azote m; • vt rayar.

strive vi esforzarse; empeñarse; disputar, contender; oponerse.

stroke n golpe m; toque (en la pintura) m; sonido (del reloj) m; plumada f; acaricia f; apoplejía f; • vt acariciar.

stroll n paseo; • vi dar un paseo.

strong adj fuerte, vigoroso, robusto; poderoso; violento; ~ly adv fuertemente, con violencia.

strongbox n cofre fuerte m.

stronghold n plaza fuerte f.

strophe n estrofa f.

structure n estructura f; edificio m.

struggle vi esforzarse; luchar; agitarse; • n lucha f.

strum vt (mus) rasguear.

strut vi pavonearse; • n contoneo m.

stub n talón m; colilla f; tronco m.

stubble n rastrojo m; cerda f.

stubborn adj obstinado, testarudo; ~ly adv obstinadamente.

stubbornness n obstinación, pertinacia f.

stucco n estuco m.

stud n corchete m; taco m; cabelleriza f.

student n estudiante m/f; • adj estudiantil.

studhorse n caballo entero m.

studio n estudio de un artista m.

studio apartment n estudio m.

studious adj estudioso; diligente; ~ly adv estudiosamente, diligentemente.

study n estudio m; aplicación f; meditación profunda f; • vt estudiar; observar; • vi estudiar; aplicarse.

stuff n materia f; material m; estofa f; • vt henchir, llenar; disecar.

stuffing n relleno m.

stuffy adj cargado; de miras estrechas.

stumble vi tropezar; • n traspié, tropiezo m.

stumbling block n tropiezo m; piedra de escándalo f.

stump n tronco m; tocón m; muñón m.

stun vt aturdir, ensordecer.

stunner n cualquier cosa que sorprende f.
stunt n vuelo acrobático m; truco publicitario m; • vt no dejar crecer.
stuntman n especialista m.
stupefy vt atontar, atolondrar.
stupendous adj estupendo, maravilloso.
stupid adj estúpido; ~**ly** adv estúpidamente.
stupidity n estupidez f.
stupor n estupor m.
sturdily adv fuertemente.
sturdiness n fuerza, fortaleza f; obstinación f.
sturdy adj fuerte, tieso, robusto; bronco, insolente.
sturgeon n esturión m.
stutter vi tartamudear.
sty n zahurda f; pocilga f.
stye n orzuelo m.
style n estilo m; moda f; • vt intitular; nombrar; estilizar.
stylish adj elegante, en buen estilo.
suave adj afable.
subdivide vt subdividir.
subdivision n subdivisión f.
subdue vt sojuzgar, sujetar; conquistar; mortificar.
subject adj sujeto; sometido a; • n sujeto m; súbdito m; tema m; • vt sujetar; exponer.
subjection n sujeción f.
subjugate vt sojuzgar, sujetar.
subjugation n sujeción f.
subjunctive n subjuntivo m.
sublet vt subarrendar.
sublimate vt sublimar.
sublime adj sublime, excelso; ~**ly** adv de modo sublime; • n sublime m.
sublimity n sublimidad f.
submachine gun n metralleta f.
submarine adj submarino; • n submarino m.
submerge vt sumergir.
submersion n sumersión f.
submission n sumisión f.
submissive adj sumiso, obsequioso; ~**ly** adv con sumisión.
submissiveness n obsequio m; sumisión f.
submit vt, (vi) someter(se).
subordinate adj subordinado, inferior; • vt subordinar.
subordination n subordinación f.
subpoena n citación f; • vt citar.
subscribe vt, vi suscribir, certificar con su firma; consentir.
subscriber n suscriptor, ra m/f.
subscription n suscripción f.
subsequent adj, ~**ly** adv subsiguiente(mente).
subservient adj subordinado; útil.
subside vi sumergirse, irse a fondo.
subsidence n derrumbamiento m.
subsidiary adj subsidiario.
subsidize vt subvencionar, dar subsidios.
subsidy n subvención f; subsidio, socorro m.
subsist vi subsistir; existir.
subsistence n existencia f; subsistencia f.
substance n substancia f; entidad f; esencia f.
substantial adj substancial; real, material; substancioso; fuerte; ~**ly** adv substancialmente.
substantiate vt hacer existir.
substantive n sustantivo m.
substitute vt sustituir; • n suplente m.
substitution n sustitución f.
substratum n lecho m.
subterfuge n subterfugio m; evasión f.
subterranean adj subterráneo.
subtitle n subtítulo m.
subtle adj sútil, astuto.
subtlety n sutileza, astucia f.
subtly adv sútilmente.
subtract vt (math) sustraer.
suburb n suburbio m.

suburban adj suburbano.
subversion n subversión f.
subversive adj subversivo.
subvert vt subvertir, destruir.
subway n metro m.
succeed vt, vi seguir; conseguir, lograr, tener éxito.
success n éxito m.
successful adj próspero, dichoso; ~**ly** adv prósperamente.
succession n sucesión f; descendencia f; herencia f.
successive adj sucesivo; ~**ly** adv sucesivamente.
successor n sucesor m.
succinct adj sucinto, compendioso; ~**ly** adv con brevedad.
succulent adj suculento, jugoso.
succumb vi sucumbir.
such adj tal, semejante; ~ **as** tal como.
suck vt, vi chupar; mamar.
suckle vt amamantar.
suckling n mamantón m.
suction n (med) succión f.
sudden adj repentino, no previsto; ~**ly** adv de repente, súbitamente.
suddenness n precipitación f.
suds npl espuma de agua y jabón f.
sue vt poner por justicia; suplicar.
suede n ante m, gamuza f.
suet n sebo m.
suffer vt, vi sufrir, padecer; tolerar, permitir.
suffering n pena f; dolor m.
suffice vi bastar, ser suficiente.
sufficiency n suficiencia f; capacidad f.
sufficient adj suficiente; ~**ly** adv bastante.
suffocate vt sufocar; • vi ahogarse.
suffocation n sofocación f.
suffrage n sufragio, voto m.
suffuse vt difundir, derramar.
sugar n azúcar m; • vt azucarar.
sugar beet n remolacha f.
sugar cane n caña de azúcar f.
sugar loaf n pan de azúcar m.
sugar plum n confite m.
sugary adj azucarado.
suggest vt sugerir.
suggestion n sugestión f.
suicidal adj de suicida.
suicide n suicidio m; suicida m.
suit n conjunto m; petición f; traje m; pleito m; surtido m; • vt convenir; sentar a; adaptar.
suitable adj conforme, conveniente.
suitably adv convenientemente.
suitcase n maleta, valija f.
suite n suite f; serie f; tren m, comitiva f.
suitor n suplicante m; amante, cortejo m; pleiteante m.
sulfur n azufre m.
sulfurous adj sulfúreo, azufroso.
sulkiness n mal humor m.
sulky adj regañón, terco.
sullen adj malcontento; intratable; ~**ly** adv de mal humor; tercamente.
sullenness n mal humor m; obstinación, pertinacia, terquedad f.
sultan n sultán m.
sultana n sultana f; pasa f.
sultry adj caluroso; sofocante.
sum n suma f; total m; **to ~ up** vt sumar; recopilar; • vi hacer un resumen.
summarily adv sumariamente.
summary adj, n sumario (m).
summer n verano, estío m.
summerhouse n glorieta de jardín f.
summit n ápice m; cima f.
summon vt citar, requerir por auto de juez; convocar, convidar; (mil) intimar la rendición.

summons n citación f; requerimiento m.
sumptuous adj suntuoso; ~ly adv suntuosamente.
sun n sol m.
sunbathe vi tomar el sol.
sunburnt adj tostado por el sol, asoleado.
Sunday n domingo m.
sundial n reloj de sol, cuadrante m.
sundry adj varios, muchos, diversos.
sunflower n girasol m.
sunglasses npl gafas o antojos de sol mpl.
sunless adj sin sol; sin luz.
sunlight n luz del sol f.
sunny adj semejante al sol; soleado; brillante.
sunrise n salida del sol f; nacer del sol m.
sun roof n techo corredizo m.
sunset n puesta del sol f.
sunshade n quitasol m.
sunshine n solana f; claridad del sol f.
sunstroke n insolación f.
suntan n bronceado m.
suntan oil n aceite bronceador m.
super adj (fam) bárbaro.
superannuated adj añejado; pensionado.
superannuation n pensión, jubilación f; retiro m.
superb adj magnífico; ~ly adv magníficamente.
supercargo n (mar) sobrecargo m.
supercilious adj arrogante, altanero; ~ly adv con altivez.
superficial adj, ~ly adv superficial(mente).
superfluity n superfluidad f.
superfluous adj superfluo.
superhuman adj sobrehumano.
superintendent n superintendente m.
superior adj, n superior (m).
superiority n superioridad f.
superlative adj, n superlativo (m); ~ly adv superlativamente, en sumo grado.
supermarket n supermercado m.
supernatural n sobrenatural.
supernumerary adj supernumerario.
superpower n superpotencia f.
supersede vt sobreseer; diferir; invalidar.
supersonic adj supersónico.
superstition n superstición f.
superstitious adj supersticioso; ~ly adv supersticiosamente.
superstructure n edificio levantado sobre otra fábrica m.
supertanker n superpetrolero m.
supervene vi sobrevenir.
supervise vt inspeccionar, revistar.
supervision n superintendencia f.
supervisor n superintendente m/f.
supine adj supino; negligente.
supper n cena f.
supplant vt suplantar.
supple adj flexible, manejable; blando.
supplement n suplemento m.
supplementary adj adicional.
suppleness n flexibilidad f.
suppli(c)ant n suplicante m.
supplicate vt suplicar.
supplication n súplica, suplicación f.
supplier n distribuidor, ra m/f.
supply vt suministrar; suplir, completar; surtir; • n provisión f; suministro m.
support vt sostener; soportar, asistir; • n apoyo m.
supportable adj soportable.
supporter n partidario, ria; aficionado, da m/f.
suppose vt, vi suponer.
supposition n suposición f.
suppress vt suprimir.
suppression n supresión f.
supremacy n supremacía f.
supreme adj supremo; ~ly adv supremamente.

surcharge vt sobrecargar; • n sobretasa f.
sure adj seguro, cierto; firme; estable; to be ~ sin duda; ya se ve; ~ly adv ciertamente, seguramente, sin duda.
sureness n certeza, seguridad f.
surety n seguridad f; fiador m.
surf n (mar) resaca f.
surface n superficie f; • vt revestir; • vi salir a la superficie.
surfboard n plancha (de surf) f.
surfeit n exceso m.
surge n ola, onda f; • vi avanzar en tropel.
surgeon n cirujano, na m/f.
surgery n cirujía m.
surgical adj quirúrgico.
surliness n mal humor m.
surly adj áspero de genio.
surmise vt sospechar; • n sospecha f.
surmount vt sobrepujar.
surmountable adj superable.
surname n apellido, sobrenombre m.
surpass vt sobresalir, sobrepujar, exceder, aventajar.
surpassing adj sobresaliente.
surplice n sobrepelliz f.
surplus n excedente m; sobrante m; • adj sobrante.
surprise vt sorprender; • n sorpresa f.
surprising adj sorprendente.
surrender vt, vi rendir; ceder; rendirse; • n rendición f.
surreptitious adj subrepticio; ~ly adv subrepticiamente.
surrogate vt subrogar; • n subrogado m.
surrogate mother n madre portadora f.
surround vt circundar, cercar, rodear.
survey vt inspeccionar, examinar; apear; • n inspección f; apeo (de tierras) m.
survive vi sobrevivir; • vt sobrevivir a.
survivor n sobreviviente m/f.
susceptibility n susceptibilidad f.
susceptible adj susceptible.
suspect vt, vi sospechar; • n sospechoso, sa m/f.
suspend vt suspender.
suspense n suspense m; detención f; incertidumbre f.
suspension n suspensión f.
suspension bridge n puente colgante o colgado m.
suspicion n sospecha f.
suspicious adj suspicaz; ~ly adv sospechosamente.
suspiciousness n suspicacia f.
sustain vt sostener, sustentar, mantener; apoyar; sufrir.
sustenance n sostenimiento, sustento m.
suture n sutura, costura f.
swab n algodón m; frotis m invar.
swaddle vt fajar.
swaddling-clothes npl pañales mpl.
swagger vi baladronear.
swallow n golondrina f; • vt tragar, engullir.
swamp n pantano m.
swampy adj pantanoso.
swan n cisne m.
swap vt canjear; • n intercambio m.
swarm n enjambre m; gentío m; hormiguero m; • vi enjambrar; hormiguear de gente; abundar.
swarthy adj atezado.
swarthiness n tez morena f.
swashbuckling adj fanfarrón.
swath n tranco m.
swathe vt fajar; • n faja f.
sway vt mover; • vi ladearse, inclinarse; • n balanceo m; poder, imperio, influjo m.
swear vt, vi jurar; hacer jurar; juramentar.
sweat n sudor m; • vi sudar; trabajar con fatiga.
sweater, sweatshirt n suéter m.
sweep vt, vi barrer; arrebatar; deshollinar; pasar o tocar ligeramente; oscilar; • n barredura f; vuelta f; giro m.
sweeping adj rápido; ~s pl barreduras fpl.
sweepstake n lotería f.

sweet *adj* dulce, grato, gustoso; suave; oloroso; melodioso; hermoso; amable; ● *adv* dulcemente, suavemente; ● *n* dulce, caramelo *m*.

sweetbread *n* mellejas de ternera *fpl*.

sweeten *vt* endulzar; suavizar; aplacar; perfumar.

sweetener *n* edulcorante *m*.

sweetheart *n* novio, via *m/f*; querida *f*.

sweetmeats *npl* dulces secos *mpl*.

sweetness *n* dulzura, suavidad *f*.

swell *vi* hincharse; ensoberbecerse; embravecerse; ● *vt* hinchar, inflar, agravar; ● *n* marejada *f*; ● *adj (fam)* estupendo, fenomenal.

swelling *n* hinchazón *f*; tumor *m*.

swelter *vi* ahogarse de calor.

swerve *vi* vagar; desviarse.

swift *adj* veloz, ligero, rápido; ● *n* vencejo, *m*.

swiftly *adv* velozmente.

swiftness *n* velocidad, rapidez *f*.

swill *vt* beber con exceso; ● *n* bazofia *f*.

swim *vi* nadar; abundar en; ● *vt* pasar a nado; ● *n* nadada *f*.

swimming *n* natación *f*; vértigo *m*.

swimming pool *n* piscina *f*.

swimsuit *n* traje de baño *m*.

swindle *vt* estafar.

swindler *n* trampista *m*.

swine *n* puerco, cochino *m*.

swing *vi* balancear, columpiarse; vibrar; agitarse; ● *vt* columpiar; balancear; girar; ● *n* vibración *f*; balanceo *m*.

swinging *adj (fam)* alegre.

swinging door *n* puerta giratoria *f*.

swirl *n* hacer remolinos el agua.

switch *n* varilla *f*; interruptor *m*; *(rail)* aguja *f*; ● *vt* cambiar de; to ~ off apagar; parar; to ~ on encender, prender.

switchboard *n* centralita (de teléfonos) *f*.

swivel *vt* girar.

swoon *vi* desmayarse; ● *n* desmayo, deliquio, pasmo *m*.

swoop *vi* calarse; ● *n* calada; redada *f*; in one ~ de un golpe.

sword *n* espada *f*.

swordfish *n* pez espada *f*.

swordsman *n* guerrero, soldado *m*.

sycamore *n* sicomoro *m* (árbol).

sycophant *n* sicofante *m*.

syllabic *adj* silábico.

syllable *n* sílaba *f*.

syllabus *n* programa de estudios *m*.

syllogism *n* silogismo *m*.

sylph *n* silfio *m*; sílfida *f*.

symbol *n* símbolo *m*.

symbolic(al) *adj* simbólico.

symbolize *vt* simbolizar.

symmetrical *adj* simétrico; ~ly *adv* con simetría.

symmetry *n* simetría *f*.

sympathetic *adj* simpático; ~ally *adv* simpáticamente.

sympathize *vi* compadecerse.

sympathy *n* simpatía *f*.

symphony *n* sinfonía *f*.

symposium *n* simposio *m*.

symptom *n* síntoma *m*.

synagogue *n* sinagoga *f*.

synchronism *n* sincronismo *m*.

syndicate *n* sindicato *m*.

syndrome *n* síndrome *m*.

synod *n* sínodo *m*.

synonym *n* sinónimo *m*.

synonymous *adj* sinónimo; ~ly *adv* con sinonimia.

synopsis *n* sinopsis *f*; sumario *m*.

synoptical *adj* sinóptico.

syntax *n* sintaxis *f*.

synthesis *n* síntesis *f*.

syringe *n* jeringa, lavativa *f*; ● *vt* jeringar.

system *n* sistema *m*.

systematic *adj* sistemático; ~ally *adv* sistemáticamente.

systems analyst *n* analista de sistemas *m/f*.

T

tab *n* lengüeta *f*; etiqueta *f*.

tabernacle *n* tabernáculo *m*.

table *n* mesa *f*; tabla *f*; ● *vt* apuntar en forma sinóptica; poner sobre la mesa; ~ d'hôte menú *m*.

tablecloth *n* mantel *m*.

tablespoon n cuchara para comer *f*.

tablet *n* tableta *f*; pastilla *f*; comprimido *m*.

table tennis *n* ping-pong *m*.

taboo *adj* tabú; ● *n* tabú *m*; ● *vt* interdecir.

tabular *adj* reducido a índices.

tacit *adj* tácito; ~ly *adv* tácitamente.

taciturn *adj* taciturno, callado.

tack *n* tachuela *f*; bordo *m*; ● *vt* atar; pegar; ● *vi* virar.

tackle *n* todo género de instrumentos *o* aparejos *m*; placaje *m*; *(mar)* cordaje *m*, jarcia *f*.

tact *n* tacto *m*.

tactician *n* táctico *m*.

tactics *npl* táctica *f*.

tadpole *n* ranilla *f*; sapillo *m*.

taffeta *n* tafetán *m*.

tag *n* herrete *m*; ● *vt* herretear.

tail *n* cola *f*; rabo *m*; ● *vt* vigilar a.

tailgate *n* puerta trasera *f*.

tailor *n* sastre *m*.

tailoring *n* corte *m*.

tailor-made *adj* hecho a la medida.

tailwind *n* viento de cola *m*.

taint *vt* tachar, manchar; viciar; ● *n* mancha *f*.

tainted *adj* contaminado; manchado.

take *vt* tomar, coger, asir; recibir, aceptar; pillar; prender; admitir; entender; ● *vi* prender el fuego; to ~ away quitar; llevar; to ~ back devolver; retractar; to ~ down derribar; apuntar; to ~ in entender, abarcar; acoger; to ~ off *vi* despegar; *vt* quitar; imitar; to ~ on aceptar; contratar; desafiar; to ~ out sacar; quitar; to ~ to encariñarse con; to ~ up acortar; ocupar; dedicarse a; ● *n* toma *f*.

takeoff *n* despegue *m*.

takeover *n* absorción *f*.

takings *npl* ingresos *mpl*.

talc *n* talco *m*.

talent *n* talento *m*; capacidad *f*.

talented *adj* talentoso.

talisman *n* talismán *m*.

talk *vi* hablar, conversar; charlar; ● *n* habla *f*; charla *f*; fama *f*.

talkative *adj* locuaz.

talk show *n* programa magazine *m*.

tall *adj* alto, elevado; robusto.

tally *vi* corresponder.

talon *n* garra de ave de rapiña *f*.

tambourine *n* pandereta *f*.

tame *adj* amansado, domado, domesticado; ~ly *adv* mansamente; bajamente; ● *vt* domar, domesticar.

tameness *n* domesticidad *f*; sumisión *f*.

tamper *vi* tocar.

tampon *n* tampón *m*.

tan *vt* broncear; ● *vi* ponerse moreno; ● *n* bronceado *m*.

tang *n* sabor fuerte *m*.

tangent *n* tangente *f*.

tangerine *n* mandarina *f*.

tangible *adj* tangible.

tangle *vt* enredar, embrollar.

tank *n* cisterna *f*; aljibe *m*.

tanker *n* buque cisterna *m*; camión cisterna *m*.

tanned *adj* bronceado.

tantalizing *adj* tentador.

tantamount *adj* equivalente.

tantrum *n* rabieta *f*.
tap *vt* tocar ligeramente; utilizar; intervenir; • *n* palmada suave *f*; toque ligero *m*; espita *f*.
tape *n* cinta *f*; • *vt* grabar.
tape measure *n* metro *m*.
taper *n* cirio *m*.
tape recorder *n* grabadora *f*.
tapestry *n* tapiz *m*; tapicería *f*.
tar *n* brea *f*.
target *n* blanco *m* (para tirar).
tariff *n* tarifa *f*.
tarmac *n* pista *f*.
tarnish *vt* deslustrar.
tarpaulin *n* alquitranado *m*.
tarragon *n* (*bot*) estragón *m*.
tart *adj* acedo, acre; • *n* tarta, torta *f*.
tartan *n* tela escocesa *f*.
tartar *n* tártaro *m*.
task *n* tarea *f*.
tassel *n* borlita *f*.
taste *n* gusto *m*; sabor *m*; saboreo *m*; ensayo *m*; • *vt*, *vi* gustar; probar; experimentar; agradar; tener sabor.
tasteful *adj* sabroso; ~**ly** *adv* sabrosamente.
tasteless *adj* insípido, sin sabor.
tasty *adj* sabroso.
tattoo *n* tatuaje *m*; • *vt* tatuar.
taunt *vt* mofar; ridiculizar; • *n* mofa, burla *f*.
Taurus *n* Tauro *m*.
taut *adj* tieso.
tautological *adj* tautológico.
tautology *n* tautología *f*.
tawdry *adj* jarifo, vistoso, chabacano.
tax *n* impuesto *m*; contribución *f*; • *vt* gravar; poner a prueba.
taxable *adj* sujeto a impuestos.
taxation *n* imposición de impuestos *f*.
tax collector *n* recaudador *m*.
tax-free *adj* libre de impuestos.
taxi *n* taxi *m*; • *vi* rodar por la pista.
taxi driver *n* taxista *m*.
taxi stand *n* parada de taxis *f*.
tax payer *n* contribuyente *m*.
tax relief *n* desgravación fiscal *f*.
tax return *n* declaración de la renta *f*.
tea *n* té *m*.
teach *vt* enseñar, instruir; • *vi* enseñar.
teacher *n* profesor, ra *m/f*; maestro, tra *m/f*.
teaching *n* enseñanza *f*.
teacup *n* taza para el té *f*.
teak *n* teca *f* (árbol).
team *n* equipo *m*.
teamster *n* camionero *m*.
teamwork *n* trabajo de equipo *m*.
teapot *n* tetera *f*.
tear *vt* despedazar, rasgar; **to ~ up** hacer trizas.
tear *n* lágrima *f*; gota *f*.
tearful *adj* lloroso; ~**ly** *adv* con lloro.
tear gas *n* gas lacrimógeno *m*.
tease *vt* tomar el pelo.
tea-service, tea-set *n* servicio para el té *m*.
teaspoon *n* cucharita *f*.
teat *n* ubre, teta *f*.
technical *adj* técnico.
technicality *n* detalle técnico *m*.
technician *n* técnico *m*.
technique *n* técnica *f*.
technological *adj* tecnológico.
technology *n* tecnología *f*.
teddy (bear) *n* osito de felpa *m*.
tedious *adj* tedioso, fastidioso; ~**ly** *adv* fastidiosamente.
tedium *n* tedio, fastidio *m*.
tee *n* tee *m*.
teem *vi* rebosar de.

teenage *adj* juvenil; ~**r** *n* adolescente *m/f*.
teens *npl* años desde 13 hasta 20 años.
tee-shirt *n* camiseta *f*.
teeth *npl* de tooth.
teethe *vi* echar los dientes.
teetotal *adj* moderado, sobrio.
teetotaler *n* hombre sobrio *m*.
telegram *n* telegrama *m*.
telegraph *n* telégrafo *m*.
telegraphic *adj* telegráfico.
telegraphy *n* telegrafía *f*.
telepathy *n* telepatía *f*.
telephone *n* teléfono *m*.
telephone booth *n* cabina telefónica *f*.
telephone call *n* llamada telefónica *f*.
telephone directory *n* guía *f*.
telephone number *n* número de teléfono *m*.
telescope *n* telescopio *m*.
telescopic *adj* telescópico.
televise *vt* televisar.
television *n* televisión *f*.
television set *n* televisor *m*.
telex *n* télex *m*; *vt*, *vi* enviar un télex.
tell *vi* decir; informar, contar.
teller *n* cajero, ra *m/f*.
telling *adj* que hace impresión.
telltale *adj* indicador.
temper *vt* templar, moderar; • *n* mal genio *m*.
temperament *n* temperamento *m*.
temperance *n* templanza, moderación *f*.
temperate *adj* templado, moderado, sobrio.
temperature *n* temperatura *f*.
tempest *n* tempestad *f*.
tempestuous *adj* tempestuoso.
template *n* plantilla *f*.
temple *n* templo *m*; sien *f*.
temporarily *adv* temporalmente.
temporary *adj* temporal.
tempt *vt* tentar; provocar.
temptation *n* tentación *f*.
tempting *adj* tentador.
ten *adj*, *n* diez.
tenable *adj* defendible.
tenacious *adj*, ~**ly** *adv* tenaz(mente).
tenacity *n* tenacidad *f*; porfía *f*.
tenancy *n* tenencia *f*.
tenant *n* arrendador, inquilino *m*.
tend *vt* guardar, velar; • *vi* tener tendencia a.
tendency *n* tendencia *f*.
tender *adj* tierno, delicado; sensible; ~**ly** *adv* tiernamente; • *n* oferta *f*; • *vt* ofrecer; estimar.
tenderness *n* ternura *f*.
tendon *n* tendón *m*.
tenement *n* casa de pisos *f*.
tenet *n* dogma *m*; aserción *f*.
tennis *n* tenis *m*.
tennis court *n* cancha de tenis *f*.
tennis player *n* tenista *m/f*.
tennis racket *n* raqueta de tenis *f*.
tennis shoes *npl* zapatillas de tenis *fpl*.
tenor *n* (*mus*) tenor *m*; contenido *m*; substancia *f*.
tense *adj* tieso, tenso; • *n* (*gr*) tiempo *m*.
tension *n* tensión, tirantez *f*.
tent *n* tienda de campaña *f*.
tentacle *n* tentáculo *m*.
tentative *adj* de ensayo, de prueba; ~**ly** *adv* como prueba.
tenth *adj*, *n* décimo.
tenuous *adj* tenue.
tenure *n* tenencia *f*.
tepid *adj* tibio.
term *n* término *m*; dicción *f*; vocablo *m*; condición, estipulación *f*; • *vt* nombrar, llamar.

terminal *adj* mortal; • *n* terminal *m*; terminal *f*.
terminate *vt* terminar.
termination *n* terminación, conclusión *f*.
terminus *n* terminal *f*.
terrace *n* terraza *f*.
terrain *n* terreno *m*.
terrestrial *adj* terrestre, terreno.
terrible *adj* terrible.
terribly *adv* terriblemente.
terrier *n* terrier *m*.
terrific *adj* fantástico; maravilloso.
terrify *vt* aterrar, espantar.
territorial *adj* territorial.
territory *n* territorio, distrito *m*.
terror *n* terror *m*.
terrorism *n* terrorismo *m*.
terrorist *n* terrorista *m/f*.
terrorize *vt* aterrorizar.
terse *adj* terso, pulido.
test *n* examen *m*; prueba *f*; • *vt* probar; examinar.
testament *n* testamento *m*.
tester *n* ensayador *m*.
testicles *npl* testículos *mpl*.
testify *vt* testificar, atestiguar.
testimonial *n* atestación *f*.
testimony *n* testimonio *m*.
test pilot *n* piloto de prueba *m*.
test tube *n* probeta *f*.
testy *adj* tétrico.
tetanus *n* tétano *m*.
tether *vt* atar.
text *n* texto *m*.
textbook *n* libro de texto *m*.
textiles *npl* textiles *mpl*.
textual *adj* textual.
texture *n* textura *f*; tejido *m*.
than *adv* que, de.
thank *vt* agradecer, dar gracias.
thankful *adj* grato, agradecido; ~ly *adv* con gratitud.
thankfulness *n* gratitud *f*.
thankless *adj* ingrato.
thanks *npl* gracias *fpl*.
Thanksgiving *n* día de acción de gracias *m*.
that *pn* aquel, aquello, aquella; que; este; • *conj* porque; para que; so ~ de modo que.
thatch *n* techo de paja *m*; • *vt* techar con paja.
thaw *n* deshielo *m*; • *vi* deshelarse.
the *art* el, la, lo; los, las.
theater *n* teatro *m*.
theater-goer *n* aficionado al teatro *m*.
theatrical *adj* teatral.
theft *n* robo *m*.
their *pn* su, suyo, suya; de ellos, de ellas; ~s el suyo, la suya, los suyos, las suyas; de ellos, de ellas.
them *pn* los, las, les; ellos, ellas.
theme *n* tema *m*.
themselves *pn pl* ellos mismos, ellas mismas; sí mismos; se.
then *adv* entonces, después; en tal caso; • *conj* en ese caso; • *adj* entonces; now and ~ de vez en cuando.
theologic(al) *adj* teológico.
theologian *n* teólogo *m*.
theology *n* teología *f*.
theorem *n* teorema *m*.
theoretic(al) *adj* teórico; ~ly *adv* teóricamente.
theorist *n* teórico *m*.
theorize *vt* teorizar.
theory *n* teoría *f*.
therapeutics *n* terapéutica *f*.
therapist *n* terapeuta *m*.
therapy *n* terapia *f*.
there *adv* allí, allá.
thereabout(s) *adv* por ahí, acerca de.

thereafter *adv* después; según.
thereby *adv* así; de ese modo.
therefore *adv* por eso, por lo tanto.
thermal *adj* termal.
thermal printer *n* termoimpresora *f*.
thermometer *n* termómetro *m*.
thermostat *n* termostato *m*.
thesaurus *n* tesoro *m*.
these *pn pl* estos, estas.
thesis *n* tesis *f*.
they *pn pl* ellos, ellas.
thick *adj* espeso, denso; grueso; torpe.
thicken *vi* espesar, condensar; condensarse.
thicket *n* espesura de un bosque *f*.
thickness *n* espesor *m*.
thickset *adj* plantado muy espeso; rechoncho.
thickskinned *adj* duro de pellejo.
thief *n* ladrón *m*.
thigh *n* muslo *m*.
thimble *n* dedal *m*.
thin *adj* delgado, delicado, flaco; claro; • *vt* atenuar; adelgazar; aclarar.
thing *n* cosa *f*; objeto *m*; chisme *m*.
think *vi* pensar, imaginar, meditar, considerar; creer, juzgar; to ~ over reflexionar; to ~ up imaginar.
thinker *n* pensador *m*.
thinking *n* pensamiento *m*; juicio *m*; opinión *f*.
third *adj* tercero; • *n* tercio *m*; ~ly *adv* en tercer lugar.
third rate *adj* mediocre.
thirst *n* sed *f*.
thirsty *adj* sediento.
thirteen *adj, n* trece.
thirteenth *adj, n* décimotercio.
thirtieth *adj, n* trigésimo.
thirty *adj, n* treinta.
this *adj* este, esta, esto; • *pn* éste, ésta, esto.
thistle *n* cardo *m*.
thorn *n* espino *m*; espina *f*.
thorny *adj* espinoso; arduo.
thorough *prep* por, por medio; • *adj* entero, perfecto; ~ly *adv* enteramente, profundamente.
thoroughbred *adj* de sangre, de casta.
thoroughfare *n* paso, tránsito *m*.
those *pn pl* ésos, ésas; aquéllos, aquéllas; • *adj* esos, esas; aquellos, aquellas.
though *conj* aunque, no obstante; • *adv* sin embargo.
thought *n* pensamiento, juicio *m*; opinión *f*; cuidado *m*.
thoughtful *adj* pensativo.
thoughtless *adj* descuidado; insensato; ~ly *adv* descuidadamente, sin reflexión.
thousand *adj, n* mil.
thousandth *adj, n* milésimo.
thrash *vt* golpear; derrotar.
thread *n* hilo *m*; rosca *f*; • *vt* enhebrar.
threadbare *adj* raído, muy usado.
threat *n* amenaza *f*.
threaten *vt* amenazar.
three *adj, n* tres.
three-dimensional *adj* tridimensional.
three-ply *adj* triple.
threshold *n* umbral *m*.
thrifty *adj* económico.
thrill *vt* emocionar; • *n* emoción *f*.
thriller *n* película o novela de suspense *f*.
thrive *vi* prosperar; crecer.
throat *n* garganta *f*.
throb *vi* palpitar; vibrar; dar punzadas.
throne *n* trono *m*.
throng *n* tropel de gente *m*; • *vt* venir en tropel.
throttle *n* acelerador *m*; • *vt* estrangular.
through *prep* por; durante; mediante; • *adj* directo; • *adv* completamente.

throughout *prep* por todo; ● *adv* en todas partes.
throw *vt* echar, arrojar, tirar, lanzar; ● *n* tiro *m*; golpe *m*; to ~ away tirar; to ~ off desechar; to ~ out tirar; to ~ up vomitar.
throwaway *adj* desechable.
thru = through.
thrush *n* tordo *m* (ave).
thrust *vt* empujar, introducir; ● *n* empuje *m*.
thud *n* ruido sordo *m*.
thug *n* gamberro *m*.
thumb *n* pulgar *m*.
thumbtack *n* chinche *m*.
thump *n* golpe *m*; ● *vt*, *vi* golpear.
thunder *n* trueno *m*; ● *vi* tronar.
thunderbolt *n* rayo *m*.
thunderclap *n* trueno *m*.
thunderstorm *n* tormenta *f*.
thundery *adj* tormentoso.
Thursday *n* jueves *m*.
thus *adv* así, de este modo.
thwart *vt* frustrar.
thyme *n* (*bot*) tomillo *m*.
thyroid *n* tiroides *m invar*.
tiara *n* tiara *f*.
tic *n* tic *m*.
tick *n* tictac *m*; palomita *f*; ● *vt* marcar; to ~ over girar en marcha; ir tirando.
ticket *n* billete, boleto *m*; etiqueta *f*; tarjeta *f*.
ticket collector *n* (*rail*) revisor *m*.
ticket office *n* boletería *f*; despacho de boletos *m*.
tickle *vt* hacer cosquillas.
ticklish *adj* cosquilloso.
tidal *adj* (*mar*) de marea.
tidal wave *n* maremoto *m*.
tidbit *n* golosina *f*; pedazo *m*.
tide *n* curso *m*; marea *f*.
tidy *adj* ordenado; arreglado; aseado.
tie *vt* anudar, atar; ● *vi* empatar; to ~ up envolver; atar; amarrar; concluir; ● *n* atadura *f*; lazo *m*; empate *m*.
tier *n* grada *f*; piso *m*.
tiger *n* tigre *m*.
tight *adj* tirante, tieso, tenso; cerrado; apretado; ● *adv* muy fuerte.
tighten *vt* tirar, estirar.
tightfisted *adj* tacaño.
tightly *adv* muy fuerte.
tightrope *n* cuerda floja *f*.
tigress *n* tigra *f*.
tile *n* teja *f*; baldosa *f*; azulejo *m*; ● *vt* tejar.
tiled *adj* embaldosado.
till *n* caja *f*; ● *vt* cultivar, labrar.
tiller *n* caña del timón *f*.
tilt *vt* inclinar; ● *vi* inclinarse.
timber *n* madera de construcción *f*; árboles *mpl*.
time *n* tiempo; época *f*; hora *f*; momento *m*; (*mus*) compás *m*; in ~ a tiempo; from ~ to ~ de vez en cuando; ● *vt* medir el tiempo; cronometrar.
time bomb *n* bomba de efecto retardado *f*.
time lag *n* desfase *m*.
timeless *adj* eterno.
timely *adj* oportuno.
time off *n* tiempo libre *m*.
timer *n* interruptor *m*; programador horario *m*.
time scale *n* escala de tiempo *f*.
time zone *n* huso horario *m*.
timid *adj* tímido, temeroso; ~ly *adv* con timidez.
timidity *n* timidez *f*.
timing *n* cronometraje *m*.
tin *n* estaño *m*; hojalata *f*.
tinfoil *n* papel de estaño *m*.
tinge *n* matiz *m*.
tingle *vi* zumbar los oídos; latir, punzar.

tingling *n* zumbido de oídos *m*; latido *m*.
tinker *n* calderero remendón *m*; gitano *m*.
tinkle *vi* tintinear.
tinplate *n* hojalata *f*.
tinsel *n* oropel *m*.
tint *n* tinte *m*; ● *vt* teñir.
tinted *adj* teñido; ahumado.
tiny *adj* pequeño, chico.
tip *n* punta, extremidad *f*; propina *f*; consejo *m*; ● *vt* dar una propina a; inclinar; vaciar.
tip-off *n* advertencia *f*.
tipsy *adj* alegre.
tiptop *adj* excelente, el *o* lo mejor.
tirade *n* inventiva *f*.
tire *n* neumático *m*; llanta *f*; ● *vt* cansar, fatigar; ● *vi* cansarse; fastidiarse.
tireless *adj* incansable.
tire pressure *n* presión de las llantas *f*.
tiresome *adj* tedioso, molesto.
tiring *adj* cansado.
tissue *n* tejido *m*; pañuelo de papel *m*.
tissue paper *n* papel de seda *f*.
titillate *vt* estimular.
title *n* título *m*.
title deed *n* derecho de propiedad *m*.
title page *n* portada *f*.
titter *vi* sonreírse; ● *n* sonrisa *f*.
titular *adj* titular.
to *prep* a; para; por; de; hasta; en; con; que.
toad *n* sapo *m*.
toadstool *n* (*bot*) hongovejín *m*.
toast *vt* tostar; brindar; ● *n* tostada *f*; brindis *m*.
toaster *n* tostadora *f*.
tobacco *n* tabaco *m*.
tobacconist *n* tabaquero *m*.
tobacco pouch *n* petaca *f*.
tobacco shop *n* tabaquería *f*.
toboggan *n* tobogán *m*.
today *adv* hoy.
toddler *n* niño que empieza a andar *m*.
toddy *n* ponche *m*.
toe *n* dedo del pie *m*; punta *f*.
together *adv* juntamente, juntos; al mismo tiempo.
toil *vi* fatigarse, trabajar mucho; afanarse; ● *n* trabajo *m*; fatiga *f*; afán *m*.
toilet *n* servicios *mpl*; sanitario *m*; ● *adj* de aseo.
toilet bag *n* esponjera *f*.
toilet bowl *n* taza de retrete *f*.
toilet paper *n* papel higiénico *m*.
toiletries *npl* artículos de aseo *mpl*.
token *n* señal *f*; muestra *f*; recuerdo *m*; vale *m*; ficha *f*.
tolerable *adj* soportable; pasable.
tolerance *n* tolerancia *f*.
tolerant *adj* tolerante.
tolerate *vt* tolerar.
toll *n* peaje *m*; número de víctimas *m*; ● *vi* doblar.
tomato *n* tomate *m*.
tomb *n* tumba *f*; sepulcro *m*.
tomboy *n* muchachota *f*.
tombstone *n* piedra sepulcral *f*.
tomcat *n* gato *m*.
tomorrow *adv*, *n* mañana *f*.
ton *n* tonelada *f*.
tone *n* tono de la voz *m*; acento *m*; ● *vi* armonizar; to ~ down suavizar.
tone-deaf *adj* que no tiene oído musical.
tongs *npl* tenacillas *fpl*.
tongue *n* lengua *f*.
tongue-tied *adj* mudo.
tongue-twister *n* trabalenguas *m invar*.
tonic *n* (*med*) tónico.
tonight *adv*, *n* esta tarde (*f*).

tonnage *n* porte de un buque *m*.
tonsil *n* amígdala *f*.
tonsure *n* tonsura *f*.
too *adv* demasiado; también.
tool *n* herramienta *f*; utensilio *m*.
tool box *n* caja de herramientas *f*.
toot *vi* tocar la bocina.
tooth *n* diente *m*.
toothache *n* dolor de muelas *m*.
toothbrush *n* cepillo de dientes *m*.
toothless *adj* desdentado.
toothpaste *n* pasta dentífrica *f*.
toothpick *n* palillo *m*.
top *n* cima, cumbre *f*; último grado *m*; lo alto; superficie *f*; tapa *f*; cabeza *f*; ● *adj* de arriba; primero; ● *vt* elevarse por encima; sobrepujar, exceder; **to ~ off** llenar.
topaz *n* topacio *m*.
top floor *n* último piso *m*.
top-heavy *adj* inestable.
topic *n* tema *m*; **~al** *adv* actual.
topless *adj* topless.
top-level *adj* al más alto nivel.
topmost *adj* lo más alto.
topographic(al) *adj* topográfico.
topography *n* topografía *f*.
topple *vt* derribar; ● *vi* volcarse.
top-secret *adj* de alto secreto.
topsy-turvy *adv* al revés.
torch *n* antorcha *f*.
torment *vt* atormentar; ● *n* tormento *m*.
tornado *n* huracán *m*.
torrent *n* torrente *m*.
torrid *adj* apasionado.
tortoise *n* tortuga *f*.
tortoiseshell *adj* de carey.
tortuous *adj* tortuoso, sinuoso.
torture *n* tortura *f*; ● *vt* atormentar.
toss *vt* tirar, lanzar, arrojar; agitar, sacudir.
total *adj* total, entero; **~ly** *adv* totalmente.
totalitarian *adj* totalitario.
totality *n* totalidad *f*.
totter *vi* vacilar.
touch *vt* tocar, palpar; **to ~ on** aludir a; **to ~ up** retocar; ● *n* contacto *m*; tacto *m*; toque *m*; prueba *f*.
touch-and-go *adj* arriesgado.
touchdown *n* aterrizaje *m*; ensayo *m*.
touched *adj* commovido; chiflado.
touching *adj* patético, conmovedor.
touchstone *n* piedra de toque *f*.
touchwood *n* yesca *f*.
touchy *adj* quisquilloso.
tough *adj* duro; difícil; resistente; fuerte; ● *n* gorila *m*.
toughen *vt* endurecer.
toupée *n* tupé *m*.
tour *n* viaje *m*; visita *f*; ● *vt* visitar.
touring *n* viajes turísticos *mpl*.
tourism *n* turismo *m*.
tourist *n* turista *m/f*.
tourist office *n* oficina de turismo *f*.
tournament *n* torneo *m*.
tow *n* remolque *m*; ● *vt* remolcar.
toward(s) *prep*, *adv* hacia, con dirección a; cerca de, respecto a.
towel *n* toalla *f*.
toweling *n* felpa *f*.
towel rack *n* toallero *m*.
tower *n* torre *m*.
towering *adj* imponente.
town *n* ciudad *f*.
town clerk *n* secretario del ayuntamiento *m*.
town hall *n* ayuntamiento *m*.
towrope *n* cable de remolque *m*.

toy *n* juguete *m*.
toyshop *n* juguetería *f*.
trace *n* huella, pisada *f*; ● *vt* trazar, delinear; encontrar.
track *n* vestigio *m*; huella *f*; camino *m*; vía *f*; pista *f*; canción *f*; ● *vt* rastrear.
tracksuit *n* chandal *m*.
tract *n* región, comarca *f*; serie *f*; tratado *m*.
traction *n* tracción *f*.
trade *n* comercio, tráfico *m*; negocio, trato *m*; ocupación *f*; ● *vi* comerciar, traficar.
trade fair *n* feria comercial *f*.
trademark *n* marca de fábrica *f*.
trade name *n* marca registrada *f*.
trader *n* comerciante, traficante *m*.
tradesman *n* tendero *m*.
trade(s) union *n* sindicato *m*.
trade unionist *n* sindicalista *m/f*.
trading *n* comercio *m*; ● *adj* comercial.
tradition *n* tradición *f*
traditional *adj* tradicional.
traffic *n* tráfico *m*; tránsito *m*; ● *vi* traficar, comerciar.
traffic circle *n* glorieta *f*.
traffic jam *n* embotellamiento *m*.
trafficker *n* traficante, comerciante *m*.
traffic lights *npl* semáforo *m*.
tragedy *n* tragedia *f*.
tragic *adj* trágico; **~ally** *adv* trágicamente.
tragicomedy *n* tragicomedia *f*.
trail *vt*, *vi* rastrear; arrastrar; ● *n* rastro *m*; pista *f*; cola *f*.
trailer *n* remolque *m*; caravana *f*; avance *m*.
trailer truck *n* trailer *m*.
train *vt* entrenar; amaestrar, enseñar, criar, adiestrar; disciplinar; ● *n* tren *m*; cola *f*; serie *f*.
trained *adj* cualificado; amaestrado.
trainee *n* aprendiz *m*.
trainer *n* entrenador *m*.
training *n* entrenamiento *m*; formación *f*.
trait *n* rasgo *m*.
traitor *n* traidor *m*.
tramp *n* vagabundo *m*; (*sl*) puta *f*; ● *vi* andar pesadamente; ● *vt* pisotear.
trample *vt* pisotear.
trampoline *n* trampolín *m*.
trance *n* rapto *m*; éxtasis *m*.
tranquil *adj* tranquilo.
tranquilize *vt* tranquilizar.
tranquilizer *n* tranquilizante *m*.
transact *vt* negociar.
transaction *n* transacción *f*; negociación *f*.
transatlantic *adj* transatlántico.
transcend *vt* trascender, pasar; exceder.
transcription *n* traslado *m*; copia *f*.
transfer *vt* transferir, trasladar; ● *n* transferencia *f*; traspaso *m*; calcomanía *f*.
transform *vt* transformar.
transformation *n* transformación *f*.
transfusion *n* transfusión *f*.
transient *adj* pasajero, transitorio.
transit *n* tránsito *m*.
transition *n* tránsito *m*; transición *f*.
transitional *adj* de transición.
transitive *adj* transitivo.
translate *vt* traducir.
translation *n* traducción *f*.
translator *n* traductor, ra *m/f*.
transmission *n* transmisión *f*.
transmit *vt* transmitir.
transmitter *n* transmisor *m*; emisora *f*.
transparency *n* transparencia *f*.
transparent *adj* transparente, diáfano.
transpire *vi* resultar; ocurrir.
transplant *vt* trasplantar; ● *n* trasplante *m*.

transport *vt* transportar; ● *n* transporte *m*.
transportation *n* transporte *m*.
trap *n* trampa *f*; ● *vt* hacer caer en la trampa, bloquear.
trap door *n* puerta disimulada *f*; escotillón *m*.
trapeze *n* trapecio *m*.
trappings *npl* adornos *mpl*.
trash *n* pacotilla *f*; tonterías *fpl*.
trash can *n* balde de la basura *m*.
trashy *adj* vil, despreciable, de ningún valor.
travel *vi* viajar; ● *vt* recorrer; ● *n* viaje *m*.
travel agency *n* agencia de viajes *f*.
travel agent *n* agente de viajes *m*.
traveler *n* viajante, viajero, ra *m/f*.
traveler's check *n* cheque de viajero *m*.
traveling *n* viajes *mpl*.
traveling sickness *n* mareo *m*.
travesty *n* parodia *f*.
trawler *n* pesquero de arrastre *m*.
tray *n* bandeja *f*; cajón *m*.
treacherous *adj* traidor, pérfido.
treachery *n* traición *f*.
tread *vi* pisar; pistoear; ● *n* pisada *f*; ruido de pasos *m*; banda de rodadura *f*.
treason *n* traición *n*; **high** ~ delito de lesa majestad *f*.
treasure *n* tesoro *m*; ● *vt* atesorar.
treasurer *n* tesorero *m*.
treat *vt* tratar; regalar; ● *n* regalo *m*; placer *m*.
treatise *n* tratado *m*.
treatment *n* trato *m*.
treaty *n* tratado *m*.
treble *adj* triple; ● *vt, vi* triplicar(se); ● *n (mus)* tiple *m*.
treble clef *n* clave de sol *f*.
tree *n* árbol *m*.
trek *n* caminata *f*; expedición *f*.
trellis *n* enrejado *m*.
tremble *vi* temblar.
trembling *n* temor *m*; trino *m*.
tremendous *adj* tremendo; enorme; estupendo.
tremor *n* temblor *m*.
trench *n* foso *m*; *(mil)* trinchera *f*.
trend *n* tendencia *f*; curso *m*; moda *f*.
trendy *adj* de moda.
trepidation *n* inquietud *f*.
trespass *vt* transpasar, violar.
tress *n* trenza *f*; rizo de pelo *m*.
trestle *n* caballete de serrador *m*.
trial *n* proceso *m*; prueba *f*; ensayo *m*; desgracia *f*.
triangle *n* triángulo *m*.
triangular *adj* triangular.
tribal *adj* tribal.
tribe *n* tribu *f*; raza, casta *f*.
tribulation *n* tribulación *f*.
tribunal *n* tribunal *m*.
tributary *adj, n* tributario *m*.
tribute *n* tributo *m*.
trice *n* momento, tris *m*.
trick *n* engaño, fraude *m*; burla *f*; baza *f* (en el juego de naipes); ● *vt* engañar.
trickery *n* engaño *m*.
trickle *vi* gotear; ● *n* reguero *m*.
tricky *adj* difícil; delicado.
tricycle *n* triciclo *m*.
trifle *n* bagatela, niñería *f*; ● *vi* bobear; juguetear.
trifling *adj* frívolo, inútil.
trigger *n* gatillo *m*; **to ~ off** *vt* desencadenar.
trigonometry *n* trigonometría *f*.
trill *n* trino *m*; ● *vi* trinar.
trim *adj* aseado; en buen estado; arreglado; ● *vt* arreglar; recortar; adornar.
trimmings *npl* accesorios *mpl*.
Trinity *n* Trinidad *f*.
trinket *n* joya, alhaja *f*; adorno *m*.

trio *n (mus)* trío *m*.
trip *vt* hacer caer; ● *vi* tropezar; resbalar; **to ~ up** *vi* caerse; *vt* hacer caer; ● *n* resbalón *m*; viaje corto *m*.
tripe *n* callos *mpl*; bobadas *fpl*.
triple *adj* triple; ● *vt* triplicar.
triplets *npl* trillizos *mpl*.
triplicate *n* triplicado *m*.
tripod *n* trípode *m*.
trite *adj* trivial; usado.
triumph *n* triunfo *m*; ● *vi* triunfar.
triumphal *adj* triunfal.
triumphant *adj* triunfante; victorioso; ~**ly** *adv* en triunfo.
trivia *npl* trivialidades *fpl*.
trivial *adj* trivial, vulgar; ~**ly** *adv* trivialmente.
triviality *n* trivialidad *f*.
trolley *n* carrito *m*.
trombone *n* trombón *m*.
troop *n* grupo *m*; ~**s** *npl* tropas *fpl*.
trooper *n* soldado a caballo *m*.
trophy *n* trofeo *m*.
tropical *adj* trópico.
trot *n* trote *m*; ● *vi* trotar.
trouble *vt* afligir; molestar; ● *n* problema *m*; disturbio *m*; inquietud *f*; aflicción, pena *f*.
troubled *adj* preocupado; agitado.
troublemaker *n* agitador *m*.
troubleshooter *n* conciliador *m*.
troublesome *adj* molesto.
trough *n* abrevadero *m*; comedero *m*.
troupe *n* grupo *m*.
trousers *npl* pantalones *mpl*.
trout *n* trucha *f*.
trowel *n* paleta *f*.
truce *n* tregua *f*.
truck *n* camión *m*; vagón *m*.
truck driver *n* camionero *m*.
truck farm *n* huerto de hortalizas *m*.
truculent *adj* truculento, cruel.
trudge *vi* andar con afán; afanarse.
true *adj* verdadero, cierto; sincero; exacto.
truelove *n* novio, via *m/f*.
truffle *n* trufa *f*.
truly *adv* en verdad; sinceramente.
trump *n* triunfo (en el juego de naipes) *m*.
trumpet *n* trompeta *f*.
trunk *n* baúl, cofre *m*; trompa *f*.
truss *n* braguero *m*; ● *vt* atar; espetar.
trust *n* confianza *f*; trust *m*; fideicomiso *m*; ● *vt* tener confianza en; confiar algo a.
trusted *adj* de confianza.
trustee *n* fideicomisario, curador *m*.
trustful *adj* fiel; confiado.
trustily *adj* fielmente.
trusting *adj* confiado.
trustworthy *adj* digno de confianza.
trusty *adj* fiel, leal; seguro.
truth *n* verdad *f*; fidelidad *f*; realidad *f*; **in ~** en verdad.
truthful *adj* verídico; veraz.
truthfulness *n* veracidad *f*.
try *vt* examinar, ensayar, probar; experimentar; tentar; intentar; juzgar; ● *vi* probar; **to ~ on** probarse; **to ~ out** probar; ● *n* tentativa *f*; ensayo *m*.
trying *adj* pesado; cansado.
tub *n* balde, cubo *m*; tina *f*.
tuba *n* tuba *f*.
tube *n* tubo, cañón, cañuto *m*.
tuberculosis *n* tuberculosis *f invar*.
tubing *n* cañería *f*.
tuck *n* pliegue *m*; ● *vt* poner.
tucker *vt* cansar.
Tuesday *n* martes *m*.
tuft *n* mechón *m*; manojo *m*.

tug *vt* remolcar; • *n* remolcador *m*.
tuition *n* matrícula *f*.
tulip *n* tulipán *m*.
tumble *vi* caer, hundirse; revolcarse; • *vt* revolver; volcar; • *n* caída *f*; vuelco *m*.
tumbledown *adj* destartalado.
tumbler *n* vaso *m*.
tummy *n* barriga *f*.
tumor *n* tumor *m*.
tumultuous *adj* tumultuoso.
tuna *n* atún *m*.
tune *n* tono *m*; armonía *f*; aria *f*; • *vt* afinar; sintonizar.
tuneful *adj* armonioso, acorde, melodioso.
tuner *n* sintonizador *m*.
tunic *n* túnica *f*.
tuning fork *n* (*mus*) horquilla tónica *f*.
tunnel *n* túnel *m*; • *vt* construir un túnel.
turban *n* turbante *m*.
turbine *n* turbina *f*.
turbulence *n* turbulencia, confusión *f*.
turbulent *adj* turbulento, tumultuoso.
tureen *n* sopera *f*.
turf *n* césped *m*; • *vt* cubrir con césped.
turgid *adj* pesado.
turkey *n* pavo *m*.
turmoil *n* disturbio *m*; baraúnda *f*.
turn *vi* volver; cambiar; girar; dar vueltas; volverse a, mudarse, transformarse; to ~ around volverse; girar; to ~ back volverse; to ~ down rechazar; doblar; to ~ in acostarse; to ~ off *vi* desviarse; *vt* apagar; parar; to ~ on encender, prender; poner en marcha; to ~ out apagar; to ~ over *vi* volverse; *vt* volver; to ~ up *vi* llegar; aparecer; *vt* subir; • *n* vuelta *f*; giro *m*; rodeo *m*; turno *m*; vez *f*; inclinación *f*.
turncoat *n* desertor, renegado *m*.
turning *n* vuelta *f*.
turnip *n* nabo *m*.
turn-off *n* salida *f*.
turnout *n* concurrencia *f*.
turnover *n* facturación *f*.
turnpike *n* autopista de peaje *f*.
turnstile *n* torniquete *m*.
turntable *n* plato *m*.
turpentine *n* trementina *f*.
turquoise *n* turquesa *f*.
turret *n* torrecilla *f*.
turtle *n* galápago *m*.
turtledove *n* tórtola *f*.
tusk *n* colmillo *m*.
tussle *n* pelea *f*.
tutor *n* tutor *m*; profesor *m*; • *vt* enseñar, instruir.
tuxedo *n* smóking *m*.
twang *n* gangueo *m*; sonido agudo *m*.
tweezers *npl* tenacillas *fpl*.
twelfth *adj*, *n* duodécimo.
twelve *adj*, *n* doce.
twentieth *adj*, *n* vigésimo.
twenty *adj*, *n* veinte.
twice *adv* dos veces.
twig *n* ramita *f*; • *vi* caer en la cuenta.
twilight *n* crepúsculo *m*.
twin *n* gemelo *m*.
twine *vi* entrelazarse; caracolear; • *n* bramante *m*.
twinge *vt* punzar, pellizcar; • *n* dolor agudo *o* punzante *m*; remordimiento *m*.
twinkle *vi* centellear; parpadear.
twirl *vt* dar vueltas a; • *vi* piruetear; • *n* rotación *f*.
twist *vt* torcer, retorcer; entretejer; • *vi* serpentear; • *n* torsión *f*; vuelta *f*; doblez *f*.
twit (*sl*) *n* tonto *m*.
twitch *vi* moverse nerviosamente; • *n* pellizco *m*.
twitter *vi* gorjear; • *n* gorjeo *m*.

two *adj*, *n* dos.
two-door *adj* de dos puertas.
two-faced *adj* falso.
twofold *adj* doble, duplicado; • *adv* al doble.
two-seater *n* avión *o* coche de dos plazas *m*.
twosome *n* pareja *f*.
tycoon *n* magnate *m*.
type *n* tipo *m*; letra *f*; modelo *m*; • *vt* escribir a máquina.
typecast *adj* encasillado.
typeface *n* tipo *m*.
typescript *n* texto, mecanografiado *m*.
typewriter *n* máquina de escribir *f*.
typewritten *adj* mecanografiado.
typical *adj* típico.
tyrannical *adj* tiránico.
tyranny *n* tiranía *f*; crueldad *f*.
tyrant *n* tirano *m*.

U

ubiquitous *adj* ubicuo.
udder *n* ubre *f*.
ugh *excl* ¡uf!
ugliness *n* fealdad *f*.
ugly *adj* feo; peligroso.
ulcer *n* úlcera *f*.
ulterior *adj* ulterior.
ultimate *adj* último; ~ly *adv* al final; a fin de cuentas.
ultimatum *n* ultimátum *m*.
ultramarine *n* ultramar *m*; • *adj* ultramarino.
ultrasound *n* ultrasonido *m*.
umbilical cord *n* cordón umbilical *m*.
umbrella *n* paraguas *m invar*.
umpire *n* árbitro *m*.
umpteen *adj* enésimos.
unable *adj* incapaz.
unaccompanied *adj* solo, sin acompañamiento.
unaccomplished *adj* incompleto, no acabado.
unaccountable *adj* inexplicable, extraño.
unaccountably *adv* extrañamente.
unaccustomed *adj* desacostumbrado, desusado.
unacknowledged *adj* desconocido; negado.
unacquainted *adj* desconocido; ignorado.
unadorned *adj* sin adorno.
unadulterated *adj* genuino, puro; sin mezcla.
unaffected *adj* sincero, sin afectación.
unaided *adj* sin ayuda.
unaltered *adj* invariado.
unambitious *adj* no ambicioso.
unanimity *n* unanimidad *f*.
unanimous *adj* unánime; ~ly *adv* unánimemente.
unanswerable *adj* incontrovertible, incontestable.
unanswered *adj* no respondido.
unapproachable *adj* inaccesible.
unarmed *adj* inerme, desarmado.
unassuming *adj* nada presuntuoso, modesto.
unattached *adj* independiente; disponible.
unattainable *adj* inasequible.
unattended *adj* sin atender.
unauthorized *adj* no autorizado.
unavoidable *adj* inevitable.
unavoidably *adv* inevitablemente.
unaware *adj* desatento.
unawares *adv* inadvertidamente; de improviso.
unbalanced *adj* desequilibrado; trastornado.
unbearable *adj* intolerable.
unbecoming *adj* indecente, indecoroso.
unbelievable *adj* increíble.
unbend *vi* relajarse; • *vt* enderezar.
unbiased *adj* imparcial.

unblemished *adj* sin mancha, sin tacha, irreprensible.
unborn *adj* no nacido.
unbreakable *adj* irrompible.
unbroken *adj* intacto; indómito; entero; no batido.
unbutton *vt* desabotonar.
uncalled-for *adj* inmerecido.
uncanny *adj* extraordinario.
unceasing *adj* sin cesar, continuo.
unceremonious *adj* brusco.
uncertain *adj* incierto, dudoso.
uncertainty *n* incertidumbre *f*.
unchangeable *adj* inmutable.
unchanged *adj* no alterado.
unchanging *adj* inalterable, immutable.
uncharitable *adj* nada caritativo, duro.
unchecked *adj* desenfrenado.
unchristian *adj* poco cristiano.
uncivil *adj* grosero, descortés.
uncivilized *adj* tosco, salvaje, no civilizado.
uncle *n* tío.
uncomfortable *adj* incómodo; desconsolado; desagradable.
uncomfortably *adv* desconsoladamente; incómodamente; tristemente.
uncommon *adj* raro, extraordinario.
uncompromising *adj* irreconciliable.
unconcerned *adj* indiferente.
unconditional *adj* sin condiciones, absoluto.
unconfined *adj* libre, ilimitado.
unconfirmed *adj* irresoluto, sin resolución, indeciso.
unconnected *adj* inconexo.
unconquerable *adj* invencible, insuperable.
unconscious *adj* inconsciente; **~ly** *adv* sin conocimiento *o* conciencia de las cosas.
unconstrained *adj* libre, voluntario.
uncontrollable *adj* irresistible; desenfrenado.
unconventional *adj* poco convencional.
unconvincing *adj* no convincente.
uncork *vt* destapar.
uncorrected *adj* incorrecto, no corregido.
uncouth *adj* grosero.
uncover *vt* descubrir.
uncultivated *adj* inculto.
uncut *adj* no cortado, entero.
undamaged *adj* ileso, libre de daño.
undaunted *adj* intrépido.
undecided *adj* indeciso.
undefiled *adj* impoluto, puro.
undeniable *adj* innegable, incontestable; **~bly** *adv* indubitablemente.
under *prep* debajo de; menos de; según; ● *adv* debajo.
under-age *adj* menor de edad.
undercharge *vt* cobrar de menos.
underclothing *n* ropa íntima *f*.
undercoat *n* primera mano *f*.
undercover *adj* clandestino.
undercurrent *n* tendencia oculta *f*.
undercut *vt* vender más barato que.
underdeveloped *adj* subdesarrollado.
underdog *n* desvalido *m*.
underdone *adj* poco cocido.
underestimate *vt* subestimar.
undergo *vt* sufrir; sostener.
undergraduate *n* estudiante *m*.
underground *n* movimiento clandestino *m*.
undergrowth *n* soto, monte *m*.
underhand *adv* clandestinamente; ● *adj* secreto, clandestino.
underlie *vi* estar debajo.
underline *vt* subrayar.
undermine *vt* minar.
underneath *adv* debajo; ● *prep* debajo de.
underpaid *adj* mal pagado.
underprivileged *adj* desvalido.

underrate *vt* menospreciar.
undersecretary *n* subsecretario *m*.
undershirt *n* camiseta *f*.
undershorts *npl* calzoncillos *mpl*.
underside *n* revés *m*.
understand *vt* entender, comprender.
understandable *adj* comprensible.
understanding *n* entendimiento *m*; inteligencia *f*; conocimiento *m*; correspondencia *f*; ● *adj* comprensivo.
understatement *n* subestimación *f*; modestia *f*.
undertake *vt, vi* emprender.
undertaking *n* empresa *f*; empeño *m*.
undervalue *vt* menospreciar.
underwater *adj* submarino; ● *adv* bajo el agua.
underwear *n* ropa íntima *f*.
underworld *n* hampa *f*.
underwrite *vt* suscribir; asegurar contra riesgos.
underwriter *n* asegurador *m*.
undeserved *adj* no merecido; **~ly** *adv* sin haberlo merecido.
undeserving *adj* indigno.
undesirable *adj* indeseable.
undetermined *adj* indeterminado, indeciso.
undigested *adj* indigesto.
undiminished *adj* entero, no disminuido.
undisciplined *adj* indisciplinado.
undisguised *adj* sin disfraz, cándido, sincero.
undismayed *adj* intrépido.
undisputed *adj* incontestable.
undisturbed *adj* quieto, tranquilo.
undivided *adj* indiviso, entero.
undo *vt* deshacer, destar.
undoing *n* ruina *f*.
undoubted *adj* indudable; **~ly** *adv* indudablemente.
undress *vi* desnudarse.
undue *adj* indebido; injusto.
undulating *adj* ondulante.
unduly *adv* indebidamente.
undying *adj* inmortal.
unearth *vt* desenterrar.
unearthly *adj* inverosímil.
uneasy *adj* inquieto, desasosegado; incómodo.
uneducated *adj* ignorante.
unemployed *adj* parado.
unemployment *n* paro *m*.
unending *adj* interminable.
unenlightened *adj* no iluminado.
unenviable *adj* lo que no debe envidiarse.
unequal *adj* , **~ly** *adv* desigual(mente).
unequaled *adj* incomparable.
unerring *adj* , **~ly** *adv* infalible(mente).
uneven *adj* desigual; impar; **~ly** *adv* desigualmente.
unexpected *adj* inesperado; inopinado; **~ly** *adv* de repente; inopinadamente.
unexplored *adj* ignorado, no descubierto.
unfailing *adj* infalible, seguro.
unfair *adj* falso; injusto; **~ly** *adv* injustamente.
unfaithful *adj* infiel, pérfido.
unfaithfulness *n* infidelidad, perfidia *f*.
unfaltering *adj* firme, asegurado.
unfamiliar *adj* desacostumbrado, poco común.
unfashionable *adj* pasado de moda; **~bly** *adv* contra la moda.
unfasten *vt* desatar, soltar, aflojar.
unfathomable *adj* insondable, impenetrable.
unfavorable *adj* no favorable.
unfeeling *adj* insensible, duro de corazón.
unfinished *adj* imperfecto, no acabado.
unfit *adj* indispuesto; incapaz.
unfold *vt* desplegar; revelar; ● *vi* abrirse.
unforeseen *adj* imprevisto.
unforgettable *adj* inolvidable.
unforgivable *adj* imperdonable.
unforgiving *adj* implacable.

unfortunate *adj* desafortunado, infeliz; ~ly *adv* por desgracia, infelizmente.
unfounded *adj* sin fundamento.
unfriendly *adj* antipático.
unfruitful *adj* estéril; infructuoso.
unfurnished *adj* sin muebles; desprovisto.
ungainly *adj* desmañado.
ungentlemanly *adj* indigno de un hombre bien criado.
ungovernable *adj* indomable, ingobernable.
ungrateful *adj* ingrato; desagradable; ~ly *adv* ingratamente.
ungrounded *adj* infundado.
unhappily *adv* infelizmente.
unhappiness *n* infelicidad *f*.
unhappy *adj* infeliz.
unharmed *adj* ileso, sano y salvo.
unhealthy *adj* malsano; enfermizo.
unheard-of *adj* inaudito, extraño, sin ejemplo.
unheeding *adj* negligente; distraído.
unhook *vt* desenganchar; descolgar; desabrochar.
unhoped(-for) *adj* inesperado.
unhurt *adj* ileso.
unicorn *n* unicornio *m*.
uniform *adj* , ~ly *adv* uniforme(mente); ● *n* uniforme *m*.
uniformity *adj* uniformidad *f*.
unify *vt* unificar.
unimaginable *adj* inimaginable.
unimpaired *adj* no disminuido, no alterado.
unimportant *adj* nada importante.
uninformed *adj* ignorante.
uninhabitable *adj* inhabitable.
uninhabited *adj* inhabitado, desierto.
uninjured *adj* ileso, no dañado.
unintelligible *adj* ininteligible.
unintelligibly *adj* de modo ininteligible.
unintentional *adj* involuntario.
uninterested *adj* desinteresado.
uninteresting *adj* poco interesante.
uninterrupted *adj* sin interrupción, continuo.
uninvited *adj* no convidado.
union *n* unión *f*; sindicato *m*.
unionist *n* unitario *m*.
unique *adj* único, uno, singular.
unison *n* unisonancia *f*.
unit *n* unidad *f*.
unitarian *n* unitario *m*.
unite *vt vi* unir(se), juntarse.
unitedly *adv* unidamente, de acuerdo.
United States (of America) *npl* Estados Unidos *mpl*.
unity *n* unidad, concordia, conformidad *f*.
universal *adj* , ~ly *adv* universal(mente).
universe *n* universo *m*.
university *n* universidad *f*.
unjust *adj* injusto; ~ly *adv* injustamente.
unkempt *adj* despeinado; descuidado.
unkind *adj* poco amable; severo.
unknowingly *adv* sin saberlo.
unknown *adj* incógnito.
unlawful *adj* ilegítimo, ilícito; ~ly *adv* ilegítimamente.
unlawfulness *n* ilegalidad *f*.
unleash *vt* desencadenar.
unless *conj* a menos que, si no.
unlicensed *adj* sin licencia.
unlike, unlikely *adj* diferente, disímil; improbable; inverosímil; ~ly *adv* improbablemente.
unlikelihood *n* inverisimilitud *f*.
unlimited *adj* ilimitado.
unlisted *adj* que no viene en la guía.
unload *vt* descargar.
unlock *vt* abrir alguna cerradura.
unluckily *adv* desafortunadamente.
unlucky *adj* desafortunado.
unmanageable *adj* inmanejable, intratable.

unmannered *adj* rudo, brutal, grosero.
unmannerly *adj* malcriado, descortés.
unmarried *adj* soltero; soltera.
unmask *vt* quitar la máscara.
unmentionable *adj* que no se puede mencionar.
unmerited *adj* desmerecido.
unmindful *adj* olvidadizo, negligente.
unmistakable *adj* evidente; ~ly *adv* con evidencia.
unmitigated *adj* absoluto.
unmoved *adj* inmoto, firme.
unnatural *adj* antinatural; perverso; afectado.
unnecessary *adj* inútil, no necesario.
unneighborly *adj* poco atento con sus vecinos; descortés.
unnoticed *adj* no observado.
unnumbered *adj* innumerable.
unobserved *adj* no observado.
unobtainable *adj* inconseguible; inexistente.
unobtrusive *adj* modesto.
unoccupied *adj* desocupado.
unoffending *adj* sencillo, inocente.
unofficial *adj* no oficial.
unorthodox *adj* heterodoxo.
unpack *vt* desempacar; desenvolver.
unpaid *adj* no pagado.
unpalatable *adj* desabrido.
unparalleled *adj* sin paralelo; sin par.
unpleasant *adj* , ~ly *adv* desagradable(mente).
unpleasantness *n* desagrado *m*.
unplug *vt* desconectar.
unpolished *adj* que no está pulido; rudo, grosero.
unpopular *adj* no popular.
unpracticed *adj* inexperto, no versado.
unprecedented *adj* sin ejemplo.
unpredictable *adj* imprevisible.
unprejudiced *adj* imparcial.
unprepared *adj* no preparado.
unprofitable *adj* inútil, vano; poco lucrativo.
unprotected *adj* desvalido, sin protección.
unpublished *adj* no publicado; inédito.
unpunished *adj* impune.
unqualified *adj* sin títulos; total.
unquestionable *adj* indubitable, indisputable; ~ly *adv* sin duda, sin disputa.
unquestioned *adj* incontestable, no preguntado.
unravel *vt* desenredar.
unread *adj* no leído; ignorante.
unreal *adj* irreal.
unrealistic *adj* poco realista.
unreasonable *adv* irracionalmente.
unreasonably *adj* irrazonable.
unregarded *adj* descuidado; despreciado.
unrelated *adj* sin relación; no de familia.
unrelenting *adj* incompasivo, inflexible.
unreliable *adj* poco fiable.
unremitting *adj* constante, incansable.
unrepentant *adj* impenitente.
unreserved *adj* sin restricción; franco; ~ly *adv* abiertamente.
unrest *n* malestar *m*; disturbios *mpl*.
unrestrained *adj* desenfrenado; ilimitado.
unripe *adj* inmaduro.
unrivaled *adj* sin rival, sin igual.
unroll *vt* desenrollar.
unruliness *n* turbulencia *f*; desenfreno *m*.
unruly *adj* desenfrenado.
unsafe *adj* no seguro, peligroso.
unsatisfactory *adj* lo que no satisface o no convence.
unsavory *adj* desabrido, insípido.
unscathed *adj* ileso.
unscrew *vt* destornillar.
unscrupulous *adj* sin escrúpulos.
unseasonable *adj* intempestivo, fuera de propósito.
unseemly *adj* indecente.

unseen *adj* invisible; que no se ha visto.
unselfish *adj* desinteresado.
unsettle *vt* perturbar.
unsettled *adj* inquieto; inestable; variable.
unshaken *adj* firme, estable.
unshaven *adj* sin afeitar.
unsightly *adj* desagradable a la vista, feo.
unskilled *adj* inhábil.
unskillful *adj* inhábil, poco mañoso.
unsociable *adj* insociable, intratable.
unspeakable *adj* inefable, indecible.
unstable *adj* instable, inconstante.
unsteadily *adv* ligeramente, inconstantemente.
unsteady *adj* inestable.
unstudied *adj* no estudiado; no premeditado.
unsuccessful *adj* infeliz, desafortunado; ~ly *adv* sin éxito.
unsuitable *adj* inapropiado; inoportuno.
unsure *adj* poco seguro.
unsympathetic *adj* poco compasivo.
untamed *adj* indomado.
untapped *adj* sin explotar.
untenable *adj* insostenible.
unthinkable *adj* inconcebible.
unthinking *adj* desatento, indiscreto.
untidiness *n* desaliño *m*.
untidy *adj* desordenado; sucio.
untie *vt* desatar, deshacer, soltar.
until *prep* hasta; • *conj* hasta que.
untimely *adj* intempestivo.
untiring *adj* incansable.
untold *adj* nunca dicho; indecible; incalculable.
untouched *adj* intacto.
untoward *adj* impropio; adverso.
untried *adj* no ensayado o probado.
untroubled *adj* no perturbado, tranquilo.
untrue *adj* falso.
untrustworthy *adj* indigno de confianza.
untruth *n* falsedad, mentira *f*.
unused *adj* inusitado, no usado.
unusual *adj* inusitado, raro; ~ly *adv* inusitadamente, raramente.
unveil *vt* quitar el velo, descubrir.
unwavering *adj* inquebrantable.
unwelcome *adj* desagradable, inoportuno.
unwell *adj* enfermizo, malo.
unwieldy *adj* pesado.
unwilling *adj* desinclinado; ~ly *adv* de mala gana.
unwillingness *n* mala gana, repugnancia *f*.
unwind *vt* desenredar, desenmarañar; • *vi* relajarse.
unwise *adj* imprudente.
unwitting *adj* inconsciente.
unworkable *adj* poco práctico.
unworthy *adj* indigno.
unwrap *vt* desenvolver.
unwritten *adj* no escrito.
up *adv* arriba, en lo alto; levantado; • *prep* hacia; hasta.
upbringing *n* educación *f*.
update *vt* poner al día.
upheaval *n* agitación *f*.
uphill *adj* difícil, penoso; • *adv* cuesta arriba.
uphold *vt* sos tener, apoyar.
upholstery *n* tapicería *f*.
upkeep *n* mantenimiento *m*.
uplift *vt* levantar.
upon *prep* sobre, encima.
upper *adj* superior; más elevado.
upper-class *adj* de la clase alta.
upper-hand *n* (*fig*) superioridad *f*.
uppermost *adj* más alto, supremo; **to be** ~ predominar.
upright *adj* derecho, perpendicular, recto; puesto en pie; honrado.
uprising *n* sublevación *f*.

uproar *n* tumulto, alboroto *m*.
uproot *vt* desarraigar.
upset *vt* trastornar; derramar, volcar; • *n* revés *m*; trastorno *m*; • *adj* molesto; revuelto.
upshot *n* remate *m*; fin *m*; conclusión *f*.
upside-down *adv* de arriba abajo.
upstairs *adv* de arriba.
upstart *n* advenedizo *m*.
uptight *adj* nervioso.
up-to-date *adj* al día.
upturn *n* mejora *f*.
upward *adj* ascendente; ~s *adv* hacia arriba.
urban *adj* urbano.
urbane *adj* cortés.
urchin *n* golfillo *m*.
urge *vt* animar; • *n* impulso *m*; deseo *m*.
urgency *n* urgencia *f*.
urgent *adj* urgente.
urinal *n* orinal *m*.
urinate *vi* orinar.
urine *n* orina *f*.
urn *n* urna *f*.
us *pn* nos; nosotros.
usage *n* tratamiento *m*; uso *m*.
use *n* uso *m*; utilidad, práctica *f*; • *vt* usar, emplear.
used *adj* usado.
useful *adj* , ~ly *adv* útil(mente).
usefulness *n* utilidad *f*.
useless *adj* inútil; ~ly *adv* inútilmente.
uselessness *n* inutilidad *f*.
user-friendly *adj* amistoso.
usher *n* ujier *m*; acomodador *m*.
usherette *n* acomodadora *f*.
usual *adj* usual, común, normal; ~ly *adv* normalmente.
usurer *n* usurero *m*.
usurp *vt* usurpar.
usury *n* usura *f*.
utensil *n* utensilio *m*.
uterus *n* útero *m*.
utility *n* utilidad *f*.
utilize *vt* utilizar.
utmost *adj* extremo, sumo; último.
utter *adj* total; todo; entero; • *vt* proferir; expresar; publicar.
utterance *n* expresión *f*.
utterly *adv* enteramente, del todo.

V

vacancy *n* cuarto libre *m*.
vacant *adj* vacío; desocupado; vacante.
vacant lot *n* solar *m*.
vacate *vt* desocupar; dejar.
vacation *n* vacaciones *fpl*.
vacationer *n* turista *m/f*.
vaccinate *vt* vacunar.
vaccination *n* vacunación *f*.
vaccine *n* vacuna *f*.
vacuous *adj* vacío.
vacuum *n* vacío *m*.
vacuum bottle *n* termo *m*.
vagina *n* vagina *f*.
vagrant *n* vagabundo.
vague *adj* vago; ~ly *adv* vagamente.
vain *adj* vano, inútil; vanidoso.
valet *n* criado *m*.
valiant *adj* valiente, valeroso.
valid *adj* válido.
valley *n* valle *m*.
valor *n* valor, aliento, brío, esfuerzo *m*.
valuable *adj* precioso; ~s *npl* cosas preciosas *fpl*.

valuation *n* tasa, valuación *f.*
value *n* valor, precio *m;* • *vt* valuar; estimar, apreciar.
valued *adj* apreciado.
valve *n* válvula *f.*
vampire *n* vampiro *m.*
van *n* camioneta *f.*
vandal *n* gamberro *m.*
vandalism *n* vandalismo *m.*
vandalize *vt* dañar.
vanguard *n* vanguardia *f.*
vanilla *n* vainilla *f.*
vanish *vi* desvanecerse, desaparecer.
vanity *n* vanidad *f.*
vanity case *n* neceser *m.*
vanquish *vt* vencer, conquistar.
vantage point *n* punto panorámico *m.*
vapor *n* vapor *m;* exhalación *f.*
variable *adj* variable; voluble.
variance *n* discordia, desavenencia *f.*
variation *n* variación *f.*
varicose vein *n* variz *f.*
varied *adj* variado.
variety *n* variedad *f.*
variety show *n* espectáculo de variedades *m.*
various *adj* vario, diverso, diferente.
varnish *n* barniz *m;* • *vt* barnizar.
vary *vt, vi* variar; cambiar.
vase *n* florero *m.*
vast *adj* vasto; inmenso.
vat *n* tina *f.*
vault *n* bóveda *f;* cueva *f;* caverna *f;* • *vt* saltar.
veal *n* ternera *f.*
veer *vi* (*mar*) virar.
vegetable *adj* vegetal; • *n* vegetal *m;* ~s *pl* legumbre *f.*
vegetable garden *n* huerta *f.*
vegetarian *n* vegetariano, na *m/f.*
vegetate *vi* vegetar.
vegetation *n* vegetación *f.*
vehemence *n* vehemencia, violencia *f.*
vehement *adj* vehemente, violento; ~ly *adv* vehementemente.
vehicle *n* vehículo *m.*
veil *n* velo *m;* • *vt* encubrir, ocultar.
vein *n* vena *f;* cavidad *f;* inclinación del ingenio *f.*
velocity *n* velocidad *f.*
velvet *n* terciopelo *m.*
vending machine *n* vendedora automática *f.*
vendor *n* vendedor *m.*
veneer *n* chapa *f;* barniz *m.*
venerable *adj* venerable.
venerate *vt* venerar, honrar.
veneration *n* veneración *f.*
venereal *adj* venéreo.
vengeance *n* venganza *f.*
venial *adj* venial.
venison *n* (carne de) venado *f.*
venom *n* veneno *m.*
venomous *adj* venenoso; ~ly *adv* venenosamente.
vent *n* respiradero *m;* salida *f;* • *vt* desahogar.
ventilate *vt* ventilar.
ventilation *n* ventilación *f.*
ventilator *n* ventilador *m.*
ventriloquist *n* ventrílocuo *m.*
venture *n* empresa *f;* • *vi* aventurarse; • *vt* aventurar, arriesgar.
venue *n* lugar de reunión *m.*
veranda(h) *n* terraza *f.*
verb *n* (*gr*) verbo *m.*
verbal *adj* verbal, literal; ~ly *adv* verbalmente.
verbatim *adv* palabra por palabra.
verbose *adj* verboso.
verdant *adj* verde.

verdict *n* (*law*) veredicto *m;* opinión *f.*
verification *n* verificación *f.*
verify *vt* verificar.
veritable *adj* verdadero.
vermin *n* bichos *mpl.*
vermouth *n* vermut *m.*
versatile *adj* versátil; polifacético.
verse *n* verso *m;* versículo *m.*
versed *adj* versado.
version *n* versión *f.*
versus *prep* contra.
vertebra *n* vértebra *f.*
vertebral, vertebrate *adj* vertebral.
vertex *n* cenit, vértice *m.*
vertical *adj* , ~ly *adv* vertical(mente).
vertigo *n* vértigo *m.*
verve *n* brío *m.*
very *adj* verdadero, real; idéntico, mismo; • *adv* muy, mucho, sumamente.
vessel *n* vasija *f;* vaso *m;* barco *m.*
vest *n* chaleco *m.*
vestibule *n* vestíbulo *m.*
vestige *n* vestigio *m.*
vestment *n* vestido *m;* vestidura *f.*
vestry *n* sacristía *f.*
veteran *adj,* *n* veterano (*m*).
veterinarian *n* veterinario *m.*
veterinary *adj* veterinario.
veto *n* veto *m;* • *vt* vedar.
vex *vt* molestar.
vexed *adj* controvertido.
via *prep* por.
viaduct *n* viaducto *m.*
vial *n* redoma, ampolleta *f.*
vibrate *vi* vibrar.
vibration *n* vibración *f.*
vicarious *adj* sustituto.
vice *n* vicio *m;* culpa *f;* tornillo *m.*
vice-chairman *n* vice-presidente *m.*
vice versa *adv* viceversa.
vicinity *n* vecindad, proximidad *f.*
vicious *adj* vicioso; ~ly *adv* de manera viciosa.
victim *n* víctima *f.*
victimize *vt* victimizar.
victor *n* vencedor *m.*
victorious *adj* victorioso.
victory *n* victoria *f.*
video *n* videofilm *m;* video cassette *f;* videograbadora *f.*
video tape *n* cinta de video *f.*
viewer *n* televidente *m/f.*
vie *vi* competir.
view *n* vista *f;* perspectiva *f;* aspecto *m;* opinión *f;* paisaje *m;* • *vt* mirar, ver; examinar.
viewfinder *n* visor de imagen *m.*
viewpoint *n* punto de vista *m.*
vigil *n* vela *f;* vigilia *f.*
vigilance *n* vigilancia *f.*
vigilant *adj* vigilante, atento.
vigor *n* vigor *m;* energía *f.*
vigorous *adj* vigoroso; ~ly *adv* vigorosamente.
vile *adj* vil, bajo; asqueroso.
vilify *vt* envilecer.
villa *n* chalet *m;* casa de campo *f.*
village *n* aldea *f.*
villager *n* aldeano *m.*
villain *n* malvado *m.*
vindicate *vt* vindicar, defender.
vindication *n* vindicación *f;* justificación *f.*
vindictive *adj* vengativo.
vine *n* vid *f.*
vinegar *n* vinagre *m.*
vineyard *n* viña *f.*

vintage *n* vendimia *f*.
vinyl *n* vinilo *m*.
viola *n* (*mus*) viola *f*.
violate *vt* violar.
violation *n* violación *f*.
violence *n* violencia *f*.
violent *adj* violento; ~**ly** *adv* violentamente.
violet *n* (*bot*) violeta *f*.
violin *n* (*mus*) violín *m*.
violinist *n* violinista *m/f*.
violoncello *n* (*mus*) violón, violoncello *m*.
viper *n* víbora *f*.
virgin *n* virgen *f*; ● *adj* virgen.
virginity *n* virginidad *f*.
Virgo *n* Virgo *f* (signo del zodíaco).
virile *adj* viril.
virility *n* virilidad *f*.
virtual *adj* , ~**ly** *adv* virtual(mente).
virtue *n* virtud *f*.
virtuous *adj* virtuoso.
virulent *adj* virulento.
virus *n* virus *m*.
visa *n* visado *m*, visa *f*.
vis-à-vis *prep* con respecto a.
viscous *adj* viscoso, glutinoso.
visibility *n* visibilidad *f*.
visible *adj* visible.
visibly *adv* visiblemente.
vision *n* vista *f*; visión *f*.
visit *vt* visitar; ● *n* visita *f*.
visitation *n* visitación, visita *f*.
visiting hours *npl* horas de visita *fpl*.
visitor *n* visitante *m/f*; turista *m/f*.
visor *n* visera *f*.
vista *n* vista, perspectiva *f*.
visual *adj* visual.
visual aid *n* medio visual *m*.
visualize *vt* imaginarse.
vital *adj* vital; esencial; imprescindible; ~**ly** *adv* vitalmente; ~**s** *npl* partes vitales *fpl*.
vitality *n* vitalidad *f*.
vital statistics *npl* medidas vitales *fpl*.
vitamin *n* vitamina *f*.
vitiate *vt* viciar, corromper.
vivacious *adj* vivaz.
vivid *adj* vivo; gráfico; intenso; ~**ly** *adv* vivamente; gráficamente.
vivisection *n* vivisección *f*.
vocabulary *n* vocabulario *m*.
vocal *adj* vocal.
vocation *n* vocación *f*; oficio *m*; carrera, profesión *f*; ~**al** *adj* profesional.
vocative *n* vocativo *m*.
vociferous *adj* vocinglero, clamoroso.
vodka *n* vodka *m*.
vogue *n* moda *f*; boga *f*.
voice *n* voz *f*; ● *vt* expresar.
void *adj* nulo; ● *n* vacío *m*.
volatile *adj* volátil; voluble.
volcanic *adj* volcánico.
volcano *n* volcán *m*.
volition *n* voluntad *f*.
volley *n* descarga *f*; salva *f*; rociada *f*; volea *f*.
volleyball *n* voleibol *m*.
volt *n* voltio *m*.
voltage *n* voltaje *m*.
voluble *adj* locuaz.
volume *n* volumen *m*; libro *m* (encuadernado).
voluntarily *adv* voluntariamente.
voluntary *adj* voluntario.
volunteer *n* voluntario *m*; ● *vi* servir como voluntario.
voluptuous *adj* voluptuoso.

vomit *vt*, *vi* vomitar; ● *n* vómito *m*.
voracious *adj* ~**ly** *adv* voraz(mente).
vortex *n* remolino, torbellino *m*.
vote *n* voto, sufragio *m*; votación *f*; ● *vt* votar.
voter *n* votante *m/f*.
voting *n* votación *f*.
voucher *n* vale *m*.
vow *n* voto *m*; ● *vi* jurar.
vowel *n* vocal *f*.
voyage *n* viaje *m*; travesía *f*.
vulgar *adj* ordinario; de mal gusto.
vulgarity *n* grosería *f*; mal gusto *m*.
vulnerable *adj* vulnerable.
vulture *n* buitre *m*.

W

wad *n* fajo *m*; bolita *f*.
waddle *vi* anadear.
wade *vi* vadear.
wading pool *n* piscina para niños *f*.
wafer *n* galleta *f*; oblea *f*.
waffle *n* gofre *m*.
waft *vt* llevar por el aire *o* por encima del agua; ● *vi* flotar.
wag *vt* menear; ● *vi* menearse.
wage *n* salario *m*.
wage earner *n* asalariado, da *m/f*.
wager *n* apuesta *f*; ● *vt* apostar.
wages *npl* salario *m*.
waggle *vt* menear.
waggon *n* carro *m*; (*rail*) vagón *m*.
wail *n* lamento, gemido *m*; ● *vi* gemir.
waist *n* cintura *f*.
waistline *n* talle *m*.
wait *vi* esperar; ● *n* espera *f*; pausa *f*.
waiter *n* camarero *m*.
waiting list *n* lista de espera *f*.
waiting room *n* sala de espera *f*.
waive *vt* suspender.
wake *vi* despertarse; ● *vt* despertar; ● *n* vela *f*; (*mar*) estela *f*.
waken *vt*, (*vi*) despertar(se).
walk *vt*, *vi* pasear, ir; andar, caminar; ● *n* paseo *m*; caminata *f*.
walker *n* paseante *m/f*.
walkie-talkie *n* walkie-talkie *m*.
walking *n* paseo *m*.
walking stick *n* bastón *m*.
walkout *n* huelga *f*.
walkover *n* (*sl*) pan comido *m*.
walkway *n* paseo *m*.
wall *n* pared *f*; muralla *f*; muro *m*.
walled *adj* amurallado.
wallet *n* cartera, billetera *f*.
wallflower *n* (*bot*) alelí doble *m*.
wallow *vi* revolcarse.
wallpaper *n* papel pintado *m*.
walnut *n* nogal *m*; nuez *f*.
walrus *n* morsa *f*.
waltz *n* vals *m* (baile).
wan *adj* pálido.
wand *n* varita mágica *f*.
wander *vt*, *vi* errar; vagar.
wane *vi* menguar.
want *vt* querer; necesitar; faltar; ● *n* necesidad *f*; falta *f*.
wanting *adj* falto, defectuoso.
wanton *adj* lascivo; juguetón.
war *n* guerra *f*.
ward *n* sala *f*; pupilo *m*.
wardrobe *n* guardarropa *f*, ropero *m*.
warehouse *n* almacén *m*.
warfare *n* guerra *f*.

warhead *n* cabeza armada *f*.
warily *adv* prudentemente.
wariness *n* cautela, prudencia *f*.
warm *adj* cálido; caliente; efusivo; ● *vt* calentar; to ~ up *vi* calentarse; entrar en calor; acalorarse; *vt* calentar.
warm-hearted *adj* afectuoso.
warmly *adv* con calor, ardientemente.
warmth *n* calor *m*.
warn *vt* avisar; advertir.
warning *n* aviso *m*.
warning light *n* luz de advertencia *f*.
warp *vi* torcerse; ● *vt* torcer; pervertir.
warrant *n* orden de detención *f*; mandamiento de registro *m*.
warranty *n* garantía *f*.
warren *n* conejero *m*.
warrior *n* guerrero, soldado *m*.
warship *n* barco de guerra *m*.
wart *n* verruga *f*.
wary *adj* cauto, prudente.
wash *vt* lavar; bañar; ● *vi* lavarse; ● *n* lavado *m*; baño *m*.
washable *adj* lavable.
washbowl *n* lavabo *m*.
washcloth *n* manopla *f*.
washer *n* arandela *f*.
washing *n* ropa sucia *f*; colada *f*.
washing machine *n* lavadora *f*.
washing-up *n* fregado *m*.
wash-out *n* (*sl*) fracaso *m*.
washroom *n* aseos *mpl*.
wasp *n* avispa *f*.
wastage *n* desgaste *m*; pérdida *f*.
waste *vt* malgastar; destruir, arruinar; perder; ● *vi* gastarse; ● *n* desperdicio *m*; destrucción *f*; despilfarro *m*; basura *f*.
wasteful *adj* destructivo; pródigo; ~ly *adv* pródigamente.
waste paper *n* papel de desecho *m*.
waste pipe *n* tubo de desagüe *m*.
watch *n* reloj *m*; centinela *f*; guardia *f*; ● *vt* mirar; ver; vigilar; tener cuidado; ● *vi* ver; montar guardia.
watchdog *n* perro guardián *m*.
watchful *adj* vigilante; ~ly *adv* cuidadosamente.
watchmaker *n* relojero *m*.
watchman *n* sereno *m*; vigilante *m*.
watchtower *n* atalaya, garita *f*.
watchword *n* santo *m*; seña *f*.
water *n* agua *f*; ● *vt* regar, humedecer, mojar; ● *vi* hacerse agua.
water closet *n* wáter *m*.
watercolor *n* acuarela *f*.
waterfall *n* cascada *f*.
water heater *n* calentador de agua *m*.
watering-can *n* regadera *f*.
water level *n* nivel del agua *m*.
waterlily *n* ninfea *f*.
water line *n* flotación *f*.
waterlogged *adj* anegado.
water main *n* cañería del agua *f*.
watermark *n* filigrana *f*.
water melon *n* sandía *f*.
watershed *n* momento crítico *m*.
watertight *adj* impermeable.
waterworks *npl* central depuradora *f*.
watery *adj* aguado; desvaído; lloroso.
watt *n* vatio *m*.
wave *n* ola, onda *f*; oleada *f*; señal *f*; ● *vi* agitar la mano; ondear; ● *vt* agitar.
wavelength *n* longitud de onda *f*.
waver *vi* vacilar, balancear.
wavering *adj* inconstante.
wavy *adj* ondulado.
wax *n* cera *f*; ● *vt* encerar; ● *vi* crecer.
wax paper *n* papel apergaminado *m*.
waxworks *n* museo de cera *m*.

way *n* camino *m*; vía *f*; ruta *f*; modo *m*; recorrido *m*; to give ~ ceder.
waylay *vt* salir al paso.
wayward *adj* caprichoso.
we *pn* nosotros, nosotras.
weak *adj* , ~ly *adv* débil(mente).
weaken *vt* debilitar.
weakling *n* persona muy delicada *f*.
weakness *n* debilidad *f*; parte flaca de una persona *f*.
wealth *n* riqueza *f*; bienes *mpl*.
wealthy *adj* rico.
wean *vt* destetar.
weapon *n* arma *f*.
wear *vt* gastar, consumir; usar, llevar; ● *vi* consumirse; to ~ away *vt* gastar; *vi* desgastarse; to ~ down gastar; agotar; to ~ off pasar; to ~ out desgastar; agotar; ● *n* uso *m*; desgaste *m*.
weariness *n* cansancio *m*; fatiga *f*; enfado *m*.
wearisome *adj* tedioso.
weary *adj* cansado, fatigado; tedioso.
weasel *n* comadreja *f*.
weather *n* tiempo *m*; ● *vt* (out) sufrir, superar.
weather-beaten *adj* endurecido a la intemperie.
weather cock *n* gallo de campanario *m*; veleta *f*.
weather forecast *n* boletín meteorológico *m*.
weave *vt* tejer; trenzar.
weaving *n* tejido *m*.
web *n* telaraña *f*; membrana *f*; red *f*.
wed *vt*, *vi* casar(se).
wedding *n* boda *f*; nupcias *fpl*; casamiento *m*.
wedding day *n* día de la boda *m*.
wedding dress *n* traje de novia *m*.
wedding present *n* regalo de boda *m*.
wedding ring *n* alianza *f*.
wedge *n* cuña *f*; ● *vt* acuñar; apretar.
wedlock *n* matrimonio *m*.
Wednesday *n* miércoles *m*.
wee *adj* pequeñito.
weed *n* mala hierba *f*; ● *vt* escardar.
weedkiller *n* herbicida *m*.
weedy *adj* lleno de malas hierbas.
week *n* semana *f*; tomorrow ~ mañana en una semana; yesterday ~ ayer hace ocho días.
weekday *n* día laborable *m*.
weekend *n* fin de semana *m*.
weekly *adj* semanal; ● *adv* semanalmente, por semana.
weep *vt*, *vi* llorar; lamentar.
weeping willow *n* sauce llorón *m*.
weigh *vt*, *vi* pesar.
weight *n* peso *m*.
weightily *adv* pesadamente.
weightlifter *n* levantador de pesas *m*.
weighty *adj* ponderoso; importante.
welcome *adj* recibido con agrado; ~! ¡bienvenido!; ● *n* bienvenida *f*; ● *vt* dar la bienvenida a.
weld *vt* soldar; ● *n* soldadura *f*.
welfare *n* prosperidad *f*; bienestar *m*; subsidio de paro *m*.
welfare state *n* estado del bienestar *m*.
well *n* fuente *f*; manantial *m*; pozo *m*; ● *adj* bueno, sano; ● *adv* bien, felizmente; favorablemente; suficientemente; convenientemente; as ~ as así como, además de, lo mismo que.
well-behaved *adj* bien educado.
well-being *n* felicidad, prosperidad *f*.
well-bred *adj* bien criado, bien educado.
well-built *adj* fornido.
well-deserved *adj* merecido.
well-dressed *adj* bien vestido.
well-known *adj* conocido.
well-mannered *adj* educado.
well-meaning *adj* bien intencionado.
well-off *adj* acomodado.

well-to-do adj acomodado.
well-wisher n amigo, partidario m.
wench n mozuela, cantonera f.
west n oeste, occidente m; ● adj occidental; ● adv hacia el oeste.
westerly, western adj occidental.
westward adv hacia el oeste.
wet adj húmedo, mojado; ● n humedad f; ● vt mojar, humedecer.
wet-nurse n ama de leche f.
wet suit n traje de buzo m.
whack vt aporrear; ● n golpe m.
whale n ballena f.
wharf n muelle m.
what pn que, qué, el que, la que, lo que; ● adj qué; ● excl ¡cómo!.
whatever pn cualquier o cualquiera cosa que, que sea.
wheat n trigo m.
wheedle vt halagar, engañar con lisonjas.
wheel n rueda f; volante m; timón m; ● vt (hacer) rodar; volver, girar; ● vi rodar.
wheelbarrow n carretilla f.
wheelchair n sillita de ruedas f.
wheel clamp n cepo m.
wheeze vi jadear.
when adv cuando; mientras que; ● conj cuando.
whenever adv cuando; cada vez que.
where adv dónde; ● conj donde; any~ en cualquier parte; every~ en todas partes.
whereabout(s) adv dónde.
whereas conj mientras que; pues que, ya que.
whereby pn por lo cual, con lo cual.
wherever adv dondequiera que.
whereupon conj con lo cual.
wherewithal npl recursos mpl.
whet vt excitar.
whether conj si.
which pn que; lo que; el que, el cual; cual; ● adj qué; cuyo.
whiff n bocanada de humo f.
while n rato m; vez f; ● conj durante; mientras; aunque.
whim n antojo, capricho m.
whimper vi sollozar, gemir.
whimsical adj caprichoso, fantástico.
whine vi llorar, lamentar; ● n quejido, lamento m.
whinny vi relinchar.
whip n azote m; látigo m; ● vt azotar; batir.
whipped cream n nata montada f.
whirl vt, vi girar; hacer girar; mover(se) rápidamente.
whirlpool n vórtice m.
whirlwind n torbellino m.
whiskey n whisky m.
whisper vi cuchichear; susurrar.
whispering n cuchicheo m; susurro m.
whistle vi silbar; ● n silbido m.
white adj blanco, pálido; cano; puro; ● n color blanco m; clara del huevo f.
white elephant n maula f.
white-hot adj incandescente.
white lie n mentirijilla f.
whiten vt, vi blanquear; emblanquecerse.
whiteness n blancura f; palidez f.
whitewash n enlucimiento m; ● vt encalar; jalbegar.
whiting n pescadilla f.
whitish adj blanquecino.
who pn quién, que.
whoever pn quienquiera, cualquiera.
whole adj todo, total; sano, entero; ● n total m; conjunto m.
wholehearted adj sincero.
wholemeal adj integral.
wholesale n venta al por mayor f.
wholesome adj sano, saludable.
wholewheat adj integral.

wholly adv enteramente.
whom pn quién; que.
whooping cough n tos ferina f.
whore n puta f.
why n por qué; ● conj por qué; ● excl ¡hombre!
wick n mecha f.
wicked adj malvado, perverso; ~ly adv malamente.
wickedness n perversidad, malignidad f.
wicker n mimbre m; ● adj tejido de mimbre.
wide adj ancho, vasto; grande; ~ly adv muy; far and ~ por todos lados.
wide-awake adj despierto.
widen vt ensanchar, extender.
wide open adj de par en par.
widespread adj extendido.
widow n viuda f.
widower n viudo m.
width n anchura f.
wield vt manejar, empuñar.
wife n esposa f; mujer f.
wig n peluca f.
wiggle vt menear; ● vi menearse.
wild adj silvestre, feroz; desierto; descabellado; salvaje.
wilderness n desierto m.
wild life n fauna f.
wildly adv violentamente; locamente; desatinadamente.
wiliness n fraude, engaño m.
will n voluntad f; testamento m; ● vt querer, desear.
willful adj deliberado; testarudo.
willfulness n obstinación f.
willing adj inclinado, dispuesto; ~ly adv de buena gana.
willingness n buena voluntad, buena gana f.
willow n sauce m (árbol).
willpower n fuerza de voluntad f.
wilt vi marchitarse.
wily adj astuto.
win vt ganar, conquistar; alcanzar; lograr.
wince vi encogerse.
winch n torno m.
wind n viento m; aliento m; pedo m.
wind vt enrollar; envolver; dar cuerda a; ● vi serpentear.
windfall n golpe de suerte m.
winding adj tortuoso.
windmill n molino de viento m.
window n ventana f.
window box n jardinera de ventana f.
window cleaner n limpiacristales m invar.
window ledge n repisa f.
window pane n cristal m.
window sill n repisa f.
windpipe n tráquea f.
windshield n parabrisas m invar.
windshield washer n lavaparabrisas m invar.
windshield wiper n limpiaparabrisas m invar.
windy adj de mucho viento.
wine n vino m.
wine cellar n bodega f.
wine glass n copa f.
wine list n lista de vinos f.
wine merchant n vinatero m.
wine-tasting n degustación de vinos f.
wing n ala f.
winged adj alado.
winger n extremo m.
wink vi guiñar; ● n pestañeo m; guiño m.
winner n ganador, ra m/f; vencedor, ra m/f.
winning post n meta f.
winter n invierno m; ● vi invernar.
winter sports npl deportes de invierno mpl.
wintry adj invernal.
wipe vt limpiar; borrar.

wire *n* alambre *m*; telegrama *m*; • *vt* instalar el alambrado en; conectar.

wiring *n* alambrado *m*.

wiry *adj* delgado y fuerte.

wisdom *n* sabiduría, prudencia *f*.

wisdom teeth *npl* muelas de juicio *fpl*.

wise *adj* sabio, docto, juicioso, prudente.

wisecrack *n* broma *f*.

wish *vt* querer, desear, anhelar; • *n* anhelo, deseo *m*.

wishful *adj* deseoso.

wisp *n* mechón *m*; voluta *f*.

wistful *adj* pensativo, atento.

wit *n* entendimiento, ingenio *m*.

witch *n* bruja, hechicera *f*.

witchcraft *n* brujería *f*; sortilegio *m*.

with *prep* con; por, de, a.

withdraw *vt* quitar; privar; retirar; • *vi* retirarse, apartarse.

withdrawal *n* retirada *f*.

withdrawn *adj* reservado.

wither *vi* marchitarse, secarse.

withhold *vt* detener, impedir, retener.

within *prep* dentro de, adentro; • *adv* interiormente; en casa.

without *prep* sin.

withstand *vt* resistir.

witless *adj* necio, tonto, falto de ingenio.

witness *n* testimonio *m*; testigo *m*; • *vt* atestiguar, testificar.

witness stand *n* tribuna de los testigos *f*.

witticism *n* ocurrencia *f*.

wittily *adv* ingeniosamente.

wittingly *adv* adrede, de propósito.

witty *adj* ingenioso, agudo, chistoso.

wizard *n* brujo, hechicero *m*.

wobble *vi* tambalearse.

woe *n* dolor *m*; miseria *f*.

woeful *adj* triste, funesto; ~ly *adv* tristemente.

wolf *n* lobo *m*; she ~ loba *f*.

woman *n* mujer *f*.

womanish *adj* mujeril.

womanly *adj* mujeril, mujeriego.

womb *n* útero *m*.

women's lib *n* la liberación de la mujer *f*.

wonder *n* milagro *m*; maravilla *f*; asombro *m*; • *vi* maravillarse de; preguntarse si.

wonderful maravilloso; ~ly *adv* maravillosamente.

wondrous *adj* maravilloso.

won't *abrev de* will not.

wont *n* uso *m*; costumbre *f*.

woo *vt* cortejar.

wood *n* bosque *m*; selva *f*; madera *f*; leña *f*.

wood alcohol *n* alcohol desnaturalizado *m*.

wood carving *n* tallado en madera *f*.

woodcut *n* estampa de madera *f*.

woodcutter *n* grabador en láminas de madera, xilógrafo *m*.

wooded *adj* arbolado.

wooden *adj* de madera.

woodland *n* arbolado *m*.

woodlouse *n* cochinilla *f*.

woodman *n* cazador *m*; guardabosque *m*.

woodpecker *n* picamaderos *m invar*.

woodwind *n* intrumento de viento de madera *m*.

woodwork *n* carpintería *f*.

woodworm *n* carcoma *f*.

wool *n* lana *f*.

woolen *adj* de lana.

woolens *npl* géneros de lana *mpl*.

wooly *adj* lanudo, lanoso.

word *n* palabra *f*; noticia *f*; • *vt* expresar; componer en escritura.

wordiness *n* verbosidad *f*.

wording *n* redacción *f*.

word processing *n* proceso de textos *m*.

word processor *n* procesador de textos *m*.

wordy *adj* verboso.

work *vi* trabajar; obrar; estar en movimiento *o* en acción; fermentar; • *vt* trabajar, labrar; fabricar, manufacturar; to ~ out *vi* salir bien; • *vt* resolver; • *n* trabajo *m*; fábrica *f*; obra *f*; empleo *m*.

workable *adj* práctico.

workaholic *n* trabajador obsesivo *m*.

worker *n* trabajador, ra *m/f*; obrero, ra *m/f*.

workforce *n* mano de obra *f*.

working-class *adj* obrero.

workman *n* labrador *m*.

workmanship *n* manufactura *f*; destreza del artífice *f*.

workmate *n* compañero de trabajo *m*.

workshop *n* taller, obrador *m*.

world *n* mundo *m*; • *adj* del mundo; mundial.

worldliness *n* vanidad mundana *f*; profanidad *f*; avaricia *f*.

worldly *adj* mundano, terreno.

worldwide *adj* mundial.

worm *n* gusano *m*; (of a screw) rosca de tornillo *f*.

worn-out *adj* gastado; rendido.

worried *adj* preocupado.

worry *vt* preocupar; *n* preocupación *f*.

worrying *adj* inquietante.

worse *adj, adv* peor; • *n* lo peor.

worship *n* culto *m*; adoración *f*; your ~ señor alcalde, señor juez; • *vt* adorar, venerar.

worst *adj* el/la peor; • *adv* peor; • *n* lo peor, lo más malo *m*.

worth *n* valor, precio *m*; mérito *m*.

worthily *adv* dignamente, convenientemente.

worthless *adj* sin valor; inútil.

worthwhile *adj* que vale la pena; loable.

worthy *adj* digno; respetable; honesto.

would-be *adj* llamado.

wound *n* herida, llaga *f*; • *vt* herir, llagar.

wrangle *vi* reñir; • *n* riña *f*.

wrap *vt* envolver.

wrath *n* ira, rabia, cólera *f*.

wreath *n* corona, guirnalda *f*.

wreck *n* naufragio *m*; ruina *f*; destrucción *f*; navío naufragado *m*; • *vt* naufragar; arruinar.

wreckage *n* restos *mpl*; escombros *mpl*.

wren *n* reyezuelo *m* (avecilla).

wrench *vt* arrancar; dislocar; torcer; • *n* llave inglesa *f*; tirón *m*.

wrest *vt* arrancar, arrebatar.

wrestle *vi* luchar; disputar.

wrestling *n* lucha *f*.

wretched *adj* infeliz, miserable.

wriggle *vi* menearse, agitarse.

wring *vt* torcer; arrancar; estrujar.

wrinkle *n* arruga *f*; • *vt* arrugar; • *vi* arrugarse.

wrist *n* muñeca *f*.

wristband *n* puño de camisa *m*.

wristwatch *n* reloj de pulsera *m*.

writ *n* escrito *m*; escritura *f*; orden *f*.

write *vt* escribir; componer; to ~ down apuntar; to ~ off borrar; desechar; to ~ up redactar.

write-off *n* pérdida total *f*.

writer *n* escritor, ra, *m/f*; autor, ra *m/f*.

writhe *vi* retorcerse.

writing *n* escritura *f*; letra *f*; obras *fpl*; escrito *m*.

writing desk *n* escritorio *m*.

writing paper *n* papel para escribir *m*.

wrong *n* injuria *f*; injusticia *f*; perjuicio *m*; error *m*; • *adj* malo; injusto; equivocado, inoportuno; falso; • *adv* mal, equivocadamente; • *vt* agraviar, injuriar.

wrongful *adj* injusto.

wrongly *adv* injustamente.

wry *adj* irónico.

X

Xmas *n* Navidad *f*.
X-ray radiografía *f*.
xylophone xilófano *m*.

Y

yacht *n* yate *m*.
yachting balandrismo *m*.
Yankee *n* yanqui *m*.
yard *n* corral *m*; yarda *f*.
yardstick criterio *m*.
yarn *n* estambre *m*; hilo de lino *m*.
yawn *vi* bostezar; ● *n* bostezo *m*.
yawning *adj* muy abierto.
yeah *adv* sí.
year *n* año *m*.
yearbook *n* anales *mpl*.
yearling *n* animal que tiene un año *m*.
yearly *adj* anual; ● *adv* anualmente, todos los años.
yearn *vi* añorar.
yearning *n* añoranza *f*.
yeast *n* levadura *f*.
yell *vi* aullar; ● *n* aullido *m*.
yellow *adj* amarillo; ● *n* color amarillo *m*.
yellowish *adj* amarillento.
yelp *vi* latir, gañir; ● *n* aullido *m*.
yes *adv*, *n* sí (*m*).
yesterday *adv*, *n* ayer (*m*).
yet *conj* sin embargo; pero; ● *adv* todavía.
yew *n* tejo *m*.
yield *vt* dar, producir; rendir; ● *vi* rendirse; ceder el paso; ● *n* producción *f*; cosecha *f*; rendimiento *m*.
yoga *n* yoga *m*.
yog(h)urt *n* yogur *m*.

yoke *n* yugo *m*.
yolk *n* yema de huevo *f*.
yonder *adv* allá.
you *pn* vosotros, tú, usted, ustedes.
young *adj* joven, mozo; ~ **er** *adj* menor.
youngster *n* jovencito, ta *m/f*; joven *m/f*.
your(s) *pn* tuyo, vuestro, suyo; **sincerely** ~s su seguro servidor.
yourself *pn* tú mismo, usted mismo, vosotros mismos, ustedes mismos.
youth *n* juventud, adolescencia *f*; joven *m*.
youthful *adj* juvenil.
youthfulness *n* juventud *f*.
yuppie *adj*, *n* yuppie *m/f*.

Z

zany *adj* estrafalario.
zap *vt* borrar.
zeal *n* celo *m*; ardor *m*.
zealous *adj* celoso.
zebra *n* cebra *f*.
zenith *n* cénit *m*.
zero *n* zero, cero *m*.
zest *n* ánimo *m*.
zigzag *n* zigzag *m*.
zinc *n* zinc *m*.
zip, zipper *n* cremallera *f*; cierre *m*.
zip code *n* código postal *m*.
zodiac *n* zodíaco *m*.
zone *n* banda, faja *f*; zona *f*.
zoo *n* zoo *m*.
zoological *adj* zoológico.
zoologist *n* zoólogo, ga *m/f*.
zoology *n* zoología *f*.
zoom *vi* zumbar.
zoom lens *n* zoom *m*.

A

a *prep* to, in, at, according to, on, by, for, of.
abacería *f* grocery.
abacero *m* grocer.
ábaco *m* abacus.
abad *m* abbot.
abadejo *m* codfish; Spanish fly.
abadesa *f* abbess.
abadia *f* abbey.
abajo *adv* under, underneath; below; ~ de *prep* under, below.
abalanzarse *vr* to rush forward.
abalorio *m* glass bead.
abanderado *m* (*mil*) ensign; standard bearer.
abandonado, da *adj* derelict; abandoned; neglected.
abandonar *vt* to abandon; to leave; ~se *vr* to give one's self up to.
abandono *m* desertion; neglect; retirement.
abanicar *vt* to fan.
abanico *m* fan.
abaratar *vt* to lower the price.
abarca *f* sandal.
abarcar *vt* to include; to monopolize.
abarrancarse *vr* to get into a jam.
abarrotado, da *adj* packed.
abarrotar *vt* to tie down; (*mar*) to stow.
abastecedor, ra *m/f* purveyor, caterer.
abastecer *vt* to purvey.
abastecimiento *m* provision; provisions *pl*.
abasto *m* supply of provisions.
abate *m* abbé.
abatido, da *adj* dejected, low-spirited; abject.
abatimiento *m* low spirits, depression.
abatir *vi* to knock down; to humble.
abdicación *f* abdication.
abdicar *vt* to abdicate.
abdomen *m* abdomen.
abdominal *adj* abdominal.
abecé *m* alphabet.
abecedario *m* alphabet; spelling book; primer.
abedul *m* birch tree.
abeja *f* bee; ~ maestra o madre, queen bee.
abejar *m* beehive.
abejarrón *m* bumblebee.
abejón *m* drone; hornet.
abejorro *m* bumblebee.
aberración *f* aberration.
abertura *f* aperture, chink, opening.
abeto *m* fir tree.
abetunado, da *adj* dark-skinned.
abierto, ta *adj* open; sincere; frank.
abigarrado, da *adj* multi-colored.
ab intestato *adj* intestate.
abismal *adj* abysmal.
abismo *m* abyss; gulf; hell.
abjuración *f* abjuration.
abjurar *vt* to abjure, to recant an oath.
ablandamiento *m* softening.
ablandar *vt*, *vi* to soften.
ablativo *m* (*gr*) ablative.
ablución *f* ablution, lotion.
abnegación *f* self-denial.
abnegado, da *adj* selfless.
abnegar *vt* to renounce.
abobado, da *adj* stultified, silly.
abobamiento *m* stupefaction.
abobar *vt* to stupefy.
abocado, da *adj* light (wine).
abocar *vt* to seize with the mouth; ~se *vr* to meet by agreement.
abochornar *vt* to swelter; ~se *vr* to shame.

abofetear *vt* to slap.
abogacía *f* legal profession.
abogado, a *m/f* lawyer; attorney.
abogar *vi* to advocate; to intercede.
abolengo *m* ancestry; inheritance from ancestors.
abolición *f* abolition, abrogation.
abolir *vt* to abolish.
abolladura *f* dent.
abollar *vt* to dent.
abollonar *vt* to emboss.
abominable *adj* abominable, cursed.
abominación *f* abomination.
abominar *vt* to detest.
abonado, da *adj* paid-up; ● *m/f* subscriber.
abonar *vt* to settle; to fertilize; to endorse; ~se *vr* to subscribe to; ● *vi* to clear up.
abono *m* payment; subscription; dung, manure.
abordaje *m* boarding.
abordar *vt* (*mar*) to board; to broach.
aborígen *m* aborigine.
aborrecer *vt* to hate, to abhor.
aborrecible *adj* hateful, detestable.
aborrecimiento *m* abhorrence, hatred.
abortar *vi* to miscarry, to have an abortion.
abortivo, va *adj* abortive.
aborto *m* abortion; monster.
abortón *m* abortion.
abotagado, da *adj* swollen.
abotinado, da *adj* tied up.
abotonar *vt* to button.
abovedado, da *adj* vaulted.
abrasar *vt* to burn; to parch; ~se *vr* to burn oneself.
abrazadera *f* cramp-iron, clasp.
abrazar *vt* to embrace; to surround; to contain.
abrazo *m* embrace.
abrebotellas *m invar* bottle opener.
abrecartas *m invar* letter opener.
abrelatas *m invar* can opener.
abrevadero *m* watering place.
abrevar *vt* to water cattle.
abreviación *f* abbreviation, abridgment; shortening.
abreviar *vt* to abridge, to cut short.
abreviatura *f* abbreviation.
abridera *f* earring.
abridor *m* opener.
abrigar *vt* to shelter; to protect; ~se *vr* to take shelter.
abrigo *m* shelter; protection, aid.
abril *m* April.
abrillantar *vt* to polish.
abrir *vt* to open; to unlock; to be open; to disclose a secret; ~se *vr* to open up; to clear up.
abrochador *m* buttonhook.
abrochar *vt* to button; to do up.
abrogar *vt* to abrogate.
abrumador, ra *adj* overwhelming; annoying.
abrumar *vt* to overwhelm.
abrupto, ta *adj* abrupt; steep.
absceso *m* abscess.
absentismo *m* absenteeism.
absolucion *f* forgiveness; absolution.
absoluto, ta *adj* absolute.
absolutorio, a *adj* absolutory.
absolver *vt* to absolve.
absorbente *adj* absorbent.
absorber *vt* to absorb.
absorcion *f* absorption; takeover.
absorto *adj* engrossed.
abstemio *adj* teetotal.
abstencion *f* abstention.
abstenerse *vr* to abstain.
abstinencia *f* abstinence.
abstinente *adj* abstinent, abstemious.

abstraccion *f* abstraction.
abstracto, ta *adj* abstract.
abstraer *vt* to abstract; ~se *vr* to be absorbed.
abstraido *adj* absent-minded.
absuelto, ta *adj* absolved.
absurdidad *f*, absurdo *m* absurdity.
absurdo *adj* absurd.
abuela *f* grandmother.
abuelo *m* grandfather; ancestor.
abulia *f* lethargy.
abultado, da *adj* bulky, large, massive.
abultar *vt* to increase, to enlarge; • *vi* to be bulky.
abundancia *f* abundance.
abundante *adj* abundant, copious.
abundar *vi* to abound.
aburrido, da *adj* weary.
aburrimiento *m* boredom.
aburrir *vt* to bore, to weary.
abusar *vt* to abuse.
abusivo, va *adj* abusive.
abuso *m* abuse.
abyección *f* abjectness.
abyecto, ta *adj* abject, wretched.
acá *adv* here.
acabado, da *adj* perfect, accomplished; old.
acabar *vt*, *vi* to finish, to complete; to achieve; to die, to
    expire; ~se *vr* to finish; to be over; to run out.
acabóse *m* the last straw.
acacia *f* acacia.
academia *f* academy; literary society.
académico, ca *m/f* academician; • *adj* academical.
acaecer *vi* to happen.
acalorado, da *adj* heated.
acalorarse *vr* to become heated.
acallar *vt* to quiet, to hush; to soften, to appease.
acampar *vt* (*mil*) to encamp.
acanalado, da *adj* grooved; fluted.
acanalar *vt* to corrugate.
acanto *m* acanthus.
acantonamiento *m* cantonment.
acantonar *vt* to billet.
acaparar *vt* to monopolize; to hoard.
acariciar *vt* to fondle, to caress.
acarrear *vt* to transport; to occasion.
acarreo *m* carriage, transportation.
acaso *m* chance; • *adv* perhaps.
acatarrarse *vr* to catch cold.
acaudalado, da *adj* rich, wealthy.
acaudalar *vt* to hoard.
acaudillar *vt* to command.
acceder *vi* to agree; to have access to.
accesible *adj* attainable; of easy access.
acceso *m* access; fit.
accesorio, ria *adj*, *m* accessory.
accidentado, da *adj* uneven; hilly; eventful.
accidental *adj* accidental, casual.
accidentarse *vr* to have an accident.
accidente *m* accident.
acción *f* action, operation; share.
accionar *vt* to work.
accionista *m* shareholder.
acebo *m* holly tree.
acebuche *m* wild olive tree.
acechanza *f* trap.
acechar *vt* to lie in ambush, to lurk.
acecho *m* ambush.
aceitar *vt* to oil.
aceite *m* oil.
aceitera *f* oilcan.
aceitoso, sa *adj* oily.
aceituna *f* olive.
aceitunado, da *adj* olive-green.

aceitunero *m* olive seller.
aceituno *m* olive tree.
aceleración *f* acceleration.
aceleradamente *adj* swiftly, hastily.
acelerador *m* gas pedal.
acelerar *vt* to accelerate; to hurry.
acelga *f* (*bot*) beet.
acento *m* accent.
acentuación *f* accentuation.
acentuar *vt* to accentuate.
aceña *f* water mill.
acepción *f* acceptation.
aceptable *adj* acceptable; worthy of acceptance.
aceptación *f* acceptation; approval.
aceptar *vt* to accept, to admit.
acequia *f* canal, channel, drain.
acera *f* sidewalk.
acerado, da *adj* steeled, made of steel; sharp; steely.
acerbo, ba *adj* rigorous, harsh; cruel.
acerca *prep* about, relating to.
acercar *vt* to move nearer; ~se *vr* to approach.
acerico *m* pincushion.
acero *m* steel.
acérrimo, ma *adj* staunch; bitter.
acertado, da *adj* correct, proper; prudent.
acertar *vt* to hit; to guess right; to turn out true; • *vi* to get it
    right.
acertijo *m* riddle.
acervo *m* heap, pile.
acetato *m* (*quim*) acetate.
aciago, ga *adj* unlucky, ominous.
acíbar *m* aloes; (*fig*) bitterness, displeasure.
acicalar *vi* to polish; ~se *vr* to dress in style.
acicate *m* spur.
acidez *f* acidity.
ácido *m* acid; ~, da, *adj* acid, sour.
acierto *m* success; solution; dexterity.
aclamación *f* acclamation.
aclamar *vt* to applaud, to acclaim.
aclaracion *f* clarification.
aclarar *vt* to clear; to brighten; to explain; to clarify; ~se *vr* to
    understand; • *vi* to clear up.
aclimatar *vt* to acclimate; ~se *vr* to become acclimated.
acobardar *vt* to intimidate.
acodarse *vr* to lean on.
acogedor, ra *adj* welcoming.
acoger *vt* to receive; to welcome; to harbor; ~se *vr* to take
    refuge.
acogida *f* reception; asylum.
acolchar *vt* to quilt; to cushion.
acólito *m* acolyte; assistant.
acometer *vt* to attack; to undertake.
acometida *f* attack, assault.
acomodadizo *adj* accommodating.
acomodado, da *adj* suitable, convenient, fit; wealthy.
acomodador, ra *m/f* usher, usherette.
acomodar *vt* to accommodate, to arrange; ~se *vr* to comply.
acomodaticio, cia *adj* accomodating; pliable.
acompañamiento *m* (*mus*) accompaniment.
acompañar *vt* to accompany; to join; (*mus*) to accompany.
acompasado, da *adj* measured; well-proportioned.
acondicionado, da *adj* conditioned.
acondicionar *vt* to arrange; to condition.
acongojar *vt* to distress.
aconsejable *adj* advisable.
aconsejar *vt* to advise; ~se *vr* to take advice.
acontecer *vi* to happen.
acontecimiento *m* event, incident.
acopio *m* gathering, storing.
acopiar *vt* to gather, to store up.
acoplamiento *m* coupling.
acoplar *vt* to couple; to fit; to connect.

acorazado, da *adj* armored; • *m* battleship.
acordado, da *adj* agreed.
acordar *vt* to agree; to remind; ~se *vr* to agree; to remember.
acorde *adj* harmonious; • *m* chord.
acordeón *m* accordion.
acordonado, da *adj* cordoned-off.
acordonar *vt* to tie up; to cordon off.
acorralar *vt* to round up; to intimidate.
acortar *vt* to abridge, to shorten; ~se *vr* to become shorter.
acosar *vt* to pursue closely; to pester.
acostado, da *adj* in bed; lying down.
acostar *vt* to put to bed; to lay down; ~se *vr* to go to bed; to lie down.
acostumbrado, da *adj* usual.
acostumbrar *vt* to accustom; • *vi* to be used to; ~se *vr* to get used to.
acotación *f* boundary mark; quotation in the margin; stage direction.
acotar *vt* to set bounds; to annotate.
ácrata *m/f* anarchist.
acre *adj* acid; sharp; • *m* acre.
acrecentamiento *m* increase.
acrecentar *vt* to increase, to augment.
acreditar *vt* to guarantee; to assure, to affirm; to authorize; to credit; ~se *vr* to become famous.
acreedor *m* creditor.
acribillar *vt* to riddle with bullets; to molest, to torment.
acriminar *vt* to accuse.
acrimonia *f* acrimony.
acrisolar *vt* to refine, to purify.
acritud *f* acrimony.
acróbata *m/f* acrobat.
acta *f* act; ~s *fpl* acts, records *pl*.
actidud *f* attitude, posture.
activar *vt* to activate; to speed up.
actividad *f* activity; liveliness.
activo, va *adj* active, diligent.
acto *m* act, action; act of a play; ceremony.
actor *m* actor; plaintiff.
actriz *f* actress.
actuación *f* action; behavior; proceedings *pl*.
actual *adj* actual, present.
actualidad *f* present; ~es *fpl* news.
actualizar *vt* to update.
actualmente *adv* at present.
actuar *vt* to work; to operate; • *vi* to work; to act.
acuarela *f* watercolor.
acuario *m* tank.
Acuario *m* Aquarius (sign of the zodiac).
acuartelamiento *m* quartering of troops.
acuartelar *vt* (*mil*) to quarter troops.
acuático, ca *adj* aquatic.
acuciar *vt* to urge on.
acuclillarse *vr* to crouch.
acuchillar *vt* to cut; to plane.
acudir *vi* to go to; to attend; to assist.
acueducto *m* aqueduct.
acuerdo *m* agreement; de ~ O.K.
acumular *vt* to accumulate, to collect.
acuñación *f* coining.
acuñar *vt* to coin, to mint; to wedge in.
acuoso, sa *adj* watery.
acurrucarse *vr* to squat; to huddle up to.
acusación *f* accusation.
acusador, ra *m/f* accuser; • *adj* accusing.
acusar *vt* to accuse; to reveal; to denounce; ~se *vr* to confess.
acusativo *m* (*gr*) accusative.
acuse *m*: ~ de recibo acknowledgment of receipt.
acústica *f* acoustics *pl*.
acústico, ca *adj* acoustic.
achacar *vt* to impute.
achacoso, sa *adj* sickly, unhealthy.

achantar *vt* (*fam*) to scare; ~se *vr* to back down.
achaparrado, da *adj* stunted; stocky.
achaque *m* ailment; excuse; subject, matter.
achicar *vt* to diminish; to humiliate; to bale a boat.
achicharrar *vt* to scorch; to overheat.
achicoria *f* (*bot*) chicory.
achisparse *vr* to get tipsy.
adagio *m* adage, proverb; (*mus*) adagio.
adalid *m* chief, commander.
adamascado, da *adj* damask.
adaptable *adj* adaptable.
adaptación *f* adaptation.
adaptador *m* adapter.
adaptar *vt* to adapt.
adecuado, da *adj* adequate, fit; appropriate.
adecuar *vt* to fit, to accommodate, to proportion.
adefesio *m* folly, nonsense.
adelantado, da *adj* advanced; fast.
adelantamiento *m* progress, improvement, advancement; passing.
adelantar *vt, vi* to advance, to accelerate; to pass; to ameliorate, to improve; ~se *vr* to advance; to outdo.
adelante *adv* forward(s); • *excl* come in!; de hoy en ~ from now on; más ~ later on; further on.
adelanto *m* advance; progress; improvement.
adelfa *f* (*bot*) rose-bay.
adelgazar *vt* to make thin *or* slender; to discuss with subtlety.
ademán *m* gesture; attitude.
además *adv* moreover, besides; ~ de besides.
adentrarse *vr* to get inside; to penetrate.
adentro *adv* in; inside.
adepto, ta *m/f* supporter.
aderezar *vt* to dress, to adorn; to prepare; to season.
aderezo *m* adorning; seasoning; arrangement.
adeudado *adj* in debt.
adeudar *vt* to owe; ~se *vr* to run into debt.
adherencia *f* adhesion, cohesion; alliance.
adherente *adj* adhering to, cohesive.
adherir *vi* to adhere to; to espouse.
adhesión *f* adhesion; cohesion.
adición *f* addition.
adicionar *vt* to add.
adicto, ta *adj* addicted, devoted to; • *m* supporter; addict.
adiestrar *vt* to guide; to teach, to instruct; ~se *vr* to practice.
adinerado, da *adj* wealthy, rich.
adiós *excl* goodbye; hello.
aditivo *m* additive.
adivinanza *f* enigma; riddle.
adivinar *vt* to foretell; to guess.
adivino, na *m/f* fortune-teller.
adjetivo *m* adjective.
adjudicación *f* adjudication.
adjudicar *vt* to adjudge; ~se *vr* to appropriate.
adjuntar *vt* to endorse.
adjunto, ta *adj* united, joined, annexed; • *m/f* assistant.
administración *f* administration.
administrador, a *m/f* administrator.
administrar *vt* to administer.
administrativo, va *adj* administrative.
admirable *adj* admirable, marvelous.
admiración *f* admiration; wonder; (*gr*) exclamation mark.
admirar *vt* to admire; to surprise; ~se *vr* to be surprised.
admisible *adj* admissible.
admisión *f* admission, acceptance.
admitir *vt* to admit; to let in; to concede; to permit.
admonición *f* warning.
adobado *m* pickled pork.
adobar *vt* to dress; to season.
adobe *m* adobe, sun-dried brick.
adobo *m* dressing; pickle sauce.
adoctrinar *vt* to indoctrinate; to teach.
adolecer *vi* to suffer from.

adolescencia f adolescence.
adolescente adj adolescent, young.
adonde conj (to) where.
adónde adv where.
adopción f adoption.
adoptar vt to adopt.
adoptivo, va adj adoptive; adopted.
adoquín m paving stone.
adoración f adoration, worship.
adorar vt to adore; to love.
adormecer vt to put to sleep; ~se vr to fall asleep.
adormidera f (bot) poppy.
adornar vt to embellish, to adorn.
adorno m adornment; ornament, decoration.
adosado, da adj semi-detached.
adquirir vt to acquire.
adquisición f acquisition.
adrede adv on purpose.
adscribir vt to appoint.
aduana f customs pl.
aduanero m customs officer; ~, ra adj customs.
aducir vt to adduce.
adueñarse vr to take possession of.
adulación f adulation.
adulador, ra m/f flatterer.
adular vt to flatter.
adulterar vt, vi to adulterate; to commit adultery.
adulterio m adultery.
adúltero, ra m/f adulterer, adulteress.
adulto, ta adj, m/f adult, grown-up.
adusto, ta adj gloomy; stern.
advenedizo m upstart.
advenimiento m arrival; accession.
adverbio m adverb.
adversario m adversary; antagonist.
adversidad f adversity; setback.
adverso, sa adj adverse.
advertencia f warning, foreword.
advertido, da adj sharp.
advertir vt to notice; to warn.
Adviento m Advent.
adyacente adj adjacent.
aéreo, rea adj aerial.
aerobic m aerobics.
aerodeslizador m hovercraft.
aerodeslizante m hovercraft.
aeromozo, za m/f air steward(ess).
aeronauta m aeronaut.
aeronáutica f aeronautics pl.
aeronave f spaceship.
aeroplano m airplane.
aeropuerto m airport.
aerosol m aerosol.
aerostática f aerostatics.
afabilidad f affability.
afable adj affable, complacent.
afán m hard work; desire.
afanar vt to harass; (col) to pinch; ~se vr to strive.
afanoso, sa adj hard, industrious.
afear vt to deform, to misshape.
afección f affection; fondness, attachment; disease.
afectación f affectation.
afectadamente adv affectedly; for appearance's sake.
afectado, da adj affected.
afectar vt to affect, to feign.
afectísimo, ma adj affectionate; ~ suyo yours truly.
afectivo, va adj fond, tender.
afecto m affection; passion; disease; ~, ta adj affectionate; disposed; reserved.
afectuoso, sa adj affectionate; moving; tender.
afeitar vt, ~se vr to shave.
afeite m make-up, rouge.

afeminado, da adj effeminate.
afeminar vt to effeminate.
aferrado, da adj stubborn.
aferrar vt to grapple, to grasp, to seize.
afianzamiento m strengthening.
afianzar vt to strengthen; to prop; ~se vr to become established.
afiche m poster.
afición f affection; liking; fans pl.
aficionado, da adj keen; ● m/f lover, devotee; amateur.
aficionar vt to inspire affection; ~se vr to grow fond of.
afiladera f grindstone.
afilado adj sharp.
afilar vt to sharpen, to grind.
afín m related; similar.
afinar vt to tune; to refine.
afincarse vr to settle.
afinidad f affinity; analogy; relationship.
afirmación f affirmation.
afirmado m road surface.
afirmar vt to secure, to fasten; to affirm, to assure.
afirmativo, va adj affirmative.
aflicción f affliction, grief.
aflictivo, va adj distressing.
afligir vt to afflict, to torment.
aflojar vt to loosen, to slacken, to relax; to relent; ● vi to grow weak; to abate; ~se vr to relax.
aflorar vi to emerge.
afluente adj flowing; ● m tributary.
afluir vi to flow.
afónico, ca adj hoarse; voiceless.
aforismo m aphorism.
afortunado, da adj fortunate, lucky.
afrancesado, da adj francophile; Frenchified.
afrenta f outrage; insult.
afrentar vt to affront; to insult.
afrontar vt to confront; to bring face to face.
afuera adv out, outside.
afueras fpl outskirts pl.
agacharse vr to stoop, to squat.
agalla f gill; ~s pl tonsils pl; tonsillitis.
agarradero m handle.
agarrado, da adj miserable, stingy.
agarrar vt to grasp, to seize; ~se vr to hold on tightly.
agarrotar vt to tie down; to squeeze tightly; to garrotte.
agasajar vt to receive and treat kindly; to regale.
agasajo m graceful reception; kindness.
ágata f agate.
agazaparse vr to crouch.
agencia f agency.
agenciarse vr to obtain.
agenda f diary.
agente m agent; policeman.
ágil adj agile.
agilidad f agility, nimbleness.
agitación f shaking; stirring; agitation.
agitanado, da adj gypsy-like.
agitar vt to wave, to move; ~se vr to get excited; to get worried.
aglomeración f crowd; jam.
aglomerar vt; ~se vr to crowd together.
agnóstico, ca adj, m/f agnostic.
agobiar vt to weigh down; to oppress; to burden.
agolparse vt to assemble in crowds.
agonía f agony.
agonizante adj dying.
agonizar vi to be dying.
agorar vt to predict.
agostar vt to parch.
agosto m August (month).
agotado, da adj exhausted; finished; sold out.
agotador, ra adj exhausting.

agotamiento *m* exhaustion.
agotar *vt* to exhaust; to drain; to misspend; to exhaust.
agraciado, da *adj* attractive; lucky.
agraciar *vt* to pardon; to reward.
agradable *adj* pleasant; lovely.
agradar *vt* to please, to gratify.
agradecer *vt* to be grateful for; to thank.
agradecido, da *adj* thankful.
agradecimiento *m* gratitude, gratefulness, thanks *pl.*
agrado *m* agreeableness, courteousness; will, pleasure; liking.
agrandar *vt* to enlarge; to exaggerate; to aggrandize; ~se *vr* to get bigger.
agrario, ria *adj* agrarian; agricultural.
agravante *f* further difficulty.
agravar *vt* to oppress; to aggrieve; to aggravate; to exaggerate; ~se *vr* to get worse.
agraviar *vt* to wrong; to offend; ~se *vr* to be aggrieved; to be piqued.
agravio *m* offense; grievance.
agredir *vt* to attack.
agregado *m* aggregate; attaché.
agregar *vt* to aggregate, to heap together; to collate; to appoint.
agresión *f* aggression, attack.
agresivo, va *adj* aggressive.
agresor *m* aggressor, assaulter.
agreste *adj* rustic; rural.
agriar *vt* to sour; to exasperate.
agrícola *adj* farming.
agricultor, ra *m/f* farmer.
agricultura *f* agriculture.
agridulce *adj* sweet and sour.
agrietarse *vr* to crack.
agrimensor *m* land-surveyor, surveyor.
agrimensura *f* land-surveying.
agrio *adj* sour, acrid; rough, craggy; sharp, rude, unpleasant.
agronomía *f* agriculture.
agropecuario, ria *adj* farming.
agrupación *f* group(ing).
agrupar *vt* to group; to cluster, to crowd.
agua *f* water; wake; slope of a roof; ~ fuerte etching; ~ bendita holy water; ~s *pl* waters *pl.*
aguacate *m* avocado pear.
aguacero *m* short heavy shower of rain.
aguachirle *f* slops *pl*
aguado, da *adj* watery.
aguador *m* water carrier.
aguafuerte *m* etching.
aguamarina *f* aqua marina (precious stone).
aguanieve *f* sleet.
aguantar *vt* to bear, to suffer; to hold up.
aguante *m* firmness; patience.
aguar *vt* to water down.
aguardar *vt* to wait for.
aguardiente *m* brandy.
aguarrás *f* turpentine.
agudeza *f* keenness, sharpness; acuteness; acidity, smartness.
agudizar *vt* to make worse; ~se *vr* to get worse.
agudo, da *adj* sharp; keen-edged; smart; fine; acute; witty; brisk.
agüero *m*; **buen/mal ~** good/bad omen.
aguijar *vt* to prick, to spur, to goad; to stimulate.
aguijón *m* sting of a bee, wasp *etc*; stimulation.
aguijonear *vt* to prick, to spur; to stimulate.
águila *f* eagle; genius.
aguileño, ña *adj* aquiline; sharp-featured.
aguilucho *m* eaglet.
aguinaldo *m* Christmas box.
aguja *f* needle; spire; hand; magnetic needle; (*ferro*) switch, siding.
agujerear *vt* to pierce, to bore.
agujero *m* hole.

agujetas *fpl* stitch; stiffness; pains from fatigue *pl.*
agustino *m* monk of the order of St Augustin.
aguzar *vt* to whet, to sharpen; to stimulate.
ahí *adv* there.
ahijada *f* goddaughter.
ahijado *m* godson.
ahijar *vt* to adopt as one's child.
ahínco *m* earnestness, eagerness.
ahogar *vt* to smother; to drown, to suffocate; to oppress; to quench; ~se *vr* to drown; to suffocate.
ahogo *m* breathlessness; financial difficulty.
ahondar *vt* to deepen; to study deeply; ● *vi* to penetrate into.
ahora *adv* now, at present; just now.
ahorcar *vt* to hang; ~se *vr* to hang oneself.
ahorrar *vt* to save; to avoid.
ahorrativo, va *adj* thrifty, saving; stingy.
ahorro *m* saving; thrift.
ahuecar *vt* to hollow, to scoop out; ~se *vr* to get pig headed.
ahumar *vt* to smoke, to cure in smoke; ~se *vr* to fill with smoke.
ahuyentar *vt* to drive off; to dispel.
airado, da *adj* angry.
airarse *vr* to get angry.
aire *m* air; wind; aspect; musical composition.
airearse *vt* to take the air.
airoso, sa *adj* airy; windy; graceful; successful.
aislado, da *adj* insulated; isolated.
aislar *vt* to insulate; to isolate.
ajar *vt* to spoil; to abuse.
ajardinado, da *adj* landscaped.
ajedrez *m* chess.
ajedrezado, da *adj* checkered.
ajenjo *m* wormwood, absinth.
ajeno, na *adj* someone else's; foreign; contrary to; ignorant; improper.
ajetrearse *vt* to exert oneself; to bustle; to toil; to fidget.
ajetreo *m* activity; bustling.
ají *m* red pepper.
ajo *m* garlic.
ajorca *f* bracelet.
ajuar *m* household furniture; trousseau.
ajustado, da *adj* tight; right; close.
ajustar *vt* to regulate, to adjust; to settle a balance; to fit; to agree on; ● *vi* to fit.
ajuste *m* agreement; accommodation; settlement; fitting.
ajusticiar *vt* to execute.
al = a el.
ala *f* wing; aisle; row, file; brim; winger.
alabanza *f* praise, applause.
alabar *vt* to praise, to applaud.
alabastro *m* alabaster; gypsum.
alacena *f* cupboard, closet.
alacrán *m* scorpion.
alado, da *adj* winged.
alambique *m* still.
alambrada *f* wire fence; wire netting.
alambrado *m* wire fence, wire netting.
alambrista *m/f* tightrope walker.
alambre *m* wire.
alameda *f* avenue; poplar grove.
álamo *m* poplar.
alano *m* mastiff.
alarde *m* show.
alargador *m* extension lead.
alargar *vt* to lengthen; to extend; to hasten; to stretch out; to spin out; ~se *vr* to get longer.
alarido *m* outcry, shout; dar ~s to howl.
alarma *f* alarm.
alarmante *adj* alarming.
alarmar *vt* to alarm.
alarmista *m* alarmist.
alazán *m* sorrel.

alba f dawn.
albacea m executor.
albahaca f (bot) sweet basil.
albañil m mason, bricklayer.
albañilería f masonry.
albarán m invoice.
albarda f saddle.
albaricoque m apricot.
albedrío m free will.
alberca f reservoir; swimming pool.
albergar vt to lodge, to harbor; ~se to shelter.
albergue m shelter; ~ de juventud youth hostel.
albóndiga f meatball.
albor m dawn; whiteness.
alborada f dawn; reveille.
alborear vi to dawn.
albornoz m burnoose; bathrobe.
alborotado, da adj restless, turbulent.
alborotar vt to stir up; ● vi to make a row; ~se to get excited; to get rough.
alboroto m noise, disturbance, riot.
alborozar vt to exhilarate; ~se vr to rejoice.
alborozo m joy.
albricias fpl good news pl.
albufera f lagoon.
álbum m album.
albumen m egg white.
alcachofa f artichoke.
alcahuete, ta m/f pimp, bawd.
alcalde m mayor.
alcaldesa f mayoress.
alcaldía f office and jurisdiction of an alcalde; mayor's office.
alcalino, na adj alkaline.
alcance m reach; bad balance.
alcancía f money box.
alcanfor m camphor.
alcantarilla m sewer; gutter.
alcanzar vt to reach; to get, to obtain; to hit; ● vi to suffice; to reach.
alcaparra f caper.
alcatraz m gannet.
alcayata f hook.
alcázar m castle, fortress.
alcoba f bedroom.
alcohol m alcohol.
alcohólico, ca adj alcoholic.
alcoholismo m alcoholism.
alcornoque m cork tree.
aldaba f knocker.
aldea f village.
aldeana f villager.
aldeano m villager; ● adj rustic.
ale excl come on!
aleación f art of alloying metals.
aleatorio, ria adj random.
aleccionar vt to instruct; to train.
alegación f allegation.
alegar vt to allege, to quote.
alegato m allegation; argument.
alegoría f allegory.
alegórico, ca adj allegorical.
alegrar vt to cheer; to poke; to liven up; ~se vr to get merry.
alegre adj happy; merry, joyful, content.
alegría f happiness; merriment.
alegrón m sudden joy; sudden flicker.
alejamiento m remoteness; removal.
alejar vt to remove; to estrange; ~se vr to go away.
aleluya f hallelujah.
alemán m German.
alentador, ra adj encouraging.
alentar vt to encourage.
alergia f allergy.

alero m gable-end; eaves.
alerta adj, f alert.
alertar vt to alert.
aleta f fin; wing; flipper; fender.
aletargarse vr to get drowsy.
aletazo m flap.
aletear vi to flutter.
aleteo m fluttering.
alevosía f treachery.
alevoso, sa adj treacherous.
alfabéticamente adv alphabetically.
alfabético, ca adj alphabetical.
alfabeto m alphabet.
alfalfa f (bot) lucerne.
alfarería f pottery.
alfarero m potter.
alféizar m window sill.
alférez m second lieutenant; ensign.
alfil m bishop (at chess).
alfiler m pin; clip; clothes pin.
alfiletero m pincushion.
alfombra f carpet; rug.
alfombrar vt to carpet.
alfombrilla f small carpet.
alforja f saddlebag, knapsack.
alga f (bot) seaweed.
algarabía f gabble, gibberish.
algarroba f (bot) carob.
algarrobo m (bot) carob tree.
algazara f din.
álgebra f algebra.
álgido, da adj chilly; crucial.
algo pn something; anything; ● adv somewhat.
algodón m cotton; cotton plant; cotton wool.
algodonero m cotton plant; dealer in cotton.
alguacil m bailiff; mounted official.
alguien pn someone; somebody; anyone, anybody.
alguno, na adj some; no, any; ● pn someone; somebody.
alhaja f jewel.
alhelí m wallflower.
aliado, da adj allied.
alianza f alliance, league; wedding ring.
aliar vt to ally; ~se vr to form an alliance.
alias adv alias.
alicaído, da adj weak; downcast.
alicates m, pl pincers, nippers pl.
aliciente m attraction, incitement.
alienación f alienation.
aliento m breath, respiration.
aligerar vt to lighten; to alleviate; to hasten; to ease.
alijo m lightening of a ship; alleviation, cache.
alimaña f pest.
alimentación f nourishment; food; grocery.
alimentar vt to feed, to nourish; ~se vr to feed.
alimenticio, cia adj food compd; nutritious.
alimento m food; ~s pl alimony.
alineación m alignment; line-up.
alinear vt to arrange in line; ~se vr to line up.
aliñar vt to adorn; to season.
aliño m dressing, ornament, decoration.
alisar vt to plane, to polish; to smoothe.
alistarse vr to enlist, to enrol.
aliviar vt to lighten; to ease, to relieve, to mollify.
alivio m alleviation, mitigation; relief; comfort.
aljibe m cistern.
alma f soul; human being.
almacén m warehouse, store; magazine.
almacenaje m storage.
almacenar vt to store, to stock up.
almanaque m almanac.
almeja f clam.
almena f battlement.

almendra f almond.
almendrado, da adj almond-like; ~ m macaroon.
almendro m almond tree.
almiar m haystack.
almíbar m syrup.
almidón f starch.
almidonado, da adj starched; affected; spruce.
almidonar vt to starch.
almirantazgo m admiralty.
almirante m admiral.
almirez m mortar.
almizcle m musk.
almohada f pillow, cushion.
almohadilla f small pillow; pad; pincushion.
almohadón m large cushion.
almorranas fpl hemorrhoids pl.
almorzar vt to have for lunch.
almuerzo m lunch.
alocado, da adj crazy; foolish, inconsiderate.
alocución f allocution.
áloe m (bot) aloes pl.
alojamiento m lodging; housing.
alojar vt to lodge; ~se vr to stay.
alondra f lark.
alpargata f rope-soled shoe.
alpinismo m mountaineering.
alpinista m/f mountaineer.
alpiste m canary seed.
alquería f farmhouse.
alquilar vt to let, to hire; to rent.
alquiler m renting; letting; hiring; rent; hire.
alquimia f alchemy.
alquimista m alchemist.
alquitrán m tar, liquid pitch.
alquitranado, da adj tarred.
alrededor adv around.
alrededores mpl surroundings pl.
alta f (mil) discharge from hospital.
altanería f haughtiness.
altanero, ra adj haughty, arrogant, vain, proud.
altar m altar; ~ mayor high altar.
altavoz m loudspeaker, amplifier.
alterable adj changeable.
alteración f alteration; disturbance, tumult.
alterar vt to alter, to change; to disturb; ~se vr to get upset.
altercado m altercation, controversy; quarrel.
alternar vt, vi to alternate.
alternativa f alternative.
alternativo, va adj alternate.
alterno, na adj alternate; alternating.
Alteza f Highness (title).
altibajos mpl ups and downs pl.
altillo m hillock.
altiplanicie f high plateau.
altísimo, ma adj extremely high, highmost; ● m the Most High, God.
altisonante, altísono, na adj high-sounding, pompous.
altitud f height; altitude.
altivez f haughtiness.
altivo, va adj haughty, proud, high-flown.
alto, ta adj high, elevated; tall; sharp; arduous, difficult; eminent; enormous; ● m height; story; highland; (mil) halt; (mus) alto; ¡~¡, !~ ahí! interj stop!
altramuz m (bot) lupin.
altura f height; depth; mountain summit; altitude; ~s pl the heavens.
alubia f kidney bean.
alucinación f hallucination.
alucinar vt to blind, to deceive; ● vi to hallucinate; ~se vr to deceive oneself, to labor under a delusion.
aludir vi to allude.
alumbrado m lighting; illumination.

alumbramiento m lighting; illumination; childbirth.
alumbrar vt to light; ● vi to give birth.
aluminio m aluminum.
alumno, na m/f student, pupil.
alunizar vi to land on the moon.
alusión f allusion, hint.
alusivo, va adj allusive.
aluvión f alluvium; flood.
alvéolo m socket; cell of a honeycomb.
alza f rise; sight.
alzacuello m dog collar.
alzada f height; appeal.
alzamiento m rise; elevation; higher bid; uprising.
alzar vt to raise, to lift up; to construct, to build; to gather (in); ~se vr to get up; to rise in rebellion; ~se con algo vr to encroach.
allá adv there; over there; then.
allanamiento m: ~ de morada burglary.
allanar vt to level, to flatten; to overcome difficulties; to pacify; to subdue; to burglarize; ~se vr to submit; to tumble down.
allegado, da adj near; ● m/f follower.
allí adv there, in that place.
ama f mistress, housewife; owner; foster mother; ~ de llaves housekeeper; ~ de leche nurse.
amabilidad f kindness; niceness.
amable adj kind, nice.
amaestrado, da adj performing.
amaestrar vt to teach, to instruct; to train.
amagar vt to threaten; to shake one's fist; to feint.
amago m threat; indication; symptom.
amalgama f amalgam.
amalgamar vt to amalgamate.
amamantar vt to suckle.
amanecer vi to dawn; al ~ at daybreak.
amanerado, da adj affected.
amansar vt to take; to soften; to subdue; ~se vr to calm down.
amante m/f lover.
amanuense m amanuensis, clerk, copyist.
amapola f (bot) poppy.
amar vt to love; to fancy.
amargar vt to make bitter; to exasperate; ~se vr to be bitter.
amargo, ga adj bitter, acrid; painful; ● m bitterness.
amargor m bitterness; sorrow, distress.
amargura f bitterness; sorrow.
amarillear vi to turn yellow.
amarillento, ta adj yellowish.
amarillo, lla adj, m yellow.
amarra f cable.
amarrar vt to moor; to tie, to fasten.
amartelar vt to court, to make love; ~se vr to fall in love with.
amartillar vt to hammer; to cock a gun or pistol.
amasar vt to knead; (fig) to arrange, to prepare, to settle.
amasijo m dough; mixed mortar; medley.
amatista f amethyst.
amatorio, ria adj relating to love.
amazona f amazon; masculine woman.
ambages mpl: sin ~ in plain language.
ámbar m amber.
ambición f ambition.
ambicionar vt to crave, to covet.
ambicioso, sa adj ambitious.
ambidextro, tra adj ambidextrous.
ambientación f setting; sound effects.
ambiente m atmosphere; environment.
ambigüedad f ambiguity.
ambiguo, gua adj ambiguous, doubtful, equivocal.
ámbito m circuit, circumference; field; scope.
ambos, bas pn both.
ambrosía f ambrosia.
ambulancia f ambulance.

ambulante *adj* traveling.
ambulatorio *m* state clinic.
ameba *f* ameba.
amedrentar *vt* to frighten, to terrify, to intimidate.
amén *f* amen, so be it; ~ de besides; except.
amenaza *f* threat.
amenazar *vt* to threaten.
amenizar *m* to make pleasant.
ameno, na *adj* pleasant, delicious; flowery (of language).
América *f* America; ~ del Norte/del Sur North/South America.
americano, na *adj*, *m/f* American.
ametralladora *m* machine gun.
amianto *m* asbestos.
amiga *f* female friend.
amigable *adj* amicable, friendly; suitable.
amigo *m* friend; comrade; lover; ~, ga *adj* friendly.
amilanar *vt* to frighten, to terrify; ~se *vr* to get scared.
aminorar *vt* to diminish; to reduce.
amistad *f* friendship.
amistoso, sa *adj* friendly, cordial.
amnesia *f* amnesia.
amnistía *f* amnesty.
amo *m* owner; boss.
amodorrarse *vr* to grow sleepy.
amohinar *vt* to annoy; ~se *vr* to sulk.
amoldar *vt* to mold; to adapt; ~se *vr* to adapt oneself.
amonestación *f* advice, admonition; ~ ones *fpl* publication of marriage banns.
amonestar *vt* to advise, to admonish; to publish banns of marriage.
amoníaco *m* ammoniac.
amor *m* love; fancy; lover; ~ mío my love; por ~ de Dios for God's sake; ~ propio self-love.
amoratado *adj* livid.
amordazar *vt* to muzzle; to gag.
amorfo, fa *adj* shapeless.
amorío *m* love affair.
amoroso, sa *adj* affectionate, loving; lovely.
amortajar *vt* to shroud.
amortiguador *m* shock absorber.
amortiguadores *mpl* suspension.
amortiguar *vt* to mortify, to deaden; to temper; to muffle.
amortización *f* repayment; redemption.
amortizar *vt* to entail an estate, to render inalienable; to pay, to liquidate, to discharge a debt.
amotinamiento *m* mutiny.
amotinar *vt* to excite rebellion; ~se *vr* to mutiny.
amparar *vt* to shelter, to favor, to protect; ~se *vr* to claim protection.
amparo *m* protection, help, support; refuge, asylum.
amperio *m* amp.
ampliación *f* amplification, enlargement.
ampliar *vt* to amplify, to enlarge, to extend, to expand.
amplificación *f* enlargement.
amplificador *m* amplifier.
amplificar *vt* to amplify.
amplio, lia *adj* ample, extensive.
amplitud *f* amplitude, extension, largeness.
ampolla *f* blister; phial, cruet.
ampuloso, sa *adj* pompous.
amputación *f* amputation.
amputar *vt* to amputate.
amueblar *vt* to furnish.
amuleto *m* amulet.
amurallar *vt* to surround with walls.
anacoreta *m* anchorite, hermit.
anacronismo *m* anachronism.
ánade *m/f* duck.
anadear *vi* to waddle.
anagrama *f* anagram.
anales *mpl* annals *f*.

analfabetismo *m* illiteracy.
analfabeto, ta *adj* illiterate.
analgésico *m* painkiller.
análisis *m* analysis.
analista *m/f* analyst.
analítico, ca *adj* analytical.
analizar *vt* to analyze.
analogía *f* analogy.
analógico, ca, análogo, ga *adj* analogous.
ananá *m* pineapple.
anaquel *m* shelf in a bookcase.
anaranjado, da *adj* orange-colored.
anarquía *f* anarchy.
anárquico, ca *adj* anarchical, confused.
anarquismo *m* anarchism.
anarquista *m/f* anarchist.
anatema *f* anathema.
anatomía *f* anatomy.
anatómico, ca *adj* anatomical.
anca *f* rump.
anciano, na *adj* old; ● *m/f* old man/woman.
ancla *f* anchor.
ancladero *m* anchorage.
anclaje *m* anchorage.
anclar *vi* to anchor.
ancho, cha *adj* broad, wide, large; ● *m* breadth, width.
anchoa *f* anchovy.
anchura *f* width, breadth.
andaderas *fpl* baby walker.
andadura *f* walk; pace; amble.
andamio *m* scaffold.
andamiaje *m* scaffolding.
andanada *f* (*mar*) broadside.
andar *vi* to go, to walk; to fare; to act, to proceed, to work, to behave; to elapse; to move; ● *vt* to go, to travel; ● *m* walk, pace.
andariego, ga *adj* wandering.
andarín *m* fast walker.
andas *fpl* stretcher.
andén *m* sidewalk; (*ferro*) platform; quayside.
andrajo *m* rag.
andrajoso, sa *adj* ragged.
andurriales *mpl* byways *pl*.
anécdota *f* anecdote.
anegar *vt* to inundate, to submerge; ~se *vr* to drown; to sink.
anejo, ja *adj* attached.
anemia *f* anemia.
anestésico *m* anesthetic.
anexar *vt* to annex, to join.
anexión *f* annexation.
anexionamiento *m* annexation.
anexo, xa *adj* annexed.
anfibio, bia *adj* amphibious.
anfiteatro *m* amphitheater.
anfitrión, ona *m/f* host(ess).
ángel *m* angel.
angelical *adj* angelical, heaven-born.
angélico, ca *adj* angelical.
angina *f* quinsy.
anglicano, na *m/f* Anglican.
anglicismo *m* anglicism.
angosto, ta *adj* narrow, close.
anguila *f* eel.
angula *f* elver.
angular *adj* angular; piedra ~ *f* cornerstone.
ángulo *m* angle, corner.
anguloso, sa *adj* angled, cornered.
angustia *f* anguish; heartache.
angustiar *vt* to cause anguish.
anhelante *adj* eager; longing.
anhelar *vi* to gasp; ● *vt* to long for.
anhelo *m* desire, longing.

anidar *vi* to nestle, to make a nest; to dwell, to inhabit.
anillo *m* ring.
ánima *f* soul.
animación *f* liveliness; activity.
animado, da *adj* lively.
animador, ra *m/f* host(ess).
animadversión *f* ill-will.
animal *adj, m* animal.
animar *vt* to animate, to liven, to comfort, to revive; ~se *vr* to cheer up.
ánimo *m* soul; courage; mind, intention, meaning, will; thought; ¡~! *excl* come on!
animosidad *f* valor, courage; boldness.
animoso, sa *adj* courageous, spirited.
aniñarse *vr* to act in a childish manner.
aniquilar *vt* to annihilate, to destroy; ~se *vr* to decline, to decay.
anís *m* aniseed; anisette.
aniversario, ria *adj* annual; ● *m* anniversary.
ano *m* anus.
anoche *adv* last night.
anochecer *vi* to grow dark; ● *m* nightfall.
anodino, na *adj* (*med*) anodyne.
anomalía *f* anomaly.
anómalo, la *adj* anomalous.
anonadar *vt* to annihilate; to lessen; ~se *vr* to humble one self.
anonimato *m* anonymity.
anónimo, ma *adj* anonymous.
anormal *adj* abnormal.
anotación *f* annotation, note.
anotar *vt* to comment, to note.
anquilosamiento *m* paralysis.
ansar *m* goose.
ansia *f* anxiety, eagerness, hankering.
ansiar *vt* to desire.
ansiedad *f* anxiety.
ansioso, sa *adj* anxious, eager.
antagónico, ca *adj* antagonistic; opposed.
antagonista *m* antagonist.
antaño *adv* formerly.
antártico, ca *adj* antarctic.
ante *m* suede; ● *prep* before; in the presence of; faced with.
anteanoche *adv* the night before last.
anteayer *adv* the day before yesterday.
antebrazo *m* forearm.
antecámara *f* antechamber.
antecedente *adj, m* antecedent.
anteceder *vt* to precede.
antecesor, ra *m/f* predecessor; forefather.
antedicho, cha *adj* aforesaid.
antelación *f*; con ~ in advance.
antemano *adv*; de ~ beforehand.
antena *f* feeler, antenna; aerial.
anteojo *m* eyeglass; ~ de larga vista telescope; ~s *pl* glasses.
antepasado, da *adj* passed, elapsed; ~s *mpl* ancestors.
antepecho *m* (*mil*) parapet; ledge.
anteponer *vt* to place in front; to prefer.
anteproyecto *m* sketch; blueprint.
anterior *adj* preceding; former.
anterioridad *f* priority; preference.
antes *prep* before; ● *adv* before; ● *conj* before.
antesala *f* antechamber.
antiaéreo, rea *adj* anti-aircraft.
antibalas *adj* bullet-proof.
antibiótico *m* antibiotic.
anticiclón *m* anticyclone.
anticipación *f* anticipation.
anticipado, da *adj* advance.
anticipar *vt* to anticipate; to forestall; to advance.
anticipo *m* advance.
anticonceptivo *m* contraceptive.

anticongelante *m* antifreeze.
anticuado, da *adj* antiquated.
anticuario *m* antiquary, antiquarian.
anticuerpo *m* antibody.
antídoto *m* antidote.
antífona *f* antiphony, anthem.
antiestético, ca *adj* unsightly.
antifaz *m* mask.
antigualla *f* monument of antiquity; antique.
antiguamente *adv* anciently, of old.
antigüedad *f* antiquity, oldness; the ancients.
antiguo, gua *adj* antique, old, ancient; ● *m* senior.
antílope *m* antelope.
antinatural *adj* unnatural.
antimonio *m* antimony.
antipatía *f* antipathy.
antipático, ca *adj* unpleasant.
antípodas *mpl* antipodes.
antirrobo *adj* anti-theft.
antisemita *adj* anti-Semitic.
antiséptico, ca *adj* antiseptic.
antítesis *f* (*gr*) antithesis.
antojadizo, za *adj* capricious, fanciful.
antojarse *vr* to long, to desire; to itch.
antojo *m* whim; longing, fancy.
antología *f* anthology.
antorcha *f* torch, taper.
antro *m* (*poet*) cavern, den, grotto.
antropófago *m* man-eater, cannibal.
antropología *f* anthropology.
anual *adj* annual.
anualidad *f* annuity.
anublar *vt* to cloud, to obscure; ~se *vr* to become clouded.
anudar *vt* to knot, to join; ~se *vr* to get into knots.
anulación *f* annulment; cancellation.
anular *vt* to annul; to revoke; to cancel; ● *adj* annular.
anunciación *f* announcement.
anunciante *m/f* advertiser.
anunciar *vt* to announce; to advertise.
anuncio *m* advertisement.
anverso *m* obverse.
anzuelo *m* hook; allurement.
añadidura *f* addition.
añadir *vt* to add.
añejo, ja *adj* old, stale, musty.
añicos *mpl* bits, small pieces; hacer ~ to shatter.
añil *m* indigo plant; indigo.
año *m* year.
añojo *m* a yearling calf.
añoranza *f* longing.
aorta *f* aorta.
aovar *vi* to lay eggs.
apabullar *vt* to squash.
apacentar *vt* to graze.
apacible *adj* affable, gentle, placid, quiet.
apaciguar *vt* to appease, to pacify, to calm.
apadrinar *vt* to support, to favor; to be godfather to.
apagado, da *adj* dull; quiet; muted; listless.
apagar *vt* to put out; to turn off; to quench, to extinguish; to damp; to destroy; to soften.
apagón *m* outage, power cut.
apalabrar *vt* to agree to; to engage.
apalancar *vt* to lever.
apalear *vt* to cane, to drub; to winnow.
apañado, da *adj* skillful; suitable.
apañar *vt* to grasp; to pick up; to patch; ~se *vr* to manage.
aparador *m* sideboard; store window.
aparato *m* apparatus; machine; ostentation, show.
aparatoso, sa *adj* showy.
aparcamiento *m* parking lot.
aparcar *vt, vi* to park.
aparcería *f* partnership in a farm (*or* other business).

aparcero, ra *m/f* partner; associate.
aparecer *vi* to appear; ~**se** *vr* to appear.
aparecido, da *m/f* ghost.
aparejar *vt* to prepare; to harness horses; to rig a ship.
aparejo *m* preparation; harness, gear; (*mar*) tackle, rigging; ~**s** *pl* tools, implements.
aparentar *vt* to look; to pretend, to deceive.
aparente *adj* apparent; convenient.
aparición *f* apparition; appearance.
apariencia *f* outward appearance.
apartadero *m* (*ferro*) siding.
apartado *m* paragraph.
apartamento *m* apartment.
apartamiento *m* isolation; separation; apartment.
apartar *vt* to separate, to divide; to remove; to sort; ~**se** *vr* to go away; to be divorced; to desist.
aparte *m* aside; new paragraph; ● *adv* apart, separately; besides; aside.
apasionado, da *adj* passionate; devoted to; fond; biased.
apasionar *vt* to excite; ~**se** *vr* to get excited.
apatía *f* apathy.
apático, ca *adj* apathetic, indifferent.
apeadero *m* stopping place; station.
apearse *vr* to dismount; to get down/out/off.
apechugar *vt* to face up to.
apedrear *vt* to stone; ● *vi* to hail.
apegarse *vr*: ~ **a** to become fond of.
apego *m* attachment, fondness.
apelación *f* (*jur*) appeal.
apelar *vi* (*jur*) to appeal; to have recourse to.
apelativo *adj* (*gr*): **nombre** ~ *m* generic name.
apelmazar *vt* to compress.
apellidar *vt* to call by name; to proclaim; ~**se** *vr* to be called.
apellido *m* surname; family name; epithet.
apenar *vt* to grieve; to embarrass; ~**se** *vr* to grieve; to be embarrassed.
apenas *adv* scarcely, hardly; ● *conj* as soon as.
apéndice *m* appendix, supplement.
apendicitis *f* appendicitis.
apercibido, da *adj* provided; ready.
apercibirse *vr* to notice.
aperitivo *m* aperitif; appetizer.
apero *m* agricultural implement.
apertura *f* aperture, opening, chink, cleft.
apesadumbrar *vt* to sadden.
apestar *vt* to infect; ● *vi* to stink of.
apetecer *vt* to fancy.
apetecible *adj* desirable; appetizing.
apetito *m* appetite.
apetitoso, sa *adj* pleasing to the taste, appetizing; tempting.
apiadarse *vr* to take pity.
ápice *m* summit, point; smallest part of a thing.
apilar *vt* to pile up; ~**se** *vr* to pile up.
apiñado, da *adj* crowded; pyramidal; pine-shaped.
apiñarse *vr* to clog, to crowd.
apio *m* (*bot*) celery.
apisonadora *f* steamroller.
apisonar *vt* to ram down.
aplacar *vt* to appease, to pacify; ~**se** *vr* to calm down.
aplanar *vt* to level, to flatten.
aplastar *vt* to flatten, to crush.
aplatanarse *vr* to get weary.
aplaudir *vt* to applaud; to extol.
aplauso *m* applause, approbation, praise.
aplazamiento *m* postponement.
aplazar *vt* to postpone.
aplicable *adj* applicable.
aplicación *f* application; effort.
aplicado, da *adj* studious, industrious.
aplicar *vt* to apply; to clasp; to attribute; ~**se** *vr* to devote oneself to.
aplique *m* wall light.

aplomo *m* self-assurance.
apocado, da *adj* timid.
Apocalipsis *m* Apocalypse.
apocamiento *m* timidity; depression.
apocar *vt* to lessen, to diminish; to contract; ~**se** *vr* to feel humiliated.
apócrifo, fa *adj* apocryphal; fabulous.
apodar *vt* to nickname.
apoderado, da *adj* powerful; ● *m* proxy, attorney; agent.
apoderar *vt* to authorize; to give the power of attorney to; ~**se** *vr* to take possession of.
apodo *m* nickname, sobriquet.
apogeo *m* peak.
apolillar *vt* to gnaw *or* eat clothes; ~**se** *vr* to be moth-eaten.
apología *f* eulogy; defense.
apoltronarse *vr* to grow lazy, to loiter.
apoplejía *f* apoplexy.
apoplético, ca *adj* apoplectic.
apoquinar *vt* (*fam*) to fork out.
aporrear *vt* to beat up.
aportar *vi* to arrive at a port; to arrive; ● *vt* to contribute.
aposentar *vt* to harbor; to put up.
aposento *m* room, apartment.
aposición *f* (*gr*) apposition.
apósito *m* external medicinal application.
aposta *adv* on purpose.
apostar *vt* to bet, to lay a wager; to post soldiers; ● *vi* to bet.
apostasía *f* apostasy.
apóstata *m* apostate.
apostatar *vi* to apostatize.
apostilla *f* marginal note; postscript.
apóstol *m* apostle.
apostolado *m* apostleship.
apostólico, ca *adj* apostolical.
apostrofar *vt* to apostrophize.
apóstrofe *m* apostrophe.
apóstrofo *m* (*gr*) apostrophe.
apostura *f* neatness.
apoteosis *f* apotheosis.
apoyar *vt* to rest; to favor, to patronize; to support; ~**se** *vr* to lean on.
apoyo *m* prop, stay, support; protection.
apreciable *adj* appreciable, valuable, respectable.
apreciar *vt* to appreciate, to estimate, to value.
aprecio *m* appreciation; esteem.
aprehender *vt* to apprehend, to seize.
aprehensión *f* apprehension, seizure.
apremiante *adj* urgent.
apremiar *vt* to press; to compel.
apremio *m* pressure, constriction; judicial compulsion.
aprender *vt* to learn; ~ **de memoria** to learn by heart.
aprendiz, za *m/f* apprentice.
aprendizaje *m* apprenticeship.
aprensión *f* apprehension.
aprensivo, va *adj* apprehensive.
apresar *vt* to seize, to grasp.
apresurado, da *adj* hasty.
apresuramiento *m* hurry.
apresurar *vt* to accelerate, to hasten, to expedite; ~**se** *vr* to hurry.
apretado, da *adj* tight; cramped; hard, difficult.
apretar *vt* to compress, to tighten; to constrain; to distress; to urge earnestly; ● *vi* to be too tight.
apretón *m* squeeze.
apretura *f* squeeze.
aprieto *m* crowd; conflict; tight spot.
aprisa *adv* quickly, swiftly, promptly.
aprisco *m* sheepfold.
aprisionar *vt* to imprison.
aprobación *f* approbation, approval.
aprobar *vt* to approve; to pass; ● *vi* to pass.
apropiación *f* appropriation, assumption.

apropiado, da *adj* appropriate.
apropiarse *vr* to appropriate.
aprovechable *adj* profitable.
aprovechado, da *adj* industrious; thrifty; selfish.
aprovechamiento *m* use; exploitation.
aprovechar *vt* to use; to exploit; to profit from; to take advantage of; ● *vi* to be useful; to progress; ~se *vr* to use; to take advantage of.
aproximación *f* approximation; closeness.
aproximado, da *adj* approximate.
aproximar *vt* to approach; ~se *vr* to approach.
aptitud *f* aptitude, fitness, ability.
apto, ta *adj* apt, fit, able; clever.
apuesta *f* bet, wager.
apuesto, ta *adj* neat.
apuntado, da *adj* pointed.
apuntador *m* prompter.
apuntalar *vt* to prop.
apuntar *vt* to aim; to level, to point at; to mark, to begin to appear *or* show itself; to prompt (theater); ~se *vr* to score; to enroll.
apunte *m* annotation; stage-prompting.
apuñalar *vt* to stab.
apurado, da *adj* poor, destitute of means, exhausted; hurried.
apurar *vt* to purify, to clear up, to verify; to exhaust; to tease and perplex; ~se *vr* to worry; to hurry.
apuro *m* want; pain, affliction; haste; jam.
aquejado, da *adj* afflicted.
aquel ~ la, ~ lo *adj* that; ~ **los, ~ las** *pl* those.
aquél, ~ la; ~ los, ~ las *pn* that (one); (*pl*) those (ones).
aquello *pn* that.
aquí *adv* here; now.
aquietar *vt* to quiet, to appease.
aquilino *adj* aquiline.
aquilón *m* north wind.
ara *f* altar.
árabe *adj*, *m/f*, *m* (*ling*) Arabic.
arabesco *m* arabesque.
arado *m* plow.
arancel *m* tariff.
arándano *m* bilberry, cranberry.
arandela *f* washer.
araña *f* spider; chandelier.
arañar *vt* to scratch; to scrape; to corrode.
arar *vt* to plow.
arbitraje *m* arbitration.
arbitrar *vt, vi* to arbitrate; to referee.
arbitrariedad *f* arbitrariness.
arbitrario, ria *adj* arbitrary.
arbitrativo, va *adj* arbitrary.
arbitrio *m* free will; arbitration.
árbitro *m* arbitrator; referee; umpire.
árbol *m* tree; (*mar*) mast; shaft.
arbolado, da *adj* forested; wooded; ● *m* woodland.
arboladura *f* masting, masts.
arbolar *vt* to hoist, to set upright.
arboleda *f* grove.
arbusto *m* shrub.
arca *f* chest, wooden box.
arcada *f* arch; arcade; ~s *pl* retching.
arcaico, ca *adj* archaic.
arcaísmo *m* archaism.
arcángel *m* archangel.
arce *m* maple tree.
arcilla *f* clay.
arcilloso, sa *adj* clayey.
arcipreste *m* archpriest.
arco *m* arc, arch; fiddle-bow; hoop; ~ **iris** rainbow.
archipiélago *m* archipelago.
archivador *m* filing cabinet.
archivar *vt* to file.
archivero, archivista *m* keeper of records, archivist.

archivo *m* file(s); archives.
arder *vi* to burn, to blaze.
ardid *m* stratagem, artifice, cunning.
ardiente *adj* ardent, burning, passionate; active, fiery.
ardilla *f* squirrel.
ardor *m* heat; valor, vivacity, fieriness, fervor.
ardoroso, sa *adj* fiery, restless.
arduo, dua *adj* arduous, difficult; high.
área *f* area.
arena *f* sand; grit; arena.
arenal *m* sandy ground.
arenga *f* harangue, speech.
arengar *vi* to harangue.
arenisca *f* sandstone; grit.
arenoso, sa *adj* sandy; arenaceous.
arenque *m* herring; ~ **ahumado** red herring.
argamasa *f* mortar, cement for building.
argamasar *vt* to mix mortar.
argolla *f* large ring.
argot *m* slang.
argucia *f* subtlety.
argüir *vi* to argue, to dispute, to oppose; ● *vt* to deduce; to argue; to imply.
argumentación *f* argumentation.
argumentar *vt, vi* to argue, to dispute; to conclude.
argumento *m* argument.
aria *f* (*mus*) aria, tune, air.
aridez *f* drought, want of rain.
árido, da *adj* dry; barren.
Aries *m* Aries, the Ram (sign of the zodiac).
ariete *m* battering ram.
ario, a *adj* Aryan.
arisco, ca *adj* fierce, rude, intractable.
aristocracia *f* aristocracy.
aristócrata *m* aristocrat.
aristocrático, ca *adj* aristocratic.
aritmética *f* arithmetic.
arlequín *m* harlequin, buffoon.
arma *f* weapon, arms.
armada *f* fleet, armada.
armadillo *m* armadillo.
armado, da *adj* armed; reinforced.
armador *m* shipowner; privateer; jacket, jerkin.
armadura *f* armor; framework; skeleton; armature.
armamento *m* armament.
armar *vt* to man; to arm, to fit up; ~ **la** to kick up a fuss.
armario *m* clothes closet; cupboard.
armatoste *m* hulk; contraption.
armazón *f* chassis; skeleton; frame.
armería *f* arsenal; heraldry; gunsmith's.
armero *m* gunsmith.
armiño *m* ermine.
armisticio *m* armistice.
armonía *f* harmony.
armonioso, sa *adj* harmonious.
armonizar *vt* to harmonize; to reconcile.
arnés *m* harness; gear, trapping.
aro *m* ring; earring.
aroma *m* aroma; fragrance.
aromático, ca *adj* aromatic.
arpa *f* harp.
arpegio *m* (*mus*) arpeggio.
arpía *f* (*poet*) shrew.
arpillera *f* sackcloth.
arpón *m* harpoon.
arqueado, da *adj* arched, vaulted.
arquear *vt* to arch; to bend.
arqueo *m* arching; gauging of a ship.
arqueología *f* archeology.
arquero *m* archer.
arqueta *f* small trunk.
arquetipo *m* archetype.

arquitecto *m* architect.
arquitectónico, ca *adj* architectonic.
arquitectura *f* architecture.
arrabal *m* suburb; slum.
arrabalero *m* suburbanite.
arraigado *adj* deep-rooted; established.
arraigar *vi* to root; to establish; ● *vt* to establish; ~se *vr* to take root; to settle.
arrancar *vt* to pull up by the roots; to pull out; to wrest; to extract; ● *vi* to start; to move.
arranque *m* sudden start; start; outburst.
arras *fpl* security.
arrasar *vt* to demolish, to destroy.
arrastrado, da *adj* miserable, painstaking; servile.
arrastrar *vt*, *vi* to creep, to crawl; to drag; to lead a trump at cards; ~se *vr* to crawl; to grovel.
arrastre *m* dragging.
¡arre! (*excl*) gee!, go on!
arrear *vt* to drive on; ● *vi* to hurry along.
arrebañar *vt* to scrape together, to pick up.
arrebatado, da *adj* rapid, violent, impetuous; rash, inconsiderate.
arrebatar *vt* to carry off, to snatch; to enrapture.
arrebato *m* fury; rapture.
arrebol *m* rouge.
arrebujar *vt* to crumple; to wrap up.
arrecife *m* reef.
arrecirse *vr* to grow stiff with cold.
arreglado *adj* neat; regular, moderate.
arreglar *vt* to regulate; to tidy; to adjust; ~se *vr* to come to an understanding.
arreglo *m* rule, order; agreement;·arrangement.
arrellanarse *vr* to sit at ease; to make oneself comfortable.
arremangar *vt* to roll up; ~se *vr* to roll up one's sleeves.
arremeter *vt* to assail, to attack; to seize suddenly.
arremetida *f* attack, assault.
arrendador *m* landlord.
arrendamiento *m* leasing; hire; lease.
arrendar *vt* to rent, to let out, to lease.
arrendatario, ria *m/f* tenant.
arreo *m* dress, ornament; ~s *pl* harness.
arrepentido, da *adj* repentant.
arrepentimiento *m* repentance, penitence.
arrepentirse *vr* to repent.
arrestar *vt* to arrest; to imprison.
arresto *m* boldness; prison, arrest.
arriada *f* flood, overflowing.
arriar *vt* (*mar*) to lower, to strike; to pay out.
arriate *m* bed; causeway.
arriba *adv* above, over, up, high, on high, overhead; aloft.
arribada *f* arrival of a vessel in port.
arribar *vi* (*mar*) to put into harbor.
arribista *m/f* upstart.
arriendo *m* lease, farm rent.
arriero *m* muleteer.
arriesgado, da *adj* risky; daring.
arriesgar *vt* to risk, to hazard, to expose to danger; ~se *vr* to take a chance.
arrimar *vt* to approach, to draw near; (*mar*) to stow cargo; ~se *vr* to side up to; to lean on.
arrinconar *vt* to put in a corner; to lay aside.
arrobado, da *adj* enchanted.
arrobamiento *m* rapture; amazement, rapturous admiration.
arrobarse *vr* to be totally amazed, to be out of one's senses.
arrocero, ra *adj* rice-producing.
arrodillarse *vr* to kneel down.
arrogancia *f* arrogance, haughtiness.
arrogante *adj* haughty, proud, assuming; stout.
arrojadizo, za *adj* easily thrown.
arrojar *vt* to throw, to fling, to jet; to dash; to emit; to shoot, to sprout; ~se *vr* to hurl oneself.
arrojo *m* boldness, fearlessness.

arrollador, ra *adj* overwhelming.
arrollar *vt* to run over; to defeat heavily.
arropar *vt* to clothe, to dress; ~se *vr* to wrap up.
arrostrar *vt* to face up (to).
arroyo *m* stream; gutter.
arroz *m* rice.
arrozal *m* ricefield.
arruga *f* wrinkle; rumple.
arrugar *vt* to wrinkle; to rumple, to fold; ~ la frente to frown; ~se *vr* to shrivel.
arruinar *vt* to demolish; to ruin; ~se *vr* to go bankrupt.
arrullador, ra *adj* flattering, cajoling.
arrullar *vt* to lull; ● *vi* to coo.
arrullo *m* cooing of pigeons; lullaby.
arrumaco *m* caress.
arsenal *m* arsenal; dockyard.
arsénico *m* arsenic.
arte *m/f* art; skill; artfulness.
artefacto *m* appliance.
arteria *f* artery.
artero, ra *adj* dexterous, cunning, artful.
artesa *f* kneading trough.
artesanía *f* craftsmanship.
artesano *m* artisan, workman.
ártico, ca *adj* arctic, northern.
articulación *f* articulation; joint.
articulado, da *adj* articulated; jointed.
articular *vt* to articulate; to joint.
artículo *m* article; clause; point; (*gr*) article; condition.
artífice *m* artisan; artist.
artificial *adj* artificial.
artificio *m* workmanship, craft; artifice, cunning trick.
artificioso, sa *adj* skillful, ingenious; artful, cunning.
artillería *f* gunnery; artillery.
artillero *m* artilleryman.
artimaña *f* trap; cunning.
artista *m* artist; craftsman.
artístico, ca *adj* artistic.
artritis *f* arthritis.
arzobispado *m* archbishopric.
arzobispo *m* archbishop.
as *m* ace.
asa *f* handle; lever.
asado *m* roast meat; barbecue.
asador *m* spit.
asadura *f* offal.
asalariado, da *adj* salaried.
asaltador, a *m/f* assailant.
asaltante *m/f* assailant.
asaltar *vt* to storm a position; to assail.
asalto *m* assault, attack.
asamblea *f* assembly, meeting.
asar *vt* to roast.
asbesto *m* asbestos.
ascendencia *f* ascendancy; ancestry.
ascendente *adj* ascending; (*ferro*) tren ~ *m* up-train.
ascender *vi* to be promoted; to rise; ● *vt* to promote.
ascendiente *m* forefather; influence.
Ascensión *f* feast of the Ascension.
ascenso *m* promotion; ascent.
ascensor *m* elevator.
asceta *m* ascetic.
ascético, ca *adj* ascetic.
asco *m* nausea, loathing.
ascua *f* red-hot coal.
aseado, da *adj* clean, elegant, neat.
asear *vt* to clean; to tidy.
asediar *vt* to besiege; to chase.
asedio *m* siege.
asegurado, da *adj* insured.
asegurador *m* insurer.

asegurar *vt* to secure; to insure; to affirm; to bail; ~**se** *vr* to make sure.

asemejarse *vr* to be like, to resemble.

asentado, da *adj* established.

asentar *vt* to sit down; to affirm, to assure; to note; ● *vi* to suit.

asentir *vi* to acquiesce, to concede.

aseo *m* cleanliness, neatness.

aséptico, ca *adj* germ-free.

asequible *adj* attainable, obtainable.

aserción *f* assertion, affirmation.

aserradero *m* sawmill.

aserrar *vt* to saw.

aserrín *m* sawdust.

asertivo, va *adj* affirmative.

asesinar *vt* to assassinate; to murder.

asesinato *m* assassination; murder.

asesino *m* assassin; murderer.

asesor *m* counselor, assessor.

asesorar *vt* to advise; to act as consultant; ~**se** *vr* to consult.

asestar *vt* to aim, to point; to strike.

aseverar *vt* to affirm.

asfalto *m* asphalt.

asfixia *f* suffocation.

asfixiar *vt* to suffocate; ~**se** *vr* to suffocate.

así *adv* so, thus, in this manner; like this; therefore, so that; also; ~ **que** so that, therefore; **asi, asi** so-so; middling.

asidero *m* handle.

asiduidad *f* assiduousness.

asiduo, dua *adj* assiduous.

asiento *m* chair, bench, stool; seat; contract; entry; residence.

asignación *f* assignation; destination.

asignar *vt* to assign, to attribute.

asignatura *f* subject; course.

asilado, da *m/f* inmate; refugee.

asilo *m* asylum, refuge.

asimilación *f* assimilation.

asimilar *vt* to assimilate.

asimismo *adv* similarly, in the same manner.

asir *vt, vi* to grasp, to seize; to hold, to grip, to take root.

asistencia *f* audience, presence; assistance; help.

asistente *m* assistant, helper.

asistir *vi* to be present, to assist; ● *vt* to help.

asma *f* asthma.

asmático, ca *adj* asthmatic.

asno *m* ass.

asociación *f* association; partnership.

asociado *m* associate.

asociar *vt* to associate; ~**se** *vr* to associate.

asolar *vt* to destroy, to devastate.

asolear *vt* to expose to the sun; ~**se** *vr* to sunbathe.

asomar *vi* to appear; ~**se** *vr* to appear; to show up.

asombrar *vt* to amaze; to astonish; ~**se** *vr* to be amazed; to get a fright.

asombro *m* dread, terror; astonishment.

asombroso, sa *adj* astonishing, marvelous.

asomo *m* mark, token, indication; conjecture.

asonancia *f* assonance; harmony.

aspa *f* cross; sail.

aspaviento *m* astonishment; fuss.

aspecto *m* appearance; aspect.

aspereza *f* roughness; surliness.

áspero, ra *adj* rough, rugged; craggy, knotty; horrid; harsh, hard; severe, austere, gruff.

asperón *m* grindstone.

aspersión *f* aspersion, sprinkling.

áspid *m* asp.

aspiración *f* breath; pause.

aspirante *m* aspirant, aspirer.

aspirar *vt* to breathe; to aspire; (*gr*) to aspirate.

aspirina *f* aspirin.

asquear *vt* to sicken; ● *vi* to be sickening; ~**se** *vr* to feel disgusted.

asqueroso, sa *adj* disgusting.

asta *f* lance; horn; handle.

astado, da *adj* horned.

asterisco *m* asterisk.

astilla *f* chip of wood, splinter.

astillero *m* dockyard.

astral *adj* astral.

astringente *adj* astringent.

astro *m* star.

astrología *f* astrology.

astrológico, ca *adj* astrological.

astrólogo *m* astrologer.

astronauta *m/f* astronaut.

astronave *f* spaceship.

astronomía *f* astronomy.

astronómico, ca *adj* astronomical.

astrónomo *m* astronomer.

astucia *f* cunning, slyness.

astuto, ta *adj* cunning, sly, astute.

asueto *m* time off; vacation.

asumir *vt* to assume.

Asunción *f* Assumption.

asunto *m* subject, matter; affair, business.

asustar *vt* to frighten; ~**se** *vr* to be frightened.

atacar *vt* to attack, to onset.

atajo *m* short cut; tackle.

atalaya *f* watchtower.

atañer *vi* to concern.

ataque *m* attack.

atar *vt* to tie, to fasten.

atardecer *vi* to get dark; ● *m* dusk; evening.

atareado, da *adj* busy.

atascar *vt* to jam; to hinder; ~**se** *vr* to become bogged.

atasco *m* traffic jam.

ataúd *m* coffin.

ataviar *vt* to dress out, to trim, to adorn.

atavío *m* dress, ornament, finery.

ateísmo *m* atheism.

atemorizar *vt* to frighten; ~**se** *vr* to get scared.

atenazar *vt* to grip; to torment.

atención *f* attention, heedfulness; civility; observance, consideration.

atender *vi* to be attentive; to heed, to expect, to wait for; to look at; ● *vt* to attend to.

atenerse *vr* to adhere to.

atentado, da *adj* discreet, prudent, moderate; ● *m* attempt, transgression, offense.

atentamente *adv*: **le saluda** ~ Yours faithfully.

atentar *vt* to attempt; to commit.

atento, ta *adj* attentive; heedful; observing; mindful; polite, courteous, mannerly.

atenuante *adj* extenuating.

atenuar *vt* to diminish; to lessen.

ateo, a *adj*, *m/f* atheist.

aterciopelado, da *adj* velvet-like.

aterido, da *adj* frozen stiff.

aterirse *vr* to grow stiff with cold.

aterrador, a *adj* frightening.

aterrar *vt* to terrify; ~**se** *vr* to be terrified.

aterrizaje *m* landing.

aterrizar *vi* to land.

aterrorizar *vt* to frighten, to terrify.

atesorar *vt* to treasure *or* hoard up riches.

atestación *f* testimony, evidence.

atestado, da *adj* packed; ● *m* affidavit.

atestar *vt* to cram, to stuff; to attest, to witness.

atestiguar *vt* to witness, to attest.

atiborrar *vt* to stuff; ~**se** *vr* to stuff oneself.

ático *m* attic.

atildar *vt* to punctuate, to underline; to censure.

atinado, da *adj* wise; correct.

atisbar *vt* to pry, to examine closely.

atizar *vt* to stir the fire with a poker; to stir up.

atlántico, ca *adj* atlantic.

atlas *m* atlas.

atleta *m* athlete.

atlético, ca *adj* athletic.

atletismo *m* athletics.

atmósfera *f* atmosphere.

atmosférico, ca *adj* atmospheric.

atolondramiento *m* stupefaction, consternation.

atolondrar *vt* to stun, to stupefy; ~se *vr* to be stupefied.

atolladero *m* bog; obstacle; impediment.

atollar *vi* to stick; ~se *vr* to get stuck.

atómico, ca *adj* atomic.

atomizador *m* spray.

átomo *m* atom.

atónito, ta *adj* astonished, amazed.

atontado, da *adj* stunned; silly.

atontar *vt* to stun, to stupefy; ~se *vr* to grow stupid.

atormentar *vt* to torture; to harrass; to torment.

atornillar *vt* to screw on/down.

atosigar *vt* to poison; to harass, to oppress.

atracadero *m* landing-place.

atracador, a *m/f* robber.

atracar *vt* to moor; to rob; ~se *vr* to stuff oneself (with).

atracción *f* attraction.

atractivo, va *adj* attractive; magnetic; ● *m* charm.

atraer *vt* to attract, to allure.

atragantarse *vr* to stick in the throat, to choke.

atrancar *vt* to bar a door.

atrapar *vt* to trap; to nab; to deceive.

atrás *adv* backward(s); behind; previously, **hacia** ~ backward(s).

atrasado, da *adj* slow; backward; in arrears.

atrasar *vi* to be slow; ● *vt* to postpone; ~ **el reloj**, to put back a watch; ~se *vr* to stay behind; to be late.

atraso *m* backwardness; slowness; delay.

atravesado, da *adj* oblique; cross, perverse; mongrel; degenerate.

atravesar *vt* to cross; to pass over; to pierce; to go through; ~se *vr* to get in the way; to thwart.

atrayente *adj* attractive.

atreverse *vr* to dare, to venture.

atrevido, da *adj* bold, audacious, daring.

atrevimiento *m* boldness, audacity.

atribución *f* attribution, imputation.

atribuir *vt* to attribute, to ascribe; to impute.

atribular *vt* to vex, to afflict.

atributivo, va *adj* attributive.

atributo *m* attribute.

atrición *f* attrition.

atril *m* lectern; bookrest.

atrio *m* porch; portico.

atrocidad *f* atrocity.

atrochar *vi* to take a short cut.

atropellado, da *adj* hasty, precipitate.

atropellar *vt* to trample; to run down; to hurry; to insult; ~se *vr* to hurry oneself too much.

atropello *m* accident; push; outrage.

atuendo *m* attire.

atroz *adj* atrocious, heinous, cruel.

atufar *vt* to vex, to plague; ~se *vr* turn sour; to get mad.

atún *m* tunny fish.

aturdido, da *adj* hare-brained.

aturdimiento *m* stupefaction; astonishment; dullness.

aturdir *vt* to stun, to confuse; to stupefy.

atusar *vt* to smooth.

audacia *f* audacity, boldness.

audaz *adj* audacious, bold.

audible *adj* audible.

audiencia *f* audience.

auditivo, va *adj* auditive, auditory.

auditor *m* auditor.

auditorio *m* audience; auditorium.

auge *m* boom; climax.

augurar *vt* to predict.

augurio *m* omen.

aula *f* lecture room.

aullar *vi* to howl.

aullido, aúllo *m* howling.

aumentar *vt* to augment, to increase; to magnify; to put up; ● *vi* to increase; to grow larger.

aumento *m* increase; promotion, advancement.

aun *adv* even; ~ **así** even so.

aún *adv* still; yet.

aunar *vt* to unite, to assemble.

aunque *adv* though, although.

¡aupa! *excl* come on!

áureo, rea *adj* golden, gilt.

aureola *f* glory; nimbus.

auricular *m* receiver; ~es *mpl* headphones.

aurora *f* dawn.

auscultar *vt* to sound.

ausencia *f* absence.

ausentarse *vr* to go out.

ausente *adj* absent.

auspicio *m* auspice; prediction; protection.

austeridad *f* austerity.

austero, ra *adj* austere, severe.

austral *adj* southern.

autenticar *vt* to authenticate.

autenticidad *f* authenticity.

auténtico, ca *adj* authentic.

autillo *m* horned owl.

auto *m* judicial sentence; car; edict, ordinance; ~ **de fe** auto-da-fe.

autoadhesivo, va *adj* self-sealing.

autobiografía *f* autobiography.

autobús *m* bus.

autocar *m* bus.

autocracia *f* autocracy.

autócrata *m* autocrat.

autóctono, na *adj* native.

autodefensa *f* self defense.

autodeterminación *f* self determination.

autoescuela *f* driving school.

autógrafo *m* autograph.

autómata *m* automaton.

automático, ca *adj* automatic.

automatización *f* automation.

automotor *m* diesel train.

automóvil *m* automobile.

automovilismo *m* motoring; car racing.

automovilista *m/f* motorist, driver.

automovilístico, ca *adj* car *compd*.

autonomía *f* autonomy.

autónomo, ma *adj* autonomous.

autonómico, ca *adj* autonomous.

autopista *f* freeway.

autopsia *f* autopsy.

autor *m* author; maker; writer.

autora *f* authoress.

autoridad *f* authority.

autorización *f* authorization.

autorizar *vt* to authorize.

autorretrato *m* self-portrait.

autoservicio *m* self-service store; restaurant.

autostop *m* hitch-hiking.

autostopista *m/f* hitch-hiker.

autosuficiencia *f* self-sufficiency.

autovía *f* state highway.

auxiliar *vt* to aid, to help, to assist; to attend a dying person; ● *adj* auxiliary.

auxilio *m* aid, help, assistance.
aval *m* guarantee; guarantor.
avalancha *f* avalanche.
avance *m* advance, attack; trailer.
avanzada *f (mil)* vanguard.
avanzar *vt, vi* to advance.
avaricia *f* avarice.
avaricioso, sa *adj* avaricious, covetous.
avaro, ra *adj* avaricious, miserly.
avasallar *vt* to subdue, to enslave.
ave *f* bird; fowl.
avecinarse *vr* to be on the way.
avellana *f* hazelnut.
avellano *m* hazelnut tree.
ave maría *f* hail mary.
avena *f* oats *pl.*
avenencia *f* agreement, bargain; union.
avenida *f* avenue.
avenido, da *adj* agreed.
avenir *vt* to reconcile; ~**se** *vr* to reach a compromise.
aventajado, da *adj* advantageous, profitable; beautiful, excellent.
aventajar *vt* to surpass, to excel.
aventar *vt* to fan; to expel.
aventura *f* adventure, event, incident.
aventurado, da *adj* risky.
aventurar *vt* to venture, to risk.
aventurero, ra *adj* adventurous.
avergonzar *vt* to shame, to abash; ~**se** *vr* to be ashamed.
avería *f* breakdown.
averiado, da *adj* broken down; out of order.
averiarse *vr* to break down.
averiguación *f* discovery; investigation.
averiguar *vt* to inquire, to investigate, to explore.
aversión *f* aversion, dislike; abhorrence.
avestruz *m* ostrich.
aviación *f* aviation; air force.
aviador, a *m/f* aviator.
avicultura *f* poultry farming.
avidez *f* covetousness.
ávido, da *adj (poet)* greedy, covetous.
avieso, sa *adj* irregular, out of the way; mischievous, perverse.
avinagrado, da *adj* sour.
avinagrarse *vr* to go sour.
avío *m* preparation, provision.
avión *m* airplane.
avioneta *f* light aircraft.
avisado, da *adj* prudent, cautious; **mal** ~ ill advised.
avisar *vt* to inform; to warn; to advise.
aviso *m* notice; warning, hint.
avispa *f* wasp.
avispado, da *adj* lively, brisk, vivacious.
avisparse *vr* to worry.
avispero *m* wasp's nest.
avispón *m* hornet.
avistar *vt* to sight.
avituallar *vt (mil)* to supply (with food).
avivar *vt* to quicken, to enliven, to encourage.
avutarda *f* bustard, wild turkey.
axioma *m* axiom, maxim.
¡ay! *excl* alas!; ow! ¡~ **de mí!** alas! poor me!
aya *f* governess, instructress.
ayer *adv* yesterday.
ayuda *f* help, aid; support; ● *m* deputy, assistant.
ayudante *m (mil)* adjutant; assistant.
ayudar *vt* to help, to assist, to further.
ayunar *vi* to fast, to abstain from food.
ayuno *m* fasting, abstinence from food.
ayuntamiento *m* town/city hall.
azabache *m* jet.
azada *f* spade, hoe.

azafata *f* air stewardess.
azafrán *m* saffron.
azahar *m* orange *or* lemon blossom.
azar *m* unforeseen disastér, unexpected accident; fate; **por** ~ by chance; **al** ~ at random.
azaroso, sa *adj* unlucky, ominous; risky.
azogue *m* mercury.
azor *m* goshawk.
azorar *vt* to frighten, to terrify.
azotaina *f* drubbing, sound flogging.
azotar *vt* to whip, to lash.
azote *m* whip.
azotea *f* flat roof of a house.
azteca *m/f* Aztec.
azúcar *m* sugar.
azucarado, da *adj* sugared; sugary.
azucarar *vt* to sugar, to sweeten.
azucarero *m* sugar bowl.
azucena *f* white lily.
azufre *m* sulphur, brimstone.
azul *adj* blue; ~ **celeste** sky blue.
azulado, da *adj* azure, bluish.
azulejo *m* tile.
azuzar *vt* to irritate, to stir up.

B

baba *f* drivel, slaver.
babear *vi* to drivel, to slaver.
babel *m* bedlam.
babero *m* bib.
babia *f:* **estar en** ~ to be absent-minded *or* dreaming.
baboso, sa *adj* driveling, slavering.
babucha *f* slipper.
baca *f (auto)* roof rack.
bacalao *m* cod.
báculo *m* stick.
bache *m* pothole.
bachillerato *m* baccalaureate.
bagaje *m* baggage.
bagatela *f* trifle.
bahía *f* bay.
bailador, ra *m/f* dancer.
bailar *vi* to dance.
bailarín, ina *m/f* dancer.
baile *m* dance, ball.
baja *f* fall; casualty.
bajada *f* descent; inclination; slope; ebb.
bajamar *f* low tide.
bajar *vt* to lower, to let down; to lessen; to humble; to go/come down; to bend downward(s); ● *vi* to descend; to go/come down; to grow less; ~**se** *vr* to crouch; to lessen.
bajeza *f* meanness; lowliness.
bajío *m* shoal, sandbank; lowlands.
bajo, ja *adj* low; abject, despicable; common; dull (of colors); deep; humble; ● *prep* under, underneath, below; ● *adv* softly; quietly; ● *m (mus)* base; low place.
bajón *m* fall.
bala *f* bullet.
baladronada *f* boast, brag; bravado.
balance *m* hesitation; balance sheet; balance; rolling of a ship.
balancear *vt, vi* to balance; to roll; to waver; ~**se** *vr* to swing.
balancín *m* balance beam; rocker arm; seesaw; balancing pole.
balanza *f* scale; balance; judgement.
balar *vi* to bleat.
balaustrada *f* balustrade, banister.
balazo *m* shot.
balbucear *vt, vi* to stutter.
balbuciente *adj* stammering, stuttering.

balcón m balcony.

baldar vt to cripple.

balde m bucket; de ~ adv gratis, for nothing; en ~ in vain.

baldío, dia adj waste; uncultivated.

baldosa f floor; tile; flagstone.

balido m bleating, bleat.

balín m buckshot.

balística f ballistics pl.

balneario m spa.

balón m large football; bale of goods.

baloncesto m basketball.

balonmano m handball.

balonvolea m volleyball.

balsa f balsa wood; pool; raft, float; ferry.

bálsamo m balsam, balm.

baluarte m bastion; bulwark.

ballena f whale; whalebone.

ballenato m cub of a whale.

ballenero m (mar) whaler.

ballesta f crossbow; a tiro de ~ at a great distance.

ballestero m archer; crossbow-maker.

ballet m ballet.

bamba f goat; (pej) police; (bot) swelling; flabbiness.

bambolear vi to reel; ~se vr to sway.

bamboleo m reeling, staggering.

bambú m bamboo.

banana f banana, plantain.

banano m banana tree.

banasta f large basket.

banca f bench; banking.

bancario, ria adj bank(ing).

bancarrota f bankruptcy.

banco m bench; work bench; bank.

banda f band; sash; ribbon; troop; party; gang; touchline.

bandada f flock; shoal.

bandearse vr to move to and fro.

bandeja f tray, salver.

bandera f banner, standard; flag.

banderilla f small decorated dart used at a bullfight.

banderillear vt to plant banderillas in a bull's neck or shoulder.

banderillero m thrower of banderillas.

banderín m small flag, pennant.

bandido m bandit, outlaw.

bando m faction, party; edict.

bandolera f bandoleer.

bandolero m bandit.

bandurria f bandore (musical instrument resembling a lute).

banquero, ra m/f banker.

banqueta f three-legged stool; sidewalk.

banquete m banquet; formal dinner.

banquillo m dock.

bañador m swimsuit.

bañar vt to bathe; to dip; to coat (with varnish); ~se vr to bathe; to swim.

bañera f bath (tub).

bañero m lifeguard.

bañista m/f bather.

baño m bath; dip; bathtub; varnish; crust of sugar; coating.

baptista m/f Baptist.

bar m bar.

baraja f pack of cards.

barajar vt to shuffle cards; to jumble up.

baranda f rail.

barandilla f small balustrade, small railing.

baratijas fpl trifles , toys pl; trash, junk.

baratillo m secondhand goods pl; junkshop; bargain sale.

barato, ta adj cheap; de ~ gratis; • m cheapness, bargain sale; money extracted from winning gamblers.

baraúnda f noise, hurly-burly.

barba f chin; beard; ~ a ~ face to face; • m actor who impersonates old men.

barbacoa f barbecue.

barbaridad f barbarity, barbarism; outrage.

barbarie f barbarism; savagery.

barbarismo m barbarism (form of speech).

bárbaro, ra adj barbarous; cruel; rude; rough.

barbecho m first plowing, fallow land.

barbería f barber's shop.

barbero m barber.

barbilampiño, ña adj clean-shaven; (fig) inexperienced.

barbilla f (tip of the) chin.

barbo m barbel.

barbudo, da adj bearded.

barca f boat.

barco m boat; ship.

barítono m (mus) baritone.

barman m barman.

barniz m varnish; glaze.

barnizar vt to varnish.

barómetro m barometer.

barón m baron.

baronesa f baroness.

barquero m boatman.

barquilla f (mar) log; basket (of an air balloon).

barquillo m wafer; cornet, cone.

barra m bar; rod; lever; French loaf; sandbank; de ~ a ~ from place to place.

barrabasada f trick, plot.

barraca f hut.

barranco m gully, ravine; (fig) great difficulty.

barrena f drill, bit, auger.

barrenar vt to drill, to bore; (fig) to frustrate.

barrendero m sweeper, garbage man.

barreno m large drill; borehole.

barreño m tub.

barrer vt to sweep; to overwhelm.

barrera f barrier; turn-pike, claypit.

barriada f suburb, district of a city.

barricada f barricade.

barrido m sweep.

barriga f abdomen, belly.

barrigudo, da adj big-bellied.

barril m barrel; cask.

barrio m neighborhood, district,

barrizal m claypit.

barro m clay, mud.

barroco, ca adj baroque.

barrote m ironwork of doors, windows, tables; crosspiece.

barruntar vt to guess, to foresee, to conjecture.

barrunto m conjecture.

bártulos mpl gear, belongings pl.

barullo m uproar.

basamento m base.

basalto m basalt.

basar vt to base; ~se vr to be based on.

basca f squeamishness, nausea.

báscula f scales pl.

base f base, basis.

básico, ca adj basic.

basílica f basilica.

basilisco m basilisk.

bastante adj sufficient, enough; • adv quite.

bastar vi to be sufficient, to be enough.

bastardo, da adj, m/f bastard.

bastidor m embroidery frame; ~es pl scenery (on stage).

bastión m bastion.

basto, ta adj coarse, rude, unpolished.

bastón m cane, stick; truncheon; (fig) command.

bastonazo m beating.

bastos mpl clubs (one of the four suits at cards).

basura f garbage; trash; dung.

basurero m garbage man; dunghill; trashcan.

bata f dressing gown; overall; laboratory coat.

batacazo *m* noise of a fall.

batalla *f* battle, combat, fight; agitation of the mind.

batallar *vi* to battle, to fight; to fence with foils; to waver.

batallón *m* (*mil*) battalion.

batata *f* sweet potato.

bate *m* bat.

batería *m* battery; percussion.

batida *f* battue (chase).

batido, da *adj* shot (applied to silks); beaten (as roads); ● *m* milk shake.

batidora *f* food mixer, whisk.

batir *vt* to beat; to whisk; to dash; to demolish; to defeat; to strike (of the sun).

batista *f* batiste, cambric.

batuta *f* baton.

baúl *m* trunk; (*fam*) belly.

bautismal *adj* baptismal.

bautismo *m* baptism.

bautizar *vt* to baptize, to christen.

bautizo *m* baptism.

baya *f* berry.

bayeta *f* baize (kind of cloth).

bayo, ya *adj* bay (of a horse).

bayoneta *f* bayonet.

bayonetazo *m* thrust with a bayonet.

baza *f* card-trick.

bazar *m* bazaar.

bazo *m* spleen.

bazofia *f* refuse; hogwash.

be *m* baa (cry of sheep).

beatificación *f* beatification.

beatificar *vt* to beatify; to hallow, to sanctify, to make blessed.

beato, ta *adj* happy, blessed; devout; ● *m* lay brother; pious person.

bebé *m/f* baby.

bebedero *m* drinking trough; place where birds drink.

bebedizo *m* (love) potion.

bebedor, ra *m/f* (hard) drinker.

beber *vt* to drink.

bebida *f* drink, beverage.

beca *f* fellowship; grant, allowance, scholarship; sash, hood.

becada *f* woodcock.

becerro *m* yearling calf.

bedel *m* head porter, uniformed employee.

befa *f* jeer, taunt.

befarse *vr* to mock, to ridicule.

beldad *f* beauty.

belén *m* nativity scene.

bélico, ca *adj* warlike, martial.

belicoso, sa *adj* warlike; aggressive.

beligerante *adj* belligerent.

bellaco, ca *adj* artful, sly; cunning.

belladona *f* (*bot*) deadly nightshade.

belleza *f* beauty.

bello, lla *adj* beautiful, handsome; lovely; fine.

bellota *f* acorn; (*med*) Adam's apple; pomander.

bemol *m* (*mus*) flat.

bencina *f* gasoline.

bendecir *vt* to bless; to consecrate; to praise.

bendición *f* blessing, benediction.

bendito, ta *adj* saintly, blessed; simple; happy.

benedictino, benito *adj, m* Benedictine.

beneficiado *m* incumbent; beneficiary.

beneficiar *vt* to benefit; to be of benefit to.

beneficiario, ra *m/f* beneficiary.

beneficio *m* benefit, profit, advantage; benefit-night.

beneficioso, sa *adj* beneficial.

benéfico, ca *adj* beneficent, kind.

benemérito, ta *adj* worthy, meritorious.

beneplácito *m* consent, approbation.

benevolencia *f* benevolence.

benévolo, la *adj* benevolent, kind-hearted.

benigno, na *adj* benign; kind; mild.

beodo, da *adj* drunk, drunken.

berenjena *f* eggplant.

bergantín *m* (*mar*) brig.

bermejo, ja *adj* red.

berrear *vi* to low, to bellow.

berrido *m* bellowing of a calf.

berrinche *m* anger, rage, tantrum (applied to children).

berro *m* watercress.

berruga *f* wart.

berza *f* cabbage.

besamanos *m* levee; royal audience.

besamel *f* white sauce.

besar *vt* to kiss; to graze; ~se *vr* to kiss; to knock one's head against another's.

beso *m* kiss; collision of persons or things.

bestia *f* beast; animal; idiot.

bestial *adj* bestial; (*fam*) marvelous, swell.

bestialidad *f* bestiality.

besugo *m* sea bream.

besuquear *vt* to cover with kisses.

besuqueo *m* repeated kisses.

betún *m* shoe polish.

bezo *m* thick lip; proud flesh in a wound.

biberón *m* feeding bottle.

Biblia *f* Bible.

bíblico, ca *adj* biblical.

bibliófilo, la *m/f* book-lover, bookworm.

bibliografía *f* bibliography.

bibliográfico, ca *adj* bibliographical.

bibliógrafo, fa *m/f* bibliographer.

biblioteca *f* library.

bibliotecario, ra *m/f* librarian.

bicarbonato *m* bicarbonate.

bici *f* (*fam*) bike.

bicicleta *f* bicycle.

bicho *m* small animal; bug; **mal** ~ villain.

bidé *m* bidet.

bielda *f* pitchfork.

bien *m* good, benefit; profit; ~es *pl* goods, property, wealth; ● *adv* well, right; very; willingly, easily; ~ **que** *conj* although; **está** ~ very well.

bienal *adj* biennial.

bienaventuranza *f* blessedness, bliss; happiness; prosperity; ~s *pl* the Beatitudes.

bienestar *m* well-being.

bienhablado, da *adj* well-spoken.

bienhecho, cha *adj* well-shaped.

bienhechor, ra *m/f* benefactor.

bienio *m* space of two years.

bienvenida *f* welcome.

bifurcación *f* fork.

bigamia *f* bigamy.

bígamo, ma *m/f* bigamist.

bigote *m* mustache; whiskers *pl*.

bigotudo, da *adj* with a big mustache.

bikini *m* bikini.

bilingüe *adj* bilingual.

bilioso, sa *adj* bilious.

bilis *f* bile.

billar *m* billiards *pl*.

billete *m* bill, banknote; ticket; (*ferro*) ticket; ~ **sencillo** one-way ticket; ~ **de ida y vuelta** round-trip ticket.

billetero *m* pocketbook, billfold.

billón *m* billion.

bimensual *adj* twice monthly.

bimotor *m* twin-engined plane.

binario *m* binary.

binoculares *mpl* binoculars; opera glasses.

biografía *f* biography.

biógrafo, fa *m/f* biographer.

biología f biology.
biológico, ca adj biological.
biólogo, ga m/f biologist.
biombo m screen.
biopsia f biopsy.
bípedo m biped.
birlar vt to knock down at one blow; to pinch (fam).
birreta f cardinal's red cap.
bis excl encore.
bisabuela f great-grandmother.
bisabuelo m great-grandfather.
bisagra f hinge.
bisexual adj bisexual.
bisexualidad f bisexuality.
bisiesto adj: año ~ leap year.
bisnieto, ta m/f great-grandson/daughter.
bisoño, ña adj raw, inexperienced; novice.
bisonte m bison.
bistec m steak.
bisturí m scalpel.
bisutería f costume jewellery.
bizarro, rra adj brave, gallant; generous.
bizco, ca adj cross-eyed.
bizcocho m sponge cake; biscuit, ship's biscuit.
bizquear vi to squint.
blanco, ca adj white, blank; ● m whiteness; white person, blank, blank space; targetmark (to shoot at).
blancura f whiteness.
blandir vt to brandish a sword; ~se vr to swing.
blando, da soft, smooth; mild, gentle; (fam) cowardly.
blanducho, cha adj flabby.
blandura f softness; gentleness; mildness.
blanquear vt to bleach; to whitewash; to launder (money); ● vi to show white.
blanquecino, na adj whitish.
blasfemador, ra m/f blasphemer.
blasfemar vi to blaspheme.
blasfemia f blasphemy; verbal insult.
blasfemo, ma adj blasphemous; ● m blasphemer.
blasón m heraldry, honor, glory.
blasonar vt to emblazon; to blow one's own trumpet.
bledo m: no me importa un ~ I don't give a damn (sl).
blindado, da adj armor-plated; bullet-proof.
bloc m writing pad.
bloque m block.
bloquear vt to block; to blockade.
bloqueo m blockade.
blusa f blouse.
boato m ostentation, pompous show.
bobada f folly, foolishness.
bobear vt to act or talk in a stupid manner.
bobería f silliness, foolishness.
bobina f bobbin.
bobo, ba m/f idiot, fool; clown, funny man; ● adj stupid, silly.
boca f mouth; entrance, opening; mouth of a river; ~ en ~ adv by word of mouth; a pedir de ~ to one's heart's content.
bocacalle f entrance to a street.
bocadillo m sandwich, roll.
bocado m mouthful.
bocal m pitcher; mouthpiece of a trumpet.
bocamanga f cuff.
bocanada f mouthful (of liquor); gust.
bocazas m invar bigmouth.
boceto m sketch.
bocina f trumpet; megaphone; horn (of a car).
bochorno m sultry weather, scorching heat; blush.
bochornoso, sa adj sultry; shameful.
boda f wedding.
bodega f wine cellar; warehouse; bar.
bodegón m cheap restaurant; still life (in art).
bodoque m pellet; lump; (fam) idiot.

bodorrio m quiet wedding.
bofes mpl lungs, lights.
bofetada f slap (in the face).
bofetón m hard slap.
boga f fashion; (ferro) bogey; rower; rowing; estar en ~ to be fashionable.
bogar vi to row, to paddle.
bohemio m/f Bohemian.
boicot m boycott.
boicotear vt to boycott.
boina f beret.
boj m box, box tree.
bola f ball; marble; globe; slam (in cards); shoe polish; (fam) lie, fib.
bolazo m blow with a ball.
bolchevique adj Bolshevik.
bolear vi to knock balls about (billiards); ● vt to throw (a ball).
bolera f bowling alley.
bolero m bolero jacket; bolero dance.
boleta f entrance ticket; pass, permit.
boletín m bulletin; journal, review.
boleto m ticket.
boli m (fam) Biro, pen.
boliche m jack at bowls; bowls, bowling alley; dragnet.
bolígrafo m ballpoint pen.
bolillo m bobbin.
bolo m ninepin; (large) pill.
bolsa f purse; bag; pocket; sac; stock exchange.
bolsillo m pocket; purse.
bolsista m/f stockbroker.
bolso m purse.
bollo m bread roll; lump.
bomba f pump; bomb; surprise; dar a la ~ to pump; ~ de gasolina gas pump.
bombardear vt to bombard.
bombardeo m bombardment.
bombardero m bomber.
bombazo m bomb explosion; bombshell.
bombero m fireman.
bombilla f light bulb.
bombín m bowler hat.
bombo m large drum.
bombón m chocolate.
bonachón, ona adj good-natured.
bonanza f fair weather at sea; prosperity, bonanza.
bondad f goodness; kindness, courtesy.
bondadoso, sa adj good, kind.
bonete m clerical hat; college cap.
bonito, ta adj pretty, nice-looking; pretty good, passable; ● m tuna fish.
boñiga f cow dung.
bono m (financial) bond.
boqueada f act of opening the mouth; la última ~ the last gasp.
boquear vi to gape, to gasp; to breathe one's last; ● vt to pronounce, to utter a word.
boquerón m anchovy; large hole.
boquete m gap, narrow entrance.
boquiabierto, ta adj with the mouth open; gaping.
boquilla f mouthpiece of a musical instrument; nozzle.
borbollón, borbotón m bubbling; salir a borbollones to gush forth.
borda f (mar) gunwhale; hut.
bordado m embroidery.
bordadora f embroiderer.
bordar vt to embroider; to do anything very well.
borde m border; margin; (mar) board.
bordear vi (mar) to tack; ● vt to go along the edge of; to flank.
bordillo m curb.
bordo m board of a ship.
boreal adj boreal, northern.

borgoña *m* burgundy wine.
borla *f* tassel; tuft.
borona *f* millet; corn; corn bread.
borrachera *f* drunkenness; hard-drinking; spree.
borracho, cha *adj* drunk, intoxicated; blind with passion; ● *m/f* drunk, drunkard.
borrador *m* first draft; scribbling pad; eraser.
borraja *f* (*bot*) borage.
borrar *vt* to erase, to rub out; to blur; to obscure.
borrasca *f* storm, violent squall of wind; hazard, danger.
borrascoso, sa *adj* stormy.
borrego, ga *m/f* yearling lamb; simpleton, blockhead.
borrico, ca *m/f* donkey; ass; blockhead.
borrón *m* blot, blur; rough draft of a writing; first sketch of a painting; stain, tarnish; blemish.
borronear *vt* to sketch.
boscaje *m* grove, small wood; landscape (in painting).
bosque *m* forest, wood.
bosquejar *vt* to make a sketch of a painting; to make a rough model of a figure.
bosquejo *m* sketch of a painting; unfinished work.
bostezar *vi* to yawn; to gape.
bostezo *m* yawn, yawning.
bota *f* leather wine-bag; boot.
botánica *f* botany.
botánico, ca *adj* botanic.
botánico, ca, botanista *m/f* botanist.
botar *vt* to cast, to fling; to launch.
bote *m* bounce; thrust; can; boat.
botella *f* bottle.
botica *f* drugstore.
boticario, ria *m/f* pharmacist.
botijo *m* earthenware jug.
botín *m* high boot, half-boot; gaiter; booty.
botiquín *m* medicine chest.
botón *m* button; knob (of a radio *etc*); (*bot*) bud.
botonadura *f* set of buttons.
botones *m invar* bellhop.
bóveda *f* arch, vault; crypt.
boxeador *m* boxer.
boxeo *m* boxing.
boya *f* (*mar*) buoy.
boyante *adj* buoyant, floating; (*fig*) fortunate, successful.
bozal *m* muzzle.
bozo *m* down (on the upper lip or chin); headstall of a horse.
braceada *f* violent movement of the arms.
bracear *vi* to swing the arms.
bracero *m* day-laborer; farmhand.
braga *f* sling, rope; diaper; ~s *pl* breeches; panties.
bragazas *m invar* henpecked husband.
braguero *m* truss.
bragueta *f* fly, flies (of trousers).
braille *m* braille.
bramante *m* twine, string.
bramar *vi* to roar, to bellow; to storm, to bluster.
bramido *m* roar, bellow, howl.
brasa *f* live coal; **estar hecho una ~** to be very flushed.
brasero *m* brazier.
bravamente *adv* bravely, gallantly; fiercely; roughly; fine, extremely well.
bravío, vía *adj* ferocious, savage, wild; coarse; ● *m* fierceness, savageness.
bravo, va *adj* brave, valiant; bullying; savage, fierce; rough; sumptuous; excellent; fine; ! ~ ! *excl* well done!
bravura *f* ferocity; courage.
braza *f* fathom.
brazada *f* extension of the arms; armful.
brazado *m* armful.
brazal *m* armband; irrigation channel.
brazalete *m* bracelet.
brazo *m* arm; branch of a tree; enterprise; courage; **luchar a ~ partido** to fight hand-to-hand.

brea *f* pitch; tar.
brear *vt* to pitch; to tar; to abuse, to ill-treat; to play a joke on.
brebaje *m* potion.
brecha *f* (*mil*) breach; gap, opening; **batir en ~** (*mil*) to make a breach.
bregar *vi* to struggle; to quarrel; to slog away.
breva *f* early fig; early large acorn.
breve *m* papal brief; ● *f* (*mus*) breve; ● *adj* brief, short; **en ~** shortly.
brevedad *f* brevity, shortness, conciseness.
breviario *m* breviary; (*fig*) daily reading.
brezo *m* (*bot*) heather.
bribón, ona *adj* dishonest, rascally.
bribonear *vi* to be idle; to play dirty tricks.
bricolaje *m* do-it-yourself.
brida *f* bridle; clamp, flange.
bridge *m* bridge (cards).
brigada *f* brigade; squad, gang.
brigadier *m* brigadier.
brillante *adj* brilliant; bright, shining; ● *m* diamond.
brillar *vi* to shine; to sparkle, to glisten; to shine, to be outstanding.
brillo *m* brilliancy, brightness.
brincar *vi* to skip, to leap, to jump, to gambol; to fly into a passion.
brinco *m* leap, jump, bounce.
brindar *vi*: ~ **a**, ~ **por** to drink a health, to toast; ● *vt* to offer, to present.
brindis *f* toast.
brío *m* spirit, dash.
briosamente *adv* spiritedly, dashingly.
brioso, sa *adj* dashing, full of spirit; lively.
brisa *f* breeze.
brisca *f* a game at cards.
broca *f* reel; drill; shoemaker's tack.
brocado *m* gold or silver brocade; ~, **da** *adj* embroidered, like brocade.
brocal *m* rim, mouth; curb.
brocha *f* large brush; ~ **de afeitar** shaving brush.
brochada *f* brushstroke.
broche *m* clasp; brooch; cufflink.
broma *f* joke.
bromear *vi* to joke.
bromista *m/f* joker.
bronca *f* row.
bronce *m* bronze.
bronceado, da *adj* tanned; *m* bronzing, suntan.
broncearse *vr* to get a suntan.
bronco, ca *adj* rough, coarse; rude; harsh.
bronquitis *f* bronchitis.
broquel *m* shield.
brotar *vi* (*bot*) to bud, to germinate; to gush, to rush out; (*med*) to break out.
brote *m* (*bot*) shoot; (*med*) outbreak.
bruces *adv*: **a ~**, **de ~** face downwards.
bruja *f* witch.
brujería *f* witchcraft.
brujo *m* sorcerer, magician, wizard.
brújula *f* compass.
bruma *f* mist, (*mar*) sea mist.
brumoso, sa *adj* misty.
bruñido *m* polish.
bruñir *vt* to polish; to put on rouge.
brusco, ca *adj* rude; sudden; brusque.
brutal *adj* brutal, brutish; ● *m* brute.
brutalidad *f* brutality; brutal action.
bruto, ta *m* brute, beast; ~, **ta** *adj* stupid; gross; brutish.
buba *f* tumor.
bucal *adj* oral.
bucear *vi* to dive.
buceo *m* diving.
bucle *m* curl.

bucólica *f* pastoral poetry; (*fam*) food.
buche *m* craw, maw; (*fam*) guts; mouthful; crease in clothes.
budismo *m* Buddhism.
buenamente *adv* easily; willingly.
buenaventura *f* fortune, good luck.
bueno, na *adj* good, perfect; fair; fit, proper; good-looking; ¡buenos días! good morning!; ¡buenas tardes! good afternoon; ¡buenas noches! good night!; ¡~! right!
buey *m* ox, bullock.
bufa *f* joke, mock.
búfalo *m* buffalo.
bufanda *f* scarf.
bufar *vi* to choke with anger; to snort.
bufete *m* desk, writing-table; lawyer's office.
bufido *m* snorting of an animal.
bufo, fa *adj* comic; ópera ~a *f* comic opera.
bufón *m* buffoon; jester; ~, ona *adj* funny, comical.
bufonada *f* buffoonery; joke.
buhardilla *f* attic.
buho *m* owl; an unsocial person.
buhonero *m* peddler, hawker.
buitre *m* vulture.
bujía *f* candle; spark plug.
bula *f* papal bull.
bulbo *m* (*bot*) bulb.
bulboso, sa *adj* bulbous.
bulevar *m* boulevard.
bulto *m* bulk; tumor, swelling; bust; baggage.
bulla *f* confused noise, clatter; crowd; **meter ~** to make a noise.
bullicio *m* bustle; uproar.
bullicioso, sa *adj* lively, restless, noisy, busy; turbulent; boisterous.
buñuelo *m* donut; fritter.
buque *m* tonnage, capacity of a ship; hull of a ship; vessel, ship.
burbuja *f* bubble.
burbujear *vi* to bubble.
burdel *m* brothel.
burdo, da *adj* coarse, rough.
burgués, esa *adj* bourgeois.
burguesía *f* bourgeoisie.
buril *m* burin, engraver's chisel.
burla *f* trick; gibe; joke; de ~s in fun.
burlar *vt* to hoax; to defeat, to play tricks, to deceive; to frustrate; ~se *vr* to joke, to laugh at.
burlesco, ca *adj* burlesque, comical, funny.
burlón, ona *m/f* joker.
burocracia *f* bureaucracy.
burócrata *m/f* bureaucrat.
burrada *f* drove of asses; stupid action.
burro *m* ass, donkey; idiot; saw-horse.
bursátil *adj* stock-exchange.
bus *m* bus.
busca *f* search, hunt; bleeper.
buscapiés *m* crackers (fireworks).
buscar *vt* to seek, to search for; to look for *or* after; to hunt after; ● *vi* to look, to search, to seek.
buscavidas *m* prying person, busybody.
buscón *m* petty thief, small-time crook.
búsqueda *f* search.
busto *m* bust.
butaca *f* armchair; seat.
butano *m* butane.
butifarra *f* catalan sausage.
buzo *m* diver.
buzón *m* mailbox; conduit, canal; cover of a jar.

C

cabal *adj* just, exact; right; complete, accomplished.
cábalas *fpl* intrigue.
cabalgada *f* cavalcade; (*mil*) cavalry raid.
cabalgadura *f* mount-horse, beast of burden.
cabalgar *vi* to ride, to go riding.
cabalgata *f* procession.
cabalístico, ca *adj* cabalistic.
caballa *f* mackerel.
caballar *adj* equine.
caballería *f* mount, steed; cavalry; cavalry horse; chivalry; knighthood.
caballeriza *f* stable; stud; stable hands.
caballerizo *m* groom of a stable.
caballero *m* knight; gentleman; rider; horseman; horse soldier; ~ andante knight errant.
caballerosidad *f* chivalry.
caballeroso, sa *adj* noble, gentlemanlike.
caballete *m* ridge of a roof; painter's easel; trestle; bridge (of the nose).
caballo *m* horse; (at chess) knight; queen (in cards); a ~ on horseback.
cabaña *f* hut, cabin; hovel; livestock; balk (in billiards).
cabaré *m* cabaret.
cabecear *vi* to nod with sleep; to shake one's head; (*mar*) to pitch.
cabeceo *m* nod, shaking of the head.
cabecera *f* headboard; head; far end; pillow; headline; vignette.
cabecilla *m* ringleader.
cabellera *f* head of hair; wig; tail of a comet.
cabello *m* hair.
cabelludo, da *adj* hairy, shaggy.
caber *vt*, *vi* to contain, to fit.
cabestrillo *m* sling, splint.
cabestro *m* halter; bell-ox.
cabeza *f* head; chief; leader; main town, chief center.
cabezada *f* butt; nod, shake of the head.
cabezal *m* pillow; compress.
cabezón *m* collar of a shirt; opening in a garment for the head.
cabezudo, da *adj* big-headed; pig-headed.
cabida *f* room, capacity; **tener ~ con una persona** to have influence with someone.
cabildo *m* chapter (of a church); meeting of a chapter; corporation of a town.
cabina *f* cabin; telephone booth.
cabizbajo, ja, cabizcaído, da *adj* crestfallen; pensive; thoughtful.
cable *m* cable, lead, wire.
cabo *m* end, extremity; cape, headland; (*mar*) cable, rope.
cabra *f* goat.
cabrero *m* goatherd.
cabrío, a *adj* goatish.
cabriola *f* caper; gambol.
cabritilla *f* kidskin.
cabrito *m* kid.
cabrón *m* cuckold; ¡~! (*fam*) bastard! (*sl*).
cacahuete *m* peanut.
cacao *m* (*bot*) cacao tree; cocoa.
cacarear *vi* to crow; to brag, to boast.
cacareo *m* crowing of a cock, cackling of a hen; boast, brag.
cacería *f* hunting-party.
cacerola *f* pan, saucepan; casserole.
cacique *m* chief; local party boss.
caco *m* pickpocket; coward.
cacofonía *f* harsh unharmonious sound.
cacto *m* cactus.
cachalote *m* sperm whale.
cacharro *m* coarse earthen pot.
cachear *vt* to frisk.

cachemir *m* cashmere.
cacheo *m* frisking.
cachete *m* cheek; slap in the face.
cachiporra *f* truncheon.
cachivache *m* pot; piece of junk.
cacho *m* slice, piece (lemons, oranges, *etc*); horn.
cachondeo *m* (*fam*) farce.
cachondo, da *adj* randy; funny.
cachorro, ra *m/f* puppy; cub (of any animal).
cada *pn* every; each.
cadalso *m* scaffold.
cadáver *m* corpse, cadaver.
cadavérico, ca *adj* cadaverous.
cadena *f* chain; series, link; radio *or* TV network.
cadencia *f* cadence.
cadente *adj* harmonious.
cadera *f* hip.
cadete *m* (*mil*) cadet.
caducar *vi* to become senile; to expire, to lapse; to deteriorate.
caducidad *f* expiry.
caduco, ca *adj* worn out; decrepit; perishable; expired, lapsed.
caer *vi* to fall; to tumble down; to lapse; to happen; to die; ~se *vr* to fall down.
café *m* coffee; café, coffee house.
cafetera *f* coffee pot.
cafetería *f* café.
cafetero, ra *m/f* coffee merchant; café owner.
cafre *adj* savage, inhuman; rude.
cagar *vi* (*fam*) to have a shit (*sl*).
caída *f* fall, falling; slope, descent.
caimán *m* caiman, alligator.
caja *f* box, case; casket; cashbox; cash desk; supermarket check-out; ~ de ahorros savings bank; ~ de cambios gearbox.
cajero, ra *m/f* cashier, teller.
cajetilla *f* packet.
cajón *m* chest of drawers; locker.
cal *f* lime; ~ viva quick lime.
cala *f* creek, small bay; small piece of melon, *etc*; (*mar*) hold; dipstick.
calabacín *m* marrow, zucchini.
calabaza *f* pumpkin, squash.
calabozo *m* prison; cell.
calada *f* soaking; lowering of nets; puff, drag; swoop.
calado *m* openwork in metal, wood *or* linen.
calafatear *vt* (*mar*) to calk.
calamar *m* squid.
calambre *m* cramp.
calamidad *f* calamity, disaster.
calamitoso, sa *adj* calamitous, unfortunate.
calandria *f* calendra lark.
calaña *f* model, pattern.
calar *vt* to soak, to drench; to penetrate, to pierce; to see through; to lower; ~se *vr* to stall (of a car).
calavera *f* skull; madcap.
calaverada *f* ridiculous, foolish action.
calcañar *m* heel.
calcar *vt* to trace, to copy.
calcáreo, rea *adj* calcareous.
calceta *f* (knee-length) stocking.
calcetín *m* sock.
calcinar *vt* to calcine.
calcio *m* calcium.
calco *m* tracing.
calcomanía *f* transfer.
calculable *adj* calculable.
calculadora *f* calculator.
calcular *vt* to calculate, to reckon, to compute.
cálculo *m* calculation, estimate; calculus; (*med*) gallstone.
caldear *vt* to weld; to warm, to heat.

caldera *f* kettle, boiler; las ~s de Pero Botero (*fam*) hell.
calderada *f* stew.
calderilla *f* holy water fount; small change.
caldero *m* small boiler.
caldo *m* stock, broth.
caldoso, sa *adj* having too much broth *or* gravy.
calefacción *f* heating.
calendario *m* calendar.
calentador *m* heater.
calentar *vt* to warm; to heat; ~se *vr* to grow hot; to dispute.
calentura *f* fever.
calenturiento, ta *adj* feverish.
calesa *f* calash, cab.
calibre *m* caliber; (*fig*) caliber.
calidad *f* grade, quality, condition; kind.
cálido, da *adj* hot; (*fig*) warm.
caliente *adj* hot; fiery; en ~ in the heat of the moment.
califa *m* caliph.
califato *m* caliphate.
calificación *f* qualification; grade.
calificar *vt* to qualify; to assess, to mark; ~se *vr* to register as a voter.
caligrafía *f* calligraphy.
cáliz *m* chalice.
calizo, za *adj* calcareous.
calma *f* calm; calmness.
calmante *m* (*med*) sedative.
calmar *vt* to calm, to quiet, to pacify; ● *vi* to become calm.
calmoso, sa *adj* calm; tranquil.
calor *m* heat, warmth; ardor, passion.
caloría *f* calorie.
calumnia *f* calumny, slander.
calumniar *vt* to slander.
calumnioso, sa *adj* slanderous.
caluroso, sa *adj* warm, hot; lively.
calva *f* bald patch.
calvario *m* Calvary; (*fig*) debts *pl*.
calvicie *f* baldness.
calvinismo *m* Calvinism.
calvinista *m* Calvinist.
calvo, va *adj* bald; bare, barren.
calza *f* wedge.
calzado *m* footwear.
calzador *m* shoehorn.
calzar *vt* to put on shoes; to wear; to stop a wheel; ~se *vr* to put on one's shoes.
calzón *m* shorts; pants; panties.
calzonazos *m invar* stupid guy; es un ~ he is a weak-willed guy.
calzoncillos *mpl* underpants, shorts *pl*.
callado, da *adj* silent, reserved, quiet.
callandico *adv* softly, silently.
callar *vi*, ~se *vr* to be silent, to keep quiet.
calle *f* street; road.
calleja *f* lane, narrow passage.
callejear *vi* to loiter about the streets.
callejero, ra *adj* loitering.
callejón *m* alley.
callejuela *f* lane, narrow passage; subterfuge.
callista *m/f* chiropodist.
callo *m* corn; callus; ~s *pl* tripe.
callosidad *f* callosity.
calloso, sa *adj* callous; horny.
cama *f* bed, couch; hacer la ~ to make the bed.
camada *f* litter (of animals); ~ de ladrones gang of thieves.
camafeo *m* cameo.
camaleón *m* chameleon.
camandulero, ra *adj* prudish; hypocritical; sly, tricky.
cámara *f* hall; chamber; room; camera; cine camera.
camarada *m/f* comrade, companion.
camarera *f* waitress; maid.
camarero *m* waiter.

camarilla f clique; lobby.
camarín m dressing room; elevator car.
camarón m shrimp.
camarote m berth, cabin.
cambalache m exchange, swap.
cambalachear vt to exchange, to swap.
cambiable adj changeable, variable; interchangeable.
cambiar vt to exchange; to change; ● vi to change, to alter; ~se vr to move house.
cambio m change, exchange; rate of exchange; bureau de change.
cambista m exchange broker.
camelar vt to flirt with.
camello m camel.
camilla f couch; cot; stretcher.
caminante m/f traveler, walker.
caminar vi to travel; to walk, to go.
caminata f long walk; hike.
camino m road; way.
camión m truck.
camioneta f van.
camisa f shirt; chemise.
camiseta f T-shirt, vest.
camisón m nightgown.
camorra f quarrel, dispute.
camorrista m/f quarrelsome person.
campamento m (mil) encampment, camp.
campana f bell.
campanada f peal of a bell; (fig) scandal.
campanario m belfry.
campaneo m bellringing, chime.
campanero m bell founder; bellringer.
campanilla f handbell; (med) uvula.
campante adj excelling, outstanding; smug.
campánula f bellflower.
campaña f countryside; level country, plain; (mil) campaign.
campear vi to go out to pasture; to work in the fields.
campechano, na adj open.
campeón, ona m/f champion.
campeonato m championship.
campesino, na, campestre adj rural.
campiña f flat tract of cultivated farmland.
camping m camping, campsite.
campo m country; field; camp; ground; pitch.
camuflaje m camouflage.
canal m channel, canal.
canalizar vt to canalize.
canalón m large gutter.
canalla f mob, rabble.
canana f cartridge belt.
canapé f couch, sofa.
canario m canary.
canas fpl gray hair; **peinar** ~ to grow old.
canasta f basket, hamper.
canastilla f small basket.
canasto m large basket.
cancel m storm door.
cancelación f cancellation.
cancelar vt to cancel; to write off.
cáncer m cancer.
Cáncer m Cancer (sign of the zodiac).
canceroso, sa adj cancerous.
canciller m chancellor; foreign minister.
canción f song.
cancionero m songbook.
cancha f (tennis) court.
candado m padlock.
candela f candle.
candelabro m candlestick.
candente adj red-hot.
candidato, ta m/f candidate.
cándido, da adj simple, naïve; white, snowy.

candil m oil lamp.
candilejas fpl footlights pl.
candor m candor, innocence.
canela f cinnamon.
canelón m icicle.
cangrejo m crawfish, crab.
canguro m kangaroo.
caníbal m/f cannibal, man-eater.
canica f marble.
canícula f dog days pl.
canijo, ja adj weak, sickly.
canilla f shinbone; arm-bone; tap of a cask; spool.
canino, na adj canine; **hambre** ~a f ravenous hunger.
canje m exchange.
canjear vt to exchange.
cano, na adj gray-haired; white-haired.
canoa f canoe.
canon m canon; tax; royalty; rent.
canónico, ca adj canonical.
canónigo m canon, prebendary.
canonización f canonization.
canonizar vt to canonize.
canoso, sa adj gray-haired, white-haired.
cansado, da adj weary, tired; tedious, tiresome.
cansancio m tiredness, fatigue.
cansar vt to tire, to tire out; to bore; ~se vr to get tired, to grow weary.
cantable adj suitable for singing.
cantante m/f singer.
cantar m song; ● vt to sing; to chant; ● vi to sing; to chirp.
cántara f pitcher.
cantarín, ina m/f someone who sings a lot.
cántaro m pitcher; jug; **llover a** ~s to rain heavily, to pour.
cantera f quarry.
cantero m quarryman.
cántico m canticle.
cantidad f quantity; number; amount.
cantimplora f water bottle; hip flask.
cantina f buffet, refreshment room; canteen; cellar; snack bar; bar.
cantinela f ballad, song.
canto m stone; singing; song; edge.
cantón m corner; canton.
cantonear vi to loaf around.
cantor, ra m/f singer.
canuto m (fam) joint (sl), marijuana cigarette.
caña f cane, reed; stalk; shinbone; glass of beer; ~ **dulce** sugar cane.
cañada f gully; glen; sheep-walk.
cáñamo m hemp.
cañamón m hemp seed.
cañaveral m reedbed.
cañería f conduit of water, water pipe.
caño m tube, pipe; sewer.
cañón m tube, pipe; barrel; gun; canyon.
cañonazo m gunshot; (fig) bombshell.
cañonear vt to shell, to bombard.
cañoneo m shelling, gunfire.
cañonera f gunboat.
caoba f mahogany.
caos m chaos; confusion.
capa f cloak; cape; layer, stratum; cover; pretext.
capacidad f capacity; extent; talent.
capacho m hamper; big basket.
capar vt to geld; to castrate; (fig) to curtail.
caparazón m caparison.
capataz m foreman, overseer.
capaz adj capacious, capable, spacious, roomy.
capazo m large basket; carrycot.
capcionar vt to seize, to arrest.
capcioso, sa adj wily, deceitful.

capear *vt* to flourish one's cloak in front of a bull; ● *vi* (*mar*) to ride out, to weather.

capellán *m* chaplain.

capeo *m* challenging of a bull with a cloak.

caperuza *f* hood.

capilar *adj* capillary.

capilla *f* hood; cowl; chapel.

capirote *m* hood.

capital *m* capital; capital sum; ● *f* capital, capital city; ● *adj* capital; principal.

capitalismo *m* capitalism.

capitalista *m/f* capitalist.

capitalizar *vt* to capitalize.

capitán *m* captain.

capitana *f* flagship; (woman) captain (in sport).

capitanear *vt* to captain; to command.

capitanía *f* captaincy.

capitel *m* spire over the dome of a church; capital (of a column).

capitolio *m* capitol.

capitulación *f* capitulation; agreement; ~ ones *pl* marriage contract.

capitular *vi* to come to terms, to make an agreement.

capítulo *m* chapter of a cathedral; chapter (of a book).

capó *m* (*auto*) hood.

capón *m* capon.

caporal *m* chief, ringleader.

capota *f* hat, bonnet; (*auto*) top.

capote *m* greatcoat; bullfighter's cloak.

Capricornio *m* Capricorn (sign of the zodiac).

capricho *m* caprice, whim, fancy.

caprichoso, sa *adj* capricious, whimsical; obstinate.

cápsula *f* capsule.

captar *vt* to captivate; to understand; (*rad*) to tune in to, to receive.

captura *f* capture, arrest.

capturar *vt* to capture.

capucha *f* circumflex; cap, cowl, hood of a cloak.

capuchino *m* Capuchin monk; (**café**) ~ cappuccino (coffee).

capullo *m* cocoon of a silkworm; rosebud; coarse cloth made of spun silk.

caqui *m, adj* khaki.

cara *f* face; appearance; ~ a ~ face to face.

carabina *f* carbine, rifle.

carabinero *m* carabineer.

caracol *m* snail; seashell; spiral.

caracola *f* shell.

caracolear *vi* to prance about (of a horse).

carácter *m* character; quality; condition; hand-writing.

característico, ca *adj* characteristic.

caracterizar *vt* to characterize.

caradura *m/f*: es un ~ he's got a nerve.

caramba *excl* well!

carámbano *m* icicle.

carambola *f* cannon (at billiards); trick.

caramelo *m* candy.

caramente *adv* dearly.

caramillo *m* small flute; piece of gossip.

carantoña *f* hideous mask; dressed-up old woman; ~s *pl* caresses.

carátula *f* pasteboard mask; la ~ the stage.

caravana *f* caravan; tailback (of a car).

caray *excl* well!

carbón *m* coal; charcoal; carbon; carbon paper.

carbonada *f* grill; kind of pancake.

carboncillo *m* charcoal.

carbonera *f* coal tip, coal mine.

carbonería *f* coalyard.

carbonero *m* coal merchant; collier.

carbónico, ca *adj* carbonic.

carbonilla *f* coaldust.

carbonizar *vt* to carbonize.

carbono *m* (*quim*) carbon.

carbunclo, carbunco *m* carbuncle.

carburador *m* carburettor.

carcaj *m* quiver.

carcajada *f* (loud) laugh.

carcamal *m* nickname for old people.

cárcel *f* prison; jail.

carcelero *m* warder, jailor.

carcoma *f* deathwatch beetle; woodworm; anxious concern.

carcomer *vt* to gnaw, to corrode; ~se *vr* to grow worm-eaten.

carcomido, da *adj* worm-eaten.

cardar *vt* to card wool.

cardenal *m* cardinal; cardinal bird; (*med*) bruise, weal.

cardenalicio, cia *adj* belonging to a cardinal.

cárdeno, na *adj* purple; livid.

cardíaco, ca *adj* cardiac; ● *compd* heart.

cardinal *adj* cardinal, principal.

cardo *m* thistle.

carear *vt* to bring face to face; to compare; ~se *vr* to come face to face.

carecer *vi*: ~ de to want, to lack.

carencia *f* lack.

careo *m* confrontation.

carero, ra *adj* in the habit of selling things at a high price.

carestía *f* scarcity, want; famine.

careta *f* pasteboard mask.

carga *f* load, freight; cargo; (*mil*) charge; duty, obligation, tax.

cargadero *m* loading place.

cargado, da *adj* loaded; (*elec*) live.

cargador *m* loader; carrier; longshoreman.

cargamento *m* cargo.

cargar *vt* to load, to burden; to charge; ● *vi* to charge; to load (up); to lean.

cargo *m* burden, loading; employment, post; office; charge, care; obligation; accusation.

carguero *m* freighter.

cariarse *vr* to become decayed.

caricatura *f* caricature.

caricia *f* caress.

caridad *f* charity.

caries *f* (*med*) tooth decay, caries.

carilargo, ga *adj* long-faced.

carilla *f* side (of paper); beekeeper's mask.

cariño *m* fondness, tenderness; love.

cariñoso, sa *adj* affectionate; fond; loving.

caritativo, va *adj* charitable.

cariz *m* look.

carmelita *adj, m/f* Carmelite.

carmesí *adj, m* crimson.

carmín *m* carmine; rouge; lipstick.

carnada *f* bait, lure.

carnal *adj* carnal, of the flesh; primo ~ first cousin.

carnaval *m* carnival.

carne *f* flesh; meat; pulp (of fruit).

carné, carnet *m* driver's license; ~ de identidad identity card.

carnero *m* sheep, mutton.

carnicería *f* butcher's shop; carnage, slaughter.

carnicero, ra *m/f* butcher; ● *adj* carnivorous.

carnívoro, ra *adj* carnivorous.

carnoso, sa, carnudo *adj* beefy, fat; fleshy.

caro, ra *adj* dear; affectionate; expensive; ● *adv* dearly.

carótida *f* carotid artery.

carpa *f* carp (fish); tent.

carpeta *f* table cover; folder, file, portfolio.

carpintería *f* carpentry; carpenter's shop.

carpintero *m* carpenter.

carraca *f* carrack (ship); rattle.

carrasca *f*, carrasco *m* evergreen oak.

carraspera *f* hoarseness.

carrera f career; course; race; run, running; route, journey; a ~ **abierta**, at full speed.

carreta f long narrow cart.

carrete m reel, spool, bobbin.

carretera f highway.

carretero m carter, cartwright.

carretilla f carter; truck; trolley; go-cart; squib, cracker; wheel barrow.

carretón m small cart.

carril m lane (of highway); furrow.

carrillo m cheek; pulley.

carro m cart; automobile.

carrocería f bodywork, coachwork.

carromato m covered wagon, (gipsy) caravan.

carroña f carrion.

carroza f state-coach; (mar) awning.

carruaje m carriage; vehicle.

carrusel m merry-go-round.

carta f letter; map; document; playing card; menu; ~ **blanca** carte blanche; ~ **credencial** o **de creencia** credentials pl; ~ **certificada** registered letter; ~ **de crédito** credit card; ~ **verde** green card.

carta-bomba f letter-bomb.

cartapacio m notebook; folder.

cartel m placard, poster; wall chart; cartel.

cartera f satchel; purse; briefcase.

carterista m/f pickpocket.

cartero m mailman.

cartilaginoso, sa adj cartilaginous.

cartílago m cartilage.

cartilla f first reading book, primer.

cartón m cardboard, pasteboard; cartoon.

cartuchera f (mil) cartridge belt.

cartucho m (mil) cartridge.

cartuja m Carthusian order.

cartujo m Carthusian monk.

cartulina f card, pass; thin cardboard.

casa f house; home; firm, company; ~ **de campo** country house; ~ **de moneda** mint; ~ **de huéspedes** boarding house.

casaca f coat.

casación f abrogation.

casadero, ra adj marriageable.

casado, da adj married.

casamentero, ra m/f marriage-maker, matchmaker.

casamiento m marriage, wedding.

casar vt to marry; to couple; to abrogate; to annul; ~**se** vr to marry, to get married.

cascabel m small bell; rattlesnake.

cascada f cascade, waterfall.

cascanueces m invar nutcracker.

cascar vt to crack, to break into pieces; (fam) to beat; ~**se** vr to be broken open.

cáscara f rind, peel, husk, shell; bark.

cascarón m eggshell.

casco m skull; helmet; fragment; shard; hulk of a ship; crown of a hat; hoof; empty bottle, returnable bottle.

cascote m rubbish, fragments of material used in building.

casera f landlady.

caserío m country house; hamlet.

casero m landlord; janitor; ~, **ra** adj domestic; household; home-made.

caset(t)e m cassette; ● f cassette-player.

casi adv almost, nearly; ~ **nada** next to nothing; ~ **nunca** hardly ever, almost never.

casilla f hut, cabin; theater box office; square (on a chess board); pigeonhole, compartment.

casillero m (set of) pigeonholes; baggage locker.

casino m club, social club.

caso m case, occurrence, event; hap, casuality; occasion; (gr)

case; **en ese** ~ in that case; **en todo** ~ in any case; ~ **que** in case.

casorio m unwise marriage.

caspa f dandruff; scurf.

casquete m helmet.

casquillo m bottle top; tip, cap; point.

casta f caste, race, lineage; breed; kind, quality.

castaña f chestnut; demijohn.

castañar m chestnut grove.

castañetear vi to play the castanets.

castaño m chestnut tree; ~, **ña** adj chestnut (colored), brown.

castañuela f castanet.

castellano m Castilian, Spanish.

castidad f chastity.

castigar vt to castigate, to punish; to afflict.

castigo m punishment; correction; penalty.

castillo m castle.

castizo, za adj pure, thoroughbred.

casto, ta adj pure, chaste.

castor m beaver.

castrar vt to geld, to castrate; to prune; to cut the honeycombs out of beehives.

casual adj casual, accidental.

casualidad f chance, accident.

casucha f hovel; slum.

casulla f chasuble.

cata f tasting.

catacumbas f pl catacombs pl.

catador, ra m/f wine tester.

catadura f looks pl, face.

catalejo m telescope.

catalizador m catalyst.

catálogo m catalog.

cataplasma f poultice.

catapulta f catapult.

catar vt to taste; to inspect, to examine; to look at; to esteem.

catarata f (med) cataract; waterfall.

catarro m catarrh.

catarroso, sa adj catarrhal.

catástrofe f catastrophe.

catavino m small cup for tasting wine; ~**s** m/f invar winetaster; tippler.

catecismo m catechism.

cátedra f professor's chair.

catedral adj, f cathedral.

catedrático, ca m/f professor of a university.

categoría f category; rank.

categórico, ca adj categorical, decisive.

catequismo m catechism.

caterva f mob.

catolicismo m catholicism.

católico, ca adj, m/f catholic.

catorce adj, m fourteen.

catre m cot.

cauce m riverbed; (fig) channel.

caución f caution; security, bail.

caucionar vt to prevent, to guard against; (jur) to bail.

caucho m rubber; tire.

caudal m volume, flow; property, wealth; plenty.

caudaloso, sa adj carrying much water (of rivers); wealthy, rich.

caudillo m leader.

causa f cause; motive, reason; law-suit; a ~ **de** considering, because of.

causal adj causal.

causante m/f originator; ● adj causing, originating.

causar vt to cause, to produce; to occasion.

cáustico m caustic; ~, **ca** adj caustic.

cautela f caution, cautiousness.

cauteloso, sa adj cautious, wary.

cauterizar vt (med) to cauterize; to apply a drastic remedy to.

cautivar vt to take prisoner in war; to captivate, to charm.

cautiverio m captivity.

cautividad f captivity.

cautivo, va adj, m/f captive.

cauto, ta adj cautious, wary.

cava f digging and earthing of vines; wine cellar; sparkling wine.

cavar vt to dig up, to excavate; ● vi to delve into; to think profoundly.

caverna f cavern, cave.

cavernoso, sa adj cavernous.

cavidad f cavity, hollow.

cavilación f deep thought.

cavilar vt to ponder, to consider carefully.

caviloso, sa adj obsessed; suspicious.

cayada f, cayado m shepherd's crook.

caza f hunting; shooting; chase; game; ● m fighter-plane.

cazador, ra m/f hunter, huntsman; ~ furtivo poacher.

cazamoscas m invar flycatcher (bird).

cazar vt to chase, to hunt; to catch.

cazo m saucepan; ladle.

cazuela f casserole; pan.

cazurro, rra adj silent, taciturn.

cebada f barley.

cebar vt to feed animals, to fatten.

cebo m feed, food; bait, lure; priming.

cebolla f onion; bulb.

cebolleta f scallion.

cebollino m onion seed; chive.

cebón m fattened pig.

cebra f zebra.

cecear vt to pronounce s the same as c; to lisp.

cecina f dried meat; salt beef.

cedazo m sieve, strainer.

ceder vt to hand over; to transfer, to make over; to yield, to give up; ● vi to submit, to comply, to give in; to diminish, to grow less.

cedro m cedar.

cédula f certificate, document; slip of paper; bill; ~ de cambio bill of exchange.

cegar vi to grow blind; ● vt to blind; to block up.

cegato, ta adj short-sighted.

ceguera f blindness.

ceja f eyebrow; edging of clothes; (mus) bridge of a stringed instrument; brow of a hill.

cejar vi to go backward; to slacken, to give in.

celada f helmet; ambush; trick.

celador, ora m/f watchman.

celda f cell.

celdilla f cell; cavity.

celebración f celebration; praise.

celebrar vt to celebrate; to praise; ~ misa to say mass.

célebre adj famous, renowned; witty, funny.

celebridad f celebrity, fame.

celeridad f speed, velocity.

celeste adj heavenly; sky-blue.

celestial adj heavenly; delightful.

celibato m celibacy.

célibe m/f bachelor; spinster.

celo m zeal; rut (in animals).

celofán m cellophane.

celosía f lattice of a window.

celoso, sa adj zealous; jealous.

célula f cell.

celular adj cellular.

celuloide m celluloid.

cementerio m graveyard.

cemento m cement.

cena f supper.

cenador m arbor.

cenegal m quagmire.

cenagoso, sa adj miry, marshy.

cenar vt to have for dinner; ● vi to have supper, to have dinner.

cencerro m jangle, clatter.

cenicero m ashtray.

ceniciento, ta adj ash-colored.

cenit m zenith.

ceniza f ashes pl; miércoles de ~ Ash Wednesday.

censo m census; tax; ground rent; ~ electoral electoral roll.

censor, ra m/f censor, reviewer, critic.

censura f censorship; critical review; censure, blame.

censurar vt to review, to criticize; to censure, to blame.

centella f lightning; spark.

centellear vi to sparkle.

centena f hundred.

centenadas adv: a ~ by hundreds.

centenar m hundred.

centenario, ia adj centenary; ● m centennial.

centeno m rye.

centésimo, ma adj, m hundredth.

centígrado m centigrade.

centímetro m centimeter.

céntimo m cent.

centinela f sentry, guard.

central adj central; ● f head office, headquarters; (telephone) exchange.

centralización m centralization.

centralizar vt to centralize.

centrista adj centrist.

céntrico adj central.

centrífugo, ga adj centrifugal.

centro m center; ~ comercial shopping mall.

centuplicar vt to increase a hundredfold.

céntuplo, pla adj centuple, hundredfold.

ceñido, da adj tight-fitting; sparing, frugal.

ceñir vt to surround, to circle; to abbreviate, to abridge; to fit tightly.

ceño m frown.

ceñudo, da adj frowning, grim.

cepa f stock of a vine; origin of a family.

cepillar vt to brush.

cepillo m brush; plane (tool).

cepo m branch, bough; trap; snare; poor box.

cera f wax; ~s pl honeycomb.

cerámica f pottery.

cerca f enclosure; fence; ~s mpl objects placed in the foreground of a painting; ● adv near, at hand, close by; ~ de close, near.

cercanías fpl outskirts.

cercano, na adj near, close by, neighboring, adjoining.

cercar vt to enclose, to circle; to fence in.

cerciorar vt to assure, to ascertain, to affirm; ~se vr to find out.

cerco m enclosure; fence; (mil) siege.

cerdo m pig.

cereal m cereal.

cerebelo m cerebellum.

cerebro m brain.

ceremonia f ceremony.

ceremonial adj, m ceremonial.

ceremonioso, sa adj ceremonious.

cereza f cherry.

cerezo m cherry tree.

cerilla f waxtaper; ear wax; ~s pl matches, safety matches.

cerner vt to sift; ● vi to bud and blossom; to drizzle; ~se vr to hover, to swagger.

cernido m sifting.

cero m nothing, zero.

cerquita adv close by.

cerrado, da adj closed, shut; locked; overcast, cloudy; having a broad accent.

cerradura f locking-up; lock.

cerrajería f trade of a locksmith; locksmith's shop.

cerrajero *m* locksmith.
cerrar *vt*, *vi* to close, to shut; to block up; to lock; ~ **la cuenta** to close an account; ~**se** *vr* to close; to heal; to cloud over.
cerril *adj* mountainous, rough; wild, untamed.
cerro *m* hill; neck of an animal; backbone; combed flax *or* hemp; **en ~** bareback.
cerrojo *m* bolt of a door.
certamen *m* competition, contest.
certero *adj* accurate; well-aimed.
certeza, certidumbre *f* certainty.
certificación *f* certificate.
certificado *m* certificate; ~, **da** *adj* registered (of a letter).
certificar *vt* to certify, to affirm.
cervato *m* fawn.
cervecería *f* bar, brewery.
cervecero *m* brewer.
cerveza *m* beer.
cerviz *f* nape of the neck; cervix.
cesación *f* cessation, stoppage.
cesar *vt* to cease, to stop; to fire (*sl*); to remove from office; • *vi* to cease, to stop; to quit, to retire.
cese *m* suspension; dismissal.
cesión *f* cession, transfer.
césped *m* grass, lawn.
cesta *f* basket, pannier.
cestería *f* basket shop; basketwork.
cesto *m* (large) basket.
cetrino, na *adj* greenish-yellow; sallow; jaundiced, melancholic.
cetro *m* scepter.
cianuro *m* cyanide.
ciática *f* sciatica.
ciático, ca *adj* sciatic.
cicatear *vi* to be stingy, to be mean.
cicatriz *f* scar.
cicatrizar *vt* to heal.
ciclismo *m* cycling.
ciclista *m/f* cyclist.
ciclo *m* cycle.
ciclón *m* cyclone.
cicuta *f* (*bot*) hemlock.
ciegamente *adv* blindly.
ciego, ga *adj* blind.
cielo *m* sky; heaven; atmosphere; climate.
cien *adj*, *m* a hundred.
ciénaga *f* swamp.
ciencia *f* science.
cieno *m* mud, mire.
cienpiés *m invar* centipede.
científico, ca *adj* scientific.
ciento *adj*, *m* a hundred.
cierne *m*: **en ~** in blossom; **estar en ~** to be in its infancy.
cierto, ta *adj* certain, sure; right, correct; **por ~** certainly.
cierva *f* hind.
ciervo *m* deer, hart, stag; ~ **volante** stag beetle.
cierzo *m* cold northerly wind.
cifra *f* number, numeral; quantity; cipher; abbreviation.
cifrar *vt* to write in code; to abridge.
cigala *f* langoustine.
cigarra *f* cicada.
cigarrera *m* cigar case.
cigarrillo *m* cigarette.
cigarro *m* cigar; cigarette.
cigüeña *f* stork; crank of a bell.
cilicio *m* hair shirt.
cilíndrico, ca *adj* cylindrical.
cilindro *m* cylinder.
cima *f* summit; peak; top of trees.
címbalo *m* cymbal.
cimborio, cimborrio *m* cupola, dome.
cimbr(e)ar *vt* to shake, to swish, to swing; ~ **a uno** to give one a clout (with a stick); ~**se** *vr* to sway.

cimentado *m* refinement of gold.
cimentar *vt* to lay the foundation of a building; to found; to refine metals; to strengthen, to cement.
cimiento *m* foundation, groundwork of a building; basis, origin.
cinc *m* zinc.
cincel *m* chisel.
cincelar *vt* to chisel, to engrave.
cinco *adj*, *m* five.
cincuenta *adj*, *m* fifty.
cine *m* cinema.
cineasta *m/f* movie maker.
cinematográfico, ca *adj* cinematographic.
cincha *f* girth.
cinchar *vt* to girth.
cínico, ca *adj* cynical.
cinismo *m* cynicism.
cinta *f* band, ribbon; reel.
cinto *m* belt.
cintura *f* waist.
cinturón *m* belt, girdle; (*fig*) zone; ~ **de seguridad** seatbelt.
ciprés *m* cypress tree.
circo *m* circus.
circuito *m* circuit; circumference.
circulación *f* circulation; traffic.
circular *adj* circular, circulatory; • *vt* to circulate; • *vi* (*aut*) to drive.
círculo *m* circle; (*fig*) scope, compass.
circuncidar *vt* to circumcize.
circuncisión *f* circumcision.
circundar *vt* to surround, to encircle.
circunferencia *f* circumference.
circunflejo, ja *adj*: **acento ~** *m* circumflex.
circunscribir *vt* to circumscribe.
circunscripción *f* division; electoral district.
circunspección *f* circumspection.
circunspecto, ta *adj* circumspect, cautious.
circunstancia *f* circumstance.
circunstante *m/f* bystander.
circunvalacion *f*: **carretera de ~** bypass.
cirio *m* wax candle.
ciruela *f* plum; ~ **pasa** prune.
ciruelo *m* plum tree.
cirugía *f* surgery.
cirujano *m* surgeon.
cisco *m* coaldust.
cisma *m* schism; discord.
cismático, ca *adj* schismatic.
cisne *m* swan.
cisterna *f* cistern.
cisura *f* incision.
cita *f* quotation; appointment, meeting.
citación *f* quotation; (*jur*) summons.
citar *vt* to make an appointment with; to quote; (*jur*) to summon.
cítrico, ca *adj* citric; ~**s** *mpl* citric fruits.
ciudad *f* city, town.
ciudadanía *f* citizenship.
ciudadano, na *m/f* citizen; • *adj* civic.
ciudadela *f* citadel.
cívico, ca *adj* civic.
civil *adj* civil; polite, courteous; • *m* Civil Guard; civilian.
civilización *f* civilization.
civilizar *vt* to civilize.
civismo *m* public spirit, patriotism.
cizaña *f* discord.
clamar *vt* to cry out for.
clamor *m* clamor, outcry; peal of bells.
clamoroso, sa *adj* noisy, loud.
clandestino, na *adj* clandestine, secret, concealed.
clara *f* egg-white.
claraboya *f* skylight.

clarear *vi* to dawn; ~**se** *vr* to be transparent.
clarete *adj, m* claret.
claridad *f* brightness, clearness.
clarificar *vt* to brighten; to clarify.
clarín *m* bugle; bugler.
clarinete *m* clarinet; ● *m/f* clarinetist.
claro, ra *adj* clear, bright; evident, manifest; ● *m* opening; clearing (in a wood); skylight.
claroscuro *adj* light and shade (in painting).
clase *f* class, rank; order.
clásico, ca *adj* classical.
clasificación *f* classification.
clasificar *vt* to classify.
claudicar *vi* to limp; to act deceitfully; to back down.
claustro *m* cloister; faculty (of a university); womb, uterus.
cláusula *f* clause.
clausura *f* closure, closing.
clavado, da *adj* tight-fitting; nailed.
clavar *vt* to nail; to fasten in, to force in; to drive in; (*fam*) to cheat, to deceive; ~**se** *vr* to penetrate.
clave *f* key; (*mus*) clef; ● *m* harpsichord.
clavel *m* (*bot*) carnation.
clavetear *vt* to decorate with studs.
clavicordio *m* clavichord.
clavícula *f* clavicle, collar bone.
clavija *f* pin, peg.
clavo *m* nail; corn (on the feet); clove.
claxon *m* horn.
clemencia *f* clemency.
clemente *adj* clement, merciful.
cleptómano, na *m/f* kleptomaniac.
clerecía *f* clergy.
clerical *adj* clerical.
clérigo *m* priest; clergyman.
clero *m* clergy.
cliché *m* cliché; negative (of a photo).
cliente *m/f* client.
clientela *f* clientèle.
clima *m* climate.
climatizado, da *adj* air-conditioned.
clínica *f* clinic; private hospital.
clínico, ca *adj* clinical.
clip *m* paper clip.
cloaca *f* sewer.
cloquear *vi* to cluck.
club *m* club.
clueca *f* broody hen.
coacción *f* coercion, compulsion.
coactivo, va *adj* coercive.
coadjutor, ra *m/f* coadjutor, assistant.
coagular *vt*, ~**se** *vr* to coagulate; to curdle.
coágulo *m*: ~ **sanguíneo** blood clot.
coalición *f* coalition.
coartada *f* (*jur*) alibi.
coartar *vt* to limit, to restrict, to restrain.
cobalto *m* cobalt.
cobarde *adj* cowardly, timid.
cobardía *f* cowardice.
cobaya *f* guinea pig.
cobertizo *m* small shed; shelter.
cobertura *f* cover; coverage; bedspread.
cobijar *vt* to cover, to shelter.
cobra *f* cobra.
cobrador, ra *m/f* conductor/conductress; collector.
cobrar *vt* to recover; ~**se** *vr* (*med*) to come to.
cobre *m* copper; kitchen utensils; (*mus*) brass.
cobrizo, za *adj* coppery.
cobro *m* encashment; payment; recovery.
cocaína *f* cocaine.
cocción *f* cooking.
cocear *vt* to kick; (*fig*) to resist.

cocer *vt* to boil; to bake (bricks); ● *vi* to boil; to ferment; ~**se** *vr* to suffer intense pain.
cocido, da *adj* boiled; (*fig*) skilled, experienced; ● *m* stew.
cocina *f* kitchen; cooker; cookery.
cocinero, ra *m/f* cook.
coco *m* coconut; bogeyman.
cocodrilo *m* crocodile.
cochambre *m* dirty, stinking object.
cochambroso, sa *adj* nasty, filthy, stinking.
coche *m* automobile; coach, carriage; baby carriage; (*ferro*) ~ **cama** sleeping car; ~ **restaurante** dining car.
cochera *f* garage, carport, depot.
cochero *m* coachman.
cochinilla *f* woodlouse; cochineal.
cochino, na *adj* dirty, nasty, filthy; ● *m* pig.
cochiquera *f* pigsty.
codazo *m* blow given with the elbow.
codear *vt, vi* to elbow; ~**se** *vr*: ~**se con** to rub shoulders with.
códice *m* old manuscript.
codicia *m* covetousness, greediness.
codiciable *adj* covetable.
codiciar *vt* to covet, to desire.
codicilo *m* (*jur*) codicil.
codicioso, sa *adj* greedy, covetous.
código *m* code; law; set of rules.
codillo *m* knee of a four-legged animal; angle; (*tec*) elbow (joint).
codo *m* elbow.
codorniz *f* quail.
coerción *f* coercion, restraint.
coercitivo, va *adj* coercive.
coetáneo, nea *adj* contemporary.
coexistencia *f* coexistence.
coexistente *adj* coexistent.
coexistir *vi* to coexist.
cofia *f* (nurse's) cap.
cofrade *m* member (of a brotherhood).
cofradía *f* brotherhood, fraternity.
cofre *m* trunk.
cogedor *m* shovel; dustpan.
coger *vt* to catch, to take hold of, to occupy, to take up; ~**se** *vr* to catch.
cognitivo, va *adj* cognitive.
cogollo *m* heart of a lettuce, cabbage; shoot of a plant.
cogote *m* back of the neck.
cohabitar *vi* to cohabit, to live together.
cohechar *vt* to bribe, to suborn.
cohecho *m* bribery.
coherencia *f* coherence.
coherente *adj* coherent, cohesive.
cohete *m* rocket.
cohibido, da *adj* shy.
cohibir *vt* to prohibit, to restrain.
cohorte *m* cohort.
coincidencia *f* coincidence.
coincidente *adj* coincidental.
coincidir *vi* to coincide.
coito *m* intercourse, coitus.
cojear *vi* to limp, to hobble; (*fig*) to go astray.
cojera *f* lameness, limp.
cojín *m* cushion.
cojo, ja *adj* lame, crippled.
col *f* cabbage.
cola *f* tail; line; last place; glue.
colaborador, ra *m/f* collaborator.
colaborar *vi* to collaborate.
colación *f* collation, comparison; light meal.
colada *f* wash, washing; (*quim*) bleach; sheep run.
coladero *m* colander, strainer.
colador *m* sieve.
colapso *m* collapse.

colar *vt* to strain, to filter; • *vi* to ooze; ~**se en** to get into without paying.

colateral *adj* collateral.

colcha *f* bedspread, counterpane.

coichón *m* mattress.

colchoneta *f* mattress.

coleada *f* wagging of an animal's tail.

colear *vi* to wag the tail.

colección *f* collection.

coleccionar *vt* to collect.

coleccionista *m/f* collector.

colecta *f* collection (for charity).

colectar *vt* to collect taxes.

colectivo, va *adj* collective.

colector *m* collector; sewer.

colega *m/f* colleague.

colegial *m* schoolboy.

colegiala *f* schoolgirl.

colegiata *f* collegiate church.

colegio *m* college; school.

colegir *vt* to collect, to deduce; to infer.

cólera *f* bile; anger, fury, rage.

coléricamente *adv* in a rage.

colérico, ca *adj* angry, furious; bad-tempered.

colesterol *m* cholesterol.

coleta *f* pigtail.

colgadero *m* hook, hanger, peg.

colgadura *f* tapestry; hangings *pl*, drapery.

colgajo *m* tatter, rag.

colgante *adj* hanging; • *m* pendant.

colgar *vt* to hang; to suspend; to decorate with tapestry; • *vi* to be suspended.

colibrí *m* hummingbird.

cólico *m* colic.

coliflor *f* cauliflower.

colilla *f* end *or* butt of a cigarette.

colina *f* hill.

colindante *adj* neighboring.

colindar *vi* to adjoin.

coliseo *m* coliseum; opera house; theater.

colisión *f* collision; friction.

colmar *vt* to heap up; • *vi* to fulfill, to realize.

colmena *f* hive, beehive.

colmenar *m* beehive stand, beehouse.

colmillo *m* eyetooth; tusk.

colmo *m* height, summit, extreme; a ~ plentifully.

colocación *f* employment; placing; situation.

colocar *vt* to arrange, to place; to provide with a job; ~**se** *vr* to get a job.

colon *m* (*gr*) colon (:); (*med*) colon.

colonia *f* colony; silk ribbon.

colonial *adj* colonial.

colonización *f* colonization.

colonizador, a *m/f* settler; • *adj* colonizing.

colonizar *vt* to colonize.

colono *m* colonist; farmer.

coloquio *m* conversation; conference.

color *m* color, hue, dye; rouge; suit (of cards).

coloración *f* coloring, coloration.

colorado, da *adj* ruddy; red.

colorar *vt* to color; to dye.

colorear *vt* to color; to excuse.

colorete *m* rouge.

colorido *m* coloring.

colosol *adj* colossal.

columna *f* column.

columnata *f* colonnade.

columpiar(se) *vt, vr* to swing to and fro.

columpio *m* swing, seesaw.

colusión *f* collusion.

colza *f* (*bot*) rape, rape seed.

collar *m* necklace; (dog) collar.

coma *f* (*gr*) comma; • *m* (*med*) coma.

comadre *f* midwife; godmother; neighbor.

comadreja *f* weasel.

comadrón, ona *m/f* midwife.

comandancia *f* command.

comandante *m* commander.

comandar *vt* to command.

comarca *f* territory, district.

comba *f* curve; warp (of timber); skipping rope.

combar *vt* to bend; ~**se** *vr* to warp.

combate *m* combat, conflict; fighting.

combatiente *m* combatant.

combatir *vt* to combat, to fight; to attack; • *vi* to fight.

combinación *f* combination; (*quim*) compound; cocktail; scheme.

combinar *vi* to combine.

combustible *adj* combustible; • *m* combustible; fuel.

combustión *f* combustion.

comedero *m* dining room; trough.

comedia *f* comedy; play, drama.

comediante *m/f* player, actor/actress.

comedido, da *adj* moderate, restrained.

comedirse *vr* to restrain oneself.

comedor, ra *m/f* glutton; • *m* dining room.

comensal *m/f* fellow diner.

comendatorio, ria *adj* recommending, introductory (of letters).

comentar *vt* to comment on, to expound.

comentario *m* comment, remark; commentary.

comentarista *m/f* commentator.

comenzar *vi* to commence, to begin.

comer *vt* to eat; to take a piece at chess; • *vi* to have lunch.

comercial *adj* commercial.

comerciante *m/f* trader, merchant, dealer.

comerciar *vi* to trade, to do business.

comercio *m* trade, commerce; business.

comestible *adj* eatable; ~**s** *mpl* food, foodstuffs.

cometa *m* comet; • *f* kite.

cometer *vt* to commit, to charge; to entrust.

cometido *m* task.

comezón *f* itch; itching.

comicios *mpl* elections.

cómico, ca *adj* comic, comical.

comida *f* eating, food; meal; lunch.

comienzo *m* beginning.

comilón, ona *m/f* great eater, glutton; • *f* blow-out.

comillas *fpl* quotation marks.

comino *m* cumin (plant *or* seed).

comisaría *f* police station; commissariat.

comisario *m* commissioner.

comisión *f* commission; committee.

comisionado, da *m/f* commissioner; committee member.

comisionar *vt* to commission.

comité *m* committee.

comitiva *f* suite, retinue, followers.

como *adv* as; like; such as.

cómo *adv* how?, why? • *excl* what?

cómoda *f* chest of drawers.

comodidad *f* comfort; convenience; ~**es** *pl* wealth, comforts.

comodín *m* joker.

cómodo, da *adj* convenient; comfortable.

compacto, ta *adj* compact, close, dense.

compadecer *vt* to pity; ~**se** *vr* to pity; to agree with each other.

compadre *m* godfather; friend.

compaginar *vt* to arrange, to put in order; ~**se** *vr* to tally.

compañero, ra *m/f* companion, friend; comrade; partner.

compañía *f* company.

comparación *f* comparison.

comparar *vt* to compare.

comparativo, va *adj* comparative.

comparecer *vi* to appear in court.

comparsa *m/f* extra (in the theater).

compartimento *m* compartment.

compartir *vt* to divide into equal parts.

compás *m* compass; pair of compasses; (*mus*) measure, beat.

compasión *f* compassion, commiseration.

compasivo, va *adj* compassionate.

compatibilidad *f* compatibility.

compatible *adj* compatible, consistent with.

compatriota *m/f* countryman; countrywoman; fellow citizen.

compeler *vt* to compel, to constrain.

compendiar *vt* to abridge.

compendio *m* abridgment, summary.

compensación *f* compensation; recompense.

compensar *vt* to compensate; to recompense.

competencia *f* competition, rivalry; competence.

competente *adj* competent; adequate.

competer *vi* to be one's responsibility.

competición *f* competition.

competidor, ra *m/f* competitor, contestant; rival.

competir *vi* to vie; to compete with, to rival.

compilación *f* compilation.

compilador *m* compiler.

compilar *vt* to compile.

compinche *m* pal, buddy (*sl*).

complacencia *f* pleasure; indulgence.

complacer *vt* to please; ~se *vr* to be pleased with.

complaciente *adj* pleasing.

complejo *m* complex; ~, **ja** *adj* complex.

complementario, ria *adj* complementary.

complemento *m* complement, completion.

completar *vt* to complete.

completo, ta *adj* complete, perfect.

complexión *f* constitution, temperament; build.

complicado, da *adj* complicated.

complicar *vt* to complicate.

cómplice *m/f* accomplice.

complicidad *f* complicity.

complot *m* plot.

componer *vt* to compose; to constitute; to mend, to repair; to strengthen, to restore; to adorn; to adjust; to reconcile; to compose, to calm; ~se *vr*: ~se de to consist of.

comportamiento *m* behavior.

comportarse *vr* to behave.

composición *f* composition; composure, agreement; settlement.

compositor, ra *m/f* composer; compositor.

compostura *f* composition, composure; mending, repairing; discretion; modesty, demureness.

compota *f* stewed fruit.

compra *f* purchase.

comprador, ra *m/f* buyer; customer, shopper.

comprar *vt* to buy, to purchase.

comprender *vt* to include, to contain; to comprehend, to understand.

comprensible *adj* comprehensible.

comprensión *f* comprehension, understanding.

comprensivo, va *adj* comprehensive.

compresa *f* sanitary napkin.

compresión *f* compression.

comprimido *m* pill.

comprimir *vt* to compress; to repress, to restrain.

comprobante *m* receipt; voucher.

comprobar *vt* to verify, to confirm; to prove.

comprometer *vt* to compromise; to embarrass; to implicate; to put in danger; ~se *vr* to compromise oneself.

compromiso *m* compromise.

compuerta *f* hatch; sluice.

compuesto *m* compound; ~, **ta** *adj* composed; made up of.

compulsar *vt* to collate, to compare; to make an authentic copy.

compulsivo, va *adj* compulsive.

compunción *f* compunction, regret.

compungirse *vr* to feel remorseful.

computador *m*, **computadora** *f* computer.

computar *vt* to calculate, to compute.

cómputo *m* computation, calculation.

comulgar *vt* to administer communion to; ● *vi* to receive communion.

común *adj* common, usual, general; ● *m* community, public; en ~ in common.

comunal *adj* communal.

comunicación *f* communication; report.

comunicado *m* announcement.

comunicar *vt* to communicate; ~se *vr* to communicate (with each other).

comunicativo, va *adj* communicative.

comunidad *f* community.

comunión *f* communion.

comunismo *m* communism.

comunista *m/f* communist.

con *prep* with; by; ~ **que** so then, providing that.

conato *m* endeavor; effort; attempt.

concavidad *f* concavity.

cóncavo, va *adj* concave.

concebir *vt* to conceive; ● *vi* to become pregnant.

conceder *vt* to give; to grant; to concede, to allow.

concejal, la *m/f* member of a council.

concejo *m* council.

concentración *f* concentration.

concentrar *vt*, ~se *vr* to concentrate.

concéntrico, ca *adj* concentric.

concepción *f* conception; idea.

concepto *m* conceit, thought; judgment, opinion.

concerniente *adj* concerning, relating to.

concernir *v imp* to regard, to concern.

concertar *vt* to coordinate, to settle; to adjust; to agree; to arrange, to fix up; ● *vi* (*mus*) to harmonize, to be in tune.

concesión *f* concession.

concesionario *m* agent.

conciencia *f* conscience.

concienciar *vt* to make aware; ~se *vr* to become aware.

concierto *m* concert; agreement; (*mus*) concert; concerto; de ~ in agreement.

conciliación *f* conciliation, reconciliation.

conciliar *vt* to reconcile; ● *adj* belonging to councils.

conciliatorio, ra *adj* conciliatory.

concilio *m* council.

concisión *f* conciseness.

conciso, sa *adj* concise, brief.

conciudadanía *f* joint-citizenship.

conciudadano, na *m/f* fellow citizen.

cónclave *m* conclave.

concluir *vt* to conclude, to end, to complete; to infer, to deduce; ~se *vr* to conclude.

conclusión *f* conclusion.

concluyente *adj* conclusive.

concordancia *f* concordance, concord; harmony.

concordar *vi* to reconcile, to make agree; ● *vt* to agree, to correspond.

concordato *m* concordat.

concordia *f* conformity, agreement.

concretar *vt* to make concrete; to specify.

concreto, ta *adj* concrete.

concubina *f* concubine.

concubinato *m* concubinage.

concupiscencia *f* greed, lust.

concurrencia *f* concurrence; coincidence; competition; crowd, gathering.

concurrido, da *adj* busy.

concurrir *vi* to meet; to contribute; to coincide; to compete.

concursante *m/f* competitor.

concurso *m* crowd; competition; help, cooperation.

concusión *f* concussion.

concha *f* shell; tortoise-shell.

conchabar *vt* to mix, to blend; **~se** *vr* to plot, to conspire.

condado *m* county.

conde *m* earl, count.

condecoración *f* medal.

condecorar *vt* to adorn; (*mil*) to decorate.

condenable *adj* culpable.

condena *f* condemnation.

condenar *vt* to condemn; to find guilty; **~se** *vr* to blame oneself; to confess (one's guilt).

condenatorio, ria *adj* condemnatory.

condensación *f* condensation.

condensar *vt* to condense.

condesa *f* countess.

condescendencia *f* helpfulness, willingness; acquiescence; compliance.

condescender *vt* to acquiese, to comply.

condición *f* condition, quality; state; status; rank; stipulation.

condicionado, da *adj* conditioned.

condicional *adj* conditional.

condimentar *vt* to flavor, to season.

condimento *m* condiment, seasoning.

condiscípulo, la *m/f* fellow pupil, fellow student.

condolerse *vr* to sympathize.

condón *m* condom.

condonar *vt* to condone; to forgive.

conducción *f* conveyance; management; (*aut*) driving.

conducente *adj*: **~ a** leading to.

conducir *vt* to convey, to conduct; to drive; to manage; ● *vi* to drive; to lead (to); **~se** *vr* to conduct oneself.

conducta *f* conduct; behavior; management.

conducto *m* conduit, pipe, drain; (*fig*) channel.

conductor, ra *m/f* conductor, guide; (*ferro*) guard; driver.

conectado, da *adj* on-line.

conectar *vt* to connect.

conejera *f* warren, burrow.

conejo *m* rabbit.

conexión *f* connection; plug; relationship.

conexo, xa *adj* connected, related.

confabularse *vr* to conspire.

confección *f* preparation; clothing industry.

confeccionar *vt* to make up.

confederación *f* confederacy.

confederado *adj* confederate.

confederarse *vr* to confederate.

conferencia *f* conference; telephone call.

conferenciar *vi* to confer; to be in conference.

conferir *vt* to award; to compare.

confesar *vt* to confess; to admit.

confesión *f* confession.

confesionario *m* confessional.

confeso, sa *adj* (*jur*) confessed.

confesonario *m* confessional.

confesor *m* confessor.

confeti *m* confetti.

confiado, da *adj* trusting; confident; arrogant.

confianza *f* trust; confidence; conceit; familiarity; **en ~** confidential.

confiar *vt* to confide, to entrust; ● *vi* to trust.

confidencia *f* confidence.

confidencial *adj* confidential.

confidente *m/f* confidante; informer.

configurar *vt* to shape, to form.

confín *m* limit, boundary.

confinar *vt* to confine; ● *vi* to border upon.

confirmación *f* confirmation.

confirmar *vt* to confirm; to corroborate.

confiscación *f* confiscation.

confiscar *vt* to confiscate.

confite *m* candy.

confitería *f* candy store.

confitero, ra *m/f* confectioner.

confitura *f* preserve; jam.

conflagración *f* conflagration.

conflictivo, va *adj* controversial.

conflicto *m* conflict.

confluencia *f* confluence.

confluir *vi* to join (applied to rivers); to gather (applied to people).

conformar *vt* to shape; to adjust, to adapt; ● *vi* to agree; **~se** *vr* to conform, to resign oneself.

conforme *adj* alike, similar; agreed; ● *prep* according to.

conformidad *f* similarity; agreement; resignation.

conformista *m/f* conformist.

confortable *adj* comfortable.

confortar *vt* to comfort; to strengthen; to console.

confortativo, va *adj* comforting.

confraternidad *f* fraternity.

confrontación *f* confrontation.

confrontar *vt* to confront.

confundir *vt* to confound, to jumble; to confuse; **~se** *vr* to make a mistake.

confusamente *adv* confusedly.

confusión *f* confusion.

confuso, sa *adj* confused.

congelación *f* freezing.

congelado, da *adj* frozen; **~s** *mpl* frozen food.

congelador *m* freezer.

congelar *vt* to freeze; **~se** *vr* to congeal.

congeniar *vi* to get on well (with).

congestión *f* congestion.

congestionar *vt* to congest.

congoja *f* anguish, distress, grief.

congraciarse *vr* to ingratiate oneself.

congratulación *f* congratulation.

congratular *vt* to congratulate.

congregación *f* congregation, assembly.

congregar(se) *vt* (*vr*) to assemble, to meet, to collect.

congresista *m/f* delegate.

congreso *m* congress.

cónico, ca *adj* conical.

conjetura *f* conjecture, guess.

conjeturar *vt* to conjecture, to guess.

conjugación *f* (*gr*) conjugation.

conjugar *vt* (*gr*) to conjugate; to combine.

conjunción *f* conjunction.

conjuntamente *adv* together.

conjunto, ta *adj* united, joint; ● *m* whole; (*mus*) ensemble, band; team.

conjuración *f* conspiracy, plot.

conjurado, da *m/f* conspirator.

conjurar *vt* to exorcise; ● *vi* to conspire, to plot.

conjuro *m* incantation, exorcism.

conmemoración *f* commemoration.

conmemorar *vt* to commemorate.

conmigo *pn* with me.

conminación *f* threat.

conminar *vt* to threaten.

conminatorio, ria *adj* threatening.

conmiseración *f* commiseration, pity, sympathy.

conmoción *f* shock; upheaval; commotion; (*med*) concussion; disturbance.

conmovedor, ra *adj* touching.

conmover *vt* to move; to disturb.

conmutación *f* commutation, exchange.

conmutador *m* switch.

conmutar *vt* (*jur*) to commute; to exchange.

connotar *vt* to imply.

cono *m* cone.

conocedor, ra *m/f* connoisseur.

conocer *vt* to know, to understand; **~se** *vr* to know one another.

conocido, da *m/f* acquaintance.

conocimiento *m* knowledge, understanding; (*med*) consciousness; acquaintance; (*mar*) bill of lading.

conque *m* condition.
conquista *f* conquest.
conquistador *m* conqueror; ~, ra *adj* conquering.
conquistar *vt* to conquer.
consabido, da *adj* well-known; above-mentioned.
consagración *f* consecration.
consagrar *vt* to consecrate.
consanguíneo, nea *adj* related by blood.
consanguinidad *f* blood relationship.
consecución *f* acquisition; attainment.
consecuencia *f* consequence; conclusion; consistency; por ~ therefore.
consecuente *adj* consistent.
consecutivo, va *adj* consecutive.
conseguir *vt* to attain, to get, to obtain.
consejero, ra *m/f* adviser; councilor.
consejo *m* advice; council.
consenso *m* consensus.
consentido *adj* spoiled (of children).
consentimiento *m* consent.
consentir *vt* to consent to; to allow; to admit; to spoil (a child).
conserje *m* doorman; janitor.
conservación *f* conservation.
conservante *m* preservative.
conservar *vt* to conserve; to keep; to preserve fruit.
conservas *fpl* canned food.
conservatorio *m* (*mus*) conservatoire.
considerable *adj* considerable.
consideración *f* consideration; respect.
consideradamente *adv* considerately.
considerado, da *adj* respected; considerate.
considerar *vt* to consider.
consigna *f* (*mil*) watchword; order, instruction; (*ferro*) check-room.
consignación *f* consignment.
consignar *vt* to consign, to dispatch; to assign; to record, to register.
consignatario, ria *m/f* consignee.
consigo *pn* (*m*) with him; (*f*) with her; (*vd*) with you; (*reflexivo*) with oneself.
consiguiente *adj* consequent.
consistencia *f* consistence, consistency.
consistente *adj* consistent, firm, solid.
consistir *vi:* ~ en to consist of; to be due to.
consistorio *m* town council; town hall.
consocio, cia *m/f* fellow member; partner.
consola *f* control panel.
consolación *f* consolation.
consolador, ra *adj* consoling, comforting.
consolar *vt* to console, to comfort, to cheer.
consolidar *vt* to consolidate.
consomé *m* consommé.
consonancia *f* consonance.
consonante *m* rhyme; • *f* (*gr*) consonant; • *adj* consonant, harmonious.
consorcio *m* partnership.
consorte *m/f* consort, companion, partner; accomplice.
conspiración *f* conspiracy, plot.
conspirador, ra *m/f* conspirator, plotter.
conspirar *vi* to conspire, to plot.
constancia *f* constancy, steadiness.
constante *adj* constant, firm.
constar *vi* to be evident, to be certain; to be composed of, to consist of.
constatar *vt* to note; to check.
constelación *f* constellation.
consternación *f* consternation.
consternar *vt* to dismay, to shock.
constipado, da *adj:* estar ~ to have a cold.
constiparse *vr* to catch a cold.
constitución *f* constitution.

constitucional *adj* constitutional.
constituir *vt* to constitute; to establish; to appoint.
constitutivo, va *adj* constitutive, essential.
constituyente *adj* constituent.
constreñimiento *m* constraint.
constreñir *vt* to restrict; to force; (*med*) to constipate; to constrict.
constricción *f* constriction, contraction.
construcción *f* construction.
constructor, ra *m/f* builder.
construir *vt* to form, to build, to construct; to construe.
consuegro, gra *m/f* father-in-law/mother-in-law of one's son or daughter.
consuelo *m* consolation, comfort.
cónsul *m* consul.
consulado *m* consulate.
consulta *f* consultation.
consultar *vt* to consult, to ask advice.
consultivo, va *adj* consultative.
consultor, ra *m/f* adviser, consultant.
consultorio *m* (*med*) surgery.
consumación *f* consummation, finishing.
consumado, da *adj* consummate, complete, perfect, accomplished.
consumar *vt* to consummate, to finish; to carry out.
consumición *f* consumption; drink.
consumidor, ra *m/f* consumer.
consumir *vt* to consume; to burn, to use; to waste, to exhaust; ~se *vr* to waste away, to be consumed.
consumismo *m* consumerism.
consumo *m* consumption.
contabilidad *f* accounting; bookkeeping.
contable *m/f* accountant.
contacto *m* contact; (*aut*) ignition.
contado, da *adj:* ~s scarce, few; • *m:* pagar al ~ to pay (in) cash.
contador *adj* meter; accountant; counter in a café.
contaduría *f* accountancy; accountant's office.
contagiar *vt* to infect; ~se *vr* to get infected.
contagio *m* contagion.
contagioso, sa *adj* contagious.
contaminación *f* contamination, pollution.
contaminar *vt* to contaminate; to pollute; to corrupt.
contante *m* cash.
contar *vt* to count, to reckon; to tell; • *vi* to count; ~ con to rely upon.
contemplación *f* contemplation.
contemplar *vt* to look at, to contemplate, to consider; to meditate.
contemplativo, va *adj* contemplative.
contemporáneo, nea *adj* contemporary.
contemporizar *vi* to temporize.
contencioso, sa *adj* contentious; quarrelsome.
contender *vi* to contend, to compete.
contendiente *m/f* competitor.
contener *vt* to contain, to hold; to hold back; to repress; ~se *vr* to control oneself.
contenedor *m* container.
contenido, da *adj* moderate, restrained; • *m* contents *pl*.
contentar *vt* to content, to satisfy, to please; ~se *vr* to be pleased *or* satisfied.
contento, ta *adj* glad; pleased; content; • *m* contentment; (*jur*) release.
contestación *f* answer, reply.
contestador *m:* ~ automático answering machine.
contestar *vt* to answer, to reply; to prove, to corroborate.
contexto *m* context.
contienda *f* contest, dispute.
contigo *pn* with you.
contigüidad *f* contiguity.
contiguo, gua *adj* contiguous, close.
continencia *f* continence, abstinence, moderation.

continental adj continental.
continente m continent, mainland; ● adj continent.
contingencia f risk; contingency.
contingente adj contingent, accidental; ● m contingent.
continuación f continuation; sequel.
continuar vt, vi to continue.
continuidad f continuity.
continuo, nua adj continuous.
contonearse vr to walk affectedly.
contoneo m affected manner of walking.
contorno m environs pl; contour, outline; en ~ round about.
contorsión f contortion.
contra prep against, contrary to, opposite.
contraataque m counter-attack.
contrabajo m (mus) double bass; bass guitar; low bass.
contrabandista m/f smuggler.
contrabando m contraband trade, smuggling.
contracción f contraction.
contrachapado m plywood.
contradecir vt to contradict.
contradicción f contradiction.
contradictorio, ria adj contradictory, opposite to.
contraer vt to contract, to shrink; to make a bargain; ~se vr to shrink, to contract.
contrafuerte m buttress; foothill; heel-pad.
contragolpe m backlash.
contrahecho, cha adj deformed, hunchback; counterfeit, fake.
contralto m (mus) contralto.
contramaestre m (mar) boatswain; foreman.
contrapartida f (com) balancing entry.
contrapaso m back step.
contrapelo adv against the grain.
contrapesar vi to counterbalance.
contrapeso m counterpoise; counterweight.
contraponer vt to compare, to oppose.
contraposición f comparison; contrast.
contraproducente adj counterproductive.
contrapunto m (mus) counterpoint.
contrariar vt to contradict, to oppose; to vex.
contrariedad f opposition; setback; annoyance.
contrario, ria m/f opponent; ● adj contrary, opposite; por el ~ on the contrary.
contrarrestar vt to return a ball; (fig) to counteract.
contrarrevolución f counter-revolution.
contrasentido m contradiction.
contraseña f countersign; (mil) watchword.
contrastar vt to resist, to contradict; to assay metals; to verify measures and weights; ● vi to contrast.
contraste m contrast.
contrata f contract.
contratación f signing-up, hiring.
contratar vt to contract; to hire, to engage.
contratiempo m setback; accident.
contratista m contractor.
contrato m contract, agreement.
contravención f contravention.
contraveneno m antidote.
contravenir vi to contravene, to transgress; to violate.
contraventana f shutter.
contribución f contribution; tax.
contribuir vt, vi to contribute.
contribuyente m/f contributor; taxpayer.
contrincante m competitor.
contrito, ta adj contrite, penitent.
control m control.
controlador, ra m/f controller.
controlar vt to control; to check.
controversia f controversy, dispute.
contumacia f ohstinacy, stubbornness; (jur) contempt of court.

contumaz adj obstinate, stubborn; (jur) guilty of contempt of court.
contundente adj overwhelming; blunt.
contusión f bruise.
convalecencia f convalescence.
convalecer vi to recover from sickness, to convalesce.
convaleciente m/f, adj convalescent.
convalidar vt to recognize.
convencer vt to convince.
convencimiento m conviction.
convención f convention, pact.
convencional adj conventional.
conveniencia f suitability; usefulness; agreement; ~s pl property.
conveniente adj useful, suitable.
convenio m convention, agreement, treaty.
convenir vi to agree, to suit.
convento m convent, monastery, nunnery.
conventual adj monastic.
convergencia f convergence.
converger vi to converge.
conversación f conversation, talk; communication.
conversar vi to talk, to converse.
conversión f conversion, change.
converso, sa m/f convert.
convertir vt, ~se vr to convert.
convexo, xa adj convex.
convicción f conviction.
convicto, ta adj convicted (found guilty).
convidado, da m/f guest.
convidar vt to invite.
convincente adj convincing.
convite m invitation; banquet.
convivencia f living together.
convocar vt to convoke, to assemble.
convocatoria f summons; notice of a meeting.
convoy m convoy.
convulsión f convulsion.
convulsivo, va adj convulsive.
conyugal adj conjugal, married.
cónyuge m/f spouse.
coñac m brandy, cognac.
coño excl (fam) shit! (sl).
cooperar vi to cooperate.
cooperativa f cooperative.
cooperativo, va adj cooperative.
coordinadora f coordinating committee.
coordinar vt to arrange, to coordinate.
copa f cup; glass; top of a tree; crown of a hat; ~s pl hearts (at cards).
copete m quiff; pride.
copia f plenty, abundance; copy, duplicate.
copiador, ra m/f copyist; copier; libro ~ letter book.
copiar vt to copy; to imitate.
copioso, sa adj copious, abundant, plentiful.
copla f verse; (mus) popular song, folksong.
copo m small bundle; flake of snow.
copropietario, ria m/f joint owner.
cópula f copulation; conjunction; (gr) copula.
copulativo, va adj copulative.
coqueta f coquette, flirt.
coquetear vi to flirt.
coquetería f coquetry, flirtation.
coraje m courage; anger, passion.
coral m coral; choir; ● adj choral.
coraza f cuirass; armor-plating.
corazón m heart; core; de ~ willingly.
corazonada f inspiration; quick decision; presentiment.
corbata f tie.
corbeta f corvette (light vessel with three masts and square sails).
corcel m steed, charger.

corchea f (mus) quaver.
corchete m clasp; snap fastener.
corcho m cork; float (for fishing); cork bark.
cordel m cord, rope; (mar) line.
cordero m lamb; lambskin; meek, gentle person.
cordial adj cordial, affectionate; ● m cordial.
cordialidad f cordiality.
cordillera f range of mountains.
cordón m cord, string; lace; cordon.
cordura f prudence, good sense, wisdom.
corista m/f chorister.
cornada f thrust with a bull's horn.
cornadura f horns pl.
cornamenta f horns of an animal pl.
córnea f cornea.
cornear vi to butt with the horns.
córneo, ea adj horny, corneous.
corneta f bugle.
cornisa f cornice.
cornudo, da adj horned.
coro m choir; chorus.
corona f crown; coronet; top of the head; crown (of a tooth); tonsure; crown; halo.
coronación f coronation.
coronar vt to crown; to complete, to perfect.
coronario, ria adj coronary.
coronel m (mil) colonel.
coronilla f crown of the head.
corpiño m bodice.
corporación f corporation.
corporal adj corporal.
corpóreo, rea adj corporeal.
corpulencia f corpulence.
corpulento, ta adj corpulent, bulky.
Corpus m Corpus Christi day.
corral m yard; farmyard; corral; playpen.
correa f leather strap, thong; flexibility.
correaje m leather straps pl.
corrección f correction; reprehension; amendment.
correccional m reformatory.
correctivo, va adj corrective.
correcto, ta adj exact, correct.
corrector, ra m/f proof-reader.
corredizo, za adj sliding; easy to be untied.
corredor, ra adj running; ● m/f broker, runner; ● m corridor.
corregir vt to correct, to amend; to reprehend; ~se vr to reform.
correlación f correlation.
correo m post, mail; courier; mailman; a vuelta de ~ by return of post; ~s pl post office.
correoso, sa adj flexible, leathery.
correr vt to run; to flow; to travel over; to pull (a drape); ● vi to run, to rush; to flow; to blow (applied to the wind); ~se vr to be ashamed; to slide, to move; to run (of colors).
correría f incursion.
correspondencia f correspondence; communication; agreement.
corresponder vi to correspond, to answer; to be suitable; to belong; to concern; ~se vr to love one another.
correspondiente adj corresponding, suitable.
corresponsal m/f correspondent.
corretear vi to rush around; to hang about the streets.
corrida f run, dash; bullfight.
corrido, da adj expert; knowing; ashamed.
corriente f current; course, progression; (electric) current; ● adj current; common, ordinary, general; fluent; flowing, running.
corrillo m circle of persons; clique.
corro m circle of people.
corroborar vt to corroborate.
corroer vt to corrode, to erode.

corromper vt to corrupt; to rot; to turn bad; to seduce; to bribe; ● vi to stink; ~se vr to rot; to become corrupted.
corrosión f corrosion.
corrosivo, va adj corrosive.
corrupción f corruption; rot, decay.
corruptible adj corruptible.
corrupto, ta adj corrupted, corrupt.
corruptor, ra m/f corruptor, perverter.
corrusco m broken bread.
corsé f corset.
cortacésped m lawn mower.
cortado m coffee with a little milk; ~, da adj cut; sour; embarrassed.
cortadura f cut; cutting; incision; fissure; ~s pl shreds, cuttings, parings.
cortafuego m fire lane.
cortaplumas m invar penknife.
cortar vt to cut; to cut off, to curtail; to intersect; to carve; to chop; to cut (at cards); to interrupt; ~se vr to be ashamed or embarrassed; to curdle.
cortauñas m invar nail clippers.
corte m cutting; cut; section; length (of cloth); style; ● f (royal) court; the capital (city); C~s fpl Spanish Parliament.
cortedad f shortness, smallness; stupidity; bashfulness.
cortejar vt to court.
cortejo m entourage; courtship; procession; lover.
cortés, esa adj courteous, polite.
cortesana f courtesan.
cortesía f courtesy, good manners pl.
corteza f bark; peel; crust; (fig) outward appearance.
cortina f drape.
cortinaje m set of drapes for a house.
corto, ta adj short; scanty, small; stupid; bashful; a la ~a o a la larga sooner or later.
corvo, va adj bent, crooked.
corzo, za m/f roe deer, fallow deer.
cosa f thing; matter; affair; no hay tal ~ no such thing.
cosaco m cossack.
cosecha f harvest; harvest time; de su ~ of one's own invention.
cosechar vt to harvest, to reap.
coser vt to sew; to join.
cosido m stitching, sewing.
cosmético, a adj, m cosmetic.
cosmopolita adj, m cosmopolitan.
cosquillas fpl tickling; (fig) agitation.
costa f cost, price; charge; expense; coast, shore; a toda ~ at all events.
costado m side; (mil) flank; side of a ship.
costal m sack, large bag.
costalada f heavy fall.
costar vt to cost; to need.
coste m cost, expense.
costear vt to pay for.
costera f side; slope; coast.
costero, ra adj coastal; (mar) coasting.
costilla f rib; (fig) wife; cutlet; ~s pl back, shoulders.
costillar m human ribs.
costo m cost, price, expense.
costoso, sa adj costly, dear, expensive.
costra f crust; (med) scab.
costumbre f custom, habit.
costura f sewing; seam; needlework.
costurera f seamstress.
costurero m sewing box.
cota f height above sea level; number, figure.
cotejar vt to compare.
cotejo m comparison, collation.
cotidiano, na adj daily.
cotilla m/f gossip.
cotización f quotation.
cotizar vt to quote; ~se vr to sell at; to be quoted at.

coto *m* enclosure; reserve; boundary stone.
cotorra *f* magpie; small parrot; (*col*) chatterbox.
covacha *f* small cave, grotto.
coyote *m* coyote.
coyuntura *f* joint, articulation; juncture.
coz *f* kick; recoil of a gun; ebbing of a flood; (*fig*) insult.
cráneo *m* skull.
cráter *m* crater.
creación *f* creation.
creador, ra *adj* creative; ● *m/f* creator.
crear *vt* to create, to make; to establish.
crecer *vi* to grow, to increase; to rise.
creces *fpl* increase.
crecida *f* swell of rivers.
crecido, da *adj* full-grown (of a person); large; (*fig*) vain.
creciente *f* crescent (moon); (*mar*) flood tide; ● *adj* growing; crescent.
crecimiento *m* increase; growth.
credenciales *fpl* credentials.
credibilidad *f* credibility.
crédito *m* credit; belief; faith; reputation.
credo *m* creed.
credulidad *f* credulity.
crédulo, la *adj* credulous.
creencia *f* credence, belief.
creer *vt, vi* to believe; to think; to consider.
crema *f* cream; custard.
cremallera *f* zipper.
crepúsculo *m* twilight.
crespo, pa *adj* curled; angry, displeased.
crespón *m* crêpe.
cresta *f* crest (of birds).
creyente *m/f* believer.
cría *f* breeding; young.
criada *f* servant, maid.
criadero *m* (*bot*) nursery; breeding place.
criadilla *f* testicle; small loaf; truffle.
criado *m* servant; ~, da *adj* reared, brought up, bred.
criador *f* Creator; breeder.
crianza *f* breeding, rearing.
criar *vt* to create, to produce; to breed; to nurse; to breast-feed; to bring up, to raise.
criatura *f* creature; child.
criba *f* sieve.
cribar *vt* to sift.
crimen *m* crime.
criminal *adj, m/f* criminal.
criminalista *m* criminologist; criminal lawyer.
crin *f* mane, horsehair.
crío, a *m/f* (*fam*) kid.
criollo, lla *adj, m/f* Creole.
cripta *f* crypt.
crisis *f invar* crisis.
crisma *f* chrism.
crisol *m* crucible; melting pot.
crispar *vt* to set on edge; to tense up.
cristal *m* crystal; glass; pane; lens.
cristalino, na *adj* crystalline.
cristalización *f* crystallization.
cristalizar *vt* to crystallize.
cristiandad *f* Christianity.
cristianismo *m* Christianity.
cristiano, na *adj, m/f* Christian.
Cristo *m* Christ.
criterio *m* criterion.
crítica *m/f* criticism.
criticar *vt* to criticize.
crítico, ca *m/f* critic; ● *adj* critical.
croar *vi* to croak.
cromo *m* chrome.
cronica *f* chronicle; news report; feature.
crónico, ca *adj* chronic.

cronista *m/f* chronicler; reporter, columnist.
cronología *f* chronology.
cronológico, ca *adj* chronological.
cronómetro *m* stopwatch.
cruce *m* crossing; crossroads.
crucero *m* cruiser; cruise; transept; crossing; Cross (southern constellation).
crucificar *vt* to crucify; to torment.
crucifijo *m* crucifix.
crucigrama *m* crossword.
crudeza *f* unripeness; crudeness; undigested food (in the stomach).
crudo, da *adj* raw; green, unripe; crude, cruel; hard to digest.
cruel *adj* cruel.
crueldad *f* cruelty.
cruento, ta *adj* bloody, cruel.
crujido *m* crack, creak, clash, crackling.
crujiente *adj* crunchy.
crujir *vi* to crackle, to rustle.
crustáceo *m* crustacean.
cruz *f* cross; tails (of a coin).
cruzada *f* crusade.
cruzado *m* crusader; ~, da *adj* crossed.
cruzar *vt* to cross; to cross a road; (*mar*) to cruise ~se *vr* to cross; to pass each other.
cuaderna *f* fourth part; timber; rib.
cuaderno *m* notebook; exercise book; logbook.
cuadra *f* block; stable.
cuadrado, da *adj, m* square.
cuadragenario, ria *adj* forty years old.
cuadragésimo, ma *adj, m* fortieth.
cuadrangular *adj* quadrangular, four-cornered.
cuadrángulo *m* quadrangle.
cuadrante *m* quadrant; dial.
cuadrar *vt, vi* to square; to fit, to suit, to correspond.
cuadricular *adj* squared.
cuadrilátero, ra *adj, m* quadrilateral.
cuadrilla *f* party, group; gang, crew.
cuadro *m* square; picture, painting; window frame; scene; chart; (*dep*) team; executive.
cuadrúpedo, da *adj* quadruped.
cuádruple *adj* quadruple.
cuádruplo, pla *adj* quadruple, fourfold.
cuajada *f* curd.
cuajar *vt* to coagulate; to thicken; to adorn; to set; ~se *vr* to coagulate, to curdle; to set; to fill up.
cual *pn* which; who; whom; ● *adv* as; like; ● *adj* such as.
cuál *pn* which (one).
cualidad *f* quality.
cualquier *adj* any.
cualquiera *adj* anyone, someone, anybody, somebody; whoever; whichever.
cuando *adv* when; if; even; ● *conj* since; de ~ en ~ from time to time; ~ más, ~ mucho at most, at best; ~ menos at least.
cuándo *adv* when; ¿de cuándo acá? since when?
cuantía *f* quantity, amount; importance.
cuantioso, sa *adj* numerous, substantial.
cuantitativo, va *adj* quantitive.
cuanto, ta *adj* as many as, as much as, all, whatever; ● *adv* en ~ as soon as; en ~ a as regards; ~ más moreover, the more as.
cuánto *adj* what a lot of; how much?; ¿~s? how many?; ● *pn, adv* how; how much; how many.
cuarenta *adj, m* forty.
cuarentena *f* space of forty days; Lent; quarantine.
cuaresma *f* Lent.
cuarta *f* fourth; span; (*mar*) point (of the compass).
cuartear *vt* to quarter, to divide up; ~se *vr* to split into pieces.
cuartel *m* quarter, district; barracks *pl*.
cuarteta *f* (*poet*) quatrain.
cuartilla *f* fourth part; sheet of paper.

cuarto m fourth part; quarter; room, apartment; span; ~s pl cash, money; ~, ta adj fourth.

cuarzo m quartz.

cuatrero m horse thief.

cuatro adj, m four.

cuatrocientos, tas adj four hundred.

cuba f cask; tub; (fig) drunkard.

cubeta f small cask.

cúbico, ca adj cubic.

cubierta f cover; deck of a ship; (auto) hood; tire; pretext.

cubierto m cover; shelter; place at table; meal at a fixed charge.

cubil m lair.

cubilete m tumbler; dice box.

cubrecama m bedspread.

cubo m cube; bucket.

cubrir vt to cover; to disguise; to protect; to roof a building; ~se vr to become overcast.

cucaña f (fam) soft job (sl); bargain; cinch (sl).

cucaracha f cockroach.

cuclillas adv: en ~ squatting.

cuclillo m cuckoo; (fig) cuckold.

cuco m cuckoo; ~, ca adj sharp.

cucurucho m paper cornet.

cuchara f spoon.

cucharada f spoonful, ladleful.

cucharadita f teaspoonful.

cucharita f teaspoon.

cucharón m ladle; large spoon.

cuchichear vi to whisper.

cuchicheo m whispering.

cuchilla f large kitchen knife; chopping knife; blade.

cuchillada f cut; gash; ~s pl wrangles, quarrels.

cuchillo m knife.

cuchitril m pigsty.

cuello m neck; collar.

cuenca m bowl, deep valley; hollow; socket of the eye.

cuenco m earthenware bowl.

cuenta f calculation; account; check (in a restaurant); count, counting; bead; importance.

cuentista m/f storyteller.

cuento m tale, story, narrative.

cuerda f rope; string; spring.

cuerdo, da adj sane; prudent, judicious.

cuerno m horn.

cuero m hide, skin, leather.

cuerpo m body; cadaver, corpse.

cuervo m raven.

cuesta f slope, hill; slope; ir ~ abajo to go downhill; ~ arriba uphill.

cuestión f question, matter; dispute; quarrel; problem.

cuestionable adj questionable, problematical.

cuestionar vt to question, to dispute.

cueva f cave; cellar.

cuidado m care, worry, concern; charge.

cuidadoso, sa adj careful; anxious.

cuidar vt to care for; to mind, to look after.

culata f butt; breech (of a gun); hindquarters (of an animal); rear of a horse.

culebra f snake.

culinario, ria adj culinary.

culminación f culmination.

culo m backside; ass (sl); bottom.

culpa f fault, blame; guilt.

culpabilidad f guilt.

culpable adj culpable; guilty; ● m/f culprit.

culpar vt to accuse, to blame.

cultivación f cultivation, culture.

cultivar vt to cultivate.

cultivo m cultivation; crop.

culto, ta adj cultivated, cultured; refined, civilized; ● m culture; worship.

cultura f culture.

cumbre f top, summit.

cumpleaños m invar birthday.

cumplido, da adj large, plentiful; complete, perfect, courteous; ● m compliment.

cumplidor, ora adj reliable.

cumplimentar vt to compliment.

cumplimiento m fulfillment; accomplishment; completion.

cumplir vt to carry out, to fulfill; to serve (a prison sentence); to carry out (death penalty); to attain, to reach (a certain age); ~se vr to be fulfilled; to expire, to be up.

cúmulo m heap, pile.

cuna f cradle.

cundir vi to spread; to grow, to increase.

cuneta f ditch.

cuña f wedge.

cuñado, da m/f brother/sister-in-law.

cuota f share; fee.

cupo m quota.

cupón m coupon.

cúpula f cupola, dome.

cura m priest; ● f cure; treatment.

curable adj curable.

curación f cure; curing.

curandero m quack (doctor).

curar vt to cure; to treat, to dress (a wound); to salt; to dress; to tan.

curativo, va adj curative, healing.

curia f ecclesiastical court.

curiosear vt to glance at; ● vi to look round.

curiosidad f curiosity.

curioso, sa adj curious; ● m/f bystander.

currante m/f (fam) worker.

currar vi to work.

curriculum m curriculum vitae.

cursado, da adj skilled; versed.

cursar vt to frequent a place; to send, to dispatch; to study.

cursillo m short course of lectures (in a university).

cursivo, va adj italic (type).

curso m course, direction; year (at university); subject.

cursor m cursor.

curtidor m tanner.

curtidos mpl tanned leather.

curtir vt to tan leather; ~se vr to become sunburned; to become inured.

curva f curve, bend.

curvatura f curvature.

curvilíneo, nea adj curvilinear.

curvo, va curved, bent.

cuscurro m little crust of bread.

cúspide f summit, peak; apex.

custodia f custody, safekeeping; care; monstrance.

custodio m guard, keeper, watchman.

cutáneo, nea adj cutaneous.

cutícula f cuticle.

cutis m skin.

cutre adj (fam) mean, grotty (sl).

cuyo, ya pn of which, of whom, whose.

Ch

chabacano, na adj coarse, vulgar, shoddy.

chabola f shack.

chacolí m light red wine with a sharp taste.

cháchara f chitchat, chatter, idle talk.

chafar vt to crush; to ruin.

chal m shawl.

chalado, da adj crazy.

chale(t) m detached house.

chaleco m waistcoat, vest.

chalupa *f (mar)* boat, launch.
chamarra *f* sheepskin jacket.
champán *m* champagne.
champiñón *m* mushroom.
champú *m* shampoo.
chamuscar *vt* to singe, to scorch.
chamusquina *f* scorching; *(fig)* row, quarrel.
canciller *m* chancellor.
chancleta *f* slipper.
chanclo *m* clog, galosh.
chanchullo *m (fam)* fix, fiddle *(sl)*.
chanfaina *f* cheap stew.
chantaje *m* blackmail.
chanza *f* joke, jest, fun.
chapa *f* metal plate; panel; *(auto)* license plate.
chaparrón *m* heavy shower of rain.
chapotear *vt* to wet with a sponge; ● *vi* to paddle in water.
chapucear *vt* to botch, to bungle.
chapucero *m* bungler; ~, ra *adj* clumsy, crude.
chapurrar *vt* to speak (a language) badly; to mix drinks.
chapuza *f* badly done job.
chapuzarse *vr* to duck; to dive.
chaqueta *f* jacket.
charca *f* pool.
charco *m* pool; puddle.
charcutería *f* shop selling pork meat products.
charla *f* chat; talk.
charlar *vi* to chat.
charlatán, ana *m/f* chatterbox.
charlatanería *f* talkativeness.
charol *m* varnish; patent leather.
charrada *f* coarse thing; bad breeding; bad taste.
charretera *f* shoulder pad.
charro *m* coarse individual; ~, rra *adj* coarse; gaudy.
chasco *m* disappointment; fun, joke, jest.
chasis *m invar (auto)* chassis.
chasquear *vt* to crack a whip; to disappoint.
chasquido *m* crack; click.
chatarra *f* scrap.
chato, ta *adj* flat, flattish; snub-nosed.
chaval, la *m/f* lad/lass.
cheque *m* check.
chequeo *m* check-up; service.
chequera *f* checkbook.
chibo *m* kid.
chicano, na *adj* chicano.
chicle *m* chewing gum.
chico, ca *adj* little, small; ● *m/f* boy/girl.
chichal *f* corn liquor; meat.
chicharra *f* harvest fly.
chicharrón *m* (pork) crackling.
chichón *m* lump, bump.
chichonora *f* helmet.
chifla *f* whistle; hiss.
chiflado, da *adj* crazy.
chiflar *vt* to boo.
chile *m* chilli pepper.
chillar *vi* to scream, to shriek; to howl; to creak.
chillido *m* squeak, shriek; howl.
chillón, ona *adj* loud, noisy; gaudy; ● *m/f* whiner, moaner.
chimenea *f* chimney; fireplace.
china *f* pebble, porcelain; china-ware; China silk.
chinche *f* bug; thumbtack; ● *m* nuisance.
chincheta *f* thumbtack.
chinela *f* slipper.
chino, na *adj, m/f* Chinese; ● *m* Chinese language.
chiquero *m* pig sty.
chiripa *f* fluke.
chirla *f* mussel.
chirriar *vi* to hiss; to creak; to chirp.
chirrido *m* chirping of birds; squeaking.
chis *excl* sh!

chisgarabís *m (fam)* meddler.
chisme *m* tale; thingummyjig.
chismear *vt* to tell tales.
chismoso, sa *adj* gossiping; ● *m/f* gossip.
chispa *f* spark; sparkle; wit; drop (of rain); drunkenness.
chispazo *m* spark.
chispeante *adj* sparkling.
chispear *vi* to sparkle; to drizzle.
chisporrotear *vi* to crackle; to sparkle, to hiss (of liquids).
chistar *vi* to speak.
chiste *m* funny story; joke.
chistoso, sa *adj* witty, amusing, funny.
chivato *m* kid; child.
chivo, va *m/f* billy/nanny goat.
chocante *adj* startling; odd.
chocar *vi* to strike, to knock; to crash; ● *vt* to shock.
chocolate *m* chocolate.
chocolatera *f* chocolate pot.
chochear *vi* to dodder, to be senile; to dote.
choco *adj* doddering; doting.
chófer *m* driver.
chollo *m* bargain.
chopo *m (bot)* black poplar.
choque *m* shock; crash, collision; clash, conflict.
chorizo *m* pork sausage.
chorlito *m* plover.
chorrear *vi* to spout, to gush, to drip.
chorrera *f* channel; frill.
chorro *m* gush; jet; stream; a ~s abundantly.
choto *m* kid; calf.
choza *f* hut, shack.
chubasco *m* squall.
chuchería *f* trinket.
chucho *m* dog, mongrel.
chufleta *f* joke; taunt, jeer.
chulada *f* funny speech *or* action.
chulear *vi* to brag.
chuleta *f* chop.
chulo *m* rascal; pimp.
chunga *f* fun, joke; estar de ~ to be in good humor.
chunguearse *vr* to be in good humor.
chupado, da *adj* skinny; easy.
chupar *vt* to suck; to absorb.
chupete *m* pacifier.
chupetear *vi* to suck gently.
chupón, ona *m/f* swindler, sponger *(sl)*.
churro *m* fritter.
churruscarse *vr* to scorch.
churrusco *m* burnt toast.
chusco, ca *adj* pleasant, funny.
chusma *f* rabble, mob.
chuzo *m* little spear *or* spike; llover a ~s to pour heavily.

D

dactilógrafo, fa *m/f* typist.
dádiva *f* gift, present; donation.
dadivoso, sa *adj* generous, open-handed.
dado *m* die *(pl* dice).
daga *f* dagger.
¡dale! *excl* come on!
daltónico, ca *adj* color-blind.
dama *f* lady, gentlewoman; mistress; queen; actress who performs principal parts.
damasco *m* damask (stuff); damson (plum).
damasquino, na *adj* damask.
damero *m* checkers board.
damnificar *vt* to hurt, to damage, to injure.
danza *f* dance.
danzar *vi* to dance; to meddle.

danzarín m fine dancer; meddler.

dañar vt to hurt, to damage; to injure.

dañino, na adj harmful; noxious; mischievous.

daño m harm; damage, prejudice, loss.

dar vt to give; to supply, to administer, to afford; to deliver; to bestow; to strike, to beat, to knock; to communicate; ~se vr to conform to the will of another; to give oneself up to; ~se prisa vr to hurry.

dardo m dart.

datar vt to date.

dátil m (bot) date.

dativo m (gr) dative.

dato m fact.

de prep of; from; for; by; on; to; with.

deambular vi to stroll.

deán m dean.

debajo adv under, underneath, below.

debate m debate, discussion, contest, altercation.

debatir vt to debate, to argue, to discuss.

debe m (com) debit; ~ y haber debit and credit.

deber m obligation, duty; debt; ● vt to owe; to be obliged; ● vi: debe (de) it must, it should.

debidamente adv justly; duly, exactly, perfectly.

débil adj feeble, weak; sickly; frail.

debilidad f dimness; weakness.

debilitar vt to debilitate, to weaken.

débito m debt; duty.

debutar vi to make one's debut.

década f decade.

decadencia f decay, decline.

decaer vi to decay, to decline, to fade.

decaimiento m decay, decline.

decálogo m the Decalogue.

decano m senior; dean.

decantar vt to decant.

decapitación f decapitation, beheading.

decapitar vt to behead.

decena f ten.

decencia f decency.

decente adj decent, honest.

decepción f disappointment.

decidir vt to decide, to determine.

decimal adj decimal.

décimo, ma adj, m tenth.

decir vt to say, to tell, to speak; to name.

decisión f decision, determination, resolution; sentence.

decisivo, va adj decisive, final.

declamación f declamation, discourse, oration.

declamar vi to declaim, to harangue.

declaración f declaration, explanation; interpretation; (law) deposition.

declarar vt to declare, to manifest; to expound; to explain; (law) to decide; ● vi to testify; ~se vr to declare one's opinion.

declinación f declination, descent; decline.

declinar vi to decline; to decay, to degenerate; ● vt (gr) to decline.

declive m slope; decline.

decolorarse vr to become discolored.

decomiso m confiscation.

decoración f decoration.

decorado m scenery.

decorar vt to decorate; to adorn; to illustrate.

decorativo, va adj decorative.

decoro m honor, respect; circumspection; honesty; decency.

decoroso, sa adj decorous, decent.

decrecer vi to decrease.

decrépito, ta adj decrepit, crazy, worn out with age.

decrepitud f decrepitude.

decretar vt to decree, to determine.

decreto m decree, decision; judicial decree.

dechado m model of virtue and perfection.

dedal m thimble; very small drinking glass.

dedicación f dedication; consecration.

dedicar vt to dedicate, to devote, to consecrate; ~se vr to apply oneself to.

dedicatoria f dedication.

dedo m finger; toe; small bit; ~ meñique little finger; ~ pulgar thumb; ~ del corazón middle finger; ~ anular ring finger.

deducción f deduction, derivation, consequence.

deducir vt to deduce, to infer; to allege in pleading; to subtract.

defección f defection, apostasy.

defectivo, va adj defective.

defecto m defect, defectiveness.

defectuoso, sa adj defective, imperfect, faulty.

defender vt to defend, to protect; to justify, to assert, to maintain; to prohibit, to forbid; to resist, to oppose.

defensa f defense, justification, apology; guard, shelter, protection, fence.

defensiva f defensive.

defensivo m defense, safeguard; ~, va adj defensive.

defensor, ra m/f defender, protector; lawyer, counsel.

deferente adj pliant, docile, yielding.

deferir vi to defer; to yield to another's opinion; ● vt to communicate.

deficiencia f deficiency.

deficiente adj defective.

déficit m deficit.

definición f definition; decision.

definir vt to define, to describe, to explain; to decide.

definitivo, va adj definitive, positive.

deformar vt to deform; ~se vr to become deformed.

deforme adj deformed, ugly.

deformidad f deformity, ugliness; gross error.

defraudación f fraud, usurpation.

defraudar vt to defraud, to cheat; to usurp; to disturb.

defunción f death; funeral.

degeneración f degeneration; degeneracy.

degenerar vi to degenerate.

degollación f beheading.

degollar vt to behead; to destroy, to ruin.

degradación f degradation.

degradar vt to degrade; ~se vr to degrade or demean oneself.

degustar vt to taste.

dehesa f pasture ground.

deidad f deity, divinity; goddess.

dejadez f slovenliness, neglect.

dejado, da adj slovenly, idle, indolent; dejected.

dejar vt to leave, to let, to quit; to omit; to permit, to allow; to leave, to forsake; to bequeath; to pardon; ~ de vi to stop; to fail to; ~se vr to abandon oneself (to).

dejo m accent; aftertaste, tang.

del adj of the (contraction of de el).

delantal m apron.

delante adv in front; opposite; ahead; ~ de in front of, before.

delantera f front, forepart of something; advantage; forward line.

delantero, ra adj front; ● m forward.

delatar vt to accuse, to denounce.

delator m accuser, informer, denouncer.

delegación f delegation, substitution.

delegado m delegate, deputy.

delegar vt to delegate, to substitute.

deleitar vt to delight.

deletrear vt to spell; to examine; to conjecture.

delfín m dolphin; dauphin.

delgadez f thinness.

delgado, da adj thin, delicate, light; slender, lean; acute, fine, ingenious; little, scanty.

deliberación f deliberation; resolution.

deliberadamente adv deliberately.

deliberar vi to consider, to deliberate; to consult; • vt to debate.

delicadeza f tenderness, softness; delicacy, daintiness; subtlety.

delicado, da adj delicate, tender; faint; exquisite; delicious, dainty; slender, subtle.

delicia f delight, pleasure.

delicioso, sa adj delicious, delightful.

delincuencia f delinquency.

delincuente m delinquent.

delineante m/f draftsman/woman.

delinear vt to delineate, to sketch; to describe.

delinquir vi to offend.

delirante adj delirious.

delirar vi to rave; to talk nonsense.

delirio m delirium; dotage; nonsense.

delito m offense; crime.

demacrado, da adj pale and drawn.

demagogia f demagogy.

demagogo m demagogue.

demanda f demand, claim; pretension, complaint; challenge; request.

demandado, da m/f defendant.

demandante m/f claimant.

demandar vt to demand, to ask; to claim; to sue.

demarcación f demarcation; boundary line.

demarcar vt to mark out limits.

demás adj other; remaining; • pn **los/las** ~ the others, the rest; **estar** ~ to be over and above; to be useless or superfluous; **por** ~ in vain, to no purpose.

demasía f excess; arduous enterprise; rudeness; want of respect; abundance, plenty; **en** ~ excessively.

demasiado, da adj too, too much; excessive; • adv too, too much.

demencia f madness.

demente adj mad, insane.

democracia f democracy.

demócrata m democrat.

democrático, ca adj democratic.

demoler vt to demolish; to destroy.

demolición f demolition.

demonio m demon.

demora f delay; demurrage.

demorar vt to delay; • vi to linger; ~**se** vr to be delayed.

demostrable adj demonstrable.

demostración f demonstration; manifestation.

demostrar vt to prove, to demonstrate, to manifest.

demostrativo, va adj demonstrative.

denegación f denial, refusal.

denegar vt to deny, to refuse.

dengue m prudery.

denigración f defamation, stigma, disgrace.

denigrar vt to blacken; to insult.

denominación f denomination.

denominar vt to name; to designate.

denotar vt to denote, to express.

densidad f density; obscurity.

denso, sa adj dense, thick; compact.

dentado, da adj dentated, toothed; indented.

dentadura f set of teeth.

dentellada f gnashing of the teeth; nip; pinch with the teeth; a ~**s** snappishly, peevishly.

dentera f (fig) the shivers pl.

dentición f dentition, teething.

dentífrico m toothpaste.

dentista m/f dentist.

dentro adv within; • pn ~ **de** in, inside.

denuncia f denunciation; accusation; report.

denunciar vt to advise; to denounce; to report.

deparar vt to offer, to present.

departamento m department; (ferro) compartment; apartment.

dependencia f dependency, relation, affinity; dependence; office; business, affair.

depender vi to depend, to be dependent on.

dependienta f saleswoman.

dependiente m shop assistant; • adj dependent.

depilar vt to wax.

depilatorio m hair remover.

deplorable adj deplorable, lamentable.

deplorar vt to deplore.

deponer vt to depose, to declare; to displace; to deposit.

deportación f deportation.

deportar vt to deport.

deporte m sport.

deportista m/f sportsman/woman.

deportivo, va adj sports compd.

deposición f deposition; assertion, affirmation; (jur) deposition upon oath.

depositar vt to deposit, to confide; to put in any place to be kept safe.

depósito m deposit; warehouse; tank.

depravación f depravity.

depravar vt to deprave, to corrupt.

depreciar vt to depreciate.

depredador, ra adj predatory; • m predator.

depresión f depression.

deprimido, da adj depressed.

deprimir vt to depress; ~**se** vr to become depressed.

deprisa adv quickly.

depuración f purification.

depurar vt to cleanse, to purify, to filter.

derecha f right hand, right side; right.

derecho, cha adj right; straight; just; perfect; certain; • m right, justice, law; just claim; tax, duty; fee; • adv straight.

derivación f derivation; source; origin.

derivado, da adj, m derivative; • m by-product.

derivar vt, vi to derive; (mar) to deflect from the course.

derogar vt to derogate, to abolish; to reform.

derogatorio, ria adj derogatory.

derramamiento m effusion, waste; dispersion.

derramar vt to drain off water; to spread; to spill, to scatter, to waste, to shed; ~**se** vr to pour out.

derrame m spelling; overflow; discharge; leakage.

derredor m circumference, circuit; **al** ~, **en** ~ around, about.

derrengado, da adj bent, crooked.

derrengar vt to sprain.

derretir vt to melt; to consume; to thaw; ~**se** vr to melt.

derribar vt to demolish; to flatten.

derribo m demolition; ruins of a demolished building.

derrocar vt to pull down, to demolish.

derrochador m spendthrift.

derrochar vt to dissipate; to squander.

derroche m waste.

derrota f ship's course; road, path; defeat.

derrotar vt to destroy; to defeat.

derrotero m collection of sea charts; ship's course; (fig) course, way.

derruir vt to demolish.

derrumbar vt to throw down; ~**se** vr to collapse.

desabastecer vt to cut off supplies from.

desabillé m deshabille.

desabollar vt to take bulges out of.

desabotonar vt to unbutton; ~**se** vr to come undone.

desabrido, da adj tasteless, insipid; rude; unpleasant.

desabrigado, da adj uncovered; unsheltered.

desabrigar vt to uncover, to deprive of clothes or shelter.

desabrochar vt to undo; ~**se** vr to come undone.

desacatar vt to treat in a disrespectful manner.

desacato m disrespect, incivility.

desacertado, da adj mistaken; unwise; inconsiderate.

desacierto m error, gross mistake, blunder.

desaconsejado, da adj inconsiderate; ill-advised.

desaconsejar vt to advise against.

desacorde *adj* discordant.
desacostumbrado, da *adj* unusual.
desacreditar *vt* to discredit.
desacuerdo *m* blunder; disagreement; forgetfulness.
desafiar *vt* to challenge; to defy.
desafilado, da *adj* blunt.
desafinado, da *adj* out of tune.
desafinar *vi* to be out of tune.
desafío *m* challenge; struggle, contest, combat.
desaforado, da *adj* huge; disorderly, lawless, impudent.
desafortunadamente *adv* unfortunately.
desafortunado, da *adj* unfortunate, unlucky.
desafuero *m* outrage; excess.
desagradable *adj* disagreeable, unpleasant.
desagradar *vt* to displease; to pester.
desagradecido, da *adj* ungrateful.
desagradecimiento *m* ingratitude.
desagrado *m* harshness; displeasure.
desagraviar *vt* to make amends for.
desagravio *m* amends *pl*; satisfaction.
desaguar *vt* to drain; • *vi* to drain off.
desagüe *m* channel, drain; drainpipe; drainage.
desaguisado *m* outrage.
desahogado, da *adj* comfortable; roomy.
desahogar *vt* to ease; to vent; ~se *vr* to recover; to relax; to let off steam.
desahogo *m* ease, relief; freedom.
desahuciar *vt* to despair; to give up; to evict.
desahucio *m* eviction.
desairado, da *adj* disregarded, slighted.
desairar *vt* to disregard, to take no notice.
desaire *m* disdain, disrespect; unattractiveness.
desajustar *vt* to disproportion; to unbalance; ~se *vr* to get out of order.
desajuste *m* disorder; imbalance.
desalentador, ra *adj* disheartening.
desalentar *vt* to put out of breath; to discourage.
desaliento *m* dismay.
desaliño *m* slovenliness; carelessness.
desalmado, da *adj* cruel, inhuman.
desalojar *vt* to eject; to move out of; • *vi* to move out.
desamarrar *vt* to unmoor a ship; to untie; to remove.
desamor *m* indifference.
desamparado, da *adj* helpless.
desamparar *vt* to forsake, to abandon, to relinquish.
desamparo *m* abandonment; helplessness; dereliction.
desamueblar *vt* to unfurnish.
desandar *vt* to retrace, to go back the same road.
desangrar *vt* to bleed; to drain a pond; (*fig*) to exhaust one's means; ~se *vr* to lose a lot of blood.
desanimado, da *adj* downhearted.
desanimar *vt* to discourage; ~se *vr* to lose heart.
desapacible *adj* disagreeable, unpleasant, harsh.
desaparecer *vi* to disappear.
desaparecido, da *adj* missing; ~s *mpl* people missing.
desaparejar *vt* to unharness beasts; (*mar*) to unrig a ship.
desaparición *f* disappearance.
desapego *m* coolness; uninterestedness.
desapercibido, da *adj* unnoticed.
desaplicado, da *adj* lazy, careless, neglectful.
desapolillar *vt* to free from moths; ~se *vr* to get rid of the cobwebs.
desaprensivo, va *adj* unscrupulous.
desaprobación *f* disapproval.
desaprobar *vt* to disapprove; to condemn; to reject.
desaprovechado, da *adj* useless, unprofitable; backward; slack.
desaprovechar *vt* to waste, to turn to a bad use.
desarmar *vt* to disarm; to disband troops; to dismantle; (*fig*) to pacify.
desarme *m* disarmament.
desarraigar *vt* to root out; to extirpate.

desarraigo *m* eradication.
desarrapado, da *adj* ragged.
desarreglado, da *adj* untidy.
desarreglar *vt* to disorder, to upset.
desarreglo *m* disorder; untidiness.
desarrollar *vt* to develop; to unroll, to unfold; ~se *vr* to develop; to be unfolded, to open.
desarrollo *m* development.
desarropar *vt* to undress.
desarticular *vt* to take apart.
desasir *vt* to loosen, to disentangle; ~se *vr* to extricate oneself.
desasosegar *vt* to disquiet, to disturb.
desasosiego *m* restlessness; anxiety.
desastrado, da *adj* wretched, miserable; ragged.
desastre *m* disaster; misfortune.
desastroso, sa *adj* disastrous.
desatado, da *adj* untied; wild.
desatar *vt* to untie, to loose; to separate; to unriddle; ~se *vr* to come undone; to break.
desatascar *vt* to unblock; to clear.
desatender *vt* to pay no attention; to disregard.
desatinado, da *adj* foolish; extravagant; • *m* fool, madman.
desatinar *vt* to talk nonsense; to reel, to stagger.
desatino *m* blunder; nonsense.
desatornillar *vt* to unscrew.
desatrancar *vt* to unbar; to unblock.
desautorizado, da *adj* unauthorized.
desautorizar *vt* to deprive of authority; to deny.
desavenencia *f* discord, disagreement.
desavenido, da *adj* contrary, disagreeing.
desaventajado, da *adj* disadvantageous, unprofitable.
desayunar *vt* to have for breakfast; • *vi* to have breakfast; ~se *vr* to breakfast.
desayuno *m* breakfast.
desazón *f* disgust; uneasiness; annoyance.
desazonado, da *adj* ill-adapted; ill-humored.
desazonar *vt* to annoy; ~se *vr* to be annoyed; to be anxious.
desbancar *vt* to break the bank (in gambling); (*fig*) to supplant.
desbandarse *vr* to disband; to go off in all directions.
desbarajuste *m* confusion.
desbaratar *vt* to destroy.
desbarrar *vi* to talk rubbish.
desbastar *vt* to smooth; to polish; to waste.
desbloquear *vt* to unblock.
desbocado, da *adj* open-mouthed; wild (applied to a horse); foul-mouthed, indecent.
desbocarse *vr* to bolt.
desbordar *vt* to exceed; ~se *vr* to overflow.
descabalgar *vi* to dismount.
descabellado, da *adj* disheveled; disorderly; wild, unrestrained; disproportional; violent.
descabellar *vt* to ruffle.
descafeinado, da *adj* decaffeinated.
descalabrado, da *adj* wounded on the head; imprudent.
descalabrar *vt* to break or wound the head; to smash.
descalabro *m* blow; misfortune; considerable loss.
descalificar *vt* to disqualify; to discredit.
descalzar *vt*, ~se *vr* to pull off one's shoes.
descalzo, za *adj* barefooted; (*fig*) destitute.
descambiar *vt* to exchange.
descaminado, da *adj* (*fig*) misguided.
descaminar *vt* to misguide, to lead astray.
descamisado, da *adj* shirtless.
descampado, da *adj* disengaged, free, open; • *m* open space.
descansado, da *adj* rested, refreshed; quiet.
descansar *vt* to rest; • *vi* to rest; to lie down.
descansillo *m* landing.
descanso *m* rest, repose; break; interval.
descapotable *m* convertible.
descarado, da *adj* sassy, barefaced.

descararse vr to behave insolently.
descarga f unloading; volley, discharge.
descargar vt to unload, to discharge; ~**se** vr to unburden oneself.
descargo m discharge; evidence; receipt.
descarnado, da adj scrawny.
descarnar vt to strip off the flesh; to clean away the flesh from; to corrode; ~**se** vr to grow thin.
descaro m nerve.
descarriar vt to lead astray; to misdirect; ~**se** vr to lose one's way; to stray; to err.
descarrilamiento m (ferro) running off the rails, derailment.
descarrilar vi (ferro) to leave or run off the rails.
descarrío m losing of one's way.
descartar vt to discard; to dismiss; to rule out; ~**se** vr to excuse oneself.
descascarillado, da adj peeling.
descastado adj degenerate; ungrateful.
descendencia f descent, offspring.
descendente adj descending; **tren ~** m (ferro) down train.
descender vt to go down; ● vi to descend, to walk downward; to flow; to be derived from; to fall.
descendiente adj, m descending; descendant.
descenso m descent; drop.
descerrajar vt to force the lock of a door etc; to discharge firearms.
descifrar vt to decipher; to unravel.
desclavar vt to draw out nails.
descocado, da adj bold, impudent.
descolgar vt to unhang; to pick up; ~**se** vr to come down gently; to let oneself down.
descolorido, da adj pale, colorless.
descollar vi to excel, to surpass.
descomedido, da adj impudent, insolent; huge.
descompaginar vt to disarrange.
descomponer vt to discompose, to set at odds, to disconcert; (quim) to decompose.
descomposición f disagreement, discomposure; decomposition.
descompuesto, ta adj decomposed; broken.
descomunal adj uncommon; huge.
desconcertado, da adj disconcerted; bewildered.
desconcertar vt to disturb; to confound; to disconcert; ~**se** vr to be bewildered; to be upset.
desconchado, da adj peeling.
desconchar vt to peel off.
desconcierto m disorder, confusion; uncertainty.
desconectar vt to disconnect.
desconfiado, da adj diffident, mistrustful.
desconfianza f distrust; jealousy.
desconfiar vi to mistrust; to suspect.
descongelar vt to defrost.
descongestionar vt to clear.
desconocer vt to disown, to disavow; to be totally ignorant of a thing; not to know a person; not to acknowledge (a favor received).
desconocido, da adj ungrateful; disguised; unknown; ● m/f stranger.
desconocimiento m ignorance.
desconsiderado, da adj inconsiderate, imprudent.
desconsolado, da adj disconsolate; painful; sad.
desconsolar vt to distress.
desconsuelo m distress; trouble; despair.
descontado adj: **por ~** of course; **dar por ~** to take for granted.
descontar vt to discount; to deduct.
descontento m dissatisfaction, disgust.
descorazonar vt to dishearten; to discourage.
descorchar vt to uncork.
descorrer vt to draw.
descortés, esa adj impolite, rude.
descortesía f rudeness.

descoser vt to unseam; to separate; ~**se** vr to come apart at the seams.
descosido, da adj unstitched; disjointed.
descoyuntar vt to dislocate; to vex, to annoy.
descrédito m discredit.
descreído, da adj incredulous.
descremado, da adj skimmed.
describir vt to draw, to delineate; to describe.
descripción f delineation; description; inventory.
descriptivo, va adj descriptive.
descuartizar vt to quarter; to carve.
descubierto m deficit; ~, **a** adj uncovered.
descubrimiento m discovery; revelation.
descubrir vt to discover, to disclose; to uncover; to reveal; to show; ~**se** vr to reveal oneself; to take off one's hat; to confess.
descuento m discount; decrease.
¡descuida! excl don't worry!
descuidado, da adj careless, negligent.
descuidar vt to neglect; ● vi, ~**se** vr to be careless.
descuido m carelessness, negligence, forgetfulness; incivility; improper action.
desde prep since, after, from; ~ **luego** of course; ~ **entonces** since then.
desdecirse vr to retract.
desdén m disdain, scorn.
desdentado, da adj toothless.
desdentar vt to draw out teeth.
desdeñable adj contemptible, despicable.
desdeñar vt to disdain, to scorn; ~**se** vr to be disdainful.
desdeñoso, sa adj disdainful; contemptuous.
desdicha f misfortune, calamity; great poverty.
desdichado, da adj unfortunate, wretched, miserable.
desdoblar vt to unfold, to spread open.
desear vt to desire, to wish; to require, to demand.
desecación f desiccation.
desecar vt to dry up.
desechar vt to depreciate; to reject; to refuse; to throw away.
desecho m residue; ~**s** mpl rubbish.
desembalar vt to unpack.
desembarazado, da adj free.
desembarazar vt to free; to clear; ~**se** vr to get rid of.
desembarcadero m landing stage.
desembarcar vt to unload, to disembark; ● vi to disembark, to land.
desembarco m landing.
desembargo m (jur) raising an embargo.
desembarque m landing.
desembocadura f mouth.
desembocar vi to flow into.
desembolsar vt to pay out.
desembolso m expenditure.
desembragar vi to declutch.
desembuchar vt to disgorge; to tell all.
desempaquetar vt to unpack.
desempatar vt to hold a play-off.
desempate m play-off.
desempeñar vt to redeem; to extricate from debt; to fulfill any duty or promise; to acquit; ~**se** vr to get out of debt.
desempeño m redeeming a pledge; occupation.
desempleado, da adj unemployed; ● m/f unemployed person.
desempleo m unemployment.
desempolvorar vt to dust.
desencadenar vt to unchain; ~**se** vr to break loose; to burst.
desencajar vt to disjoint; to dislocate; to disconnect.
desencallar vt to refloat.
desencanto m disenchantment.
desenchufar vt to unplug.
desenfadado, da adj free, unembarrassed.
desenfado m ease; facility; calmness, relaxation.
desenfocado, da adj out of focus.
desenfrenado, da adj outrageous; ungovernable.

desenfreno *m* wildness; lack of self control.
desenganchar *vt* to unhook; to uncouple.
desengañado, da *adj* disillusioned.
desengañar *vt* to disillusion; ~se *vr* to become disillusioned.
desengaño *m* disillusionment; disappointment.
desengrasar *vt* to take out the grease.
desenhebrar *vt* to unthread; to unravel.
desenlace *m* climax; outcome.
desenmarañar *vt* to disentangle; to unravel.
desenmascarar *vt* to unmask.
desenredar *vt* to disentangle.
desenrollar *vt* to unroll.
desenroscar *vt* to untwist, to unroll.
desentenderse *vr* to feign not to understand; to pass by without noticing.
desenterrar *vt* to exhume; to dig up.
desentonar *vi* to humble; to be out of tune; to clash.
desentrañar *vt* to unravel.
desentumecer *vt* to stretch; to loosen up.
desenvainar *vt* to unsheath; to show.
desenvoltura *f* sprightliness; cheerfulness; impudence, boldness.
desenvolver *vt* to unfold, to unroll; to decipher, to unravel; to develop; ~se *vr* to develop; to cope.
desenvuelto, ta *adj* forward; natural.
deseo *m* desire, wish.
deseoso, sa *adj* anxious.
desequilibrado, da *adj* unbalanced.
deserción *f* desertion; defection.
desertar *vt* to desert; (*jur*) to abandon a cause.
desertor *m* deserter, fugitive.
desesperación *f* despair, desperation; anger, fury.
desesperado, da *adj* desperate, hopeless.
desesperar *vi*, ~se *vr* to despair; ● *vt* to make desperate.
desestabilizar *vt* to destabilize.
desestimar *vt* to disregard, to reject.
desfachatez *f* impudence.
desfalcar *vt* to embezzle.
desfalco *m* embezzlement.
desfallecer *vi* to get weak; to faint.
desfallecimiento *m* fainting.
desfasado, da *adj* old-fashioned.
desfase *m* gap.
desfavorable *adj* unfavorable.
desfigurar *vt* to disfigure, to deform; to disguise.
desfiladero *m* gorge.
desfilar *vi* (*mil*) to parade.
desfogarse *vr* to give vent to one's passion *or* anger.
desgajar *vt* to tear off; to break in pieces; ~se *vr* to be separated; to be torn in pieces.
desgana *f* disgust, loss of appetite; aversion, reluctance.
desganado, da *adj* not hungry; half-hearted; **estar** ~ to lose all pleasure in doing a thing; to lose one's appetite.
desgañitarse *vr* to scream, to bawl.
desgarrador, a *adj* heartrending.
desgarrar *vt* to tear; to shatter.
desgarro *m* tear; grief; impudence.
desgarrón *m* large tear.
desgastar *vt* to waste; to corrode; ~se *vr* to get worn out.
desgaste *m* wear (and tear).
desglosar *vt* to break down.
desgracia *f* misfortune, disgrace; accident; setback.
desgraciado, da *adj* unfortunate, unhappy, miserable; out of favor; disagreeable; ungrateful.
desgreñado, da *adj* disheveled.
desgreñar *vt* to dishevel the hair; to disorder.
desguarnecer *vt* to strip down; to dismantle.
deshabitado, da *adj* deserted, uninhabited, desolate.
deshacer *vt* to undo, to destroy; to cancel, to efface; to rout an army; to solve; to melt; to break up, to divide; to dissolve in a liquid; to violate a treaty; to diminish; to disband troops; ~se *vr* to melt; to come apart.

desharrapado, da *adj* shabby, ragged, in tatters.
deshecho, cha *adj* undone, destroyed, wasted; melted; in pieces.
deshelar *vt* to thaw; ~se *vr* to thaw, to melt.
desheredar *vt* to disinherit.
deshidratar *vt* to dehydrate.
deshielo *m* thaw.
deshilachar *vt* to ravel, to unweave.
deshilar *vt* to ravel.
deshinchar *vt* to deflate; ~se *vr* to go flat, to go down.
deshojar *vt* to strip off the leaves.
deshollinador *m* chimney sweep.
deshonesto, ta *adj* indecent.
deshonra *f* dishonor; shame.
deshonrar *vt* to affront, to insult, to defame; to dishonor.
deshonroso, sa *adj* dishonorable, indecent.
deshora *f* unseasonable time.
deshuesar *vt* to rid of bones; to stone.
desidia *f* idleness, indolence.
desierto, ta *adj* deserted, solitary; ● *m* desert, wilderness.
designación *f* designation.
designar *vt* to design, to intend; to appoint; to express, to name.
designio *m* design, purpose; road, course.
desigual *adj* unequal, unlike; uneven, craggy, cliffy.
desigualdad *f* inequality, dissimilitude; inconstancy; knottiness, unevenness.
desilusión *f* disappointment.
desilusionar *vt* to disappoint; ~se *vr* to become disillusioned.
desinfección *f* disinfection.
desinfectar *vt* to disinfect.
desinflar *vt* to deflate.
desintegración *f* disintegration.
desinterés *m* unselfishness; disinterestedness.
desinteresado, da *adj* disinterested; unselfish.
desistir *vi* to desist, to cease.
desleal *adj* disloyal; unfair.
deslealtad *f* disloyalty, breach of faith.
desleír *vt* to dilute, to dissolve.
deslenguado, da *adj* foul-mouthed, free-tongued.
desligar *vt* to separate; to loosen, to unbind; ~se *vr* to extricate oneself.
desliz *m* slip, sliding; lapse, weakness.
deslizadizo, za *adj* slippery, slippy, glib.
deslizar *vt* to slip, to slide; to speak carelessly, to go too far in conversation; ~se *vr* to slip; to skid; to flow softly; to creep in.
deslucido, da *adj* tarnished; dull; shabby.
deslucir *vt* to tarnish; to damage; to discredit.
deslumbramiento *m* glare; confusion.
deslumbrar *vt* to dazzle; to puzzle.
desmán *m* outrage; disaster; misconduct.
desmandarse *vr* to behave badly.
desmantelar *vt* to dismantle; to abandon, to forsake.
desmaquillador *m* make-up remover.
desmarañar *vt* to disentangle.
desmayado, da *adj* unconscious; dismayed, appalled; weak.
desmayar *vi* to be dispirited *or* faint-hearted; ~se *vr* to faint.
desmayo *m* unconsciousness; swoon; dismay.
desmedido, da *adj* disproportionate.
desmejorar *vt* to impair; to weaken.
desmembrar *vt* to dismember; to separate.
desmemoriado, da *adj* forgetful.
desmentir *vt* to give the lie; ~se *vr* to contradict oneself.
desmenuzar *vt* to crumble, to chip, to fritter; to examine minutely.
desmerecer *vt* to be unworthy of; ● *vi* to deteriorate.
desmesurado, da *adj* excessive; huge; immeasurable.
desmontar *vt* to level; to remove a heap of rubbish; to dismantle; ● *vi* to dismount.
desmoralización *f* demoralization.
desmoralizar *vt* to demoralize.

desmoronar *vt* to destroy little by little; ~**se** *vr* to fall into disrepair.

desnatado, da *adj* skimmed.

desnatar *vt* to skim milk; to take the choicest part.

desnaturalizar *vt* to divest of naturalization rights; ~**se** *vr* to forsake one's country.

desnivel *m* unevenness of the ground.

desnucar *vt* to break one's neck.

desnudar *vt* to undress; to strip; to discover, to reveal; ~**se** *vr* to undress.

desnudez *f* nakedness.

desnudo, da *adj* naked, bare, uncovered; ill-clothed; *(fig)* plain, evident.

desnutrición *f* malnutrition.

desnutrido, da *adj* undernourished.

desobedecer *vt, vi* to disobey.

desobediencia *f* disobedience; insubordination.

desobediente *adj* disobedient.

desocupado, da *adj* empty; at leisure.

desocupar *vt* to quit, to empty; ~**se** *vr* to retire from a business; to withdraw from an arrangement.

desodorante *m* deodorant.

desolación *f* destruction; affliction.

desolado, da *adj* desolate, disconsolate.

desolar *vt* to lay waste; to harass.

desollar *vt* to flay, to skin; *(fig)* to extort.

desorden *m* disorder, confusion.

desordenado, da *adj* disorderly; untidy.

desordenar *vt* to disorder; to untidy; ~**se** *vr* to get out of order.

desorganización *f* disorganization.

desorganizar *vt* to disorganize.

desorientar *vt* to mislead; to confuse; ~**se** *vr* to lose one's way.

desovar *vi* to spawn.

despabilado, da *adj* watchful, vigilant; wide-awake.

despabilar *vt* to snuff a candle; *(fig)* to despatch quickly; to sharpen; ~**se** *vr* to wake up.

despacio *adv* slowly, leisurely; little by little; ¡~! softly! gently!

despachar *vt* to dispatch; to expedite; to sell; to send.

despacho *m* dispatch, expedition; cabinet; office; commission; warrant, patent; expedient; a smart answer.

despachurrar *vt* to squash, to crush; to mangle.

desparejar *vt* to make unequal *or* uneven.

desparpajo *m* ease; savoir-faire.

desparramar *vt* to disseminate, to spread; to spill; to squander, to lavish; ~**se** *vr* to be dissipated.

despavorido *adj* frightened.

despectivo, va *adj* pejorative; derogatory.

despecho *m* indignation, displeasure; spite; dismay, despair; deceit; derision, scorn; a ~ de in spite of.

despedazar *vt* to tear into pieces; to mangle.

despedida *f* farewell; sacking.

despedir *vt* to discharge; to dismiss from office; to see off; ~**se** *vr* to say goodbye to.

despegado, da *adj* cold; detached.

despegar *vt* to unglue; to take off; ~**se** *vr* to come loose.

despego *m* detachment; coolness.

despegue *m* take-off.

despeinado, da *adj* disheveled.

despeinar *vt* to ruffle.

despejado, da *adj* sprightly, quick; clear.

despejar *vt* to clear away obstructions; ● *vi* to clear; ~**se** *vr* to cheer up; to clear.

despellejar *vt* to skin.

despensa *f* pantry, larder; provisions, *pl.*

despeñadero *m* precipice.

despeñar *vt* to precipitate; ~**se** *vr* to throw oneself headlong.

despepitarse *vr* to bawl.

desperdiciar *vt* to squander.

desperdicio *m* waste; ~**s** *mpl* garbage; waste.

desperdigar *vt* to separate, to scatter.

desperezarse *vr* to stretch oneself.

desperfecto *m* slight damage; flaw.

despertador *m* alarm clock.

despertar *vt* to wake up, to rouse from sleep; to excite; ● *vi* to wake up; to grow lively *or* sprightly; ~**se** *vr* to wake up.

despiadado, da *adj* heartless; merciless.

despido *m* dismissal.

despierto, ta *adj* awake; vigilant; fierce; brisk, sprightly.

despilfarrar *vt* to waste.

despilfarro *m* slovenliness; waste; mismanagement.

despintar *vt* to deface a painting; to obscure things; to mislead; ~**se** to lose its color.

despistar *vt* to mislead; to throw off the track; ~**se** *vr* to take the wrong way; to become confused.

desplante *m* bold statement; wrong stance; insolence.

desplazamiento *m* displacement.

desplazar *vt* to move; to scroll; ~**se** *vr* to travel.

desplegar *vt* to unfold, to display; to explain, to elucidate; *(mar)* to unfurl; ~**se** *vr* to blow, to open; to travel.

despliegue *m* display.

desplomarse *vr* to fall flat to the ground; to collapse.

desplumar *vt* to deplume, to fleece; to pluck.

despoblado *m* desert.

despoblar *vt* to depopulate; to desolate; ~**se** *vr* to become depopulated.

despojar *vt* to strip (of); to deprive of; ~**se** *vr* to undress.

despojo *m* plunder; loot; ~**s** *pl* giblets; remains; offal.

desposado, da *adj* newly wed.

desposar *vt* to marry, to betroth; ~**se** *vr* to be betrothed *or* married.

desposeer *vt* to dispossess.

desposeimiento *m* dispossession.

déspota *m* despot.

despótico, ca *adj* despotic.

despotismo *m* despotism.

despreciable *adj* contemptible, despicable.

despreciar *vt* to offend; to despise.

desprecio *m* scorn, contempt.

desprender *vt* to unfasten, to loosen, to separate; ~**se** *vr* to give way, to fall down; to extricate oneself.

desprendimiento *m* alienation, disinterestedness.

despreocupado, da *adj* careless; unworried.

despreocuparse *vr* to be carefree.

desprestigiar *vt* to run down.

desprevenido, da *adj* unawares, unprepared.

desproporción *f* disproportion.

desproporcionado, da *adj* disproportionate.

desproporcionar *vt* to disproportion.

despropósito *m* absurdity.

desprovisto, ta *adj* unprovided.

después *adv* after, afterwards; next.

despuntar *vt* to blunt; ● *vi* to sprout; to dawn; **al** ~ **del día** at break of day.

desquiciar *vt* to upset; to discompose; to disorder.

desquitar *vt* to retrieve a loss; ~**se** *vr* to win one's money back again; to return by giving like for like; to take revenge.

desquite *m* recovery of a loss; revenge, retaliation.

desrizar *vt* to uncurl.

destacamento *m (mil)* detachment.

destacar *vt* to emphasize; *(mil)* to detach (a body of troops); ~**se** *vr* to stand out.

destajo *m* job, piecework.

destapar *vt* to uncover; to open; ~**se** *vr* to be uncovered.

destartalado, da *adj* untidy.

destello *m* signal light; sparkle.

destemplado, da *adj* out of tune, incongruous (applied to paintings); intemperate.

desteñir *vt* to discolor; ~**se** *vr* to fade.

desternillarse *vr* to roar with laughter.

desterrar *vt* to banish; to expel, to drive away.

destetar *vt* to wean.

destete *m* weaning.
destierro *m* exile, banishment.
destilación *f* distillation.
destilar *vt*, *vi* to distill.
destinar *vt* to destine for, to intend for.
destinatario, a *m/f* addressee.
destino *m* destiny; fate, doom; destination; office.
destitución *f* destitution, abandonment.
destituir *vt* to dismiss.
destornillador *m* screwdriver.
destornillar *vt* to unscrew.
destreza *f* dexterity, cleverness, cunning, expertness, skill.
destripar *vt* to disembowel; to trample.
destronar *vt* to dethrone.
destrozar *vt* to destroy, to break into pieces; (*mil*) to defeat.
destrozo *m* destruction; (*mil*) defeat, massacre.
destrucción *f* destruction, ruin.
destructivo, va *adj* destructive.
destruir *vt* to destroy.
desunir *vt* to separate, to disunite; to cause discord.
desuso *m* disuse.
desvaído, da *adj* tall and graceless.
desvalido, da *adj* helpless, destitute.
desvalijar *vt* to rob; to burgle.
desván *m* garret.
desvanecer *vt* to dispel; ~**se** *vr* to grow vapid, to become insipid; to vanish; to be affected with giddiness.
desvanecimiento *m* pride, haughtiness; giddiness; swoon.
desvariar *vi* to be delirious.
desvarío *m* delirium; giddiness; inconstancy, caprice; extravagance.
desvelar *vt* to keep awake; ~**se** *vr* to stay awake.
desvelo *m* want of sleep, watchfulness.
desvencijado, da *adj* rickety.
desvencijar *vt* to disunite, to weaken, to divide; ~**se** *vr* to be ruptured; to come apart.
desventaja *f* disadvantage, damage.
desventura *f* misfortune, calamity.
desventurado, da *adj* unfortunate, calamitous.
desvergonzado, da *adj* impudent, shameless.
desvergonzarse *vr* to behave in an impudent manner.
desvergüenza *f* impudence; shamelessness.
desvestir *vt*, ~**se** *vr* to undress.
desviar *vt* to divert; to dissuade; to parry (at fencing); ~**se** *vr* to go off course.
desvío *m* turning away, going astray; aversion; disdain; indifference.
desvivirse *vr* to long for.
detallar *vt* to detail, to relate minutely.
detalle *m* detail.
detallista *m* retailer.
detención *f* detention; delay.
detener *vt* to stop, to detain; to arrest; to keep back; to reserve; to withhold; ~**se** *vr* to stop, to stay.
detenidamente *adv* carefully.
detenido, da *adj* detailed; sparing, niggardly; slow, inactive.
detergente *m* detergent.
deterioración *f* deterioration, damage.
deteriorar *vt* to deteriorate.
deterioro *m* deterioration.
determinación *f* determination, resolution; boldness.
determinado, da *adj* determined; resolute.
determinar *vt* to determine; ~**se** *vr* to decide.
detestable *adj* detestable.
detestar *vt* to detest, to abhor.
detonación *f* detonation.
detonar *vi* to detonate.
detractar *vt* to detract, to defame, to slander.
detrás *adv* behind; at the back, in back.
detrimento *m* detriment, damage, loss.
deuda *f* debt; fault; offense.
deudor, ra *m/f* debtor.

devaluación *f* devaluation.
devanar *vt* to reel; to wrap up.
devastación *f* devastation, desolation.
devastador, ra *adj* devastating.
devastar *vt* to desolate, to waste.
devengar *vt* to accrue.
devoción *f* devotion, piety; strong affection, ardent love.
devolución *f* return; (*jur*) devolution.
devolutivo, va *adj* (*jur*) transferable.
devolver *vt* to return; to send back; to refund; ● *vi* to be sick.
devorar *vt* to devour, to swallow up.
devoto, ta *adj* devout, pious, devotional; strongly attached.
día *m* day.
diablo *m* devil, Satan.
diablura *f* prank.
diabólico, ca *adj* diabolical; devilish.
diácono *m* deacon.
diadema *m/f* diadem; halo.
diafragma *m* diaphragm, midriff.
diagnosis *f invar* diagnosis.
diagnóstico *m* diagnosis.
diagonal *adj* diagonal.
diagrama *m* diagram.
dialecto *m* dialect.
diálogo *m* dialogue.
diamante *m* diamond.
diámetro *m* diameter.
diana *f* (*mil*) reveille; bull's-eye.
diapasón *m* (*mus*) diapason, octave.
diapositiva *f* transparency, slide.
diario *m* journal, diary; daily newspaper; daily expense; ~, **ria** *adj* daily.
diarrea *f* diarrhea.
dibujar *vt* to draw, to design.
dibujo *m* drawing, sketch, draft; description.
dicción *f* diction, style, expression.
diccionario *m* dictionary.
diciembre *m* December.
dictado *m* dictation.
dictador *m* dictator.
dictadura *f* dictatorship.
dictamen *m* opinion, notion; suggestion, insinuation; judgment.
dictar *vt* to dictate.
dicha *f* happiness, good fortune; **por** ~ by chance.
dicho *m* saying, sentence; declaration; promise of marriage; ~, **cha** *adj* said.
dichoso, sa *adj* happy, prosperous.
diecinueve *adj*, *m* nineteen.
dieciocho *adj*, *m* eighteen.
dieciséis *adj*, *m* sixteen.
diecisiete *adj*, *m* seventeen.
diente *m* tooth; fang, tusk.
diestro, tra *adj* right; dexterous, skillful, clever; sagacious, prudent; sly, cunning; ● *m* skillful fencer; halter, bridle.
diesel *adj* diesel.
dieta *f* diet, regimen; diet, assembly; daily salary of judges.
diez *adj*, *m* ten.
diezmar *vt* to decimate.
diezmo *m* tithe.
difamación *f* defamation.
difamar *vt* to defame, to libel.
difamatorio, ria *adj* defamatory, calumnious.
diferencia *f* difference.
diferencial *adj* differential, different.
diferenciar *vt* to differ, to differentiate; ~**se** *vr* to differ, to distinguish oneself.
diferente *adj* different, unlike.
diferido, da *adj* recorded.
diferir *vt* to defer, to put off; to differ.
difícil *adj* difficult.
dificultad *f* difficulty.

dificultar *vt* to raise difficulties; to render difficult.

dificultoso, sa *adj* difficult; painful.

difundir *vt* to diffuse, to spread; to divulge; ~se *vr* to spread (out).

difunto, ta *adj* dead, deceased; late.

difusión *f* diffusion.

difuso, sa *adj* diffusive, copious; large; prolix, circumstantial.

digerir *vt* to digest; to bear with patience; to adjust, to arrange; (*chem*) to digest.

digestión *f* digestion; concoction.

digestivo, va *adj* digestive.

digital *adj* digital.

dignarse *vr* to condescend, to deign.

dignidad *f* dignity, rank.

digno, na *adj* worthy; suitable.

dije *m* relic; trinket.

dilapidar *vt* to squander, to waste.

dilatación *f* dilation, extension; greatness of mind; calmness.

dilatado, da *adj* large, numerous; prolix; spacious, extensive.

dilatar *vt* to dilate, to expand; to spread out; to defer, to protract.

dilatorio, ria *adj* dilatory.

dilema *m* dilemma.

diligencia *f* diligence; affair, business; call of nature; stage-coach.

diligente *adj* diligent, assiduous, prompt, swift.

dilucidar *vt* to elucidate, to explain.

diluir *vt* to dilute.

diluviar *vi* to rain in torrents.

diluvio *m* flood, deluge, inundation; abundance.

dimensión *f* dimension; extent, capacity, bulk.

diminutivo, va *adj* diminutive.

diminuto, ta *adj* defective, faulty; minute, small.

dimisión *f* resignation.

dimitir *vt* to give up, to abdicate; ● *vi* to resign.

dinámica *f* dynamics.

dinámico, ca *adj* dynamic.

dinamita *f* dynamite.

dínamo *f* dynamo.

dinastía *f* dynasty.

dineral *m* large sum of money.

dinero *m* money.

diocesano, na *adj* diocesan.

diócesis *f* diocese.

Dios *m* God.

diosa *f* goddess.

diploma *m* diploma, patent.

diplomacia, diplomática *f* diplomacy.

diplomado, da *adj* qualified.

diplomático, ca *adj* diplomatic; ● *m/f* diplomat.

diptongo *m* diphthong.

diputación *f* deputation.

diputado *m* deputy.

diputar *vt* to depute.

dique *m* dike, dam.

dirección *f* direction; guidance, administration; steering.

directivo, va *adj* governing.

directo, ta *adj* direct, straight; apparent, evident; live.

director, ra *m/f* director; conductor; president; manager.

dirigir *vt* to direct; to conduct; to regulate, to govern; ~se *vr* to go toward; to address oneself to.

discernimiento *m* discernment.

discernir *vt* to discern, to distinguish.

disciplina *f* discipline.

discípulo *m* disciple, scholar.

disco *m* disk; record; discus; light; face of the sun *or* moon; lens of a telescope.

díscolo, la *adj* ungovernable; peevish.

disconforme *adj* differing.

discordancia *f* disagreement, discord.

discordante *adj* dissonant, discordant.

discordar *vi* to clash, to disagree.

discorde *adj* discordant; (*mus*) dissonant.

discordia *f* discord, disagreement.

discoteca *m* discotheque.

discreción *f* discretion; acuteness of mind.

discrecional *adj* discretionary.

discrepancia *f* discrepancy.

discrepar *vi* to differ.

discreto, ta *adj* discreet; ingenious, witty, eloquent.

discriminación *f* discrimination.

disculpa *f* apology, excuse.

disculpar *vt* to exculpate, to excuse, to acquit, to absolve; ~se *vr* to apologize; to excuse oneself.

discurrir *vi* to ramble about, to run to and fro; to discourse upon a subject; ● *vt* to invent, to contrive; to meditate.

discurso *m* speech; conversation; dissertation; space of time.

discusión *f* discussion.

discutir *vt, vi* to discuss.

disecar *vt* to dissect; to stuff.

disección *f* dissection.

diseminar *vt* to scatter; to disseminate, to propagate.

disentería *f* dysentery.

disentir *vi* to dissent, to disagree.

diseñador *m* designer.

diseñar *vt* to draw, to design.

diseño *m* design, draft; description; picture.

disfraz *m* mask, disguise.

disfrazar *vt* to disguise, to conceal; to cloak, to dissemble; ~se *vr* to disguise oneself as.

disfrutar *vt* to enjoy; ~se *vr* to enjoy oneself.

disgustar *vt* to disgust; to offend; ~se *vr* to be displeased, to fall out.

disgusto *m* disgust, aversion; quarrel; annoyance; grief, sorrow.

disidente *adj, m* dissident, dissenter.

disimular *vt* to hide; to tolerate.

disimulo *m* dissimulation; tolerance.

disipado, da *adj* prodigal, lavish.

disipar *vt* to dissipate, to disperse, to scatter; to lavish.

dislocación *f* dislocation.

dislocarse *vr* to be dislocated *or* put out of joint.

disminución *f* diminution.

disminuir *vt* to diminish; to decrease.

disolución *f* dissolution; liquidation.

disolver *vt* to loosen, to untie; to dissolve, to disunite; to melt, to liquefy; to interrupt.

disonancia *f* dissonance; disagreement, discord.

disparar *vt, vi* to shoot, to discharge, to fire; to let off; to throw with violence.

disparatado, da *adj* inconsistent, absurd, extravagant.

disparate *m* nonsense, absurdity, extravagance.

disparo *m* shot; discharge, explosion.

dispensar *vt* to dispense; to excuse, to dispense with; to distribute.

displicencia *f* displeasure, dislike.

disponer *vt* to arrange; to dispose, to prepare.

disponible *adj* available; disposable.

disposición *f* disposition, order; resolution; command; power, authority.

dispositivo *m* device.

dispuesto, ta *adj* disposed, fit, ready.

disputa *f* dispute, controversy.

disputar *vt, vi* to dispute, to controvert, to question; to debate, to argue.

disquete *m* floppy disk.

distancia *f* distance, interval; difference.

distanciarse *vr* to become estranged.

distante *adj* distant, far off.

distinción *f* distinction; difference; prerogative.

distinguido, da *adj* distinguished, conspicuous.

distinguir *vt* to distinguish; to discern; ~se *vr* to distinguish oneself.

distintivo *m* distinctive mark; particular attribute.

distinto, ta *adj* distinct, different; clear.
distracción *f* distraction, want of attention.
distraer *vt* to distract; ~**se** *vr* to be absent-minded, to be inattentive.
distraído, da *adj* absent, inattentive.
distribución *f* distribution, division, separation; arrangement.
distribuidor *m* distributor.
distribuir *vt* to distribute.
distrito *m* district; territory.
disturbar *vt* to disturb, to interrupt.
disturbio *m* riot; disturbance, interruption.
disuadir *vt* to dissuade.
disuasión *f* dissuasion.
diurno, na *adj* daily.
diva *f* prima donna.
divagar *vt* to digress.
diván *m* divan.
divergencia *f* divergence.
divergente *adj* divergent.
diversidad *f* diversity; variety of things.
diversificar *vt* to diversify, to vary.
diversión *f* diversion; sport, amusement; (*mil*) diversion.
diverso, sa *adj* diverse, different; several, sundry.
divertido, da *adj* amused; amusing.
divertir *vt* to divert (the attention); to amuse, to entertain; (*mil*) to draw the enemy off; ~**se** *vr* to amuse oneself.
dividir *vt* to divide, to disunite, to separate; to share out.
divieso *m* (*med*) boil.
divinidad *f* divinity.
divino, na *adj* divine, heavenly; excellent.
divisa *f* emblem.
divisar *vt* to perceive.
divisible *adj* divisible.
división *f* division; partition; separation; difference.
divorciar *vt* to divorce, to separate; ~**se** *vr* to get divorced.
divorcio *m* divorce; separation, disunion.
divulgación *f* publication; dissemination.
divulgar *vt* to publish, to divulge.
dobladillo *m* hem; cuff.
dobladura *f* fold.
doblar *vt* to double, to fold; to bend; ● *vi* to turn; to toll; ~**se** *vr* to bend, to bow, to submit.
doble *adj* double; dual; deceitful; **al** ~ doubly; ● *m* double.
doblegar *vt* to bend; ~**se** *vr* to yield.
doblez *m* crease; fold; cuff; ● *f* duplicity.
doce *adj*, *m* twelve.
docena *f* dozen.
docente *adj* teaching.
dócil *adj* docile, tractable.
docilidad *f* docility, compliance, gentleness.
doctor, ra *m/f* doctor; physician.
doctorado *m* doctorate.
doctrina *f* doctrine, instruction; science.
doctrinal *m* catechism; ● *adj* doctrinal.
documentación *f* documentation.
documento *m* document; record.
dogma *m* dogma.
dólar *m* dollar.
dolencia *f* disease, affliction.
doler *vt*, *vi* to feel pain; to ache; ~**se** *vr* to feel for the sufferings of others; to complain.
dolor *m* pain, aching, ache; affliction.
doloroso, sa *adj* painful.
domador, ra *m/f* tamer.
domar *vt* to tame; to subdue, to master.
domesticar *vt* to domesticate.
domiciliarse *vr* to establish oneself in a residence.
domicilio *m* domicile, home, abode.
dominación *f* domination; dominion, authority, power.
dominante *adj* dominant, domineering.

dominar *vt* to be fluent in; to domineer; ~**se** *vr* to moderate one's passions.
domingo *m* Sunday.
dominguero, ra *adj* done *or* worn on Sunday.
dominical *adj* Sunday.
dominio *m* dominion, domination, power, authority; domain.
donación *f* donation, gift.
donar *vt* to donate, to bestow.
donativo *m* contribution.
doncella *f* virgin, maiden; lady's maid.
donde *adv* where; **¿de dónde?** from where? **¿por dónde?** where?
dondequiera *adv* anywhere.
dorado, da *adj* gilt; golden; ● *m* gilding.
dorar *vt* to gild; (*fig*) to palliate.
dormilón, ona *m* dull, sleepy person.
dormir *vi* to sleep; ~**se** *vr* to fall asleep.
dormitorio *m* dormitory.
dorsal *adj* dorsal.
dos *adj*, *m* two.
doscientos, tas *adj pl* two hundred.
dosis *f* dose, dosis.
dotado, da *adj* gifted.
dotar *vt* to endow.
dote *f* dowry; ~**s** *pl* gifts of nature; endowments.
dragón *m* dragon; (*mil*) dragoon.
drama *m* drama.
dramático, ca *adj* dramatic.
dramatizar *vt* to dramatize.
dramaturgo *m* dramatist.
droga *f* drug; stratagem, artifice, deceit.
drogadicto, ta *m/f* drug addict.
droguería *f* hardware store.
dromedario *m* dromedary.
dubitativo, va *adj* doubtful, dubious, uncertain.
ducado *m* duchy; ducat.
ducha *f* shower; (*med*) douche.
ducharse *vr* to take a shower.
ducho, cha *adj* skilled, experienced.
duda *f* doubt; suspense; hesitation.
dudar *vt* to doubt.
dudoso, sa *adj* doubtful, dubious.
duelo *m* grief, affliction; mourning.
duende *m* elf, hobgoblin.
dueño, ña *m/f* owner; landlord/lady; employer.
dulce *adj* sweet; mild, soft, gentle, meek; ● *m* sweet, candy.
dulcificar *vt* to sweeten.
dulzura *f* sweetness; gentleness; softness.
dúo *m* (*mus*) duo, duet.
duodécimo, ma *adj* twelfth.
duplicación *f* duplication.
duplicado *m* duplicate.
duplicar *vt* to double, to duplicate; to repeat.
duplicidad *f* duplicity; falseness.
duplo *m* double.
duque *m* duke.
duquesa *f* duchess.
duración *f* duration.
duradero, ra *adj* lasting, durable.
durante *adv* during.
durar *vi* to last, to continue.
durazno *m* peach.
durazno, duraznero *m* peach tree.
dureza *f* hardness; harshness; ~ **de oído** hardness of hearing.
durmiente *adj* sleeping; ● *m* (*ferro*) sleeper, tie.
duro, ra *adj* hard; cruel; harsh, tough, rough; ● *m* dollar.
duunvir *m* a five peseta coin; ● *adv* hard.

E

e *conj* and.
ea *interj* hey! come on!; ¡~ pues! well then! let's see!
ebanista *m* cabinet-maker, carpenter.
ébano *m* ebony.
ebrio, ia *adj* drunk.
ebullición *f* boiling.
eccema *m* eczema.
eclesiástico, ca *adj* ecclesiastical.
eclipsar *vt* to eclipse, to outshine.
eclipse *m* eclipse.
eco *m* echo.
ecología *f* ecology.
economato *m* cooperative store.
economía *f* economy.
económico, ca *adj* economic(al); cheap; thrifty; financial; avaricious.
economista *m/f* economist.
ecuación *f* equation.
ecuador *m* equator.
ecuánime *adj* level-headed.
ecuestre *adj* equestrian.
ecuménico, ca *adj* ecumenical, universal.
echar *vt* to throw; to add; to fire; to pour out; to mail; to give off; to bud; ~se *vr* to lie down, to rest, to stretch out.
edad *f* age.
edecán *m* (*mil*) aide-de-camp.
edición *f* edition; publication.
edicto *m* edict.
edificación *f* construction.
edificante *adj* exemplary, instructive.
edificar *vt* to build; to construct a building.
edificio *m* building, structure.
editar *vt* to edit; to publish.
editor *m* editor; publisher.
educación *f* education; upbringing; (good) manners.
educador, ra *m/f* teacher, educator.
educando, da *m/f* pupil.
educar *vt* to educate, to instruct; to bring up.
efectivamente *adv* exactly; really; in fact.
efectivo, va *adj* effective, true, certain.
efecto *m* effect; consequence; purpose; ~s *pl* effects, goods; en ~ in fact, really.
efectuar *vt* to effect, to carry out.
efeméride *f* event (remembered on its anniversary).
efervescencia *f* effervescence, fizziness.
eficacia *f* effectiveness, efficacy.
eficaz *adj* efficient; effective.
eficiente *adj* efficient.
efigie *f* effigy, image.
efímero, ra *adj* ephemeral.
efluvio *m* outflow.
efusión *f* effusion.
efusivo, va *adj* effusive.
égloga *f* (*poet*) eclogue.
egoísmo *m* selfishness.
egoísta *m/f* self-seeker; ● *adj* selfish.
egregio, gia *adj* eminent, remarkable.
eje *m* axle; axis.
ejecución *f* execution.
ejecutar *vt* to execute, to perform; to put to death; (*jur*) to distrain, to seize.
ejecutivo, va *adj* executive; ● *m/f* executive.
ejecutor, ra *m/f* executor; (*jur*) distrainer.
ejecutoria *f* (*jur*) writ of execution.
ejecutorio, ria *adj* (*jur*) executory.
ejemplar *m* specimen; copy; example; ● *adj* exemplary.
ejemplificar *vt* to exemplify.
ejemplo *m* example; por ~ for example, for instance.
ejercer *vt* to exercise.

ejercicio *m* exercise.
ejercitación *f* exercise, practice.
ejercitar *vt* to exercise; ~se *vr* to apply oneself to the functions of an office.
ejército *m* army.
ejote *m* green bean.
el *art m* the.
él, ella, ello *pn* he, she, it.
elaboración *f* elaboration.
elaborado, da *adj* elaborate.
elaborar *vt* to elaborate.
elasticidad *f* elasticity.
elástico, ca *adj* elastic.
elección *f* election; discernment, choice.
elector, ra *m/f* elector.
electorado *m* electorate.
electoral *adj* electoral.
electricidad *f* electricity.
electricista *m/f* electrician.
eléctrico, ca *adj* electric, electrical.
electrización *f* electrification.
electrizar *vt* to electrify.
electrocutar *vt* to electrocute.
electrodomésticos *mpl* (electrical) household appliances.
electrónico, ca *adj* electronic.
electrotecnia *f* electrical engineering.
elefante *m* elephant.
elegancia *f* elegance.
elegante *adj* elegant, fine.
elegía *f* elegy.
elegir *vt* to choose, to elect.
elemental *adj* elemental; elementary.
elemento *m* element; ~s *pl* elements, rudiments, first principles.
elevación *f* elevation; highness; rise; haughtiness, pride, height; altitude.
elevar *vt* to raise; to elevate; ~se *vr* to rise; to be enraptured; to be conceited.
eliminar *vt* to eliminate, to remove.
eliminatoria *f* preliminary (round).
elipse *f* (*geom*) ellipse.
elipsis *f* (*gr*) ellipsis.
elite *f* elite.
elixir *m* elixir.
elocución *f* elocution.
elocuencia *f* eloquence.
elocuente *adj* eloquent.
elogiar *vt* to praise, to eulogize.
elogio *m* eulogy, praise.
elote *m* corn on the cob.
elucidación *f* elucidation, explanation.
eludir *vt* to elude, to escape.
emanación *f* emanation.
emanar *vi* to emanate.
emancipación *f* emancipation.
emancipar *vt* to emancipate, to set free.
embadurnar *vt* to smear, to bedaub.
embajada *f* embassy.
embajador, ra *m/f* ambassador.
embalaje *m* packing, package.
embalar *vt* to bale, to pack in bales.
embaldosar *vt* to pave with tiles.
embalsamador *m* embalmer.
embalsamar *vt* to embalm.
embalse *m* reservoir.
embarazada *f* pregnant woman; ● *adj* pregnant.
embarazar *vt* to embarrass; to make pregnant; ~se *vr* to become intricate.
embarazo *m* pregnancy; embarrassment; obstacle.
embarazoso, sa *adj* difficult, intricate, entangled.
embarcación *f* embarkation; any vessel *or* ship.
embarcadero *m* quay, wharf; port; harbor.

embarcar vt to embark; ~se vr to go on board; (fig) to get involved in a matter.

embargar vt to lay on an embargo; to impede, to restrain.

embargo m embargo; sin ~ still, however.

embarque m embarkation.

embastar vt to baste, to stitch, to tack.

embate m breakers pl, surf, surge; sudden attack.

embaucador m swindler, impostor.

embaucar vt to deceive; to trick.

embebecer vt to fascinate; ~se vr to be fascinated.

embebecimiento m amazement, astonishment; fascination.

embeber vt to soak; to saturate; • vi to shrink; ~se vr to be enraptured; to be absorbed.

embelesamiento m rapture.

embelesar vt to amaze, to astonish.

embeleso m amazement, enchantment.

embellecer vt to embellish, to beautify.

emberrincharse vr to have a tantrum.

embestida f assault, violent attack.

embestir vt to assault, to attack.

emblanquecer vt to whiten; ~se vr to grow white; to bleach.

emblema m emblem.

embobado, da adj amazed, fascinated.

embobamiento m astonishment; fascination.

embobar vt to amaze, to fascinate; ~se vr to be amazed, to stand gaping.

embobecer vt to make silly; ~se vr to get silly.

embobecimiento m silliness.

émbolo m plunger; piston.

embolsar vt to put money into a purse; to pocket.

emborrachar vt to intoxicate, to inebriate; ~se vr to get drunk.

emboscada f (mil) ambush.

emboscarse vr (mil) to lie in ambush.

embotar vt to blunt; ~se vr to go numb.

embotellamiento m traffic jam.

embotellar vt to bottle (wine).

embozado, da adj covered; covert.

embozar vt to muffle the face; (fig) to cloak, to conceal.

embozo m part of a cloak, veil or anything with which the face is muffled; covering of one's face.

embrague m clutch.

embrear vt to cover with tar or pitch.

embriagar vt to intoxicate, to inebriate; to transport, to enrapture.

embriaguez f intoxication, drunkenness; rapture, delight.

embrión m embryo.

embrollador, ra m/f troublemaker.

embrollar vt to muddle; to entangle, to embroil.

embrollo m muddle.

embromar vt to tease; to cajole, to wheedle.

embrujar vt to bewitch.

embrutecer vt to brutalize; ~se vr to get depraved.

embudo m funnel.

embuste m fraud; lie; fib.

embustero, ra m/f impostor, cheat; liar; • adj deceitful.

embutido m sausage; inlay.

embutir vt to insert; to stuff; to inlay; to cram, to eat too much.

emergencia f emergency.

emerger vi to emerge, to appear.

emético, ca adj emetic.

emigración f emigration, migration.

emigrado, da adj emigrated; • m/f emigrant.

emigrar vi to emigrate.

eminencia f eminence.

eminente adj eminent, high; excellent, conspicuous.

emisario m emissary.

emisión f emission; broadcasting; program; issue.

emisora f broadcasting station.

emitir vt to emit, to send forth; to issue; to broadcast.

emoción f emotion; feeling; excitement.

emocionante adj exciting.

emocionar vt to excite; to move, to touch.

emoliente adj emolient, softening.

emolumento m emolument.

emotivo, va adj emotional.

empacar vt to pack; to crate.

empachar vt to give indigestion; ~se vr to have indigestion.

empacho m (med) indigestion.

empachoso, sa adj indigestible.

empadronamiento m register; census.

empadronarse vr to register.

empalagar vt to sicken; to disgust.

empalago m disgust; boredom; cloying.

empalagoso, sa adj cloying; tiresome.

empalizada f (mil) palisade.

empalmadura f join; weld; splice.

empalmar vt to join.

empalme m (ferro) junction; connection.

empanada f (meat) pie.

empanar vt to cover with breadcrumbs.

empantanarse vr to get swamped; to get bogged down.

empañar vt to put a diaper on; to mist; to steam up; to tarnish one's reputation; ~se vr to steam up.

empapar vt to soak; to soak up; ~se vr to soak.

empapelar vt to paper.

empaquetar vt to pack, to parcel up.

emparedado m sandwich.

emparejar vt to level; to match, to fit, to equalize.

emparentar vi to be related by marriage.

emparrado m vine arbor.

empastar vt to paste; (med) to fill (a tooth).

empaste m (med) filling.

empatar vt to draw.

empate m draw.

empedernido, da adj inveterate; heartless.

empedernir vt to harden; ~se to be inflexible.

empedrado m paving.

empedrador m paver.

empedrar vt to pave.

empeine m instep.

empellón m push, heavy blow.

empeñado, da adj determined; pawned.

empeñar vt to pawn, to pledge; ~se vr to pledge oneself to pay debts; to get into debt; ~se en algo to insist on something.

empeño m obligation; determination; perseverance.

empeorar vt to make worse; • vi, ~se vr to grow worse.

empequeñecer vt to dwarf; (fig) to belittle.

emperador m emperor.

emperatriz f empress.

emperifollarse vt to dress oneself up.

empero conj yet, however.

emperrarse vr to get stubborn, to be obstinate.

empezar vt to begin, to start.

empinado, da adj high; proud.

empinar vt to raise; to exalt; • vi to drink much; ~se vr to stand on tiptoe; to soar.

empírico, ca adj empirical.

empirismo m empiricism.

empizarrado m slate roofing.

empizarrar vt to slate, to roof with slate.

emplasto m plaster.

emplazamiento m summons; location.

emplazar vt to summon; to locate.

empleado, da m/f official; employee.

emplear vt to employ; to occupy; to commission.

empleo m employ, employment, occupation.

empobrecer vt to reduce to poverty; • vi to become poor.

empobrecimiento m impoverishment.

empolvar vt to powder, to sprinkle powder.

empollar vt to incubate; to hatch; (fam) to swot (up).

emponzoñador, ra m/f poisoner.

emponzoñamiento *m* poisoning.
emponzoñar *vt* to poison; to taint, to corrupt.
emporio *m* emporium.
empotrado, da *adj* built-in.
empotrar *vt* to embed; to build in.
emprendedor *m* entrepreneur.
emprender *vt* to embark on; to tackle; to undertake.
empresa *f (com)* company; enterprise, undertaking.
empresario *m* manager.
empréstito *m* loan.
empujar *vt* to push, to press forward.
empuje *m* thrust; pressure; *(fig)* drive.
empujón *m* impulse, push; a ~**ones** in fits and starts.
empuñadura *f* hilt of a sword.
empuñar *vt* to clench, to grip with the fist; to clutch.
emulación *f* emulation.
emular *vt* to emulate, to rival.
emulsión *f* emulsion.
en *prep* in; for; on, upon.
enaguas *fpl* petticoat.
enajenación *f* alienation; absent-mindedness.
enajenamiento *m* alienation; absent-mindedness.
enajenar *vt* to alienate; ~**se** *vr* to fall out.
enamoradamente *adv* lovingly.
enamoradizo, za *adj* inclined to love.
enamorado, da *adj* in love, lovesick.
enamoramiento *m* falling in love.
enamorar *vt* to inspire love in; ~**se** *vr* to fall in love.
enano, na *adj* dwarfish; ● *m* dwarf.
enarbolar *vt* to hoist, to raise high.
enardecer *vt* to fire with passion, to inflame.
enarenar *vt* to fill with sand.
encabezamiento *m* heading; foreword.
encabezar *vt* to head; to put a heading to; to lead.
encabritarse *vr* to rear (of horses).
encadenamiento *m* linking together, chaining.
encadenar *vt* to chain, to link together; to connect, to unite.
encajadura *f* insertion; socket; groove.
encajar *vt* to insert, to drive in; to encase; to intrude; ● *vi* to fit (well); ~**se** *vr* to squeeze; to gatecrash.
encaje *m* encasing; joining; socket; groove; inlaid work.
encajera *f* lacemaker.
encajonamiento *m* packing into boxes, etc.
encajonar *vt* to pack up in a box.
encalabrinar *vt* to make confused; ~**se** *vr* to become obstinate.
encaladura *f* whitening, whitewash.
encalar *vt* to whitewash.
encallar *vi (mar)* to run aground.
encallecer *vi* to get corns.
encamarse *vr* to take to one's bed.
encaminar *vt* to guide, to show the way; ~**se** *vr* to take the road to.
encandilar *vt* to dazzle.
encanecer *vi* to grow gray; to grow old.
encantado, da *adj* bewitched; delighted; pleased.
encantador, ra *adj* charming; *m/f* magician.
encantamiento *m* enchantment.
encantar *vt* to enchant, to charm; *(fig)* to delight.
encanto *m* enchantment, spell, charm.
encañonar *vt* to hold up; to cover (with a gun); ● *vi* to grow feathers.
encapotar *vt* to cover with a cloak; ~**se** *vr* to be cloudy.
encapricharse *vr* to become stubborn.
encapuchar *vt* to cover with a hood.
encaramar *vt* to raise; to extoll.
encarar *vi* to face, to come face to face.
encarcelación *f* incarceration.
encarcelar *vt* to imprison.
encarecer *vt* to raise the price of; ~**se** *vr* to get dearer.
encarecimiento *m* price increase; **con** ~ insistently.

encargado, da *adj* in charge; ● *m/f* representative; person in charge.
encargar *vt* to charge, to commission.
encargo *m* charge, commission; job; order.
encariñarse *vr*: ~ **con** to grow fond of.
encarnación *f* incarnation, embodiment.
encarnado, da *adj* incarnate; flesh-colored; ● *m* flesh color.
encarnar *vt* to embody, to personify.
encarnizado, da *adj* bloodshot, inflamed; bloody, fierce.
encarrilar *vt* to put back on the rails; to put on the right track.
encasillar *vt* to pigeonhole; to typecast.
encasquetar *vt* to kindle, to light, to set on fire; to inflame; to incite; to switch on, to turn on; ~**se** *vr* to catch fire; to flare up.
encastillarse *vr* to refuse to yield.
encauzar *vt* to channel.
encebollado *m* casseroled beef *or* lamb and onions, seasoned with spice.
encenagado, da *adj* muddy, mud-stained.
encenagamiento *m* wallowing in mud.
encenagar *vt*, ~**se** *vr* to wallow in mud.
encendedor *m* lighter.
encender *vt* to kindle, to light, to set on fire; to inflame; to incite; to switch on, to turn on; ~**se** *vr* to catch fire; to flare up.
encendido, da *adj* inflamed; high-colored; ● *m* ignition (of car).
encerado *m* blackboard.
encerar *vt* to wax; to polish.
encerrar *vt* to shut up, to confine; to contain; ~**se** *vr* to withdraw from the world.
encespedar *vt* to turf.
encía *f* gum (of the teeth).
encíclica *f* encyclical.
enciclopedia *f* encyclopedia.
enciclopédico, ca *adj* encyclopedic.
encierro *m* confinement, enclosure; prison; bull-pen; penning (of bulls).
encima *adv* above, over; at the top; besides.
encina *f* evergreen oak.
encinar *m* evergreen oakwood; evergreen oak grove.
encinta *adj* pregnant.
enclaustrado, da *adj* cloistered; hidden away.
enclenque *adj* weak, sickly; ● *m* weakling.
encoger *vt* to contract, to shorten; to shrink; to discourage; ~**se** *vr* to shrink; *(fig)* to cringe.
encogidamente *adv* shyly, timidly, bashfully.
encogido, da *adj* shy, timid, bashful.
encogimiento *m* contraction; shrinkage; shyness; timidness; bashfulness.
encoladura *f* gluing.
encolar *vt* to glue.
encolerizar *vt* to provoke, to irritate; ~**se** *vr* to get angry.
encomendar *vt* to recommend; to entrust; ~**se** *vr* to entrust oneself to; to put one's trust in.
encomiar *vt* to praise.
encomienda *m* commission, charge; message; *(mil)* command; patronage, protection; parcel post.
encomio *m* eulogy, praise, commendation.
enconar *vt* to inflame, to irritate.
encono *m* ill-feeling, rancor.
enconoso, sa *adj* hurtful, prejudicial; malevolent.
encontrado, da *adj* conflicting; hostile.
encontrar *vt, vi* to meet, to encounter; to assemble, to come together; ~**se con** *vr* to meet.
encopetado, da *adj* presumptuous, boastful.
encorvadura *f* curvature; crookedness.
encorvar *vt* to bend, to curve.
encrespar *vt* to curl, to frizzle (hair); *(fig)* to anger; ~**se** *vr* to get rough (of the sea); *(fig)* to get cross.
encrucijada *f* crossroads; junction.
encuadernación *f* binding.
encuadernador, ra *m/f* bookbinder.
encuadernar *vt* to bind books.

encubiertamente adv secretly; deceitfully.

encubierto, ta adj hidden, concealed.

encubridor, ra m/f concealer, harborer; receiver of stolen goods.

encubrimiento m concealment, hiding; receiving of stolen goods.

encubrir vt to hide, to conceal.

encuentro m meeting; collision, crash; match, game.

encuesta f inquiry; opinion poll.

encumbrado, da adj high, elevated.

encumbramiento m elevation; height.

encumbrar vt to raise, to elevate; ~se vr to be raised; (fig) to become conceited.

encurtir vt to pickle.

enchapar vt to veneer.

encharcarse vr to be flooded.

enchufar vt to plug in; to connect.

enchufe m plug; socket; connection; (fam) contact, connection.

endeble adj feeble, weak.

endecasílabo, ba adj consisting of eleven syllables.

endecha f dirge, lament.

endemoniado, da adj possessed with the devil; devilish.

enderezamiento m guidance, direction.

enderezar vt to straighten out; go set right; ~se vr to stand upright.

endeudarse vr to get into debt.

endiablado, da adj devilish, diabolical; ugly.

endiosar vt to deify; ~se vr to be high and mighty.

endosar vt to endorse.

endoso m endorsement.

endrina f sloe.

endrino m blackthorn, sloe.

endulzar vt to sweeten; to soften.

endurecer vt to harden, to toughen; ~se vr to become cruel; to grow hard.

endurecidamente adv cruelly.

endurecimiento m hardness; obstinacy; hard heartedness.

enebro m (bot) juniper.

enemigo, ga adj hostile; ● m enemy.

enemistad f enmity, hatred.

enemistar vt to make an enemy; ~se vr to become enemies; to fall out.

energía f energy, power, drive; strength of will.

enérgico, ca adj energetic; forceful.

energúmeno, na m/f (fam) madman/woman.

enero m January.

enervar vt to enervate.

enfadadizo, za adj irritable, crotchety.

enfadar vt to anger, to irritate; to trouble; ~se vr to get angry.

enfado m trouble; anger.

enfadoso, sa adj annoying, troublesome.

énfasis m emphasis.

enfático, ca adj emphatic.

enfermar vi to fall ill; ● vt to make sick; to weaken.

enfermedad f illness.

enfermería f infirmary; sick bay.

enfermero, ra m/f nurse.

enfermizo, za adj infirm, sickly.

enfermo, ma adj sick, ill; ● m/f invalid, sick person; patient.

enfervorizar vt to arouse, to inflame, to incite.

enflaquecer vt to weaken, to make thin.

enflaquecimiento m loss of weight; (fig) weakening.

enfocar vt to focus; to consider (a problem).

enfoque m focus.

enfrascarse vr to be deeply embroiled.

enfrentar vt to confront; to put face to face; ~se vr to face each other; to meet (two teams).

enfrente adv over against, opposite; in front.

enfriamiento m refrigeration; (med) cold.

enfriar vt to cool, to refrigerate; ~se vr to cool down; (med) to catch a cold.

enfurecer vt to madden, to enrage; ~se vr to get rough (of the wind and sea); to become furious or enraged.

enfurruñarse vr to get sulky, to frown.

engalanar vt to adorn, to deck.

engallarse vr to be arrogant.

enganchar vt to hook, to hang up; to hitch up; to couple, to connect; to recruit into military service; ~se vr (mil) to enlist.

engañabobos m trickster; trick, trap.

engañadizo, za adj gullible, easily deceived.

engañador, ra adj cheating; deceptive; ● m/f cheat, impostor, deceiver.

engañar vt to deceive, to cheat; ~se vr to be deceived; to make a mistake.

engañifa f deceit, trick.

engaño m mistake, misunderstanding, deceit, fraud.

engañoso, sa adj deceitful, artful, false.

engarzar vt to thread; to link; to curl.

engastar vt to set, to mount.

engaste m setting, mount.

engatusamiento m deception, coaxing.

engatusar vt to coax.

engendrar vt to beget, to engender, to produce.

engendro m fetus, embryo; (fig) monstrosity; brainchild.

englobar vt to include.

engolfarse vr (mar) to sail out to sea; to be deeply involved in.

engolosinar vt to entice; ~se vr to find delight in.

engomadura f gluing.

engomar vt to glue.

engordar vt to fatten; ● vi to grow fat, to put on weight.

engorro m nuisance, bother.

engorroso, sa adj troublesome, cumbersome.

engranaje m gear; gearing.

engrandecer vt to augment, to magnify; to speak highly of; to exaggerate.

engrandecimiento m increase, aggrandizement; exaggeration.

engrasar vt to grease, to lubricate.

engreído, da adj conceited, vain.

engreimiento m presumption, vanity.

engreír vt to make proud; ~se vr to grow proud.

engrosar vt to enlarge; to increase.

engrudo m paste.

engullidor, ra m/f devourer; guzzler.

engullir vt to swallow, to gobble, to devour.

enharinar vt to cover or sprinkle with flour.

enhebrar vt to thread a needle.

enhilar vt to thread.

enhorabuena f congratulations; ● adv all right; well and good.

enhoramala adv good riddance.

enigma m enigma, riddle.

enigmático, ca adj enigmatic, dark, obscure.

enjabonar vt to soap; (fam) to tick off.

enjaezar vt to harness a horse.

enjalbegar vt to whitewash.

enjambre m swarm of bees; crowd, multitude.

enjaular vt to shut up in a cage; to imprison.

enjoyar vt to adorn with jewels.

enjuagar vt to rinse out; to wash out.

enjuague m (med) mouthwash; rinsing, rinse.

enjugar vt to dry (the tears); to wipe off.

enjuiciar vt to prosecute, to try; to pass judgment on, to judge.

enjuto, ta adj dried up; (fig) lean.

enlace m connection, link; relationship.

enladrillado m brick paving.

enladrillador m bricklayer.

enladrillar vt to pave a floor with bricks.

enlazable adj able to be fastened together.

enlazar vt to join, to unite; to tie.

enlodar vt to cover in mud; (fig) to stain.

enloquecer vt to madden, to drive crazy; ● vi to go mad.

enloquecimiento *m* madness.

enlosar *vt* to lay a floor with flags.

enlutar *vt* to put into mourning; ~**se** *vr* to go into mourning.

enmaderar *vt* to roof a house with timber.

enmarañar *vt* to entangle; to complicate; to confuse; ~**se** *vr* to become entangled; to get confused.

enmascarar *vt* to mask; ~**se** *vr* to go in disguise, to masquerade.

enmendar *vt* to correct, to reform; to repair, to compensate; to amend; ~**se** *vr* to mend one's ways.

enmienda *f* correction, amendment.

enmohecer *vt* to make moldy, to rust; ~**se** *vr* to grow moldy *or* musty; to rust.

enmudecer(se) *vt* (*vr*) to silence; to grow dumb; to be silent.

ennegrecer *vt* to blacken; to darken, to obscure.

ennoblecer *vt* to ennoble.

ennoblecimiento *m* ennoblement.

enojadizo, za *adj* peevish; short-tempered, irritable.

enojar *vt* to irritate, to make angry; to annoy; to upset; to offend; ~**se** *vr* to get angry.

enojo *m* anger, annoyance.

enojoso, sa *adj* offensive, annoying.

enorgullecerse *vr* to be proud (of).

enorme *adj* enormous, vast, huge; horrible.

enormidad *f* enormity, monstrousness.

enramar *vt* to cover with the branches of trees.

enranciarse *vr* to grow rancid.

enrarecer *vt* to thin, to rarefy.

enredadera *f* climbing plant; bindweed.

enredador, ra *m/f* gossip; troublemaker; busybody.

enredar *vt* to entangle, to ensnare, to confound, to perplex; to puzzle; to sow discord; ~**se** *vr* to get entangled; to get complicated; to get embroiled.

enredo *m* entanglement; mischievous lie; plot of a play.

enredoso, sa *adj* complicated.

enrejado *m* trellis-work.

enrejar *vt* to fix a grating to a window; to grate, to lattice.

enrevesado, da *adj* complicated.

enriquecer *vt* to enrich; to adorn; ~**se** *vr* to grow rich.

enristrar *vt* to string (garlic); to straighten out; to go straight to.

enrobustecer *vt* to strengthen.

enrojecer *vt* to redden; • *vi* to blush.

enrolar *vt* to recruit; ~**se** *vr* (*mil*) to join up.

enrollar *vt* to roll (up).

enronquecer *vt* to make hoarse; • *vi* to grow hoarse.

enroscadura *f* twist.

enroscar *vt* to twist; ~**se** *vr* to curl *or* roll up.

ensalada *f* salad.

ensaladera *f* salad bowl.

ensaladilla (rusa) *f* Russian salad.

ensalmar *vt* to set dislocated bones; to heal by spells.

ensalmo *m* enchantment, spell.

ensalzar *vt* to exalt, to aggrandize; to exaggerate.

ensamblador, ra *m/f* joiner.

ensamblar *vt* to assemble.

ensanchar *vt* to widen, to extend, to enlarge; ~**se** *vr* to expand; to assume an air of importance.

ensanche *m* dilation, augmentation; widening; expansion.

ensangrentar *vt* to stain with blood.

ensañar *vt* to irritate, to enrage; ~**se con** *vr* to treat brutally.

ensartar *vt* to string (beads, *etc*).

ensayar *vt* to test; to rehearse.

ensayo *m* test, trial; rehearsal of a play; essay.

ensenada *f* creek.

enseña *f* colours *pl*, standard.

enseñanza *f* teaching, instruction; education.

enseñar *vt* to teach, to instruct; to show.

enseres *mpl* belongings *pl*.

ensillar *vt* to saddle.

ensimismarse *vr* to be lost in thought; to become lost in thought.

ensoberbecer *vt* to make proud; ~**se** *vr* to become proud; (*mar*) to get rough.

ensordecer *vt* to deafen; • *vi* to grow deaf.

ensordecimiento *m* deafness.

ensortijamiento *m* curling the hair.

ensortijar *vt* to fix a ring in; to curl.

ensuciar *vt* to stain, to soil; to defile; ~**se** *vr* to wet oneself; to dirty oneself.

ensueño *m* fantasy; daydream; illusion.

entablar *vt* to board (up); to strike up (conversation).

entablillar *vt* (*med*) to put in a splint.

entallar *vt* to tailor (a suit); • *vi* to fit.

ente *m* organization; entity, being; (*fam*) odd character.

entendederas *fpl* understanding, brains.

entender *vt, vi* to understand, to comprehend; to remark, to take notice of; to reason, to think; **a mi** ~ in my opinion; ~**se** *vr* to understand each other.

entendido, da *adj* understood; wise, learned, knowing.

entendimiento *m* understanding, knowledge, judgment.

enteramente *adv* entirely, completely.

enterar *vt* to inform; to instruct; ~**se** *vr* to find out.

entereza *f* entireness, integrity; firmness of mind.

enternecer *vt* to soften; to move (to pity); ~**se** *vr* to be moved.

enternecimiento *m* compassion, pity.

entero, ra *adj* entire; perfect, complete; honest; resolute; **por** ~ entirely, completely.

enterrador *m* gravedigger.

enterrar *vt* to inter, to bury.

entibiar *vt* to cool.

entidad *f* entity; company; body; society.

entierro *m* burial; funeral.

entoldar *vt* to cover with an awning.

entomología *f* entomology.

entonación *f* modulation; intonation; (*fig*) presumption, pride.

entonar *vt* to tune, to intonate; to intone; to tone; • *vi* to be in tune; ~**se** *vr* to give oneself airs.

entonces *adv* then, at that time.

entontecer *vt* to fool; • *vi*, ~**se** *vr* to get silly.

entontecimiento *m* silliness.

entornar *vt* to half close.

entorpecer *vt* to dull; to make lethargic; to hinder; to delay.

entorpecimiento *m* numbness; lethargy.

entrada *f* entrance, entry; (*com*) receipts *pl*; entrée; ticket (for cinema, theatre *etc*).

entrambos, bas *pn pl* both.

entrampar *vt* to trap, to snare; to mess up; to burden with debts; ~**se** *vr* get into debt.

entrañable *adj* intimate, affectionate.

entrañas *fpl* entrails, intestines *pl*.

entrante *adj* coming, next.

entrar *vt, vi* to enter, to go in; to commence.

entre *prep* between; among(st); in; ~ **manos** in hand.

entreabrir *vt* to half open a door, to leave it ajar.

entrecano, na *adj* gray-black, grayish.

entrecejo *m* the space between the eyebrows; frown.

entrecortado, da *adj* faltering; difficult.

entredicho *m* (*jur*) injunction; **estar en** ~ to be banned; **poner en** ~ to cast doubt on.

entrega *f* delivery; installment.

entregar *vt* to deliver; to hand over; ~**se** *vr* to surrender; to devote oneself.

entrelazar *vt* to interlace.

entremedias *adv* in the meantime.

entremeses *mpl* hors d'oeuvres.

entremeter *or* **entrometer** *vt* to put one thing between others; ~**se** *vr* to interfere, to meddle.

entremetido *or* **entrometido** *m* meddler, interferer; ~, **da** *adj* meddling, interfering.

entremetimiento *m* insertion; meddling.

entrenador, ra *m/f* trainer, coach.

entrenarse *vr* to train.

entreoír *vt* to hear without perfectly understanding what is said, to half hear.

entrepaño *m* panel.

entrepierna *f* crotch.

entresaca *f* thinning out (of trees).

entresacar *vt* to thin out; to sift, to separate.

entresuelo *m* entresol; mezzanine.

entretanto *adv* meanwhile.

entretejer *vt* to interweave.

entretela *f* interfacing, stiffening, interlining.

entretener *vt* to amuse; to entertain, to divert; to hold up; to maintain; ~se *vr* to amuse oneself; to linger.

entretenido, da *adj* pleasant, amusing, entertaining.

entretenimiento *m* amusement, entertainment.

entrever *vt* to have a glimpse of.

entreverado, da *adj* patchy; streaky.

entrevista *f* interview.

entrevistar *vt* to interview; ~se *vr* to have an interview.

entristecer *vt* to sadden.

entroncar *vi* to be related *or* connected.

entronización *f* enthronement.

entronizar *vt* to enthrone.

entumecer *vt* to swell; to numb; ~se *vr* to become numb.

entumecido, da *adj* numb, stiff.

entumecimiento *m* numbness.

enturbiar *vt* to make cloudy; to obscure, to confound; ~se *vr* to become cloudy; (*fig*) to get confused.

entusiasmar *vt* to excite, to fill with enthusiasm; to delight.

entusiasmo *m* enthusiasm.

entusiasta *m/f* enthusiast.

enumeración *f* enumeration, counting over.

enumerar *vt* to enumerate.

enunciación *f*, **enunciado** *m/f* enunciation, declaration.

enunciar *vt* to enunciate, to declare.

envainar *vt* to sheathe, to sheath.

envalentonar *vt* to give courage to; ~se *vr* to boast.

envanecer *vt* to make vain; to swell with pride; ~se *vr* to become proud.

envaramiento *m* stiffness, numbness.

envarar *vt* to numb.

envasar *vt* to pack; to bottle; to can.

envase *m* packing; bottling; canning; container; package; bottle; can.

envejecer *vt* to make old; • *vi*, ~se *vr* to grow old.

envenenador, ra *m/f* poisoner.

envenenar *vt* to poison; to embitter.

envenenamiento *m* poisoning.

envergadura *f* (*fig*) scope.

envés *m* wrong side (of material).

enviado, da *m/f* envoy, messenger.

enviar *vt* to send, to transmit, to convey, to dispatch.

enviciar *vt* to vitiate, to corrupt; ~se *vr* to get corrupted.

envidia *f* envy; jealousy.

envidiable *adj* enviable.

envidiar *vi* to envy, to grudge; to be jealous of.

envidioso, sa *adj* envious; jealous.

envilecer *vt* to vilify, to debase; ~se *vr* to degrade oneself.

envío *m* (*com*) dispatch, remittance of goods; consignment.

enviudar *vi* to become a widower *or* widow.

envoltorio *m* bundle of clothes.

envoltura *f* cover; wrapping.

envolver *vt* to involve; to wrap up.

enyesar *vt* to plaster; (*med*) to put in a plaster cast.

enzarzarse *vr* to get involved in a dispute; to get oneself into trouble.

épico, ca *adj* epic.

epicúreo, rea *adj* epicurean.

epidemia *f* epidemic.

epidémico, ca *adj* epidemic.

epidermis *f* epidermis, cuticle.

Epifanía *f* Epiphany.

epígrafe *f* epigraph, inscription; motto; headline.

epigrama *m* epigram.

epilepsia *f* epilepsy.

epílogo *m* epilog(ue).

episcopado *m* episcopacy; bishopric.

episcopal *adj* episcopal.

episódico, ca *adj* episodic.

episodio *m* episode, installment.

epístola *f* epistle, letter.

epistolar *adj* epistolary.

epistolario *m* collected letters *pl*.

epitafio *m* epitaph.

epíteto *m* epithet.

epítome *m* epitome; compendium.

época *f* epoch; period, time.

epopeya *f* epic.

equidad *f* equity, honesty; impartiality, justice.

equidistar *vi* to be equidistant.

equilátero, ra *adj* equilateral.

equilibrar *vt* to poise; to balance.

equilibrio *m* balance, equilibrium.

equinoccial *adj* equinoctial.

equinoccio *m* equinox.

equipaje *m* baggage; equipment.

equipar *vt* to fit out, to equip, to furnish.

equipararse *vr*: ~ **con** to be on a level with.

equipo *m* equipment; team, shift.

equitación *f* horsemanship; riding.

equitativo, va *adj* equitable; just.

equivalencia *f* equivalence.

equivalente *adj* equivalent.

equivaler *vi* to be of equal value.

equivocación *f* mistake, error, misunderstanding.

equivocado, da *adj* mistaken, wrong.

equivocar *vt* to mistake; ~se *vr* to make a mistake, to be wrong.

equívoco, ca *adj* equivocal, ambiguous; • *m* equivocation; quibble.

era *f* era, age; threshing floor.

erario *m* treasury, public funds *pl*.

erección *f* foundation, establishment; erection, elevation.

erguir *vt* to erect, to raise up straight; ~se *vr* to straighten up.

erial *m* fallow land.

erigir *vt* to erect, to raise, to build; to establish.

erizamiento *m* standing on end (of hair, *etc*).

erizarse *vr* to bristle; to stand on end.

erizo *m* hedgehog; ~ **de mar** sea urchin.

ermita *f* hermitage.

ermitaño *m* hermit.

erosionar *vt* to erode.

erótico, ca *adj* erotic.

erotismo *m* eroticism.

errante *adj* errant; stray; roving.

errar *vi* to be mistaken; to wander.

errata *f* misprint.

erre *adv*: ~ **que** ~ obstinately.

erróneo, nea *adj* erroneous.

error *m* error, mistake, fault.

eructar *vi* to belch, to burp.

eructo *m* belch, burp.

erudición *f* erudition, learning.

erudito, ta *adj* learned, scholarly.

erupción *f* eruption, outbreak.

esbelto, ta *adj* slim, slender.

esbirro *m* bailiff; henchman; killer.

esbozo *m* outline.

escabechar *vt* to marinate, to pickle.

escabeche *m* pickle; pickled fish.

escabel *m* footstool.

escabrosidad *f* unevenness, roughness; harshness.

escabroso, sa *adj* rough, uneven; craggy; rude, risqué, blue.

escabullirse *vr* to escape, to evade; to slip through one's fingers.

escafandra *f* diving suit; space suit.

escala *f* ladder; (*mus*) scale; stopover.

escalador, ra *m/f* climber.

escalar *vt* to climb.

escaldado, da *adj* cautious, suspicious, wary.

escaldar *vt* to scald.

escalera *f* staircase; ladder.

escalfar *vt* to poach eggs.

escalofríos *mpl* shivers.

escalofriante *adj* chilling.

escalón *m* step of a stair; rung.

escama *f* fish scale.

escamado, da *adj* wary, cautious.

escamar *vt* to take off the scales; ~**se** *vr* to flake off; to become suspicious.

escamoso, sa *adj* scaly.

escamotear *vt* to swipe; to make disappear.

escampar *vi* to stop raining.

escanciador *m* wine waiter; cupbearer.

escanciar *vt* to pour wine.

escandalizar *vt* to scandalize; ~**se** *vr* to be shocked.

escándalo *m* scandal; uproar.

escandaloso, sa *adj* scandalous; shocking.

escaño *m* bench with a back; seat (parliament).

escapada *f* escape, flight.

escapar *vi* to escape; ~**se** *vr* to get away; to leak (water etc).

escaparate *m* shop window; closet.

escapatoria *f* escape, flight; excuse.

escape *m* escape, flight; leak; exhaust (of motor); **a todo** ~ at full speed.

escapulario *m* scapulary.

escarabajo *m* beetle.

escaramuza *f* skirmish; dispute, quarrel.

escaramuzar *vt* to skirmish.

escarbadura *f* act and effect of scratching.

escarbar *vt* to scratch the earth (as hens do); to inquire into.

escarcha *f* white frost.

escarchar *vi* to be frosty.

escardador *m* weeding hoe.

escardillo *m* small weeding hoe.

escarlata *adj* scarlet.

escarlatina *f* scarlet fever.

escarmentar *vi* to learn one's lesson; ● *vt* to punish severely.

escarmiento *m* warning, caution; punishment.

escarnecer *vt* to mock, to ridicule.

escarnio *m* jibe, ridicule.

escarola *f* (*bot*) endive.

escarpa *f* slope; escarpment.

escarpado, da *adj* sloped, craggy.

escarpín *m* sock; pump (shoe).

escasear *vi* to be scarce.

escasez *f* shortage; poverty.

escaso, sa *adj* small, short, little; sparing; scarce; scanty.

escatimar *vt* to curtail, to lessen; to be scanty with.

escena *f* stage; scene.

escenario *m* stage; set.

escepticismo *m* skepticism.

escéptico, ca *adj* skeptic, skeptical.

esclarecer *vt* to lighten; to illuminate; to illustrate; to shed light on (problem *etc*).

esclarecido, da *adj* illustrious, noble.

esclarecimiento *m* clarification; enlightenment.

esclavina *f* short cloak, cape.

esclavitud *f* slavery, servitude.

esclavizar *vt* to enslave.

esclavo, va *m/f* slave, captive.

esclusa *f* sluice, floodgate.

escoba *f* broom, brush.

escobazo *m* blow given with a broom.

escobilla *f* brush; small broom.

escocer *vt* to sting, to burn; ~**se** *vr* to chafe.

escoger *vt* to choose, to select.

escolar *m/f* schoolboy/girl; ● *adj* scholastic.

escolástico, ca *adj* scholastic; ● *m* schoolman.

escollo *m* reef, rock.

escolta *f* escort.

escoltar *vt* to escort.

escombros *mpl* garbage; debris.

esconder *vt* to hide, to conceal; ~**se** *vr* to be hidden.

escondidas, escondidillas *adv*: **a** ~ in a secret manner.

escondite *m* hiding place; **juego de** ~ hide-and-seek.

escondrijo *m* hiding place.

escopeta *f* shotgun; **a tiro de** ~ within gunshot.

escopetazo *m* gunshot; gunshot wound.

escopetero *m* gunsmith.

escoplo *m* chisel.

escorbuto *m* scurvy.

escoria *f* dross; scum; dregs.

escoriación *f* incrustation.

escoriarse *vr* to get skinned.

Escorpio *m* Scorpio (sign of the zodiac).

escorpión *m* scorpion.

escotado, da *adj* low-cut.

escotadura *f* low neck(line).

escotar *vt* to cut low in front.

escote *m* low neck (of a dress).

escotilla *f* (*mar*) hatchway.

escozor *m* smart; burning pain, sting(ing).

escriba *m* scribe (among the Hebrews).

escribanía *f* clerk's office; writing desk.

escribano *m* court clerk; notary.

escribiente *m* copyist.

escribir *vt* to write; to spell.

escrito *m* document; manuscript, text.

escritor, ra *m/f* writer, author.

escritorio *m* writing desk; office, study.

escritura *f* writing; deed.

escrúpulo *m* doubt, scruple, scrupulousness.

escrupulosidad *f* scrupulousness.

escrupuloso, sa *adj* scrupulous; exact.

escrutar *vt* to examine; to count (ballot papers).

escrutinio *m* scrutiny, inquiry.

escrutiñador *m* scrutinizer, inquirer.

escuadra *f* square; squadron.

escuadrar *vt* to square.

escuadrón *m* squadron.

escuálido, da *adj* skinny; squalid.

escucha *f* listening (-in); ● *m* scout.

escuchar *vt* to listen, to heed.

escudar *vt* to shield; to guard from danger; ~**se** *vr* to protect oneself.

escudero *m* squire; page.

escudilla *f* bowl.

escudo *m* shield.

escudriñamiento *m* investigation, scrutiny.

escudriñar *vt* to search, to pry into; to examine.

escuela *f* school.

escueto, ta *adj* plain; simple.

esculpir *vt* to sculpt.

escultor, ra *m/f* sculptor, sculptress.

escultura *f* sculpture.

escupidera *f* cuspidor.

escupidura *f* spit.

escupir *vt* to spit.

escurreplatos *m invar* plate rack.

escurridizo, za *adj* slippery.

escurrir *vt* to drain; to drip; ● *vi* to wring out; ~**se** *vr* to slip away; to slip, to slide.

ese, esa, eso that.

esencia *f* essence.

esencial *adj* essential; principal.

esfera *f* sphere; globe.

esférico, ca *adj* spherical.
esferoide *f* spheroid.
esfinge *m* sphinx.
esforzado, da *adj* strong, vigorous, valiant.
esforzarse *vr* to exert oneself, to make an effort.
esfuerzo *m* effort.
esfumarse *vr* to fade away.
esgrima *f* fencing.
esgrimidor *m* fencer.
esgrimir *vi* to fence.
esguince *m* (*med*) sprain.
eslabón *m* link of a chain; steel; shackle.
eslabonar *vt* to link; to unite.
esmaltador *m* enameler.
esmaltar *vt* to enamel.
esmalte *m* enamel.
esmerado, da *adj* careful, neat.
esmeralda *m* emerald.
esmerar *vt* to polish; ~se *vr* to exercise great care; to work hard.
esmeril *m* emery.
esmerillar *vt* to polish with emery.
esmero *m* careful attention, great care.
esnob *adj* snobbish; posh; ● *m/f* snob.
esófago *m* esophagus; throat.
espabilar *vt* to wake up; ~se *vr* to wake up; (*fig*) to get a move on.
espacial *adj* space *compd*.
espaciar *vt* to spread out; to space (out).
espacio *m* space; (radio *or* TV) program.
espaciosidad *f* spaciousness, capacity.
espacioso, sa *adj* spacious, roomy.
espada *f* sword; ace of spades.
espadachín *m* bully.
espadaña *f* (*bot*) bullrush.
espadín *m* small short sword.
espaguetis *mpl* spaghetti.
espalda *f* back, back-part; ~s *fpl* shoulders.
espaldilla *f* shoulder blade.
espantadizo, za *adj* timid, easily frightened.
espantajo *m* scarecrow; bogeyman.
espantapájaros *m invar* scarecrow.
espantar *vt* to frighten; to chase *or* drive away.
espanto *m* fright; menace, threat; astonishment.
espantoso, sa *adj* frightful, dreadful; amazing.
español, la *adj* Spanish; ● *m/f* Spaniard; ● *m* Spanish language.
esparadrapo *m* adhesive tape.
esparcir *vt* to scatter; to divulge; ~se *vr* to amuse oneself.
espáfrago *m* asparagus.
esparto *m* (*bot*) esparto.
espasmo *m* spasm.
espátula *f* spatula.
especia *f* spice.
especial *adj* special, particular; en ~ especially.
especialidad *f* specialty.
especie *f* species; kind, sort; matter.
especificación *f* specification.
especificar *vt* to specify.
específico, ca *adj* specific.
espectáculo *m* spectacle; show.
espectador, ra *m/f* spectator.
espectro *m* specter, phantom, ghost, apparition.
especulación *f* speculation, contemplation; venture.
especulador, ra *m/f* speculator.
especular *vt* to speculate.
especulativo, va *adj* speculative; thoughtful.
espejismo *m* mirage.
espejo *m* mirror.
espeluznante *adj* horrifying.
espera *f* stay, waiting; (*law*) respite, adjournment, delay.
esperanza *f* hope.

esperanzar *vt* to give hope.
esperar *vt* to hope; to expect, to wait for.
esperma *f* sperm.
espesar *vt* to thicken, to condense; ~se *vr* to grow thick, to solidify.
espeso, sa *adj* thick, dense.
espesor *m* thickness.
espesura *f* thickness, density, solidity.
espía *m/f* spy.
espiar *vt* to spy.
espiga *f* ear (of corn).
espigón *m* ear of corn; sting; (*mar*) breakwater.
espina *f* thorn; fishbone.
espinaca *f* (*bot*) spinach.
espinazo *m* spine, backbone.
espinilla *f* shinbone.
espino *m* hawthorn.
espinoso, sa *adj* thorny; dangerous.
espionaje *m* spying, espionage.
espiral *adj*, *f* spiral.
espirar *vt* to exhale.
espíritu *m* spirit, soul; mind; intelligence; el E~ Santo the Holy Ghost; ~s *pl* demons, hobgoblins *pl*.
espiritual *adj* spiritual; ghostly.
espiritualidad *f* spirituality.
espiritualizar *vt* to spiritualize.
esplendidez *f* splendor, magnificence.
espléndido, da *adj* splendid, magnificent; brilliant.
esplendor *m* splendor.
espliego *m* (*bot*) lavender.
espolear *vt* to spur, to instigate, to incite.
espolón *m* spur (of a cock); spur (of a mountain range); sea wall; jetty; (*mar*) buttress.
espolvorear *vt* to sprinkle.
espondeo *m* (*poet*) spondee.
esponja *f* sponge.
esponjar *vt* to sponge; ~se *vr* to be puffed up with pride.
esponjoso, sa *adj* spongy.
esponsales *mpl* betrothal.
espontaneidad *f* spontaneity.
espontáneo, nea *adj* spontaneous.
esposa *f* wife.
esposar *vt* to handcuff.
esposas *fpl* handcuffs *pl*.
esposo *m* husband.
espuela *f* spur; stimulus; (*bot*) larkspur.
espuerta *f* pannier, basket.
espulgar *vt* to delouse; to get rid of fleas; to examine closely.
espuma *f* froth, foam.
espumadera *f* skimmer.
espumajear *vi* to foam at the mouth.
espumar *vt* to skim, to take off the scum.
espumarajo *m* foam, froth (from the mouth).
espumoso, sa *adj* frothy, foamy; sparkling (wine).
espurio, ria *adj* spurious; adulterated; illegitimate.
esputo *m* spit, saliva.
esqueje *m* cutting (of plant).
esquela *f* note, slip of paper.
esqueleto *m* skeleton.
esquema *m* scheme; diagram; plan.
esquí *m* ski; skiing.
esquiar *vt* to ski.
esquife *m* skiff, small boat.
esquilador *m* sheep-shearer.
esquilar *vt* to shear sheep.
esquina *f* corner, angle.
esquinado, da *adj* cornered, angled.
esquinar *vt* to form a corner with.
esquirol *m* blackleg.
esquivar *vt* to shun, to avoid, to evade.
esquivez *f* disdain; shyness.
esquivo, va *adj* scornful; shy, reserved.

estabilidad f stability.
estable adj stable.
establecer vt to establish.
establecimiento m establishment.
establo m stable.
estaca f stake; stick; post.
estacada f fence, fencing; stockade.
estacazo m blow given with a stick.
estación f season of the year; station; railroad station, terminus; ~ **de autobuses** bus station; ~ **de servicio** service station.
estacional adj seasonal.
estacionamiento m parking; (mil) stationing.
estacionar vt to park; (mil) to station.
estacionario, ria adj stationary.
estadio m phase; stadium.
estadista m statesman; statistician.
estadística f statistics pl.
estadístico, ca adj statistical.
estado m state, condition.
Estados Unidos mpl United States (of America).
estafa f trick, fraud.
estafador, ra m/f swindler, racketeer.
estafar vt to deceive, to defraud.
estafeta f post office.
estallar vi to crack, to burst; to break out.
estallido m explosion; (fig) outbreak.
estambre m stamen of flowers.
estamento m estate; body; layer; class.
estameña f serge.
estampa f print; engraving; appearance.
estampado, da adj printed; ● m printing; print; stamping.
estampar vt to print.
estampida f stampede.
estampido m report of a gun; crack.
estampilla f seal, stamp.
estancar vt to check a current; to monopolize; to prohibit, to suspend; ~**se** vr to stagnate.
estancia f stay; bedroom; ranch; (poet) stanza.
estanco m tobacconist's (shop); ~, **ca** adj watertight.
estándar adj, m standard.
estandarizar vt to standardize.
estandarte m banner, standard.
estanque m pond, pool; reservoir.
estanquero, ra m/f tobacconist.
estante m shelf (for books).
estantería f shelves, shelving.
estaño m tin.
estar vi to be; to be in a place.
estatal adj state compd.
estática f statics pl.
estático, ca adj static.
estatua f statue.
estatura f stature.
estatuto m statute, law.
este m east; ~, **esta, esto** pn this.
estera f mat.
estercolar vt to manure.
estercolero m dunghill.
estéreo adj invar, m stereo.
estereotipar vt to stereotype.
estereotipo m stereotype.
estéril adj sterile, infertile.
esterilidad f sterility, infertility.
esterilla f mat.
esterlina adj: **libra** ~ pound sterling.
estético, ca adj esthetic; ● f esthetics.
estiércol m dung; manure.
estilar(se) vi (vr) to be in fashion; to be used.
estilo m style; fashion; stroke (in swimming).
estima f esteem.
estimable adj estimable, worthy of esteem.

estimación f estimation, valuation.
estimar vt to estimate, to value; to esteem; to judge; to think.
estimulante adj stimulating; ● m stimulant.
estimular vt to stimulate, to excite, to goad.
estímulo m stimulus.
estío m summer.
estipendiario m stipendiary.
estipulación f stipulation.
estipular vt to stipulate.
estirado, da adj stretched tight; (fig) pompous.
estirar vt to stretch out.
estirón m pulling; tugging; **dar un** ~ to grow rapidly.
estirpe f race, origin, stock.
estival adj summer compd.
estocada f stab.
estofa f: **de baja** ~ poor quality.
estofado m stew.
estola f stole.
estolidez f stupidity.
estólido, da adj stupid.
estomacal adj stomachic.
estómago m stomach.
estopa f tow.
estoque m rapier, sword.
estorbar vt to hinder; (fig) to bother; ● vi to be in the way.
estorbo m obstacle, hindrance, impediment.
estornudar vi to sneeze.
estornudo m sneeze.
estrada f highway.
estrado m drawing room; stage, platform.
estrafalario, ria adj slovenly; eccentric.
estrago m ruin, destruction; havoc.
estrambótico, ca adj eccentric, odd.
estrangulador, ra m/f strangler.
estrangulamiento m bottleneck.
estrangular vt to strangle; (med) to strangulate.
estraperlo m black market.
estratagema f stratagem, trick.
estrategia f strategy.
estratégico, ca adj strategic(al).
estrato m stratum, layer.
estraza f rag; **papel de** ~ brown paper.
estrechar vt to tighten; to contract, to constrain; to compress; ~**se** vr to grow narrow; to embrace; ~ **la mano** to shake hands.
estrechez f straitness, narrowness; shortage of money.
estrecho m straits pl; ~, **cha** adj narrow, close; tight; intimate; rigid, austere; short (of money).
estrella f star.
estrellado, da adj starry; **huevos** ~**s** fried eggs.
estrellar vt to dash to pieces; ~**se** vr to smash; to crash; to fail.
estremecer vt to shake, to make tremble; ~**se** vr to shake, to tremble.
estremecimiento m trembling, shaking.
estrenar vt to wear for the first time; to move into (a house); to show (a film) for the first time; ~**se** vr to make one's debut.
estreñido, da adj constipated.
estreñimiento m constipation.
estrépito m noise, racket, fuss.
estrepitoso, sa adj noisy.
estribar vi: ~ **en** to prop; to be based on; to be supported.
estribillo m chorus.
estribo m buttress; stirrup; running board; **perder los** ~**s** to fly off the handle (fam).
estribor m (mar) starboard.
estricto, ta adj strict; severe.
estrofa f (poet) verse, strophe.
estropajo m scourer.
estropajoso, sa adj tough, leathery; despicable; mean; stammering.
estropear vt to spoil; to damage; ~**se** vr to get damaged.

estructura f structure.
estruendo m clamor, noise; confusion, uproar; pomp, ostentation.
estrujar vt to press, to squeeze.
estrujón m pressing, squeezing.
estuario m estuary.
estuche m case (for scissors, etc); sheath.
estudiante m/f student.
estudiantil adj student compd.
estudiar vt to study.
estudio m study; studio; ~s mpl studies; learning.
estudioso, sa adj studious.
estufa f heater, fire.
estufilla f muff; small stove.
estupefacción f stupefaction.
estupefaciente m narcotic.
estupefacto adj speechless; thunderstruck.
estupendo, da adj terrific, marvelous.
estupidez f stupidity.
estúpido adj stupid.
estupor m stupor; astonishment.
estupro m rape.
etapa f stage; stopping place; (fig) phase.
etcétera adv et cetera, and so on.
éter m ether.
etéreo, rea adj ethereal.
eternidad f eternity.
eternizar vt to eternalize, to perpetuate.
eterno, na adj eternal.
ética f ethics.
ético, ca adj ethical, moral.
etimología f etymology.
etimológico, ca adj etymological.
etiqueta f etiquette, formality; ticket, label.
Eucaristía f Eucharist.
eufemismo m euphemism.
euforia f euphoria.
evacuación f evacuation.
evacuar vt to evacuate, to empty.
evadir vt to evade, to escape.
evaluar vt to evaluate.
evangélico, ca adj evangelical.
evangelio m gospel.
evangelista m evangelist; gospeler.
evangelizar vt to evangelize.
evaporar vt to evaporate; ~se vr to vanish.
evasión f evasion, escape.
evasivo, va adj evasive; ● f excuse.
eventual adj possible; temporary, casual (worker).
evidencia f evidence, proof.
evidente adj evident, clear, manifest.
evitable adj avoidable.
evitar vt to avoid.
evocación f evocation; invocation.
evocar vt to call out; to invoke.
evolución f evolution, development; change; (mil) maneuver.
evolucionar vi to evolve.
ex adj ex.
exacción f exaction; extortion.
exacerbar vt to exacerbate, to irritate.
exactamente adv exactly.
exactitud f exactness.
exacto, ta adj exact, punctual, accurate.
exageración f exaggeration.
exagerar vt to exaggerate.
exaltación f exaltation, elation.
exaltar vt to exalt, to elevate; to praise, to extoll; ~se vr to get excited.
examen m exam, examination, test, inquiry.
examinador m examiner.
examinar vt to examine.
exánime adj lifeless, weak.

exasperación f exasperation.
exasperar vt to exasperate, to irritate.
excavación f excavation.
excavadora f excavator.
excavar vt to excavate, to dig out.
excedente adj excessive, exceeding.
exceder vt to exceed, to surpass, to excel, to outdo.
excelencia f excellence.
Excelencia f Excellency (title).
excelente adj excellent.
excelso, sa adj elevated, sublime, lofty.
excentricidad f eccentricity.
excéntrico, ca adj eccentric.
excepción f exception.
excepto adv excepting, except (for).
exceptuar vt to except, to exempt.
excesivo, va adj excessive.
exceso m excess.
excitación f excitement; excitation.
excitar vt to excite; ~se vr to get excited.
exclamación f exclamation.
exclamar vt to exclaim, to cry out.
excluir vt to exclude.
exclusión f exclusion.
exclusiva f exclusive; (com) sole right.
exclusivamente, exclusive adv exclusively.
exclusivo, va adj exclusive.
excomulgar vt to excommunicate.
excomunión f excommunication.
excremento m excrement.
excursión f excursion, trip.
excusa f excuse, apology.
excusable adj excusable.
excusado m toilet.
excusar vt to excuse; to exempt from; to avoid; ~se vr to apologize.
execrable adj execrable, abhorrent.
execrar vt to execrate, to curse.
exención f exemption, immunity, privilege.
exento, ta adj exempt, free.
exequias fpl funeral rites, obsequies.
exhalación f exhalation; fumes, vapor.
exhalar vt to exhale; to give off; to heave (a sigh).
exhausto, ta adj exhausted.
exhibición f exhibition, display.
exhibir vt to exhibit.
exhortación f exhortation.
exhortar vt to exhort.
exhumación f exhumation.
exhumar vt to disinter, to exhume.
exigencia f demand, requirement.
exigir vt to demand, to require.
exiguo, gua adj meager, small.
exiliado, da adj exiled; ● m/f exile.
exilio m exile.
eximir vt to exempt, to free, to excuse.
existencia f existence, being.
existente adj existing, in existence.
existir vi to exist, to be.
éxito m outcome; success; (mus etc) hit; **tener ~** to be successful.
exoneración f exoneration.
exonerar vt to exonerate.
exorbitante adj exhorbitant, excessive.
exorcismo m exorcism.
exorcista m exorcist.
exorcizar vt to exorcize.
exótico, ca adj exotic.
expandir vt to expand.
expansión f expansion, extension.
expansivo, va adj expansive.
expatriarse vr to emigrate; to go into exile.

expectativa f expectation; prospect.
expectoración f expectoration.
expectorar vt to expectorate.
expedición f expedition.
expedicionario adj expeditionary.
expediente m expedient; means; (jur) proceedings; dossier, file.
expedir vt to send, to forward, to dispatch.
expeditivo, va adj expeditious.
expedito, ta adj speedy; clear, free.
expeler vt to expel.
expensas fpl: a ~ de at the expense of.
experiencia f experience; trial.
experimentado, da adj experienced, expert.
experimental adj experimental.
experimentar vt to experience; to experiment with.
experimento m experiment, trial.
experto, ta adj expert, experienced.
expiación f expiation; purification.
expiar vt to atone for; to purify.
expiatorio, ria adj expiatory.
expirar vt to expire.
explanada f esplanade.
explayarse vr to speak at length.
explicación f explanation.
explicar vt to explain, to expound; ~se vr to explain oneself.
explícito, ta adj explicit.
exploración f exploration.
explorador, ra m/f explorer.
explorar vt to explore.
explosión f explosion.
explotación f exploitation; running.
explotar vt to exploit; to run; ● vi to explode.
exponente m (mat) exponent.
exponer vt to expose; to explain.
exportación f export; exports pl.
exportar vt to export.
exposición f exposure; exhibition; explanation; account.
expresar vt to express.
expresión f expression.
expresivo, va adj expressive; energetic.
expreso, sa adj express, clear, specific; fast (train).
express m (ferro) express train.
exprimidor m squeezer.
exprimir vt to squeeze out.
ex profeso adv on purpose.
expropriar vt to expropriate.
expuesto, ta adj exposed; on display.
expulsar vt to expel, to drive out.
expulsión f expulsion.
exquisito, ta adj exquisite, excellent.
éxtasis m ecstasy, enthusiasm.
extático, ca adj ecstatic.
extender vt to extend, to stretch out; ~se vr to extend; to spread.
extensión f extension; extent.
extensivo, va adj extensive.
extenso, sa adj extensive.
extenuación f emaciation, debility, exhaustion.
extenuar vt to exhaust, to debilitate.
exterior adj exterior, external; ● m exterior, outward appearance.
exteriormente adv externally.
exterminador m exterminator.
exterminar vt to exterminate.
exterminio m extermination.
externo, na adj external, outward; ● m/f day pupil.
extinción f extinction.
extinguir vt to wipe out; to extinguish.
extintor m (fire) extinguisher.
extirpación f extirpation, extermination.
extirpar vt to extirpate, to root out.

extorsión f extortion.
extra adj invar extra; good quality; ● m/f extra; ● m bonus.
extracción f extraction.
extracto m extract.
extraer vt to extract.
extranjero, ra m/f stranger, foreigner; ● adj foreign, alien.
extrañar vt to find strange; to miss; ~se vr to be surprised; to grow apart.
extrañeza f strangeness; surprise.
extraño, ña adj foreign; rare; singular, strange, odd.
extraordinario, ria adj extraordinary, uncommon, odd.
extravagancia f extravagance.
extravagante adj extravagant.
extraviado, da adj lost, missing.
extraviar vt to mislead; ~se vr to lose one's way.
extravío m deviation; loss.
extremado, da adj extreme; accomplished.
extremaunción f extreme unction.
extremidad f extremity, brim; tip; ~es fpl extremities.
extremo, ma adj extreme, last; ● m extreme, highest degree; en ~, por ~ extremely.
extrínseco, ca adj extrinsic, external.
extrovertido, da adj, m/f extrovert.
exuberancia f exuberance, luxuriance.

F

fábrica f factory.
fabricación f manufacture; production.
fabricante m/f fabricator, manufacturer.
fabricar vt to build, to construct; to manufacture; (fig) to fabricate.
fabril adj manufacturing, industrial.
fábula f fable; fiction; rumor, common talk.
fabulista m/f writer of fables.
fabuloso, sa adj fabulous, fictitious.
facción f (political) faction; feature.
faccioso, sa adj factious, turbulent.
fácil adj facile, easy.
facilidad f facility, easiness.
facilitar vt to facilitate.
fácilmente adv easily.
facineroso adj wicked, criminal.
facsímil m facsimile, fax.
factible adj feasible, practicable.
factor m (mat) factor; (com) factor, agent.
factoría f agency; factory.
factura f invoice.
facultad f faculty.
facultativo, va adj optional; ● m/f doctor, practitioner.
facha f appearance, aspect, face.
fachada f façade, face, front.
faena f hard work, task, job.
faisán m pheasant.
faja f band, fillet; strip (of land); corset.
fajo m bundle; wad.
falacia f fallacy, fraud.
falange f phalanx.
falaz adj deceitful, fraudulent; falacious.
falda f skirt; lap; flap; train; slope, hillside.
faldero, ra adj: hombre ~ ladies' man; perrillo ~ lap-dog.
faldón m coat-tails; skirt.
falible adj fallible.
falsamente adv falsely.
falsario, ria adj falsifying, forging.
falsear vt to falsify, to counterfeit.
falsedad f falsehood; untruth, fib; hypocrisy.
falsete m (téc) plug; bung; (mus) falsetto.
falsificación f falsification.
falsificador, ra m/f forger, counterfeiter.

falsificar vt to falsify, to forge, to counterfeit.
falso, sa adj false, untrue; deceitful; fake.
falta f fault, defect; want; flaw, mistake; (dep) foul.
faltar vi to be wanting; to fail; not to fulfill one's promise; to need; to be missing.
falto, ta adj wanting, deficient, lacking; miserable, wretched.
faltriquera f pocket.
fallar vt (jur) to pronounce sentence, to judge; ● vi to fail.
fallecer vi to die.
fallecimiento m decease, death.
fallido, da adj unsuccessful, frustrated.
fallo m judgment, sentence; failure.
fama f fame; reputation, name.
famélico, ca adj starving.
familia f family.
familiar adj familiar, homely, domestic; ● m/f relative, relation.
familiaridad f familiarity.
familiarizarse vr: ~ con to familiarize oneself with.
famoso, sa adj famous.
fanático, ca adj fanatical; enthusiastic; ● m/f fanatic; fan.
fandango m fandango (lively Spanish dance).
fanfarrón m bully, braggart.
fanfarronada f boast, brag.
fanfarronear vi to bully, to brag.
fanfarronería f boast, brag.
fango m mire, mud.
fangoso, sa adj muddy, miry.
fantasía f fancy; fantasy; caprice; presumption.
fantasma f phantom, ghost.
fantástico, ca adj fantastic, whimsical; presumptuous.
fardo m bale, parcel.
farfullar vi to talk stammeringly.
farisaico, ca adj pharisaical; hypocritical.
fariseo m pharisee; hypocrite.
farmacéutico, ca adj pharmaceutical; ● m/f pharmacist.
farmacia f pharmacy.
faro m (mar) lighthouse; (auto) headlamp; floodlight.
farol m lantern.
farola f street light.
farsa f farce.
farsante m fraud, fake.
fascículo m part, installment.
fascinación f fascination.
fascinar vt to fascinate; to enchant.
fascismo m fascism.
fase f phase.
fastidiar vt to annoy, to offend; to spoil.
fastidio m annoyance; boredom; disgust.
fastidioso, sa adj annoying; tedious.
fatal adj fatal; mortal; awful.
fatalidad f fatality, mischance, ill-luck.
fatalismo m fatalism.
fatalista m/f fatalist.
fatiga f weariness, fatigue.
fatigar vt to fatigue, to tire, to harass.
fatigoso, sa adj tiresome, troublesome.
fatuidad f fatuity, foolishness, silliness.
fatuo, tua adj fatuous, stupid, foolish; conceited.
fauces fpl jaws, gullet.
fausto, ta adj happy, fortunate; ● m splendor, pomp.
favor m favor, protection, good turn.
favorable adj favorable, advantageous.
favorecer vt to favor, to protect.
favorito, ta adj favorite.
faz f face.
fe f faith, belief.
fealdad f ugliness.
febrero m February.
febril adj feverish.
fecundar vt to fertilize.
fecundidad f fecundity, fertility.

fecundo, da adj fruitful, fertile.
fecha f date (of a letter etc).
fechar vt to date.
fechoría f action, exploit.
federación f federation.
felicidad f happiness.
felicitar vt to congratulate.
feligrés, esa m/f parishioner.
feliz adj happy, fortunate.
felpa f plush; toweling.
felpudo m doormat.
femenil adj feminine, womanly.
femenino, na adj feminine, female.
feminista adj, m/f feminist.
fenómeno m phenomenon; (fig) freak, accident; ● adj (fam) great (sl), marvelous.
feo, ea adj ugly; bad, nasty.
feracidad f productivity, fertility.
feraz adj fertile, fruitful.
féretro m bier, casket.
feria f fair, rest day; village market.
fermentación f fermentation.
fermentar vi to ferment.
fermento m ferment; leaven.
ferocidad f ferocity, wildness; cruelty.
feroz adj ferocious, cruel, savage.
ferretería f hardware store.
ferrocarril m railroad.
ferroviario, ria adj rail compd.
fértil adj fertile, fruitful.
fertilidad f fertility, fruitfulness.
fertilizar vt to fertilize.
férula f ferule; (med) splint.
ferviente adj fervent, ardent.
fervor m fervor, zeal, ardor.
fervoroso, sa adj fervent, ardent, passionate.
festejar vt to feast; to court, to woo.
festejo m courtship; feast.
festín m feast.
festividad f festivity.
festivo, va adj festive, merry; witty; día ~ holiday.
festón m garland; festoon.
festonear vt to ornament with garlands.
fétido, da adj fetid, stinking.
feto m fetus.
feudal adj feudal.
fiable adj trustworthy; reliable.
fiador, ra m/f surety, guarantor; (com) backer.
fiambre m cold meat.
fiambrera f dinner pail.
fianza f (jur) surety.
fiar vt to entrust, to confide; to bail; to sell on credit; to buy on credit; ● vi to trust.
fibra f fiber.
fibroso, sa adj fibrous.
ficción f fiction.
ficticio, cia adj fictitious.
ficha f token, counter (at games); (index) card.
fidedigno, na adj reliable, trustworthy.
fideicomisario, ria m/f trustee.
fideicomiso f trust.
fidelidad f fidelity; loyalty.
fideos mpl noodles.
fiebre f fever.
fiel adj faithful, loyal; los ~es mpl the faithful.
fieltro m felt.
fiera f wild beast.
fiereza f fierceness, cruelty, ferocity.
fiero, ra adj fierce, cruel, ferocious; rough, harsh.
fiesta f party; festivity; ~s pl holidays, vacations.
figura f figure, shape.
figurado, da adj figurative.

figurar vt to figure; ~**se** vr to fancy, to imagine.
figurilla f ridiculous little figure.
fijador m fixative; gel (for the hair).
fijar vt to fix, to fasten; ~**se** vr to become fixed; to establish oneself; ~**se en** to notice.
fijo, ja adj fixed, firm; settled, permanent.
fila f row, line; (mil) rank; **en** ~ in a line, in a row.
filamento m filament.
filantropía f philanthropy.
filántropo, pa m/f philanthropist.
filete m fillet; fillet steak.
filiación f filiation; personal description, particulars.
filial adj filial; ● f (com) subsidiary.
filibustero m freebooter.
filigrana f filigree.
filmar vt to film.
filo m edge, blade.
filología f philology.
filológico, ca adj philological.
filólogo, ga m/f philologist.
filosofar vi to philosophize.
filosofía f philosophy.
filosófico, ca adj philosophical.
filósofo, fa m/f philosopher.
filtración f filtration.
filtrar vt to filter, to strain.
filtro m filter.
fin m end, termination, conclusion; aim, purpose; **al** ~ at last; **en** ~ (fig) well then; **por** ~ finally, lastly.
final adj final; ● m end, termination, conclusion; ● f (dep) final.
finalizar vt to finish, to conclude; ● vi to be finished.
finalmente adv finally, at last.
financiar vt to finance.
finca f land, property, real estate; country house; farm.
fineza f fineness, perfection; elegance; courtesy; small gift.
fingido, da adj feigned, fake, sham.
fingimiento m simulation, pretense.
fingir vt to feign, to fake; to invent; to imitate; ● vi to pretend; ~**se** vr to pretend to be.
finito, ta adj finite.
fino, na adj fine, pure; slender; polite; acute; (of sherry) dry.
finura f fineness.
firma f signature; (com) company.
firmamento m firmament, sky, heaven.
firmar vt to sign.
firme adj firm, stable, strong, secure; constant, resolute; ● m road surface.
firmeza f firmness, stability, constancy.
fiscal adj fiscal; ● m/f district attorney.
fiscalía f office and business of the district attorney.
fiscalizar vt to inspect; to criticize.
fisco m treasury, exchequer.
fisgar vt to pry into.
fisgón, ona m/f prying person, snooper (sl).
física f physics.
físico, ca adj physical; ● m/f physicist; ● m physique.
fisonomía f physiognomy.
fisonomista m/f: **ser buen** ~ to have a good memory for faces.
flaco, ca adj lean, skinny; feeble.
flagelación f flagellation.
flagrante adj flagrant.
flamante adj flaming, bright; brand-new.
flan m crème caramel.
flanco m flank.
flanquear vt (mil) to flank.
flaquear vi to flag; to weaken.
flaqueza f thinness, leanness, feebleness, weakness.
flato m (med) flatulence; depression.
flatulento, ta adj flatulent.
flauta f (mus) flute.
flautista m/f flute player, flautist.

flecha f arrow.
fleco m fringe.
flema f phlegm.
flemático, ca adj phlegmatic.
flemón m ulcer in the gums.
flequillo m fringe (of hair), bangs pl.
fletar vt to freight a ship.
flete m (mar) freight; charter.
flexibilidad f flexibility.
flexible adj flexible, compliant; docile.
flojedad f feebleness, laxity, laziness, negligence.
flojera f: **me da** ~ I can't be bothered.
flojo, ja adj loose; flexible, lax, slack; lazy.
flor f flower.
florecer vi to blossom.
florero m vase.
floresta f wood, grove; beauty spot.
florete m fencing foil.
florido, da adj full of flowers; in bloom; choice.
florista m/f florist.
flota f fleet.
flotador m float; rubber ring.
flotante adj floating.
flotar vi to float.
flote m: **a** ~ afloat.
flotilla f small fleet, flotilla.
fluctuación f fluctuation; uncertainty.
fluctuar vi to fluctuate; to waver.
fluidez f fluidity; fluency.
fluido, da adj fluid; (fig) fluent; ● m fluid.
fluir vi to flow.
flujo m flux; flow; ~ **de sangre** (med) loss of blood.
fluvial adj fluvial, river.
foca f seal.
foco m focus; center; source; floodlight; (light) bulb.
fofo, fa adj spongy, soft, bland.
fogata f blaze; bonfire.
fogón m stove; hearth.
fogonazo m flash, explosion.
fogosidad f dash, verve, fieriness.
fogoso, sa adj fiery, ardent, fervent; impetuous, boisterous.
follaje m foliage.
folletista m/f pamphleteer.
folleto m pamphlet; folder, brochure.
follón m (fam) mess; fuss.
fomentar vt to encourage, to foment.
fomento m promotion.
fonda f hotel, inn, boarding house.
fondeadero m anchorage.
fondear vi to cast anchor.
fondista m/f innkeeper.
fondo m bottom; back; background; space; ~**s** stock, funds, capital; **a** ~ perfectly, completely.
fontanería f plumbing.
fontanero, ra m/f plumber.
forajido m outlaw.
foral adj belonging to the statute law of a country.
forastero, ra adj strange, exotic; ● m/f stranger.
forcejear vi to struggle.
forense adj forensic.
forjador, ra m/f framer, forger.
forjadura f forging.
forjar vt to forge; to frame; to invent.
forma f form, shape, pattern; (med) fitness; (dep) form; means, method; **de** ~ **que** in such a manner that.
formación f formation; form, figure; education; training.
formal adj formal; proper, genuine; serious, grave.
formalidad f formality; gravity.
formalizar vt (jur) to formalize; to regularize; ~**se** vr to be regularized.
formar vt to form, to shape.
formidable adj formidable, dreadful; terrific (sl).

fórmula f formula.
formulario m formulary.
fornicación f fornication.
fornicador m fornicator.
fornicar vi to commit fornication.
fornido, da adj well-built.
foro m court of justice; forum.
forraje m forage.
forrajear vt to forage.
forrar vt to line, to face, to cover.
forro m lining; book jacket.
fortalecer vt to fortify, to strengthen.
fortaleza f courage; strength, vigor; (mil) fortress, stronghold.
fortificación f fortification.
fortificar vt to strengthen; to fortify a place.
fortín m (mil) small fort.
fortuito, ta adj fortuitous.
fortuna f fortune; wealth.
forzar vt to force.
forzoso, sa adj indispensable, necessary.
forzudo, da adj strong, vigorous.
fosa f grave; pit.
fósforo m phosphorus; ~s pl matches.
fósil adj, m fossil.
foso vt pit; moat, ditch, fosse.
foto f photo.
fotocopia f photocopy.
fotografía f photography; photograph.
fotógrafo, fa m/f photographer.
frac m evening coat, dress coat.
fracasar vi to fail.
fracaso m failure.
fracción f fraction.
fractura f fracture.
fracturar vt to break a bone.
fragancia f fragrance, sweetness of smell.
fragante adj fragrant, scented.
fragata f (mar) frigate.
frágil adj fragile, frail.
fragilidad f fragility, brittleness; frailty.
fragmento m fragment.
fragosidad f roughness; denseness.
fragoso, sa adj craggy, rough, uneven.
fragua f forge.
fraguar vt to forge; to contrive; ● vi to solidify, to harden.
fraile m friar, monk.
frambuesa f raspberry.
francés, sa adj French; ● m French language; ● m/f Frenchman/woman.
franco, ca adj frank; candid; free, gratis.
franela f flannel; undershirt.
franja f fringe.
franquear vt to clear; to overcome; to stamp letters; ~se to unbosom oneself.
franqueo m postage.
franqueza f frankness.
franquicia f immunity from taxes.
frasco m flask.
frase f phrase.
fraternal adj fraternal, brotherly.
fraternidad f fraternity, brotherhood.
fratricida m/f fratricide.
fratricidio m fratricide.
fraude m fraud, deceit, cheat.
fraudulento, ta adj fraudulent, deceitful.
frazada f blanket.
frecuencia f frequency.
frecuentar vt to frequent.
frecuente adj frequent.
fregadero m (kitchen) sink.
fregado m scouring, scrubbing; (fig) intrigue; underhand work.

fregar vt to scrub; to wash up.
fregona f mop; skivvy.
freír vt to fry.
frenar vt to brake; (fig) to check.
frenesí m frenzy.
frenético, ca adj frantic, frenzied, wild.
frenillo m speech impediment.
freno m bit; brake; (fig) check.
frente f front; face; ~ a ~ face to face; en ~ opposite; (mil) front; ● m forehead.
fresa f strawberry.
fresal m strawberry plant; ground bearing strawberry plants.
fresco, ca adj fresh, cool; new; ruddy; ● m fresh air; ● m/f (fam) shameless person; impudent person.
frescura f freshness; frankness; cheek, nerve.
fresno m ash tree.
frialdad f coldness; indifference.
fricción f friction.
friega f rubbing; nuisance.
frígido, da adj frigid.
frigorífico m fridge.
frijol m kidney bean.
frío, fría adj cold; indifferent; ● m cold; indifference.
friolento, ta adj chilly.
friolera f trifle.
friso m frieze; wainscot.
fritada f dish of fried meat or fish.
frito, ta adj fried.
frivolidad f frivolity.
frívolo, la adj frivolous.
frondosidad f foliage.
frondoso, sa adj leafy.
frontera f frontier.
fronterizo, za adj frontier compd; bordering.
frontón m (dep) pelota court; pelota.
frotación, frotadura f friction, rubbing.
frotar vt to rub.
fructífero, ra adj fruit-bearing, fruitful.
fructificar vt to bear fruit; to come to fruition.
fructuoso, sa adj fruitful.
frugal adj frugal, sparing.
frugalidad f frugality, parsimony.
fruncir vt to pleat; to knit; to contract; ~ las cejas to knit the eyebrows.
frustrar vt to frustrate.
fruta f fruit; ~ del tiempo seasonal fruit.
frutal m fruit tree.
frutera f fruit dish.
frutero, ra m/f fruiterer; ● m fruit basket.
frutilla f strawberry.
fruto m fruit; benefit, profit.
fuego m fire.
fuelle m bellows pl.
fuente f fountain; spring; source; large dish.
fuera adv out(side); away; except, save; ¡~! out of the way!
fuero m statute law of a country; jurisdiction.
fuerte m (mil) fortification, fort; forte; ● adj vigorous, tough; strong; loud; heavy; ● adv strongly; hard.
fuerza f force, strength; (elec) power; violence; a ~ de by dint of; ~s pl troops.
fuga f flight, escape; leak (of gas).
fugarse vr to escape, to flee.
fugaz adj fleeting.
fugitivo, va adj, m/f fugitive.
fulano, na m/f so-and-so, what's-his-name/what's-her-name.
fulgurar vi to flash.
fulminar vt to fulminate; ● vi to explode.
fullería f cheating.
fullero m cardsharper, cheat.
fumador, ra m/f smoker.
fumar vt, vi to smoke.
fumigación f fumigation.

funámbulista m/f tightrope walker.
función f function; duties pl; show, performance.
funcionar vi to function; to work (of a machine).
funcionario, ria m/f official; civil servant.
funda f case, sheath; ~ de almohada pillowcase.
fundación f foundation.
fundador, ra m/f founder.
fundamental adj fundamental.
fundamento m foundation, groundwork; reason, cause.
fundar vt to found; to establish, to ground.
fundición f fusion; foundry.
fundir vt to fuse; to melt, to smelt; (com) to merge; to bankrupt; (elec) to fuse, to blow.
fúnebre adj mournful, sad; funereal.
funeral m funeral; ~es mpl funeral, obsequies.
funerario, ria adj funeral, funereal.
funesto, ta adj ill-fated, unfortunate; fatal.
furgón m wagon.
furgoneta f pick-up (truck).
furia f fury, rage.
furibundo, da adj furious, frenzied.
furioso, sa adj furious.
furor m fury, rage.
furtivamente adv furtively.
furtivo, va adj furtive.
furúnculo m (med) boil.
fusible m fuse.
fusil m rifle.
fusilar vt to shoot.
fusilero m rifleman.
fusión f fusion; (com) merger.
fusta f riding crop.
fútbol m football.
futbolista m/f footballer.
fútil adj futile, trifling.
futilidad f futility.
futuro, ra adj, m future.

G

gabán m overcoat.
gabardina f gabardine, raincoat.
gabarra f (mar) lighter (boat).
gabinete m (pol) cabinet, study; office (of solicitors etc).
gaceta f gazette.
gachas fpl porridge, pap.
gacho, cha adj curved, bent downward.
gafas fpl glasses, spectacles.
gafe m jinx.
gaita f bagpipe; flageolet.
gaitero, ra m/f bagpiper, bagpipe player.
gaje m: los ~s del oficio occupational hazards.
gajo m segment (of orange).
gala f full dress; (fig) cream, flower; ~s pl finery; **hacer ~ de** to display, to show off.
galán m lover; handsome young man; (teat) male lead.
galante adj gallant.
galanteador m lover.
galantear vt to court, to woo.
galanteo m gallantry, courtship.
galantería f gallantry; politeness; compliment.
galápago m tortoise.
galardón m reward, prize.
galardonar vt to reward, to recompense.
galaxia f galaxy.
galbana f laziness, idleness.
galeón m (mar) galleon.
galera f (mar) galley; wagon; type-galley.
galería f gallery.
galgo m greyhound.

galón m (mil) stripe; braid; gallon.
galopar vi to gallop.
galope m gallop.
galvánico, ca adj galvanic.
galvanismo m galvanism.
gallardete m (mar) pennant, streamer.
gallardía f fineness, elegance, gracefulness; dash.
gallardo, da adj graceful, elegant, brave, daring.
galleta f cookie.
gallina f hen; ● m/f (fig) coward; ~ ciega blindman's buff.
gallinero m henhouse, coop; poulterer; (teat) top gallery; hubbub.
gallineta f woodcock (bird).
gallo m cock.
gama f (mus) scale; (fig) range, gamut; doe.
gamba f shrimp.
gamberro, rra m/f hooligan.
gamo m buck of the fallow deer.
gamuza f chamois.
gana f desire, wish; appetite; will, longing; **de buena ~** with pleasure, voluntarily; **de mala ~** unwillingly, with reluctance.
ganadería f cattle raising; cattle; livestock.
ganadero m rancher; dealer in cattle.
ganado m livestock, cattle; ~ **mayor** horses and mules; ~ **menor** sheep, goats and pigs.
ganancia f gain, profit, increase.
ganancial adj lucrative.
ganar vt to gain, to win, to earn; ● vi to win.
gancho m hook; crook.
gandul adj, m/f layabout.
ganga f bargain.
gangoso, sa adj nasal.
gangrena f gangrene.
gangrenarse vr to become gangrenous.
gangrenoso, sa adj gangrenous.
ganso, sa m/f gander; goose; (fam) idiot.
garabatear or **garapatear** vi, vt to scrawl, to scribble.
garabatos mpl scrawling letters or characters.
garaje m garage.
garante m/f guarantor; ● adj responsible.
garantía f warranty, guarantee.
garañón m jackass, male donkey.
garapiñar vt to freeze; to ice.
garbanzo m chickpea, garbanzo.
garbo m gracefulness, elegance, stylishness; generosity.
garboso, sa adj graceful; elegant, stylish; generous.
garduña f marten.
gargajo m phlegm, spit.
garganta f throat, gullet; instep; neck (of a bottle); narrow pass between mountains or rivers.
gargantilla f necklace.
gárgara f noise made by gargling.
gargarismo m gargling, gargle.
gargarizar vi to gargle.
garita f (mil) sentry box; (ferro) signal box.
garra f claw, talon, paw.
garrafa f carafe; (gas) cylinder.
garrafal adj great, vast, huge.
garrapata f tick (insect).
garrotazo m blow with a stick or club.
garrote m stick, club, cudgel; (jur) garrotte.
garrotillo m (med) croup.
garrucha f pulley.
garza f heron.
garzo, za adj blue-eyed.
gas m gas.
gasa f gauze.
gaseoso, sa adj fizzy; ● f lemonade.
gasfitero, ra m/f plumber.
gasoil m diesel (oil).
gasolina f gas(oline).

gasolinera *f* gas station.
gasómetro *m* gasometer.
gastador, ra *m/f* spendthrift.
gastar *vt* to spend; to expend; to waste; to wear away; to use up; ~**se** *vr* to wear out; to waste.
gasto *m* expense, expenditure; use.
gastronomía *f* gastronomy.
gata *f* she-cat; a ~**s** on all fours.
gatear *vi* to go on all fours.
gatera *f* cat hole.
gatillazo *m* click of the trigger in firing.
gatillo *m* trigger of a gun; *(med)* dental forceps.
gato *m* cat; jack.
gatuno, na *adj* catlike, feline.
gaveta *f* drawer of a desk, locker.
gavilán *m* sparrow hawk.
gavilla *f* sheaf of corn.
gaviota *f* seagull.
gay *(fam) adj invar,* *m* gay *(sl),* homosexual.
gazapo *m* young rabbit; lie.
gazmoñada, gazmoñería *f* prudery, hypocrisy.
gazmoñero, ra, gazmoño, ña *adj* hypocritical.
gaznate *m* throttle, wind pipe.
gazpacho *m* a Spanish cold tomato soup.
gazuza *f* ravenous hunger.
gelatina *f* jelly; gelatine.
gemelo, la *m/f* twin.
gemido *m* groan, moan, howl.
Géminis *m* Gemini (sign of the zodiac).
gemir *vi* to groan, to moan.
genciana *f (bot)* gentian.
gendarme *m* gendarme, policeman.
gendarmería *f* gendarmery, police.
genealogía *f* genealogy.
genealógico, ca *adj* genealogical.
generación *f* generation; progeny, race.
general *m* general; ● *adj* general; **en** ~ generally, in general.
generalidad *f* generality.
generalizar *vt* to generalize.
generalmente *adv* generally.
genérico, ca *adj* generic.
género *m* genus; kind, type; gender; cloth, material; ~**s** *pl* goods, commodities.
generosidad *f* generosity.
generoso, sa *adj* noble, generous.
Génesis *f* Genesis.
genial *adj* inspired, brilliant; genial.
genio *m* nature, character, genius.
genital *adj* genital; ~**es** *mpl* genitals.
genitivo *m (gr)* genitive case.
gente *f* people; nation; family.
gentil *m/f* pagan, heathen; ● *adj* elegant, graceful, charming.
gentileza *f* grace; charm; politeness.
gentilhombre *m* gentleman.
gentío *m* crowd, throng.
genuflexión *f* genuflection.
genuino, na *adj* genuine, pure.
geografía *f* geography.
geográfico, ca *adj* geographical.
geógrafo, fa *m/f* geographer.
geología *f* geology.
geometría *f* geometry.
geométrico, ca *adj* geometrical, geometric.
geranio *m (bot)* geranium.
gerente *m/f* manager; director.
geriatría *f (med)* geriatrics.
germen *m* germ, bud; source, origin.
germinar *vi* to germinate, to bud.
gerundio *m (gr)* gerund.
gesticular *vi* to gesticulate.
gestión *f* management; negociation.
gesto *m* face; grimace; gesture.

giganta *f* giantess.
gigante *m* giant; ● *adj* gigantic.
gigantesco, ca *adj* gigantic, giant.
gilipollas *(fam) adj invar* stupid; ● *m/f invar* wimp *(sl).*
gimnasia *f* gymnastics.
gimnasio *m* gymnasium.
gimnasta *m/f* gymnast.
gimnástico, ca *adj* gymnastic.
ginebra *f* gin.
ginecólogo, ga *m/f* gynecologist.
gira *f* trip, tour.
girar *vt* to turn around; to swivel; *(com)* to draw, to issue; ● *vi* to go round, to revolve; *(com)* to do business; to draw.
giratorio, ria *adj* revolving.
girasol *m* sunflower.
giro *m* turning round; tendency; change; *(com)* draft.
gitano, na *m/f* gipsy.
glacial *adj* icy.
glaciar *m* glacier.
glándula *f* gland.
glandular *adj* glandular.
globo *m* globe; sphere; orb; balloon; ~ **aerostático** air balloon.
glóbulo *m* globule; corpuscle.
gloria *f* glory.
gloriarse *vr* to glory in, to pride in; to take delight in.
glorieta *f* bower, arbor; traffic circle.
glorificación *f* glorification; praise.
glorificar *vt* to glorify.
glorioso, sa *adj* glorious.
glosa *f* gloss; comment.
glosar *vt* to gloss; to comment on.
glotón, ona *m/f* glutton.
glotonería *f* gluttony.
gobernación *f* government.
gobernador, ra *m/f* governor.
gobernar *vt* to govern; to regulate; to direct.
gobierno *m* government.
goce *m* enjoyment.
gol *m* goal.
goleta *f* schooner.
golf *m* golf.
golfa *f (fam)* slut.
golfo *m* gulf, bay; *(fam)* urchin; lout.
golondrina *f* swallow.
golosina *f* dainty, titbit; candy.
goloso, sa *adj* sweet-toothed.
golpe *m* blow, stroke, hit; knock; clash; coup; **de** ~ suddenly.
golpear *vt* to beat, to knock; to punch.
goma *f* gum; rubber; elastic.
gomosidad *f* gumminess, viscosity.
gomoso, sa *adj* gummy, viscous.
góndola *f* gondola; *(ferro)* freight truck.
gondolero *m* gondolier.
gordiflón, ona *m/f* very fat person.
gordo, da *adj* fat, plump, big-bellied; first, main; *(fam)* enormous.
gordura *f* grease; fatness, corpulence, obesity.
gorgojo *m* grub, weevil.
gorgorito *m* trill, warble.
gorila *m* gorilla.
gorjear *vi* to twitter, to chirp.
gorjeo *m* chirping.
gorra *f* cap, bonnet; *(mil)* bearskin.
gorrión *m* sparrow.
gorro *m* cap; bonnet.
gorrón, ona *m/f* scrounger.
gota *f* drop; *(med)* gout.
gotear *vt* to drip; to drizzle.
gotera *f* leak.
gótico, ca *adj* Gothic.
gotoso, sa *adj* gouty.

gozar vt to enjoy, to have, to possess; **~se** vr to enjoy oneself, to rejoice.

gozne m hinge.

gozo m joy, pleasure.

gozoso, sa adj joyful, cheerful, content, glad, pleased.

grabación f recording.

grabado m engraving.

grabador m engraver.

grabadora f tape recorder.

grabar vt to engrave; to record.

gracejo m wit, charm; gracefulness.

gracia f grace, gracefulness; wit; ¡(**muchas**) **~s!** thanks (very much); **tener ~** to be funny.

gracioso, sa adj graceful, beautiful; funny, pleasing; ● m comic character.

grada f step of a staircase; tier, row; **~s** pl seats of a stadium or theatre.

gradería f (flight of) steps; row of seats.

grado m step; degree; **de buen ~** willingly.

graduación f graduation; (mil) rank.

gradual adj gradual.

graduar vt to graduate.

gráfico, ca adj graphic; ● m diagram; ● f graph.

graja f rook.

grajo m rook (bird).

grama f grass.

gramática f grammar.

gramatical adj grammatical.

gramático m grammarian.

gramo m gram.

gran adj = **grande**.

grana f grain; scarlet.

granada f (mil) grenade; pomegranate.

granadero m (mil) grenadier.

granadilla f passionflower; passion fruit.

granado m pomegranate tree.

granate m garnet (precious stone).

grande adj great; big; tall; grand; ● m/f adult.

grandeza f greatness; grandeur; size.

grandiosidad f greatness, grandeur; magnificence.

grandioso, sa adj grand, magnificent.

granel adv: **a ~** in bulk.

granero m granary.

granito m granite.

granizada f hail; hailstorm; shower, volley.

granizado m iced drink.

granizar vi to hail.

granizo m hail.

granja f farm.

grano m grain.

granuja m/f rogue; urchin.

grapa f staple; clamp.

grasa f suet, fat; grease.

grasiento, ta adj greasy; rusty, filthy.

gratificación f gratification, recompense.

gratificar vt to gratify, to reward, to recompense.

gratis adj free.

gratitud f gratitude, gratefulness.

grato, ta adj pleasant, agreeable.

gratuito, ta adj gratuitous; free.

gravamen m charge, obligation; nuisance; tax.

gravar vt to burden; (com) to tax.

grave adj weighty, heavy; grave, important; serious.

gravedad f gravity; graveness.

gravemente adv gravely, seriously.

gravilla f gravel.

gravitación f gravitation.

gravitar vt to gravitate; to weigh down on.

gravoso, sa adj onerous, burdensome; costly.

graznar vi to croak; to cackle; to quack.

graznido m croak, cackle.

greda f clay.

gremio m union; society; company, guild, corporation.

greña f tangle; shock of hair.

greñudo, da, adj disheveled.

gresca f clatter, outcry, confusion; wrangle, quarrel.

grieta f crevice, crack, chink.

grifo m faucet; gas station.

grilletes mpl shackles, fetters.

grillo m cricket; bud, shoot; **~s** pl fetters, irons.

grima f disgust; annoyance.

gripe f flu, influenza.

gris adj gray.

gritar vi to cry out, to shout, to yell.

gritería f shouting, clamor, uproar.

grito m shout, cry, scream.

grosella f redcurrant; **~ negra** blackcurrant.

grosellero m currant bush.

grosería f coarseness, rudeness; vulgar comment.

grosero, ra adj coarse, rude, bad-mannered.

grosor m thickness.

grotesco, ca adj grotesque.

grúa f crane (machine); derrick.

grueso, sa adj thick; bulky; large; coarse; ● m bulk.

grulla f crane (bird).

grumo m clot; curd.

grumoso, sa adj clotted.

gruñido m grunt, grunting; growl.

gruñidor, ra m/f grunter, mumbler; (fig) grumbler.

gruñir vi to grunt; to grumble; to creak (of hinges etc).

grupa f rump.

grupo m group.

gruta f grotto.

guadaña f scythe.

guagua f baby; bus.

gualdrapa f trappings (of a horse); tatter, rag.

guantada f slap.

guante m glove.

guapo, pa adj good-looking; handsome, smart.

guarda m/f guard, keeper; ● f custody, keeping.

guardaagujas m invar (ferro) switchman, pointsman.

guardabosque m gamekeeper; ranger.

guardacostas m coastguard vessel.

guardaespaldas m/f invar bodyguard.

guardafuegos m invar fireguard, fender.

guardameta m/f goalkeeper.

guardapolvo m dust cover; coveralls pl.

guardar vt to keep, to preserve; to save (money); to guard; **~se** vr to be on one's guard, to avoid, to abstain from.

guardarropa f closet; checkroom.

guardia f guard; (mar) watch; care, custody; ● m/f guard; policeman/woman; (mil) guardsman.

guardián, ana m/f keeper; guardian.

guardilla f garret, attic.

guarecer vt to protect; to shelter; **~se** vr to take refuge.

guarida f den, lair; shelter; hiding place.

guarismo m figure, numeral.

guarnecer vt to provide, to equip; to reinforce; to garnish, to set (in gold etc); to adorn.

guarnición f trimming; gold setting; sword guard; garnish; (mil) garrison.

guasa f joke.

guasón, na m/f joker, jester.

gubernativo, va adj governmental.

guedeja f lock of hair.

guerra f war; hostility.

guerrear vi to fight, to wage war.

guerrero, ra m/f warrior; ● adj martial, warlike.

guerrilla f guerrilla warfare.

guía m/f guide; ● f guidebook.

guiar vt to guide; (auto) to steer.

guijarral m stony place.

guijarro m pebble.

guillotina f guillotine.

guillotinar *vt* to guillotine.
guinda *f* cherry.
guindal *m* cherry tree.
guindilla *f* chilli pepper.
guiñapo *m* tatter, rag; rogue.
guiñar *vt* to wink.
guión *m* hyphen (in writing); script (of film).
guirigay *m* gibberish, confused language.
guirnalda *f* garland, wreath.
guisado *m* stew.
guisante *m* (bot) pea.
guisar *vt* to cook.
guiso *m* seasoning; cooked dish; stew.
guisote *m* hash, poor quality stew.
guitarra *f* guitar.
guitarrista *m/f* guitar player.
gula *f* gluttony.
gusano *m* maggot, worm.
gustar *vt* to taste; to sample; ● *vi* to like, to love; to please, to be pleasing.
gusto *m* taste; pleasure, delight; liking.
gustosamente *adv* gladly, with pleasure.
gustoso, sa *adj* pleasant; tasty.
gutural *adj* guttural.

H

haba *f* (bot) bean.
haber *vt* to get, to lay hands on; to occur; ● *v imp*: **hay** there is, there are; ● *v aux* to have; to have; ~**se** *vr*: **habérselas con uno** to have it out with somebody; ● *m* income, salary, assets; (com) credit.
habichuela *f* kidney bean.
hábil *adj* able, clever, skillful, dexterous, apt.
habilidad *f* ability, ableness, dexterity, aptitude.
habilitación *f* entitlement, qualification.
habilitar *vt* to qualify, to enable; to finance.
habitable *adj* inhabitable.
habitación *f* habitation, abode, lodging, dwelling, residence; room.
habitante *m/f* inhabitant, occupant.
habitar *vt* to inhabit, to reside.
hábito *m* dress, habit; custom.
habitual *adj* habitual, customary.
habituar *vt* to accustom; ~**se** *vr* to become accustomed to.
habla *f* speech; language; dialect.
hablador, ra *m/f* talkative person.
habladuría *f* rumor; ~**s** *pl* gossip.
hablante *adj* speaking; ● *m/f* speaker.
hablar *vt* to speak; to talk.
hacedor, ra *m/f* maker, author.
hacendado *m* landowner; rancher.
hacendoso, sa *adj* industrious.
hacer *vt* to make, to do, to put into practice; to perform; to effect; to prepare; to imagine; to force; (mat) to amount to, to make; ● *vi* to act, to behave; ~**se** *vr* to become.
hacia *adv* toward; about; ~ **arriba/abajo** up(ward)/down(ward).
hacienda *f* property; large farm; ranch; **H~** Treasury.
hacinar *vt* to stack or pile up; to hoard.
hacha *f* torch; ax, hatchet.
hachazo *m* blow with an ax.
hada *f* fairy.
hado *m* fate, destiny.
halagar *vt* to cajole, to flatter.
halago *m* cajolery; pleasure.
halagüeño *adj* attractive, flattering.
halcón *m* falcon.
halconero *m* falconer.
hálito *m* breath; gentle breeze.

hallar *vt* to find; to meet with; to discover; ~**se** *vr* to find oneself, to be.
hallazgo *m* finding, discovery.
hamaca *f* hammock.
hambre *f* hunger; famine; longing.
hambriento, ta *adj* hungry; starved.
hamburguesa *f* hamburger.
haragán, ana *m/f* idler, good-for-nothing.
haraganear *vt* to idle, to loiter.
haraganería *f* idleness, laziness.
harapo *m* rag, tatter.
haraposo *adj* ragged.
harina *f* flour.
harinoso, sa *adj* floury.
hartar *vt* to satiate; to glut; to tire, to sicken; ~**se** *vr* to gorge oneself (with food); to get fed up.
harto, ta *adj* full; fed up; ● *adv* enough.
hartura *f* surfeit; plenty, abundance.
hasta *prep* up to; down to; until, as far as; ● *adv* even.
hastío *m* loathing; disgust; boredom.
hatajo *m* lot, collection.
hato *m* clothes *pl*; herd of cattle, flock of sheep; provisions *pl*; crowd, gang, collection.
haya *f* beech tree.
haz *m* bunch, bundle; beam (of light).
hazaña *f* exploit, achievement.
hazmerreír *m invar* ridiculous person, laughing stock.
hebilla *f* buckle.
hebra *f* thread; vein of minerals or metals; grain of wood.
hebraico, ca *adj* belonging to the Hebrews.
hebraísmo *m* Hebraism.
hebreo, ea *m/f* Hebrew; Israeli; ● *m* Hebrew language; ● *adj* Hebrew; Israeli.
hectárea *f* hectare.
hechicería *f* witchcraft; charm.
hechicero, ra *adj* charming, bewitching; ● *m/f* sorcerer/sorceress.
hechizar *vt* to bewitch; to enchant; to charm.
hechizo *m* bewitchment, enchantment.
hecho, cha *adj* made, done; mature; ready-to-wear; cooked; ● *m* action; act; fact; matter; event.
hechura *f* form, shape, fashion; making; workmanship; creature.
heder *vi* to stink, to smell badly.
hediondez *f* strong stench.
hediondo, da *adj* fetid, stinking.
hedor *m* stench, stink.
helada *f* frost; freeze-up.
helado, da *adj* frozen; glacial, icy; astonished; astounded; ● *m* ice cream.
helar *vt*, *vi* to congeal; to freeze; to astonish, to amaze; ~**se** *vr* to be frozen; to turn into ice; to congeal.
helecho *m* fern.
hélice *f* helix; propeller.
helicóptero *m* helicopter.
hembra *f* female.
hemisferio *m* hemisphere.
hemorragia *f* hemorrhage.
hemorroides *fpl* hemorrhoids, piles.
henchir *vt* to fill up; ~**se** *vr* to fill or stuff oneself.
hendedura or **hendidura** *f* fissure, chink, crevice.
hender *vt* to crack, to split; to go through; to open a passage.
heno *m* hay.
heraldo *m* herald.
herborizar *vt* to pick herbs; to collect plants.
heredad *f* patrimony, inherited property; farm.
heredar *vt* to inherit.
heredera *f* heiress.
heredero *m* heir.
hereditario, ria *adj* hereditary.
hereje *m/f* heretic.
herejía *f* heresy.

herencia f inheritance, heritage, heredity.
herida f wound, injury.
herido, da adj wounded, hurt.
herir vt to wound, to hurt; to beat, to strike; to affect, to touch, to move; to offend.
hermafrodita m hermaphrodite.
hermana f sister.
hermanar vt to match, to suit, to harmonize.
hermanastra f step-sister, half-sister.
hermanastro m step-brother, half-brother.
hermandad f fraternity; brotherhood.
hermano m brother; ~, na, adj matched; resembling.
hermético, ca adj hermetic, watertight.
hermoso, sa adj beautiful, handsome, lovely; large, robust.
hermosura f beauty.
hernia f hernia, rupture.
héroe m hero.
heroicidad f heroism, heroic deed.
heroico, ca adj heroic.
heroína f heroine; heroin (drug).
heroísmo m heroism.
herpes m herpes; ● fpl (med) shingles.
herrador m farrier, blacksmith.
herradura f horseshoe.
herramienta f tool.
herrar vt to shoe horses.
herrería f ironworks; forge.
herrero m smith.
hervidero m boiling; unrest; swarm.
hervir vt, vi to boil; to cook; ● to boil; to bubble; to seethe.
hervor m boiling; fervor, passion.
heterogeneidad f heterogeneousness.
heterogéneo, nea adj heterogeneous.
heterosexual adj, m/f heterosexual.
heterosexualidad f heterosexuality.
hexámetro m hexameter.
hez f lee, dregs pl.
hidalgo m hidalgo, nobleman.
hidalguía f nobility.
hidra f hydra.
hidráulica f hydraulics.
hidráulico, ca adj hydraulic.
hidrofobia f hydrophobia.
hidrógeno m (quim) hydrogen.
hiedra f ivy.
hiel f gall, bile.
hielo m frost, ice.
hiena f hyena.
hierba f grass; herb.
hierro m iron.
hígado m liver; (fig) courage, pluck.
higiene f hygiene.
higiénico, ca adj hygienic.
higo m fig.
higuera f fig tree.
hijastro, tra m/f stepson/daughter.
hijo, ja m/f son/daughter; child; offspring.
hilandero, ra m/f spinner.
hilar vt to spin.
hilera f row, line, file.
hilo m thread; wire.
hilván m basting.
hilvanar vt to baste, to tack; to perform in a hurry.
himno m hymn.
hincapié m: hacer ~ en to emphasize.
hincar vt to thrust in, to drive in.
hincha m/f (fam) fan, rooter.
hinchado, da adj swollen; vain, arrogant.
hinchar vt to swell; to inflate; (fig) to exaggerate; ~se vr to swell; to become vain.
hinchazón f swelling, lump.
hinojo m (bot) fennel.

hipar vi to hiccup.
hipérbola f hyperbola, section of a cone.
hipérbole f hyperbole, exaggeration.
hiperbólico, ca adj hyperbolical.
hiper(mercado) m hypermarket, superstore.
hipnotismo m hypnotism.
hipo m hiccups.
hipocondría f hypochondria.
hipocondríaco, ca adj hypochondriac.
hipocresía f hypocrisy.
hipócrita adj hypocritical; ● m/f hypocrite.
hipódromo m racetrack.
hipopótamo m hippopotamus.
hipoteca f mortgage.
hipotecar vt to mortgage.
hipotecario, ria adj belonging to a mortgage.
hipótesis f hypothesis.
hipotético, ca adj hypothetical.
hisopo m (bot) hyssop; water sprinkler; paintbrush.
histeria f hysteria.
histérico, ca adj hysterical.
historia f history; tale, story.
historiador, ra m/f historian.
histórico, ca adj historical, historic.
historieta f short story, short novel; comic strip.
hito m landmark; boundary post; target.
hocico m snout; meter el ~ en todo to meddle in everything.
hogar m hearth, fireplace; (fig) house, home; family life.
hogaza f large loaf of bread.
hoguera f bonfire; blaze.
hoja f leaf; petal; sheet of paper; blade.
hojalata f tin (plate).
hojaldre f puff pastry.
hojarasca f dead leaves pl; trash.
hojear vt to turn the pages of a book.
¡hola! excl hello!
holgado, da adj loose, wide, baggy; at leisure; idle, unoccupied, well-off; well-to-do.
holgar vi to rest; to be out of work; to be superfluous.
holgazán, ana m/f idler; slacker, loafer.
holgazanear vt to idle, to loaf around, to lounge.
holgazanería f idleness, laziness.
holgura f looseness, bagginess; leisure; comfort; enjoyment.
hollín m soot.
holocausto m holocaust.
hombre m man; human being.
hombrera f shoulder pad.
hombro m shoulder.
hombruno, na adj manlike, virile, manly.
homenaje m homage.
homicida m/f murderer; ● adj homicidal, murderous.
homicidio m murder.
homilía f homily.
homogeneidad f homogeneity.
homogéneo, nea adj homogeneous.
homólogo, ga adj homologous; synonymous.
homosexual adj, m/f homosexual.
honda f sling.
hondazo m throw with a sling.
hondero m slinger.
hondo, da adj profound, deep.
hondonada f dale, hollow; ravine.
hondura f depth, profundity.
honestidad f honesty, modesty; decency.
honesto, ta adj honest; modest.
hongo m mushroom; fungus.
honor m honor.
honorable adj honorable.
honorario, ria adj honorary; ~s mpl fees.
honorífico, ca adj creditable, honorable.
honra f honor, reverence; self-esteem; reputation; integrity; ~s funebres pl funeral honors.

honradez f honesty, integrity.
honrado, da adj honest, honorable, reputable.
honrar vt to honor.
honroso, sa adj honorable; respectable; honest.
hora f hour; time.
horadar vt to drill, to bore.
horario, ria adj hourly, hour compd; • m timetable.
horca f gallows; pitchfork.
horcajadas, horcajadillas adv: a ~ astride.
horchata f tiger-nut milk.
horizontal adj horizontal.
horizonte m horizon.
horma f mold, form.
hormiga f ant.
hormigón m concrete.
hormiguear vi to itch; to swarm, to team.
hormiguero m anthill; place swarming with people.
hormona f hormone.
hornada f batch.
horno m oven; furnace.
horóscopo m horoscope.
horquilla f pitchfork; hairpin.
horrendo, da adj horrible; frightful.
hórreo m granary.
horrible adj horrid, horrible.
horripilante adj hair-raising.
horror m horror, fright; atrocity.
horrorizar vt to cause horror; ~se vr to be terrified.
horroroso, sa adj horrid, hideous, frightful.
hortaliza f vegetable.
hortelano, na m/f gardener, truck farmer.
hortera m shop assistant; (fig) coarse person.
hosco, ca adj sullen, gloomy.
hospedaje m board and lodging.
hospedar vt to put up, to lodge, to entertain.
hospedería f inn; guest room; hospice.
hospedero, ra m/f landlord/lady; host/hostess.
hospicio m orphanage; hospice.
hospital m hospital.
hospitalario, ria adj hospitable.
hospitalidad f hospitality.
hostal m small hotel.
hostelería f hotel business or trade.
hostería f inn, tavern, hostelry.
hostia f host; wafer; (fam) whack (sl), punch.
hostigar vt to lash, to whip; to trouble, to pester, to bore.
hostil adj hostile, adverse.
hostilidad f hostility.
hostilizar vt (mil) to harry, to harass.
hotel m hotel.
hoy adv today, now, nowadays; de ~ en adelante from now on, henceforward.
hoya f hole, pit.
hoyo m hole, pit, excavation.
hoz f sickle; gorge.
hozar vt to grub (of pigs).
hucha f money-box.
hueco, ca adj hollow, concave; empty; vain, ostentatious; • m interval; gap, hole; vacancy.
huelga f strike.
huella f track, footstep.
huérfano, na adj, m/f orphan.
huero, ra adj empty; addled.
huerta f market garden; irrigated region.
huerto m orchard; kitchen-garden.
hueso m bone; stone, core.
huésped, da m/f guest, lodger; inn-keeper.
hueste f army; crowd.
huesudo, da adj bony.
huevera f eggcup.
huevo m egg.
huida f flight, escape.

huir vi to flee, to escape.
hule m oilcloth.
humanidad f humanity; corpulence; ~es pl humanities pl.
humano, na adj human; humane, kind.
humareda f cloud of smoke.
humeante adj smoking, steaming.
humear vi to smoke.
humedad f humidity, moisture, wetness.
humedecer vt to moisten, to wet, to soak.
húmedo, da adj humid, wet, moist, damp.
humildad f humility; humbleness; submission.
humilde adj humble.
humillación f humiliation, submission.
humillar vt to humble; to subdue; ~se vr to humble oneself.
humo m smoke; fumes pl.
humor m mood, temper; humor.
hundir vt to submerge; to sink; to ruin; ~se vr to sink, to go to the bottom; to collapse; to be ruined.
huracán m hurricane.
huraño, ña adj shy; unsociable.
hurgar vt to stir; to poke.
hufón m ferret; (fig) shy person; busybody.
huronear vt to ferret out.
hurtadillas adv: a ~ by stealth.
hurtar vt to steal, to rob.
hurto m theft, robbery.
húsar m hussar.
husmear vt to scent; to pry.
huso m spindle.

I

ictericia f jaundice.
ida f departure, going; (viaje de) ~ outward journey; ~ y vuelta round trip; ~s y venidas coming and going.
idea f idea; scheme.
ideal adj ideal.
idealmente adv ideally.
idear vt to conceive; to think, to contrive.
ídem pn ditto.
idéntico, ca adj identical.
identidad f identity.
identificar vt to identify.
ideología f ideology.
idilio m idyll.
idioma m language.
idiosincrasia f idiosyncrasy.
idiota m/f idiot.
idiotez f idiocy.
idólatra m/f idolater.
idolatrar vt to idolize; to worship.
idolatría f idolatry.
ídolo m idol.
idoneidad f aptitude, fitness.
idóneo, nea adj suitable, fit.
iglesia f church.
ignominia f ignominy, infamy.
ignominioso, sa adj ignominious.
ignorancia f ignorance.
ignorante adj ignorant; uninformed.
ignorar vt to be ignorant of, not to know.
igual adj equal, similar; the same; al ~ equally.
igualar vt to equalize, to equal; to match; to level off; ~se vr to be equal; to agree.
igualdad f equality.
igualmente adv equally.
ijar m flank.
ilegal adj illegal, unlawful.
ilegalidad f illegality.
ilegitimidad f illegitimacy.

ilegítimo, ma *adj* illegal; illegitimate.
ileso, sa *adj* unhurt.
ilícito, ta *adj* illicit, unlawful.
ilimitado, da *adj* unlimited.
iluminación *f* illumination.
iluminar *vt* to illumine, to illuminate, to enlighten.
ilusión *f* illusion; hope; hacerse ~ones to build up one's hopes.
ilusionista *m/f* conjurer.
iluso, sa *adj* easily deceived.
ilusorio, ria *adj* illusory.
ilustración *f* illustration; enlightenment.
ilustrar *vt* to illustrate; to instruct.
ilustre *adj* illustrious, famous.
imagen *f* image.
imaginable *adj* imaginable.
imaginación *f* imagination, fancy.
imaginar *vt* to imagine; to think up; *vi*, ~se *vr* to imagine.
imán *m* magnet.
imbécil *m/f* imbecile, idiot.
imbecilidad *f* imbecility.
imbuir *vt* to imbue; to infuse.
imitable *adj* imitable.
imitación *f* imitation; a ~ de in imitation of.
imitador, ra *m/f* imitator.
imitar *vt* to imitate, to copy; to counterfeit.
impaciencia *f* impatience.
impacientar *vt* to make impatient; to irritate.
impaciente *adj* impatient.
impacto *m* impact.
impar *adj* odd.
imparcial *adj* impartial.
imparcialidad *f* impartiality.
impasibilidad *f* impassivity.
impasible *adj* impassive.
impavidez *f* intrepidity; cheekiness.
impávido, da *adj* dauntless, intrepid; cheeky.
impecable *adj* impeccable.
impedimento *f* impediment, obstacle.
impedir *vt* to impede, to hinder; to prevent.
impeler *vt* to drive, to propel; to impel; to incite, to stimulate.
impenetrable *adj* impenetrable, impervious; incomprehensible.
impenitente *adj* impenitent.
impensado, da *adj* impenitent.
imperativo, va *adj*, *m* imperative.
imperceptible *adj* imperceptible.
imperdible *m* safety pin.
imperdonable *adj* unforgivable.
imperfección *f* imperfection.
imperfecto, ta *adj* imperfect.
imperial *adj* imperial.
impericia *f* lack of experience.
imperio *m* empire.
imperioso, sa *adj* imperious; arrogant, haughty; urgent.
impermeable *adj* waterproof; ● *m* raincoat.
impermutable *adj* immutable.
impersonal *adj* impersonal.
impertérrito, ta *adj* intrepid, fearless.
impertinencia *f* impertinence; irrelevance.
impertinente *adj* not pertinent; touchy; impertinent.
imperturbable *adj* imperturbable; unruffled.
ímpetu *m* impetus; impetuosity.
impetuoso, sa *adj* impetuous.
implacable *adj* implacable, inexorable.
implicación *f* implication.
implicar *vt* to implicate, to involve.
implícito, ta *adj* implicit.
implorar *vt* to beg, to implore.
imponderable *adj* imponderable; (*fig*) priceless.
imponer *vt* to impose to command; ~se *vr* to assert oneself; to prevail.

impopular *adj* unpopular.
importación *f* importing; imports.
importancia *f* importance; significance, weight; size.
importante *adj* important, considerable.
importar *vi* to be important, to matter; ● *vt* to import; to be worth.
importe *m* amount, cost.
importunar *vt* to bother, to pester.
importunidad *f* pestering; annoyance.
importuno, na *adj* annoying; unreasonable.
imposibilidad *f* impossibility.
imposibilitar *vt* to make impossible.
imposible *adj* impossible; extremely difficult; slovenly.
imposición *f* imposition; tax; deposit.
impostor, ra *m/f* impostor, fraud.
impostura *f* imposture, deceit, cheat.
impotencia *f* impotence.
impotente *adj* impotent.
impracticable *adj* impracticable, unworkable.
imprecación *f* curse.
imprecar *vt* to curse.
imprecatorio, ria *adj* containing curses, full of evil wishes.
impreciso, sa *adj* imprecise, vague.
impregnarse *vr* to be impregnated.
imprenta *f* printing; press; printing office.
imprescindible *adj* essential.
impresión *f* impression; stamp; print; edition.
impresionante *adj* impressive; marvelous; tremendous.
impresionar *vt* to move; to impress; ~se *vr* to be impressed; to be moved.
impreso *m* printed paper; printed book.
impresor *m* printer.
imprevisto, ta *adj* unforeseen, unexpected.
imprimir *vt* to print; to imprint; to stamp.
improbable *adj* improbable, unlikely.
improperio *m* insult, taunt.
impropio, pia *adj* improper; unfit; unbecoming.
improvisar *vt* to extemporize, to improvize.
improviso, sa *adj*: de ~ unexpectedly.
imprudencia *f* imprudence; indiscretion; carelessness.
imprudente *adj* imprudent; indiscreet; unwise.
impudencia *f* shamelessness.
impudente *adj* shameless.
impúdico, ca *adj* shameless; lecherous.
impuesto, ta *adj* imposed; ● *m* tax, duty.
impugnación *f* opposition, contradiction.
impugnar *vt* to impugne, to oppose.
impulsivo, va *adj* impulsive.
impulso *m* impulse; thrust; (*fig*) impulse.
impune *adj* unpunished.
impunidad *f* impunity.
impureza *f* impurity.
impuro, ra *adj* impure, foul.
imputable *adj* attributable to, chargeable.
imputar *vt* to impute, to attribute.
inaccesible *adj* inaccessible.
inacción *f* inaction; inactivity.
inadmisible *adj* inadmissible.
inadvertencia *f* carelessness, inadvertence.
inadvertido, da *adj* unnoticed.
inagotable *adj* inexhaustible.
inaguantable *adj* unbearable, intolerable.
inalterable *adj* unalterable.
inapelable *adj* without appeal.
inapreciable *adj* imperceptible; invaluable.
inaudito, ta *adj* unheard of.
inauguración *f* inauguration, opening.
inaugurar *vt* to inaugurate.
incalculable *adj* incalculable.
incandescente *adj* incandescent.
incansable *adj* untiring, tireless.
incapacidad *f* incapacity, inability.

incapaz *adj* incapable, unable.
incauto, ta *adj* incautious, unwary.
incendiar *vt* to kindle, to set on fire.
incendiario, ria *m, adj* incendiary.
incendio *m* fire.
incentivo *m* incentive.
incertidumbre *f* doubt, uncertainty.
incesante *adj* incessant, continual.
incesto *m* incest.
incestuoso, sa *adj* incestuous.
incidencia *f* incidence; incident.
incidente *m* incident.
incidir *vi* to fall upon; to influence, to affect.
incienso *m* incense.
incierto, ta *adj* uncertain, doubtful.
incineración *f* incineration; cremation.
incipiente *adj* incipient.
incisión *f* incision, cut.
incisivo, va *adj* incisive.
inciso *m* (*gr*) comma.
incitación *f* incitement.
incitar *vt* to incite, to excite.
incivil *adj* rude, uncivil.
inclemencia *f* inclemency, severity; inclemency (of the weather).
inclinación *f* inclination.
inclinar *vt* to incline; to nod, to bow (the head); ~se *vr* to bow; to stoop.
incluir *vt* to include, to comprise; to incorporate; to enclose.
inclusión *f* inclusion.
inclusive *adv* inclusive.
incluso, sa *adj* included; • *adv* inclusively; even.
incógnito, ta *adj* unknown; de ~ incognito.
incoherencia *f* incoherence.
incoherent *adj* incoherent.
incombustible *adj* incombustible, fireproof.
incomodar *vt* to inconvenience; to bother, to annoy.
incomodidad *f* inconvenience; annoyance; discomfort.
incómodo, da *adj* uncomfortable; annoying; inconvenient.
incomparable *adj* incomparable, matchless.
incompatibilidad *f* incompatibility.
incompatible *adj* incompatible.
incompetencia *f* incompetence.
incompetente *adj* incompetent.
incompleto, ta *adj* incomplete.
incomprehensible *adj* incomprehensible.
incomunicación *f* isolation; lack of communication.
incomunicado, da *adj* isolated, cut off; in solitary confinement.
inconcebible *adj* inconceivable.
incondicional *adj* unconditional; wholehearted; staunch.
inconexo, xa *adj* unconnected, disconnected.
inconfundible *adj* unmistakable.
incongruencia *adj* incongruity, incongruence.
incongruo, grua *adj* incongruous.
inconmensurable *adj* immeasurable.
inconsciencia *f* unconsciousness; thoughtlessness.
inconsciente *adj* unconscious; thoughtless.
inconsecuencia *f* inconsequence.
inconsiderado, da *adj* inconsiderate, thoughtless.
inconsolable *adj* inconsolable.
inconstancia *f* inconstancy, unsteadiness.
inconstante *adj* inconstant, variable, fickle.
incontestable *adj* indisputable, incontrovertible, undeniable.
incontinencia *f* incontinence.
incontinente *adj* incontinent.
inconveniencia *f* inconvenience; impoliteness; unsuitability.
inconveniente *adj* inconvenient, unsuitable; impolite.
incorporación *f* incorporation, involvement.
incorporar *vt* to incorporate; ~se *vr* to sit up; to join (an organization), to become incorporated.
incorrecto, ta *adj* incorrect.

incorregible *adj* incorrigible.
incorruptible *adj* incorruptible.
incredulidad *f* incredulity.
incrédulo, la *adj* incredulous.
increíble *adj* incredible.
incremento *m* increment, increase; growth; rise.
increpar *vt* to reprehend, to reprimand.
incruento, ta *adj* bloodless.
inculcar *vt* to inculcate.
inculpar *vt* to accuse, to blame.
inculto, ta *adj* uncultivated; uneducated; uncouth.
incumbencia *f* obligation; duty.
incumbir *vi* to be incumbent upon one.
incurable *adj* incurable; irremediable.
incurrir *vi*: ~ en to incur; to commit (a crime).
incursión *f* incursion, raid.
indagación *f* search, inquiry.
indagar *vt* to search, to inquire.
indebido, da *adj* undue, illegal, unlawful.
indecencia *f* indecency.
indecente *adj* indecent.
indecible *adj* unspeakable, unutterable.
indecisión *f* hesitation, indecision.
indeciso, sa *adj* hesitant; undecided.
indecoroso, sa *adj* unseemly, unbecoming.
indefectible *adj* unfailing.
indefenso, sa *adj* defenseless.
indefinible *adj* indefinable.
indefinido, da *adj* indefinite.
indeleble *adj* indelible.
indemnización *f* indemnification, compensation.
indemnizar *vt* to indemnify, to compensate.
independencia *f* independence.
independiente *adj* independent.
indestructible *adj* indestructible.
indeterminado, da *adj* indeterminate; indefinite.
indicación *f* indication.
indicador *m* indicator; gauge.
indicar *vt* to indicate.
indicativo, va *adj, m* indicative.
índice *m* ratio, rate; hand of a watch *or* clock; index, table of contents; catalog; forefinger, index finger.
indicio *m* indication, mark; sign, token; clue.
indiferencia *f* indifference, apathy.
indiferente *adj* indifferent.
indígena *adj* indigenous, native; • *m/f* native.
indigencia *f* indigence, poverty, need.
indigente *adj* indigent, poor, destitute.
indigestión *f* indigestion.
indigesto, ta *adj* undigested; indigestible.
indignación *f* indignation, anger.
indignar *vt* to irritate, to provoke, to tease; ~se *vr*: ~ por to get indignant about.
indigno, na *adj* unworthy, contemptible, low.
indirecta *f* innuendo, hint.
indirecto, ta *adj* indirect.
indisciplinado, da *adj* undisciplined.
indiscreción *f* indiscretion, tactlessness; gaffe.
indiscreto, ta *adj* indiscreet, tactless.
indisoluble *adj* indissoluble.
indispensable *adj* indispensable.
indisponer *vt* to spoil, to upset; to make ill; ~se *vr* to fall ill.
indisposición *f* indisposition, slight illness.
indispuesto, ta *adj* indisposed.
indisputable *adj* indisputable, incontrovertible.
indistinto, ta *adj* indistinct.
individual *adj* individual; single (of a room); • *m* (*dep*) singles.
individualidad *f* individuality.
individualizar *vt* to specify individually.
individuo *m* individual.
indivisible *adj* indivisible.
indocilidad *f* disobedience.

índole f disposition, nature, character; soft, kind.
indolencia f indolence, laziness.
indolente adj indolent, lazy.
indómito, ta adj untamed, ungoverned.
inducción f induction, persuasion.
inducir vt to induce, to persuade.
inductivo, va adj inductive.
indudable adj undoubted; unquestionable.
indulgencia f indulgence.
indulgente adj indulgent.
indultar vt to pardon; to exempt.
indulto m pardon; exemption.
industria f industry; skill.
industrial adj industrial.
inédito, ta adj unpublished; (fig) new.
inefable adj ineffable, unspeakable, indescribable.
ineficacia f inefficacy.
ineficaz adj ineffective; inefficient.
ineptitud f inability, unfitness, ineptitude.
inepto, ta adj inept, unfit, useless.
inercia f inertia, inactivity.
inerme adj unarmed; defenseless.
inerte adj inert, dull, sluggish, motionless.
inescrutable adj inscrutable.
inesperado, da adj unexpected, unforeseen.
inestable adj unstable.
inestimable adj inestimable.
inevitable adj unavoidable.
inexactitud f inaccuracy.
inexacto, ta adj inaccurate, untrue.
inexorable adj inexorable.
inexperto, ta adj inexperienced.
infalibilidad f infallibility.
infalible adj infallible.
infame adj infamous.
infancia f infancy, childhood.
infanta f infant, princess.
infante m infante; prince; (mil) infantryman.
infantería f infantry.
infanticida m infanticide (person).
infanticidio m infanticide (murder).
infantil adj infantile; childlike; children's.
infarto m heart attack.
infatigable adj tireless, untiring.
infección f infection.
infectar vt to infect.
infeliz adj unhappy, unfortunate.
inferior adj inferior.
inferioridad f inferiority.
inferir vt to infer.
infernal adj infernal, hellish.
infestar vt to harass; to infest.
infidelidad f infidelity; unfaithfulness.
infiel adj unfaithful; disloyal; inaccurate.
infierno m hell.
infiltración f infiltration.
infiltrarse vr to infiltrate.
ínfimo, ma adj lowest; of very poor quality.
infinidad f infinity, immensity.
infinitivo m (gr) infinitive.
infinito, ta adj infinite, immense.
inflación f inflation.
inflamable adj flammable.
inflamación f ignition; inflammation.
inflamar vt to inflame; to excite, to arouse; ~se vr to catch fire.
inflamatorio, ria adj inflammatory.
inflar vt to inflate, to blow up; (fig) to exaggerate.
inflexibilidad f inflexibility.
inflexible adj inflexible.
influencia f influence.
influir vt to influence.

influjo m influence.
información f information; news; (mil) intelligence; investigation, judicial inquiry.
informal adj irregular, incorrect; untrustworthy; informal.
informalidad f irregularity; untrustworthiness; informality.
informar vt to inform; to reveal, to make known; • vi to report; (jur) to plead; to inform; ~se vr to find out.
informática f computer science, information technology.
informe m report, statement; piece of information, account; • adj shapeless, formless.
infortunio m misfortune, ill luck.
infracción f infraction; breach, infringement.
infractor, ra m/f offender.
infructuoso, sa adj fruitless, unproductive, unprofitable.
infundado, da adj groundless.
infundir vt to infuse, to instill.
infusión f infusion.
infuso, sa adj infused, introduced.
ingeniar vt to devise; ~se vr: ~ para to manage to.
ingeniero, ra m/f engineer.
ingenio m talent; wit; ingenuity; engine; ~ de azúcar sugar mill.
ingenioso, sa adj ingenious, clever; witty.
ingenuidad f ingenuousness; candor, frankness.
ingenuo, nua adj ingenuous.
ingerir vt to ingest; to swallow; to consume.
ingle f groin.
inglés, esa adj English; • m English language; • m/f Englishman/woman.
ingratitud f ingratitude, unthankfulness.
ingrato, ta adj ungrateful, thankless; disagreeable.
ingrediente m ingredient.
ingresar vt to deposit; • vi to come in.
ingreso m entry; admission; ~s mpl income; takings.
inhabilitar vt to disqualify, to disable.
inhabitable adj uninhabitable.
inherente adj inherent.
inhibición f inhibition.
inhibir vt to inhibit, to restrain.
inhumano, na adj inhuman.
inicial adj, f initial.
iniciar vt to initiate; to begin.
iniciativa f initiative.
inimaginable adj unimaginable, inconceivable.
inimitable adj inimitable.
ininteligible adj unintelligible.
iniquidad f iniquity, injustice.
injertar vt to graft.
injerto m graft.
injuria f offense; insult.
injuriar vt to insult, to wrong.
injurioso, sa adj insulting; offensive.
injusticia f injustice.
injusto, ta adj unjust.
inmaculado, da adj immaculate.
inmadurez f immaturity.
inmediaciones fpl neighborhood.
inmediatamente adv immediately, at once.
inmediato, ta adj immediate.
inmemorial adj immemorial.
inmensidad f immensity.
inmenso, sa adj immense, infinite.
inmensurable adj immeasurable.
inmigración f immigration.
inminente adj imminent.
inmobiliario, ria adj real-estate compd; • f estate agency.
inmoral adj immoral.
inmortal adj immortal.
inmortalidad f immortality.
inmortalizar vt to immortalize.
inmóvil adj immovable.
inmovilidad f immobility.

inmueble *m* property; ● *adj*: **bienes ~s** real estate.
inmundicia *f* nastiness, filth.
inmundo, da *adj* filthy, dirty; nasty.
inmune *adj* (*med*) immune, free, exempt.
inmunidad *f* immunity, exemption.
inmutabilidad *f* immutability.
inmutable *adj* immutable.
inmutarse *vr* to turn pale.
innato, ta *adj* inborn, innate.
innecesario, ria *adj* unnecessary.
innegable *adj* undeniable, incontrovertible.
innovación *f* innovation.
innovador, ra *m/f* innovator.
innovar *vt* to innovate.
innumerable *adj* innumerable, countless.
inocencia *f* innocence.
inocentada *f* practical joke.
inocente *adj* innocent.
inoculación *f* inoculation.
inocular *vt* to inoculate.
inodoro *m* toilet.
inofensivo, va *adj* harmless.
inolvidable *adj* unforgettable.
inopinado, da *adj* unexpected.
inoxidable *adj*: **acero ~** stainless steel.
inquietar *vt* to worry, to disturb; **~se** *vr* to worry, to get worried.
inquieto, ta *adj* anxious, worried.
inquietud *f* inquietude, anxiety.
inquilino, na *m/f* tenant; lodger.
inquirir *vt* to inquire into, to investigate.
insaciable *adj* insatiable.
insalubre *adj* unhealthy.
insalubridad *f* unhealthiness.
insano, na *adj* insane, mad.
inscribir *vt* to inscribe; to list, to register.
inscripción *f* inscription; enrolment, registration.
insecticida *m* insecticide.
insecto *m* insect.
inseguridad *f* insecurity.
insensatez *f* stupidity, folly.
insensato, ta *adj* senseless, stupid, mad.
insensibilidad *f* insensitivity; callousness.
insensible *adj* insensitive; imperceptible; numb.
insensiblemente *adv* insensitively; imperceptibly.
inseparable *adj* inseparable.
inserción *f* insertion.
insertar *vt* to insert.
inservible *adj* useless.
insidioso, sa *adj* insidious.
insigne *adj* notable.
insignificante *adj* insignificant.
insignia *f* badge; **~s** *pl* insignia.
insinuación *f* insinuation.
insinuar *vt* to insinuate; **~se** *vr*: **~ en** to worm one's way into.
insipidez *f* insipidness.
insípido, da *adj* insipid.
insistencia *f* persistence, insistence.
insistir *vi* to insist.
insolación *f* (*med*) sunstroke.
insolencia *f* insolence, rudeness, effrontery.
insolente *adj* insolent, rude.
insólito, ta *adj* unusual.
insolvencia *f* insolvency.
insolvente *adj* insolvent.
insomnio *m* insomnia.
insondable *adj* unfathomable; inscrutable.
insoportable *adj* unbearable.
inspección *f* inspection, survey, check.
inspeccionar *vt* to inspect, to supervise.
inspector, ra *m/f* inspector, superintendent.
inspiración *f* inspiration.

inspirar *vt* to inspire; (*med*) to inhale.
instalación *f* installation.
instalar *vt* to install.
instancia *f* instance.
instantáneo, nea *adj* instantaneous; ● *f* snap(shot); **café ~** instant coffee.
instante *m* instant; **al ~** immediately, instantly.
instar *vt* to press, to urge.
instigación *f* instigation.
instigar *vt* to instigate.
instinto *m* instinct.
institución *f* institution.
instituir *vt* to institute.
instituto *m* institute.
institutriz *f* governess.
instrucción *f* instruction.
instructivo, va *adj* instructive; educational.
instructor, ra *m/f* instructor, teacher.
instruir *vt* to instruct, to teach.
instrumento *m* instrument; tool, implement.
insuficiencia *f* lack, inadequacy.
insuficiente *adj* insufficient, inadequate.
insufrible *adj* insufferable, insupportable.
insulso, sa *adj* insipid; dull.
insultar *vt* to insult.
insulto *m* insult.
insuperable *adj* insuperable, insurmountable.
insurgente *m/f* insurgent.
insurrección *f* insurrection.
intacto, ta *adj* untouched; entire; intact.
integral *adj* integral, whole; **pan ~** wholewheat bread.
integrar *vt* to make up; to integrate.
integridad *f* integrity; completeness.
íntegro, gra *adj* integral, entire.
intelectual *adj*, *m/f* intellectual.
inteligencia *f* intelligence; understanding.
inteligente *adj* intelligent.
inteligible *adj* intelligible.
intemperie *f*: **a la ~** out in the open.
intempestivo, va *adj* untimely.
intención *f* intention, purpose, plan.
intencionado, da *adj* meaningful; deliberate.
intendencia *f* administration, management.
intendente *m* manager.
intensidad *f* intensity; strength.
intenso, sa *adj* intense, strong; deep.
intentar *vt* to try; to attempt.
intento *m* intent, purpose, attempt.
intercalación *f* insertion.
intercalar *vt* to insert.
intercambio *m* exchange, swap.
interceder *vi* to intercede.
interceptar *vt* to intercept.
intercesión *f* intercession, mediation.
intercesor, ra *m/f* intercessor, mediator.
interés *m* interest; share, part; concern, advantage; profit.
interesado, da *adj* interested, prejudiced; mercenary.
interesante *adj* interesting, useful, convenient.
interesar *vt*, *vi* to be of interest to, to interest; **~se** *vr*: **~ en** *o* **por** to take an interest in.
interferir *vt* to interfere with; to jam (a telephone); ● *vi* to interfere.
interfono *m* intercom.
interinidad *f* temporary holding of office.
interino, na *adj* provisional, temporary; ● *m/f* temporary holder of a post; stand-in.
interior *adj* interior, internal; ● *m* interior, inside.
interioridad *f* inwardness.
interjección *f* (*gr*) interjection.
interlocutor, ra *m/f* speaker.
intermediar *vt* to interpose.
intermedio, dia *adj* intermediate; ● *m* interval.

interminable *adj* interminable, endless.
intermitente *adj* intermittent; *m (auto)* indicator.
internacional *adj* international.
internado *m* boarding school.
internar *vt* to intern, to commit; ~se *vr* to penetrate.
interno, na *adj* interior, internal; ● *m/f* boarder.
interpelación *f* interpellation, appeal, plea.
interpelar *vt* to appeal to.
interpolar *vt* to interpolate; to interrupt.
interponer *vt* to interpose, to put in.
interposición *f* insertion; interjection.
interpretación *f* interpretation.
interpretar *vt* to interpret, to explain; *(teat)* to perform; to translate.
intérprete *m/f* interpreter, translator; *(teat)* performer.
interrogación *f* interrogation; question mark.
interrogante *adj* questioning.
interrogar *vt* to interrogate.
interrogatorio *m* questioning; *(jur)* examination; questionnaire.
interrumpir *vt* to interrupt.
interrupción *f* interruption.
interruptor *m* switch.
intervalo *m* interval.
intervención *f* supervision, control; *(com)* auditing; *(med)* operation; intervention.
intervenir *vt* to control, to supervise; *(com)* to audit; *(med)* to operate on; ● *vi* to participate, to intervene.
interventor, ra *m/f* inspector; *(com)* auditor.
interviú *f* interview.
intestino, na *adj* internal, interior; ● *m* intestine.
intimar *vt* to intimate; ● *vi* to become friendly.
intimidad *f* intimacy; private life.
intimidar *vt* intimidate.
íntimo, ma *adj* internal, innermost; intimate, private.
intolerable *adj* intolerable, insufferable.
intolerancia *f* intolerance.
intolerante *adj* intolerant.
intranquilizarse *vr* to get anxious *or* worried.
intranquilo, la *adj* worried.
intransigente *adj* intransigent.
intransitable *adj* impassable.
intransitivo, va *adj (gr)* intransitive.
intratable *adj* intractable, difficult.
intrepidez *f* intrepidity; fearlessness.
intrépido, da *adj* intrepid, daring.
intriga *f* intrigue.
intrigante *m/f* intriguer.
intrigar *vt, vi* to intrigue.
intrínseco, ca *adj* intrinsic.
introducción *f* introduction.
introducir *vt* to introduce; to insert.
introductor *m* introducer.
introvertido, da *adj, m/f* introvert.
intrusión *f* intrusion.
intruso, sa *adj* intrusive; ● *m/f* intruder.
intuición *f* intuition.
intuitivo, va *adj* intuitive.
inundación *f* inundation, flood(ing).
inundar *vt* to inundate, to overflow; to flood.
inusitado, da *adj* unusual.
inútil *adj* useless.
inutilidad *f* uselessness.
inutilizar *vt* to render useless.
invadir *vt (mil)* to invade; to overrun.
invalidar *vt* to invalidate, to render null and void.
inválido, da *adj* invalid, null; ● *m/f* invalid.
invariable *adj* invariable.
invasión *f* invasion.
invasor, ra *adj* invading; ● *m/f* invader.
invencible *adj* invincible.
invención *f* invention.

inventar *vt* to invent.
inventario *m* inventory.
invento *m* invention.
inventor, ra *m/f* inventor.
invernadero *m* greenhouse.
invernar *vi* to pass the winter.
inverosímil *adj* unlikely, improbable.
inverosimilitud *f* unlikeliness, improbability.
inversión *f (com)* investment; inversion.
inverso, sa *adj* inverse; inverted; contrary.
invertir *vt (com)* to invest; to invert.
investidura *f* investiture.
investigación *f* investigation, research.
investigar *vt* to investigate; to do research into.
investir *vt* to confer.
invicto, ta *adj* unconquerable.
invierno *m* winter.
inviolabilidad *f* inviolability.
inviolable *adj* inviolable.
invisible *adj* invisible.
invitado, da *m/f* guest.
invitar *vt* to invite; to entice; to pay for.
invocación *f* invocation.
invocar *vt* to invoke.
involuntario, ria *adj* involuntary.
invulnerable *adj* invulnerable.
inyección *f* injection.
ir *vi* to go, to walk; to travel; ~se *vr* to go away, to depart.
ira *f* anger, wrath.
iracundo, da *adj* irate; irascible.
iris *m* iris (of the eye); **arco ~** rainbow.
ironía *f* irony.
irónico, ca *adj* ironic(al).
irracional *adj* irrational.
irradiación *f* irradiation.
irrazonable *adj* unreasonable.
irreal *adj* unreal.
irreconciliable *adj* irreconcilable.
irreflexión *f* rashness, thoughtlessness.
irregular *adj* irregular, abnormal.
irregularidad *f* irregularity, abnormality.
irremediable *adj* irremediable; incurable.
irremisible *adj* irretrievable, unpardonable.
irreparable *adj* irreparable.
irresistible *adj* irresistible.
irresoluto, ta *adj* irresolute, hesitant.
irreverencia *f* irreverence; disrespect.
irreverente *adj* irreverent; disrespectful.
irrevocable *adj* irrevocable.
irrisorio, ria *adj* derisory, ridiculous.
irritación *f* irritation.
irritar *vt* to irritate, to exasperate; to stir up; to inflame.
irrupción *f* irruption, invasion.
isla *f* isle, island.
islote *m* small island.
istmo *m* isthmus.
italiano, na *adj* Italian; ● *m* Italian language; ● *m/f* Italian.
ítem *m* item.
itinerario *m* itinerary.
izar *vt (mar)* to hoist.
izquierdo, da *adj* left; left-handed; ● *f* left; left(wing).

J

jabalí *m* wild boar.
jabalina *f* wild sow; *(dep)* javelin.
jabón *m* soap.
jabonar *vt* to soap.
jaca *f* pony.
jacinto *m* hyacinth.

jactancia f boasting.
jactancioso, sa adj boastful.
jactarse vr to boast.
jadear vi to pant.
jaguar m jaguar.
jalea f jelly.
jaleo m racket, uproar.
jalón m pull, tug.
jamás adv never; para siempre ~ for ever.
jamón m ham; ~ de York cooked ham; ~ serrano cured ham.
jaque m check (at game of chess); ~ mate checkmate.
jaqueca f migraine.
jarabe m syrup.
jarcia f (mar) ropes pl, rigging.
jardín m garden.
jardinería f gardening.
jardinero, ra m/f gardener.
jarra f jug, jar, pitcher; en ~s, de ~s with arms placed akimbo; with hands to the sides.
jarro m jug.
jarrón m vase.
jaspe m jasper.
jaspear vt to marble, to speckle.
jaula f cage; cell for mad people.
jauría f pack of hounds.
jazmín m jasmin.
jefatura f: ~ de policía police headquarters.
jefe m chief, head, leader; (ferro) ~ de tren guard, conductor.
jengibre m ginger.
jerarquía f hierarchy.
jerárquico adj hierarchical.
jerga f coarse cloth; jargon.
jergón m coarse mattress.
jerigonza f jargon, gibberish.
jeringa f syringe.
jeroglífico, ca adj hieroglyphic; • m hieroglyph, hieroglyphic.
jersey m sweater, pullover.
Jesucristo m Jesus Christ.
jesuita m Jesuit.
jesuítico, ca adj jesuitical.
jibia f cuttlefish.
jícara f small cup (for chocolate).
jilguero m goldfinch.
jinete, ta m/f horseman/woman, rider.
jipijapa m straw hat.
jirafa f giraffe.
jirón m rag, shred.
jocosidad f humor, jokiness.
jocoso, sa adj good-humored.
jornada f journey; day's journey; working day.
jornal m day's wage.
jornalero m laborer.
joroba f hump; • m/f hunchback.
jorobado, da adj hunchbacked.
jorobar vt to pester, to annoy.
jota f jot, iota; Spanish dance.
joven adj young; • m/f youth; young woman.
jovial adj jovial, cheerful.
jovialidad f joviality, cheerfulness.
joya f jewel.
joyería f jeweler's shop.
joyero m jeweler.
juanete m (med) bunion.
jubilación f retirement.
jubilado, da adj retired; • m/f senior citizen.
jubilar vt to pension off; to superannuate; to discard; ~se vr to retire.
jubileo m jubilee.
júbilo m joy, rejoicing.
judaico, ca adj Judaic, Jewish.
judaísmo m Judaism.

judía f bean; ~ verde French bean.
judicatura f judicature; office of a judge.
judicial adj judicial.
judío, día adj Jewish; • m/f Jew/Jewess.
juego m play, amusement, sport; game, gambling.
juerga f binge; party.
jueves m Thursday.
juez m/f judge.
jugada f playing of a card; stroke, shot.
jugador, ra m/f player; gambler.
jugar vt, vi to play, to sport, to gamble.
jugarreta f bad play, unskillful playing.
jugo m sap, juice.
jugoso, sa adj juicy, succulent.
juguete m toy, plaything.
juguetear vi to play.
juguetón, ona adj playful.
juicio m judgment, reason; sanity; opinion.
juicioso, sa adj judicious, prudent.
julio m July.
junco m (bot) rush; junk (small Chinese ship).
jungla f jungle.
junio m June.
junta f congress, assembly, council, meeting.
juntamente adv jointly; at the same time.
juntar vt to join, to unite; ~se vr to meet, to assemble; to draw closer.
junto, ta adj joined; united; near; adjacent; ~s together; • adv: todo ~ all at once.
juntura f junction; joint.
Júpiter m Jupiter (planet).
jurado m jury; juror, juryman; member of a panel.
juramento m oath; curse.
jurar vt, vi to swear.
jurídico, ca adj lawful, legal, juridical.
jurisdicción f jurisdiction; district.
jurisprudencia f jurisprudence.
jurista m/f jurist, lawyer.
justa f joust, tournament.
justamente adv justly, just.
justicia f justice; equity.
justificación f justification.
justificante m voucher; receipt.
justificar vt to justify.
justo, ta adj just; fair, right; exact, correct; tight; • adv exactly, precisely; just in time.
juvenil adj youthful.
juventud f youthfulness, youth; young people pl.
juzgado m tribunal; court.
juzgar vt, vi to judge.

K

kilogramo m kilogram.
kilometraje m distance in kilometers, mileage.
kilómetro m kilometer.
kilovatio m kilowatt.
kiosco m kiosk.

L

la pn the; • pn her; you; it.
laberinto m labyrinth.
labia f fluency; (fam) the gift of the gab (sl).
labio m lip; edge.
labor f labor, task; needlework; farm work; plowing.
laboratorio m laboratory.
laboriosidad f laboriousness.

laborioso, sa *adj* laborious; hard-working.
labrado, da *adj* worked; carved; wrought; ● *m* cultivated land.
labrador, ra *m/f* farmer; peasant.
labranza *f* farming; cultivation; farmland.
labrar *vt* to work; to carve; to farm; (*fig*) to bring about.
labriego, ga *m/f* peasant.
laca *f* lacquer; hairspray.
lacayo *m* lackey, footman.
lacerar *vt* to tear to pieces, to lacerate.
lacio, cia *adj* faded, withered; languid; lank (hair).
lacónico, ca *adj* laconic.
laconismo *m* laconic style, terseness.
lacra *f* scar; blot, blemish.
lacrar *vt* to seal (with sealing wax).
lacre *m* sealing wax.
lactancia *f* lactation; breast-feeding.
lácteo, tea *adj*: **productos ~s** dairy products.
ladear *vt* to move to one side; to incline; **~se** *vr* to lean; to tilt.
ladera *f* slope.
ladino, na *adj* cunning, crafty.
lado *m* side; faction, party; favor, protection; (*mil*) flank; **al ~ de** beside; **poner a un ~** to put aside; **por todos ~s** on all sides.
ladrar *vt* to bark.
ladrido *m* barking.
ladrillo *m* brick.
ladrón, ona *m/f* thief, robber.
lagar *m* wine press.
lagartija *f* (small) lizard.
lagarto *m* lizard.
lago *m* lake.
lágrima *f* tear.
lagrimal *m* corner of the eye.
lagrimoso, sa *adj* weeping, shedding tears.
laguna *f* lake; lagoon; gap.
laico, ca *adj* lay.
lamedura *f* licking.
lamentable *adj* lamentable, deplorable, pitiable.
lamentación *f* lamentation.
lamentar *vt* to be sorry about; to lament, to regret; ● *vi*, **~se** *vr* to lament, to complain, to mourn.
lamento *m* lament.
lamer *vt* to lick, to lap.
lámina *f* plate, sheet of metal; engraving.
lámpara *f* lamp.
lamparilla *f* nightlight.
lamparón *m* grease spot.
lampiño, ña *adj* beardless.
lamprea *f* lamprey (fish).
lana *f* wool.
lance *m* cast, throw; move, play (in a game); event, incident.
lancero *m* (*mil*) lancer.
lancha *f* barge, lighter; launch.
langosta *f* locust; lobster.
langostino *m* crayfish.
languidez *f* langor.
lánguido, da *adj* languid, faint, weak.
lanudo, da *adj* wooly, fleecy.
lanza *f* lance, spear.
lanzada *f* stroke with a lance.
lanzadera *f* shuttle.
lanzamiento *m* throwing; (*mar, com*) launch, launching.
lanzar *vt* to throw; (*dep*) to bowl, to pitch, to launch, to fling; (*jur*) to evict.
lapicero *m* ballpoint pen.
lápida *f* flat stone, tablet.
lapidario *m*; **~, ria,** *adj* lapidary.
lápiz *m* pencil; mechanical pencil.
lapso *m* interval; error.
lapsus *m* error, mistake.
largamente *adv* for a long time.

largar *vt* to loosen, to slacken; to let go; to launch; to throw out; **~se** *vr* (*fam*) to beat it (*sl*).
largo, ga *adj* long; lengthy, generous; copious; **a la ~a** in the end, eventually.
largueza *f* liberality, generosity.
largura *f* length.
laringe *f* larynx.
laringitis *f* laryngitis.
lascivia *f* lasciviousness; lewdness.
lascivo, va *adj* lascivious; lewd.
láser *m* laser.
lasitud *f* lassitude, weariness.
lástima *f* compassion, pity; shame.
lastimar *vt* to hurt; to wound; to feel pity for; **~se** *vr* to hurt oneself.
lastimero, ra *adj* pitiful, pathetic.
lastimoso, sa *adj* pathetic, mournful.
lastrar *vt* to ballast a ship.
lastre *m* ballast; good sense.
lata *f* tin; can; (*fam*) nuisance.
lateral *adj* lateral.
latido *m* (heart)beat.
latifundio *m* large estate.
latigazo *m* lash, crack of a whip.
látigo *m* whip.
latín *m* Latin.
latinizar *vt* to latinize.
latino, na *adj* Latin.
latir *vi* to beat, to palpitate.
latitud *f* latitude.
latón *m* brass.
latoso, sa *adj* annoying; boring.
latrocinio *m* theft, robbery.
laúd *f* lute (musical instrument).
laudable *adj* laudable, praiseworthy.
láudano *m* laudanum.
laureado, da *adj* honored; ● *m* laureate.
laurel *m* (*bot*) laurel; reward.
lava *f* lava.
lavabo *m* washbasin; washroom.
lavadero *m* washing place; laundry.
lavado *m* washing; laundry.
lavadora *f* washing machine.
lavanda *f* lavender.
lavandera *f* laundress.
lavandería *f* laundry; **~ automática** launderette.
lavaplatos *m invar* dishwasher.
lavar *vt* to wash; to wipe away; **~se** *vr* to wash oneself.
lavativa *f* (*med*) enema; (*fig*) nuisance.
laxante *m* (*med*) laxative.
laxitud *f* laxity; laxness; slackness.
laxo, xa *adj* lax, slack.
lazada *f* bow, knot.
lazarillo *m*: **perro ~** guide dog.
lazo *m* knot, bow; snare, trap; tie; bond.
le *pn* him, you; (*dativo*) to him, to her, to it, to you.
leal *adj* loyal; faithful.
lealtad *f* loyalty.
lebrel *m* greyhound.
lebrillo *m* glazed earthenware pan.
lección *f* reading; lesson; lecture; class.
lector, ra *m/f* reader.
lectura *f* reading.
leche *f* milk.
lechera *f* milkmaid, dairymaid; milk churn.
lechería *f* dairy.
lecho *m* bed; layer.
lechón *m* suckling pig.
lechuga *f* lettuce.
lechuza *f* owl.
leer *vt* to read.
legado *m* bequest; legate; legacy.

legajo *m* file.
legal *adj* legal; trustworthy.
legalidad *f* legality.
legalización *f* legalization.
legalizar *vt* to legalize.
legaña *f* sleep (in eyes).
legar *vt* to leave (to), to bequeath.
legible *adj* legible.
legión *f* legion.
legionario, ria *adj* legionary.
legislación *f* legislation.
legislador, ra *m/f* legislator, lawmaker.
legislar *vt* to legislate.
legislativo, va *adj* legislative.
legislatura *f* legislature.
legitimar *vt* to legitimize.
legitimidad *f* legitimacy.
legítimo, ma *adj* legitimate, lawful; authentic.
legua *f* league.
legumbres *fpl* pulses.
leído, da *adj* well-read.
lejano, na *adj* distant, remote, far.
lejía *f* bleach.
lejos *adv* at a great distance, far off.
lelo, la *adj* stupid, ignorant; ● *m/f* idiot.
lema *m* motto; slogan.
lencería *f* linen, drapery.
lengua *f* tongue; language.
lenguado *m* sole.
lenguaje *m* language.
lente *m/f* lens.
lenteja *f* lentil.
lentilla *f* contact lens.
lentitud *f* slowness.
lento, ta *adj* slow.
leña *f* wood, timber.
leñador *m* woodman, woodcutter.
leño *m* block, log; trunk of a tree.
leñoso, sa *adj* woody.
Leo *m* Leo (sign of the zodiac).
león *m* lion.
leona *f* lioness.
leonado, da *adj* lion-colored, tawny.
leopardo *m* leopard.
leotardos *mpl* tights.
lepra *f* leprosy.
leproso, sa *adj* leprous; ● *m/f* leper.
lerdo, da *adj* slow, heavy; dull; slow-witted.
lesbiana *adj, f* lesbian.
lesión *f* hurt, damage, wound; injury.
letal *adj* mortal, deadly.
letanía *f* litany.
letárgico, ca *adj* lethargic.
letargo *m* lethargy.
letra *f* letter; handwriting; printing type; draft of a song; bill, draft; ~s *pl* letters, learning.
letrado, da *adj* learned, lettered; ● *m/f* lawyer; counsel.
letrero *m* sign; label.
letrina *f* latrine.
leucemia *f* leukemia.
leva *m* (*mar*) weighing anchor; (*mil*) levy.
levadizo, za *adj* that can be lifted *or* raised; **puente** ~ drawbridge.
levadura *f* yeast; brewer's yeast.
levantamiento *m* raising; insurrection.
levantar *vt* to raise, to lift up; to build; to elevate; to hearten, to cheer up; ~se *vr* to get up; to stand up.
levante *m* Levant; east; east wind.
leve *adj* light; trivial.
levita *f* greatcoat, frockcoat.
léxico *m* vocabulary.
ley *f* law; standard (for metal).

leyenda *f* legend.
liar *vt* to tie, to bind; to confuse.
libelo *m* petition; satire, lampoon.
libélula *f* dragonfly.
liberación *f* liberation; release.
liberal *adj* liberal, generous; ● *m/f* liberal.
liberalidad *f* liiberality, generosity.
libertad *f* liberty, freedom.
libertador, ra *m/f* liberator.
libertar *vt* to free, to set at liberty; to exempt, to clear from an obligation *or* debt.
libertinaje *m* licentiousness.
libertino, na *m/f* permissive person.
libra *f* pound; ~ **esterlina** a pound sterling.
Libra *f* Libra (sign of the zodiac).
librar *vt* to free, to deliver; (*com*) to draw; to make out (a check); (*jur*) to exempt; to fight (a battle); ~se *vr* to escape.
libre *adj* free; exempt; vacant.
libremente *adv* freely.
librería *f* bookshop.
librero, ra *m/f* bookseller.
libreta *f* notebook; ~ **de ahorros** savings book.
libro *m* book.
licencia *f* permission, license; licentiousness.
licenciado, da *adj* licensed; ● *m/f* graduate.
licenciar *vt* to permit, to allow; to license; to discharge; to confer a degree upon; ~se *vr* to graduate.
licencioso, sa *adj* licentious, dissolute.
liceo *m* lyceum; high school.
lícitamente *adv* lawfully, licitly.
lícito, ta *adj* lawful, fair; permissible.
licor *m* liquor.
licuadora *f* blender.
lid *m* contest, fight; dispute.
líder *m/f* leader.
liderazgo *m* leadership.
liebre *f* hare.
lienzo *f* linen; canvas; face *or* front of a building.
liga *f* garter; birdlime; league; coalition; alloy.
ligadura *f* (*med*, *mus*) ligature; binding; bond, tie.
ligamento *m* ligament; tie; bond.
ligar *vt* to tie, to bind, to fasten; ● *vi* to mix, blend; (*fam*) to pick up; ~se *vr* to commit oneself.
ligazón *f* union, connection.
ligereza *f* lightness; swiftness; agility; superficiality.
ligero, ra *adj* light, swift; agile; superficial.
liguero *m* garter belt.
lija *f* dogfish; sandpaper.
lijar *vt* to smooth, to sandpaper.
lila *f* lilac.
lima *f* file.
limadura *f* filing.
limar *vt* to file; to polish.
limitación *f* limitation, restriction.
limitado, da *adj* limited.
limitar *vt* to limit; to restrict; to cut down.
límite *m* limit, boundary.
limítrofe *adj* neighboring, bordering.
limón *m* lemon.
limonada *f* lemonade.
limonar *m* plantation of lemon trees.
limosna *f* alms, charity.
limpiabotas *m/f invar* shoeshine boy/girl.
limpiaparabrisas *m invar* windshield wiper.
limpiar *vt* to cleanse, to purify; to clean; to polish; (*fig*) to clean up.
limpieza *f* cleanliness, cleaning; cleansing; polishing; purity.
limpio, pia *adj* clean; neat; pure.
linaje *m* lineage, family, descent.
linaza *f* linseed.
lince *m* lynx.
linchar *vt* to lynch.

lindar *vt* to be adjacent.
linde *m* landmark, boundary.
lindero *m* edge; landmark, boundary.
lindo, da *adj* pretty, lovely.
línea *f* line; cable; outline.
lineal *adj* linear.
lingote *m* ingot.
lingüista *m/f* linguist.
lino *m* flax.
linterna *f* lantern, lamp; flashlight.
lío *m* bundle, parcel; (*fam*) muddle, mess.
liquidación *f* liquidation.
liquidar *vt* to liquidate; to settle accounts.
líquido, da *adj* liquid.
lira *f* (*mus*)lyre.
lirio *m* (*bot*) iris.
lirón *m* dormouse; (*fig*) sleepyhead.
lisiado, da *adj* injured; ● *m/f* cripple.
lisiar *vt* to injure; to hurt.
liso, sa *adj* plain, even, flat, smooth.
lisonja *f* adulation, flattery.
lisonjear *vt* to flatter.
lisonjero, ra *m/f* flatterer; ● *adj* flattering; pleasing.
lista *f* school register, list, catalog; menu.
listo, ta *adj* ready; smart, clever.
listón *m* ribbon; strip (of wood or metal).
litera *f* berth; bunk, bunk bed.
literal *adj* literal.
literario, ria *adj* literary.
literato, ta *adj* literary; ● *m/f* writer, literary person; ~s *pl* literati.
literatura *f* literature.
litigar *vt* to fight; ● *vi* (*jur*) to go to law; (*fig*) to dispute.
litigio *m* lawsuit.
litografía *f* lithography.
litográfico, ca *adj* lithographic.
litoral *adj* coastal; ● *m* coast.
litro *m* liter (measure).
liturgia *f* liturgy.
litúrgico, ca *adj* liturgical.
liviandad *f* fickleness; triviality; lightness.
liviano, na *adj* light; fickle; trivial.
lívido, da *adj* livid.
lo *pn* it; ● *art* the.
loable *adj* laudable.
loar *vt* to praise.
lobato *m* young wolf.
lobo *m* wolf.
lóbrego, ga *adj* murky, dark, gloomy.
lóbulo *m* lobe.
local *adj* local; ● *m* place, site.
localidad *f* locality; location.
localizar *vt* to localize.
loción *f* lotion.
loco, ca *adj* mad; ● *m/f* mad person.
locomotora *f* locomotive.
locuacidad *f* loquacity.
locuaz *adj* loquacious, talkative.
locución *f* expression.
locura *f* madness, folly.
locutor, ra *m/f* (*rad*) announcer; (*TV*) newsreader.
locutorio *m* telephone booth.
lodazal *m* muddy place.
lodo *m* mud, mire.
logaritmo *m* logarithm.
lógica *f* logic.
lógico, ca *adj* logical.
lograr *vt* to achieve; to gain, to obtain.
logro *m* achievement, success.
loma *f* hillock.
lombarda *f* red cabbage.
lombriz *f* worm.

lomo *m* loin; back (of an animal), spine of a book; **llevar** *o* **traer a** ~ to carry on the back.
lona *f* canvas.
loncha *or* **lonja** *f* slice; rasher.
longaniza *f* pork sausage.
longitud *f* length; longitude.
lonja *f*: ~ **de pescado** fish market.
loro *m* parrot.
losa *f* flagstone.
lote *m* lot, portion.
lotería *f* lottery.
loza *f* crockery.
lozanía *f* luxuriance, lushness; vigor; self-assurance.
lozano, na *adj* luxuriant; sprightly.
lubricante *m* lubricant.
lucero *m* morning star, bright star.
lúcido, da *adj* lucid.
luciérnaga *f* glowworm.
lucimiento *m* splendor, luster; brightness.
lucir *vt* to light (up); to show off; ● *vi* to shine; ~**se** *vr* to make a fool of oneself.
lucrativo, va *adj* lucrative.
lucro *m* gain, profit.
lucha *f* struggle, fight.
luchador, ra *m/f* fighter; ● *m* wrestler.
luchar *vt* to wrestle, to struggle.
luego *adv* next; afterward; **desde** ~ of course. 5-27-20
lugar *m* place, spot; village; reason; **en** ~ **de** instead of, in lieu of.
lugareño, ña *adj*, *m/f* belonging to a village; inhabitant of a village.
lugarteniente *m* deputy.
lúgubre *adj* sad, gloomy; lugubrious, dismal.
lujo *m* luxury; abundance.
lujoso, sa *adj* showy, profuse, lavish, sumptuous.
lujuria *f* lust.
lujurioso, sa *adj* lustful, lewd.
lumbre *f* fire; light.
lumbrera *f* luminary; skylight.
luminaria *f* illumination.
luminoso, sa *adj* luminous, shining.
luna *f* moon; glass plate for mirrors; lens.
lunar *m* mole, spot; ● *adj* lunar.
lunático, ca *adj* lunatic.
lunes *m* Monday.
lupa *f* magnifying glass.
lupanar *m* brothel.
lustre *m* gloss, luster; splendor.
lustro *m* lustrum (space of five years).
lustroso, sa *adj* bright, brilliant.
luteranismo *m* Lutheranism.
luterano, na *adj*, *m/f* Lutheran.
luto *m* mourning (dress); grief.
luz *f* light.

LL

llaga *f* wound, sore.
llama *f* flame; llama (animal).
llamada *f* call.
llamador *m* door-knocker.
llamamiento *m* call.
llamar *vt* to call; to name, to summon; to call, to telephone; ● *vi* to knock at the door; to call, to telephone; ~**se** *vr* to be named.
llamarada *f* sudden blaze of fire; outburst.
llamativo, va *adj* showy, loud (color).
llano, na *adj* plain, even, level, smooth; clear, evident; ● *m* level field.
llanta *f* (wheel) rim; tire; inner (tube).

llanto m flood of tears, crying.
llanura f evenness, level; plain, prairie.
llave f key; ~ **maestra** master key.
llavero m keyring.
llegada f arrival, coming.
llegar vi to arrive; to reach; ~**se** vr to come near, to approach.
llenar vt to fill; to cover; to fill out (a form); to satisfy, to fulfill; ~**se** vr to fulfill; to gorge oneself.
lleno, na adj full, full up; complete.
llevadero, ra adj tolerable.
llevar vt to take; to wear; to carry, to convey, to transport; to drive; to carry (money); to lead; to bear; ~**se** vr to carry off, to take away.
llorar vt, vi to weep, to cry.
lloriquear vt to whine.
lloro m weeping, crying.
llorón, na m/f tearful person; crybaby.
lloroso, sa adj mournful, full of tears.
llover vi to rain.
lloviznar vi to drizzle.
lluvia f rain.
lluvioso, sa adj rainy.

M

macarrones mpl macaroni.
macedonia f: ~ **de frutas** fruit salad.
macerar vt to macerate, to soften.
maceta f flowerpot.
macilento, ta adj lean, haggard; withered.
macizo, za adj massive, solid; ● m mass, chunk.
machacar vt to pound, to crush; ● vi to insist, to go on.
machacón, ona adj wearisome, tedious.
machete m machete, cutlass.
machista adj, m sexist.
macho adj male; (fig) virile; ● m male; (fig) he-man.
machucar vt to pound, to bruise.
madeja f skein of thread; mop of hair.
madera f timber, wood.
madero m beam of timber.
madrastra f stepmother.
madraza f very fond mother.
madre f mother; womb.
madreperla f mother-of-pearl.
madreselva f honeysuckle.
madrigal m madrigal.
madriguera f burrow; den.
madrina f godmother.
madroño m strawberry plant.
madrugada f dawn; **de** ~ at day break.
madrugador, ra m/f early riser.
madrugar vi to get up early; to anticipate, to get ahead.
madurar vt to ripen; ● vi to ripen, to grow ripe; to mature.
madurez f maturity; ripeness; wisdom.
maduro, ra adj ripe, mature.
maestra f mistress; schoolmistress; teacher.
maestría f mastery, skill.
maestro m master; teacher; ~, **tra** adj masterly, skilled; principal.
magia f magic.
mágico, ca adj magical.
magisterio m teaching; teaching profession; teachers pl.
magistrado, da m/f magistrate.
magistral adj magisterial; masterly.
magistratura f magistracy.
magnanimidad f magnanimity.
magnánimo, ma adj magnanimous.
magnate m magnate.
magnético, ca adj magnetic.
magnetismo m magnetism.

magnetizar vt to magnetize.
magnetofón or **magnetófono** m tape recorder.
magnetofónico, ca adj: **cinta magnetofónica** recording tape.
magnificencia f magnificence, splendor.
magnífico, ca adj magnificent, splendid.
magnitud f magnitude.
mago, ga m/f magician.
magro, gra adj thin, lean; meager.
magulladura f bruise.
magullar vt to bruise; to damage; to bash (sl).
mahometano, na m/f, adj Mohammedan.
mahometanismo m Mohammedanism.
mahonesa or **mayonesa** m mayonnaise.
maíz m corn, Indian corn.
maizal m cornfield.
majada f sheepfold.
majadería f absurdity; silliness.
majadero, ra adj dull, silly, stupid; ● m idiot.
majestad f majesty.
majestuoso, sa adj majestic.
majo, ja adj nice; attractive; smart.
majuelo m vine newly planted; hawthorn.
mal m evil, hurt, harm, damage; misfortune; illness; ● adj (used only before masculine nouns) bad.
malamente adv badly.
malaria f malaria.
malcriado, da adj rude, ill-behaved; naughty; spoiled.
maldad f wickedness.
maldecir vt to curse.
maldición f curse.
maldito, ta adj wicked; damned, cursed.
malear vt to damage, to corrupt.
malecón m pier.
maledicencia f slander, scandal.
maleducado, da adj bad-mannered, rude.
maleficio m curse, spell; witchcraft.
maléfico, ca adj harmful, damaging, evil.
malestar m discomfort; (fig) uneasiness; unrest.
maleta f suitcase; (auto) trunk.
maletera f (auto) trunk.
malevolencia f malevolence.
malévolo, la adj malevolent.
maleza f weeds; thicket.
malgastar vt to waste, to ruin.
malhablado, da adj foul-mouthed.
malhechor, ra m/f malefactor; criminal.
malhumorado, da adj cross, bad-tempered.
malicia f malice, wickedness; suspicion; cunning.
malicioso, sa adj malicious, wicked, evil; sly, crafty; spiteful.
malignidad f (med) malignancy; evil nature; malice.
maligno, na adj malignant, malicious.
malo, la adj bad, ill, wicked; ● m/f villain.
malograr vt to spoil; to upset (a plan); to waste; ~**se** vr to fail; to die early.
malparado, da adj: **salir** ~ to come off badly.
malparida f woman who has had a miscarriage.
malparir vi to miscarry.
malsano, na adj unhealthy.
malteada f milk shake.
maltratamiento m ill-treatment.
maltratar vt to ill treat, to abuse, to mistreat.
malva f (bot) mallow.
malvado, da adj wicked, villainous.
malversación f embezzlement.
malversador, ra m/f embezzler.
malversar vt to embezzle.
malla f mesh, network; ~**s** fpl leotard.
mama teat; breast.
mamá f (fam) mom, mamma.
mamar vt, vi to suck.
mamarrachada f ridiculous sight.
mamarracho m sight.

mamífero *m* mammal.
mamón, ona *m/f* baby which is breast fed.
mampara *f* partition; screen.
mampostería *f* masonry; rubblework.
maná *m* manna.
manada *f* flock, herd, pack; crowd.
manantial *m* source, spring; origin.
manar *vt* to run with, to flow; ● *vi* to spring from; to flow; to abound.
mancilla *f* spot, blemish.
manco, ca *adj* one-armed; one-handed; maimed; faulty.
mancomunar *vt* to associate, to unite; to make jointly responsible.
mancomunidad *f* union, fellowship; community; (*jur*) joint responsibility.
mancha *f* stain, spot.
manchado, da *adj* spotted.
manchar *vt* to stain, to soil.
mandado *m* command; errand, message.
mandamiento *m* order, command; commandment.
mandar *vt* to command, to order; to bequeath; to send.
mandarín *m* mandarin.
mandarina *f* tangerine.
mandatario, ria *m/f* agent; leader.
mandato *m* mandate, order; term of office.
mandíbula *f* jaw.
mandil *m* apron.
mando *m* command, authority, power; term of office.
mandón, ona *adj* bossy, domineering.
manecilla *f* small hand (of a watch *or* meter); book-clasp.
manejable *adj* manageable.
manejar *vt* to manage; to operate; to handle; (*auto*) to drive; ~se *vr* to manage; to behave.
manejo *m* management; handling; driving; confidence.
manera *f* manner, way; fashion; kind.
manga *f* sleeve; hose.
mango *m* handle; mango.
mangonear *vi* to interfere; to boss people about.
manguera *f* hose; pipe.
manguito *m* muff.
maní *m* peanut.
manía *f* mania; craze; dislike; spite.
maniatar *vt* to tie the hands of, to handcuff.
maniático, ca *adj* maniac, mad, frantic; ● *m/f* maniac.
manicomio *m* insane asylum.
manicura *f* manicure.
manifestación *f* manifestation; show; demonstration; mass meeting.
manifestar *vt* to manifest, to declare.
manifiesto, ta *adj* manifest, open, clear; ● *m* manifesto.
manija *f* handle.
maniobra *f* maneuvering; handling; (*mil*) maneuver.
maniobrar *vt* to maneuvre; to handle.
manipulación *f* manipulation.
manipular *vt* to manipulate.
maniquí *m* dummy; ● *m/f* model.
manirroto, ta *adj* lavish, extravagant.
manivela *f* crank.
manjar *m* (tasty) dish.
mano *f* hand; hand of a clock *or* watch; foot, paw (of an animal); coat (of paint); lot, series; first hand at play; a ~ by hand; a ~s llenas liberally, generously.
manojo *m* handful, bunch.
manopla *f* glove; face cloth.
manosear *vt* to handle; to mess up.
manoseo *m* handling.
manotazo *m* slap, smack.
manoteo *m* gesticulation.
mansalva *f*: a ~ *adv* indiscriminately.
mansedumbre *f* meekness, gentleness.
mansión *f* mansion.
manso, sa *adj* tame; gentle, soft.

manta *f* blanket.
manteca *f* fat; ~ de cerdo lard.
mantecado *m* cake eaten at Christmas; ice cream.
mantecoso, sa *adj* greasy.
mantel *m* tablecloth.
mantelería *f* table linen.
mantener *vt* to maintain, to support; to nourish; to keep; ~se *vr* to hold one's ground; to support oneself.
mantenimiento *m* maintenance; subsistence.
mantequilla *f* butter.
mantilla *f* mantilla (head covering for women); ~s *pl* baby clothes.
manto *m* mantle; cloak, robe.
mantón *m* shawl.
manual *adj* manual; ● *m* manual, handbook.
manufactura *f* manufacture.
manufacturar *vt* to manufacture.
manuscrito *m* manuscript; ● *adj* handwritten.
manutención *f* support, maintenance.
manzana *f* apple.
manzanilla *f* camomile; camomile tea; manzanilla sherry.
manzano *m* apple tree.
maña *f* handiness, dexterity, cleverness, cunning; habit *or* custom; trick.
mañana *f* morning; ● *adv* tomorrow.
mañoso, sa *adj* skilful, handy; cunning.
mapa *m* map.
mapamundi *f* map of the world.
maquillaje *m* make-up; making up.
maquillar *vt* to make up; ~se *vr* to put on make-up.
máquina *f* machine; (*ferro*) engine; camera; (*fig*) machinery; plan, project.
maquinación *f* machination.
maquinador, ra *m/f* schemer, plotter.
maquinalmente *adv* mechanically.
maquinar *vt, vi* to machinate; to conspire.
maquinaria *f* machinery; mechanism.
maquinilla *f*: ~ de afeitar razor.
maquinista *m* (*ferro*) engineer; operator; (*mar*) engineer.
mar *m/f* sea.
maraña *f* shrub, thicket; tangle.
maravilla *f* wonder.
maravillar *vt* to astonish, to amaze; ~se *vr* to be amazed, to be astonished.
maravilloso, sa *adj* wonderful, marvelous.
marca *f* mark; stamp; (*com*) make, brand.
marcado, da *adj* strong, marked.
marcador *m* scoreboard; scorer.
marcar *vt* to mark; to dial; to score; to record; to set (the hair); ● *vi* to score; to dial.
marcial *adj* martial, warlike.
marciano, na *adj* martian.
marco *m* frame; framework; (*dep*) goalposts *pl*.
marcha *f* march; running; gear; speed; (*fig*) progress.
marchar *vi* to go; to work; ~se *vr* to go away.
marchitar *vt* to wither; to fade.
marchito, ta *adj* faded, withered.
marea *f* tide.
marear *vt* (*mar*) to sail, to navigate; to annoy, to upset; ~se *vr* to feel sick; to feel faint; to feel dizzy.
marejada *f* swell, heavy sea, surge.
mareo *m* sick feeling; dizziness; nuisance.
marfil *m* ivory.
margarina *f* margarine.
margarita *f* daisy.
margen *m* margin; border; ● *f* bank (of river).
marginal *adj* marginal.
marginar *vt* to exclude; to leave margins (on a page); to make notes in the margin.
marica *m* (*fam*) sissy.
maricón *m* (*fam*) queer (*sl*).
marido *m* husband.

mariguana or **marihuana** f cannabis.
marimacho f (fam) mannish woman.
marina f navy.
marinero, ra adj sea compd; seaworthy; ● m sailor.
marino, na adj marine; ● m sailor, seaman.
marioneta f puppet.
mariposa f butterfly.
mariquita f ladybug.
mariscal m marshal.
mariscos mpl invar shellfish.
marital adj marital.
marítimo, ma adj maritime, marine.
marmita f pot.
mármol m marble.
marmóreo, rea adj marbled, marble.
marmota f marmot.
maroma f rope.
marqués m marquis.
marquesa f marchioness.
marrano m pig, boar.
marrón adj brown.
marrullería f plausibility; plausible excuse; ~s pl cajolery.
marrullero, ra adj crafty, cunning.
marta f marten, sable.
martes m Tuesday.
martillar vt to hammer.
martillo m hammer.
mártir m/f martyr.
martirio m martyrdom.
martirizar vt to martyr.
marxismo m Marxism.
marxista adj, m/f Marxist.
marzo m March.
mas adv but, yet.
más adv more; most; besides, moreover; a ~ **tardar** at latest; sin ~ **ni** ~ without more ado.
masa f dough, paste; mortar; mass.
masacre m massacre.
masaje m massage.
mascar vt to chew.
máscara m/f masked person; ● f mask.
mascarada f masquerade.
mascarilla f (med) mask.
masculino adj masculine, male.
mascullar vt to mumble, to mutter.
masivo, va adj mass, en masse.
masoquista m/f masochist.
masticación f mastication.
masticar vt to masticate, to chew.
mástil m (mar) mast.
mastín m mastiff.
masturbación f masturbation.
masturbarse vr to masturbate.
mata f shrub; sprig, blade; grove, group of trees; mop of hair.
matadero m slaughterhouse.
matador, ra adj killing; ● m/f killer; ● m bullfighter.
matanza f slaughtering; massacre.
matar vt to kill; to execute; to murder; ~se vr to kill oneself, to commit suicide.
matasanos m invar quack (doctor).
matasellos m invar postmark.
mate m checkmate; ● adj matt.
matemáticas fpl mathematics.
matemático, ca adj mathematical; ● m/f mathematician.
materia m matter, materials pl; subject.
material adj material, physical; ● m equipment, materials pl.
materialidad f outward appearance.
materialismo m materialism.
materialista m/f materialist.
maternal adj maternal, motherly.
maternidad f motherhood, motherliness.
materno, na adj maternal, motherly.

matinal adj morning compd.
matiz m shade of color; shading.
matizar vt to mix colors; to tinge, to tint.
matón m bully.
matorral m shrub, thicket.
matraca f rattle.
matricida m/f matricide (person).
matricidio m matricide (murder).
matrícula f register, list; (auto) registration number; license plate.
matricular vt to register, to enroll.
matrimonial adj matrimonial.
matrimonio m marriage, matrimony.
matriz f matrix; womb; mold, form.
matrona f matron.
matutino, na adj morning.
maullar vt to mew.
maullido m mew of a cat.
mausoleo m mausoleum.
máxima f maxim.
máxime adv principally.
máximo, ma adj maximum; top; highest.
mayo m May.
mayonesa = mahonesa.
mayor adj main, chief; (mus) major; biggest; eldest; greater, larger; elderly; ● m chief, boss; adult; al por ~ wholesale; ~es mpl forefathers.
mayoral m foreman.
mayordomo m steward.
mayoría f majority, greater part; ~ **de edad** coming of age.
mayorista m/f wholesaler.
mayormente adv principally, chiefly.
mayúsculo, la adj (fig) tremendous; ● f capital letter.
maza f club; mace.
mazada f blow with a club.
mazapán m marzipan.
mazmorra f dungeon.
mazo m bunch; club, mallet; bat.
mazorca f ear of corn.
me pn me; to me.
mear vi (fam) to pee, to piss (sl).
mecánica f mechanics pl.
mecánico, ca adj mechanical; ● m/f mechanic.
mecanismo m mechanism.
mecanografía f typewriting.
mecanógrafo, fa adj typist.
mecate m rope.
mecedora f rocking chair.
mecer vt to rock; to dandle a child.
mecha f wick; fuse.
mechar vt to lard; to stuff.
mechero m (cigarette) lighter.
mechón m lock of hair; large bundle of threads or fibers.
medalla f medal.
medallón m medallion.
media f stocking; sock; average.
mediación f mediation, intervention.
mediado, da adj half full; half complete; a ~s **de** in the middle of.
mediador, ra m/f mediator; go between.
medianero, ra adj dividing; adjacent.
mediano, na adj medium, middling; mediocre.
medianoche f midnight.
mediante adv by means of.
mediar vi to intervene; to mediate.
medicación f medication.
medicamento m medicine.
medicina f medicine.
medicinal adj medicinal.
médico, ca adj medical; ● m/f doctor.
medida f measure.

medio, dia *adj* half; **a medias** partly; ● *m* middle; average; way, mean; medium.
mediocre *adj* middling, moderate, mediocre.
mediocridad *f* mediocrity.
mediodía *m* noon, midday.
medir *vt* to measure; ~**se** *vr* to be moderate.
meditación *f* meditation.
meditar *vt* to meditate.
mediterráneo, nea *adj* Mediterranean.
medrar *vi* to grow, to thrive, to prosper; to improve.
medroso, sa *adj* fearful, timid.
médula *f* marrow; essence, substance; pith.
medusa *f* jellyfish.
megáfono *m* megaphone.
mejilla *f* cheek.
mejillón *m* mussel.
mejor *adj, adv* better; best.
mejora *f* improvement.
mejorar *vt* to improve, to ameliorate, to enhance; ● *vi* to improve; (*med*) to recover, to grow well from a disease *or* calamity; ~**se** *vr* to improve, to grow better.
mejoría *f* improvement; recovery.
melancolía *f* melancholy.
melancólico, ca *adj* melancholy, sad, gloomy.
melena *f* long hair, loose hair, mane.
melenudo, da *adj* long-haired.
melindroso, sa *adj* prudish, finicky.
melocotón *m* peach.
melodía *f* melody.
melodioso, sa *adj* melodious.
melodrama *f* melodrama.
melón *m* melon.
melosidad *f* sweetness.
meloso, sa *adj* honied; mellow.
mella *f* notch in edged tools; gap.
mellado, da *adj* jagged; gap-toothed.
mellar *vt* to notch.
mellizo, za *adj, m/f* twin.
membrana *f* membrane.
membranoso, sa *adj* membranous.
membrete *m* letter head.
membrillo *m* quince tree; quince.
membrudo, da *adj* strong, robust; burly.
memorable *adj* memorable.
memorándum *m* notebook; memorandum.
memoria *f* memory; report; record; ~**s** *pl* memoirs.
memorial *m* memorial; petition.
mención *f* mention.
mencionar *vt* to mention.
mendigar *vt* to beg.
mendigo, ga *m/f* beggar.
mendrugo *m* crust.
menear *vt* to move from place to place; (*fig*) to handle; ~**se** *vr* to move, to shake, to sway.
meneo *m* movement; shake; swaying.
menester *m* necessity, need, want; ~**es** *pl* duties.
menesteroso, sa *adj* needy.
menestra *f* vegetable soup *or* stew.
menguante *f* decreasing.
menguar *vi* to diminish; to discredit.
menopausia *f* menopause.
menor *m/f* young person, juvenile; ● *adj* less, smaller, minor; **al por** ~ retail.
menoría *f*: **a** ~ retail.
menos *adv* less; least; **a lo** ~ *o* **por lo** ~ at least; ● *prep* except; minus.
menoscabar *vt* to damage; to harm; to lessen; to discredit.
menoscabo *m* damage; harm; loss.
menospreciar *vt* to undervalue; to despise, to scorn.
menosprecio *m* contempt, scorn; undervaluation.
mensaje *m* message.
mensajero, ra *m/f* messenger.

menstruación *f* menstruation.
mensual *adj* monthly.
menta *f* mint.
mental *adj* mental, intellectual.
mentar *vt* to mention.
mente *f* mind, understanding.
mentecato, ta *adj* silly, stupid; ● *m/f* idiot.
mentir *vt* to feign; to pretend; ● *vi* to lie.
mentira *f* lie, falsehood.
mentiroso, sa *adj* lying; ● *m/f* liar.
menú *m* menu; set meal.
menudencia *f* trifle, small thing; minuteness; ~**s** *pl* odds and ends.
menudillos *mpl* giblets.
menudo, da *adj* small; minute; petty, insignificant; **a** ~ frequently, often.
meñique *m* little finger.
meollo *m* marrow; (*fig*) core.
mequetrefe *m* good-for-nothing; busybody.
meramente *adv* merely, solely.
mercader *m* dealer, trader.
mercadería *f* commodity, merchandise; trade.
mercado *m* market; marketplace.
mercancía *f* commodity; ~**s** *fpl* goods, merchandise.
mercantil *adj* commercial, mercantile.
mercenario, ria *adj* mercenary; ● *m* mercenary; laborer.
mercería *f* notions *pl*; notions store; drapery.
mercurio *m* mercury.
merecedor, ra *adj* deserving.
merecer *vt* to deserve, to merit.
merecido, da *adj* deserved.
merendar *vi* to have tea; to have a picnic.
merengue *m* meringue.
meridiano *m* meridian.
meridional *adj* southern.
merienda *f* (light) tea; afternoon snack; picnic.
mérito *m* merit; worth, value.
meritorio, ria *adj* meritorious.
merluza *f* hake.
merma *f* waste, leakage.
mermar *vi* to waste, to diminish.
mermelada *f* jam.
mero *m* pollack (fish); ~, **ra** *adj* mere, pure.
merodeador *m* (*mil*) marauder.
merodear *vi* to pillage, to go marauding.
mes *m* month.
mesa *f* table; desk; plateau; ~ **redonda** round table.
meseta *f* meseta, tableland.
mesón *m* inn.
mestizo, za *adj* of mixed race; crossbred; ● *m/f* half-caste.
mesura *f* gravity; politeness; moderation.
mesurado, da *adj* moderate; dignified; courteous.
meta *f* goal; finish.
metafísica *f* metaphysics *pl*.
metafísico, ca *adj* metaphysical.
metáfora *f* metaphor.
metafórico, ca *adj* metaphorical.
metal *m* metal; (*mus*) brass; timbre of the voice.
metálico, ca *adj* metallic.
metalurgia *f* metallurgy.
metamorfosis *f* metamorphosis, transformation.
meteoro *m* meteor.
meteorología *f* meteorology.
meter *vt* to place, to put; to insert, to put in; to involve; to make, to cause; ~**se** *vr* to meddle, to interfere.
metódico, ca *adj* methodical.
método *m* method.
metralla *f* (*mil*) shrapnel.
metralleta *f* submachine-gun.
métrico, ca *adj* metric.
metro *m* meter; subway.
metrópoli *f* metropolis; mother country.

mezcla f mixture, medley.
mezclar vt to mix; ~**se** vr to mix; to mingle.
mezquindad f meanness; pettiness; wretchedness.
mezquino, na adj mean; small-minded, petty; wretched.
mezquita f mosque.
mi adj my.
mí pn me; myself.
microbio m microbe.
microbús m minibus.
micrófono m microphone.
microordenador m microcomputer.
microscópico, ca adj microscopic.
microscopio m microscope.
miedo m fear, dread.
miel f honey.
miembro m member.
mientras adv meanwhile; ● conj while; as long as.
miércoles m Wednesday.
mierda f (fam) shit (sl).
mies f harvest.
miga f crumb; ~**s** pl fried breadcrumbs.
migaja f scrap, crumb.
migración f migration.
mijo m (bot) millet.
mil m one thousand.
milagro m miracle, wonder.
milagroso, sa adj miraculous.
milano m kite (bird).
milésimo, ma adj, m thousandth.
mili f: **hacer la ~** (fam) to do one's military service.
milicia f militia; military service.
miliciano m militiaman.
milímetro m millimeter.
militante adj militant.
militar adj military; ● vi to serve in the army; (fig) to be a member of a party.
milla f mile.
millar m thousand.
millón m million.
millonario, ria m/f millionaire.
mimar vt to spoil, pamper.
mimbre m wicker.
mímica f sign language; mimicry.
mimo m caress; spoiling; mime.
mimoso, sa adj spoilt, pampered, delicate, fond.
mina f mine; underground passage.
minar vt to undermine; to mine.
mineral m mineral; ● adj mineral.
mineralogía f mineralogy.
minero, ra m/f miner.
miniatura f miniature.
minifalda f miniskirt.
mínimo, ma adj minimum.
ministerio m ministry.
ministro, ra m/f minister.
minoría f minority.
minucioso, sa adj meticulous; very detailed.
minúsculo, la adj minute; ● f small letter.
minusválido, da adj (physically) handicapped; ● m/f (physically) handicapped person.
minuta f minute, first draft; menu.
minutero m minute hand of a watch or clock.
minuto m minute.
mío, mía adj mine.
miope adj short-sighted.
mira f sight of a gun; (fig) aim.
mirada f glance; gaze.
mirador m viewpoint, vantage point.
miramiento m consideration; circumspection.
mirar vt to look at; to observe; to consider; ● vi to look; ~**se** vr to look at oneself; to look at one another.
mirilla f peephole.

mirlo m blackbird.
mirón, ona m/f spectator, onlooker, bystander; voyeur.
misa f mass; ~ **del gallo** midnight mass.
misal m missal.
misantropía f misanthropy.
misántropo, pa m/f misanthropist.
miserable adj miserable; mean; squalid (place); (fam) despicable; ● m/f rotter.
miseria f misery; poverty; meanness; squalor.
misericordia f mercy.
misil m missile.
misión f mission.
misionero, ra m/f missionary.
mismo, ma adj same; very.
misterio m mystery.
misterioso, sa adj mysterious.
mística f mysticism.
místico, ca adj mystic, mystical.
mitad f half; middle.
mitigación f mitigation.
mitigar vt to mitigate.
mitin m (political) rally.
mito m myth.
mitología f mythology.
mitológico, ca adj mythological.
mitones mpl mittens.
mixto, ta adj mixed.
mobiliario m furniture.
moción f motion.
moco m snot (sl), mucus.
mochila f backpack.
mochuelo m red owl.
moda f fashion, style.
modales mpl manners.
modalidad f kind, variety.
modelar vt to model, to form.
modelo m model, pattern.
moderación f moderation.
moderado, da adj moderate.
moderar vt to moderate.
moderno, na adj modern.
modestia f modesty, decency.
modesto, ta adj modest.
módico, ca adj moderate.
modificación f modification.
modificar vt to modify.
modisto, ta m/f dressmaker.
modo m mode, method, manner.
modorra f drowsiness.
modulación f modulation.
modular vt to modulate.
mofa f mockery.
mofarse vr: ~ **de** to mock, to scoff at.
moflete m fat cheek.
moho m rust; mold, mildew.
mohoso, sa adj moldy, musty.
mojar vt to wet, to moisten; ~**se** vr to get wet.
mojigato adj hypocritical.
mojón m landmark.
molde m mold; pattern; model.
moldura f molding.
mole f bulk; pile.
molécula f molecule.
moler vt to grind, to pound; to tire out; to annoy, to bore.
molestar vt to annoy, to bother; to trouble; ● vi to be a nuisance.
molestia f trouble; inconvenience; (med) discomfort.
molesto, ta adj annoying; inconvenient; uncomfortable; annoyed.
molinero m miller.
molinillo m: ~ **de café** coffee grinder.
molino m mill.

momentáneo, nea *adj* momentary.
momento *m* moment.
momia *f* mummy.
monacal *adj* monastic.
monaguillo *m* acolyte.
monarca *m/f* monarch.
monarquía *f* monarchy.
monárquico, ca *adj* monarchical; • *m/f* royalist, monarchist.
monasterio *m* monastery, convent.
monástico, ca *adj* monastic.
mondadientes *m invar* toothpick.
mondar *vt* to clean, to cleanse; to peel; ~**se** *vr*: ~ **de risa** (*fam*) to split one's sides laughing.
mondo, da *adj* clean, pure; ~ **y lirondo** bare, plain; pure and simple.
moneda *f* money, currency; coin.
monedero *m* purse.
monería *f* funny face; mimicry; prank; trifle.
monetario, ria *adj* monetary, financial.
monitor *m* monitor.
monje *m*, **monja** *f* monk; nun.
mono, na *adj* lovely, pretty, nice; • *m/f* monkey, ape; • *mpl* dungarees; coveralls.
monólogo *m* monolog.
monopolio *m* monopoly.
monopolista *m* monopolist, monopolizer.
monosílabo, ba *adj* monosyllabic.
monotonía *f* monotony.
monótono, na *adj* monotonous.
monstruo *m* monster.
monstruosidad *f* monstrosity.
monstruoso, sa *adj* monstrous.
monta *f* amount, sum total.
montaje *m* assembly; décor (of theater); montage.
montaña *f* mountain.
montañés, esa *adj* mountain *compd*; • *m/f* highlander.
montañoso, sa *adj* mountainous.
montar *vi* to mount, to get on (a bicycle, horse *etc*); to assemble, to put together; to overlap; to set up (a business); to beat, to whip (in cooking); • *vi* to mount; to ride; to amount to.
montaraz *adj* mountainous; wild, untamed.
monte *m* mountain; woodland; ~ **alto** forest; ~ **bajo** scrub.
montería *f* hunting, chase.
montés, esa *adj* wild, untamed.
montón *m* heap, pile; mass; **a** ~**ones**, abundantly, by the score.
montura *f* mount; saddle.
monumento *m* monument.
monzón *m* monsoon.
moño *m* bun.
moquillo *m* distemper (disease in dogs).
mora *f* blackberry.
morada *f* home, abode, residence.
morado, da *adj* violet, purple.
morador, ra *m/f* inhabitant, lodger.
moral *m* mulberry tree; • *f* morals, ethics *pl*; • *adj* moral.
moraleja *f* moral.
moralidad *f* morality.
moralista *m/f* moralist.
moralizar *vi* to moralize.
moralmente *adv* morally.
morar *vi* to inhabit, to dwell.
moratoria *f* moratorium.
mórbido, da *adj* morbid, diseased.
morboso, sa *adj* diseased, morbid.
morcilla *f* black pudding.
mordacidad *f* sharpness, pungency.
mordaz *adj* biting, scathing; pungent.
mordaza *f* gag; clamp.
mordedura *f* bite.
morder *vt* to bite; to nibble; to corrode, to eat away.

mordisco *m* bite.
moreno, na *adj* brown; swarthy; dark-skinned.
moribundo, da *adj* dying.
morigeración *f* temperance.
morir *vi* to die, to expire; to die down; ~**se** *vr* to die; (*fig*) to be dying.
morisco, ca *adj* Moorish.
moro, ra *adj* Moorish.
morosidad *f* slowness, sluggishness, dilatoriness.
moroso, sa *adj* slow, sluggish; (*com*) slow to pay up.
morral *m* haversack.
morriña *f* depression; sadness.
morro *m* snout; nose (of car, plane *etc*).
morsa *f* walrus.
mortaja *f* shroud; mortise; cigarette paper.
mortal *adj* mortal; fatal, deadly.
mortalidad *f* mortality.
mortandad *f* death toll.
mortero *m* mortar (cannon).
mortífero, ra *adj* deadly, fatal.
mortificación *f* mortification.
mortificar *vt* to mortify.
mortuorio *m* mortuary.
moruno, na *adj* Moorish.
mosca *f* fly.
moscardón *m* botfly, blowfly; pest (*fam*), bore.
moscatel *adj* muscatel.
moscón *m* pest (*fam*), bore.
mosquearse *vr* (*fam*) to get cross; (*fam*) to take offense.
mosquetero *m* musketeer.
mosquitero *m* mosquito net.
mosquito *m* gnat, mosquito.
mostaza *f* mustard.
mosto *m* must, new wine.
mostrador *m* counter.
mostrar *vt* to show, to exhibit; to explain; ~**se** *vr* to appear, to show oneself.
mota *f* speck, tiny piece; dot; defect *or* fault.
mote *m* nickname.
motejar *vt* to nickname.
motín *m* revolt; mutiny.
motivar *vt* to motivate; to explain, to justify.
motivo *m* motive, cause, reason.
moto (*fam*) *or* **motocicleta** *f* motorcycle.
motor *m* engine, motor.
motriz *adj* driving motive.
movedizo, za *adj* movable; variable, changeable; fickle.
mover *vt* to move; to shake; to drive; (*fig*) to cause; ~**se** *vr* to move; (*fig*) to get a move on.
móvil *adj* mobile; moving; • *m* motive, movable.
movilidad *f* mobility.
movimiento *m* movement, motion.
mozo, za *adj* young; • *m/f* youth, young man/girl; waiter; waitress.
muchacho, a *m/f* boy/girl; • *f* maid (servant).
muchedumbre *f* crowd.
mucho, cha *adj* a lot of, much; • *adv* much, a lot, long.
muda *f* change of clothes.
mudable *adj* changeable, variable, mutable.
mudanza *f* change; move.
mudar *vt* to change; to shed; • *vi* to change; ~**se** *vr* to change one's clothes; to change house.
mudo, da *adj* dumb; silent, mute.
mueble *m* piece of furniture; ~**s** *mpl* furniture.
mueca *f* grimace, funny face.
muela *f* tooth, molar.
muelle *m* spring; regulator; quay, wharf.
muérdago *m* (*bot*) mistletoe.
muerte *f* death.
muerto *m* corpse; ~, **ta** *adj* dead.
muesca *f* notch, groove.

muestra f pattern; indication; demonstration; proof; sample; token; model.
mugido m lowing.
mugir vi to low, to bellow.
mugre m dirt, filth.
mugriento, ta adj greasy, dirty, filthy.
mujer f woman.
mulato adj mulatto.
muleta f crutch.
mulo, la m/f mule.
multa f fine, penalty.
multar vt to fine.
múltiple adj multiple; ~s many, numerous.
multiplicación f multiplication.
multiplicado m (mat) multiplicand.
multiplicar vt to multiply.
multiplicidad f multiplicity.
multitud f multitude, great number.
mullido, da adj soft; springy.
mundano, na adj mundane, worldly.
mundial adj world-wide; world compd.
mundo m world.
munición f ammunition.
municipio m town council; municipality.
municipal adj municipal.
muñeca f wrist; child's doll.
muñeco m puppet; figure.
muñón m stump.
muralla f rampart, wall.
murciélago m bat.
murmullo m murmur, mutter.
murmuración f backbiting, gossip.
murmurador, ra m/f detractor, backbiter.
murmurar vi to murmur; to gossip; to backbite.
muro m wall.
muscular adj muscular.
músculo m muscle.
muselina f muslin.
museo m museum.
musgo m moss.
música f music.
musical adj musical.
músico, ca m/f musician; ● adj musical.
muslo m thigh.
mustio, tia adj parched, withered; sad, sorrowful.
mutabilidad f mutability.
mutación f mutation, change.
mutilación f mutilation.
mutilar vt to mutilate, to maim.
mutuo, tua adj mutual, reciprocal.
mutuamente adv mutually.
muy adv very; too; greatly; ~ **ilustre** most illustrious.

N

nabo m turnip.
nácar m mother-of-pearl, nacre.
nacarado, da adj mother-of-pearl; pearl-colored.
nacer vi to be born, to bud, to shoot (of plants); to rise; to grow.
nacido, da adj born; **recién** ~ newborn.
nacimiento m birth; Nativity.
nación f nation.
nacional adj national.
nacionalidad f nationality.
nacionalizar vt to nationalize; ~se to become naturalized.
nada f nothing; ● adv no way, not at all, by no means.
nadador, ra m/f swimmer.
nadar vi to swim.
nadie pn nobody, no one.

nado adv: **a** ~ afloat.
nafta f gas.
naipe m playing card.
nalgas fpl buttocks.
naranja f orange.
naranjada f orangeade.
naranjal m orange grove.
naranjo m orange tree.
narciso m (bot) daffodil; narcissus flower; fop.
narcótico, ca adj narcotic; ● m drug, narcotic.
nardo m spikenard.
narigón, ona or **narigudo, da** adj big-nosed.
nariz f nose; sense of smell.
narración f narration.
narrar vt to narrate, to tell.
narrativa f narrative; story.
nata f cream.
natación f swimming.
natal adj natal, native.
natalicio m birthday.
natillas fpl custard.
natividad f nativity.
nativo, va adj, m/f native.
natural m temper; natural disposition; native; ● adj natural, native; common, usual; **al** ~ unaffectedly.
naturaleza f nature.
naturalidad f naturalness.
naturalista m naturalist.
naturalizar vi to naturalize; ~se vr to become naturalized; to become acclimated.
naturalmente adv in a natural way; ¡~! of course!
naufragar vi to be shipwrecked; to suffer ruin in one's affairs.
naufragio m shipwreck.
náufrago, ga adj shipwrecked.
nauseabundo, da adj nauseating.
náuseas fpl nauseousness, nausea.
náutica f navigation.
navaja f penknife; razor.
naval adj naval.
nave f ship; nave.
navegable adj navigable.
navegación f navigation; sea journey.
navegante m navigator.
navegar vt, vi to navigate; to sail; to fly.
navidad f Christmas.
navideño, ña adj Christmas compd.
navío m ship.
nazi adj, m/f Nazi.
neblina f mist, fine rain, drizzle.
nebuloso, sa adj misty, cloudy, nebulous, foggy, hazy, drizzling; ● f nebula.
necedad f gross ignorance, stupidity; imprudence.
necesario, ria adj necessary.
neceser m toilet bag; holdall.
necesidad f necessity, need, want.
necesitado, da adj necessitous, needy.
necesitar vt to need; ● vi to want, to need.
necio, cia adj ignorant, stupid, foolish; imprudent.
necrología f obituary.
nectarina f nectarine.
néctar m nectar.
nefando, da adj base, nefarious, abominable.
nefasto, ta adj unlucky.
negación f negation; denial.
negado, da adj incapable, unfit.
negar vt to deny; to refuse; ~se vr to refuse to do a thing.
negativo, va adj, m negative; ● f negative; refusal.
negligencia f negligence.
negligente adj negligent, careless, heedless.
negociación f negotiation; commerce.
negociante m/f trader, dealer.
negociar vt, vi to negotiate.

negocio m business, affair; transaction; firm; place of business.

negro, gra adj black; awful; ● m black; ● m/f Black.

negrura f blackness.

negruzco, ca adj blackish.

nene m, **nena** f baby.

nenúfar m water lily.

neófito m neophyte.

nervio m nerve.

nervioso, sa adj nervous.

neto, ta adj neat, pure, net.

neumático, ca adj pneumatic; ● m tire.

neutral adj neutral, neuter.

neutralidad f neutrality.

neutralizar vt to neutralize; to counteract.

neutro, tra adj neutral, neuter.

neutrón m neutron.

nevada f heavy fall of snow.

nevar vi to snow.

nevera f icebox.

nevería f ice-cream parlor.

nexo m link.

ni conj neither, nor.

nicho m niche.

nido m nest; hiding place.

niebla f fog, mist.

nieta f granddaughter.

nieto m grandson.

nieve f snow.

nigromancia f necromancy.

nimiedad f small-mindedness; triviality.

nimio, mia adj trivial.

ninfa f nymph.

ningún, ninguno, na adj no; ● pn nobody, none, not one; neither.

niña f little girl; pupil, apple of the eye.

niñera f nursemaid.

niñería f childishness, childish action.

niñero, ra adj fond of children.

niñez f childhood.

niño, ña adj childish; ● m boy, child; ● f girl, child; infant; desde ~ from infancy, from a child.

níspera f or **níspero** m medlar.

nitidez f clarity; brightness; sharpness.

nitrato m (quim) nitrate.

nitrógeno m nitrogen.

nivel m level; standard; height; a ~ perfectly level.

niveladora f bulldozer.

nivelar vt to level; to even up; to balance.

no adv no; not; ● excl no!

noble adj noble, illustrious, generous.

nobleza f nobleness, nobility.

noción f notion, idea.

nocivo, va adj harmful.

nocturno, na adj nocturnal, nightly; ● m nocturne.

noche f night; evening; darkness; ~ buena Christmas eve; ~ vieja New Year's Eve; ¡buenas ~s! good night!

nodriza f nurse.

nogal m walnut tree.

nómada adj nomadic; ● m/f nomad.

nombramiento m nomination; appointment.

nombrar vt to name; to nominate, to appoint.

nombre m name; title; reputation.

nomenclatura f nomenclature.

nómina f list; (com) payroll.

nominador m nominator.

nominal adj nominal.

nominativo m (gr) nominative.

non adj odd, uneven; ● m odd number.

nonagenario, ria adj ninety years old; ● m/f nonagenarian.

no obstante adv nevertheless, notwithstanding.

nor(d)este adj northeast, northeastern; ● m northeast.

nórdico, ca adj northern; Nordic.

noria f water wheel; Ferris wheel.

normal adj normal; usual.

normalizar vt to normalize; to standardize; ~se vr to return to normal.

noroeste adj northwest, northwestern; ● m northwest.

norte adj north, northern; ● m north; (fig) rule, guide.

nos pn us; to us; for us; from us; to ourselves.

nosotros, tras pn we, us.

nostalgia f homesickness.

nota f note, notice, remark; mark.

notable adj notable, remarkable.

notar vt to note, to mark; to remark; ~se vr to be obvious.

notaría f profession of a notary; notary's office.

notario m notary.

noticia f notice, knowledge, information, note; news.

noticiario m newsreel; news bulletin.

noticiero m news bulletin.

notificación f notification.

notificar vt to notify, to inform.

notoriedad f notoriety.

notorio, ria adj notorious.

novato, ta adj inexperienced; ● m/f beginner.

novecientos, tas adj nine hundred.

novedad f novelty, modernness; newness; piece of news; change.

novela f novel.

novelero, ra adj highly imaginative.

novelesco, ca adj fictional; romantic; fantastic.

noveno, na adj ninth.

noventa adj, m ninety.

novia f bride; girlfriend; fiancée.

noviazgo m engagement.

novicio m novice.

noviembre m November.

novilla f heifer.

novillada f drove of young bulls; fight of young bulls.

novillo m young bull or ox.

novio m bridegroom; boyfriend; fiancé.

nubarrón m large cloud.

nube f cloud.

nublado, da adj cloudy; ● m storm cloud.

nublarse vr to grow dark.

nuca f nape, scruff of the neck.

nuclear adj nuclear.

núcleo m core; nucleus.

nudillo m knuckle.

nudo m knot.

nuera f daughter-in-law.

nuestro, tra adj our; ● pn ours.

nuevamente adv again; anew.

nueve m, adj nine.

nuevo, va adj new, modern, fresh; ● f piece of news; ¿qué hay de ~? is there any news? what news?

nuez f nut; walnut; Adam's apple; ~ moscada nutmeg.

nulidad f incompetence; nullity.

nulo, la adj useless; drawn; null.

numeración f numeration.

numerador m numerator.

numeral m numeral.

numerar vt to number, to numerate, to count.

numérico, ca adj numerical.

número m number; cipher.

numeroso, sa adj numerous.

nunca adv never.

nuncio m nuncio.

nupcial adj nuptial.

nupcias fpl nuptials, wedding.

nutria f otter.

nutrición f nutrition.

nutrir vt to nourish; to feed.

nutritivo, va adj nutritive, nourishing.

nylon m nylon.

Ñ

ñato, ta adj snubnosed.
ñoño, ña adj insipid; spineless; silly.
ñoñería f insipidness.

O

o conj or; either.
oasis m invar oasis.
obcecación f obduracy.
obcecar vt to blind; to darken.
obedecer vt to obey.
obediencia f obedience.
obediente adj obedient.
obelisco m obelisk.
obertura f (mus) overture.
obesidad f obesity.
obeso, sa adj obese, fat.
obispado m bishopric; episcopate.
obispo m bishop.
objeción f objection, opposition, exception.
objetar vt to object, to oppose.
objetivo, va adj, m objective.
objeto m object; aim.
oblea f wafer.
oblicuo, cua adj oblique.
obligación f obligation; (com) bond.
obligar vt to force; ~se vr to bind oneself.
obligatorio, ria adj obligatory.
oblongo, ga adj oblong.
oboe m oboe.
obra f work; building, construction; play; por ~ de thanks to.
obrar vt to work; to operate, to act; to put into practice; ● vi to behave; to have an effect.
obrero, ra adj working; labor compd; ● m/f workman; laborer.
obscenidad f obscenity.
obsceno, na adj obscene.
obsequiar vt to present with; to lavish attention on.
obsequio m gift; courtesy.
obsequioso, sa adj obsequious, compliant, officious.
observación f observation; remark.
observador m observer, observator.
observancia f observance.
observar vt to observe; to notice.
observatorio m observatory.
obsesión f obsession.
obsesionar vt to obsess.
obstáculo m obstacle, impediment, hindrance.
obstar vi to oppose, to obstruct, to hinder.
obstetricia f obstetrics.
obstinación f obstinacy, stubbornness.
obstinado, da adj obstinate.
obstinarse vr to be obstinate; ~ en to persist in.
obstrucción f obstruction.
obstruir vt to obstruct; ~se vr to be blocked up, to be obstructed.
obtener vt to obtain; to gain.
obtuso, sa adj obtuse, blunt.
obús m (mil) shell.
obviar vt to obviate, to remove.
obvio, via adj obvious, evident.
ocasión f occasion, opportunity.
ocasional adj occasional.
ocasionar vt to cause, to occasion.

ocaso m (fig) decline.
occidental adj occidental, western.
occidente m occident, west.
océano m ocean.
ocio m leisure; pastime.
ociosidad f idleness, leisure.
ocioso, sa adj idle; useless.
ocre m ocher.
octavilla f pamphlet.
octavo, va adj eighth.
octogenario, ria adj, m/f octogenarian.
octubre m October.
ocular adj ocular; eye (compd).
oculista m/f oculist.
ocultar vt to hide, to conceal.
oculto, ta adj hidden, concealed, secret.
ocupación f occupation; business, employment.
ocupado, da adj busy; occupied; engaged.
ocupar vt to occupy, to hold an office; ~se vr: ~ de o en to concern oneself with; to look after.
ocurrencia f event; bright idea.
ocurrir vi to occur, to happen.
ochenta m, adj eighty.
ocho m, adj eight.
ochocientos m, adj eight hundred.
oda f ode.
odiar vt to hate; ~se vr to hate one another.
odio m hatred.
odioso, sa adj odious, hateful.
odontólogo, ga m/f dentist.
odorífero, ra adj odoriferous, fragrant.
oeste m west.
ofender vt to offend, to injure ~se vr to be vexed; to take offense.
ofensa f offense, injury.
ofensivo, va adj offensive, injurious.
ofensor m offender.
oferta f offer; offering.
oficial adj official; ● m officer; official.
oficiar vt to officiate, to minister (of clergymen, etc).
oficina f office.
oficio m office, employment, occupation, ministry; function; trade, business; ~s pl divine service.
oficiosidad f diligence; officiousness; importunity.
oficioso, sa adj officious, diligent; unofficial, informal.
ofimática f office automation.
ofrecer vt to offer; to present; to exhibit; ~se vr to offer, to occur, to present itself.
ofrecimiento m offer, promise.
ofrenda f offering, oblation.
ofrendar vt to offer, to contribute.
oftalmólogo, ga m/f ophthalmologist.
ofuscación f dimness of sight; obfuscation.
ofuscar vt to darken, to render obscure; to bewilder.
oídas fpl: de ~ by hearsay.
oído m hearing; ear.
oír vt, vi to hear; to listen.
ojal m buttonhole.
¡ojalá! conj if only . . . !, would that . . . !
ojeada f glance.
ojear vt to eye, to view; to glance.
ojera f bag under the eyes.
ojeriza f spite, grudge, ill-will.
ojo m eye; sight; eye of a needle; arch of a bridge.
ola f wave.
oleada f surge; violent emotion.
oleaje m succession of waves, sea swell.
óleo m oil.
oler vt to smell, to scent; ● vi to smell; to smack of.
olfatear vt to smell; (fig) to sniff out.
olfato m sense of smell.
oligarquía f oligarchy.

oligárquico, ca *adj* oligarchical.
olimpíada *f:*las O~s the Olympics.
olímpico, ca *adj* olympic.
oliva *f* olive.
olivar *m* olive grove.
olivo *m* olive tree.
olmo *m* elm tree.
olor *m* smell, odor, scent.
oloroso, sa *adj* fragrant, odorous.
olvidadizo, za *adj* forgetful.
olvidar *vt* to forget.
olvido *m* forgetfulness.
olla *f* pan; stew; ~ podrida dish composed of different boiled
   meats and vegetables; ~ a presión *o* exprés pressure cooker.
ombligo *m* navel.
omisión *f* omission.
omitir *vt* to omit.
omnipotencia *f* omnipotence, almightiness.
omnipotente *adj* omnipotent, almighty.
once *m, adj* eleven.
onda *f* wave.
ondear *vt* to undulate; to fluctuate.
ondulado, da *adj* wavy.
oneroso, sa *adj* burdensome.
opacidad *f* opacity, gloom, darkness.
opaco, ca *adj* opaque, dark.
opción *f* option, choice.
ópera *f* opera.
operación *f* operation.
operador, ra *m/f* operator; projectionist; cameraman.
operar *vi* to operate, to act.
opinar *vt* to think; ● *vi* to give one's opinion.
opinión *f* opinion.
opio *m* opium.
oponente *m/f* opponent.
oponer *vt* to oppose; ~se *vr* to oppose, to be opposite.
oportunidad *f* opportunity.
oportunismo *m* opportunism.
oportuno, na *adj* seasonable, opportune.
oposición *f* opposition.
oposiciones *fpl* public examinations.
opositor *m* opposer, opponent; candidate.
opresión *f* oppression.
opresivo, va *adj* oppressive.
opresor *m* oppressor.
oprimir *vt* to oppress; to crush, to press, to squeeze.
optar *vt* to choose, to elect.
optativo, va *adj* optional.
óptica *f* optics.
óptico, ca *adj* optical; ● *m/f* optician.
optimista *m/f* optimist.
óptimo, ma *adj* best.
opuesto, ta *adj* opposite, contrary, adverse.
opulencia *f* wealth, riches *pl*.
opulento, ta *adj* opulent, wealthy.
oración *f* oration, speech; prayer.
orador *m* orator.
oral *adj* oral.
orangután *m* orangutan.
orar *vi* to pray.
oratoria *f* oratory, rhetorical skill.
órbita *f* orbit.
orden *m/f* order; ~ del día order of the day; ~es sagradas
   holy orders.
ordenación *f* arrangement; ordination; edict, ordinance.
ordenado, da *adj* methodical; orderly.
ordenador *m* computer.
ordenanza *f* order; statute, ordinance; ordination.
ordenar *vt* to arrange; to order; to ordain; ~se *vr* to take holy
   orders.
ordeñar *vt* to milk.
ordinal *adj* ordinal.

ordinario, ria *adj* ordinary, common; de ~ regularly, commonly, ordinarily.
orégano *m* oregano.
oreja *f* ear.
orejera *f* earflap.
orfanato *m* orphanage.
orfandad *f* orphanhood.
orgánico, ca *adj* organic; harmonious.
organigrama *m* flowchart.
organismo *m* organism; organization.
organista *m/f* organist.
organización *f* organization; arrangement.
organizar *vt* to organize.
órgano *m* organ.
orgasmo *m* orgasm.
orgía *f* orgy.
orgullo *m* pride, haughtiness.
orgulloso, sa *adj* proud, haughty.
orientación *f* position; direction.
oriental *adj* oriental, eastern.
orientar *vt* to orient; to point; to direct; to guide; ~se *vr* to
   get one's bearings; to decide on a course of action.
oriente *m* orient.
orificio *m* orifice, mouth, aperture.
origen *m* origin, source; native country; family, extraction.
original *adj* original, primitive; ● *m* original, first copy.
originalidad *f* originality.
originar *vt, vi* to originate.
originario, ria *adj* original.
orilla *f* limit, border, margin; edge of cloth; shore.
orín *m* rust.
orina *f* urine.
orinal *m* chamber pot.
orinar *vi* to pass water.
oriundo, da *adj*: ~ de native of.
ornamento *m* ornament, embellishment.
ornitología *f* bird watching.
oro *m* gold; ~s *pl* diamonds (at cards).
orquesta *f* orchestra.
orquídea *f* orchid.
ortiga *f* (*bot*) nettle.
ortodoxia *f* orthodoxy.
ortodoxo, xa *adj* orthodox.
ortografía *f* orthography.
ortográfico, ca *adj* orthographical.
oruga *f* (*bot*) caterpillar.
orza *f* jar.
orzuelo *m* (*med*) stye.
os *pn* you; to you.
osa *f* she-bear; O~ Mayor/Menor Great/Little Bear.
osadamente *adv* boldly, daringly.
osadía *f* boldness, intrepidity; zeal, fervor.
osamenta *f* skeleton.
osar *vi* to dare, to venture.
oscilación *f* oscillation.
oscilar *vi* to oscillate.
oscurecer *vt* to obscure, to darken; ● *vi* to grow dark; ~se *vr*
   to disappear.
oscuridad *f* obscurity; darkness.
oscuro, ra *adj* obscure, dark.
osificarse *vr* to ossify.
oso *m* bear; ~ blanco polar bear.
ostensible *adj* ostensible, apparent.
ostentación *f* ostentation, ambitious display, show.
ostentar *vt* to show; ● *vi* to boast, to brag.
ostentoso, sa *adj* sumptuous, ostentatious.
ostra *f* oyster.
otitis *f* earache.
otoñal *adj* fall, autumnal.
otoño *m* fall, autumn.
otorgamiento *m* granting; execution.
otorgar *vt* to concede; to grant.

otorrino, na *or* **otorrinolaringólogo, ga** *m/f* ear, nose and throat specialist.
otro, tra *adj* another, other.
ovación *f* ovation.
ovalado, da *adj* oval.
óvalo *m* oval.
ovario *m* ovary.
oveja *f* sheep.
overol *m* coveralls *pl*.
ovillo *m* ball of wool.
ovíparo, ra *adj* oviparous, egg-bearing.
ovulación *f* ovulation.
óvulo *m* ovum.
oxidación *f* rusting.
oxidar *vt* to rust; **~se** *vr* to go rusty.
óxido *f* (*quim*) oxide.
oxígeno *m* (*quim*) oxygen.
oyente *m/f* listener, hearer.

P

pabellón *m* pavilion; summer house; block, section.
pábilo *m* wick; snuff of a candle.
pacer *vt* to pasture, to graze.
paciencia *f* patience.
paciente *adj*, *m* patient.
pacificación *f* pacification.
pacificar *vt* to pacify, to appease.
pacífico, ca *adj* pacific, peaceful.
pacotilla *f*: **de ~** third-rate; cheap.
pactar *vt* to covenant, to contract, to stipulate.
pacto *m* contract, pact.
padecer *vt* to suffer; to sustain an injury; to put up with.
padecimiento *m* suffering, sufferance.
padrastro *m* stepfather.
padrazo *m* over-indulgent father.
padre *m* father; **~s** *pl* parents.
padrino *m* godfather.
padrón *m* census; register; pattern; model.
paella *f* paella, dish of rice with shellfish, meat, *etc.*
paga *f* payment, fee.
pagadero, ra *adj* payable.
paganismo *m* paganism, heathenism.
pagano, na *adj*, *m/f* heathen, pagan.
pagar *vt* to pay; to pay for; (*fig*) to repay; ● *vi* to pay.
pagaré *m* bond, note of hand, promissory note, I.O.U. (I owe you).
página *f* page.
pago *m* payment; reward.
país *m* country, region.
paisaje *m* landscape.
paisano, na *adj* of the same country; ● *m/f* fellow countryman/woman.
paja *f* straw; (*fig*) trash.
pajar *m* straw loft.
pajarita *f* bow tie.
pájaro *m* bird; sly, acute fellow.
pajarraco *m* large bird; cunning fellow.
paje *m* page.
pajita *f* (drinking) straw.
pajizo, za *adj* straw-colored.
pala *f* shovel.
palabra *f* word; **de ~** by word of mouth.
palabrota *f* swearword.
palaciego, ga *adj* pertaining *or* relating to the palace; ● *m* courtier.
palacio *m* palace.
paladar *m* palate; taste, relish.
paladear *vt* to taste.
palanca *f* lever.

palangana *f* basin.
palco *m* box in a theater.
paleta *f* bat; palette; trowel.
paleto, ta *m/f* rustic.
paliar *vt* to mitigate.
paliativo, va *adj*, *m* palliative.
palidecer *vi* to turn pale.
palidez *f* paleness, wanness.
pálido, da *adj* pallid, pale.
palillo small stick; toothpick.
paliza *f* beating, thrashing.
palma *f* palm tree; palm of the hand; palm leaf.
palmada *f* slap, clap; **~s** *pl* clapping of hands, applause.
palmatoria *f* candlestick; cane.
palmear *vi* to slap; to clap.
palmera *f* palm tree.
palmeta *f* cane.
palmo *m* palm; small amount.
palmotear *vi* to slap; to applaud.
palmoteo *m* clapping of hands.
palo *m* stick; cudgel; blow given with a stick; post; mast; bat; suit at cards; **~s** *pl* masting.
paloma *f* pigeon, dove; **~ torcaz** ring dove; **~ zorita** wood pigeon.
palomar *m* pigeon house.
palomilla *f* moth; wing nut; angle iron.
palomino *m* young pigeon.
palomitas *fpl* popcorn.
palpable *adj* palpable, evident.
palpar *vt* to feel, to touch, to grope.
palpitación *f* palpitation, panting.
palpitante *adj* palpitating; (*fig*) burning.
palta *f* avocado (pear).
paludismo *m* malaria.
palpitar *vi* to palpitate.
palurdo, da *adj* rustic, clownish, rude.
pampa *f* pampa(s), prairie.
pámpano *m* vine branch.
pamplina *f* futility, trifle.
pan *m* bread; loaf; food in general.
pana *f* corduroy.
panacea *f* panacea, universal medicine.
panadería *f* baker's (shop).
panadero *m* baker.
panal *m* honeycomb; sweet rusk.
pancarta *f* placard.
panda *m* panda.
pandereta *f* tambourine.
pandilla *f* group; gang; clique.
panegírico, ca *adj* panegyrical; ● *m* eulogy.
panel *m* panel.
panfleto *m* pamphlet.
pánico *m* panic.
panorama *m* panorama.
pantalón *m* *or* **pantalones** *mpl* pants; trousers.
pantalla *f* screen; lampshade.
pantano *m* marsh; reservoir; obstacle, difficulty.
pantanoso, sa *adj* marshy, fenny, boggy.
panteísta *f* pantheist.
panteón *m*: **~ familiar** family tomb.
pantera *f* panther.
pantomima *f* pantomime.
pantorrilla *f* calf (of the leg).
pantufla *m* slipper.
panza *f* belly, paunch.
panzada *f* bellyful of food.
panzudo, da *adj* big-bellied.
pañal *m* diaper.
paño *m* cloth; piece of cloth; duster, rag.
pañuelo *m* handkerchief.
papa *f* potato; ● *m*: **el P~** the Pope.
papá *m* (*fam*) dad, pop.

papada f double chin.
papagayo m parrot.
papal adj papal.
papanatas m invar (fam) simpleton.
paparrucha f piece of nonsense.
papaya f papaya.
papel m paper; writing; part acted in a play; ~ **de estraza** brown paper; ~ **sellado** stamped paper.
papeleo m red tape.
papelera f writing desk; waste basket.
papelería f stationer's (shop).
papeleta f slip of paper; ballot paper; report.
paperas fpl mumps.
papilla f baby food.
papista m papist.
paquete m packet; parcel; package tour.
par adj equal, alike, even; **sin** ~ matchless; ● m pair; couple; peer.
para prep for, to, in order to, toward, to the end that.
parabién m congratulation; felicitation.
parábola f parable; parabola.
parabólico, ca adj parabolic(al).
parabrisas m invar windshield.
paracaídas m invar parachute.
paracaidista m/f parachutist; (mil) paratrooper.
parachoques m invar bumper; shock absorber.
parada f halt; suspension; pause; stop; shutdown; stopping place; ~ **de autobús** bus stop.
paradero m halting place; term, end.
parado, da adj motionless; at a standstill; stopped; standing (up); unemployed.
paradoja f paradox.
parador m parador, state-owned hotel.
parafrasear vt to paraphrase.
paráfrasis f invar paraphrase.
paraguas m invar umbrella.
paraíso m paradise.
paraje m place, spot.
paralelo, la adj, m/f parallel.
paralítico, ca adj paralytic, palsied.
paralizar vt to paralyze; ~**se** vr to become paralyzed; (fig) to come to a standstill.
páramo m desert, wilderness.
parangón m paragon, model, comparison.
paranoico, ca m/f paranoiac.
parapeto m parapet.
parar vi to stop, to halt; ● vt to stop, to detain; **sin** ~ instantly, without delay; ~**se** vr to stop, to halt; to stand up.
pararrayos m invar lightning-rod, conductor.
parásito m parasite (fig); sponger.
parasol m parasol.
parcela f piece of ground.
parcial adj partial.
parcialidad f prejudice; bias.
parco, ca adj sober, moderate.
parche m patch.
pardo, da adj gray.
parear vt to match, to pair, to couple.
parecer m opinion, advice, counsel; countenance, air, mien; ● vi to appear; to seem; ~**se** vr to resemble.
parecido, da adj resembling, like.
pared f wall; ~ **medianera** party-wall.
pareja f pair, couple, brace; accouplement.
parejo, ja adj equal; even.
parentela f parentage, kindred.
parentesco m relationship.
paréntesis m parenthesis.
parida f a woman who has recently given birth.
paridad f parity, equality.
pariente, ta m/f relative, relation.
parir vt to give birth to; ● vi to give birth.
parking m parking lot.

parlamentar vi to parley.
parlamentario, ria m/f member of parliament; ● adj parliamentary.
parlamento m parliament.
parlanchín, ina adj, m/f chatterer, jabberer.
parlotear vi to prattle, to chatter, to gossip.
paro m strike; unemployment.
parodia f parody.
parpadear vi to blink; to flicker.
párpado m eyelid.
parque m park.
parquímetro m parking meter.
parra f vine raised on stakes or nailed to a wall.
párrafo m paragraph.
parricida m/f parricide (person).
parricidio m parricide (murder).
parrilla f grill; grille.
párroco m parish priest.
parroquia f parish; customers pl.
parroquial adj parochial.
parroquiano m parishioner; customer; ~, **na** adj parochial.
parsimonia f parsimony.
parte m message; report; ● f part; side; party; **de ocho días a esta** ~ within these last eight days; **de** ~ **a** ~ from side to side, through.
partera f midwife.
partición f partition, division.
participación f participation.
participante m/f participant.
participar vt, vi to participate, to partake.
partícipe adj participant, sharing.
participio m participle.
partícula f particle.
particular adj particular, special; ● m private individual; peculiar matter or subject treated upon.
particularidad f particularity.
particularizar vt, vr to particularize; to distinguish; to specify.
partida f departure; party; item in an account; parcel; game.
partidario, ria adj partisan; ● m/f supporter.
partido m party; match; team.
partidor m parter, divider.
partir vt to part, to divide, to separate, to cut; to break; ● vi to depart; ~**se** vr to break (in two etc).
parto m birth.
parvulario m nursery school.
pasa f raisin.
pasada f passage, passing; **de** ~ on the way, in passing.
pasadizo m narrow passage; narrow, covered way.
pasado, da adj past; bad; overdone; out of date; ● m past; ~ **mañana** the day after tomorrow; **la semana pasada** last week.
pasador m bolt; hair slide; grip.
pasaje m passage; fare; passengers.
pasajero, ra adj transient, transitory, fugitive; ● m/f traveler, passenger.
pasamanos m invar (hand)rail; banisters.
pasamontañas m invar balaclava helmet.
pasaporte m passport.
pasar vt to pass; to surpass; to suffer; to strain; to dissemble; ● vi to pass; to happen; ~**se** vr to go over to another party; to go bad/off.
pasarela f footbridge; gangway.
pasatiempo m pastime, amusement.
Pascua f Passover; Easter.
pase m pass; showing; permit.
paseante m walker.
pasear vt, vi to walk; to walk about; ~**se** vr to walk.
paseo m walk.
pasillo m passage.
pasión f passion.
pasionaria f passionflower.
pasivo, va adj passive.

pasmar *vt* to amaze; to numb; to chill; ~**se** *vr* to be astonished.
pasmo *m* astonishment, amazement.
pasmoso, sa *adj* marvelous, wonderful.
paso *m* pace, step; passage; manner of walking; flight of steps; accident; (*ferro*) ~ **a nivel** railroad crossing; **al** ~ on the way, in passing.
pasota *adj, m/f* (*fam*) dropout; **ser un** ~ not to care about anything.
pasta *f* paste; dough; pastry; (*fam*) dough; ~**s** *pl* pastries; pasta; ~ **de dientes** toothpaste.
pastar *vt* to pasture, to graze.
pastel *m* cake; pie; crayon for drawing.
pastelería *f* cake shop.
pasteurizado, da *adj* pasteurized.
pastilla *f* bar (of soap); tablet, pill.
pasto *m* pasture; pasture-ground; **a** ~ abundantly.
pastor *m* shepherd; pastor.
pastoso, sa *adj* mellow, doughy.
pata *f* leg (of animal *or* furniture); foot; **a la** ~ **coja** hopscotch (children's play); **a** ~ (*fam*) on foot; **meter la** ~ to put one's foot in it.
patada *f* kick.
patalear *vi* to kick about violently.
pataleo *m* act of stamping one's foot.
pataleta *f* fit; swoon.
patán *m* clown, churl, countryman.
patata *f* potato.
patatús *m* swoon, fainting fit.
paté *m* pâté.
patear *vt* to kick; to stamp on.
patente *adj* patent, manifest, evident; ● *f* patent; warrant.
paternal *adj* paternal, fatherly.
paternidad *f* paternity, fatherhood.
paterno, na *adj* paternal, fatherly.
patético, ca *adj* pathetic.
patíbulo *m* gallows *pl*.
patillas *fpl* sideburns.
patín *m* skate; runner.
patinaje *m* skating.
patinar *vi* to skate; to skid; (*fam*) to blunder.
patio *m* courtyard; playground (in schools).
patizambo, ba *adj* bandy-legged.
pato *m* duck.
patochada *f* blunder, nonsense, folly.
patología *f* pathology.
patológico, ca *adj* pathological.
patoso, sa *adj* (*fam*) clumsy.
patraña *f* lie.
patria *f* native country.
patriarca *m* patriarch.
patriarcado *m* patriarchate.
patriarcal *adj* patriarchal.
patrimonial *adj* patrimonial.
patrimonio *m* patrimony.
patrio, tria *adj* native, paternal.
patriota *m/f* patriot.
patriótico, ca *adj* patriotic.
patriotismo *m* patriotism.
patrocinar *vt* to sponsor; to back, to support.
patrocinio *m* sponsorship; backing, support.
patrón, ona *m/f* boss, master/mistress; landlord/lady; patron saint; ● *m* pattern.
patronal *adj*: **la clase** ~ management.
patronato *m* patronage, sponsorship; trust, foundation.
patronímico *m* patronymic.
patrulla *f* patrol.
patrullar *vi* to patrol, camp *or* garrison.
paulatino, na *adj* slowly, by degrees.
pausa *f* pause; repose.
pausado, da *adj* slow, deliberate; calm, quiet, paused.
pausar *vi* to pause.

pauta *f* guideline.
pavesa *f* embers, hot cinders.
pavía *f* peach with hard stone.
pavimento *m* pavement, paving.
pavo *m* turkey; ~ **real** peacock.
pavonearse *vr* to strut, to walk with affected dignity.
pavor *m* dread, terror.
pavoroso, sa *adj* awful, formidable.
payaso, sa *m/f* clown.
payo, ya *m/f* non-gypsy (for a gypsy).
paz *f* peace; tranquillity, ease.
peaje *m* toll.
peana *f* pedestal; footstool.
peatón *m* pedestrian.
peca *f* freckle, spot.
pecado *m* sin.
pecador, ra *m/f* sinner.
pecaminoso, sa *adj* sinful.
pecar *vi* to sin.
pecoso, sa *adj* freckled.
peculiar *adj* peculiar, special.
pecuniario, ria *adj* pecuniary.
pecho *m* chest; breast(s); teat; bosom; (*fig*) courage, valor; **dar el** ~ to suckle; **tomar a** ~ to take to heart.
pechuga *f* breast of a fowl; (*fam*) bosom.
pedagogía *f* pedagogy.
pedagógico, ca *adj* pedagogic.
pedagogo *m* pedagogue.
pedal *m* pedal.
pedalear *vi* to pedal.
pedante *adj* pedantic; ● *m/f* pedant.
pedantería *f* pedantry.
pedazo *m* piece, bit.
pedernal *m* flint.
pedestal *m* pedestal, foot.
pediatra *m/f* pediatrician.
pedicuro, ra *m/f* chiropodist.
pedido *m* (*com*) order; request.
pedir *vt* to ask for; to petition, to beg, to order; to need, to solicit; ● *vi* to ask.
pedo *m* (*fam*) fart (*sl*).
pedrada *f* throw of a stone.
pedregal *m* place full of stones.
pedregoso, sa *adj* stony.
pedrería *f* collection of precious stones.
pedrisco *m* hailstone.
pedrusco *m* rough piece of stone.
pegadizo, za *adj* clammy, sticky; catchy; contagious.
pegajoso, sa *adj* sticky, viscous; contagious; attractive.
pegamento *m* glue.
pegar *vt* to cement; to join, to unite; to beat; ~ **fuego** to set fire to; ● *vi* to stick; to match; ~**se** *vr* to intrude, to steal in.
pegatina *f* sticker.
pegote *m* sticking plaster; intruder, hanger-on, sponger.
peinado *m* hairstyle.
peinar *vt* to comb; to style.
peine *m* comb.
peineta *f* convex comb for women.
peladilla *f* sugared almond, burnt almond; small pebble.
pelado, da *adj* peeled; shorn; bare; broke; ● *m* (*fam*) haircut.
peladura *f* peeling; plucking.
pelaje *m* fur coat; (*fig*) appearance.
pelar *vt* to cut hair; to strip off feathers; to peel; ~**se** *vr* to peel off; to have one's hair cut.
peldaño *m* step of a flight of stairs.
pelea *f* battle, fight; quarrel.
pelear *vt* to fight, to combat; ~**se** *vr* to scuffle.
pelele *m* dummy; man of straw.
peletería *f* fur store.
peletero *m* furrier.
peliagudo, da *adj* furry; arduous, difficult.
pelícano *m* pelican.

película f film; pellicle.
peligrar vi to be in danger; to risk.
peligro m danger, risk, peril.
peligroso, sa adj dangerous, perilous.
pelirrojo, ja m/f redhead; • adj red-haired.
pelma or **pelmazo, za** m/f (fam) pain (in the neck).
pelo m hair; pile; flaw (in precious stones).
pelón, ona adj hairless, bald.
pelota f ball.
pelotazo m blow with a ball.
pelotera f quarrel.
pelotón m large ball; (mil) platoon.
peluca f wig.
peluche m: **muñeco de** ~ soft toy.
peludo, da adj hairy.
peluquería f hairdresser's; barber's (shop).
peluquero m hairdresser; barber.
pelusa f bloom on fruit; fluff.
pellejo m skin, hide; pelt; peel; wine skin, leather bag for wine; oilskin; drunkard.
pelliza f fur jacket.
pellizcar vt to pinch.
pellizco m pinch; nip; small bit; (fig) remorse.
pena f punishment, pain; **a duras** ~s with great difficulty or trouble.
penacho m tuft on the heads of some birds; crest.
penal adj penal.
penalidad f suffering, trouble; hardship; penalty.
penalti or **penalty** m penalty (kick).
penar vi to suffer pain; • vt to chastise.
pendencia f quarrel, dispute.
pendenciero, ra adj quarrelsome.
pender vi to be pending, to hang over; to depend.
pendiente f slope, declivity; • m earring; • adj pending, unsettled.
pendón m standard; banner.
péndulo m pendulum.
pene m penis.
penetración f penetration; complete intelligence.
penetrante adj deep; sharp; piercing; searching; biting.
penetrar vt to penetrate.
penicilina f penicillin.
península f peninsula.
penique m penny.
penitencia f penitence; penalty, fine.
penitenciaría f prison.
penitenciario m penitentiary.
penitente adj penitent, repentant; • m penitent.
penoso, sa adj painful.
pensador, ra m/f thinker.
pensamiento m thought, thinking.
pensar vi to think.
pensativo, va adj pensive, thoughtful.
pensión f guest-house; pension; toil.
pensionista m/f pensioner; lodger.
Pentecostés m Pentecost, Whitsuntide.
penúltimo, ma adj penultimate, last but one.
penumbra f half-light.
penuria f penury, poverty, neediness, extreme want.
peña f rock, large stone.
peñasco m large rock.
peñón m rocky mountain.
peón m day laborer; foot soldier; pawn (at chess).
peonía f (bot) peony.
peonza f spinning top.
peor adj, adv worse; worse and worse.
pepinillo m gherkin.
pepino m cucumber.
pepita f kernel; pip.
pepitoria f fricassée.
pequeñez f littleness; triviality.
pequeño, ña adj little, small; young.

pera f pear.
peral m pear tree.
percance m perquisite; bad luck, setback.
percatarse vr: ~ **de** to notice.
percepción f perception, notion.
perceptible adj perceptible, perceivable.
percibir vt to receive; to perceive, to comprehend.
percusión f percussion.
percha f coat hook; coat hanger; perch.
perder vt to lose; to waste; to miss; ~**se** vr to go astray; to be lost; to be spoiled.
perdición f losing of a thing; perdition, ruin, loss.
pérdida f loss, damage; object lost.
perdido, da adj lost, strayed.
perdigón m young partridge; ~**ones** pl hailshot.
perdiz f partridge.
perdón m pardon; mercy; ¡~! sorry!
perdonable adj pardonable.
perdonar vt to pardon, to forgive; to excuse.
perdurable adj perpetual, everlasting.
perdurar vi to last; to still exist.
perecedero, ra adj perishable.
perecer vi to perish, to die; to shatter (an object).
peregrinación f pilgrimage.
peregrinar vi to go on a pilgrimage.
peregrino, na adj (fig) strange; • m pilgrim.
perejil m parsley.
perenne adj perennial, perpetual.
perentorio, ria adj peremptory, decisive.
pereza f laziness, idleness.
perezoso, sa adj lazy, idle.
perfección f perfection.
perfeccionar vt to perfect, to complete, to finish.
perfecto, ta adj perfect, complete.
perfidia f perfidy.
pérfido, da adj perfidious.
perfil m profile.
perfilado, da adj well-formed, delicate (of features).
perfilar vt to draw profiles; to outline; ~**se** vr to show up against.
perforar vt to perforate; to drill; to punch a hole in; • vi to drill.
perfumador m perfumer.
perfumar vt to perfume.
perfume m perfume.
perfumería f perfumery.
pergamino m parchment.
pericia f skill, knowledge, connoisseurship.
periferia f periphery; outskirts.
periférico m beltway.
perífrasis f periphrasis, circumlocution.
perímetro m circumference, perimeter.
periódico, ca adj periodical; • m newspaper.
periodista m/f journalist.
período m period.
peripecia f vicissitude; sudden change.
peripuesto, ta adj dressed up, very spruce.
periquito m budgie.
perito, ta adj skillful, experienced; • m/f expert; skilled worker; technician.
perjudicar vt to prejudice, to injure, to hurt, to damage.
perjudicial adj prejudicial, damaging.
perjuicio m damage, harm.
perjurar vi to perjure, to swear falsely; to swear.
perjurio m perjury, false oath.
perjuro, ra adj perjured; • m/f perjurer.
perla f pearl; **de** ~**s** fine.
permanecer vi to stay; to continue to be.
permanencia f permanence; stay.
permanente adj permanent.
permiso m permission, leave, license.
permitir vt to permit, to allow.

permuta f permutation, exchange.
permutar vt to exchange, to permute.
pernera f trouser leg.
pernicioso, sa adj pernicious, destructive; wicked.
pernio m hinge.
perno m bolt.
pernoctar vi to spend the night.
pero m kind of apple; ● conj but, yet.
perogrullada f truism, platitude.
perol m large metal pan.
perorata f harangue, speech.
perpendicular adj perpendicular.
perpetrar vt to perpetrate, to commit a crime.
perpetuar vt to perpetuate.
perpetuidad f perpetuity.
perpetuo, tua adj perpetual.
perplejidad f perplexity.
perplejo, ja adj perplexed.
perra f bitch; (fam) money.
perrera f kennel.
perro m dog.
persecución f persecution; toil, trouble, fatigue.
perseguidor m persecutor.
perseguir vt to pursue; to persecute; to chase after.
perseverancia f perseverance, constancy.
perseverante adj persistant.
perseverar vi to persevere, to persist.
persiana f (Venetian) blind.
persignarse vr to make the sign of the cross.
persistencia f persistence, steadiness.
persistir vi to persist.
persona f person; de ~ a ~ from person to person.
personaje m celebrity; character.
personal adj personal; single; ● m personnel.
personalidad f personality.
personarse vr to appear in person.
personificar vt to personify.
perspectiva f perspective; view; outlook.
perspicacia f perspicacity, clear-sightedness.
perspicaz adj perspicacious, quick-sighted.
persuadir vt to persuade; ~se vr to be persuaded.
persuasión f persuasion.
persuasivo, va adj persuasive.
pertenecer vi to belong to, to appertain, to concern.
pertenencia f ownership; ~s pl possessions.
perteneciente adj: ~ a belonging to.
pértiga f long pole or rod.
pertinacia f pertinacity, obstinacy, stubbornness.
pertinaz adj pertinacious, obstinate.
pertinente adj relevant; appropriate.
pertrechar vt to supply a place with ammunition and other warlike stores; to dispose, to arrange, to prepare; ~se vr to be provided with the necessary defensive stores and arms.
pertrechos mpl tools, instruments; ammunition, warlike stores.
perturbación f perturbation; disturbance.
perturbado, da adj mentally unbalanced.
perturbador m disturber.
perturbar vt to perturb, to disturb.
perversidad f perversity.
perversión f perversion; depravation, corruption.
perverso, sa adj perverse, extremely wicked.
pervertido, da adj perverted; ● m/f pervert.
pervertir vt to pervert, to corrupt.
pesa f weight.
pesadez f heaviness; gravity, weight; slowness; peevishness, fretfulness; trouble, fatigue.
pesadilla f nightmare.
pesado, da adj peevish, troublesome, cumbersome; tedious; heavy, weighty.
pesadumbre f weightiness, gravity; quarrel, dispute; grief, trouble.

pésame m message of condolence.
pesar m sorrow, grief; repentance; a ~ de in spite of, notwithstanding; ● vi to weigh; to repent; ● vt to weigh.
pesario m pessary.
pesaroso, sa adj sorrowful, full of repentance; restless, uneasy.
pesca f fishing, fishery.
pescadería f fish market.
pescado m fish (in general).
pescador m fisher, fisherman.
pescar vt to fish, to catch fish; ● vi to fish.
pescuezo m neck.
pesebre m crib, manger.
peseta f peseta.
pesimista m pessimist.
pésimo, ma adj very bad.
peso m weight, heaviness; balance-scales.
pespunte m back-stitching.
pesquero, ra adj fishing compd.
pesquisa f inquiry, examination.
pestaña f eyelash.
pestañear vi to blink.
pestañeo m blink.
peste f pest, plague, pestilence.
pesticida m pesticide.
pestífero, ra adj pestilential.
pestilencia f pestilence.
pestillo m bolt.
petaca f covered hamper; tobacco pouch.
pétalo m petal.
petardo m petard; cheat, fraud, imposition.
petate m straw-bed; sleeping mat of the Indians; (mar) sailors' beddings on board; (mar) passengers' baggage; poor fellow.
petición f petition, demand.
peto m breastplate; bodice.
petrificar(se) vt, vr to petrify.
petróleo m oil, petroleum.
petrolero, ra adj petroleum compd; ● m (oil) tanker; (com) oil man.
petulancia f petulance, insolence.
petulante adj petulant, insolent.
peyorativo, va adj pejorative.
pez m fish; ● f pitch.
pezón m nipple.
pezuña f hoof.
piadoso, sa adj pious, mild, merciful; moderate.
pianista m/f pianist.
piano m piano.
piar vi to squeak, to chirp.
piara f herd of swine; flock of ewes.
pibe, ba m/f boy/girl.
pica f pike.
picacho m sharp point.
picadero m riding school.
picadillo m minced meat.
picado, da adj pricked; minced, chopped; bad (tooth); cross.
picador m riding master; picador.
picadura f prick; puncture.
picante adj hot; racy, spicy.
picapedrero m stonecutter.
picaporte m doorhandle; latch.
picar vt to prick; to sting, to mince; to nibble; to itch; ~se vr to be piqued; to take offense; to be moth-eaten; to begin to rot.
picardía f roguery; deceit, malice; lewdness.
picaresco, ca adj roguish; picaresque.
pícaro, ra adj roguish; mischievous, malicious; sly; ● m/f rogue, knave.
picazón f itching, prurience; displeasure.
pico m beak; bill, nib; peak; pick-ax.
picotazo m peck of a bird.
picotear vt to peck (of birds).

picudo, da *adj* beaked; sharp-pointed.
pichón *m* young pigeon.
pie *m* foot; leg; basis; trunk (of trees); foundation; occasion; a
  ~ on foot.
piedad *f* piety; mercy, pity.
piedra *f* stone.
piel *f* skin; hide; peel.
pienso *m* fodder.
pierna *f* leg.
pieza *f* piece; room.
pigmeo, mea *m, adj* pigmy.
pijama *m* pajamas *pl*.
pila *f* battery; trough; font; sink; pile, heap; **nombre de ~**
  first name.
pilar *m* basin; pillar.
píldora *f* pill.
pileta *f* basin; swimming pool.
pilotaje *m* pilotage.
piloto *m* pilot.
piltrafa *f* piece of meat that is nearly all skin.
pillaje *m* pillage, plunder.
pillar *vt* to pillage, to plunder, to foray, to seize; to catch onto;
  to catch.
pillo, lla *m, adj* rascal, scoundrel.
pimentón *m* paprika.
pimienta *f* pepper.
pimiento *m* pepper, pimiento.
pinacoteca *f* art gallery.
pináculo *m* pinnacle.
pinar *m* grove of pines.
pincel *m* paintbrush.
pincelada *f* dash with a paintbrush.
pinchar *vt* to prick; to puncture.
pinchazo *m* prick; puncture; (*fig*) prod.
pinchito *m* shish kebab.
pincho *m* thorn; snack.
pingajo *m* rag, tatter.
ping-pong *m* table tennis.
pingüe *adj* fat, greasy; fertile.
pingüino *m* penguin.
pino *m* (*bot*) pine.
pinta *f* spot, blemish, scar; mark on playing cards; pint.
pintado, da *adj* painted, mottled; **venir ~** to fit exactly.
pintar *vt* to paint, to picture; to describe; to exaggerate; ● *vi*
  to paint; (*fam*) to count, to be important; **~se** *vr* to paint
  one's face.
pintarrajear *vt* to daub.
pintarrajo *m* daub.
pintor *m* painter.
pintoresco, ca *adj* picturesque.
pintura *f* painting.
pinza *f* claw; clothes peg; pincers *pl*; **~s** *pl* tweezers.
piña *f* pineapple; fir cone; group.
piñón *m* pine nut; pinion.
pío, pía *adj* pious, devout; merciful.
piojo *m* louse; troublesome hanger-on.
piojoso, sa *adj* lousy; miserable, stingy.
pionero, ra *adj* pioneering; *m/f* pioneer.
pipa *f* pipe; sunflower seed.
pipí *m* (*fam*): **hacer ~** to have to go (wee-wee).
pique *m* pique, offense taken; rivalry; **echar a ~** to sink a
  ship; **a ~** in danger, on the point of; steep (shore).
piquete *m* slight prick *or* sting; picket.
pira *f* funeral pile.
piragua *f* canoe.
piragüismo *m* canoeing.
piramidal *adj* pyramidal.
pirámide *f* pyramid.
pirata *m* pirate.
piropo *m* compliment, flattery.
pirotecnia *f* fireworks *pl*.
pirueta *f* pirouette.

pisada *f* footstep; footprint.
pisar *vt* to tread, to trample; to stamp on the ground; to
  hammer down; ● *vi* to tread, to walk.
piscina *f* swimming pool.
Piscis *m* Pisces (sign of the zodiac).
piso *m* apartment; tread, trampling; floor, pavement; floor,
  story.
pisotear *vt* to trample, to tread under foot.
pista *f* trace, footprint; clue.
pisto *m* thick broth.
pistola *f* pistol.
pistolera *f* pistol holster.
pistolero, ra *m/f* gunman/woman, gangster.
pistoletazo *m* pistol shot.
pistón *m* piston; (musical) key.
pita *f* (*bot*) agave.
pitar *vt* to blow; to whistle at; ● *vi* to whistle; to toot one's
  horn; to smoke.
pitillo *m* cigarette.
pito *m* whistle, horn.
pitón *m* python.
pitonisa *f* sorceress, enchantress.
pitorreo *m* joke; **estar de ~** to be joking.
pizarra *f* slate.
pizarral *m* slate quarry, slate pit.
pizca *f* mite; pinch.
placa *f* plate; badge.
placentero, ra *adj* joyful, merry.
placer *m* pleasure, delight; ● *vt* to please.
plácido, da *adj* placid.
plaga *f* plague.
plagar *vt* to plague, to torment.
plagio *m* plagiarism.
plan *m* plan; design, plot.
plana *f* trowel; page (of a book); level; **~ mayor** (*mil*) staff.
plancha *f* plate; iron; gangway.
planchar *vt* to iron.
planeador *m* glider.
planear *vt* to plan; ● *vi* to glide.
planeta *m* planet.
planetario *adj* planetary.
planicie *f* plain.
planificación *f* planning; **~ familiar** family planning.
planisferio *m* planisphere.
plano, na *adj* plain, level, flat; ● *m* plan, ground plot; **~
  inclinado** (*ferro*) dead level.
planta *f* plant; plantation.
plantación *f* plantation.
plantar *vt* to plant; to fix upright; to strike *or* hit a blow; to
  found, to establish; **~se** *vr* to stand upright.
plantear *vt* to plan, to trace.
plantilla *f* personnel; insole of a shoe.
plantón *m* long wait; (*mil*) sentry.
plañir *vi* to lament, to grieve, to bewail.
plasmar *vt* to mold; to represent.
plasta *f* paste, soft clay; mess.
plástico, ca *adj* plastic; ● *m* plastic; ● *f* (art of) sculpture.
plata *f* silver; plate (wrought silver); cash; **en ~** briefly.
plataforma *f* platform; **~ giratoria** (*ferro*) turnplate, turntable.
plátano *m* banana; plane tree.
plateado, da *adj* silvered; plated.
platería *f* silversmith's shop; trade of silversmith.
plática *f* discourse, conversation.
platicar *vi* to converse.
platillo *m* saucer; **~s** *pl* cymbals; **~ volador** *o* **volante** flying
  saucer.
platino *m* platinum; **~s** *pl* contact points.
plato *m* dish; plate.
platónico, ca *adj* platonic.
plausible *adj* plausible.
playa *f* beach.

playera f T-shirt; ~s pl canvas shoes.
plaza f square; place; office, employment; room; seat.
plazo m term; installment; expiry date.
pleamar f (mar) high water.
plebe f common people, populace.
plebeyo, ya adj plebeian; ● m commoner.
plebiscito m plebiscite.
plegable adj pliable; folding.
plegar vt to fold, to plait.
plegaria f prayer.
pleitear vi to plead, to litigate.
pleito m contract, bargain; dispute, controversy, debate; law-
suit.
plenamente adv fully, completely.
plenario, ria adj complete, full.
plenilunio m full moon.
plenipotenciario m plenipotentiary.
plenitud f fullness, abundance.
pleno, na adj full; complete; ● m plenum.
pliego m sheet of paper.
pliegue m fold, plait.
plisado, da adj pleated; ● m pleating.
plomero m plumber.
plomizo, za adj leaden.
plomo m lead; a ~ perpendicularly.
pluma f feather, plume.
plumaje m plumage; plume.
plumero m bunch of feathers; feather duster.
plumón m felt-tip pen; marker; down.
plural adj (gr) plural.
pluralidad f plurality.
población f population; town.
poblado m town, village, inhabited place.
poblador m populator, founder.
poblar vt to populate, to people; to fill, to occupy.
pobre adj poor.
pobreza f poverty, poorness.
pocilga f pig sty.
pocillo m coffee cup.
pócima or poción f potion.
poco, ca adj little, scanty; few; ● adv little; ~ a ~ gently;
little by little; ● m a small part.
poda f pruning of trees.
podadera f pruning knife.
podar vt to prune.
podenco m hound.
poder m power, authority; command; force; ● vi to be able; to
possess the power of doing or performing.
poderío m power, authority; wealth, riches pl.
poderoso, sa adj powerful; eminent, excellent.
podredumbre f putrid matter; grief.
podrido, da adj rotten, bad; (fig) rotten.
podrir or pudrir vt to rot, to putrefy; ~se vr to rot, to decay.
poema m poem.
poesía f poetry.
poeta m poet.
poético, ca adj poetical.
poetisa f poetess.
poetizar vt to poetize.
polar adj polar.
polea f pulley; (mar) tackle-block.
polémica f polemic.
polémico, ca adj polemical.
polen m pollen.
policía f police; ● m/f policeman/woman.
polideportivo m sports center or complex.
poligamia f polygamy.
polígamo m polygamist.
polígono m polygon.
polilla f moth.
polio f polio.
pólipo m polypus.

politécnico adj polytechnical.
politeísmo m polytheism.
política f politics; policy.
político, ca adj political; ● m/f politician.
póliza f written order; policy.
polizón m stowaway.
polo m pole; ice lolly; polo; polo neck.
polución f pollution.
polvareda f cloud of dust.
polvera f powder compact.
polvo m powder, dust.
pólvora f gunpowder.
polvoriento, ta adj dusty.
polvorín m powder reduced to the finest dust; powder flask.
pollera f skirt.
pollería f poulterer's (shop).
pollo m chicken.
pomada f cream, ointment.
pomelo m grapefruit.
pómez f: piedra ~ pumice stone.
pompa f pomp; bubble.
pomposo, sa adj pompous.
pómulo m cheekbone.
ponche m punch.
poncho, cha adj soft, mild; ● m sleeveless dress.
ponderación f pondering, considering; exaggeration.
ponderar vt to ponder, to weigh; to exaggerate.
ponedero, ra adj egg-laying; capable of being laid or placed; ●
m nest; nest egg.
poner vt to put, to place; to impose; to lay eggs; ~se vr to
oppose; to set (of stars); to become.
poniente m west; west wind.
pontificado m pontificate.
pontífice m Pope, pontiff.
pontificio, cia adj pontifical.
pontón m pontoon.
ponzoña f poison.
ponzoñoso, sa adj poisonous.
popa f (mar) poop, stern.
populacho m populace, mob.
popular adj popular.
popularidad f popularity.
popularizarse vr to become popular.
populoso, sa adj populous.
poquedad f paucity, littleness; cowardice.
por prep for, by, about; by means of; through; on account of.
porcelana f porcelain, china.
porcentaje m percentage.
porción f part, portion; lot.
porcuno, na adj hoggish.
pordiosero, ra m/f beggar.
porfiar vt to dispute obstinately; to persist in a pursuit.
pormenor m detail.
pornografía f pornography.
poro m pore.
porosidad f porosity.
poroso, sa adj porous.
porque conj because; since; so that.
porqué m cause, reason.
porquería f nastiness, foulness; brutishness, rudeness; trifle;
dirty action.
porqueriza f pig sty.
porra f cudgel.
porrillo : a ~ adv copiously, abundantly.
porrón m spouted wine jar.
portada f portal, porch; frontispiece.
portador, ra m/f carrier, porter.
portaequipajes m invar trunk (in car); baggage rack.
portal m porch.
portamonedas m invar purse.
portarse vr to behave.
portátil adj portable.

porta(a)viones *m invar* aircraft carrier.
portavoz *m/f* spokesman/woman.
portazo *m* bang of a door; banging a door in one's face.
porte *m* transportation (charges); deportment, demeanor, conduct.
portento *m* prodigy, portent.
portentoso, sa *adj* prodigious, marvelous, strange.
portería *f* porter's office; goal.
portero *m* porter, gatekeeper.
portezuela *f* little door.
pórtico *m* portico, porch, lobby.
portilla *f or* **portillo** *m* aperture in a wall; gate; gap, breach.
portón *m* inner door of a house.
porvenir *m* future.
pos *prep*: en ~ after, behind; in pursuit of.
posada *f* shelter; inn, hotel.
posaderas *fpl* buttocks.
posadero *m* innkeeper.
posar *vi* to sit, to pose; ● *vt* to lay down a burden; ~se *vr* to settle; to perch; to land.
posdata *f* postscript.
pose *f* pose.
poseedor, ra *m/f* owner, possessor; holder.
poseer *vt* to hold, to possess.
poseído, da *adj* possessed by the devil.
posesión *f* possession.
posesivo, va *adj* possessive.
posesor, ra *m/f* possessor.
posibilidad *f* possibility.
posibilitar *vt* to make possible; to make feasible.
posible *adj* possible.
posición *f* position; posture; situation.
positivo, va *adj* positive.
poso *m* sediment, dregs *pl*.
posponer *vt* to postpone.
posta *f*: a ~ on purpose, on stage.
postal *adj* postal; ● *f* postcard.
poste *m* post, pillar.
póster *m* poster.
postergación *f* missing out, putting back, passing over.
postergar *vt* to leave behind; to postpone.
posteridad *f* posterity.
posterior *adj* posterior.
posterioridad *f*: con ~ subsequently, later.
postigo *m* wicket; postern; pane *or* sash of a window.
postizo, za *adj* artificial (not natural); ● *m* false hair.
postor *m* bidder at a public sale; bettor.
postración *f* prostration.
postrar *vt* to humble, to humiliate; ~se *vr* to prostrate oneself.
postre *m* dessert.
postrer, postrero, ra *adj* last, hindermost.
postrimería *f* last portion *or* last years of life.
póstumo, ma *adj* posthumous.
postura *f* posture, position; attitude; bet, wager; agreement, convention.
potable *adj* drinkable.
potaje *m* pottage; drink made up of several ingredients; medley of various useless things.
pote *m* pot, jar; flower pot.
potencia *f* power; mightiness.
potencial *m* potential.
potentado *m* potentate, prince.
potente *adj* potent, powerful, mighty.
potestad *f* power, dominion; jurisidiction.
potro, ra *m/f* colt; foal.
poyo *m* bench (near the street-door).
pozo *m* well.
práctica *f* practice.
practicable *adj* practicable, feasible.
practicante *m* practicer; practitioner.
practicar *vt* to practice.

práctico, ca *adj* practical; skillful, experienced.
pradera *f* meadow.
prado *m* lawn, meadow.
pragmático, ca *adj* pragmatic.
preámbulo *m* preamble; circumlocution.
prebenda *f* prebend.
precario, ria *adj* precarious.
precaución *f* precaution.
precaver *vt* to prevent, to guard against.
precedencia *f* precedence; preference; superiority.
precedente *adj* precedent, foregoing.
preceder *vt* to precede, to go before.
precepto *m* precept, order.
preceptor *m* master, teacher, preceptor.
preciado, da *adj* esteemed, valued.
preciarse *vr* to boast, to take pride in.
precinto *m* seal.
precio *m* price, value.
preciosidad *f* excellence, preciousness.
precioso, sa *adj* precious; (*fam*) beautiful.
precipicio *m* precipice; violent, sudden fall; ruin, destruction.
precipitación *f* precipitation, rush.
precipitado, da *adj* precipitate, headlong, hasty.
precipitar *vt* to precipitate; ~se *vr* to act hastily; to rush.
precisamente *adv* precisely; exactly.
precisar *vt* to compel, to oblige, to need.
precisión *f* necessity, compulsion; preciseness.
preciso, sa *adj* necessary, requisite; precise, exact; abstracted.
precocidad *f* precocity.
preconizar *vt* to proclaim; to recommend.
precoz *adj* precocious.
precursor, ra *m/f* harbinger, forerunner.
predecesor, ra *m/f* predecessor.
predecir *vt* to foretell.
predestinación *f* predestination.
predestinar *vt* to predestine.
predicación *f* preaching, sermon.
predicado *m* predicate.
predicador *m* preacher.
predicar *vt* to preach.
predicción *f* prediction.
predilección *f* predilection.
predilecto, ta *adj* darling, favorite.
predisponer *vt* to predispose; to prejudice.
predisposición *f* inclination; prejudice.
predominar *vt* to predominate, to prevail; to command.
predominio *m* predominant power, superiority.
preeminencia *f* pre-eminence, superiority.
preeminente *adj* pre-eminent, superior.
preescolar *adj* pre-school.
preexistencia *f* pre-existence.
preexistente *adj* pre-existent.
preexistir *vt* to pre-exist, to exist before.
prefabricado, da *adj* prefabricated.
prefacio *m* preface.
prefecto *m* prefect.
prefectura *f* prefecture.
preferencia *f* preference.
preferible *adj* preferable.
preferir *vt* to prefer.
prefijar *vt* to prefix; to fix beforehand.
pregón *m* proclamation; hue and cry.
pregonar *vt* to proclaim.
pregonero *m* town crier.
pregunta *f* question; inquiry.
preguntar *vt* to ask; to question, to demand; to inquire.
preguntón, ona *m/f* inquisitive person.
prehistórico, ca *adj* prehistoric.
prejuicio *m* prejudgment; preconception; prejudice.
prelado *m* prelate.
preliminar *adj, m* preliminary.

preludio m prelude.
prematuro, ra adj premature, precocious.
premeditación f premeditation, forethought.
premeditar vt to premeditate, to think out.
premiar vt to reward, to remunerate.
premio m reward, recompense; premium.
premisa f premise.
premura f narrowness, pressure, haste, hurry.
prenatal adj pre-natal.
prenda f pledge; garment; sweetheart; person or thing dearly loved; ~s pl accomplishments, talents.
prendar vt to enchant; ~se vr: ~ de uno to fall in love with someone.
prendedor m brooch.
prender vt to seize, to catch, to lay hold of; to imprison; • vi to take root; ~se vr to catch fire.
prendimiento m seizure; capture.
prensa f press.
prensar vt to press.
preñado, da adj pregnant.
preñez f pregnancy.
preocupación f worry, preoccupation.
preocupado, da adj worried; anxious.
preocupar(se) vt (vr) to worry.
preparación f preparation.
preparador, ra m/f trainer.
preparar vt to prepare; ~se vr to be prepared.
preparativo, va adj preparatory, preliminary, qualifying; • m preparation.
preparatorio, ria adj preparatory.
preponderancia f preponderance.
preponderar vi to preponderate, to prevail.
preposición f (gr) preposition.
prepucio m foreskin.
prerrogativa f prerogative, privilege.
presa f capture, seizure; dike, dam.
presagiar vt to presage, to forebode.
presagio m omen.
presbítero m priest, clergyman.
presciencia f prescience, foreknowledge.
prescindir vi: ~ de to do without; to dispense with.
prescribir vt to prescribe.
prescripción f prescription.
presencia f presence.
presenciar vt to attend; to be present at; to witness.
presentación f presentation.
presentador, ra m/f (rad, TV) presenter.
presentar vt to present; to introduce; to offer; to show; ~se vr to present oneself; to appear; to run (as candidate); to apply.
presente m present, gift; • adj present.
presentemente adv presently, now.
presentimiento m presentiment.
presentir vt to have a premonition.
preservación f preservation.
preservar vt to preserve, to defend.
preservativo m condom, sheath.
presidencia f presidency.
presidente m president.
presidiario m convict.
presidio m penitentiary, prison.
presidir vt to preside at.
presilla f clip; loop in clothes.
presión f pressure, pressing.
presionar vt to press; (fig) to put pressure on.
preso, sa m/f prisoner.
prestado, da adj on loan; pedir ~ to borrow.
prestamista m borrower, lender.
préstamo m loan.
prestar vt to lend.
presteza f quickness, haste, speed.
prestigio m prestige.
presto, ta adj quick, prompt, ready; • adv soon, quickly.

presumible adj presumable.
presumido, da adj presumptous, arrogant.
presumir vt to presume, to conjecture; • vi to be conceited.
presunción f presumption, conjecture; conceit.
presunto, ta adj supposed; so-called.
presuntuoso, sa adj presumptuous.
presuponer vt to presuppose.
presupuesto m presumed cost; budget.
presuroso, sa adj hasty, prompt, quick; nimble.
pretencioso, sa adj pretentious.
pretender vt to pretend, to claim; to try, to attempt.
pretendiente m pretender; suitor.
pretensión f pretension.
pretérito, ta adj (gr) preterit, past.
pretextar vt to find a pretext or pretense.
pretexto m pretext, pretense.
prevalacer vi to prevail; to outshine; to take root.
prevención f disposition, preparation; supply of provisions; foresight; prevention; (mil) police guard.
prevenido, da adj prepared; careful, cautious, foreseeing.
prevenir vt to prepare; to foresee, to foreknow; to prevent; to warn; ~se vr to be prepared; to be predisposed.
preventivo, va adj preventive.
prever vt to foresee, to forecast.
previo, via adj previous.
previsión f foresight, prevision, forecast.
previsor, ra adj far-sighted.
prima f bonus; female cousin.
primacía f priority; primacy.
primado m primate.
primario, ria adj primary.
primavera f spring (the season).
primeramente adv in the first place, mainly.
primer = primero
primero, ra adj first, prior, former; • adv first, rather, sooner.
primicia f first fruits pl.
primitivo, va adj primitive, original.
primo, ma m cousin.
primogénito, ta adj, m/f first-born.
primogenitura f primogeniture.
primor m beauty; dexterity, ability.
primordial adj basic, fundamental.
primoroso, sa adj neat, elegant, fine, excellent; handsome.
princesa f princess.
principal adj, m principal, chief.
príncipe m prince.
principiante m beginner, learner.
principiar vt to commence, to begin.
principio m beginning, commencement; principle.
pringoso, sa adj greasy; sticky.
pringue m/f grease, lard.
prioridad f priority.
prisa f speed; hurry; urgency; promptness.
prisión f prison; imprisonment.
prisionero m prisoner.
prisma m prism.
prismáticos mpl binoculars.
privación f deprivation, want.
privado, da adj private; particular.
privar vt to deprive; to prohibit; ~se vr to deprive oneself.
privativo, va adj private, one's own; particular, peculiar.
privilegiado, da adj privileged; very good.
privilegiar vt to privilege.
privilegio m privilege.
pro m/f profit, benefit, advantage.
proa f (mar) prow.
probabilidad f probability, likelihood.
probable adj probable, likely.
probado, da adj proved, tried.
probador m fitting room.
probar vt to try; to prove; to taste; • vi to try.
probeta f test tube.

problema m problem.
problemático, ca adj problematical.
procedencia m derivation.
procedente adj reasonable; proper; ~ **de** coming from.
proceder m procedure; ● vi to proceed, to go on; to act.
procedimiento m proceeding; legal procedure.
procesado, da m/f accused.
procesador m: ~ **de textos** word processor.
procesar vt to put on trial.
procesión f procession.
proceso m process, lawsuit.
proclama f proclamation, publication.
proclamación f proclamation; acclamation.
proclamar vt to proclaim.
procreación f procreation, generation.
procrear vt to procreate, to generate.
procurador m procurer; attorney; proctor.
procurar vt to try; to obtain; to produce.
prodigalidad f plenty, abundance.
prodigar vt to waste, to lavish.
prodigio m prodigy, monster.
prodigioso, sa adj prodigious, monstrous; exquisite, excellent.
pródigo, ga adj prodigal.
producción f production.
producir vt to produce; (jur) to produce as evidence; ~**se** vr to come about; to arise, to be made; to break out.
productividad f productivity.
productivo, va adj productive.
producto m product.
productor, ra adj productive; ● m/f producer.
proeza f prowess, valor, bravery.
profanación f desecration.
profanar vt to profane, to desecrate.
profano, na adj profane.
profecía f prophecy.
profesar vt to profess, to practice.
profesión f profession.
profesional adj, m/f professional.
profeso, sa adj professed.
profesor, ra m/f teacher.
profesorado m teaching profession.
profeta m prophet.
profético, ca adj prophetic.
profetizar vt to prophesy.
prófugo m fugitive.
profundidad f profundity, profoundness; depth; grandeur.
profundizar vt to go deeply into; to deepen; to penetrate.
profundo, da adj profound.
profusamente adv profusely.
profusión f profusion, prodigality.
progenie f progeny, race, generation, offspring.
progenitor m progenitor, ancestor, forefather.
programa m program.
programación f programming.
programador, ra m/f programmer.
programar vt to program.
progresar vi to progress.
progresión f progression.
progresista adj, m/f progressive.
progreso m progress.
progresivo, va adj progressive.
prohibición f prohibition, ban.
prohibir vt to prohibit, to forbid, to hinder.
prójimo m fellow creature; neighbor.
prole f offspring, progeny, race.
proletariado m proletariat.
proletario, ria adj proletarian.
proliferación f proliferation.
proliferar vi to proliferate.
prolífico, ca adj prolific.
prolijidad f prolixity; minute attention to detail.

prolojo, ja adj prolix, tedious.
prólogo m prolog(ue).
prolongación f prolongation.
prolongar vt to prolong.
promedio m average; middle.
promesa f promise.
prometer vt to promise, to assure; ~**se** vr to get engaged.
prometido, da adj promised; engaged; ● m/f fiancé/fiancée.
prominencia f protuberance.
prominente adj prominent, jutting out.
promiscuo, cua adj promiscuous, confusedly mingled; ambiguous.
promoción f promotion.
promontorio m promontory, cape.
promotor m promoter, forwarder.
promover vt to promote, to advance; to stir up.
promulgación f promulgation.
promulgar vt to promulgate, to publish.
pronombre m (gr) pronoun.
pronosticar vt to predict, to foretell, to conjecture.
pronóstico m prediction; forecast.
prontitud f promptness.
pronto, ta adj prompt, ready; ● adv promptly.
pronunciación f pronunciation.
pronunciamiento m (jur) publication; insurrection, sedition.
pronunciar vt to pronounce; to deliver; ~**se** vr to rebel.
propagación f propagation; extension.
propagador, ra m/f propagator.
propaganda f propaganda; advertising.
propagar vt to propagate.
propasar vt to go beyond, to exceed.
propender vi to incline.
propensión f propensity, inclination.
propenso, sa adj prone, inclined.
propiamente adv properly; really.
propiciar vt to favor; to cause.
propiciatorio, ria adj, m propitiatory.
propicio, cia adj propitious.
propiedad f property, possession; right of property; propriety.
propietario, ria adj, m/f proprietor.
propina f tip.
propinar vt to hit; to give.
propio, pia adj proper; own; typical; very.
proponer vt to propose.
proporción f proportion; symmetry.
proporcionado, da adj proportionate, fit, comfortable.
proporcional adj proportional.
proporcionar vt to provide; to adjust, to adapt.
proposición f proposition.
propósito m aim; purpose; a ~ on purpose.
propuesta f proposal, offer; representation.
propulsar vt to propel; (fig) to promote.
prórroga f prolongation; extension; extra time.
prorrogable adj extendable.
prorrogar vt to extend; to postpone.
prorrumpir vi to break forth, to burst forth.
prosa f prose.
prosaico, ca adj prosaic.
proscribir vt to proscribe, to outlaw.
proscripción f proscription.
proscrito, ta adj banned.
prosecución f continuation.
proseguir vt to continue; ● vi to continue, to go on.
prospección f exploration; prospecting.
prospecto m prospectus.
prosperar vi to prosper, to thrive.
prosperidad f prosperity.
próspero, ra adj prosperous.
prostíbulo m house of prostitution.
prostitución f prostitution.
prostituir vt to prostitute.

prostituta f prostitute.
protagonista m/f protagonist.
protagonizar vt to take the chief rôle in.
protección f protection.
protector m to protect.
proteger vt protector.
proteína f protein.
protesta f protest.
protestante m Protestant.
protestar vt to protest; to make public declaration of faith; ●
  vi to protest.
protocolo m protocol.
prototipo m prototype.
provecho m profit; advantage.
provechoso, sa adj profitable; advantageous.
proveedor, ra m/f purveyor.
proveer vt to provide; to provision; to decree.
provenir vi to arise, to proceed; to issue.
proverbial adj proverbial.
proverbio m proverb; ~s pl Book of Proverbs.
providencia f providence; foresight; divine providence.
providencial adj providential.
provincia f province.
provincial adj, m provincial.
provinciano, na adj provincial; country compd.
provisión f provision; store.
provisional adj provisional.
provisionalmente adv provisionally.
provocación f provocation.
provocador, ra adj provocative.
provocar vt to provoke; to lead to; to excite.
provocativo, va adj provocative.
próximamente adv soon.
proximidad f proximity, closeness.
próximo, ma adj next, near; neighboring; close.
proyección f projection; showing; influence.
proyectar vt to throw; to cast; to screen; to plan.
proyectil m projectile, missile.
proyecto m plan; project.
proyector m projector.
prudencia f prudence, wisdom.
prudente adj prudent.
prueba f proof, reason, argument; token; experiment, essay,
  attempt; relish, taste.
prurito m prurience, itching.
psicoanálisis m psychoanalysis.
psicología f psychology.
psicólogo, ga m/f psychologist.
psiquiatra m/f psychiatrist.
psiquiátrico, ca adj psychiatric.
psíquico, ca adj psychic(al).
púa f sharp point, prickle; shoot; pick.
pubertad f puberty.
publicación f publication.
publicar vt to publish, to proclaim.
publicidad f publicity.
público, ca a, m public.
puchero m earthen pot; stew.
púdico, ca adj chaste, pure.
pudiente adj rich, opulent.
pudor m bashfulness.
pudrir vt to rot; to upset; ~se vr to decay, to rot.
pueblo m town, village; population; populace.
puente m bridge.
puerco, ca adj nasty, filthy, dirty; rude, coarse; ● m pig, hog;
  ~ espín porcupine.
pueril adj childish.
puerilidad f puerility.
puerro m leek.
puerta f door, doorway, gateway; ~ trasera back door.
puerto m port, harbor, haven; narrow pass.
pues adv then, therefore; well; ¡~! well, then.

puesto m place; particular spot; post, employment; barracks;
  stand.
púgil m boxer.
pugilato m boxing.
pugna f combat, battle.
pugnar vi to fight, to combat; to struggle.
pujante adj powerful, strong, robust, stout, strapping.
pujanza f power, strength.
pujar vt to outbid; to strain.
pulcritud f beauty.
pulcro, cra adj beautiful; affected.
pulga f flea; **tener malas ~s** to be easily piqued; to be ill-
  tempered.
pulgada f inch.
pulgar m thumb.
pulir vt to polish; to put the last touches to.
pulmón m lung.
pulmonía f inflammation of the lungs.
pulpa f pulp; soft part (of fruit).
pulpería f small grocery store.
púlpito m pulpit.
pulpo m octopus.
pulsación f pulsation.
pulsador m push button.
pulsar vt to touch; to play; to press.
pulsera f bracelet.
pulso m pulse; wrist; firmness or steadiness of the hand.
pulular vi to swarm.
pulverización f pulverization.
pulverizador m spray gun.
pulverizar vt to pulverize.
pulla f smart repartee; obscene expression.
puna f (med) mountain sickness.
pungir vt to punch, to prick.
punición f punishment, chastisement.
punitivo, va adj punitive.
punta f point; end; truce.
puntada f stitch.
puntal m prop, stay, buttress.
puntapié m kick.
puntear vt to tick; to pluck the guitar; to stitch.
puntería f aiming.
puntero m pointer; ~, ra adj leading.
puntiagudo, da adj sharp-pointed.
puntilla f narrow lace edging; de ~s on tiptoe.
punto m point; end; spot; stitch.
puntuación f punctuation.
puntual adj punctual, exact; reliable.
puntualidad f punctuality.
puntualizar vt to fix; to specify.
puntuar vt to punctuate; to evaluate.
punzada f prick, sting; pain; compunction.
punzante adj sharp.
punzar vt to punch, to prick, to sting.
punzón m punch.
puñado m handful.
puñal m dagger.
puñalada f stab.
puñetazo m punch.
puño m fist; handful; wrist-band; cuff; handle.
pupila f eyeball, pupil.
pupitre m desk.
puré m puree; (thick) soup; ~ de patatas mashed potatoes.
pureza f purity, chastity.
purga f purge.
purgante m purgative.
purgar vt to purge, to purify; to atone, to expiate.
purgativo, va adj purgative, purging.
purgatorio m purgatory.
purificación f purification.
purificador, ra m/f purifier; ● adj purificatory.
purificar vt to purify.

purismo *m* purism.
purista *m* purist.
puritano, na *adj* puritanical; • *m/f* Puritan.
puro, ra *adj* pure, mere; clear; genuine; incorrupt.
púrpura *f* purple.
purpúreo, rea *adj* purple.
purulento, ta *adj* purulent.
pus *m* pus.
pusilánime *adj* pusillanimous, fainthearted.
pusilanimidad *f* pusillanimity.
pústula *f* pustule, pimple.
puta *f* whore.
putrefacción *f* putrefaction.
pútrido, da *adj* putrid, rotten.

Q

que that; who; which; what; than.
qué *adj* what?; which?; • *pn* what?; how . . . ?
quebrada *f* broken, uneven ground.
quebradero *m* breaker; ~ de cabeza worry.
quebradizo, za *adj* brittle, flexible.
quebrado *m* (*mat*) fraction.
quebradura *f* fracture; rupture, hernia.
quebrantamiento *m* fracture, rupture; breaking; weariness, fatigue; violation of the law.
quebrantar *vt* to break, to crack, to burst; to pound, to grind; to violate; to fatigue; to weaken.
quebranto *m* weakness; great loss, severe damage.
quebrar *vt* to break, to transgress a law, to violate; • *vi* to go bankrupt; ~se *vr* to break into pieces, to be ruptured.
queda *f* resting-time; (*mil*) tattoo.
quedar *vi* to stay; ~se *vr* to remain.
quedo, da *adj* quiet, still; • *adv* softly, gently.
quehacer *m* task.
queja *f* complaint.
quejarse *vr* to complain of.
quejido *m* complaint.
quejoso, sa *adj* complaining, querulous.
quejumbroso, sa *adj* complaining, plaintive.
quema *f* burning, combustion, fire.
quemador *m* burner.
quemadura *f* mark made by fire, burn.
quemar *vt* to burn; to kindle; • *vi* to be too hot; ~se *vr* to be parched with heat; to burn oneself.
quemarropa *f*: a ~ *adv* point-blank.
quemazón *f* burn; itch.
querella *f* charge; dispute; complaint.
querellarse *vr* to complain; to file a complaint.
querer *vt* to wish, to desire; to will; to love; • *m* will, desire.
querido, da *adj* dear, beloved; • *m/f* darling; lover; ~ mío *o* ~da mía my dear, my love, my darling.
querubín *m* cherub.
quesería *f* dairy.
queso *m* cheese.
quicio *m* hook, hinge (of a door).
quiebra *f* crack, fracture; bankruptcy; slump.
quien *pn* who.
quién *pn* who, whom.
quienquiera *adj* whoever.
quieto, ta *adj* still, peaceable.
quietud *f* quietness, peace, tranquillity, calmness.
quijada *f* jaw, jawbone.
quijotada *f* quixotic action.
quijote *m* quixotic person.
quijotesco, ca *adj* quixotic.
quilate *m* carat.
quilla *f* keel.
quimera *f* chimera.
quimérico, ca *adj* chimerical, fantastic.

química *f* chemistry.
químico, ca *m/f* chemist; • *adj* chemical.
quina *f* Peruvian bark.
quincalla *f* hardware.
quince *adj*, *m* fifteen; fifteenth.
quincena *f* fortnight, two weeks.
quiniela *f* football pools *pl*; ~s *pl* pools coupon.
quinientos, tas *adj* five hundred.
quinina *f* quinine.
quinquenal *adj* quinquennial.
quinquenio *m* space of five years.
quinqui *m* delinquent.
quinta *f* country house; levy, drafting of soldiers.
quintaesencia *f* quintessence.
quintilla *f* (*poet*) metrical composition of five verses.
quinto *adj* fifth; • *m* fifth; drafted soldier.
quíntuplo, pla *adj* quintuple, fivefold.
quiosco *m* bandstand; news stand.
quiromancia *f* palmistry.
quirúrgico, ca *adj* surgical.
quisquilloso, sa *adj* difficult, touchy, peevish, irritable.
quiste *m* cyst.
quitaesmalte *m* nail-polish remover.
quitamanchas *m invar* stain remover.
quitanieves *m invar* snowplow.
quitar *vt* to take away, to remove; to take off; to relieve; to annul; ~se *vr* to take off (clothes *etc*); to withdraw.
quitasol *m* parasol.
quitapón : de ~ *adv* detachable, removable.
quizá, quizás *adv* perhaps.

R

rabadilla *f* rump, croup.
rábano *m* radish.
rabia *f* rage, fury.
rabiar *vi* to be furious, to rage.
rabieta *f* touchiness, petulance, bad temper.
rabino *m* rabbi.
rabioso, sa *adj* rabid; furious.
rabo *m* tail.
racial *adj* racial, race *compd*.
racimo *m* bunch of grapes.
raciocinio *m* reasoning; argument.
ración *f* ration.
racional *adj* rational; reasonable.
racionalidad *f* rationality.
racionar *vt* to ration (out).
racismo *m* racialism.
racha *f* gust of wind; buena/mala ~ spell of good/bad luck.
radar *m* radar.
radiacion *f* radiation.
radiactivo, va *or* radioactivo, va *adj* radioactive.
radiador *m* radiator.
radiante *adj* radiant.
radiar *vi* (*poet*) to radiate.
radicación *f* taking root; becoming rooted (of a habit).
radical *adj* radical.
radicar *vt* to take root; ~se *vr* to establish oneself.
radio *f* radio; radio (set); • *m* radius; ray.
radiografía *f* x-ray.
radioterapia *f* radiotherapy.
raer *vt* to scrape, to grate; to erase.
ráfaga *f* gust; flash; burst.
raído, da *adj* scraped; worn-out; impudent.
raíz *f* root; base, basis; origin; bienes raíces *pl* landed property.
raja *f* splinter, chip of wood; chink, fissure.
rajar *vt* to split, to chop, to cleave.
rajatabla *f*: a ~ *adv* strictly.

ralea f race, breed; species.
ralo, la adj thin, rare.
ralladura f small particles taken off by grating.
rallar vt to grate.
rama f branch (of a tree, of a family); printer's chase, form.
ramadán m Mohammedan Lent.
ramaje m branches.
rambla f avenue.
ramera f whore, prostitute.
ramificación f ramification.
ramificarse vr to ramify.
ramillete m bunch.
ramo m branch of a tree.
rampa f ramp.
rampante adj rampant.
rana f frog.
rancio, cia adj rank, rancid.
ranchero m rancher; smallholder.
rancho f grub; ranch; small farm.
rango m rank, standing.
ranúnculo m (bot) crowfoot.
ranura f groove; slot.
rapacidad f rapacity.
rapadura f shaving; baldness.
rapar vt to shave; to plunder.
rapaz, za adj rapacious; ● m/f young boy or girl.
rape m shaving; monk fish.
rapé m snuff.
rapidez f speed, rapidity.
rápido, da adj quick, rapid, swift.
rapiña f robbery.
raptar vt to kidnap.
rapto m kidnaping; ecstasy, rapture; ravishment.
raqueta f racket.
raquítico, ca adj stunted; (fig) inadequate.
rareza f rarity, rareness.
raro, ra adj rare, scarce, extraordinary.
ras m: a ~ de level with; a ~ de tierra at ground level.
rasar vt to level.
rascacielos m invar skyscraper.
rascar vt to scratch, to scrape.
rasero m strickle.
rasgar vt to tear, to rip.
rasgo m dash, stroke; grand or magnanimous action; ~s pl features.
rasguear vi to form bold strokes with a pen; (mus) to strum.
rasguñar vt to scratch, to scrape.
rasguño m scratch.
raso m satin; glade; ~, sa adj plain; flat; al ~ in the open air.
raspa f beard of an ear of corn; backbone of fish; stalk of grapes; rasp.
raspadura f filing, scraping; filings pl.
raspar vt to scrape, to rasp.
rastra f rake; a ~s by dragging.
rastreador m tracker.
rastrear vt to trace; to inquire into; ● vi to skim along close to the ground (of birds).
rastrero, ra adj creeping; low, humble, cringing, reptile.
rastrillar vt to rake.
rastrillo m rake.
rastro m track; rake; trace.
rastrojera f stubble ground.
rastrojo m stubble.
rasurador m or rasuradora f electric shaver.
rasurarse vr to shave.
rata f rat.
ratería f larceny, petty theft.
ratero, ra adj creeping, mean, vile; ● m/f pickpocket; burglar.
ratificación f ratification.
ratificar vt to ratify, to approve of.
rato m moment; a ~s perdidos in leisure time.
ratón m mouse.

ratonera f mousetrap.
raudal m torrent.
raya f stroke; line; part; frontier; ray, roach (fish).
rayado, da adj ruled; crossed; striped; rifled (of fire arms).
rayar vt to line; to cross out; to underline; to cross; to rifle.
rayo m ray, beam of light.
rayón m rayon.
raza f race, lineage; quality.
razón f reason; right; reasonableness; account, calculation.
razonable adj reasonable.
razonado, da adj rational, prudent.
razonamiento m reasoning, discourse.
razonar vi to reason, to discourse; to talk.
reacción f reaction.
reaccionar vi to react.
reaccionario, ria adj reactionary.
reacio, cia adj stubborn.
reactor m reactor.
reajuste m readjustment.
real adj real, actual; royal; ● m camp.
realce m embossment; flash; luster, splendor.
realengo, ga adj royal, kingly.
realidad f reality; sincerity.
realista m realist; royalist.
realizador, ra m/f producer (in TV etc).
realizar vt to realize; to achieve; to undertake.
realmente adv really, actually.
realzar vt to raise, to elevate; to emboss; to heighten.
reanimar vt to cheer, to encourage, to reanimate.
reanudar vt to renew; to resume.
reaparición f reappearance.
reasumir vt to retake, to resume.
reata f collar, leash; string of horses.
rebaja f abatement, deduction; ~s pl sale.
rebajar vt to abate, to lessen, to diminish; to lower.
rebanada f slice.
rebaño m flock of sheep, herd of cattle.
rebasar vt to exceed.
rebatir vt to resist; to parry, to ward off; to refute; to repress.
rebeca f cardigan.
rebelarse vr to revolt; to rebel; to resist.
rebelde m/f rebel; ● adj rebellious.
rebeldía f rebelliousness, disobedience; (jur) contumacy; en ~ by default.
rebelión f rebellion, revolt.
rebosar vi to run over, to overflow; to abound.
rebotar vt to bounce; to clinch; to repel; ● vi to rebound.
rebote m rebound; de ~ on the rebound.
rebozado, da adj fried in batter or breadcrumbs.
rebozar vt to wrap up; to fry in batter or breadcrumbs.
rebullir vi to stir, to begin to move.
rebuscado, da adj affected; recherché; far-fetched.
rebuznar vi to bray.
rebuzno m braying of an ass.
recabar vt to obtain by entreaty.
recado m message; gift.
recaer vi to fall back.
recaída f relapse.
recalcar vt to stress, to emphasize.
recalcitrante adj recalcitrant.
recalentamiento m overheating.
recalentar vt to heat again; to overheat.
recámara f bedroom.
recambio m spare; refill.
recapacitar vt to reflect.
recapitulación f recapitulation.
recapitular vt to recapitulate.
recargado, da adj overloaded.
recargar vt to overload; to recharge; to charge again; to remand to prison.
recargo m extra load; new charge or accusation.
recatado, da adj prudent, circumspect, modest.

recato *m* prudence, circumspection; modesty; bashfulness.
recaudación *f* take; recovery of debts; collector's office.
recaudador *m* tax collector.
recaudar *vt* to gather; to obtain; to recover.
recelar *vt* to fear, to suspect, to doubt.
recelo *m* dread, suspicion, mistrust.
receloso, sa *adj* mistrustful, shy.
recepción *f* reception.
recepcionista *m/f* receptionist.
receptáculo *m* receptacle.
receptor *m* receiver; investigating official.
recesión *f* (*com*) recession.
receta *f* recipe; prescription.
recetar *vt* to prescribe.
recetario *m* register of prescriptions.
recibidor *m* entrance hall.
recibimiento *m* reception, receipt.
recibir *vt* to accept, to receive; to let in; to go to meet; ~**se** *vr* to qualify.
recibo *m* receipt.
recién *adv* recently, lately.
reciente *adj* recent, new, fresh; modern.
recinto *m* precinct, district.
recio, cia *adj* stout, strong, robust; coarse, thick; rude; arduous, rigid; • *adv* strongly, stoutly; **hablar** ~ to talk loud.
recipiente *m* container.
reciprocidad *f* reciprocity.
recíproco, ca *adj* reciprocal, mutual.
recitación *f* recitation.
recital *m* recital; reading.
recitar *vt* to recite.
recitativo, va *adj* recitative.
reclamación *f* claim; reclamation; protest.
reclamar *vt* to claim.
reclamo *m* claim; advertisement; attraction; decoy-bird; catchword (in printing).
reclinar *vt* to recline; ~**se** *vr* to lean back.
recluir *vt* to shut up.
reclusión *f* seclusion; prison.
recluta *f* recruitment; • *m* recruit.
reclutador *m* recruitment officer.
reclutar *vt* to recruit.
recobrar *vt* to recover; ~**se** *vr* to recover from sickness.
recodo *m* corner *or* angle jutting out.
recogedor *m* scraper (instrument).
recoger *vt* to collect; to retake, to take back; to get; to gather; to shelter; to compile; ~**se** *vr* to take shelter *or* refuge; to retire; to withdraw from the world.
recogido, da *adj* retired, secluded; quiet.
recogimiento *m* collection, retreat, shelter; abstraction from all worldly concerns.
recolección *f* summary; recollection.
recomendación *f* recommendation.
recomendar *vt* to recommend.
recompensa *f* compensation; recompense, reward.
recompensar *vt* to recompense, to reward.
recomponer *vt* to recompose; to mend.
reconcentrar *vt* to concentrate on.
reconciliación *f* reconciliation.
reconciliar *vt* to reconcile; ~**se** *vr* to make one's peace.
recóndito, ta *adj* recondite, secret, concealed.
reconfortar *vt* to comfort.
reconocer *vt* to recognize; to examine closely; to acknowledge; to consider; (*mil*) to reconnoiter.
reconocido, da *adj* recognized; grateful.
reconocimiento *m* recognition; acknowledgment; gratitude; confession; search; submission; inquiry.
reconquista *f* reconquest.
reconquistar *vt* to reconquer.
reconstituyente *m* tonic.
reconstruir *vt* to reconstruct.
reconvenir *vt* to retort, to recriminate.

reconversión *f*: ~ **industrial** industrial rationalization.
recopilación *f* summary, abridgment.
recopilador *m* compiler.
recopilar *vt* to compile.
récord *adj invar* record.
recordar *vt* to remember; to remind; • *vi* to remember.
recorrer *vt* to run over, to peruse; to cover.
recortar *vt* to cut out.
recorte *m* cutting; trimming.
recostar *vt* to lean against, to recline; ~**se** *vr* to lie down.
recoveco *m* cubby hole; bend.
recrear *vt* to amuse, to delight, to entertain.
recreativo, va *adj* recreational.
recreo *m* recreation; playtime (at school).
recriminación *f* recrimination.
recriminar *vt* to recriminate.
recrudecer *vt, vi or* **recrudecerse** *vr* to worsen.
recrudecimiento *m* upsurge.
rectángulo, la *adj* rectangular; • *m* rectangle.
rectificación *f* rectification.
rectificar *vt* to rectify.
rectilíneo, nea *adj* rectilinear.
rectitud *f* straightness; rectitude; justness, honesty; exactitude.
recto, ta *adj* straight, right; just, honest; • *m* rectum; • *f* straight line.
rector, ra *m/f* superior of a community *or* establishment; rector (of a university); curate, rector; • *adj* governing.
rectorado *m* rectorship.
rectoría *f* rectory; rectorship.
recua *f* drove of beasts of burden.
recuadro *m* box; inset.
recuento *m* inventory.
recuerdo *m* souvenir, memory.
recular *vi* to fall back, to recoil.
recuperable *adj* recoverable.
recuperación *f* recovery.
recuperar *vt* to recover; ~**se** *vr* to recover from sickness.
recurrir *vt* to recur.
recurso *m* recourse.
recusación *f* refusal.
recusar *vt* to refuse; to refuse to admit.
rechazar *vt* to refuse; to repulse; to contradict.
rechazo *m* rebound; denial; recoil.
rechifla *f* booing; (*fig*) derision.
rechiflar *vt* to boo.
rechinar *vi* to gnash the teeth.
rechistar *vi*: **sin** ~ without a murmur.
rechoncho, cha *adj* chubby.
red *f* net; network; snare.
redacción *f* editing; editor's office.
redactar *vt* to draft; to edit.
redactor *m* editor.
redada *f*: ~ **policial** police raid.
redecilla *f* hairnet.
rededor *m* environs; **al** ~ round about.
redención *f* redemption.
redentor, ra *m/f* redeemer.
redescubrir *vt* to rediscover.
redicho, cha *adj* affected.
redil *m* sheepfold.
redimible *adj* redeemable.
redimir *vt* to redeem, to ransom.
rédito *m* revenue, rent.
redoblado, da *adj* redoubled; stout and thick; reinforced.
redoblar *vt* to redouble; to rivet.
redoble *m* doubling, repetition; (*mil*) roll of a drum.
redomado, da *adj* sly; utter.
redondear *vt* to round.
redondel *m* circle; traffic circle.
redondez *f* roundness, circular form.
redondo, da *adj* round; complete.

reducción f reduction.
reducible adj reducible, convertible.
reducido, da adj reduced; limited; small.
reducir adj to reduce; to limit; ~**se** vr to diminish.
reducto m (mil) redoubt.
redundancia f superfluity, redundancy, excess.
redundar vi to redound; to contribute.
reelegir vt to re-elect, to elect again.
reembolsar vt to refund; to reimburse.
reembolso m reimbursement; refund; **contra** ~ C.O.D.
reemplazar vt to replace, to restore.
reemplazo m replacing; reserve.
reenganchar vt (mil) to re-enlist; ~**se** vr to enlist again.
referencia f reference.
referéndum m referendum.
referir vt to refer, to relate, to report; ~**se** vr to refer to, to relate to.
refilón m: **de** ~ adv obliquely.
refinado, da adj refined; subtle, artful.
refinar vt to refine.
refinería f refinery.
reflejar vt to reflect.
reflejo m reflex; reflection.
reflexión f meditation, reflection.
reflexionar vt to reflect on; ● vi to reflect, to meditate.
reflexivo, va adj reflexive; thoughtful.
reflujo m reflux, ebb; **flujo y** ~ the tides pl.
reforma f reform; correction; repair.
reformar vt to reform, to correct, to restore; ~**se** vr to mend, to have one's manners reformed or corrected.
reformatorio m reformatory.
reforzar vt to strengthen, to fortify; to encourage.
refracción f refraction.
refractario, ria adj refractory.
refrán m proverb.
refregar vt to scrub.
refrenar vt to refrain; to check.
refrendar vt to countersign; to approve.
refrescante adj refreshing.
refrescar vt to refresh; ● vi to cool down; ~**se** vr to get cooler; to go out for a breath of fresh air.
refresco m refreshment.
refriega f affray, skirmish, fray.
refrigerador m or **refrigeradora** f icebox.
refrigerar vt to cool, to refresh, to refrigerate; to comfort.
refrigerio m refrigeration, refreshment; consolation, comfort.
refuerzo m reinforcement.
refugiado, da m/f refugee.
refugiar vt to shelter; ~**se** vr to take refuge.
refugio m refuge, asylum.
refulgir vi to shine.
refunfuñar vi to snarl, to growl, to grumble.
refutación f refutation.
refutar vt to refute.
regadera f watering can.
regadío m irrigated land.
regalar vt to give (as present); to give away; to pamper; to caress.
regalía f regalia; bonus; royalty; privilege.
regaliz m licorice.
regalo m present, gift; pleasure; comfort.
regañadientes: a ~ adv reluctantly.
regañar vt to scold; ●vi to growl, to grumble; to quarrel.
regañón, ona adj snarling, growling, grumbling; troublesome.
regar vt to water, to irrigate.
regata f irrigating ditch; regatta.
regatear vt (com) to bargain over; to be mean with; ● vi to haggle; to dribble (in sport).
regateo m act of haggling or bartering; dodge.
regazo m lap.
regencia f regency.

regeneración f regeneration.
regenerar vt to regenerate.
regentar vt to rule; to govern.
regente m regent; manager.
régimen m regime, management; diet; (gr) rules of verbs.
regimiento m regime; (mil) regiment.
regio, gia adj royal, kingly.
región f region.
regir vt to rule, to govern, to direct; ● vi to apply.
registrador m registrar; controller.
registrar vt to survey, to inspect; to examine; to record, to enter in a register; ~**se** vr to register; to happen.
registro m examining; enrolling office; register; registration.
regla f rule, ruler; period.
reglamentar vt to regulate.
reglamentario, ria adj statutory.
reglamento m regulation; by-law.
regocijar vt to gladden; ~**se** vr to rejoice.
regocijo m joy, pleasure, merriment, rejoicing.
regodearse vr to be delighted; to trifle, to play the fool; to joke, to jest.
regodeo m joy, merriment.
regordete adj chubby, plump.
regresar vi to return, to go back.
regreso m return, regression.
reguero m small rivulet; trickling line of spilt liquid; drain, gutter.
regulación f regulation.
regulador, ra m/f regulator; knob, control.
regular vt to regulate, to adjust; ● adj regular; ordinary.
regularidad f regularity.
regularizar vt to regularize.
rehabilitación f rehabilitation.
rehabilitar vt to rehabilitate.
rehacer vt to repair, to make again; to redo; ~**se** vr to recover; (mil) to rally.
rehén m hostage.
rehuir vt to avoid.
rehusar vt to refuse, to decline.
reimpresión f reprint.
reimprimir vt to reprint.
reina f queen.
reinado m reign.
reinante adj (fig) prevailing.
reinar vi to reign, to govern.
reincidencia f relapse.
reincidir vi to relapse, to fall back.
reino m kingdom, reign.
reintegración f reintegration, restoration.
reintegrar vt to reintegrate, to restore; ~**se** vr to be reinstated or restored.
reintegro m reintegration.
reír(se) vi (vr) to laugh.
reiteración f repetition, reiteration.
reiterar vt to reiterate, to repeat.
reivindicación f claim; vindication.
reivindicar vt to claim.
reja f plowshare; lattice, grating.
rejilla f grating, grille; vent; baggage rack.
rejoneador m mounted bullfighter.
rejonear vt to spear bulls.
rejuvenecer vt, vi to rejuvenate.
relación f relation; relationship; report; account.
relacionar vt to relate.
relajación f relaxation; remission; laxity.
relajar vt to relax, to slacken; ~**se** vr to relax.
relamerse vr to lick one's lips; to relish.
relamido, da adj affected, overdressed.
relámpago m flash of lightning.
relampaguear vi to flash.
relatar vt to relate, to tell.
relativo, va adj relative.

relato *m* story; recital.

relax *m*: hacer ~ to relax.

releer *vt* to reread.

relegación *f* relegation, exile.

relegar *vt* to relegate, to banish; to exile.

relente *m* evening dew.

relevante *adj* excellent, great, eminent.

relevar *vt* to emboss, to work in relief; to exonerate; to relieve; to assist.

relievo *m* (*mil*) relief.

relicario *m* reliquary.

relieve *m* relief; (*fig*) prominence.

religión *f* religion.

religiosidad *f* religiousness.

religioso, sa *adj* religious, pious.

relinchar *vi* to neigh.

relincho *m* neigh, neighing.

reliquia *f* residue, remains; saintly relic.

reloj *m* clock, watch.

relojero *m* watchmaker.

relucir *vi* to shine, to glitter; to excel, to be brilliant.

relumbrar *vi* to sparkle, to shine.

rellano *m* landing (of stairs).

rellenar *vt* to fill up; to stuff.

relleno, na *adj* satiated, full up; stuffed; • *m* stuffing.

remachar *vt* to rivet; (*fig*) to drive home.

remanente *m* remainder; (*com*) balance; surplus.

remangar *vt* to roll up.

remansarse *vr* to obstruct the course of a stream.

remanso *m* stagnant water; quiet place.

remar *vi* to row.

rematadamente *adv* entirely, totally.

rematado, da *adj* utter, complete.

rematar *vt* to terminate, to finish; to sell of cheaply; • *vi* to end.

remate *m* end, conclusion; shot; tip; last *or* best bid.

remedar *vt* to copy, to imitate, to mimic.

remediable *adj* remediable.

remediar *vt* to remedy; to assist, to help; to free from danger; to avoid.

remedio *m* amendment, correction; resource; refuge.

remedo *m* imitation, copy.

remendar *vt* to patch, to mend; to correct.

remero *m* rower, oarsman.

remesa *f* shipment; remittance.

remiendo *m* patch; mend.

remilgado, da *adj* prim; affected.

remilgo *m* affected nicety *or* gravity.

reminiscencia *f* reminiscence, recollection.

remiso, sa *adj* remiss, careless, indolent.

remitente *m* sender.

remitir *vt* to remit, to send; to pardon a fault; to suspend, to put off; • *vi*, ~se *vr* to slacken.

remo *m* oar; rowing.

remojar *vt* to steep; to dunk.

remojo *m* steeping, soaking.

remolacha *f* beet.

remolcar *vt* to tow.

remolino *m* whirlwind; whirlpool; crowd.

remolón, ona *adj* stubborn; lazy.

remolque *m* tow, towing; tow rope.

remontar *vt* to mend; ~se *vr* to tower, to soar.

remorder *vt* to disturb.

remordimiento *m* remorse.

remoto, ta *adj* remote, distant, far.

remover *vt* to stir; to move around.

remozar *vt* to rejuvenate; to renovate.

remuneración *f* remuneration, recompense.

remunerador, ra *m/f* remunerator.

remunerar *vt* to reward, to remunerate.

renacer *vi* to be born again; to revive.

renacimiento *m* regeneration; rebirth.

renacuajo *m* tadpole.

renal *adj* renal, kidney *compd*.

rencilla *f* quarrel.

rencor *m* rancor, grudge.

rencoroso, sa *adj* rancorous.

rendición *f* surrender; profit.

rendido, da *adj* submissive; exhausted.

rendija *f* crevice, crack, cleft.

rendimiento *m* output; efficiency.

rendir *vt* to subject, to subdue; ~se *vr* to yield; to surrender; to be tired out.

renegado *m* apostate; wicked person.

renegar *vt* to deny, to disown; to detest, to abhor; • *vi* to apostatize; to blaspheme, to curse.

renglón *m* line; item.

renombrado, da *adj* renowned.

renombre *m* renown.

renovación *f* renovation, renewal.

renovar *vt* to renew, to renovate, to reform.

renquear *vi* to limp.

renta *f* rent, income; profit.

renuncia *f* renunciation, resignation.

renunciar *vt* to renounce; • *vi* to resign.

reñido, da *adj* at variance, at odds; hard-fought.

reñir *vt, vi* to wrangle, to quarrel; to scold, to chide.

reo *m* offender, criminal.

reojo *m*: mirar de ~ to look at furtively.

reparación *f* reparation, repair.

reparar *vt* to repair; to consider, to observe; • *vi* to notice; to parry; to pass (at cards).

reparo *m* repair, reparation; consideration; difficulty.

repartición *f* distribution.

repartidor *m/f* distributor; assessor of taxes.

repartir *vt* to distribute; to deliver.

reparto *m* distribution; delivery; cost; real estate development.

repasar *vt* to repass; to revise; to check; to mend.

repaso *m* revision; checkup.

repatriar *vt* to repatriate.

repecho *m* slope.

repelente *adj* repellent, repulsive.

repeler *vt* to repel; to refute, to reject.

repente : de ~ *adv* suddenly.

repentino, na *adj* sudden, unforeseen.

repercusión *f* reverberation.

repercutir *vi* to reverberate; to rebound.

repertorio *m* repertory, index; list.

repetición *f* repetition; (*mus*) encore.

repetidor, ra *m/f* repeater.

repetir *vt, vi* to repeat.

repicar *vt* to chime, to ring.

repique *m* chime.

repiquetear *vt* to ring merrily.

repisa *f* pedestal *or* stand; shelf; windowsill.

replegar *vt* to redouble; to fold over; ~se *vr* (*mil*) to fall back.

repleto, ta *adj* replete, very full.

réplica *f* reply, answer; repartee.

replicar *vi* to reply.

repoblación *f* repopulation; restocking; ~ forestal reafforestation.

repoblar *vt* to repopulate; to reafforest.

repollo *m* cabbage.

reponer *vt* to replace; to restore; ~se *vr* to recover lost health *or* property.

reportaje *m* report, article.

reportero, ra *m/f* reporter.

reposado, da *adj* quiet, peaceful; settled (wine).

reposar *vi* to rest, to repose.

reposición *f* replacement; remake.

reposo *m* rest, repose.

repostería *f* confectioner's (shop).

repostero *m* confectioner.

reprender *vt* to reprehend, to blame.
represa *f* dam; lake.
represalia *f* reprisal, reprise.
representación *f* representation; authority.
representante *m/f* representative; understudy (stage).
representar *vt* to represent; to play on the stage; to look.
representativo, va *adj* representative.
represión *f* repression.
reprimenda *f* reprimand.
reprimir *vt* to repress, to refrain, to contain.
reprobable *adj* reprehensible.
reprobación *f* reprobation, reproof.
reprobar *vt* to reject, to condemn, to upbraid.
réprobo *m* reprobate.
reprochar *vt* to reproach.
reproche *m* reproach.
reproducción *f* reproduction.
reproducir *vt* to reproduce.
reptil *m* reptile.
república *f* republic.
republicano, na *adj, m/f* republican.
repudiar *vt* to repudiate.
repudio *m* repudiation.
repuesto *m* supply; spare part.
repugnancia *f* reluctance, repugnance.
repugnante *adj* repugnant.
repugnar *vt* to disgust.
repulsa *f* refusal.
repulsar *vt* to reject, to decline, to refuse.
repulsión *f* repulsion.
repulsivo, va *adj* repulsive.
reputación *f* reputation, renown.
reputar to consider.
requebrar *vt* to woo, to court.
requerimiento *m* request, requisition; intimation; summons.
requerir *vt* to intimate, to notify; to request, to require, to need; to summon.
requesón *m* cottage-cheese.
requiebro *m* endearing expression.
réquiem *m* requiem.
requisa *f* inspection; (*mil*) requisition.
requisito *m* requisite.
res *f* head of cattle.
resabio *m* (unpleasant) aftertaste; vicious habit, bad custom.
resaca *f* surge, surf; (*fig*) backlash; (*fam*) hangover.
resaltar *vi* to rebound; to jut out; to be evident; to stand out.
resarcimiento *m* compensation, reparation.
resarcir *vt* to compensate, to make amends.
resbaladizo, za *adj* slippery.
resbalar(se) *vi* (*vr*) to slip, to slide.
resbalón *m* slip, sliding.
rescatar *vt* to ransom, to redeem.
rescate *m* ransom.
rescindir *vt* to rescind, to annul.
rescisión *f* rescission, revocation.
rescoldo *m* embers, cinders *pl*.
resecarse *vr* to dry up.
reseco, ca *adj* very dry.
resentido, da *adj* resentful.
resentimiento *m* resentment.
resentirse *vr* to suffer; to resent.
reseña *f* review; account.
reseñar *vt* to describe; to review.
reserva *f* reserve; reservation.
reservado, da *adj* reserved, cautious, circumspect.
reservar *vt* to keep; to reserve; ~**se** *vr* to preserve oneself; to keep to oneself.
resfriado *m* cold.
resfriarse *vr* to catch cold.
resguardar *vt* to preserve, to defend; ~**se** *vr* to be on one's guard.
resguardo *m* guard, security, safety; voucher; receipt.

residencia *f* residence.
residente *adj* residing, resident; ● *m/f* resident.
residir *vi* to reside, to dwell.
residuo *m* residue, remainder.
resignación *f* resignation.
resignadamente *adv* resignedly.
resignarse *vr* to resign oneself.
resina *f* resin.
resinoso, sa *adj* resinous.
resistencia *f* resistance, opposition.
resistente *adj* strong; resistant.
resistir *vi, vt* to resist, to oppose; to put up with.
resma *f* ream (of paper).
resol *m* glare of the sun.
resollar *vi* to wheeze; to take breath.
resolución *f* resolution, boldness; decision.
resolver *vt* to resolve, to decide; to analyze; ~**se** *vr* to resolve, to determine.
resonar *vi* to resound.
resoplar *vi* to snore; to snort.
resoplido *m* heavy breathing.
resorte *m* spring.
respaldar *vt* to endorse; ~**se** *vr* to recline against a chair or bench.
respaldo *m* backing; endorsement; back of a seat.
respectivo, va *adj* respective.
respecto *m* relation, respect; **al** ~ on this matter.
respetable *adj* respectable.
respetar *vt* to respect; to revere.
respeto *m* respect, regard, consideration; homage.
respetuoso, sa *adj* respectful.
respingar *vi* to shy.
respingo *m* start; jump.
respiración *f* respiration, breathing.
respiradero *m* vent, breathing hole; rest, repose.
respirar *vi* to breathe.
respiratorio, ria *adj* respiratory.
respiro *m* breathing; (*fig*) respite.
resplandecer *vi* to shine; to glisten.
resplandeciente *adj* resplendent.
resplandor *m* splendor, brilliance.
responder *vt, vi* to answer; to re-echo; to correspond; to be responsible for.
respondón, ona *adj* ever ready to reply; sassy.
responsable *adj* responsible, accountable, answerable.
responsabilidad *f* responsibility.
responsabilizarse *vr* to take charge.
responso *m* response for the dead.
respuesta *f* answer, reply.
resquemor *m* resentment.
resquicio *m* crack, cleft; (*fig*) chance.
restablecer *vt* to re-establish; ~**se** *vr* to recover.
restablecimiento *m* re-establishment.
restallar *vi* to smack, to click.
restante *adj* remaining.
restar *vt* to subtract; to take away; ● *vi* to be left.
restauración *f* restoration.
restaurante *m* restaurant.
restaurar *vt* to restore.
restitución *f* restitution.
restituir *vt* to restore; to return.
resto *m* remainder, rest.
restregar *vt* to scrub, to rub.
restricción *f* restriction, limitation.
restringir *vt* to restrain, to restrict, to limit.
resucitar *vt* to resuscitate, to revive; to renew.
resuello *m* breath, breathing; shortness of breath.
resuelto, ta *adj* resolute, determined, prompt.
resultado *m* result, consequence.
resultar *vi* to be; to turn out; to amount to.
resumen *m* summary.
resumidamente *adv* summarily.

resumir *vt* to abridge; to sum up; to summarize.
resurrección *f* resurrection, revival.
retablo *m* picture drawn on a board; splendid altarpiece.
retaguardia *f* rearguard.
retahíla *f* file, range, series.
retal *m* remnant.
retar *vt* to challenge.
retardar *vt* to retard, to delay.
retardo *m* delay.
retazo *m* remnant; cutting.
retención *f* retention.
retener *vt* to retain, to keep back.
retentiva *f* memory.
reticencia *f* reticence.
retina *f* retina.
retintín *f* tinkling sound; affected tone of voice.
retirada *f* (*mil*) retreat; withdrawal; recall.
retirar *vt* to withdraw, to retire; to remove; ~**se** *vr* to retire, to retreat; to go to bed.
retiro *m* retreat, retirement; pension.
reto *m* challenge; threat, menace.
retocar *vt* to retouch; to mend; to finish any work completely.
retoñar *vi* to sprout.
retoño *m* sprout; offspring.
retoque *m* finishing stroke; retouching.
retorcer *vt* to twist; to wring.
retorcimiento *m* twisting, contortion.
retórica *f* rhetoric.
retórico, ca *adj* rhetorical; ● *f* rhetoric; affectedness.
retornar *vt, vi* to return.
retorno *m* return; barter, exchange.
retortero : **andar al** ~ to hover about.
retortijón *m* twisting; ~ **de tripas** stomach cramp.
retozar *vi* to frisk, to skip.
retozo *m* romp.
retozón, ona *adj* wanton, romping.
retracción *f* retraction.
retractar *vt* to retract.
retraer *vt* to draw back; to dissuade; ~**se** *vr* to take refuge; to flee.
retraído, da *adj* shy.
retransmisión *f* broadcast.
retransmitir *vt* to broadcast; to relay; to retransmit.
retrasado, da *adj* late; (*med*) mentally retarded; backward.
retraso *m* delay; slowness; backwardness; lateness; (*ferro*) **el tren ha tenido** ~ the train is overdue *or* late.
retratar *vt* to portray; to photograph; to describe.
retrato *m* portrait, effigy.
retreta *f* (*mil*) retreat, tattoo.
retrete *m* toilet, washroom.
retribución *f* retribution.
retribuir *vt* to repay.
retroacción *f* retroaction.
retroactivo, va *adj* retroactive.
retroceder *vi* to go backward, to fly back; to back down.
retrógrado, da *adj* retrograde; reactionary.
retrospectivo, va *adj* retrospective.
retrovisor *m* rear-view mirror.
retumbar *vi* to resound, to jingle.
reuma *f* rheumatism.
reumático, ca *adj* rheumatic.
reumatismo *m* rheumatism.
reunión *f* reunion, meeting.
reunir *vt* to reunite, to unite; ~**se** *vr* to gather, to meet.
revalidación *f* confirmation, ratification.
revalidar *vt* to ratify, to confirm.
revancha *f* revenge.
revelación *f* revelation.
revelado *m* developing.
revelar *vt* to reveal; to develop (photographs).
reventar *vi* to burst, to crack; to explode; to toil, to drudge.
reventón *m* (*auto*) flat.

reverberación *f* reverberation.
reverberar *vi* to reverberate.
reverdecer *vi* to grow green again; to revive.
reverencia *f* reverence, respect, veneration.
reverenciar *vt* to venerate, to revere.
reverendo, da *adj* reverend.
reverente *adj* respectful, reverent.
reverso *m* reverse.
revés *m* back; wrong side; disappointment, setback.
revestir *vt* to dress, to put on; to coat, to cover.
revisar *vt* to revise, to review.
revisión *f* revision.
revisor *m* inspector; ticket collector.
revista *f* review, revision.
revivir *vi* to revive.
revocación *f* revocation.
revocar *vt* to revoke.
revolcarse *vr* to wallow.
revolotear *vi* to flutter.
revoloteo *m* fluttering.
revoltijo *m* confusion, disorder.
revoltoso, sa *adj* rebellious, unruly.
revolución *f* revolution.
revolucionario, ria *adj, m/f* revolutionary.
revolver *vt* to move about, to turn around; to mess up; to revolve; ~**se** *vr* to turn round; to change (of the weather).
revólver *m* revolver.
revuelo *m* fluttering; (*fig*) commotion.
revuelta *f* turn; disturbance, revolt.
rey *m* king; king (in cards *or* chess).
reyerta *f* quarrel, brawl.
rezagar *vt* to leave behind; to defer; ~**se** *vr* to remain behind.
rezar *vi* to pray, to say one's prayers.
rezo *m* prayer.
rezongar *vi* to grumble.
rezumar *vt* to ooze, to leak.
ría *f* estuary.
riada *f* flood.
ribera *f* shore, bank.
ribereño, ña *adj* belonging to the seashore *or* bank of a river.
ribete *m* trimming; seam, border.
ribetear *vt* to hem, to border.
ricino *m*: **aceite de** ~ castor oil.
rico, ca *adj* rich; delicious; lovely, cute.
ridiculez *f* absurdity.
ridiculizar *vt* to ridicule.
ridículo, la *adj* ridiculous.
riego *m* irrigation.
riel *m* rail.
rienda *f* rein of a bridle; **dar** ~ **suelta** to give free rein to.
riesgo *m* danger, risk.
rifa *f* raffle, lottery.
rifar *vt* to raffle.
rifle *m* rifle.
rigidez *f* rigidity.
rígido, da *adj* rigid, inflexible; severe.
rigor *m* rigor.
riguroso, sa *adj* rigorous.
rima *f* rhyme.
rimar *vi* to rhyme.
rimbombante *adj* pompous.
rímel *or* **rímmel** *m* mascara.
rincón *m* inside corner.
rinoceronte *m* rhinoceros.
riña *f* quarrel, dispute.
riñón *m* kidney.
río *m* river, stream.
rioja *m* rioja (wine).
riqueza *f* riches *pl*, wealth.
risa *f* laugh, laughter.
risco *m* steep rock.
risible *adj* risible, laughable.

risotada f loud laugh.
ristra f string.
risueño, na adj smiling.
rítmico, ca adj rhythmical.
ritmo m rhythm.
rito m rite, ceremony.
ritual adj, m ritual.
rival adj, m/f rival, competitor.
rivalidad f rivalry.
rivalizar vi to rival, to vie with.
rizado, da adj curly.
rizar vt to curl hair.
rizo m curl; ripple (on water).
robar vt to rob, to steal; to break into.
roble m oak tree.
robledal m oakwood.
robo m robbery, theft.
robot m robot.
robustez f robustness.
robusto, ta adj robust, strong.
roca f rock.
rocalla f pebbles pl.
roce m rub; brush; friction.
rociada f sprinkling, spray, shower.
rociar vt to sprinkle; to spray.
rocín m nag, hack; stupid person.
rocío m dew.
rocoso, sa adj rocky.
rodada f rut, track of a wheel.
rodadura f act of rolling.
rodaja f slice.
rodaje m filming; en ~ (auto) running in.
rodar vi to roll.
rodear vi to make a detour; ● vt to surround, to enclose.
rodeo m detour; subterfuge; evasion; rodeo.
rodilla f knee; de ~s on one's knees.
rodillo m roller.
roedor, ra adj gnawing; ● m rodent.
roedura f gnawing.
roer vt to gnaw, to corrode.
rogar vt, vi to ask for; to beg, to entreat; to pray.
rogativa f supplication, prayer.
rojez f redness.
rojizo, za adj reddish.
rojo, ja adj red; ruddy.
rol m list, roll, catalog; role.
rollizo, za adj round; plump, chubby.
rollo m roll; coil.
romance m Romance language; Spanish language; romance.
romancero m collection of romances or ballads.
romanticismo m romanticism.
romántico, ca adj romantic.
rombo m rhomb.
romboide m rhomboid.
romería f pilgrimage.
romero m (bot) rosemary.
romo, ma adj blunt; snub-nosed.
rompecabezas m invar riddle; jigsaw.
romper vt to break, to tear up; to wear out; to break up land;
    ● vi to break (of waves); to break through.
rompimiento m tearing, breaking; crack.
ron m rum.
roncar vi to snore; to roar.
ronco, ca adj hoarse; husky; raucous.
roncha f wheal, bruise.
ronda f night patrol; round (of drinks, cards etc).
rondar vt, vi to patrol; to prowl around.
ronquera f hoarseness.
ronquido m snore; roar.
ronzal m halter.
ronronear vi to purr.
roña f scab, mange; grime; rust.

roñoso, sa adj filthy; mean.
ropa f clothes; clothing; dress.
ropaje m gown, robes; drapery.
ropero m linen cupboard; closet.
rosa f rose; birthmark.
rosado, da adj pink; rosy.
rosal m rosebush.
rosario m rosary.
rosca f thread of a screw; coil, spiral.
rosetón m rosette; rose window.
rosquilla f donut-shaped fritter.
rostro m face.
rotación f rotation.
roto, ta adj broken, destroyed; debauched.
rótula f kneecap; ball-and-socket joint.
rotulador m felt-tip pen.
rotular vt to inscribe, to label.
rótulo m inscription; label, ticket; placard, poster.
rotundo, da adj round; emphatic.
rotura f breaking, crack, tear.
roturar vt to plow.
rozadura f graze, scratch.
rozar vt to rub; to chafe; to nibble the grass; to scrape; to
    touch lightly.
rubí m ruby.
rubicundo, da adj reddish, rubicund.
rubio, bia adj fair-haired, blond(e); ● m/f blond/blonde.
rubor m blush; bashfulness.
rúbrica f red mark; flourish at the end of a signature; title,
    heading, rubric.
rubricar vt to sign with a flourish; to sign and seal.
rudeza f roughness, rudeness; stupidity.
rudimento m principle; beginning; ~s pl rudiments.
rudo, da adj rough, coarse; plain, simple; stupid.
rueca f distaff.
rueda f wheel; circle; slice, round.
ruedo m rotation; border, selvage; arena, bullring.
ruego m request, entreaty.
rufián m pimp, pander; lout.
rugby m rugby.
rugido m roar.
rugir vi to roar, to bellow.
rugoso, sa adj wrinkled.
ruibarbo m rhubarb.
ruido m noise, sound; din, row; fuss.
ruidoso, sa adj noisy, loud.
ruin adj mean, despicable; stingy.
ruina f ruin, collapse, downfall, destruction; ~s pl ruins.
ruindad f meanness, lowness; mean act.
ruinoso, sa adj ruinous, disastrous.
ruiseñor m nightingale.
ruleta f roulette.
rulo m curler.
rumba f rumba.
rumbo m (mar) course, bearing; road, route, way; course of
    events, pomp, ostentation.
rumboso, sa adj generous, lavish.
rumiante m ruminant.
rumiar vt to chew; ● vi to ruminate.
rumor m rumor; murmur.
runrún m rumor; sound of voices, whirr.
ruptura f rupture.
rural adj rural.
rusticidad f rusticity; coarseness.
rústico, ca adj rustic; ● m/f peasant.
ruta f route, itinerary.
rutina f routine, habit formed from custom.

S

sábado m Saturday; Sabbath.
sábana f sheet; altar cloth.
sabandija f bug, insect.
sabañón m chilblain.
sabelotodo m/f invar know-all.
saber vt to know; to find out, to learn; to experience; ● vi: ~ a to taste of; ● m learning, knowledge.
sabiduría f learning, knowledge, wisdom.
sabiendas adv: a ~ knowingly.
sabihondo, da adj know-all, pedantic.
sabio, bia adj sage, wise; ● m/f sage, a wise person.
sablazo m sword wound; (fam) sponging, scrounging.
sable m saber, cutlass.
sabor m taste, savor, flavor.
saborear vt to savor, to taste; to enjoy.
sabotaje m sabotage.
saboteador, ora m/f saboteur.
sabotear vt to sabotage.
sabroso, sa adj tasty, delicious; pleasant; salted.
sabueso m bloodhound.
sacacorchos m invar corkscrew.
sacapuntas m invar pencil sharpener.
sacar vt to take out, to extract; to get out; to bring out (a book etc); to take off (clothes); to receive, to get; (dep) to serve.
sacarina f saccharin(e).
sacerdotal adj priestly.
sacerdote m priest.
sacerdotisa f priestess.
saciar vt to satiate.
saciedad f satiety.
saco m bag, sack; jacket.
sacramental adj sacramental.
sacramento m sacrament.
sacrificar vt to sacrifice.
sacrificio m sacrifice.
sacrilegio m sacrilege.
sacrílego, ga adj sacrilegious.
sacristán m sacristan, sexton.
sacristía f sacristy, vestry.
sacro, cra adj holy, sacred.
sacrosanto, ta adj very holy.
sacudida f shake, jerk.
sacudir vt to shake, to jerk; to beat, to hit.
sádico, ca adj sadistic; ● m/f sadist.
sadismo m sadism.
saeta f arrow, dart.
sagacidad f shrewdness, cleverness, sagacity.
sagaz adj shrewd, clever, sagacious.
Sagitario m Sagittarius (sign of the Zodiac).
sagrado, da adj sacred, holy.
sagrario m shrine; tabernacle.
sainete m (teat) farce; flavor, relish; seasoning.
sal f salt.
sala f large room; (teat) house, auditorium; public hall; (jur) court; (med) ward.
salado, da adj salted; witty, amusing.
salamandra f salamander.
salar vt to salt.
salarial adj wage compd, salary compd.
salario m salary.
salazón f salting.
salchicha f sausage.
salchichón m (salami-type) sausage.
saldar vt to pay; to sell off; (fig) to settle.
saldo m settlement; balance; remainder; ~s pl sale.
saledizo, za adj salient, projecting.
salero m salt cellar.
saleroso adj witty, amusing.

salida f exit, way out; leaving, departure; production, output; (com) sale; sales outlet.
saliente adj projecting; rising; (fig) outstanding.
salina f saltworks, salt mine.
salino, na adj saline.
salir vi to go out, to leave; to depart, to set out; to appear; to turn out, to prove; ~se vr to escape, to leak.
salitre m saltpeter.
saliva f saliva.
salmo m psalm.
salmón m salmon.
salmonete m red mullet.
salmuera f brine.
salobre adj brackish, salty.
salón m living room, lounge; public hall.
salpicadero m dashboard.
salpicar vt to sprinkle, to splash, to spatter.
salpicón m salmagundi.
salpimentar vt to season with pepper and salt.
salsa f sauce.
salsera f sauce boat; gravy boat.
saltamontes m invar grasshopper.
saltar vt to jump, to leap; to skip, to miss out; ● vi to leap, to jump; to bounce; (fig) to explode, to blow up.
salteador m highwayman; holdup man.
saltear vt to rob in a holdup; to assault; to sauté.
saltimbanqui m/f acrobat.
salto m leap, jump.
saltón, ona adj bulging; protruding.
salubre adj healthy.
salubridad f healthiness.
salud f health.
saludable adj healthy.
saludar vt to greet; (mil) to salute.
saludo m greeting.
salutación f salutation, greeting.
salva f (mil) salute with firearms.
salvación f salvation; rescue.
salvado m bran.
salvaguardar vt to safeguard.
salvaguardia m safeguard.
salvaje adj savage.
salvajismo m savagery.
salvar vt to save; to rescue; to overcome; to cross, to jump across; to cover, to travel; to exclude; ~se vr to escape from danger.
salvavidas adj invar: bote/chaleco/cinturón ~ lifeboat/life jacket/life belt.
salvia f (bot) sage.
salvo, va adj safe; ● adv saving, excepting.
salvoconducto m safe-conduct.
san adj saint.
sanamente adv healthily.
sanar vt, vi to heal.
sanatorio m sanatorium; nursing home.
sanción f sanction.
sancionar vt to sanction.
sandalia f sandal.
sándalo m sandal, sandalwood.
sandez f folly, stupidity.
sandía f watermelon.
sandwich m sandwich.
saneamiento m sanitation.
sanear vt to drain.
sangrar vt, vi to bleed.
sangre f blood; a ~ fría in cold blood; a ~ y fuego without mercy.
sangría f sangria (drink); bleeding.
sangriento, ta adj bloody, blood-stained, gory; cruel.
sanguijuela f leech.
sanguinario, ria adj bloodthirsty, cruel.
sanguíneo, nea adj blood compd.

sanidad f sanitation; health.
sanitario, ria adj sanitary; health; ~s mpl washroom.
sano, na adj healthy, fit; intact, sound.
santiamén m: en un ~ in no time at all.
santidad f sanctity.
santificar vt to sanctify; to make holy.
santiguarse vr to make the sign of the cross.
santo, ta adj holy; sacred; ● m/f saint; ~ y seña watchword.
santuario m sanctuary.
saña f anger, passion.
sañudo, da adj furious, enraged.
sapo m toad.
saque m (dep) serve, service (in tennis); throw-in (in soccer).
saqueador, ra m/f ransacker, looter.
saquear vt to ransack, to plunder.
saqueo m looting; sacking.
sarampión m measles pl.
sarao m evening party, soirée.
sarcasmo m sarcasm.
sarcástico, ca adj sarcastic.
sarcófago m sarcophagus.
sardina f sardine.
sardónico, ca adj sardonic; ironical.
sargento m sergeant.
sarmiento m vine shoot.
sarna f itch; mange; (med) scabies.
sarnoso, sa adj itchy, scabby, mangy.
sarpullido m (med) rash.
sarro m (med) tartar.
sarta f string of beads etc; string, row.
sartén f frying pan.
sastre m tailor.
sastrería f tailor's shop.
Satanás m Satan.
satélite m satellite.
sátira f satire.
satírico, ca adj satirical.
satirizar vt to satirize.
sátiro m satyr.
satisfacción f satisfaction; apology.
satisfacer vt to satisfy; to pay (a debt); ~se vr to satisfy oneself; to take revenge.
satisfactorio, ria adj satisfactory.
satisfecho, cha adj satisfied.
saturación f (quim) saturation.
sauce m (bot) willow.
saúco m (bot) elder.
sauna f sauna.
savia f sap.
saxofón m saxophone.
sazonado, da adj flavored, seasoned.
sazonar vt to ripen; to season.
se pn reflexivo: himself; herself; itself; yourself; themselves; yourselves; each other, one another; oneself.
sebo m fat, grease.
seboso, sa adj fat, greasy.
secador m: ~ de pelo hairdryer.
secadora f tumble dryer.
secamente adv dryly, curtly.
secano m dry, arable land which is not irrigated.
secar vt to dry; ~se vr to dry up; to dry oneself.
sección f section.
seco, ca adj dry; dried up; skinny; cold (of character); brusque, sharp; bare.
secretaría f secretariat.
secretario, ria m/f secretary.
secreto, ta adj secret; hidden; ● m secret; secrecy.
secta f sect.
sectario, ria adj, m/f sectarian.
sector m sector.
secuela f sequel; consequence.
secuencia f sequence.

secuestrar vt to kidnap; to confiscate.
secuestro m kidnaping; confiscation.
secular adj secular.
secularización f secularization.
secularizar vt to secularize.
secundar vt to second.
secundario, ria adj secondary.
sed f thirst; **tener** ~ to be thirsty.
seda f silk.
sedal m fishing line.
sedante m sedative.
sede f see; seat; headquarters pl.
sedentario, ria adj sedentary.
sedición f sedition.
sedicioso, sa adj seditious, mutinous.
sediento, ta adj thirsty; eager.
sedoso, sa adj silky.
seducción f seduction.
seducir vt to seduce; to bribe; to charm, to attract.
seductor, ra adj seductive; charming; attractive; ● m/f seducer.
segador, ra m/f reaper, harvester.
segadora-trilladora f combine harvester.
segar vt to reap, to mow, to harvest.
seglar adj secular, lay.
segmento m segment.
segregación f segregation, separation.
segregar vt to segregate, to separate.
seguido, da adj continuous, successive, long-lasting; ● adv straight (on); after; often.
seguidor, ra m/f follower; supporter.
seguimiento m pursuit; continuation.
seguir vt to follow, to pursue; to continue; ● vi to follow; to carry on; ~se vr to follow, to ensue.
según prep according to.
segundo, da adj second; ● m second (of time).
seguramente adv surely; for sure.
seguridad f security, certainty, safety; confidence; stability.
seguro, ra adj safe, secure, sure, certain; firm, constant; ● adv for sure; ● m safety device; insurance; safety, certainty.
seis adj, m six, sixth.
seiscientos, tas adj six hundred.
seísmo m earthquake.
selección f selection, choice.
seleccionar vt to select, to choose.
selecto, ta adj select, choice.
selva f forest.
sellar vt to seal; to stamp (a document).
sello m seal; stamp.
semáforo m traffic lights pl; signal.
semana f week.
semanal adj weekly.
semanario, ria m weekly (magazine).
semblante m face; (fig) look; appearance.
sembrado m sown field.
sembrar vt to sow; to sprinkle, to scatter.
semejante adj similar, like; ● m fellow man.
semejanza f resemblance, likeness.
semejar vi to resemble; ~se vr to look alike.
semen m semen.
semental m stud.
sementera f sowing; land sown with seed.
semestral adj half-yearly.
semicircular adj semicircular.
semicírculo m semicircle.
semifinal f semifinal.
semilla f seed.
semillero m seedplot.
seminario m seedbed; seminary.
seminarista m student who boards and is instructed in a seminary.
sémola f semolina.

sempiterno, na *adj* everlasting.
senado *m* senate.
senador, ra *m/f* senator.
sencillez *f* plainness; simplicity; naturalness.
sencillo, lla *adj* simple; natural; unaffected; single.
senda *f*, **sendero** *m* path, footpath.
senil *adj* senile.
seno *m* bosom; lap; womb; hole, cavity; sinus; ~s *pl* breasts.
sensación *f* sensation, feeling; sense.
sensacional *adj* sensational.
sensato, ta *adj* sensible.
sensibilidad *f* sensibility; sensitivity.
sensible *adj* sensitive; perceptible, appreciable; regrettable.
sensitivo, va *adj* sense, sensitive.
sensorial *adj* sensorial, sensory.
sensual *adj* sensuous; sensual, sexy.
sensualidad *f* sensuousness; sensuality; sexiness.
sentado, da *adj* seated; sedate; settled.
sentar *vt* to seat; (*fig*) to establish; • *vi* to suit; ~se *vr* to sit down.
sentencia *f* (*jur*) sentence; opinion; saying.
sentenciar *vt* (*jur*) to sentence, to pass judgment; • *vi* to give one's opinion.
sentencioso, sa *adj* sententious.
sentido *m* sense; feeling; meaning; ~, **da** *adj* regrettable; sensitive.
sentimental *adj* sentimental.
sentimiento *m* feeling, emotion, sentiment; sympathy; regret, grief.
sentir *vt* to feel; to hear, to perceive; to sense; to suffer from; to regret, to be sorry for; ~se *vr* to feel; to feel pain; to crack (of walls *etc*); • *m* opinion, judgement.
seña *f* sign, mark, token; signal; (*mil*) password; ~s *pl* address.
señal *f* sign, token; symptom; signal; landmark; (*com*) deposit.
señalado, da *adj* distinct; special, distinguished, notable.
señalar *vt* to stamp, to mark; to signpost; to point out; to fix, to settle; ~se *vr* to distinguish oneself, to excel.
señor *m* man; gentleman; master; Mr; sir.
señora *f* lady; Mrs; madam; wife.
señorita *f* Miss; young lady.
señorito *m* young gentleman; rich kid.
señuelo *m* decoy; bait, lure.
separable *adj* separable.
separación *f* separation.
separar *vt* to separate; ~se *vr* to separate; to come away, to come apart; to withdraw.
septentrional *adj* north, northern.
se(p)tiembre *m* September.
séptimo, ma *adj* seventh.
sepulcral *adj* sepulchral.
sepulcro *m* sepulcher, grave, tomb.
sepultar *vt* to bury, to inter.
sepultura *f* sepulture, interment.
sepulturero *m* gravedigger, sexton.
sequedad *f* dryness; brusqueness.
sequía *f* dryness; thirst; drought.
séquito *m* retinue, suite; group of supporters; aftermath.
ser *vi* to be; to exist; to come from; to be made of; to belong to; • *m* being.
serenarse *vr* to calm down.
serenata *f* (*mus*) serenade.
serenidad *f* serenity.
sereno *m* night watchman; ~, **na** *adj* serene, calm, quiet.
serial *m* serial.
serie *f* series; sequence.
seriedad *f* seriousness; gravity; reliability; sincerity.
serio, ria *adj* serious; grave; reliable.
sermón *m* sermon.
sermonear *vt* to lecture; • *vi* to sermonize.
serpentear *vi* to wriggle; to wind, to snake.

serpentina *f* streamer.
serpiente *f* snake.
serranía *f* range of mountains, mountainous country.
serrano, na *m/f* highlander.
serrar *vt* to saw.
serrín *m* sawdust.
serrucho *m* handsaw.
servible *adj* serviceable.
servicial *adj* helpful, obliging.
servicio *m* service; service charge; service, set of dishes; ~s *pl* toilet, washroom.
servidor, ra *m/f* servant.
servidumbre *f* servitude; servants *pl*, staff.
servil *adj* servile.
servilleta *f* napkin, serviette.
servir *vt* to serve; to wait on; • *vi* to serve; to be of use; to be in service; ~se *vr* to serve oneself, to help oneself; to deign, to please; to make use of.
sesenta *m, adj* sixty; sixtieth.
sesentón, ona *m/f* person of about sixty years of age.
sesgar *vt* to slope, to slant.
sesgo *m* slope.
sesión *f* session; sitting; performance; showing.
seso *m* brain.
sestear *vi* to take a nap.
sesudo, da *adj* sensible, prudent.
seta *f* mushroom.
setecientos, tas *adj* seven hundred.
setenta *adj, m* seventy.
setiembre *m* September.
seto *m* fence, enclosure, hedge.
seudo . . . *pref* pseudo. . . .
seudónimo *m* pseudonym.
severidad *f* severity.
severo, ra *adj* severe, strict; grave, serious.
sexagenario, ria *adj* sixty years old.
sexagésimo, ma *adj* sixtieth.
sexenio *m* space of six years.
sexo *m* sex.
sexto, ta *adj, m* sixth.
sexual *adj* sexual.
si *conj* whether.
sí *adv* yes; certainly; indeed; • *pn* oneself; himself; herself; itself; yourself; themselves; yourselves; each other.
siderúrgico, ca *adj* iron and steel *compd*; • *f*: **la siderúrgica** the iron and steel industry.
sidra *f* cider.
siega *f* harvest, mowing.
siembra *f* sowing time.
siempre *adv* always; all the time; ever; still; ~ **jamás** for ever and ever.
sien *f* temple (of the head).
sierra *f* saw; range of mountains.
siervo, va *m/f* slave.
siesta *f* siesta, afternoon nap.
siete *adj, m* seven.
sietemesino, na *adj* born seven months after conception; premature; (*fig*) half-witted.
sífilis *f* syphilis.
sifón *m* syphon; soda.
sigilo *m* secrecy.
sigiloso, sa *adj* reserved; silent.
sigla *f* acronym; abbreviation.
siglo *m* century.
significación *f* significance, meaning.
significado *m* significance, meaning.
significar *vt* to signify, to mean; to make known, to express.
significativo, va *adj* significant.
signo *m* sign, mark.
siguiente *adj* following, successive, next.
sílaba *f* syllable.
silbar *vt* to hiss; • *vi* to whistle.

silbato *m* whistle.
silbido, silbo *m* hiss, whistling.
silencio *m* silence; ¡~! silence! quiet!
silencioso, sa *adj* silent.
silo *m* silo; underground store for wheat.
silogismo *m* syllogism.
silueta *f* silhouette; outline; figure.
silvestre *adj* wild, uncultivated; rustic.
silla *f* chair; saddle; seat; ~ de ruedas wheelchair.
sillón *m* armchair, easy chair; rocking chair.
sima *f* abyss; pothole, cavern.
simbólico, ca *adj* symbolic(al).
simbolizar *vt* to symbolize.
símbolo *m* symbol.
simetría *f* symmetry.
simétrico, ca *adj* symmetrical.
simiente *f* seed.
similar *adj* similar.
similitud *f* similarity, similitude.
simio *m* ape.
simpatía *f* liking; kindness; solidarity; affection.
simpático, ca *adj* pleasant; kind.
simpatizante *m/f* sympathizer.
simpatizar *vi*: ~ con to get on well with.
simple *adj* single; simple, easy; mere, sheer, silly; ● *m/f* simpleton.
simpleza *f* simpleness, silliness.
simplicidad *f* simplicity.
simplificar *vt* to simplify.
simulación *f* simulation.
simulacro *m* simulachrum, idol.
simuladamente *adv* deceptively, hypocritically.
simular *vt* to simulate.
simultaneidad *f* simultaneity.
simultáneo, nea *adj* simultaneous.
sin *prep* without.
sinagoga *f* synagogue.
sinceridad *f* sincerity.
sincero, ra *adj* sincere.
síncope *f* (*med*) syncope, fainting fit.
sincronizar *vt* to synchronize.
sindical *adj* union *compd*.
sindicato *m* trade(s) union; syndicate.
sinfín *m*: un ~ de a great many.
sinfonía *f* symphony.
singular *adj* singular; exceptional; peculiar, odd.
singularidad *f* singularity.
singularizar *vt* to distinguish; to singularize; ~se *vr* to distinguish oneself, to stand out.
siniestro, tra *adj* left; (*fig*) sinister; ● *m* accident.
sinnúmero *m* = sinfín.
sino *conj* but; except; save; only; ● *m* fate.
sinónimo, ma *adj* synonymous; ● *m* synonym.
sinsabor *m* unpleasantness; disgust.
sintaxis *f* syntax.
síntesis *f* synthesis.
sintético, ca *adj* synthetic.
sintetizar *vt* synthesize.
síntoma *m* symptom.
sinuosidad *f* sinuosity; curve, wave.
sinuoso, sa *adj* sinuous; wavy.
sinvergüenza *m/f* rogue.
siquiera *conj* even if, even though; ● *adv* at least.
sirena *f* siren; mermaid.
sirviente, ta *m/f* servant.
sisa *f* petty theft; cut, percentage.
sisear *vt, vi* to hiss.
sistema *m* system.
sistemático, ca *adj* systematic.
sitiar *vt* to besiege.
sitio *m* place; spot; site, location; room, space; job, post; (*mil*) siege, blockade.

situación *f* situation, position; standing.
situar *vt* to place, to situate; to invest; ~se *vr* to be established in place *or* business.
slip *m* pants *pl*, briefs *pl*.
smoking *m* tuxedo.
sobaco *m* armpit, armhole.
sobar *vt* to handle, to soften; to knead; to massage, to rub hard; to rumple clothes; to fondle.
soberanía *f* sovereignty.
soberano, na *adj*, *m/f* sovereign.
soberbia *f* pride, haughtiness; magnificence.
soberbio, bia *adj* proud, haughty; magnificent.
sobornar *vt* to suborn, to bribe.
soborno *m* subornation, bribe.
sobra *f* surplus, excess; de ~ spare, surplus, extra.
sobradamente *adv* too; amply.
sobrante *adj* remaining; ● *m* surplus, remainder.
sobrar *vt* to exceed, to surpass; ● *vi* to be more than enough; to remain, to be left.
sobrasada *f* pork sausage spread.
sobre *prep* on; on top of; above, over; more than; besides; ● *m* envelope.
sobreabundancia *f* superabundance.
sobreabundar *vi* to superabound.
sobrecarga *f* extra load; (*com*) surcharge.
sobrecargar *vt* to overload; (*com*) to surcharge.
sobrecoger *vt* to surprise.
sobredosis *f* overdose.
sobreentender *vt* to deduce; ~se *vr*: se sobreentiende que . . . it is implied that.
sobrehumano, na *adj* superhuman.
sobrellevar *vt* to suffer, to tolerate.
sobremanera *adv* excessively.
sobremesa *f*: de ~ immediately after dinner.
sobrenatural *adj* supernatural.
sobrenaturalmente *adv* supernaturally.
sobrenombre *m* nickname.
sobrepasar *vt* to surpass.
sobreponer *vt* to put one thing over *or* on another; ~se *vr* to pull through.
sobresaliente *adj* projecting; (*fig*) outstanding.
sobresalir *vi* to project; (*fig*) to stand out.
sobresaltar *vt* to frighten.
sobresalto *m* start, scare; sudden shock.
sobreseer *vt*: ~ una causa (*jur*) to stay a case; ● *vi*: ~ de to desist from.
sobreseimiento *m* dismissal, suspension.
sobrevenir *vi* to happen, to come unexpectedly; to supervene.
sobreviviente *adj* surviving; ● *m/f* survivor.
sobrevivir *vi* to survive.
sobrevolar *vt* to fly over.
sobriedad *f* sobriety.
sobrino, na *m/f* nephew/niece.
sobrio, ria *adj* sober, frugal.
socarrón, ona *adj* sarcastic, ironical.
socarronería *f* sarcasm, irony.
socavar *vt* to undermine.
socavón *m* hole.
sociabilidad *f* sociability.
sociable *adj* sociable.
social *adj* social.
socialdemócrata *m/f* social democrat.
socialista *adj*, *m/f* socialist.
sociedad *f* society.
socio, cia *m/f* associate, member.
sociología *f* sociology.
sociólogo, ga *m/f* sociologist.
socorrer *vt* to help.
socorrido, da *adj* well stocked, supplied.
socorrista *m/f* first aider; lifeguard.
socorro *m* help, aid, assistance, relief.
soda *f* soda; soda water.

sodomía f sodomy.
sodomita m sodomite.
soez adj dirty, obscene.
sofá m sofa.
sofisma m sophism.
sofista m/f sophist.
sofisticación f sophistication.
sofocar vt to suffocate.
soga f rope.
soja f soy.
sojuzgar vt to conquer, to subdue.
sol m sun; sunshine, sunlight.
solamente adv only, solely.
solapa f lapel.
solapado, da adj cunning, crafty, artful.
solar m building lot; real estate; ancestral home of a family; ● adj solar.
solariego, ga adj belonging to the ancestral home of a family.
solaz m recreation, relaxation; solace, consolation.
solazar vt to provide relaxation for; to comfort.
soldada f wages pl.
soldadesca f military profession.
soldado m/f soldier; ~ **raso** private.
soldador m welder; soldering iron.
soldadura f soldering; solder.
soldar vt to solder; to weld; to unite.
soleado, da adj sunny.
soledad f solitude; loneliness.
solemne adj solemn; impressive, grand.
solemnidad f solemnity.
solemnizar vt to solemnize, to praise.
soler vi to be accustomed to, to be in the habit of.
solfeo m (mus) solfa.
solicitar vt to ask for, to seek; to apply for (a job); to canvass for; to chase after, to pursue.
solícito, ta adj diligent; solicitous.
solicitud f care, solicitude; request, petition.
solidaridad f solidarity.
solidario, ria adj joint; mutually binding.
solidez f solidity.
sólido, da adj solid.
soliloquio m soliloquy, monolog(ue).
solista m/f soloist.
solitario, ria adj solitary; ● m solitaire; ● m/f hermit.
solo m (mus) solo; ~**la** adj alone, single; **a solas** alone, unaided; **sólo** adv only.
solomillo m sirloin.
solsticio m solstice.
soltar vt to untie, to loosen; to set free, to let out; ~**se** vr to get loose; to come undone.
soltero, ra m/f bachelor/single woman; ● adj single, unmarried.
soltura f looseness, slackness; agility, activity; fluency.
soluble adj soluble; solvable.
solución f solution; (teat) dénouement.
solucionar vt to solve; to resolve.
solvente adj, m solvent.
sollozar vi to sob.
sollozo m sob.
sombra f shade, shadow.
sombrear vt to shade.
sombrero m hat.
sombrilla f parasol.
sombrío, bría adj shady, gloomy; sad.
somero, ra adj superficial.
someter vt to conquer (a country); to subject to one's will; to submit; to subdue; ~**se** vr to give in, to submit.
sometimiento m submission.
somnífero m sleeping pill.
somnolencia f sleepiness, drowsiness.
son m sound; rumor.
sonado, da adj celebrated; famous; generally reported.

sonaja f (mus) timbrel.
sonajero m (mus) small timbrel.
sonámbulo, la m/f sleep-walker; somnambulist.
sonar vt to ring; ● vi to sound; to make a noise; to be pronounced; to be talked of; to sound familiar; ~**se** vr to blow one's nose.
sonata f (mus) sonata.
sonda f sounding; (med) probe.
sondear vt (mar) to sound; to probe; to bore.
sondeo m sounding; boring; (fig) poll.
soneto m sonnet.
sónico, ca adj sonic.
sonido m sound.
sonoro, ra adj sonorous.
sonreír(se) vi (vr) to smile.
sonrisa f smile.
sonrojarse vr to blush.
sonrojo m blush.
sonsacar vt to pump a secret out of a person.
sonsonete m tapping noise; monotonous voice.
soñador, ra m/f dreamer.
soñar vt, vi to dream.
soñoliento, ta adj sleepy, drowsy.
sopa f soup; sop.
sopapo m punch, thump.
sopera f soup dish.
sopero m soup plate.
sopetón m: **de ~** suddenly.
soplar vt to blow away, to blow off; to blow up, to inflate; ● vi to blow, to puff.
soplete m blowlamp.
soplo m blowing; puff of wind; (fam) tip-off.
soplón, ona m/f telltale.
sopor m drowsiness, sleepiness.
soporífero, ra adj soporific; ● m sleeping pill.
soportable adj tolerable, bearable.
soportal m portico.
soportar vt to suffer, to tolerate; to support.
sorber vt to sip; to inhale; to swallow; to absorb.
sorbete m sherbet; iced fruit drink.
sorbo m sip; gulp, swallow.
sordera f deafness.
sordidez f sordidness, dirtiness; meanness.
sórdido, da adj sordid; dirty; mean.
sorda, da adj deaf; silent, quiet; ● m/f deaf person.
sordomudo, da adj deaf and dumb.
sorna f slyness; sarcasm; slowness.
soroche m mountain sickness.
sorprender vt to surprise.
sorpresa f surprise.
sortear vt to draw or cast lots; to raffle; to avoid.
sorteo m draw; raffle.
sortija f ring; ringlet, curl.
sortilegio m sorcery.
sosegado, da adj quiet, peaceful.
sosegar vt to appease, to calm; ● vi to rest.
sosería f insipidness; dullness.
sosiego m tranquillity, calmness.
soslayar vt to do or place a thing obliquely.
soslayo adv: **al o de ~** obliquely, sideways.
soso, sa adj insipid, tasteless; dull.
sospecha f suspicion.
sospechar vt to suspect.
sospechoso, sa adj suspicious; suspect; ● m/f suspect.
sostén m support; bra; sustenance.
sostener vt to sustain, to maintain; ~**se** vr to support or maintain oneself; to contrive, to remain.
sostenimiento m support; maintenance; sustenance.
sota f knave (at cards).
sotana f cassock.
sótano m basement, cellar.
sotavento m (mar) leeward, lee.

soto *m* grove, thicket.

status *m invar* status.

su *pn* his, her, its, one's; **sus** their; your.

suave *adj* smooth, soft, delicate; gentle, mild, meek.

suavidad *f* softness, sweetness; suavity.

suavizar *vt* to soften.

subalterno, na *adj* secondary; auxiliary.

subasta *f* auction.

subastar *vt* to sell by auction.

subcampeón, ona *m/f* runner-up.

subconsciente *adj*, *m* subconscious.

subdesarrollado, da *adj* underdeveloped.

subdesarrollo *m* underdevelopment.

subdirector, ora *m/f* assistant director.

súbdito, ta *adj*, *m/f* subject.

subdividir *vt* to subdivide.

subdivisión *f* subdivision.

subestimar *vt* to underestimate.

subida *f* mounting; ascent, rise in value *or* price.

subido, da *adj* deep-colored; high (price).

subir *vt* to raise, to lift up; to go up; to climb; ● to ascend, to climb; to increase, to swell; to get in, to get on, to board; to rise (in price).

súbito, ta *adj* sudden, hasty, unforeseen.

subjetivo, va *adj* subjective.

subjuntivo *m* (*gr*) subjunctive.

sublevación *f* sedition, revolt.

sublevar *vt* to excite a rebellion; to incite a revolt; ~**se** *vr* to revolt.

sublime *adj* sublime.

sublimidad *f* sublimity.

submarino, na *adj* underwater; ● *m* submarine.

subnormal *adj* subnormal; ● *m/f* subnormal person.

subordinación *f* subordination.

subrayar *vt* to underline.

subrepticio, cia *adj* surreptitious.

subsanar *vt* to excuse; to mend, to repair; to overcome.

subsidio *m* subsidy, aid; benefit, allowance.

subsistencia *f* subsistence.

subsistir *vi* to subsist.

su(b)stancia *f* substance.

su(b)stancial *adj* substantial.

su(b)stancioso, sa *adj* substantial, nutritious.

su(b)stracción *f* removal; (*mat*) subtraction.

su(b)straer *vt* to remove; (*mat*) to subtract; ~**se** *vr* to avoid; to withdraw.

subterfugio *f* subterfuge.

subterráneo, nea *adj* subterranean; underground; ● *m* underground passage; (*ferro*) subway.

suburbio *m* slum quarter; suburbs *pl*.

subvencionar *vt* to subsidize.

subversión *f* subversion, overthrow.

subversivo, va *adj* subversive.

subvertir *vt* to subvert, to overthrow.

subyugar *vt* to subdue, to subjugate.

sucedáneo, nea *adj* substitute; ● *m* substitute (food).

suceder *vt, vi* to succeed, to inherit; to happen.

sucesión *f* succession; issue, offspring; inheritance.

sucesivamente *adv*: **y así** ~ and so on.

sucesivo, va *adj* successive.

suceso *m* event; incident.

sucesor, ra *m/f* successor; heir.

suciedad *f* dirtiness, filthiness; dirt.

sucinto, ta *adj* succinct, concise.

sucio, cia *adj* dirty, filthy; obscene; dishonest.

suculento, ta *adj* succulent, juicy.

sucumbir *vt* to succumb.

sucursal *f* branch (office).

sudar *vt, vi* to sweat.

sudeste *m* southeast.

sudoeste *m* southwest.

sudor *m* sweat.

sudorífico, ca *adj* sweaty.

suegra *f* mother-in-law.

suegro *m* father-in-law.

suela *f* sole of the shoe.

sueldo *m* wages *pl*, salary.

suelo *m* ground; floor; soil, surface.

suelto, ta *adj* loose; free; detached; swift; ● *m* loose change.

sueño *m* sleep; dream.

suero *m* (*med*) serum; whey.

suerte *f* fate, destiny, chance, lot, fortune, good luck; kind, sort.

suéter *m* sweater.

suficiencia *f* sufficiency, competence, fitness.

suficiente *adj* enough, sufficient; fit, capable.

sufragar *vt* to aid, to assist.

sufragio *m* vote, suffrage; aid, assistance.

sufrible *adj* bearable.

sufrido, da *adj* long-suffering, patient; hard-wearing.

sufrimiento *m* suffering; patience.

sufrir *vt* to suffer, to bear, to put up with; to support.

sugerencia *f* suggestion.

sugerir *vt* to suggest.

sugestión *f* suggestion.

suicida *adj* suicidal; ● *m/f* suicide; suicidal person.

suicidio *m* suicide.

sujeción *f* subjection.

sujetador *m* fastener; bra.

sujetar *vt* to fasten, to hold down; to subdue; to subject; ~**se** *vr* to subject oneself.

sujeto, ta *adj* fastened, secure; subject, liable; ● *m* subject; individual.

sulfúrico *adj* sulfuric.

sultán *m* sultan.

sultana *f* sultana.

suma *f* total, sum; adding up; summary.

sumamente *adv* extremely.

sumar *vt* to add, to sum up; to collect, to gather; ● *vi* to add up.

sumario, ria *adj* brief, concise; ● *m* summary.

sumergir *vt* to submerge, to sink, to immerse.

sumidero *m* sewer, drain.

suministrador, ra *m/f* provider, supplier.

suministrar *vt* to supply, to furnish.

sumir *vt* to sink, to submerge; (*fig*) to plunge.

sumisión *f* submission.

sumiso, sa *adj* submissive, docile.

sumo, ma *adj* great, extreme; highest, greatest; **a lo** ~ at most.

suntuosidad *f* sumptuousness.

suntuoso, sa *adj* sumptuous.

súper *f* three-star (gasoline).

superable *adj* surmountable.

superabundancia *f* superabundance.

superabundar *vi* to superabound.

superar *vt* to surpass; to overcome; to exceed, to go beyond.

superficial *adj* superficial; shallow.

superficie *f* surface; area.

superfluo, lua *adj* superfluous.

superintendencia *f* supervision.

superintendente *m/f* superintendent, supervisor; floorwalker.

superior *adj* superior; upper; higher; better; ● *m/f* superior.

superioridad *f* superiority.

superlativo, va *adj*, *m* (*gr*) superlative.

supermercado *m* supermarket.

superstición *f* superstition.

supersticioso, sa *adj* superstitious.

supervisor, ra *m/f* supervisor.

supervivencia *f* survival.

superviviente *m/f* survivor; ● *adj* surviving.

suplantación *f* supplanting.

suplantar *vt* to supplant.

suplemento *m* supplement.

suplente *m/f* substitute.
supletorio, ria *adj* supplementary.
súplica *f* petition, request, supplication.
suplicante *adj, m/f* applicant; supplicant.
suplicar *vt* to beg (for), to plead (for); to beg, to plead with.
suplicio *m* torture.
suplir *vt* to supply; to make good, to make up for; to replace.
suponer *vt* to suppose; ● *vi* to have authority.
suposición *f* supposition; authority.
supremo, ma *adj* supreme.
supresión *f* suppression; abolition; removal; deletion.
suprimir *vt* to suppress; to abolish; to remove; to delete.
supuesto *m* assumption; ~, **ta** *adj* supposed; ~ **que** *conj* since, granted that.
supuración *f* suppuration.
supurar *vt* to suppurate.
sur *m* south; south wind.
surcar *vt* to furrow; to cut, to score.
surco *m* furrow; groove.
surgir *vi* to emerge; to crop up.
surtido *m* assortment, supply.
surtir *vt* to supply, to furnish, to provide; ● *vi* to spout, to spurt.
susceptible *adj* susceptible; impressionable.
suscitar *vt* to excite, to stir up.
suscribir *vt* to sign; to subscribe to.
suscripción *f* subscription.
suscriptor, ra *m/f* subscriber.
susodicho, cha *adj* above-mentioned.
suspender *vt* to suspend, to hang up; to stop; to fail (an exam etc).
suspensión *f* suspension; stoppage.
suspenso, sa *adj* hanging; suspended, failed.
suspicacia *f* suspicion, mistrust.
suspicaz *adj* suspicious, distrustful.
suspirar *vi* to sigh.
suspiro *m* sigh.
sustancia *f* = **substancia**.
sustancial *adj* = **substancial**.
sustancioso *adj* = **substancioso**.
sustantivo, va *adj, m* (*gr*) substantive, noun.
sustentar *vt* to sustain; to support, to nourish.
sustento *m* food, sustenance; support.
sustitución *f* substitution.
sustituir *vt* to substitute.
sustituto, ta *adj, m/f* substitute.
susto *m* fright, scare.
sustracción *f* = **substracción**.
sustraer *vt* = **substraer**.
susurrar *vi* to whisper; to murmur; to rustle; ~**se** *vr* to be whispered about.
susurro *m* whisper, murmur.
sutil *adj* subtle; thin; delicate; very soft; keen, observant.
sutileza *f* subtlety; thinness; keenness.
suyo, ya *adj* his, hers, theirs, one's; his, her, its own, one's own *or* their own; **de** ~ per se; **los** ~**s** *mpl* his own, near friends, relations, family, supporters.

T

tabaco *m* tobacco; (*fam*) cigarettes *pl*.
tábano *m* horsefly.
taberna *f* bar, tavern.
tabernero, ra *m/f* barman/barmaid, bartender.
tabicar *vt* to wall up.
tabique *m* thin wall; partition wall.
tabla *f* board; shelf; plank; slab; index of a book; bed of earth in a garden.
tablado *m* scaffold; platform; stage.

tablero *m* plank, board; chessboard; draft-board; (*auto*) dash-board; bulletin board; gambling den.
tableta *f* tablet; (chocolate) bar.
tablilla *f* small board; (*med*) splint.
tablón *m* plank; beam; ~ **de anuncios** bulletin board.
tabú *m* taboo.
taburete *m* stool.
tacañería *f* meanness; craftiness.
tacaño, ña *adj* mean, stingy; crafty.
tácito, ta *adj* tacit, silent; implied.
taciturno, na *adj* tacit, silent; sulky.
taco *m* stopper, plug; heel (of a shoe); wad; book of coupons; billiard cue.
tacón *m* heel.
taconear *vi* to stamp with one's heels; to walk on one's heels.
taconeo *m* stamping of the heels in dancing.
táctica *f* tactics *pl*.
tacto *m* touch, feeling; tact.
tacha *f* fault, defect; small nail.
tachar *vt* to find fault with; to cross out, to erase.
tachuela *f* tack, nail.
tafetán *m* taffeta.
tafilete *m* morocco leather.
tahona *f* bakery.
tahur *m* gambler; cheat.
taimado, da *adj* sly, cunning, crafty.
tajada *f* slice; (*med*) hoarseness.
tajante *adj* sharp.
tajar *vt* to cut, to chop, to slice.
tajo *m* cut, incision; cleft, sheer drop; working area; chopping-block.
tal *adj* such; **con** ~ **que** provided that; **no hay** ~ no such thing.
tala *f* felling of trees.
taladrar *vt* to bore, to pierce.
taladro *m* drill; borer, gimlet.
talante *m* mood; appearance; aspect; will.
talar *vt* to fell trees; to desolate.
talco *m* talk.
talega *f* or **talego** *m* bag; bagful.
talento *m* talent.
talismán *m* talisman.
talón *m* heel; receipt; check.
talonario *m* checkbook; receipt book.
talla *f* raised work; sculpture; stature, size; measure of anything; hand, draw, turn (at cards).
tallado, da *adj* cut, carved, engraved.
tallador *m* engraver.
tallar *vt* to cut, to chop; to carve in wood; to engrave; to measure.
tallarines *mpl* noodles.
talle *m* shape, size, proportion; waist.
taller *m* workshop, laboratory.
tallo *m* shoot, sprout.
tamaño *m* size, shape, bulk.
tamarindo *m* tamarind tree.
tambalearse *vr* to stagger, to waver.
tambaleo *m* staggering, reeling.
también *adv* also, likewise; as well; besides.
tambor *m* drum; drummer; eardrum.
tamborilear *vi* to drum.
tamborilero *m* drummer.
tamiz *m* fine sieve.
tampoco *adv* neither, nor.
tampón *m* tampon.
tan *adv* so.
tanda *f* turn; rotation; task; gang; number of persons employed in a work.
tangente *f* tangent.
tangible *adj* tangible.
tanque *m* tank; tanker.

tantear vt to reckon (up); to measure, to proportion; to consider; to examine.

tanteo m computation, calculation; valuation; test; scoring.

tanto m certain sum or quantity; point; goal; ~, **ta** adj so much, as much; very great; ● adv so much, as much; so long, as long.

tañido m tune; sound; clink.

tapa f lid, cover; snack; ~ **de los sesos** skull.

tapadera f lid of a pot, cover.

tapar vt to stop up, to cover; to conceal, to hide.

taparrabo m loincloth.

tapete m table cover.

tapia f wall.

tapiar vt to brick up with a wall; to stop up a passage.

tapicería f tapestry; upholstery; upholsterer's shop.

tapicero m tapestry-maker; upholsterer.

tapiz m tapestry; carpet.

tapizar vt to upholster.

tapón m cork, plug, bung.

taquigrafía f shorthand writing.

taquilla f booking office; takings pl.

taquillero, ra m/f ticket clerk.

tara f tare.

tarántula f tarantula.

tardanza f slowness, delay.

tardar vi to delay; to take a long time; to be late.

tarde f afternoon; evening; ● adv late.

tardío, dia adj late; slow, tardy.

tardo, da adj sluggish, tardy.

tarea f task.

tarifa f tariff; price list.

tarima f platform; step.

tarjeta f visiting-card, card; ~ **postal** postcard.

tarro m pot.

tarta f tart; cake.

tartamudear vi to stutter, to stammer.

tartamudo, da adj stammering.

tarugo m wooden peg or pin.

tasa f rate; measure, rule; valuation.

tasación f valuation, appraisal.

tasador m appraiser.

tasar vt to appraise, to value.

tasca f (fam) pub, bar.

tatarabuelo m great-great-grandfather.

tataranieto m great-great-grandson.

tatuaje m tattoo; tattooing.

tatuar vt to tattoo.

taurino, na adj bullfighting compd.

Tauro m Taurus (sign of the zodiac).

taxi m taxi.

taxista m/f taxi driver.

taza f cup; basin of a fountain.

té m (bot) tea.

te pn you.

tea f torch.

teatral adj theatrical.

teatro m theater, playhouse.

tebeo m comic.

tecla f key of an organ or pianoforte.

teclado m keyboard.

técnico, ca adj technical.

tecnología f technology.

techo m roof; ceiling.

techumbre f upper roof, ceiling.

tedio m boredom, dislike, abhorrence.

teja f tile.

tejado m roof covered with tiles.

tejanos mpl jeans.

tejar vt to tile.

tejedor m weaver.

tejemaneje m artfulness, cleverness; restlessness.

tejer vt to weave.

tejido m texture, web.

tejo m quoit; yew tree.

tejón m badger.

tela f cloth; material.

telar m loom.

telaraña f cobweb.

tele f (fam) tube.

telefax m invar fax; fax (machine).

telefonear vt to telephone.

telefónico, ca adj telephone compd.

teléfono m (tele)phone.

telegráfico, ca adj telegraphic.

telégrafo m telegraph.

telegrama m telegram.

telescopio m telescope.

televidente m/f viewer.

televisar vt to televise.

televisión f television.

televisor m television set.

télex m telex.

telón m curtain, drape.

tema m theme.

temblar vi to tremble.

temblón, ona adj tremulous, shaking.

temblor m trembling; earthquake.

temer vt to fear, to doubt; ● vi to be afraid.

temerario, ria adj rash.

temeridad f temerity, imprudence.

temeroso, sa adj timid; frightful.

temible adj dreadful, terrible.

temor m dread, fear.

témpano m ice-floe.

temperamento m temperament.

temperatura f temperature.

tempestad f tempest, storm; violent commotion.

tempestuoso, sa adj tempestuous, stormy.

templado, da adj temperate, tempered.

templanza f temperance, moderation; temperature.

templar vt to temper, to moderate, to cool; to tune; ~**se** vr to be moderate.

temple m temperature; tempera; temperament; tuning; **al** ~ painted in distemper.

templo m temple.

temporada f time, season; epoch, period.

temporal adj temporary, temporal; ● m tempest, storm.

temprano, na adj early, anticipated; ● adv very early, prematurely.

tenacillas fpl small tongs.

tenacidad f tenacity; obstinacy.

tenaz adj tenacious; stubborn.

tenaza(s) f (pl) tongs, pincers.

tenazmente adv tenaciously; obstinately.

tendedero m clothes line.

tendencia f tendency.

tender vt to stretch out, to expand, to extend; to hang out; to lay; ~**se** vr to stretch oneself out.

tenderete m stall; display of goods.

tendero, ra m/f shop-keeper.

tendido, da adj lying down; hanging; ● m row of seats for the spectators at a bullfight.

tendón m tendon, sinew.

tenebroso, sa adj dark, obscure.

tenedor m holder, keeper, tenant; fork.

tenencia f possession; tenancy; tenure.

tener vt to take, to hold; to possess; to have; ~**se** vr to take care not to fall; to stop, to halt; to resist; to adhere.

tenia f tapeworm.

teniente m lieutenant.

tenis m tennis.

tenista m/f tennis player.

tenor m meaning; (mus) tenor.

tensar vt to tauten; to draw.

tensión *f* tension.
tenso, sa *adj* tense.
tentación *f* temptation.
tentador, ra *m/f* tempter.
tentar *vt* to touch; to try; to grope; to tempt; to attempt.
tentativa *f* attempt, trial.
tentempié *m* (*fam*) snack.
tenue *adj* thin, tenuous, slender.
tenuidad *f* slenderness, weakness; trifle.
teñir *vt* to tinge, to dye.
teología *f* theology, divinity.
teológico, ca *adj* theological.
teólogo *m* theologian, divine.
teorema *f* theorem.
teoría, teórica *f* theory.
teórico, ca *adj* theoretical.
terapéutico, ca *adj* therapeutic.
terapia *f* therapy.
tercermundista *adj* Third World *compd.*
tercer(o), ra *adj* third; ● *m* (*jur*) third party.
terceto *m* (*mus*) trio.
terciar *vt* to put on sideways; to divide into three parts; to plow the third time; ● *vi* to mediate; to take part.
tercio, cia *adj* third; ● *m* third part.
terciopelo *m* velvet.
terco, ca *adj* obstinate.
tergiversación *f* distortion, evasion.
tergiversar *vt* to distort.
termal *adj* thermal.
termas *fpl* thermal waters.
terminación *f* termination; conclusion; last syllable of a word.
terminal *adj*, *m/f* terminal.
terminante *adj* decisive; categorical.
terminar *vt* to finish; to end; to terminate; ● *vi* to end; to stop.
término *m* term; end; boundary; limit; terminus.
terminología *f* terminology.
termodinámico, ca *adj* thermodynamic.
termómetro *m* thermometer.
termo(s) *m* flask.
termostato *m* thermostat.
ternero, ra *m/f* calf; veal; heifer.
ternilla *f* gristle.
ternilloso, sa *adj* gristly.
terno *m* three-piece suit.
ternura *f* tenderness.
terquedad *f* stubbornness, obstinacy.
terrado *m* terrace.
terraplén *m* terrace, platform.
terrateniente *m/f* landowner.
terraza *f* balcony; (flat) roof; terrace (in fields).
terremoto *m* earthquake.
terrenal *adj* terrestrial, earthly.
terreno, na *adj* earthly, terrestrial; ● *m* land, ground, field.
terrestre *adj* terrestrial.
terrible *adj* terrible, dreadful; ferocious.
territorial *adj* territorial.
territorio *m* territory.
terrón *m* clod of earth; lump; ~**ones** *pl* landed property.
terror *m* terror, dread.
terrorismo *m* terrorism.
terrorista *m/f* terrorist.
terso, sa *adj* smooth, glossy.
tersura *f* smoothness, purity.
tertulia *f* club, assembly, circle.
tesis *f invar* thesis.
tesón *m* tenacity, firmness.
tesorero *m* treasurer.
tesoro *m* treasure; exchequer.
testamentaría *f* testamentary execution.
testamentario *m* executor of a will; ~, **ria** *adj* testamentary.
testamento *m* will, testament.
testar *vt*, *vi* to make one's will; to bequeath.

testarudo, da *adj* obstinate.
testículo *m* testicle; ~**s** *pl* genitals.
testificación *f* attestation.
testificar *vt* to attest, to witness.
testigo *m* witness, deponent.
testimoniar *vt* to attest, to bear witness.
testimonio *m* testimony.
teta *f* teat.
tétanos *m* tetanus.
tetera *f* teapot.
tetilla *f* nipple; teat (of a bottle).
tétrico, ca *adj* gloomy, sullen, surly.
textil *adj* textile.
texto *m* text.
textual *adj* textual.
textura *f* texture.
tez *f* complexion, hue.
ti *pn* you; yourself.
tía *f* aunt; (*fam*) bird.
tiara *f* tiara.
tibieza *f* lukewarmness.
tibio, bia *adj* lukewarm.
tiburón *m* shark.
tiempo *m* time; term; weather; (*gr*) tense; occasion, opportunity; season.
tienda *f* tent; awning; tilt; shop.
tiento *m* touch; circumspection; a ~ *or* a **tientas** gropingly.
tierno, na *adj* tender.
tierra *f* earth; land, ground; native country.
tieso, sa *adj* stiff, hard, firm; robust; valiant; stubborn.
tiesto *m* large earthen pot.
tifón *m* typhoon.
tifus *m* typhus.
tigre *m* tiger.
tijeras *fpl* scissors.
tijeretada *f* cut with scissors, clip.
tijereta *f* earwig.
tijeretear *vt* to cut with scissors.
tildar *vt* to brand, to stigmatize.
tilde *f* tilde (ñ).
tilo *m* lime tree.
timar *vt* to steal; to swindle.
timbrar *vt* to stamp.
timbre *m* stamp; bell; timbre; stamp duty.
timidez *f* timidity.
tímido, da *adj* timid, cowardly.
timo *m* swindle.
timón *m* helm, rudder.
tímpano *m* ear-drum; small drum.
tina *f* tub; bath (tub).
tinaja *f* large earthen jar.
tinglado *m* shed; trick; intrigue.
tinieblas *fpl* darkness; shadows.
tino *m* skill; judgment, prudence.
tinta *f* tint; ink; dye; color.
tinte *m* tint, dye; dry cleaner's.
tintero *m* inkwell.
tinto, ta *adj* dyed; ● *m* red wine.
tintorería *f* dry cleaner's.
tintura *f* tincture; dyeing.
tiña *f* scab.
tiñoso, sa *adj* scabby, scurvy; niggardly.
tío *m* uncle; (*fam*) guy.
tiovivo *m* merry-go-round.
típico, ca *adj* typical.
tiple *m* (*mus*) treble; ● *f* soprano.
tipo *m* type; norm; pattern; guy.
tipografía *f* typography.
tipográfico, ca *adj* typographical.
tipógrafo *m* printer.
tiquet *m* ticket; cash slip.
tiquismiquis *m invar* fussy person.

tira f abundance; strip.
tirabuzón m curl.
tirachinas m invar catapult.
tirado, da adj dirt-cheap; (fam) very easy; ● f cast; distance; series; edition.
tirador m handle.
tiranía f tyranny.
tiránico, ca adj tyrannical.
tiranizar vt to tyrannize.
tirano, na m/f tyrant.
tirante m joist; stay; strap; brace; ● adj taut, extended, drawn.
tirantez f tension; tautness.
tirar vt to throw; to pull; to draw; to drop; to tend, to aim at; ● vi to shoot; to pull; to go; to tend to.
tirita f Band-Aid, (sticking) plaster.
tiritar vi to shiver.
tiritona f shiver, shaking with cold.
tiro m throw, shot; prank; set of coach-horses; **errar el ~** to miss (at shooting).
tirón m pull, haul, tug.
tirotear vt to shoot at.
tiroteo m shooting, sharpshooting.
tirria f antipathy.
tísico, ca adj consumptive.
tisis f tuberculosis.
títere m puppet; ridiculous little fellow.
titiritero m puppeteer.
titubear vi to stammer; to stagger; to hesitate.
titubeo m staggering; hesitation.
titular adj titular; ● m/f occupant; ● m headline; ● vt to title; **~se** vr to obtain a title.
título m title; name; **a ~** on pretense, under pretext.
tiza f chalk.
tiznar vt to smut; to tarnish.
tizne m soot, smut of coal.
tiznón m spot, stain.
tizón m half-burnt wood.
toalla f towel.
tobillo m ankle.
tobogán m toboggan; roller-coaster; slide.
toca f headdress.
tocadiscos m invar record player.
tocado m headdress, headgear.
tocador m dressing table; ladies' room.
tocante (a) prep concerning, relating to.
tocar vt to touch; to strike; (mus) to play; to ring a bell; ● vi to belong; to concern; to knock; to call at; to be a duty or obligation.
tocayo, ya adj namesake.
tocino m bacon.
todavía adv even; yet, still.
todo, da adj all, entire; every; ● pn everything, all; ● m whole.
todopoderoso, sa adj almighty.
toga f toga; gown.
toldo m awning; parasol.
tolerable adj tolerable.
tolerancia f tolerance, indulgence.
tolerante adj tolerant.
tolerar vt to tolerate, to suffer.
toma f taking; dose; **~ (de corriente)** socket.
tomar vt to take, to seize, to grasp; to understand, to interpret; to perceive; to drink; to acquire; ● vi to drink; to take.
tomate m tomato.
tomavistas m invar movie camera.
tomillo m thyme.
tomo m bulk; tome; volume.
ton m: **sin ~ ni son** without rhyme or reason.
tonada f tune, melody.
tonadilla f interlude of music; short tune.
tonalidad f tone.

tonel m cask, barrel.
tonelada f ton; (mar) tonnage duty.
tónico, ca adj tonic, strengthening; ● m tonic; ● f (mus) tonic; (fig) keynote.
tonificar vt to tone up.
tono m tone.
tontada f nonsense.
tontear vi to talk nonsense, to act foolishly.
tontería f foolery, nonsense.
tonto, ta adj stupid, foolish.
topacio m topaz.
topar vt to run into; to find.
tope m butt; scuffle; **~s** pl (ferro) buffers.
topera f molehill.
tópico, ca adj topical.
topo m mole; stumbler.
topografía f topography.
topográfico, ca adj topographical.
toque m touch; bell-ringing; crisis.
toquilla f head-scarf; shawl.
tórax m thorax.
torbellino m whirlwind.
torcedura f twisting.
torcer vt to twist, to curve; to turn; to sprain; ● vi to turn off; **~se** vr to bend; to go wrong.
torcido, da adj oblique; crooked.
torcimiento m bending, deflection; circumlocution.
tordo m thrush; **~, da** adj speckled black and white.
torear vt to avoid; to tease; ● vi to fight bulls.
toreo m bullfighting.
torero m bullfighter.
toril m place where bulls are shut up until brought out.
tormenta f storm, tempest.
tormento m torment, pain, anguish; torture.
tornar vt, vi to return; to restore; to repeat; **~se** vr to become.
tornasolado adj iridescent; shimmering.
torneo m tournament.
tornillo m screw.
torniquete m turnstile; (med) tourniquet.
torno m winch; revolution.
toro m bull.
toronja f grapefruit.
torpe adj dull, heavy; stupid.
torpedo m torpedo.
torpeza f heaviness, dullness; torpor; stupidity.
torre f tower; turret; steeple of a church.
torrefacto, ta adj roasted.
torrente m torrent.
tórrido, da adj torrid, parched, hot.
torrija f French toast.
torso m torso.
torta f cake; (fam) slap.
tortícolis f invar stiff neck.
tortilla f omelet; pancake.
tórtola f turtledove.
tortuga f tortoise.
tortuoso, sa adj tortuous, circuitous.
tortura f torture.
torvo, va adj stern, grim.
tos f cough.
toscamente adv coarsely, grossly.
tosco, ca adj coarse, ill-bred, clumsy.
toser vi to cough.
tostada f slice of toast.
tostado, da adj parched, sunburnt; light-yellow, light-brown.
tostador m toaster.
tostar vt to toast, to roast.
total m whole, totality; ● adj total, entire; ● adv in short.
totalidad f totality.
totalitario, ria adj totalitarian.
tóxico, ca adj toxic; ● m poison.
toxicómano, na m/f drug addict.

tozudo, da *adj* obstinate.
traba *f* obstacle, impediment; trammel, fetter.
trabajador, ra *adj* working; • *m/f* worker.
trabajar *vt* to work, to labor; to persuade; to push; • *vi* to strive.
trabajo *m* work, labor, toil; difficulty; ~s *pl* troubles.
trabajoso, sa *adj* laborious; painful.
trabalenguas *m invar* tongue twister.
trabar *vt* to join, to unite; to take hold of; to fetter, to shackle.
trabucarse *vr* to mistake.
tracción *f* traction; ~ **delantera/trasera** front-wheel/rear-wheel drive.
tractor *m* tractor.
tradición *f* tradition.
traducción *f* version, translation.
traducir *vt* to translate.
traductor *m* translator.
traer *vt* to bring, to carry, to attract; to persuade; to wear; to cause.
traficante *m* merchant, dealer.
traficar *vt* to trade, to do business, to deal (in).
tráfico *m* traffic, trade.
tragaldabas *m/f invar* glutton.
tragaluz *m* skylight.
tragaperras *m o f invar* slot machine.
tragar *vt* to swallow; to swallow up.
tragedia *f* tragedy.
trágico, ca *adj* tragic, tragical.
trago *m* drink; gulp, adversity, misfortune.
tragón, ona *adj* gluttonous.
traición *f* treason.
traicionar *vt* to betray.
traicionero, ra *adj* treacherous.
traidor *m* traitor; ~, **ra** *adj* treacherous.
traje *m* suit; dress; costume.
trajín *m* haulage; (*fam*) bustle.
trajinar *vt* to carry; • *vi* to bustle about; to travel around.
trama *f* plot; woof.
tramar *vt* to weave; to plot.
tramitar *vt* to transact; to negotiate; to handle.
trámite *m* path; (*jur*) procedure.
tramo *m* section; piece of ground; flight of stairs.
tramoya *f* scene, theatrical decoration; trick.
tramoyista *m* scene-painter; swindler.
trampa *f* trap, snare; trapdoor; fraud.
trampear *vi, vt* to swindle, to deceive.
trampolín *m* trampoline; diving board.
tramposo, sa *adj* deceitful, swindling.
tranca *f* bar, crossbeam.
trance *m* danger; last stage of life; trance.
tranco *m* long step *or* stride.
tranquilidad *f* tranquillity; repose, heart's ease.
tranquilizar *vt* to calm; to reassure.
tranquilo, la *adj* tranquil, calm, quiet.
transacción *f* transaction.
transbordador *m* ferry.
transbordar *vt* to transfer.
transbordo *m* transfer; **hacer** ~ to change (trains).
transcribir *vt* to transcribe, to copy.
transcurrir *vi* to pass; to turn out.
transcurso *m*: ~ **del tiempo** course of time.
transeúnte *adj* transitory; • *m* passer-by.
transferencia *f* transference; (*com*) transfer.
transferir *vt* to transfer; to defer.
transfiguración *f* transformation, transfiguration.
transformación *f* transformation.
transformador *m* transformer.
transformar *vt* to transform; ~**se** *vr* to change one's sentiments *or* manners.
tránsfuga, tránsfugo *m* deserter, fugitive.
transfusión *f* transfusion.
transgresión *f* transgression.

transgresor *m* transgressor.
transición *f* transition.
transido, da *adj* worn out with anguish; overcome.
transigir *vi* to compromise.
transistor *m* transistor.
transitar *vi* to travel, to pass by a place.
transitivo, va *adj* transitive.
tránsito *m* passage; transition; road, way; change, removal; death of holy *or* virtuous persons.
transitorio, ria *adj* transitory.
transmisión *f* transmission; transfer; broadcast.
transmitir *vt* to transmit; to broadcast.
transmutación *f* transmutation.
transmutar *vt* to transmute.
transparencia *f* transparency; clearness; slide.
transparentarse *vr* to be transparent; to shine through.
transparente *adj* transparent.
transpiración *f* perspiration; transpiration.
transpirar *vt* to perspire; to transpire.
transportar *vt* to transport, to convey.
transporte *m* transportation.
transposición *f* transposition, transposal.
transversal *adj* transverse; collateral.
tranvía *m* tram.
trapacería *f* fraud, deceit.
trapacero, ra *adj* deceitful.
trapecio *m* trapeze.
trapecista *m/f* trapeze artist.
trapero, ra *m/f* dealer in rags.
trapicheo *m* (*fam*) fiddle.
trapo *m* rag, tatter.
tráquea *f* windpipe.
traqueteo *m* rattling.
tras *prep* after, behind.
trascendencia *f* transcendency; penetration.
trascendental *adj* transcendental.
trascender *vt* to come out; to go beyond; to rise above.
trasegar *vt* to move about; to decant.
trasero, ra *adj* back; • *m* bottom.
trasfondo *m* background.
trasgredir *vt* to contravene.
trashumante *adj* migrating.
trasiego *m* removal; decanting of liquors.
trasladar *vt* to transport; to transfer; to postpone; to transcribe, to copy; ~**se** *vr* to move.
traslado *m* move; removal.
traslucirse *vr* to be transparent; to conjecture.
trasluz *m* reflected light.
trasnochar *vi* to watch, to sit up the whole night.
traspapelarse *vr* to get mislaid among other papers.
traspasar *vt* to remove, to transport; to transfix, to pierce; to return; to exceed the proper bounds; to trespass; to transfer.
traspaso *m* transfer, sale.
traspié *m* trip; slip, stumble.
trasplantar *vt* to transplant.
trasplante *m* transplant.
trasquilar *vt* to shear sheep; to clip.
trasquilón *m* cut of the shears; hair badly cut.
traste *m* fret of a guitar; **dar al** ~ **con algo** to ruin something.
trastear *vt* to move furniture.
trastero *m* lumber room.
trastienda *f* back room behind a shop.
trasto *m* piece of junk; useless person.
trastornado, da *adj* crazy.
trastornar *vt* to overthrow, to overturn; to confuse; ~**se** *vr* to go crazy.
trastorno *m* overturning; confusion.
trastrocar *vt* to invert the order of things.
tratable *adj* friendly.
tratado *m* treaty, convention; treatise.
tratamiento *m* treatment; style of address.
tratante *m* dealer.

tratar *vt* to traffic, to trade; to use; to treat; to handle; to address; ~se *vr* to treat each other.
trato *m* treatment; manner, address; trade, traffic; conversation; (*com*) agreement.
trauma *m* trauma.
través *m* (*fig*) reverse; **de** *o* **al** ~ across, crossways; **a** ~ **de** *prep* across; over; through.
travesaño *m* crosstimber; transom.
travesía *f* crossing; cross-street; trajectory; (*mar*) side wind.
travesura *f* wit; wickedness.
travieso, sa *adj* restless, uneasy, fidgety; turbulent; lively; naughty.
trayecto *m* road; journey, stretch; course.
trayectoria *f* trajectory; path.
traza *f* first sketch; trace, outline; project; manner; means; appearance.
trazar *vt* to plan out; to project; to trace.
trazo *m* sketch, plan, design.
trébedes *fpl* trivet, tripod.
trébol *m* trefoil, clover.
trece *adj, m* thirteen; thirteenth.
trecho *m* space, distance of time *or* place; **a** ~**s** at intervals.
tregua *f* truce, cessation of hostilities.
treinta *adj, m* thirty.
tremendo, da *adj* terrible, formidable; awful, grand.
tremolar *vt* to hoist the colors; to wave.
trémulo, la *adj* tremulous, trembling.
tren *m* train, retinue; show, ostentation; (*ferro*) train; ~ **de gran velocidad** fast *or* express train; ~ **de mercancías** freight train, luggage-train.
trenza *f* braided hair, plaited silk.
trenzar *vt* to braid.
trepar *vi* to climb, to crawl.
tres *adj, m* three.
tresillo *m* three-piece suite; (*mus*) triplet.
treta *f* thrust in fencing; trick.
triangular *adj* triangular.
triángulo *m* triangle.
tribu *f* tribe.
tribulación *f* tribulation, affliction.
tribuna *f* tribune.
tribunal *m* tribunal, court of justice.
tributar *vt* to pay; to contribute to; to pay homage and respect.
tributario, ria *adj* tributary.
tributo *m* tribute.
tricolor *adj* tricolored.
tricotar *vi* to knit.
tridente *m* trident.
trienal *adj* triennial.
trienio *m* space of three years.
trigal *m* wheat field.
trigésimo, ma *adj, m* thirtieth.
trigo *m* wheat.
trigueño, ña *adj* corn-colored; olive-skinned.
trillado, da *adj* beaten; trite, stale, hackneyed; **camino** ~ common routine.
trilladora *f* threshing machine.
trillar *vt* to thresh.
trimestral *adj* quarterly; termly.
trimestre *m* space of three months.
trinar *vi* to trill, to quaver; to be angry.
trincar *vt* to tie up; to pinion.
trinchante *m* carver; carving knife.
trinchar *vt* to carve, to divide meat.
trinchera *f* trench, entrenchment.
trineo *m* sledge.
Trinidad *f* Trinity.
trino *m* trill.
trío *m* (*mus*) trio.
tripa *f* gut, tripe, intestine.
triple *adj* triple, treble.

triplicar *vt* to treble.
trípode *m* tripod, trivet.
tripulación *f* crew.
tripulante *m/f* crewman/woman.
tripular *vt* to man; to drive.
triquiñuela *f* trick.
triquitraque *m* clack, clatter, clashing.
tris *m invar*: **estar en un** ~ **de** to be on the point of.
triste *adj* sad, mournful, melancholy.
tristeza *f* sadness, mourning.
trituración *f* pulverization.
triturar *vt* to reduce to powder, to grind, to pound.
triunfal *adj* triumphal.
triunfar *vi* to triumph; to trump at cards.
triunfo *m* triumph; trump (at cards).
trivial *adj* frequented, beaten; vulgar, trivial.
trivialidad *f* vulgarity.
triza *f*: **hacer** ~**s** to smash to bits; to tear to shreds.
trocar *vt* to exchange.
trocha *f* short cut.
troche: a ~ **y moche** *adv* helter-skelter.
trofeo *m* trophy.
tromba *f* whirlwind.
trombón *m* trombone.
trombosis *f invar* thrombosis.
trompa *f* trumpet; proboscis; large top.
trompazo *m* heavy blow; accident.
trompeta *f* trumpet; ● *m* trumpeter.
trompetilla *f* small trumpet; speaking-trumpet.
trompicón *m* stumble.
trompo *m* spinning top.
tronar *vi* to thunder; to rage.
troncar *vt* to truncate, to mutilate.
tronco *m* trunk; log of wood; stock.
tronchar *vt* to cut off; to shatter; to tire out.
troncho *m* sprig, stem *or* stalk.
tronera *m* loophole; small window; pocket of a billiard table.
trono *m* throne.
tropa *f* troop.
tropel *m* confused noise; hurry, bustle, confusion, heap of things; crowd; **en** ~ in a tumultuous and confused manner.
tropelía *f* outrage.
tropezar *vi* to stumble; to meet accidentally.
tropezón, ona *adj* stumbling; **a** ~**ones** impeded and obstructed; ● *m* trip.
tropical *adj* tropical.
trópico *m* tropic.
tropiezo *m* stumble, trip; obstacle; slip, fault; quarrel; dispute.
trotamundos *m invar* globetrotter.
trotar *vi* to trot.
trote *m* trot; traveling.
trovador, ra *m/f* troubadour.
trozo *m* piece.
truco *m* knack; trick.
trucha *f* trout.
trueno *m* thunderclap.
trueque *m* exchange.
trufa *f* truffle.
truhán *adj* rogue.
truncado, da *adj* truncated.
truncamiento *m* truncation.
truncar *vt* to truncate, to maim.
tu *adj* your.
tú *pn* you.
tubérculo *m* tuber.
tuberculosis *f* tuberculosis.
tubería *f* pipe; pipeline.
tubo *m* tube.
tuerca *f* screw.
tuerto, ta *adj* one-eyed; squint-eyed; ● *m/f* one-eyed person.
tuétano *m* marrow.

tufarada *f* strong scent *or* smell.
tufo *m* warm vapor arising from the earth; offensive smell.
tugurio *m* slum.
tul *m* tulle.
tulipán *m* tulip.
tullido, da *adj* crippled, maimed.
tumba *f* tomb.
tumbar *vt* to knock down; ● *vi* to tumble (to fall down); ~**se** *vr* to lie down to sleep.
tumbo *m* fall; jolt.
tumbona *f* easy chair; beach chair.
tumor *m* tumor, growth.
túmulo *m* tomb, sepulchral monument.
tumulto *m* tumult, uproar.
tumultuoso, sa *adj* tumultuous.
tuna *f* student music group.
tunda *f* beating.
túnel *m* tunnel.
túnica *f* tunic.
tuno *m* rogue.
tupé *m* toupée.
tupido, da *adj* dense.
tupir *vt* to press close; ~**se** *vr* to stuff oneself with eating and drinking.
turbación *f* perturbation, confusion, trouble, disorder.
turbado, da *adj* disturbed.
turbante *m* turban.
turbar *vt* to disturb, to trouble; ~**se** *vr* to be disturbed.
turbina *f* turbine.
turbio, bia *adj* muddy, troubled.
turbulencia *f* turbulence, disturbance.
turbulento, ta *adj* muddy; turbulent.
turismo *m* tourism.
turista *m/f* tourist.
turístico, ca *adj* tourist.
turnar *vi* to alternate.
turno *m* turn; shift; opportunity.
turquesa *f* turquoise.
turrón *m* nougat (almond cake).
tutear *vt* to address as 'tú'.
tutela *f* guardianship, tutelage.
tutelar *adj* tutelar, tutelary.
tutor *m* guardian, tutor.
tutora *f* tutoress.
tutoría *f* tutelage.
tuyo, ya *adj* yours; ~**s** *pl* friends and relations of the party addressed.

U

u *conj* or (instead of *o* before an *o* or *ho*).
ubicar *vt* to place; ~**se** to be located.
ubre *f* udder.
ufanarse *vr* to boast.
ufano, na *adj* haughty, arrogant.
ujier *m* usher.
úlcera *f* ulcer.
ulcerar *vi* to ulcerate.
ulterior *adj* ulterior, farther, further.
últimamente *adv* lately.
ultimar *vt* to finalize; to finish.
ultimátum *m* ultimatum.
último, ma *adj* last; latest; bottom; top.
ultrajar *vt* to outrage; to despise; to abuse.
ultraje *m* outrage.
ultramar *adj*, *m* overseas.
ultramarinos *mpl* groceries.
ultrasónico, ca *adj* ultrasonic.
umbilical *adj* umbilical.
umbral *m* threshold.

un, una *art* a, an; ● *adj*, *m* one (for **uno**).
unánime *adj* unanimous.
unanimidad *f* unanimity.
unción *f* unction; extreme *or* last unction.
ungir *vt* to anoint.
ungüento *m* ointment.
únicamente *adv* only, simply.
único, ca *adj* only; singular, unique.
unicornio *m* unicorn.
unidad *f* unity; unit; conformity, union.
unificar *vt* to unite.
uniformar *vt* to make uniform.
uniforme *adj* uniform; ● *m* (*mil*) uniform, regimentals *pl*.
uniformidad *f* uniformity.
unilateral *adj* unilateral.
unión *f* union.
unir *vt* to join, to unite; to mingle, to bind, to tie; ~**se** *vr* to associate.
unísono, na *adj* unison.
universal *adj* universal.
universidad *f* universality; university.
universitario, ria *adj* university; ● *m/f* student.
universo *m* universe.
uno *m* one; ~, **na** *adj* one; sole, only; ~ **a otro** one another; ~ **a** ~ one by one; **a una** jointly together.
untar *vt* to anoint; to grease; (*fam*) to bribe.
uña *f* nail; hoof; claw, talon; pointed hook of instruments.
¡upa! up! up!
urbanidad *f* urbanity, politeness.
uranio *m* uranium.
urbanismo *m* town planning.
urbanización *f* housing development.
urbano, na *adj* urban.
urdimbre *f* warp; intrigue.
urdir *vt* to warp; to contrive.
urgencia *f* urgency; emergency; need, necessity.
urgente *adj* urgent.
urgentemente *adv* urgently.
urgir *vi* to be urgent.
urinario, ria *adj* urinary; ● *m* urinal.
urna *f* urn; ballot box.
urraca *f* magpie.
usado, da *adj* used; experienced; worn.
usanza *f* usage, use, custom.
usar *vt* to use, to make use of; to wear; ~**se** *vr* to be used.
uso *m* use, service; custom; mode.
usted *pn* you.
usuario *m* user.
usufructo *m* (*jur*) usufruct, use.
usura *f* usury.
usurario, ria *adj* usurious.
usurero *m* usurer.
usurpación *f* usurpation.
usurpar *vt* to usurp.
utensilio *m* utensil.
uterino, na *adj* uterine.
útero *m* uterus, womb.
útil *adj* useful, profitable; ● *m* utility.
utilidad *f* utility.
utilizar *vt* to use; to make useful.
utopía *f* Utopia.
utópico, ca Utopian.
uva *f* grape.

V

vaca *f* cow; beef.
vacaciones *fpl* vacation; holidays *pl*.
vacante *adj* vacant; ● *f* vacancy.

vaciar *vt* to empty, to clear; to mold; • *vi* to fall, to decrease (of waters); ~**se** *vr* to empty.

vacilación *f* hesitation; irresolution.

vacilar *vi* to hesitate; to falter; to fail.

vacío, cia *adj* void, empty; unoccupied; concave; vain; presumptuous; • *m* vacuum; emptiness.

vacuna *f* vaccine.

vacunar *vt* to vaccinate.

vacuno, na *adj* bovine, cow.

vadear *vt* to wade, to ford.

vagabundo, da *adj* wandering; • *m* bum.

vagancia *f* vagrancy.

vagar *vi* to rove *or* loiter about; to wander.

vagido *m* cry of a child; convulsive sob.

vagina *f* vagina.

vago, ga *adj* vagrant; restless; vague.

vagón *m (ferro)* wagon; carriage; ~ **de mercancías** freight car.

vaguear *vi* to rove, to loiter; to wander.

vahído *m* vertigo, giddiness.

vaho *m* steam, vapor.

vaina *f* scabbard of a sword; pod, husk.

vainilla *f (bot)* vanilla.

vaivén *m* fluctuation, instability; giddiness.

vajilla *f* crockery.

vale *m* farewell; promissory note, I.O.U.

valedero, ra *adj* valid, efficacious, binding.

valentía *f* valor, courage.

valentón *m* braggart.

valentonada *f* brag, boast.

valer *vi* to be valuable, to be deserving; to cost; to be valid; to be worth; to produce; to be equivalent to; to be current; • *vt* to protect, to favor; ~**se** *vr* to employ, to make use of; to have recourse to.

valeroso, sa *adj* valiant, brave; strong, powerful.

valía *f* valuation; worth.

validar *vt* to validate.

validez *f* validity, stability.

válido, da *adj* valid.

valiente *adj* robust, vigorous; valiant, brave; boasting.

valija *f* suitcase.

valioso, sa *adj* valuable.

valor *m* value, price; validity; force; power; courage; valor.

valoración *f* valuation.

valor(e)ar *vt* to value; to evaluate.

valuación *f* valuation.

vals *m invar* waltz.

válvula *f* valve.

valla *f* fence; hurdle; barricade.

vallar *vt* to fence in.

valle *m* valley.

vampiro *m* vampire.

vanagloriarse *vr* to boast.

vandalismo *m* vandalism.

vándalo, la *m, adj* vandal.

vanguardia *f* vanguard.

vanidad *f* vanity; ostentation.

vanidoso, sa *adj* vain, showy; haughty, self-conceited.

vano, na *adj* vain; useless, frivolous; arrogant; futile; **en ~** in vain.

vapor *m* vapor, steam; breath.

vaporizador *m* atomizer.

vaporizar *vt* to vaporize.

vaporoso, sa *adj* vaporous.

vapular *vt* to whip, to flog.

vaquerizo, za *adj* cattle; • *m* cow-herd.

vaquero *m* cow-herd; ~, **ra** *adj* belonging to cowman; ~**s** *mpl* jeans.

vara *f* rod; pole, staff; stick.

variable *adj* variable, changeable.

variación *f* variation.

variado, da *adj* varied; variegated.

variar *vt* to vary; to modify; to change; • *vi* to vary.

varices *fpl* varicose veins.

variedad *f* variety; inconstancy.

varilla *f* small rod; curtain-rod; spindle, pivot.

vario, ria *adj* varied, different; vague; variegated; ~**s** *pl* some; several.

varón *m* man, male.

varonil *adj* male, masculine; manful.

vasco, ca *adj, m/f* Basque.

vascuence *m* Basque.

vaselina *f* Vaseline.

vasija *f* vessel.

vaso *m* glass; vessel; vase.

vástago *m* bud, shoot; offspring.

vasto, ta *adj* vast, huge.

vaticinar *vt* to divine, to foretell.

vaticinio *m* prophecy.

vatio *m* watt.

vecindad *f* inhabitants of a place; neighborhood.

vecindario *m* number of inhabitants of a place; neighborhood.

vecino, na *adj* neighboring; near; • *m* neighbor, inhabitant.

veda *f* prohibition.

vedar *vt* to prohibit, to forbid; to impede.

vegetación *f* vegetation.

vegetal *adj* vegetable.

vegetar *vi* to vegetate.

vegetariano, na *adj* vegetarian.

vehemencia *f* vehemence, force.

vehemente *adj* vehement, violent.

vehículo *m* vehicle.

veinte *adj, m* twenty.

veintena *f* twentieth part; score.

vejación *f* vexation; embarrassment.

vejar *vt* to vex; to humiliate.

vejestorio *m* old man.

vejez *f* old age.

vejiga *f* bladder.

vela *f* watch; watchfulness; night-guard; candle; sail; **hacerse a la ~** to set sail.

velado, da *adj* veiled; blurred; • *f* soirée.

velador *m* watchman; careful observer; candlestick; pedestal table.

velar *vi* to stay awake; to be attentive; • *vt* to guard, to watch.

veleidad *f* feeble will; inconstancy.

velero, ra *adj* swift sailing.

veleta *f* weather cock.

velo *m* veil; pretext.

velocidad *f* speed; velocity.

velocímetro *m* speedometer.

veloz(mente) *adj (adv)* swift(ly), fast.

vello *m* down; gossamer; short downy hair.

vellón *m* fleece.

velludo, da *adj* shaggy, wooly.

vena *f* vein, blood vessel.

venado *m* deer; venison.

vencedor, ra *m/f* conqueror, victor, winner.

vencer *vt* to defeat; to conquer, to vanquish; • *vi* to win; to expire.

vencido, da *adj* defeated; due.

vencimiento *m* victory; maturity.

vendal *f* bandage.

vendaja *m* bandage, dressing of wounds.

vendar *vt* to bandage; to hoodwink.

vendaval *m* gale.

vendedor, ra *m/f* seller.

vender *vt* to sell.

vendimia *f* grape harvest; vintage.

vendimiador, ra *m/f* vintager.

vendimiar *vt* to harvest; to gather the vintage.

veneno *m* poison, venom.

venenoso, sa *adj* venomous, poisonous.

venerable *adj* venerable.

veneración *f* veneration, worship.

venerar *vt* to venerate, to worship.
venéreo, rea *adj* venereal.
venganza *f* revenge, vengeance.
vengar *vt* to revenge, to avenge; ~**se** *vr* to take revenge.
vengativo, va *adj* revengeful.
venia *f* pardon; leave, permission; bow.
venial *adj* venial.
venida *f* arrival; return; overflow of a river.
venidero, ra *adj* future; ~**s** *mpl* posterity.
venir *vi* to come, to arrive; to follow, to succeed; to happen; to spring from; ~**se** *vr* to ferment.
venta *f* sale.
ventaja *f* advantage.
ventajoso, sa *adj* advantageous.
ventana *f* window; window-shutter; nostril.
ventanilla *f* window.
ventarrón *m* violent wind.
ventilación *f* ventilation; draft.
ventilar *vt* to ventilate; to fan; to discuss.
ventisca *f*, **ventisco** *m* snowstorm.
ventiscar *vi* to drift, to lie in drifts (snow).
ventisquero *m* snowdrift; ~**s** *pl* glaciers.
ventolera *f* gust; pride, loftiness.
ventosidad *f* flatulence.
ventoso, sa *adj* windy; flatulent.
ventrículo *m* ventricle.
ventrílocuo *m* ventriloquist.
ventura *f* happiness; luck, chance, fortune; **por** ~ by chance.
venturoso, sa *adj* lucky, fortunate, happy.
Venus *f* evening star.
ver *vt* to see, to look at; to observe; to visit; ● *vi* to understand; to see; ~**se** *vr* to be seen; to be conspicuous; to find oneself; to have a bone to pick with someone; ● *m* sense of sight; appearance.
vera *f* edge; bank.
veracidad *f* truth; veracity.
veranear *vi* to spend the summer vacation.
veraneo *m* summer holiday.
veraniego, ga *adj* summer.
verano *m* summer.
veras *fpl* truth, sincerity; **de** ~ in truth, really.
veraz *adj* truthful.
verbal *adj* verbal.
verbena *f* fair; dance.
verbo *m* word, term; (*gr*) verb.
verbosidad *f* verbosity.
verdad *f* truth, veracity, reality, reliability.
verdaderamente *adv* truly, in fact.
verdadero, ra *adj* true, real; sincere.
verde *m*, *adj* green.
verdear, verdecer *vi* to turn green.
verdín *m* bright green; verdure.
verdor *m* greenness; verdure; youth.
verdoso, sa *adj* greenish, greeny.
verdugo *m* hangman; very cruel person.
verdulero, ra *m/f* greengrocer.
verdura *f* verdure; vegetables, greens; vigor.
vereda *f* path; sidewalk.
veredicto *m* verdict.
vergel *m* orchard.
vergonzoso, sa *adj* bashful, shamefaced.
vergüenza *f* shame; bashfulness; confusion.
vericueto *m* rough road.
verídico, ca *adj* truthful.
verificación *f* verification.
verificar *vt* to check; to verify; ~**se** *vr* to happen.
verisímil *adj* probable.
verja *f* grate, lattice.
vermut *m* vermouth.
verosímil *adj* likely; credible.
verosimilitud *f* likeliness; credibility.
verraco *m* boar.

verruga *f* wart, pimple.
versado, da *adj* versed.
versátil *adj* versatile.
versículo *m* versicle; verse of a chapter.
versificar *vt* to versify.
versión *f* translation, version.
verso *m* verse.
vértebra *f* vertebra.
vertedero *m* sewer, drain; tip.
verter *vt* to pour; to spill; to empty; ● *vi* to flow.
vertical *adj* vertical.
vértice *m* vertex, zenith; crown of the head.
vertiente *f* slope; waterfall, cascade.
vertiginoso, sa *adj* giddy.
vértigo *m* giddiness, vertigo.
vesícula *f* blister.
vespertino, na *adj* evening.
vestíbulo *m* vestibule, lobby; foyer.
vestido *m* dress, clothes *pl*.
vestidura *f* dress; clothing.
vestigio *m* vestige, footstep; trace.
vestimenta *f* clothing.
vestir *vt* to put on; to wear; to dress; to adorn; to cloak, to disguise; ● *vi* to dress; ~**se** to get dressed.
vestuario *m* clothes; uniform; vestry; locker room.
veta *f* vein (in mines, wood, *etc*); streak; grain.
vetado, da *adj* striped, veined.
vetar *vt* to veto.
veterano, na *adj* experienced, long practised; ● *m* veteran, old soldier.
veterinario, ria *m/f* vet; ● *f* veterinary science.
veto *m* veto.
vez *f* time, turn, return; **cada** ~ each time; **una** ~ once; **a veces** sometimes, by turns.
vía *f* way, road, route; mode, manner, method; (*ferro*) railroad, line.
viajante *m* sales representative.
viajar *vi* to travel.
viaje *m* journey, voyage, travel.
viajero *m* traveler.
vial *adj* road.
viático *m* viaticum; travel allowance.
víbora *f* viper.
vibración *f* vibration.
vibrador *m* vibrator.
vibrante *adj* vibrant.
vibrar *vt*, *vi* to vibrate.
vicaría *f* vicarship; vicarage.
vice . . . *pref* vice . . . deputy . . .
vicealmirante *m* vice-admiral.
viceconsulado *m* vice-consulate.
vicepresidente *m/f* vice-president.
viciar *vt* to vitiate, to corrupt; to annul; to deprave.
vicio *m* vice.
vicioso, sa *adj* vicious; depraved.
vicisitud *f* vicissitude.
víctima *f* victim; sacrifice.
victoria *f* victory.
victorioso, sa *adj* victorious.
vicuña *m* vicuna.
vid *f* (*bot*) vine.
vida *f* life.
vidriado *m* glazed earthenware, crockery.
vídeo *m* video.
vidriar *vt* to glaze.
vidriera *f* stained-glass window; shop window.
vidriero *m* glazier.
vidrio *m* glass.
vidrioso, sa *adj* glassy, brittle; slippery; very delicate.
vieira *f* scallop.
viejo, ja *adj* old; ancient, antiquated.
viento *m* wind; air.

vientre *m* belly.
viernes *m* Friday; **V~ Santo** Good Friday.
viga *f* beam; girder.
vigencia *f* validity.
vigente *adj* in force.
vigésimo, ma *adj, m* twentieth.
vigía *f* (*mar*) lookout; ● *m* watchman.
vigilancia *f* vigilance, watchfulness.
vigilante *adj* watchful, vigilant.
vigilar *vt* to watch over; ● *vi* to keep watch.
vigilia *f* vigil; watch.
vigor *m* vigor, strength.
vigoroso, sa *adj* vigorous.
vil *adj* mean, sordid, low; worthless; infamous; ungrateful.
vileza *f* meanness, lowness; abjectness.
vilipendiar *vt* to despise, to revile.
vilo: en ~ *adv* in the air; in suspense.
villa *f* villa; small town.
villancico *m* Christmas carol.
villano, na *adj* rustic, clownish; villanous; ● *m* villain; rustic.
villorio *m* miserable little hamlet; shanty town.
vinagre *m* vinegar.
vinagrera *f* vinegar cruet.
vinagreta *f* vinaigrette.
vinculación *f* link; linking.
vincular *vt* to link.
vínculo *m* tie, link, chain; entail.
vindicación *f* revenge.
vindicar *vt* to revenge.
vindicativo, va *adj* vindictive.
vinicultura *f* wine growing.
vino *m* wine; **~ tinto** red wine.
viña *f* vineyard.
viñedo *m* vineyard.
viñeta *f* vignette.
viola *f* viola.
violación *f* violation; rape.
violado, da *adj* violet-colored; violated.
violador, ra *m/f* rapist; violator; profaner.
violar *vt* to rape; to violate; to profane.
violencia *f* violence.
violentar *vt* to force.
violento, ta *adj* violent, forced; absurd.
violeta *f* violet.
violín *m* violin, fiddle.
violinista *m* violinist.
violón *m* double bass.
violoncelo *m* violoncello.
viperino, na *adj* viperish.
viraje *m* turn; bend.
virar *vi* to swerve.
virgen *m/f* virgin.
virginidad *f* virginity, maidenhood.
Virgo *f* Virgo (sign of the zodiac).
viril *adj* virile, manly.
virilidad *f* virility, manhood.
virrey *m* viceroy.
virtual *adj* virtual.
virtud *f* virtue.
virtuoso, sa *adj* virtuous.
viruela *f* smallpox.
virulencia *f* virulence.
virulento, ta *adj* virulent.
virus *m invar* virus.
visa *f*, **visado** *m* visa.
viscosidad *f* viscosity.
viscoso, sa *adj* viscous, glutinous.
visera *f* visor.
visibilidad *f* visibility.
visible *adj* visible; apparent.
visillos *mpl* lace curtains.
visión *f* sight, vision; fantasy.

visionario, ria *adj* visionary.
visita *f* visit; visitor.
visitar *vt* to visit.
vislumbrar *vt* to catch a glimpse; to perceive indistinctly.
visón *m* mink.
víspera *f* eve; evening before; **~s** *pl* vespers.
vista *f* sight, view; vision; eye; (eye)sight; appearance; looks; prospect; intention, purpose; (*jur*) trial; ● *m* customs officer.
vistazo *m* glance.
visto : ~ que *conj* considering that.
vistoso, sa *adj* colorful, attractive, lively.
visual *adj* visual.
vital *adj* life *compd*; living *compd*; vital.
vitalicio, cia *adj* for life.
vitalidad *f* vitality.
vitamina *f* vitamin.
viticultor, ra *m/f* wine grower.
viticultura *f* wine growing.
vitorear *vt* to shout, to applaud.
vítreo, trea *adj* vitreous.
vitriolo *m* vitriol.
vitrina *f* showcase.
vituperación *f* condemnation; censure.
vituperar *vt* to condemn, to censure.
vituperio *m* condemnation, censure; insult.
viuda *f* widow.
viudedad *f* widowhood; widow's pension.
viudez *f* widowhood.
viudo *m* widower.
vivacidad *f* vivacity, liveliness.
vivamente *adv* in lively fashion.
vivaracho, cha *adj* lively, sprightly; bright.
vivaz *adj* lively.
víveres *mpl* provisions.
vivero *m* nursery (for plants); fish farm.
viveza *f* liveliness; sharpness (of mind).
vividor, ra *adj* (*pey*) sharp, clever; unscrupulous.
vivienda *f* housing; apartment.
viviente *adj* living.
vivificar *vt* to vivify, to enliven.
vivíparo, ra *adj* viviparous.
vivir *vt* to live through; to go through; ● *vi* to live; to last.
vivo, va *adj* living; lively; **al ~** to the life; very realistically.
vizconde *m* viscount.
vocablo *m* word, term.
vocabulario *m* vocabulary.
vocación *f* vocation.
vocacional *adj* vocational.
vocal *f* vowel; ● *m/f* member (of a committee); ● *adj* vocal, oral.
vocativo *m* (*gr*) vocative.
vocear *vt* to cry, to shout to, to cheer, to shriek; ● *vi* to yell.
vocería *f*, **vocerío** *m* shouting.
vociferar *vt* to shout; to proclaim in a loud voice; ● *vi* to yell.
vodka *m or f* vodka.
volador, ra *adj* flying; fast.
volandas : en ~ *adv* in the air; (*fig*) swiftly.
volante *adj* flying; ● *m* (*auto*) steering wheel; note; pamphlet; shuttlecock.
volar *vi* to fly; to pass swiftly (of time); to rush, to hurry; ● *vt* to blow up, to explode.
volatería *f* fowling; fowls *pl*.
volátil *adj* volatile; changeable.
volatilizar *vt* to volatilize, to vaporize.
volcán *m* volcano.
volcánico *adj* volcanic.
volcar *vt* to upset, to overturn; to make giddy; to empty out; to exasperate; **~se** *vr* to tip over.
voleíbol *m* volleyball.
voleo *m* volley.
volquete *m* tipcart; dump truck.
voltaje *m* voltage.

voltear *vt* to turn over; to overturn; ● *vi* to roll over, to tumble.
voltereta *f* tumble; somersault.
voltio *m* volt.
voluble *adj* unpredictable; fickle.
volumen *m* volume; size.
voluminoso, sa *adj* voluminous.
voluntad *f* will, willpower; wish, desire.
voluntario, ria *adj* voluntary; ● *m/f* volunteer.
voluptuoso, sa *adj* voluptuous.
volver *vt* to turn (over); to turn upside down; to turn inside out; ● *vi* to return, to go back; ~**se** *vr* to turn around.
vomitar *vt, vi* to vomit.
vómito *m* vomiting; vomit.
vomitona *f* violent vomiting.
voracidad *f* voracity.
voraz(mente) *adj, (adv)* voracious(ly).
vórtice *m* whirlpool.
vos *pn* you.
vosotros, tras *pn pl* you.
votación *f* voting; vote.
votar *vi* to vow; to vote.
voto *m* vow; vote; opinion, advice; swearword; curse; ~**s** *pl* good wishes.
voz *f* voice; shout; rumor; word, term.
vuelco *m* overturning.
vuelo *m* flight; wing; projection of a building; ruffle, frill; **cazar al ~** to catch in flight; **~ charter** charter flight.
vuelta *f* turn; circuit; return; row of stitches; cuff; change; bend, curve; reverse, other side; return journey.
vuestro, tra *adj* your; ● *pn* yours.
vulgar *adj* vulgar, common.
vulgaridad *f* vulgar, common.
vulgaridad *f* vulgarity; commonness.
vulgo *m* common people, mob.
vulnerable *adj* vulnerable.

W

wáter *m* toilet.
whisky *m* whisky.

X

xenofobia *f* xenophobia.
xilófono *m* xylophone.
xilógrafo *m* xylographer, wood engraver.

Y

y *conj* and.
ya *adv* already; now; immediately; at once; soon; ● *conj*: ~ **que** since, seeing that; ¡~! of course!, sure!
yacer *vi* to lie, to lie down.
yacimiento *m* deposit.
yanqui *m/f* Yankee.
yate *m* yacht, sailboat.
yedra *f* ivy.
yegua *f* mare.
yema *f* bud, leaf; yolk; ~ **del dedo** tip of the finger.
yermo *m* waste land, wilderness; ~, **ma** *adj* waste; *(fig)* barren.
yerno *m* son-in-law.
yerro *m* error, mistake, fault.
yerto, ta *adj* stiff, inflexible; rigid.

yesca *f* tinder.
yeso *m* gypsum; plaster; ~ **mate** plaster of Paris.
yo *pn* I; ~ **mismo** I myself.
yodo *m* iodine.
yogur *m* yogurt.
yugo *m* yoke.
yugular *adj* jugular.
yunque *m* anvil.
yunta *f* yoke; ~**s** *pl* couple, pair.
yute *m* jute.
yuxtaponer *vt* to juxtapose.
yuxtaposición *f* juxtaposition.

Z

zafar *vt* to loosen, to untie; to lighten a ship; ~**se** *vr* to escape; to avoid; to free oneself from trouble.
zafio, fia *adj* uncouth, coarse.
zafiro *m* sapphire.
zaga *f* rear; **a la ~** behind.
zagal, la *m/f* boy/girl.
zaguán *m* porch, hall.
zaherir *vt* to criticize; to upbraid.
zahorí *m* clairvoyant.
zalamería *f* flattery.
zalamero, ra *adj* flattering; ● *m/f* wheedler.
zamarra *f* sheepskin; sheepskin jacket.
zambo, ba *adj* knock-kneed.
zambomba *f* rural drum.
zambullida *f* plunge, dive; dipping, submersion.
zambullirse *vr* to plunge into water, to dive.
zampar *vt* to gobble down; to put away hurriedly; ~**se** *vr* to thrust oneself suddenly into any place; to crash, to hurtle.
zanahoria *f* carrot.
zancada *f* stride.
zancadilla *f* trip; trick.
zanco *m* stilt.
zancudo, da *adj* longlegged; ● *m* mosquito.
zángano *m* drone; idler, slacker.
zanja *f* ditch, trench.
zanjar *vt* to dig ditches; *(fig)* to surmount; to resolve.
zapador *m (mil)* sapper.
zapar *vt, vi* to sap, to mine.
zapata *f* boot; ~ **de freno** *(auto)* brake shoe.
zapatazo *m* blow with a shoe.
zapatear *vt* to tap with the shoe; to beat time with the sole of the shoe.
zapatería *f* shoemaking; shoe shop; shoe factory.
zapatero *m* shoemaker; ~ **de viejo** cobbler.
zapatilla *f* slipper; pump(shoe); *(dep)* trainer, training shoe.
zapato *m* shoe.
zar *m* czar.
zarandear *vt* to shake vigorously.
zarcillo *m* earring; tendril.
zarpa *f* dirt on clothes; claw.
zarpar *vi* to weigh anchor.
zarpazo *m* thud.
zarrapastroso, sa *adj* shabby, rough-looking.
zarza *f* bramble.
zarzal *m* bramble patch.
zarzamora *f* blackberry.
zarzuela *f* Spanish light opera.
zigzag *adj* zigzag.
zigzaguear *vi* to zigzag.
zinc *m* zinc.
zócalo *m* plinth, base; baseboard.
zodíaco *m* zodiac.
zona *f* zone; area, belt.
zoo *m* zoo.
zoología *f* zoology.

zoológico, ca *adj* zoological.
zoólogo, ga *m/f* zoologist.
zopenco, ca *adj* dull, very stupid.
zoquete *m* block; crust of bread; (*fam*) blockhead.
zorra *f* fox; vixen; (*fam*) whore, tart (*sl*).
zorro *m* male fox; cunning person.
zozobra *f* (*mar*) capsizing; uneasiness, anxiety.
zozobrar *vt* (*mar*) to founder; to capsize; (*fig*) to fail; to be anxious.
zueco *m* wooden shoe; clog.
zumba *f* banter, teasing; beating.

zumbar *vt* to hit; ● *vi* to buzz; ~se *vr* to hit each other.
zumbido *m* humming, buzzing sound.
zumbón, ona *adj* waggish, funny, teasing.
zumo *m* juice.
zurcir *vt* to darn; (*fig*) to join, to unite; to hatch lies.
zurdo, da *adj* left; left-handed.
zurra *f* flogging; drudgery.
zurrar *vt* (*fam*) to flog, to lay into; (*fig*) to criticize harshly.
zurrón *m* pouch.
zutano, na *m/f* so-and-so; ~ y fulano such and such a one, so and so.

Verbos Irregulares en Ingles

	Pretérito	Participio de pasado		Pretérito	Participio de pasado
arise	arose	arisen	find	found	found
awake	awoke	awaked, awoken	flee	fled	fled
			fling	flung	flung
be [I am, you/we/they are, he/she/it is, *gerundio* being]			fly [he/she/it flies]		
	was, were	been		flew	flown
bear	bore	borne	forbid	forbade	forbidden
beat	beat	beaten	forecast	forecast	forecast
become	became	become	foresee	foresaw	foreseen
begin	began	begun	forget	forgot	forgotten
behold	beheld	beheld	forgive	forgave	forgiven
bend	bent	bent	forsake	forsook	forsaken
beseech	besought, beseeched	besought, beseeched	freeze	froze	frozen
			get	got	got, gotten
beset	beset	beset	give	gave	given
bet	bet, betted	bet, betted	go [he/she/it goes]		
bid	bade, bid	bade, bid, bidden		went	gone
bite	bit	bitten	grind	ground	ground
bleed	bled	bled	grow	grew	grown
bless	blessed	blessed, blest	hang	hung,	hung,
blow	blew	blown		hanged	hanged
break	broke	broken	have [I/you/we/they have, he/she/it has, *gerundio* having]		
breed	bred	bred		had	had
bring	brought	brought	hear	heard	heard
build	built	built	hide	hid	hidden
burn	burnt, burned	burnt, burned	hit	hit	hit
			hold	held	held
burst	burst	burst	hurt	hurt	hurt
buy	bought	bought	keep	kept	kept
can	could	(been able)	knee	knelt, kneeled	knelt, kneeled
cast	cast	cast			
catch	caught	caught	know	knew	known
choose	chose	chosen	lay	laid	laid
cling	cling	clung	lead	led	led
come	came	come	lean	leant, leaned	leant, leaned
cost	cost	cost			
creep	crept	crept	leap	leapt, leaped	leapt, leaped
cut	cut	cut			
deal	dealt	dealt	learn	learnt, learned	learnt, learned
dig	dug	dug			
do [he/she/it does]			leave	left	left
	did	done	lend	lent	lent
draw	drew	drawn	let	let	let
dream	dreamed, dreamt	dreamed, dreamt	lie [*gerundio* lying]		
				lay	lain
drink	drank	drunk	light	lighted, lit	lighted, lit
drive	drove	driven			
dwell	dwelt, dwelled	dwelt, dwelled	lose	lost	lost
			make	made	made
eat	ate	eaten	may	might	–
fall	fell	fallen	mean	meant	meant
feed	fed	fed	meet	met	met
feel	felt	felt	mistake	mistook	mistaken
fight	fought	fought	mow	mowed	mowed, mown

	Pretérito	Participio de pasado		Pretérito	Participio de pasado
must	(had to)	(had to)	spin	spun	spun
overcome	overcame	overcome	spit	spat	spat
pay	paid	paid	split	split	split
put	put	put	spoil	spoilt, spoiled	spoilt, spoiled
quit	quit, quitted	quit, quitted	spread	spread	spread
read	read	read	spring	sprang	sprung
rid	rid	rid	stand	stood	stood
ride	rode	ridden	steal	stole	stolen
ring	rang	rung	stick	stuck	stuck
rise	rose	risen	sting	stung	stung
run	ran	run	stink	stank	stunk
saw	sawed	sawn	stride	dtrode	stridden
say	said	said	strike	struck	struck
see	saw	seen	strive	strove	striven
seek	sought	sought	swear	swore	sworn
sell	sold	sold	sweep	swept	swept
send	sent	sent	swell	swelled	swelled, swollen
set	set	set	swim	swam	swum
sew	sewed	sewn	swing	swung	swung
shake	shook	shaken	take	took	taken
shall	should	–	teach	taught	taught
shear	sheared	sheared, shorn	tear	tore	torn
shed	shed	shed	tell	told	told
shine	shone	shone	think	thought	thought
shoot	shot	shot	throw	threw	thrown
show	showed	shown, showed	thrust	thrust	thrust
shrink	shrank	shrunk	tread	trod	trodden
shut	shut	shut	understand	understood	understood
sing	sang	sung	upset	upset	upset
sink	sank	sunk	wake	woke	woken
sit	sat	sat	wear	wore	worn
slay	slew	slain	weave	wove, weaved	wove, weaved
sleep	slept	slept	wed	wed, wedded	wed, wedded
slide	slid	slid	weep	wept	wept
sling	slung	slung	win	won	won
smell	smelt, smelled	smelt, smelled	wind	wound	wound
sow	sowed	sown-sowed	withdraw	withdrew	withdrawn
speak	spoke	spoken	withhold	withheld	withheld
speed	sped, speeded	sped, speeded	withstand	withstood	withstood
spell	spelt, spelled	spelt,	wring	wrung	wrung
spend	spent	spent	write	wrote	written
spill	spilt, spilled	spilt, spilled			

Spanish Verbs

REGULAR

comprar	temer	partir
to buy	*to fear*	*to divide*

Gerund

compr **ando**	tem **iendo**	part **iendo**

Part participle

compr **ado**	tem **ido**	part **ido**

Present indicative

compr **o**	tem **o**	part **o**
compr **as**	tem **es**	part **es**
compr **a**	tem **e**	part **e**
compr **amos**	tem **emos**	part **imos**
compr **áis**	tem **éis**	part **ís**
compr **an**	tem **en**	part **en**

Imperfect indicative

compr **aba**	tem **ía**	part **ía**
compr **abas**	tem **ías**	part **ías**
compr **aba**	tem **ía**	part **ía**
compr **ábamos**	tem **íamos**	part **íamos**
compr **abais**	tem **íais**	part **íais**
compr **aban**	tem **ían**	part **ían**

Past absolute (or preterit)

compr **é**	tem **í**	part **í**
compr **aste**	tem **iste**	part **iste**
compr **ó**	tem **ió**	part **ió**
compr **amos**	tem **imos**	part **imos**
compr **asteis**	tem **isteis**	part **isteis**
compr **aron**	tem **ieron**	part **ieron**

Future

compr **aré**	tem **eré**	part **iré**
compr **arás**	tem **erás**	part **irás**
compr **ará**	tem **erá**	part **irá**
compr **aremos**	tem **eremos**	part **iremos**
compr **aréis**	tem **eréis**	part **iréis**
compr **arán**	tem **erán**	part **irán**

Conditional

compr **aría**	tem **ería**	part **iría**
compr **arías**	tem **erías**	part **irías**
compr **aría**	tem **ería**	part **iría**
compr **aríamos**	tem **eríamos**	part **iríamos**
compr **aríais**	tem **eríais**	part **iríais**
compr **arían**	tem **erían**	part **irían**

Imperative

compr **a**	tem **e**	part **e**
compr **e**	tem **a**	part **a**
compr **emos**	tem **amos**	part **amos**
compr **ad**	tem **ed**	part **id**
compr **en**	tem **an**	part **an**

Present subjunctive

compr **e**	tem **a**	part **a**
compr **es**	tem **as**	part **as**
compr **e**	tem **a**	part **a**
compr **emos**	tem **amos**	part **amos**
compr **éis**	tem **áis**	part **áis**
compr **en**	tem **an**	part **an**

Imperfect subjunctive

compr **ara**	tem **iera**	part **iera**
ase	**iese**	**iese**
compr **aras**	tem **ieras**	part **ieras**
ases	**ieses**	**ieses**
compr **ara**	tem **iera**	part **iera**
ase	**iese**	**iese**
compr **áramos**	tem **iéramos**	part **iéramos**
ásemos	**iésemos**	**iésemos**
compr **arais**	tem **ierais**	part **ierais**
aseis	**ieseis**	**ieseis**
compr **aran**	tem **ieran**	part **ieran**
asen	**iesen**	**iesen**

AUXILIARY VERBS

Infinitive

haber	ser	tener	estar
to have	*to be*	*to have*	*to be*

Gerund

habiendo	siendo	teniendo	estando

Past participle

habido	sido	tenido	estado

Present indicative

he	soy	tengo	estoy
has	eres	tienes	estás
ha	es	tiene	está
hemos	somos	tenemos	estamos
habéis	sois	tenéis	estáis
han	son	tienen	están

Imperfect indicative

había	era	tenía	estaba
habías	eras	tenías	estabas
había	era	tenía	estaba
habíamos	éramos	teníamos	estábamos
habíais	erais	teníais	estabais
habían	eran	tenían	estaban

Past absolute (or preterit)

hube	fui	tuve	estuve
hubiste	fuiste	tuviste	estuviste
hubo	fue	tuvo	estuvo
hubimos	fuimos	tuvimos	estuvimos
hubisteis	fuisteis	tuvisteis	estuvisteis
hubieron	fueron	tuvieron	estuvieron

Future

habré	seré	tendré	estaré
habrás	serás	tendrás	estarás
habrá	será	tendrá	estará
habremos	seremos	tendremos	estaremos
habréis	seréis	tendréis	estaréis
habrán	serán	tendrán	estarán

Conditional

habría	sería	tendría	estaría
habrías	serías	tendrías	estarías
habría	sería	tendría	estaría
habríamos	seríamos	tendríamos	estaríamos
habríais	seríais	tendríais	estaríais
habrían	serían	tendrían	estarían

Imperative

-	sé (tu)	ten (tu)	está (tu)

Present subjunctive

haya	sea	tenga	esté
hayas	seas	tengas	estés
haya	sea	tenga	esté
hayamos	seamos	tengamos	estemos
hayáis	seáis	tengáis	estéis
hayan	sean	tengan	estén

Imperfect subjunctive

hubiera	fuera	tuviera	estuviera
iese	ese	iese	iese
hubieras	fueras	tuvieras	estuvieras
ieses	eses	ieses	ieses
hubiera	fuera	tuviera	estuviera
iese	ese	iese	iese
hubiéramos	fuéramos	tuviéramos	estuviéramos
iésemos	ésemos	iésemos	iésemos
hubierais	fuerais	tuvierais	estuvierais
ieseis	eseis	ieseis	ieseis
hubieran	fueran	tuvieran	estuvieran
iesen	esen	iesen	iesen

OTHER IRREGULAR AND SEMI- IRREGULAR VERBS:

Tenses containing irregular forms

acertar (stressed 'e' becomes 'ie'); *present indicative*: acierto, aciertas, acierta, acertamos, acertáis, aciertan; *imperative*: acierta; *present subjunctive*: acierte, aciertes, acierte, acertemos, acertéis, acierten.

acordar (stressed 'o' becomes 'ue'); *present indicative*: acuerdo, acuerdas, acuerda, acordamos, acordáis, acuerdan; *imperative*: acuerda; *present subjunctive*: acuerde, acuerdes, acuerde, acordemos, acordéis, acuerden.

advertir *see* sentir

agradecer, aparecer *see* conocer.

aprobar *see* acordar.

atravesar *see* acertar.

caber (irregular); *gerund*: cabiendo; *present indicative*: quepo, cabes, cabe, cabemos, cabéis, caben; *past absolute*: cupe, cupiste, cupo, cupimos, cupisteis, cupieron; *future* cabré *etc*; *conditional*: cabría *etc*; *present subjunctive*: quepa, quepas, quepa, quepamos, quepáis, quepan. *Imperfect subjunctive*: cupiera *etc;*

caer (unstressed 'i' between vowels becomes 'y'); *gerund*: cayendo; *present indicative*: caigo, caes, cae, caemos, caéis, caen; *past absolute*: caí, caíste, cayó, caímos, caísteis, cayeron; *present subjunctive*: caiga etc; *imperfect subjunctive* cayera *etc*.

calentar, cerrar *see* acertar.

conocer ('c' becomes 'zc' before 'a' and 'o'); *gerund*: conociendo *present indicative*: conozco, conoces, conoce, conocemos, conocéis, conocen; *past absolute*: conocí, conociste, conoció, conocimos, conocisteis, conocieron; *present subjunctive*: conozca, conoczcas, conozca, conozcamos, conozcáis, conozcan.

contar, costar *see* acordar

dar (irregular); *gerund*: dando; *present indicative*: doy, das, da, damos, dais, dan; *past absolute*: di, diste, dio, dimos, disteis, dieron; *present subjunctive*: dé. des, dé, demos, deis, den; *imerfect subjunctive*: diera etc.

decir (irregular); *gerund*: diciendo; *past participle*: dicho; *present indicative*: digo, dices, dice, decimos, decís, dicen; *past absolute*: diji, dijiste, dijo, dijimos, dijisteis, dijeron; *future*: diré *etc*; *conditional*: diría etc; *imperative*: de; *present subjunctive*: diga etc; *imperfect subjunctive*: dijera *etc*.

despertar *see* acertar

divertir *see* sentir

dormir (stressed 'o' becomes 'ue'; 'o' becomes 'u' in gerund, past absolute 3rd person singular, and present subjunctive 1st and 2nd persons plural); *gerund*: durmiendo; *present indicative*: duermo, duermes, duerme, dormimos, dormís, duermen; *past absolute*: dormí, dormiste, durmió, dormimos, dormisteis, durmieron; *imperative*: duerme; *present subjunctive*: duerma, duermas, duerma, durmamos, durmáis, duerman; *imperfect subjunctive*: durmiera *etc*.

empezar *see* acetar.

entender *see* perder

hacer (irregular); *gerund*: haciendo; *past participle*: hecho; *present indicative*: hago, haces, hace, hacemos, hacéis, hacen; *past absolute*: hice, hiciste, hizo, hicimos, hicisteis, hicieron; *future*: haré *etc*; *conditional*: haría *etc*; *imperative*: haz; *present subjunctive*: haga etc; *imperfect subjunctive*: hiciera *etc*.

huir ('y' is added before endings not beginning with 'i'); *gerund*: huyendo; *present indicative*: huyo, huyes, huye, huimos, huís, huyen; *past absolute*: huí, huiste, huyó, huimos, huisteis, huyeron; *present subjunctive*: huya, huyas, huya, huyamos, huyáis, huyan.

instruir *see* huir

ir (irregular); *gerund*: yendo; *present indicative*: voy, vas, va, vamos, vais, van; *imperfect indicative*: iba, ibas, iba, íbamos, ibais, iban; *past absolute*: fui, fuiste, fue, fuimos, fuisteis, fueron; *imperative*: ve; *present subjunctive*: vaya, vayas, vaya, vayamos, vayáis, vayan; *imperfect subjunctive*: fuera etc.

jugar (stressed 'u' becomes 'ue'; 'g' becomes 'gu' before 'e'); *present indicative*: juego, juegas, juega, jugamos, jugáis, juegan; *past absolute*: jugué, jugaste, jugó, jugamos, jugasteis, jugaron; *imperative*: juega; *present subjunctive*: juegue, juegues, juguemos, juguéis, jueguen.

leer (unstressed 'i' between vowels becomes 'y') ; *gerund*: leyendo; *past absolute*: leí, leiste, leyó, leímos, leísteis, leyeron; *imperfect subjunctive*: leyera *etc*.

morir *see* dormir.

mostrar *see* acordar.

mover (stressed 'o' becomes 'ue'); *gerund*: moviendo; *present indicative*: muevo, mueves, mueve, movemos, movéis, mueven; *past absolute*: moví, moviste, movió, movimos, movisteis, movieron; *imperative*: mueve; *present subjunctive*: mueva, muevas, mueva, movamos, mováis, muevan.

negar *see* acertar.

ofrecer *see* conocer.

oir (irregular); *gerund*: oyendo; *past participle*: oído; *present indicative*: oigo, oyes, oye, oímos, oís, oyen; *past absolute*: oí, oíste, oyó, oímos, oísteis, oyeron; *imperative*: oye; *present subjunctive*: oiga, oigas, oiga, oigamos, oigáis, oigan; *imperfect subjunctive*: oyera *etc*.

oler *gerund*: oliendo; *present indicative*: huelo, hueles, huele, olemos, oléis, heulen; *past absolute*: olí, oliste, olió, olimos, olisteis, olieron; *imperative*: huele; *present subjunctive*: huela, huelas, huela, olamos, oláis, huelan.

parecer *see* conocer

pedir ('e' becomes 'i' [1] when stressed; [2] in the past absolute 3rd person singular and present subjunctive 1st and 2nd persons plural); *gerund*: pidiendo; *present indicative*: pido, pides, pide, pedimos, pedís, piden; *past absolute*: peí, pediste, pidió, pedimos, pedisteis, pidieron; *imperative*: pide; *present subjunctive*: pida, pidas, pida, pidamos, pidáis, pidan; *imperfect subjunctive*: pidiera, *etc*.

pensar *see* acertar.

perder (stressed 'e' becomes 'ie'); *gerund*: perdiendo; *present indicative*: pierdo, pierdes, pierde, perdemos, perdéis, pierden; *past absolute*: perdí, perdiste, perdió, perdemos, perdisteis, perdieron; *imperative*: pierde; *present subjunctive*: pierda, pierdas, pierda, perdamos, perdáis, pierdan.

poder (irregular); *gerund*: pudiendo; *present indicative*: puedo, puedes, puede, podemos, podéis, pueden; *past absolute*: pude, pudiste, pudo, pudimos, pudisteis, pudieron; *future*: podré *etc*; *conditional*: podría *etc*;

imperative: puede; *present subjunctive*: pueda, puedas, pueda, podamos, podáis, puedan; *imperfect subjunctive*: pudiera *etc*.

poner (irregular)*; gerund*: poniendo; *past participle*: puesto; *present indicative*: pongo, pones, pone, ponemos, ponéis, ponen; *past absolute*: puse, pusiste, puso, pusimos, pusisteis, pusieron; *future*: pondré *etc*; *conditional*: pondría *etc*; *imperative*: pon; *present subjunctive*: ponga, pongas, ponga, pongamos, pongáis, pongan; *imperfect subjunctive*: pusiera *etc*.

preferir *see* **sentir**.

querer (irregular)*; gerund*: queriendo; *present indicative*; quiero, quieres, quiere, queremos, queréis, quieren; *past absolute*: quise, quisiste, quiso, quisimos, quisisteis, quisieron; *future*: querré *etc*; *conditional*: querría *etc*; *imperative*: quiere; *present subjunctive*: quiera, quieras, quiera, queramos, queráis, quieran; *imperfect subjunctive*: quisiera *etc*.

reir (irregular); *gerund*: riendo; *past participle*: reído; *present indicative*: río, ríes, ríe, reímos, reís, ríen; *past absolute*: reí, reíste, rió, reímos, reísteis, rieron; *imperative*: ríe; *present subjunctive*: ría, rías, ría, riamos, riáis, rían; *imperfect subjunctive*: riera *etc*.

repetir *see* **pedir**.

rogar *see* **acordar**.

saber (irregular)*; gerund*: sabiendo; *present indicative*: sé, sabes, sabe, sabemos, sabéis, saben; *past absolute*: supe, supiste, supo, supimos, supisteis, supieron; *future*: sabré *etc*; *conditional*: sabría *etc*; *present subjunctive*: sepa, sepas, sepa, sepamos, sepáis, sepan; *imperfect subjunctive*: supiera *etc*.

salir (irregular); *present indicative*: salgo, sales, sale, salimos, salís, salen; *past absolute*: sali, saliste, salió, salimos, salisteis, salieron; *future*: saldré *etc*; *conditional*: saldría etc; *imperative*: sal; *present subjunctive*: salga, salgas, salga, salgamos, salgáis, salgan.

seguir *gerund*: siguiendo; *present indicative*: sigo, sigues, sigue, seguimos, seguís, siguen; *past absolute*: seguí, seguiste, siguió, seguimos, seguisteis, siguieron;

imperative: sigue; *present subjunctive*: siga *etc*; *imperfect subjunctive*: siguiera *etc*.

sentar *see* **acertar**.

sentir (stressed 'e' becomes 'ie'; 'e' becomes 'i' in past absolute 3rd person singular and present subjunctive 1st and 2nd persons plural)*; gerund*: sintiendo; *present indicative*: siento, sientes, sienta, sentimos, sentís, sienten; *past absolute*: sentí, sentiste, sintió, sentimos, sentisteis, sintieron; *imperative*: siente; *present subjunctive*: sienta, sientas, sienta, sintamos, sintáis, sientan; *imperfect subjunctive*: sintiera *etc*.

servir *see* **perdir**.

sonar *see* **acordar**.

traer (irregular)*; gerund*: trayendo; *past participle*: traído; *present indicative*: traigo, traes, trae, traemos, traéis, traen; *past absolute*: traje, trajiste, trajo, trajimos, trajisteis, trajeron; *present subjunctive*: traiga, traigas, traiga, traigamos, traigáis, traigan; *imperfect subjunctive*: trajera *etc*.

valer (irregular) *gerund*: valiendo; *present indicative*: valgo, vales, vale, valemos, valéis, valen; *past absolute*: valí, valiste, valió, valimos, valisteis, valieron; *future*: valdré *etc*; *conditional*: valdría *etc*; *imperative*: vale; *present subjunctive*: valga, valgas, valga, valgamos, valgáis, valgan.

venir (irregular)*; gerund*: viniendo; *present indicative*: vengo, vienes, viene, venimos, venís, vienen; *past absolute*: vine, viniste, vino, vinimos, vinisteis, vinieron; *future*: vendré *etc*; *conditional*: vendría *etc*; *imperative*: ven; *present subjunctive*: venga, vengas, venga, vengamos, vengáis, vengan; *imperfect subjunctive*: viniera *etc*.

ver (irregular)*; gerund*: viendo; *past participle*: visto; *present indicative*: veo, ves, ve, vemos, veis, ven; *imperfect indicative*: veía, veías, veía, *etc*; *past absolute*: vi, viste, vio, vimos, visteis, vieron; *present subjunctive*: vea, veas, vea, veamos, veáis, vean.

vestir *see* **pedir**.

volver *see* **mover**.